Knowlesville II
The Corey Story

Judson M. Corey

Copyright ©2003 Judson M. Corey

All rights reserved. No part of this book may be reproduced, stored in a retrieval system, or transmitted in any form or by any means without prior written permission from the publisher, or, in the case of photocopying or other reprographic copying, permission from ACCESS (Canadian Copyright Licensing Agency), 1 Yonge Street, Suite 1900, Toronto, Ontario M5E 1E5

Designed and produced by:
Ken Spink, Inspiration Graphics,
61 Union Street, Saint John, New Brunswick E2L 1A2.

Printed and bound in Canada.

First Edition April 2003.

National Library of Canada Cataloguing in Publication

Corey, Judson M. (Judson Malcolm), 1923-
    Knowlesville II : the Corey story / Judson M. Corey.

Includes bibliographical references.
ISBN 0-9692176-1-7

    1. Corey family. 2. Knowlesville (N.B.)--History. I. Title.

FC2495 K59 Z48 2003   929'.2'0971   C2003-901276-X
F1044.K59C67 2003

A sequel to:
The Story of Knowlesville. The Community and its People
(Published in 1985. ISBN 0-9692176-09)

Front Cover:
Detail from an 1876 map of Knowlesville and surrounding area,
Carleton County, New Brunswick, by Roe & Colby, St. John (1876 spelling), N.B.
Reproduced with permission of the New Brunswick Museum.

Photos of the author's grandparents; Alfred Elisha Corey and his wife, Eloma Lucretia Kierstead.

Detail of an original letter written by Ira Corey on October 22, 1922, to his daughter Erma

TABLE OF CONTENTS

Dedication..ix

Acknowledgements..x

Preface..xi

CHAPTER I.
Homesteaders in Knowlesville................................15

CHAPTER II.
Scattering of the Corey family................................39

CHAPTER III.
"Carry me back" to:
Knowlesville—a home, a family, a pioneer farm..........47
Esdraelon—water wheels, mills, store........................53
Highlands—a church, people, cemetery.....................66

CHAPTER IV.
Home-coming
Ira Corey..81
Judson A. Corey...85
Sarah Louise Corey Fletcher.......................................89
Two Baptist Denominations Unite...............................90
A Circuit Pastor..99

CHAPTER V.
Stones and Stories
Knowlesville—a diamond rock..................................108
Highlands—a church and a cemetery.......................115
Glassville—Greetings to Knowlesville........................116

CHAPTER VI.
The last decade on the Corey homestead 1912-1922
Marriage: Ira and Nellie...121

Births: Wilfred, Bob, Alice, Norman,
    Tom, and Claude..122
A boy ill with pneumonia..128

CHAPTER VII.
The Hemphill farm and grandpa's last eight years

Norman recovers...135
Grandmother Lucretia passes...................................136
Haying, and pressing..137
Ira's letter: Little Clearwater......................................138
Grandpa Alfred: work at home.................................141
Logging at home and on Skedaddle Ridge...............143
Grandpa Alfred passes...154

CHAPTER VIII.
Mina McBrine branch of the Corey family

Erma Corey: visiting and teaching.............................159
East Glassville...168
Alma, Glenna, Ferne and Fred..................................171
Passing of Eb and Mina..174
Children and Grandchildren......................................176

CHAPTER IX.
Alma Corey Miller and family

Knowlesville and Glassville families..........................213
Scotland, Saint John, New Jerusalem........................214
Hugh Miller and family come to Glassville..............216
Alma and R. James and children:
    Maude, Jimmie, Will, Kathleen, Wilma.........217
Romance in Glassville..224
Alma's passing, 1915..227
Scattering: Nova Scotia and U.S.A............................228
MacNearney's: Edwin, Janet, John, Douglas,
    Alice, Lynn, Paula, Eric..................................254
Williams: Gail and Linda...263
Hoveys: Jean, Kathleen, June, Carolyn, Marilyn.........274

CHAPTER X.
Charles H.S. Corey and family

Maine: marriage to Elizabeth Thuber.........................294

Campobello Island: Lighthouse; North Road:
    fishing, farming..295
Visit of Erma and Glenna...298
Children: Ivan, Edith and Noel.................................302
Grandchildren..312

CHAPTER XI.
Judson Albert Corey and Family
Knowlesville, socializing..343
Maine: work; preparing for ministry..........................344
Marriage to Alice Howlett.
    Return to Knowlesville with children............345
Ministry: Highlands, Biggar Ridge, Knowlesville,
    Windsor, Rusagonis, Campobello,
    Hoyt Station, Mactaquac,
    Doaktown, Rusagonis.
    Wilson's Beach: last ministry.
Biographies of their children: Alberta, Earle, Annie,
    Esther, Alfred, David, Edna and Mildred.......346
Grandchildren..366

CHAPTER XII.
Ida Corey McBrine and Family
Ida m. Bill McBrine in Glassville................................401
Living in Knowlesville and Glassville........................403
Moves to Maine and New York.................................410
Iron workers and skyscrapers....................................415
Biographies of Clara, Jud, Nessie, Nellie,
    Vola,Kathleen, George, Lucretia,
    Leland and Lorne, their children and
    granchildren...419

CHAPTER XIII.
Sarah Corey Fletcher and family
Home-coming and Hunting.......................................509
Business and Politics..515

CHAPTER XIV.
Alberta Jerusha Corey
Albert Jerusha Corey..517
New Brunswick to New York....................................518

The curtain opens in Brooklyn, NY.
A happy reunion..519

Chapter XV.
Laversa Corey Garns
Home-coming to Knowlesville....................................521
Maine: work and romance..522
Maryland: home and family......................................526
Two sons and seven daughters,
    their children and grandchildren..................527

Chapter XVI.
1877 Ira Thomas Corey 1957
"What was your father like?"......................................537
Orderliness and Discipline..539
Freedom, accountability and learning.....................541
Charisma; commanding voice.................................542
Calm and nonchalant...543
Surgery and home treatment; stories.........................544
Western Canada..547
Sunday School in Knowlesville..................................549
A pact made on a river..551
Stories and Songs...552

Chapter XVII.
Growing up on the E. Knowlesville Farm
Passing of two grandfathers.
Change at beginning of the 30's................................553
Winter: a little leisure..554
Boys at play..556
Baskets of Learning—a story....................................557
Spring: new life, running sap,
    planting time, whistles..................................558
Summer: strawberries, haying,
    turnips, potatoes..562
Goings and Comings..563
Our own amusement..564
Argyle picnic..565
Autumn: harvest, digging, ploughing........................567
Christmas...570
Poem: "We Lived Here"...571

Chapter XVIII.
Ira T. Corey branch of the descendants of Alfred and Lucretia Corey

Ira Corey m. Nellie Brown Kenney
Nellie and Arthur Kenney..575
Murray Arthur Kenney and family..............................576
Nellie Corey: biography...578
Erma Corey Shaw and family.....................................584
Descendants of Nellie and Ira Corey.
    Wilfred James Corey and family......................601
    John Robert Corey and family.........................606
    Alice Corey McKenzie and family...................617
    Norman Redlon Corey and family...................624
    Thomas Wallace Corey and family..................627
    Claude Eugene Corey and family....................635
    Judson Malcolm Corey and family.................648
    Warren Allan Corey and family......................654
    Ira Keith Corey...661
Anna Kathleen Corey..669
Shirley Joyce Corey...679
Gordon Neil Corey..686

Chapter XIX.
In grateful memory of Margaret Eveline Corey....695

Chapter XX.
Home and belonging
My family experience..701
A story of near loss..703
Enlarged belonging..705

Chapter XXI.
Memorials and Remembering
Flashbacks in E. Knowlesville.......................................707
Graves in Golden Ridge: tour with Lorne Craig..........709
Values of Memorials and Monuments.........................710
Names of ministers of Knowlesville Church................712
Knowlesville-Armond War Memorial..........................714
Work of committee..715
Unveiling: church and legion....................................... 715

Names of servicemen:
    1914-18, 1939-45, 1950..............................716
Yearly service at monument.........................719

Genealogies..721
Genealogy notes...750

About the author..752

This book is dedicated to

Erma Eleanor Corey Shaw
1903-1993

From Erma came the idea for this book. In her last two years she expressed the desire to leave our family, biographies of our grandparents, Alfred and Lucretia Corey, and of their nine children, i.e., our father's siblings.

Erma had many abilities to give to biographical production: a long and vivid memory, a talent for story telling, a sense of history and a love of family. Her many contributions of stories and biographical data are distributed throughout this book. It is our hope that in some measure her desire to preserve the memory of out forebearers for succeeding generations is herein fulfilled.

ACKNOWLEDGEMENTS

The writer acknowledges help from many family relatives and friends in gathering stories and data, and in many other ways.

Family members in several family branches have helped compile and print the extensive genealogies that are included in the branch biographies: Merna Wheeler, Lynn Fiske, Marilyn and Peter Hicks, Judy Corey, Neil Rempel, Kaye Thompson, Joe McBrine, Alice Long, Margaret Monroe, and Garry Corey.

Family members in several branches have made contributions, which with added interest, have made a fund of $4,000 towards the cost of production and printing.

PREFACE

This book begins with the story of a person known to the writer: Alfred Elisha Corey, and his wife Eloma Lucretia Kierstead. It traces their many descendants and tells their stories. My grandmother, Lucretia, I did not know. She died the year before I was born. Alfred Corey, I knew only until I was age seven. Nevertheless, I had an acquaintance with him that I count fortunate; and I have memories that are indelible.

To try to portray the kind of person I perceived Alfred Corey to be, I'll relate a story:

One summer day my brother Warren and I, absorbed in our boyish play, and letting our imaginations lead us, decided to build horse stalls among the lilac bushes. To make the partitions between the stalls we needed boards. We found them very near – on Grandpa's entry platform, at the front door of the farmhouse. The front room of the farmhouse was his domain. There he kept his belongings; there he slept; there he had his own stove. Over that platform he brought his firewood. Through that entry he could retreat from the activities and sounds of the many boys in the family. The boards on Grandpa's platform were not nailed; they lay loose. We took them and propped them, on edge, against the lilac shrubs. Soon we became absorbed in imagining that we were horses in our stalls. Then we heard Grandpa's steps approaching, and his voice sounding. Warren still remembers Grandpa's words calling us: "Come here! I'm not going to hurt you." Then the call to account: "Where are the boards from my steps?" Without hesitation, we promptly replaced Grandpa's boards. Grandpa taught us a lesson about infringing on another person's territory.

The incident has been remembered for more than seven decades. It occurred perhaps in 1930, the last summer our grandfather lived, in which case I was age 7 and Warren was 5, or possibly it occurred in summer of 1929 in which case I was 6, and Warren only 4. More than six decades later, sitting at Saint John Airport, waiting for Warren's flight to British Columbia, he recalled the full speech and the dramatic incident. Margaret and I listened with rapt attention. It all came back on my memory screen also.

The incident gives us a glimpse into the personality of Alfred Corey. He knew how to assert and how to confront. He needed no course in assertiveness His assertiveness could be precise and pointed, yet clear and gentle and tailored to youngsters. You will not be surprised to learn, further into this book, that he served as a sheriff and as a fish warden.

I'm glad to have known Alfred Corey, and that two of my brothers still living, Warren, and our elder brother Norman, also knew him. We have recounted some of our memories and have gathered the memories that others have shared with us. A storyteller who left us a treasure of memories was Erma Corey Shaw who grew up in the home of Alfred and Lucretia Corey. I'm glad also to have been able to tell the stories of the descendants of Alfred Corey and Lucretia Kierstead. Thanks to many descendants and spouses who have shared their stories and those of their close relatives. Thanks also to the people in every branch of the Corey family who have had part in gathering, compiling and printing the extensive genealogies.

CHAPTER I

ALFRED AND LUCRETIA COREY: HOMESTEADERS IN KNOWLESVILLE

About the year 1874 Alfred and Lucretia Corey with five children: Mina, Alma, Charles, Judson and Ida, arrived in Knowlesville, a community then only in its second decade of settlement. They claimed lot 27 in range 3, a 100-acre portion intersected by The Cold Stream. The appearance and condition of the property that was to be their home for the next half century is described in words Alfred often spoke in later years, "When I came here it was all green forest."

What did Alfred and Lucretia Corey bring with them to Knowlesville? We surmise very little other than their five eldest children, then ages 2 to 9. We'll guess they had a horse, or perhaps two, and a wagon to carry them and their household utensils. Undoubtedly Alfred had an axe and a few other tools. They must have been faced with many uncertainties. However, they were not alone or unbefriended. The pioneer families who had come from Nova Scotia in 1861 had landed in a forest and had learned to carve homes from its trees. The pioneers had brought from Nova Scotia, ship's canvass to provide temporary shelters while they worked at building log houses.

The Corey family, arriving in the next decade, also had to carve a home out of the forest. Their first task was to clear enough to build a log house on lot 27, in range 3. Where would they live while their shelter was being erected? The land grant map shows "Ira T. Corey" on lot 27. We wonder why it was not registered "Alfred Corey". Granddaughter, Erma Corey Shaw, thought there was an existing cabin in the neighbourhood that provided the Coreys a temporary shelter. Residents of new settlements valued neighbours and befriended newcomers.

It is likely that the Coreys received a warm welcome, and help in building a cabin. It is possible that the established families helped the new family to complete their log home as quickly as possible. Then Alfred set to work cutting trees and clearing land for farming.

Who were their neighbours? Probably their nearest neighbours were the pioneer families who had come from Nova Scotia in 1861.

    Albert Cook   Thomas Spinney
    Rev. Cyril Doucette Eleazor Wheaton
    Jeremiah Frost   Jacob Whitehouse
    John Gayton   Joseph Whitehouse
    Thomas Gayton*   Alexander Campbell*
    Morris Hobbs   David Campbell*
    Prince Kenney   Robert Ricker
    Webster Simms

*These three returned to Nova Scotia[1]

By 1874, we deduce, quite a number of new families had joined the pioneers in building a new community. The 1871 census shows the following families in the Parish of Aberdeen:

Family-Names-Sex-Age-Country/Province of Birth-Religion-Origin-Profession/Occupation

AVERY-John-m-44-England-Methodist-English-Farmer
-Julia-f-45-N.B.-Methodist-Irish-
-Margaret-f-24-N.B.-Methodist-English-
-William-m-22-N.B.-Methodist-English-Farmer
-Alice-f-18-N.B.-Methodist-English-
-Augusta-f-16-N.B.-Methodist-English-
-John-m-14-N.B.-Methodist-English-
-Arthur-m-12-N.B.-Methodist-English-

-Emma-f-8-N.B.-Methodist-English-
-Ella-f-6-N.B.-Methodist-English-
-Charles-m-3-N.B.-Methodist-English-
BERRY-Richard-m-23-N.B.-Church Of England-Irish-Farmer
-James-m-23-N.B.-Church Of England-Irish-Farmer
BRANSCOMB-Noble-m-33-N.B.-Methodist-English-Farmer
-Abigail-f-26-N.B.-Methodist-Irish-
-Helen-f-5-N.B.-Methodist-English-
-Charles-m-3-N.B.-Methodist—
-John-m-9/12-N.B.-Methodist—
COOK-Albert-m-33-N.B.-Free Christian Baptist-English-Farmer
-Sophie-f-29-N.B.-Free Christian Baptist-English-
-Franklin-m-7-N.B.-Free Christian Baptist-English-
-Annie-f-6-N.B.-Free Christian Baptist-English-
-John-m-3-N.B.-Free Christian Baptist-English-
ELMS-Samuel-m-45-N.B.-Free Christian Baptist-German-Farmer
-Charlotte-f-48-N.B.-Free Christian Baptist-German-
-Elizabeth-f-19-N.B.-Free Christian Baptist-German-
-William-m-17-N.B.-Free Christian Baptist-German-
FRAZER-Isaac-m-34-N.B.—Scottish-Farmer
-Elizabeth-f-29-N.B.—Irish-
-Abner-m-3-N.B.—Scottish-
GAYTON-John-m-55-N.S.-Free Christian Baptist-Irish-Farmer
-Abigail-f-51-N.S.-Free Christian Baptist-Irish-
-John-m-20-N.S.-Free Christian Baptist-Irish-Farmer
some list Ebenezer-Edgar-m-18-N.S.-Free Christian Baptist-Irish-"
-Joseph-m-16-N.S.-Free Christian Baptist-Irish-"
-Nehemiah-m-14-N.S.-Free Christian Baptist-Irish-"
-Samuel-m-12-N.S. -Free Christian Baptist-Irish-
-Charles-m-9-N.S.-Free Christian Baptist-Irish-
GILLMOR-Wellington-m-55-N.B.-Church of England-Irish-Mill Owner
-Lizzie-f-55-N.B.-Church of England-Irish -

-Charlie-m-28-N.B.-Church of England-Irish-Mill Man
-Edward-m-25-N.B.-Church of England-Irish-"
-Matilda-f-23-N.B.-Church of England-Irish-
-Alexander-M-22-N.B.-Church of England-Irish-"
-Ruth-f-19-N.B.-Church of England-Irish-
-Margaret-f-17-N.B.-Church of England-Irish-
-Sulasta-f-15-N.B.-Church of England-Irish-
-Ada-f-14-N.B.-Church of England-Irish-
-Maude-f-11-N.B.-Church of England-Irish-
-George-m-9-N.B.-Church of England-Irish-
HEADSTRONG-Matthew-m-21-N.B.-Church of England-Irish-Labourer
HOBBS-Maurice-m-62-N.S.-Church of England-English-Farmer
-Abigail-f-60-N.S.-Church of England-English-
-Mary-f-22-N.S.-Church of England-English-
-Sophia-f-16-N.S.-Church of England-English-
-Harris-m-33-N.S.-Church of England-English-
-Jane-f-29-N.B.-Church of England-English-
-May-f-2-N.B.-Church of England-English-
-James-m-1-N.B.-Church of England-English-
IRVING-John-m-20-N.B.-Church of England-Irish-Labourer
JONES-Iviathou-m-33-N.B.-Free Christian Baptist-English-Farmer
-Annie-f-26-N.S.-Free Christian Baptist-English-
KENNEY-Prince-m-41-N.S.-Free Christian Baptist-English-Farmer
-Lucy-f-45-N.S.-Free Christian Baptist-English-
-Roland-m-16-N.S.-Free Christian Baptist-English-
-Alden-m-15-N.S.-Free Christian Baptist-English-
-Isaac-m-14-N.S.-Free Christian Baptist-English-
-Helen-f-12-N.S.-Free Christian Baptist-English-
-Robert-m-10-N.S.-Free Christian Baptist-English-
-Naomi-f-5-N.B.-Free Christian Baptist-English-
-William-m-3-N.B.-Free Christian Baptist-English-
(Grandmother)-Kenney-f-64-N.S.-Free Christian Baptist-

English-
MORRISON-Hugh-m-70-Scotland-Presbyterian-Scottish-
-Rachel-f-65-N.S.-Church of Scotland-Scottish-
-Roderick-m-21-N.B.-Presbyterian-Scottish-
MOREHOUSE-William-m-48-N.B.-Free Christian Baptist-English-Farmer
-Emaline-f-48-N.B.-Free Christian Baptist-Portuguese-
-Ummogene-f-4-N.B.-Free Christian Baptist-English-
McDERMID-Angus-m-46-N.B.-Baptist-Scottish-Farmer
-Elizabeth-f-40-N.B.-Baptist-Irish-
-James-m-13-N.B.-Baptist-Scottish-
-Angus-m-12-N.B.-Baptist-Scottish-
-Mary-f-9-N.B.-Baptist-Scottish-
-Agnes-f-7-N.B.-Baptist-Scottish-
-Helen-f-3-N.B.-Baptist-Scottish-
-Joseph-m-2-N.B.-Baptist-Scottish-
-Annie-f-5/12-N.B.-Baptist-Scottish-
McEWING-George-m-26-N.B.-Presbyterian-Irish-Labourer
McFARLANE-James-m-6-N.B.-Presbyterian/Church of Scotland-Scottish-
-George-m-3-N.B.-Presbyterian/Church of Scotland-Scottish-
McLACHLAN-John-m-33-N.B.-Presbyterian/Church of Scotland-Scottish-Farmer
-Margaret-f-33-N.B.-Presbyterian/Church of Scotland-Scottish-
-Newton-m-7-N.B.-Presbyterian/Church of Scotland-Scottish-
-Ella-f-5-N.B.-Presbyterian/Church of Scotland-Scottish-
-Lillie-f-10/12-N.B.-Presbyterian/Church of Scotland-Scottish-
McKENZIE-Alexander-m-39-Scotland-Methodist-Scottish-Farmer
-Jane-f-35-Scotland-Methodist-Scottish-
-Charles-m-l0-Scotland-Methodist-Scottish-
-George-m-ll-Scotland-Methodist-Scottish-
-Barbara-f-9-Scotland-Methodist-Scottish-
-Harry-m-7-N.B.-Methodist-Scottish-
-Alexander-m-5-N.B.-Methodist-Scottish-

-Christina-f-3-N.B.-Methodist-Scottish-
-Albert-m-1-N.B.-Methodist-Scottish-
?-Alexander-m-29-Scotland-Presbyterian-Scottish-Farmer
PATTERSON-Lachlan-m-44-Scotland-Presbyterian-Scottish-Farmer
-Sarah-f-37-Germany-Presbyterian-German-
-Alexander-m-l0-N.S.-Presbyterian-Scottish-
-Margaret-f-8-N.B.-Presbyterian-Scottish-
-John-m-5-N.B.-Presbyterian-Scottish-
-Sarah-f-3-N.B.-Presbyterian-Scottish-
-Lachlan-m-2-N.B.-Presbyterian-Scottish-
PRICE-Alfred-m-41-N.B.-Free Christian Baptist-Irish-Farmer
-Sarah-f-35-N.B.-Free Christian Baptist-Irish-
-Gideon-m-13-N.B.-Free Christian Baptist-Irish-
-Charles-m-11-N.B.-Free Christian Baptist-Irish-
-Heber-m-9-N.B.-Free Christian Baptist-Irish-
-Roland-m-7-N.B.-Free Christian Baptist-Irish-
-Frank-m-5-N.B.-Free Christian Baptist-Irish-
-Annie-f-3-N.B.-Free Christian Baptist-Irish-
-Kelson-m-l0/12-N.B.-Free Christian Baptist-Irish-
RICKER-Robert-m-60-N.S.-Free Christian Baptist-French-Farmer
-Sarah-f-56-N.S.-Free Christian Baptist-English-
-Biron-m-25-N.S.-Free Christian Baptist-French-
-Whitfield-m-23-N.S.-Free Christian Baptist-French-
TOVEY-William-m-69-Ireland-Church of England-Irish-Farmer
-Sarah-f-65-Scotland-Presbyterian-Scottish-
-Elizabeth-f-30-N.B.-Church of England-Irish-
TWEEDIE-William-m-47-Scotland-Presbyterian/Church of Scotland-Scottish-Farmer
-Elizabeth-f-37-N.B.-Presbyterian/Church .of Scotland-Irish-
WHEATON-Eleazor-m-45-N.S.-Free Christian Baptist-English-Farmer
-Adelia-f-34-N.S.-Free Christian Baptist-English-

-Oscar-m-17-N.S.-Free Christian Baptist-English-Farmer
-Anabelle-f-16-N.S.-Free Christian Baptist-English-
-George-m-13-N.S.-Free Christian Baptist-English-
-Hubert-m-12-N.S.-Free Christian Baptist-English-
-Willie-m-7—Free Christian Baptist-English-
-Helen-f-6—Free Christian Baptist-English-
-Martha-f-3—Free Christian Baptist-English-
-Emma-f-4/12—Free Christian Baptist-English-
WILSON-James-m-73-Scotland-Presbyterian/Church of Scotland-Scottish-Farmer
-Elspet-f-69-Scotland-Presbyterian/Church of Scotland-Scottish-
-Alexander-m-26-Scotland-Presbyterian/Church of Scotland-Scottish-
-Charles-m-24-Scotland-Presbyterian/Church of Scotland-Scottish-
-Barbara-f-29-England-Presbyterian/Church of Scotland-Scottish-
-Hans-m-22-Scotland-Presbyterian/Church of Scotland-Scottish-
-Elsie-f-12-Scotland-Presbyterian/Church of Scotland-Scottish-
WHITEHOUSE-Jacob-m-46-N.S.-Free Christian Baptist-English-Farmer
-Susan-f-42-N.S.-Free Christian Baptist-English-
-Ada-f-22-N.S.-Free Christian Baptist-English-
-James-m-20-N.S.-Free Christian Baptist-English-Farmer
-Theolia-f-16-N.S.-Free Christian Baptist-English-
-Morris-m-14-N.S.-Free Christian Baptist-English-
-Helen-f-12-N.S.-Free Christian Baptist-English-
-Adeline-f-7—Free Christian Baptist-English-
-Mary-f-6-N.B.-Free Christian Baptist-English-
-Armina-f-3-N.B.-Free Christian Baptist-English-
-Jacob-m-1/12-N.B.-Free Christian Baptist-English-
WHITEHOUSE-Joseph-m-57-N.S.-Free Christian Baptist-English-Farmer
-Susanah-f-51-N.S.-Free Christian Baptist-English-
-Marcy-f-22-N.S.-Free Christian Baptist-English-
-Prince-m-21-N.S.-Free Christian Baptist-English-Farmer

-Delphy-f-14-N.S.-Free Christian Baptist-English-
-Thomas-m-12-N.S.-Free Christian Baptist-English-
-Agnes-f-10-N.S.-Free Christian Baptist-English-

Community and Family Origins of Alfred and Lucretia

Having described Alfred Corey's arrival as a homesteader in Knowlesville, and having listed many other homesteaders who might have been his neighbours, we now go back a little way in history. We inquire whence came this man of venture, courage and pioneering perseverance? We gather a few glimpses of the life of Alfred and Lucretia before they came to Knowlesville.

The most vivid and the most extensive of preserved memories of our grandparents come from their granddaughter, Erma Corey Shaw. Here is a paraphrase of recollections she shared:

> "When I was growing up with my grandparents, Alfred and Lucretia Corey in Knowlesville, New Brunswick, Canada, I heard them make frequent mention of places in Queens County — New Canaan, Canaan River, Canaan Forks, and Forkstream; and places in Kings County — Havelock, Head of Millstream, Cornhill, Anagance, Apohaqui, Kierstead Mountain, and Cole's Island."

The memories of New Canaan and Havelock area that Alfred Corey shared with his granddaughter, Erma, and that she kept alive, have made us aware that New Canaan and surrounding area was Grandfather's first home. We can affirm that Alfred Elisha Corey was born and grew up in the New Canaan/Havelock region of New Brunswick. Alfred's origin in that region is substantiated by other data, such as the census records cited below. The place of his birth and youth is clearly established; the specifics of his connection with the Coreys of New Canaan, however, are not so clear.

Do we need to search out our connection with the Coreys of New Canaan? Strictly speaking, no, especially considering that the purpose of this book is not to trace our ancestry back in history. Rather it is to move forward, telling the story of Alfred Corey, describing his remarkable life for his many descendants and telling their interesting stories. Nevertheless, there are some good reasons compelling us, the descendants of Alfred Corey, to make some attempt to answer questions about how we connect with other branches of the extensive Corey family.

One reason is because some of us, especially in New Brunswick, are often asked, "Are you related to Coreys of ...., various areas of New Brunswick. More specifically, I and others of Alfred's descendants have often been asked about our relationship with the Coreys of New Canaan and vicinity.

Now there is another compelling reason for us to make attempts to clarify our origins and our connections with other Corey branches. A new book, "<u>Our Corey Heritage</u>, the Descendants of Gideon Corey of New Canaan, New Brunswick," written by Dale T. Lahey of Guelph, Ontario, and Dana Ryder of Standish, Maine, was published in Guelph in 1997. Alfred Corey and his descendants are included in this book. We appreciate being included in that significant larger history of Coreys. I, the writer of this book, have collaborated with Dale Lahey, and have contributed extensive data on the genealogies and biographies of the Alfred line.

Having recognized reasons for attempting to establish Alfred's connection with the many families of Coreys who originated in and fanned out from the region of New Canaan, we must also recognize some difficulties. One difficulty is that Alfred himself seems not to have left many specific statements about his connections, except for mentioning a few names. Erma remembered very well that he spoke of Zebulon and Margaret Ann

Corey as a brother and a sister. We know now that they are children of Elisha Clarke Corey (17.......circa. 18??). I think he also mentioned Bridget as his mother's name. These clues point definitely to our connection with the family of Elisha Clarke Corey. Furthermore, Alfred's middle name is Elisha.

However, there are some difficulties in the way of placing Alfred in a specific and indisputable place in the family tree of Elisha Clarke Corey. I am trying to honestly recognize these difficulties; e.g. some lists of the children of Elisha and Bridget Corey do not include the name of Alfred. I cite, e.g: R.H. Corey, <u>Historical Sketch of the First Settlers of New Canaan</u>. This "sketch" has a section on Coreys, starting with Gideon Corey, a Loyalist who, on May 18, 1783, arrived in Parrtown, now Saint John, N.B., with his wife Abigail Clark. R.H. Corey's "sketch" tells us further: Gideon and Abigail Corey were among a group of Loyalists who came to New Brunswick from Rhode Island, a New England colony, following the close of the Revolutionary War, and who settled along the Saint John River at various places, e.g., Long Reach and Hampstead.

Gideon and Abigail Corey moved from the Saint John River, near Hampstead, to New Canaan about 1793. This "sketch"[2] states: "To this couple were born five sons and four daughters whose names are:

    Elisha Clark Corey, m. Bridget Wright
    Thomas Corey, m. Miss Wiggins
    Gardner Corey, m. Elizabeth Humphreys
    William Corey, m. Elizabeth McDonald
    Daniel, d. when a young man
    Abigail Corey, m. Stephen Ryder
    Hannah Corey, m. Edward Price
    Betsey Corey, m. John Humphreys

    Esther Corey, never married[3]

Monument in New Canaan Cemetery

R.H. Corey says further "The above Elias Clarke Corey (who must be intended for Elisha) had four sons and four daughters." He names only three sons: Zebulon, John and William. He does not mention Alfred. He names four daughters: Eliza, Sarah, Margaret and Rachel. He also omits Abigail, who is on other lists.

We recognize that Alfred has been given little mention in the records, and not a very definite place in the Corey family tree. This lack of recognition has left a vacuum into which speculation has moved to fill the void. Some persons related to the Coreys of New Canaan and region have sometimes told us stories about our origins. We didn't know whether to give credence to them. Recently discussions among some of Alfred's descendants, and research in connection with writing this book, has demanded that we make some inquiry into those stories. Our inquiry and research has brought no documentation to those stories. We have, therefore, decided that they lack sufficient evidence even to be mentioned.

We have chosen rather to focus on data rather than speculation. One reliable record is the New Brunswick census. The 1851 census for Studholm Parish, Kings Co., shows Alfred in the home of Rachel Perry, a daughter of Elisha Corey. Here we have printed the data for easier reading:

Here we have printed the data for easier reading:

	Sex	Relationship	Age
House Charles Perry	M.	H. husband	22
Rachel Perry	F.	W. wife	21
Prissuline Perry F.	D.	daughter	1
Alfred Corey	M.	Se. servant	10

Alfred Corey is recorded again in the 1861 census, Brunswick Parish, Queens County.

The ages recorded for Alfred in 1851 and 1861 agree exactly with other records of his age, and with family memories. Dale T. Lahey described Alfred's 1861 situation:

> "In the 1861 census, Alfred, his age given as 20, was living in New Canaan, in close association with several related families, including Sarah Ann Corey Clarke, daughter of Elisha; and Zebulon Corey, son of Elisha."

Citing these census records, and other data from his research, Dale T. Lahey concludes:

> "There is little doubt that Alfred belongs to the family of Elisha Clarke Corey, but there is

considerable speculation as to his parentage, stemming from the possibility that Elisha may have died as early as 1836.[4]

"However, from the first, Alfred was treated as Elisha's son. He was given Elisha's first name as his middle name. He later told his granddaughter Erma Corey Shaw that his mother's name was Bridget, and that he had a brother called Zebulon, and a sister called Margaret Ann. He appears in the 1851 Studholm Census, his age given as ten, living in the home of Rachel and Charles Perry, and Rachel was a daughter of Elisha Corey.....

"His earliest associations, then, are with Elisha's family: Bridget, Rachel, Sarah Ann, Margaret, Zebulon, and Margaret Ann. Certainly Elisha Corey's family raised the boy, treated him as a son and brother, and generally took responsibility for him as a child.

"Speculation about Alfred's parentage is pointless and leads nowhere. The facts themselves speak simply enough — Alfred was born a Corey, lived as a Corey, died as a Corey. His descendants proudly bear the name of Corey. That is enough."[5]

Alfred Corey married at age 21, a local girl, Lucretia Kierstead, age 20. Lucretia was tenth of thirteen children born to David and Sarah Blakney Kierstead. Lucretia must have left home early. In the 1861 census of Brunswick Parish, Kings Co., she is listed in the household (#42), of James and Phoebe Cromwell. She is listed: "Kierstead, Lucretia, Servant, age 17, Free Baptist."

Alfred Elisha Corey who lived in Queens and Kings Counties, born February 13, 1841, and Eloma Lucretia

Kierstead of Kierstead Mountain, Kings Co., born January 13, 1842 were married on December 12, 1862.

Dale T. Lahey has stated: "Alfred Corey married Eloma Lucretia Kierstead. She was of Kierstead Mountain, Kings County, and the marriage probably took place there. This again places Alfred in the general vicinity of New Canaan-Havelock."[6] Dates are well established by granddaughter, Erma and others, by oral history and family records.

After their marriage they must have lived in several places in both Kings and Queens Counties. Perhaps they moved to wherever work was available. In these counties four children were born: Marintha, who lived only one year; and Mina, Alma and Charles.[7] The child of whom most memory is preserved was their first son, born July 26, 1868. They named him Charles Haddon Spurgeon Corey, after the Baptist orator, Charles Haddon Spurgeon, who was then preaching in Newington Tabernacle, England, and whose fame had spread over the English-speaking world.

> ".....Charles Haddon Spurgeon was heard, during his ministry, by millions of men and women, who found in him the chief incitement of their lives to virtue and charity, to the patient endurance of pain, and to steadfast faith in God and immortality. The words he uttered week after week in that Newington Tabernacle, built especially to seat the large and enthusiastic crowds that flocked each Sabbath to hear him, were taken down and printed and scattered broadcast over the English-speaking world to serve as moral and religious nourishment to countless homes in England and America."[8]

Naming their first son after the great spiritual leader was

probably an indication of how attuned Alfred and Lucretia were to what was happening in the world. Living in an obscure place in New Brunswick, they apparently did not miss news of the great preacher in London. It appears also to be an indication of their religious commitment.

Sometime in the two-year period following the birth of Charles, Alfred and Lucretia and their three eldest children moved to Maine. The family lived in Houlton and Hodgdon. They apparently made lasting friendships though their sojourn in Maine was brief. Two children were born in Maine: Judson Albert, August 1, 1870, and Ida May, b. May 26, 1872. Sometime after the birth of Ida, Alfred and Lucretia Corey, with their children then numbering five, returned to New Brunswick, Canada. The family lived in Woodstock, N.B., for a short time, either before going to Maine or immediately on returning to New Brunswick.

Sometime between 1872 and 1874, the Corey family began homesteading in the newly opened settlement of Knowlesville, New Brunswick. We can only establish the family's move to Knowlesville as sometime between the birth of Ida, 1872, and the birth of Sadie, on February 7, 1875. Sadie Louise was the first of the Corey children born in Knowlesville. Considering Sadie's birth date in February, it is highly unlikely that their move could have been later than the summer of 1874.

In Knowlesville, after building a log house, Alfred Corey's next task was to cut down more trees and clear enough land to begin pioneer farming, i.e., growing a garden and some small crops. A reliable crop was green beans. They planted beans on Ida's birthday, May 26th, and began harvesting them on Charles' birthday, July 26th. This became a yearly ritual.[9]

With hard work and simple joys the Corey Homestead was established. It was to remain the home of the Coreys for almost half a century. In that home the family increased. Besides Sadie, four children were born in Knowlesville: Ira

Thomas, March 3, 1877; Alberta, March 11, 1879; Laversa, July 1, 1882, and Erminnie, February 23, 1885. The last born, Erminnie, like the first born, only survived about one year.

New Church

Before the birth of their last two children, Alfred and Lucretia took part in the birth of a new church! The seminal meeting took place in January 1880 when a group, mostly couples, from Knowlesville and neighbouring communities, gathered at the home of Mr. and Mrs. Alfred Price, in Knowlesville. Under the leadership of Rev. Amos H. Hayward, the group "organized the Knowlesville and Glassville Baptist Church.....consisting of the following persons," as charter members:

>Mrs. James Armstrong
>Robert and Mrs. McElhinney
>Alfred and Lucretia Corey
>Mrs. Murdock McKenzie
>James Dickey
>Alfred and Mrs. Price
>Morris and Abigail Hobbs
>Edward H. and Mrs. Smith
>James and Mrs. Humphrey
>Phoebe Smith
>Mrs. Angus McDermid
>"17 in all"
>Edward H. Smith was chosen deacon
>and Alfred Price, clerk.[10]

On June 25, 1882, they organized a "Sabbath School." Attendance is recorded for five Sundays in July, and two in August. Highest number of "scholars" was 25; the lowest was 11. Alfred Corey was a trustee when, on September 20, 1891, the congregation dedicated a new house of worship under the name, Highlands Baptist Church.

Though Lucretia and Alfred must have been very busy at home with clearing land and growing food, and with the nurturing of their children, they took time not only for church involvement but also for other community participation.

Temperance Lodge

On October 1, 1886 a "Lodge of Good Templars" was organized at a meeting in "F. B. Church", i.e. Free Baptist Church in Knowlesville. Among the 28 charter members were: Mr. and Mrs. Alfred Corey and three of their children: Alma, Ida and Charles; also Lucretia Corey's sister-in-law, Mrs. John Kierstead. Alfred was elected chaplain; Ida was elected "L.H.S." Alfred was also appointed by the Chief Templar to two committees: finance; and care of the sick. Judson Corey must have also joined at an early meeting. On November 20, 1886, he was named on a "committee of entertainment for next meeting". On November 27, 1886, Judson Corey and Mrs. Corey, his mother, were named to opposite sides for the next meeting's debate: "Resolved that there is more true enjoyment in pursuit than in possession." The debate must have been memorable half a century later. James Hobbs was still quoting the resolution as a rationalization for remaining single.

Other debates indicate much fun, e.g., the subject of a later debate:

> "Resolved that a dirty good-natured woman is preferable to a clean cross one."[11]

Apparently the promotion of temperance was carried out with much fun, and also with much social interchange.

The foregoing accounts of participation in the religious

and social life of the community seem to suggest that Alfred must have been at home in Knowlesville a significant portion of the time. Also later events seem to indicate that Alfred soon became valued and appreciated in the community in many practical ways. However there is another aspect of his work life.

For economic reasons he was periodically absent from the farm, sometimes quite far from home. There was very little cash income connected with pioneer homesteading, hence, Alfred sought seasonal employment outside the community. One seasonal job he had was in the hemlock bark industry at Forest City, near the border of Maine. They cut down hemlock trees and harvested the bark to be used in tanneries. It appears Alfred started that work while the family lived in Woodstock, which is much nearer to Forest City, and continued it periodically, after they moved to Knowlesville.[12]

Many of the seasonal jobs were near enough to be reached by walking. Erma said that Grandpa had no hesitation about walking several miles. One job, however, was at too great a distance to be reached by foot. One summer Alfred went to Ontario looking for work. He mentioned landing in Toronto, presumably by train. Evidently, before leaving New Brunswick he had worked on the building of a bridge, and had not waited to receive his pay, but hoped Lucretia would receive it. Here is his letter, long preserved by Erma:

Muskoka   August 10 (year not stated)

Missis Corey
     I set down to let you know where I am. I am at Mr. Cockfield today. I landed in Toronto Monday, the 4th.
     I have been a cruising this week. I have not found anything better than New Brunswick. Do not sell anything until you hear from me

again. I leave here tomorrow. Do not write —- I send you another letter in a few days. Let me know how you are getting along and if you got the money from the Bridge yet. I could write a lot more but dinner is almost ready. No more at present.

    I remain your affectionate husband,
            Alfred Corey

P.S. I think I will be home this fall. I do not like this place.

  The letter leaves us wondering if the family had considered the possibility of moving to Ontario if he had found rewarding work: ("Do not sell anything...") Apparently he did not see the prospect of a lasting job, at least that he liked. Part of the summer and fall, it appears, were long enough to be there: "I will be home this fall." One point is clear. He much preferred New Brunswick.

Sheriff

  We have a story about one job that Alfred had in his own neighbourhood. It must have been predicated on the expectation that he could usually be found at home or not far away. Grandpa served as sheriff from 1900 - 1905. This engagement in the enforcement of law and order was probably not very remunerative. Erma thought he was paid only when he was called on a case. However, it indicates Alfred's versatility and also that he apparently had a natural ability to deal with people.

  One episode in his line of duty was treasured by the family and told with delight especially by his son, Judson A. Corey:

  Father was called to a scene of domestic violence. The

husband had reportedly stabbed his wife in the abdomen. Covering the stab wound with her hand, and holding her entrails in, she had run to the house of a neighbour who sent for the Sheriff. When Sheriff Corey arrived at the family home, the accused was sitting waving the blood-red knife. Father nonchalantly chose a chair facing him, quietly relaxed, took his pipe and his plug of tobacco from his pocket, and felt his pockets for his jack knife. Not finding it, he said to the offender, "Let me have your knife to cut my tobacco." Without hesitation he handed over the knife. Alfred folded it and put it in his pocket. Then he said to the accused, "Now I want you to come quietly with me." He climbed into the buggy beside Alfred. They drove quietly away together.

Skills and Occupations

Though Alfred apparently had no more than elementary school learning, he was quick to learn practical skills. He became versatile and pursued a variety of extra jobs in the community and further away to try to provide a large and growing family with some extras beyond the produce of the farm. Perhaps Alfred wanted for his children more education than he had opportunity to receive. Thanks to both Alfred and Lucretia for basic provisions and good parenting, their children all received a basic education at the local school. Thanks also to the community for providing the school.

The first school building in central Knowlesville was completed in 1874, the probable year of the arrival of the Corey family. Over the last two decades of the 19th century all nine of the Corey children attended that school, less than a mile from their home. Their names are recorded in the school census from 1878 - 1897.[13]

Only this brief data have we found recorded of the Coreys in Knowlesville School. However, we also have two oral stories. Ira liked to tell his boys about his school days. Two episodes he related repeatedly to his youngsters. The first provides a peek through a bullet hole into the school. It also illustrates that the school was not without some excitement, and the teacher not without some discipline problems.

It seems that the big boys went to school in winter when there wasn't so much work on the farms. One winter they must have started giving the teacher an unusually hard time. He decided to take drastic measures. One morning he pulled two revolvers out of his desk. He laid one at this end and one at that end of his desktop. Then he picked up one of them and fired a thunderous shot right through the west wall above the heads of the pupils. Then followed silence and a trouble-free time for the teacher.

As a youngster, I was both spellbound and flabbergasted by that story, knowing that it would not be an acceptable mode of keeping order. However it also seemed to indicate that the authority of the teacher was to be recognized. In retrospect it also seems to indicate that a tendency toward unruliness is not entirely new.

That story may suggest that at times the big boys put it over on the teacher. The second story, in contrast, seems to illustrate that the teacher outwitted the boys, and also that he was not without some humour and that he had good rapport.

One afternoon he gave them a question: If ten bushels of oats came to $30.00, what would a 700-lb hog come to? If a boy got the answer he was to write it on his slate and show it to the teacher without disclosing it to the others. He would then be allowed to go home. Some boys filled both sides of their slates with figures and were still very frustrated in not arriving at the answer: The hog would come to the trough. The teacher was Ed Jewett. He was at the school in 1894 and 1895.[14] My father would have been only aged seven and eight in those years, too young, probably, to have been one of the boys in that episode. Father seemed glad to have the story end with the teacher the winner. Maybe the story was intended as a lesson for us in authority.

It seems that Ed Jewett boarded with the Coreys and Father seemed to like him a lot. Through him he also learned a lesson about guns that he never ceased to emphasize. Repeatedly he told us, "Never point a gun at anybody even if it is empty." Once he disclosed the story behind that injunction. In a play episode he had chased the teacher with a .22 calibre rifle until he took refuge in his bedroom and sat on his bed. Thinking the rifle was empty, Father aimed it. The teacher shouted, "Oh Ira, don't shoot," and threw himself down flat on the bed. Ira pulled the trigger and a bullet went in the wall where Ed's head would have been if he hadn't flung himself down. The lesson was unforgettable: — "Never point a gun, even a toy gun, at anybody."

Alfred and Lucretia's youngsters received from the Knowlesville School a basic education that fitted them for a self-supporting life. What would they do then? Could they remain on the farm or at least in the community that had nurtured them? When not away on a seasonal job Alfred worked hard to make the most of pioneer farming. This progressed with much hard work; we shall learn more about it in Chapter III.

Knowlesville

The community progressed in many ways in the last four decades of the 19th century. For example, a market opened in Glassville offering cash income for Knowlesville farm families. The Dispatch, in June 1895, reported, "Most people in Knowlesville are selling their milk to the cheese factory in Glassville." Farmers put their milk in large cans that held several gallons. A team and wagon went from farm to farm collecting the milk. Elmer LaPage still has one of the cans.[15]

However, while there was progress in farming it seems there was still little remunerative employment for young men and even less for young single women. Hence, a custom developed of young people seeking work outside the community. All too soon Lucretia and Alfred had to watch their offspring, soon after leaving school, begin, one by one, to leave home in search of work. All nine of their children at some point in early life, went to New England to seek employment. However it seems there was never a "goodbye" but only a "so-long". Alfred and Lucretia kept an open door policy and a welcome mat. Their children knew they could return again and again. A home was still there for them when they needed one.

1   J.M. Corey, The Story of Knowlesville, p. 7, 25

2   Rowland H. Corey, op.cit., May 1947, Forward, and p.16f.

3   Elsewhere this name is replaced by Elizabeth

4   Stanley Corey, in a letter to Erma Shaw, Sept. 18, 1979, stated, "Elisha Clark Corey was supposed to have died about 1836....Of course the approximate date of death may be wrong."

5   Lahey, Dale T., and Ryder, Dana C., Our Corey Heritage, (Guelph, Ontario: Datel Publishing, 1997), p.43.

6   Ibid., p.44

7   See The Story of Knowlesville, p. 36 ff.

8   Orations of British Orators, Revised edition, Vol. II (New York and London: The Co-operative Publication Society) Revised Edition, Vol.II, p. 392.

9   Erma Corey Shaw

10   Aberdeen Baptist Church, loose pp.#1 to 3; also bound record book, p.43, and p.18. More in Chapters III and IV.

11 Record book, p. 207

12 From granddaughter, Erma

13 See, <u>The Story of Knowlesville</u>, p. 89.

14 Ibid., p.88

15 <u>Ibid</u>., p. 98; See also, <u>A History of the Glassville Settlement</u>, p. 174.

CHAPTER II

SCATTERING OF THE COREY FAMILY

Lucretia had often watched Alfred depart from Knowlesville for jobs afield, in pursuit of a little cash to bring home for a growing family. As their children matured they had to watch them also go afield to obtain employment. However, in their departures from home it was not only the pattern of their father that they were following. There was an established custom of young people of Knowlesville and vicinity leaving New Brunswick for employment, at least temporarily:

> "It appears that almost from the beginning of the community in the 1860's and lasting throughout most of the remainder of the century, some residents of Knowlesville, especially young women, went to Massachusetts for seasonal employment, especially in winter...Some Knowlesville families still treasure photographs of family members bearing the name of a studio in Lowell or Boston."[1]

For the Coreys, as for neighbouring families, scattering of the youth began almost as soon as they were mature enough to seek employment.

Charles H.S. Corey

Of the Corey siblings, perhaps the earliest to go to Maine to work was Charles. He is the one of whose sojourn in Maine we have the earliest mention.

Work and social life in Lewiston proved to be favourable

for Charles. There, he joined a music group that gathered, evenings, at a hotel to play their instruments, for entertainment. Charles played the fiddle.

At the hotel was another New Brunswicker, a girl from Campobello Island named Elizabeth Thurber. She was an employee. Thus in a happy happenstance Charles and Elizabeth met. On November 10, 1891, Charles and Elizabeth were married in Lewiston by Rev. S.A. Blaisdell. Witnesses were Miss Helen Blaisdell and Miss Genie Wilbur. Years later, Elizabeth told her children and grandchildren, "The first time I saw him he was playing the fiddle."[2]

Though they were apparently meaningfully involved in Lewiston, Charles and Elizabeth came back to New Brunswick by 1896. Their first son, Ivan, was born in Knowlesville on February 29, 1896.[3]

Judson A. Corey

Judson Albert Corey also went to Maine sometime in the 1890's. Perhaps he went while his brother Charles was still there. There are indications that Judson A. Corey lived and worked in Maine for some years during the 1890's. Some of his work was in the logging industry.[4] He also worked in a shoe factory in Lewiston.

As Lewiston had been for Charles a happy meeting place, so it proved to be for his brother also. There Judson met Alice Howlett, who was also from New Brunswick, whence she had earlier immigrated from England. Alice and Judson were married in Lewiston about 1899.[5]

Apparently the first sojourn of Judson and Alice in Maine continued until after their first two children were born. Their first daughter, Alberta Lois, was born there on December 20, 1900, and their first son, Earle Howlett, on February 27, 1902. They returned to New Brunswick before the birth of their third child, Annie. She was born May 25, 1903, at the home of Judson's sister, Ida McBrine, in Knowlesville.

Soon after the birth of Annie the family returned to Maine. That decision was not simply in pursuit of work. There was another definite purpose — to prepare for the Christian ministry.[6]

In later years my father, Ira, spoke in admiration of his brother's preparation for the ministry: "Jud worked in the day time, and attended night school." He didn't tell us then how intimately he was acquainted with his brother's work and study. In 1903 Ira also went to Maine. That was early in his first marriage, i.e., to Emily Graham. It is a story of family caring.

Soon after the birth of their daughter, Emily began to suffer from TB. Ira was advised to seek a more favourable climate for Emily, his bride of one year. In an effort to nurture Emily's health, the couple, with their baby, went to Lewiston, Maine, in 1903 and lived at the home of Ira's brother, Judson A. Corey. It must have been soon after Judson and Alice returned to Maine, in 1903, that they were joined by Ira and Emily

Laversa's Venture

By 1903 Laversa Corey, youngest sister of Judson and Ira, was also in Lewiston. She may have arrived before Ira and Emily. Thus Lewiston became a gathering point for Coreys. Three siblings were there at the same time, each with a personal reason/purpose in coming.

More than half a century later, in 1957, the writer was on a visit to Hagerstown with Aunt Laversa and some of her family. Then she told me what brought her to Lewiston: "There was no work for young women in Knowlesville. When I left home I first went to Houlton, Maine. After working there for a while, I went to Lewiston, where my brother Judson A. Corey and family were living."[7]

Laversa made no mention of Ira in Lewiston or Auburn that the writer can recall. This may suggest that Laversa arrived there before Ira. A letter from Emily Corey written in Auburn, Maine, and addressed to her mother-in-law, Lucretia Corey, in Knowlesville, confirms the presence of the three Corey siblings in Auburn.

The letter says, in part:

> "Jud and Ira are both...well as I guess Laversa is too. I saw her yesterday to Church. She was looking fine. Ira and I were over to their room one evening last week. Luther was.....sick that night but he is alright now."[8]

Emily's letter is not dated but her report of the visit to Laversa and Luther indicates that it was after their marriage. Laversa Corey and Luther Garns were married in Auburn, Maine, on December 14, 1903[9]. Another clue to the date is in Emily's description of the babies: "No, the babies don't either one of them creep yet but Alice's baby (Annie, same age as Erma) sits alone. Mine will sit a little while but not so I can leave her sitting alone." This indicates babies under one year. Erma was one year old in May 1904. The probable date of the letter is winter of 1904.

It appears that the stay of Ira, Emily and Erma in Auburn/Lewiston was only a year or less. Here is Erma's account:

> "In the spring of 1904, following one winter in Lewiston, Maine, my father took my mother and me to Campobello Island, having been advised that the climate there might be more favourable to my mother's failing health. All three of us stayed with my Uncle Charles and Aunt Elizabeth Corey who were, at that time, keep-

ing the lighthouse. At Head Harbour Lighthouse my mother died of tuberculosis, June 14, 1904."[10]

The strength of family ties is demonstrated in these and other instances of hospitality to one another.

Judson and Alice

Judson and Alice Corey lived in Maine for several years. Their fourth child, Esther Lucretia, was born in Maine on February 10, 1905. Sometime between the birth of Esther and their next child, Alfred, the family went to Campobello. They too were seeking a more favourable climate. Judson A. Corey had double pleurisy, followed by lung surgery, in Auburn/Lewiston. Then he came up to Campobello to recover. Again we see the strength of family ties. They stayed with Aunt Lizzie and Uncle Charles Corey in their house near the Head Harbour light. Their fifth child, Alfred, was born on Campobello, November 17, 1906.

We don't know how long the J.A. Corey family stayed on Campobello. We know they returned to Maine. Their next child, David, was born in Auburn, June 30, 1908.

The sojourn in Auburn/Lewiston was long remembered by family members. The writer recalls a trip he and Marion Corey made on September 28, 1959 from Gardner, Massachusetts to New Brunswick. Annie Haines was a passenger with us as far as Bangor, Maine. As we passed through Lewiston, Annie said, "There is the shoe factory where my father worked." The Judson A. Corey family remained in Maine until spring of 1910 when they returned to Knowlesville, N.B.[11] Thus the three sons all returned to their native province.

All six daughters of Alfred and Lucretia Corey, at some time, also worked in the U.S.A. The three youngest, Sadie, Alberta and Laversa, all married in the U.S.A. and became per-

Judson A. and Alice Corey with Earle, Alberta, Annie and Esther in Lewiston, c.1905

manent residents. The three eldest, Mina, Alma and Ida, have left us few references to their work in the U.S.A. We have only Erma's memory:

> "Years later Aunt Mina told me the instruction she received on leaving home: 'Don't speak to strangers. Don't take candy from strangers; it might contain a pill. Don't go out on streets alone."

This instruction was from a woman, apparently of travel experience. It was intended to safeguard against "the white slave trade".

The three eldest daughters, apparently after only short sojourns in the U.S.A., returned to New Brunswick, married, and settled close to home. All nine children of Alfred and Lucretia married.

1   J.M. Corey, The Story of Knowlesville, p. 98.

2   Story from Lalia Morehouse, granddaughter. She still has the marriage certificate.

3   Lalia says this birthplace was family knowledge.

4   See story in Chapter XI

5   See Chapter XI

6   See Chapter XI

7   See also The Story of Knowlesville, p. 174

8   Emily was the mother of Erma Corey Shaw. The letter was preserved and treasured by Erma for most of her lifetime.

9   Miriam Garns, The Garns Family Roots, 1987. "Marriage Record of Luther W. Garns at Auburn, Maine", p.43.

10   The story is expanded in Chapter X

11   The story continues in Chapter IV

CHAPTER III

"CARRY ME BACK" TO:

Knowlesville — a home, a family, a pioneer farm
Esdraelon - waterwheels, mills and a store
Highlands - a church and its people

In early summer, 1904, a one-year old girl named Erma was carried to Knowlesville by her father, Ira Corey, and carried into the home of her grandparents, Alfred and Lucretia Corey, then ages 63 and 62. Almost from the time of her birth the little girl had been on the move, as we learned from the stories of the sojourns of Ira and Emily in Chapter II. The sad story of the loss of her mother is related in Chapter II. Later, Erma summarized it:

"Tuberculosis claimed the life of my mother on Campobello Island, June 14, 1904."

Thus the baby girl was left in need of a home and loving care. It was a case of mutual need. The nine children of Alfred and Lucretia had scattered quite early in life — some far away.
Interestingly, Erma arrived at the home of Alfred and Lucretia the year following the departure from home of their youngest, Laversa. She lived at home quite a while after the rest had gone. By 1903 she was working in Maine.[1] When their last child had departed quietness descended upon their home. Then the poet Gray's memorable lines could perhaps have described the situation of Lucretia and Alfred:

"For them no more the blazing hearth shall burn,
Or busy housewife ply her evening care:
No children run to lisp their sire's return,

Or climb his knees the envied kiss to share."2

However, Alfred and Lucretia were not alone for very long. The period of calm and quiet was short. Soon they experienced again the joy of a running child.

The story of Erma's coming into the care of her grandparents in Knowlesville is a mixture of loss and gain, of pathos and pleasure, of tragedy and triumph, of orphanage and warm, affectionate, care. Erma's feelings could be paraphrased:

"Although I was half-orphaned when I was only three weeks past one year old, I never felt unwanted. My father, Ira, soon found a home for me."

The story of the loss of her mother was explained to Erma as soon as she was old enough to comprehend. A loss was transformed into warm and positive memories — memories of always being wanted and appreciated. Eighty-eight years after her arrival in Knowlesville, Erma shared those precious memories with the writer as contributions for this book. One of her memories was an image of her grandparents' home in Knowlesville. When the baby Erma arrived Alfred and Lucretia were living in a frame house, still quite new. It had been built to replace their earlier home, a log house that Alfred had built when the Corey family arrived in Knowlesville. The log house had sheltered them all the while their children were growing up. Sometime after 1889, the year their second daughter, Alma, married, they had the new frame house built. It stood on the lower side of the road, i.e., the opposite side from the old log house.

The plans for the frame house were drawn by James Miller, Sr., husband of Alma. "Grandma said, 'Jim Miller framed this house'." We can speculate that the lumber for the frame house and barn came from Esdraelon. Vella Scott said that the Gillmor woodworking factory supplied all doors, windows and frames for the area.

Ironically, "By the time the new house was built most of the family were gone. Only two girls were left: Berta and Laversa. From her remarkable memory, which stretched from

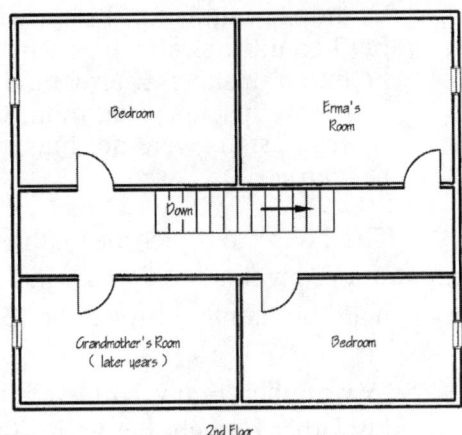

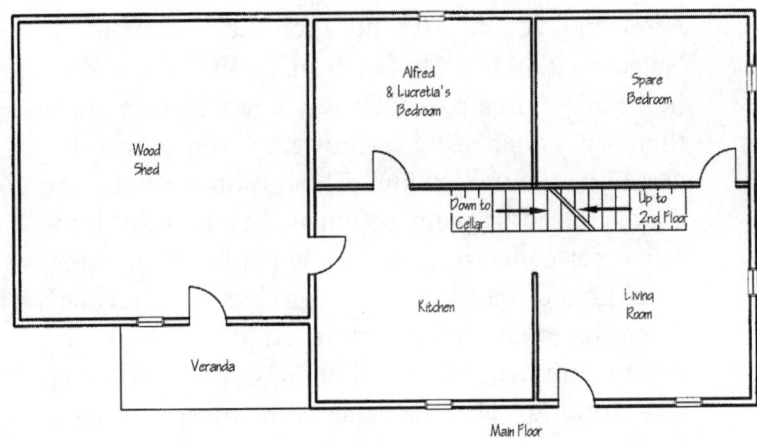

Alfred & Lucretia Corey's Homestead
Knowlesville, NB

early childhood past her 90th birthday, Erma described her grandparents' frame house. From her description we have drawn a floor plan.

> "The house had two bedrooms on the first floor. One was off the living room. It was a spare bedroom. The other was off the kitchen. Grandma and Grandpa occupied it. I slept with them until I was so big I couldn't sleep with them anymore. Then I had a bedroom upstairs. Later Grandma also moved to a bedroom upstairs. That room was finished. The other rooms upstairs were not finished until after my father re-married."

The house to which her father brought her at age one became more precious to Erma when she grew old enough to comprehend her family history. She recalled:

> "My mother, Emily, had lived in that house, briefly. My father brought her there as a bride in July 1902. They lived there until December, when she finished her school year in Armond; then they moved to Nackawick, N.B.[3] My father made that house his home again, in a part-time way when he brought me there right after he was widowed. Coming back home was quite natural for him. Though his early life was characterized by many sojourns; he never did leave home permanently. However, when he brought me there he did not then move in to live there regularly. From that point he often pursued jobs around the region, and hence boarded in Glassville or wherever he was working. Thus he came home mostly on visits, and I soon became attached to my grandparents."

A Memorable Evening; A Parting

"One evening my father spent with me and my grandparents at the Corey home in Knowlesville, I vividly remember, though I was then two months short of three years old. It was the eve of my father's departure for Western Canada in March 1906. At the fireside in the Corey homestead sat Grandma and Grandpa holding me on his lap. Across the room sat my father, Ira. He tried to coax me to come to his knee. I clung to Grandpa. Early next morning Grandpa hitched his mare, Bess, to his sleigh and drove my father, with one suitcase, to the Ricker farm. Byron and son Wilmot had owned two farms in the neighbourhood where Roy Hemphill and Edmund Hemphill currently live. The Rickers had sold their farms to James Hobbs and Fred Hemphill and were moving to Alliance, Alberta. Ira Corey accompanied the Ricker families. They went by long sled to Hartland Station where they put horses and belongings in boxcars. They rode the train to Alberta. There Ira worked on their farm for at least one spring and summer.[4]. My father's return from Western Canada in October 1908 was a sweet homecoming. Again, however, his stay at home with my grandparents and me was short. Soon he resumed his pattern of working and boarding in other neighbourhoods. Hence my attachment to my grandparents held strongly."

Little girl living with grandparents on their pioneer farm in Knowlesville was mutually beneficial. Erma gladdened their old age; they gave her warmth and affection, which filled a great need in her life and translated into appreciation and treasured memories. That affection for Erma was also expressed by her aunts and uncles and cousins.

Relatives in the Neighbourhood

"Until I was 4 or 5 years old, my aunt, Ida McBrine and family lived on the farm next to my grandfather's, on the south side. We often visited them in the evenings. A fond memory I have is of my grandfather carrying me pick-a-back when I was too sleepy to walk home from Aunt Ida's."

The home life and the visits with relatives added to Erma's treasured memories. So did her observations of her grandfather at work in the fields:

"I remember some of my grandfather's earliest farm work with little machinery. In the field between the highway and the Coldstream, he sowed buckwheat. Carrying the seed grain in a basket hung from his shoulder, he scattered it by handful as he crossed the field. To keep his crossings straight and at regular intervals, he stuck a pole in the ground at each side of the field. He hung a white flag to each pole. These were guideposts. When he reached the other side of the field he moved the pole the width of the next strip to be seeded. He also sowed oats and wheat."

After seed time, Grandpa cut his hay — in early days, by hand. Before I grew up he had a mowing machine, pulled by his team of horses. In late August and September Grandpa harvested his grain: oats, buckwheat and wheat. In his time, there were no binders, or dump reapers; combines were not invented until long after. He cut all his grain with a scythe.

Harvesting buckwheat required special care. The kernels attached so delicately to the stalks that they would fall off with a slight jar. Grandpa cut it with a hand scythe to which was attached a cradle to catch the falling stalks. If they were allowed to fall to the ground, the kernels would fall off and be lost in the soil. As an added measure to prevent kernels falling, he cut the buckwheat when it was wet with early morning dew. After the bunches of cut grain dried he lifted them carefully onto his wagon. A load cover in the bottom of the rack caught falling kernels. Grandpa thrashed all his grain with a flail. Thus he separated the kernels from the straw and chaff. He stored the grain in his granary. He raked up much of the straw and stored it in his barn for bedding, i.e., litter for all the farm animals.

Some of the straw, however, went to a much loftier purpose, thanks to a special skill possessed by Grandma. After Grandpa cut the grain, and before he raked the straw, she went to the field and selected some choice straws to later make hats for herself and her daughters. For color she used a dye called copperice which had a blue tint.

Grain to Grist Mills

"After harvest Grandpa took his grain to the grist mills to be ground. In the early 1900's there were two grist mills within reach of Knowlesville: a buckwheat mill in Esdraelon, only about four miles away, and a wheat mill at Bristol, three times the distance or more. Both mills had interesting histories.

Esdraelon

Grandfather, Alfred Corey, on his way to Knowlesville as a settler about the year 1874, assuming that he followed a route up the Coldstream, must have been pleasantly greeted at one point by the sound of much activity and by pleasant aromas. The sound was from the turning of waterwheels, the hum of saws, and the grinding of millstones. The smell was of pine and spruce boards and cedar shingles. There on the bank of the Coldstream was a centre of industry — a village soon thereafter to be given the biblical name, Esdraelon. To Joseph Farley goes the credit for being the entrepreneur of the first mill on the Cold Stream, near its confluence with Hamilton Brook. T.C.L. Kechum wrote, "As early as 1860 a mill had been built by one Joseph N. Farley on the Coldstream...."[5]. Thus the mill had been built, or was being built, by the time of the land survey in the area afterwards called Knowlesville. The survey was in 1860.[6] Thus the first mill at Esdraelon predates the opening of the settlements of both Knowlesville and Glassville, both about 1861.

In the early 1860's Mr. Farley was joined by another ambitious man, Wellington Gillmor, a son of Arthur Hill Gillmor, a native of Ireland, who emigrated from Belfast to Machias, Maine, in 1786. Some of A.H. Gillmor's descendants came to Charlotte Co., N.B. where they "became involved in the lumber trade." Wellington Gillmor grew up in Charlotte County, then an area of logging, saw mills, shipbuilding, and export of lumber. He worked in sawmills and shipyards along the coast of the Bay of Fundy and up into Kent County. In Shediac he met and married Eliza Frances Smith, whose family was acquainted with the Hannington family.[7]

When Wellington Gillmore came to Farley Mills he was probably about age 45. The 1871 census lists him as then age 55. On that list are 10 children of Wellington and Lizzie ranging in age from 28 to 9.[8] The oldest, Caroline, is not listed. Was she perhaps already married to Daniel George Hannington? Most, or perhaps all of the Gillmore children must have been born before the family came to Esdraelon. For a time, Mr. Gillmor worked for and with Mr. Farley[9]."By 1863 Mr. Wellington Gillmor, from St. Stephen, was proprietor of the mill and making improvements on it."[10] He completed the sawmill and built a shingle mill, a woodworking factory and a gristmill, all driven by water wheels. Thus, there were, for a time, four water wheels on the Coldstream.[11] Mr. Gillmor's family became involved: e.g., Jethro Milbury, son-in-law, husband of Maude Gillmor, ran the woodworking factory,

Wellington Hannington, a grandson of Wellington Gillmor, ran a blacksmith shop.[12] In time, Gillmors also had a store at the foot of the hill, and a post office.

The village was originally called Farley Mills and was changed to Esdraelon. Who changed the name is not certain. Annie Dyer's research notes state: "The place was called Farley Mills until 1876, when Farley himself gave it the biblical name, Esdraelon." Belle Elliott stated: "As I understood it, the Gillmors chose the name Esdraelon from the Bible because it meant Beautiful Valley."[13] The place was also called Gilmor, for a time. I find that name, spelled thus, on a Road and Bridge Map published by the D.O.H. of New Brunswick.[14] The name has prevailed, at least for the road. My father, when supervising roadwork, frequently spoke of "the Gillmor Road". Now the name has become permanent by two road signs, one at Roy Hemphill's end of the road, the other at its juncture with the road from Windsor.

Wellington Gillmor had four sons: Charles, Edward, Alexander, and George. It is said that the three oldest brothers went to British Columbia and enterprised in lumber. George, the youngest, remained in Esdraelon and became the operator of the mills there.

About 1910 George expanded his business to Juniper where "he acquired cutting rights" and built another sawmill.[15] The road from Glassville then extended only as far as Biggar Ridge. George had a road built. He sent two teams of horses through, one driven by a Hartsgrove.[16] In the Juniper enterprise George Gillmor had a partner: George Foster, from Lansdowne. Paul Foster of Florenceville recalls stories from his mother and his father, Talmadge, who was a cousin of George Foster. They visited the camps at Juniper to fish, gather blueberries and enjoy close-up views of moose.

Gillmor and Foster remained only four years in the Juniper operation. In 1914 they sold their mill to Flemming and Gibson. The name "Foster", however, long remained in Juniper. Gordon Corey remembers the "Foster barn" where Flemmings stabled their horses and stored hay and oats. The Gillmor mills at Esdraelon were also sold. George Gillmor, like his brothers, moved to British Columbia.

About 1911, the gristmill was acquired by William McIntosh, who also purchased the Edward Gillmor house, near the end of the bridge at Esdraelon. William McIntosh also acquired the general store that stood at the foot of the hill in Esdraelon. He bought the store from George Foss who was married to Wellington Gillmor's daughter, Margaret. William McIntosh died in 1915. His widow, the former Mary Shaw, managed the mill for many years. Her brother, Dan Shaw, operated it the rest of his life.[17] The gristmill also had a wool carding machine.[18]

The Gillmor sawmill at Esdraelon and a large block of land were sold to Henry Smith, who employed two crews and thus operated the mill day and night, under water power, until 1922. Then a swelling flood on June 10th carried the mill on its platform, to the Crandlemire Bridge above Bannon. The flood was so strong that at Hartland it pushed the railway bridge about a foot. It also damaged Sayer's Mill. Undaunted, Henry Smith loaded the mill on a sloven wagon pulled by horses. He brought it back up to Esdraelon and set it up on the flat near the bridge to Gordonsville. That was in the fall of 1922. Mr. Smith acquired more land from Scott's at Esdraelon. He ran the mill with a steam engine until about 1927.[19]

Roy Hemphill dates the Smith mill operation by the dates of the milling developments of his father, Fred Hemphill. Roy said, "In 1923 Father was putting in a turning lathe for peeve stocks. In 1928 he added a sawmill. About that time Smith's mill ceased operating."

Henry Smith had a series of stationery engineers: Harry Campbell, father of Ford Campbell; Tom Morgan, Cecil

Whitehouse, and Eddy Speakman. Eddy was a young orphan boy brought from England by George Gillmor. Eddy began working for his board. Being too short to operate the saw levers, George built him a platform. Thus started a long career in milling for Eddy. Later he went to Saint John and took a course in stationery engineering. Then he worked for Flemming and Gibson in Juniper at the time Sandy Brown was also working there. Later Eddy was back in Esdraelon.[20]

The sawmill, shingle mill and woodworking factory in Esdraelon were relatively short-lived. The gristmill had a much longer life: beginning before my Grandfather came to Knowlesville, and lasting into the time of his grandsons and great grandsons. Over three or four generations of farmers of Knowlesville, around Glassville and Windsor — even as far away as Golden Ridge, took their grain to Esdraelon.

A trip to that mill with a load of buckwheat to be ground and oats to be mashed was a fun time for the boys. When the team pulled up to the unloading zone the boys helped lift the bags of grain from their wagon or sled onto the platform — a kind of a wharf. From there they lifted them onto a trolley. Rails ran from the platform to the mill, some yards away. The loaded trolley was pushed over the rails to the point where the bags could be poured into the hopper. The rails were not in the original mill design. The mill had been built conveniently over the dam. Later, a spring freshet cut a new channel and moved the stream so that a wagon or sled had to unload farther from the mill hopper.

The mill mashed oats to make them more digestible for livestock. It ground buckwheat kernels, separated the meal from the bran and discarded the hulls. When the writer was a teenager, Eddy Speakman, who was then operating the mill for Mrs. MacIntosh, found an ingenious use for the hulls. He rigged up a stove with a steel barrel above it. Slowly the barrel funnelled the hulls into the firebox. Thus the little hut was warmed. There, men waiting for their grist to be ground, steeped their tea and ate their lunches.

Before leaving the village, there was often a stop at the general store, then being run by Jimmie and Rose Bell. Mrs. MacIntosh had sold the store to them. Rose was a daughter of Ruth Gillmor Banks, and sister of Pearl Scott, Vella's mother.[21] At the store we might have one or more 100-lb bags of buckwheat meal to be applied to the cost of flour, sugar, molasses, lard, tea and kerosene. Jimmie also paid five cents, later ten cents, for a rabbit, which would buy a chocolate bar. He paid twenty-five cents for a calf hide. Then the whole party could have a treat. The rabbits went to fox farms; the hides to a tannery.

Esdraelon in History

The name Esdraelon, goes back several centuries B.C. Descriptions of the ancient Esdraelon, by Bible scholars, may perhaps give us some clues of why the name was given to our village of mills and of trade in grain and other commodities. The ancient Esdraelon was a plain or valley with the foothills of mountains sloping toward it. It was "well watered, fertile", and served as "a magnet to draw the interest" of its surrounding areas, including Galilee. It was "of sufficient extent and fertility to be the granary for the entire region."[22] Also see <u>The Abingdon Bible Commentary</u>, 1929, p. 55. Much of this applies to our Esdraelon. Though its fertility was in trees, rather than agriculture, it served as the granary in providing the milling of the grain, which was indeed essential to the lives of our parents and grandparents. Carleton County was called the Buckwheat County.

From the buckwheat meal my grandmother made pancakes; also buckwheat cakes for the children.[23] My mother made the same use of buckwheat meal; most families in the area did. She fried them, over a hot wood fire in the morning while the men and boys were milking, and often again at suppertime. Many families ate pancakes with molasses, or maple syrup or fried pork twice a day, morning and evening. Roy Hemphill said they sometimes had pancakes three times a day. Over about three generations the gristmill at Esdraelon supplied the tables of many families.

  Esdraelon served other needs also, far into the 20th century. For example, in the 20's Hartley Carle had a sawmill there, and in the early 30's Lewis Carle had a shingle mill there.[24] The gristmill and the store continued through changes in proprietors and operators into W.W.II and beyond. Roy Hemphill remembers shopping and buying gasoline there during the wartime rationing. Mrs. Edward Scott who took over the store from her sister, Rose Bell, was obliging in allowing them to get gas and bring the coupon on the next trip. Freddy Scott worked with his mother in the store.

  The last proprietor of the store was Bud Craig of Hartland who operated it for a short while after W.W.II. The last proprietor of the gristmill was Raymond Dickinson. He acquired it soon after W.W.II. He changed from waterpower to a diesel engine. The decline of the gristmill, it seems, was related to the change in both crop and diet. The local farmers stopped growing buckwheat. It required a very fertile piece of ground. Some said it depleted the soil. The families discontinued eating pancakes, except for special occasions.

  The last man to hammer red-hot iron on the anvil at Esdraelon was Frank, son of Wellington Hannington. The blacksmith shop fell into ruin. The store burned. The millstones that had, for many years, turned in opposite directions crushing grain between them, stopped turning. Vella Scott has one of the huge stones covering her well. Let a verse from Thomas Gray pay tribute to all who enterprised and laboured in Esdraelon:

"Let not ambition mock their useful toil,
Their homely joys, and destiny obscure;
Nor grandeur hear with a disdainful smile,
The short and simple annals of the poor."[25]

Though the wheels, the saws, the stones and the stores of Esdraelon have gone silent, there is still interest in the place, even among people in faraway places. Mrs. Belle Butler Elliott of 16 Harlon St., Manchester, Ct., has given us a poem entitled "Esdraelon". She wrote: "This was written on the occasion when my husband and I took my mother back to the place of her birth. When my mother wanted to obtain Social Security, she had to have a birth certificate. All documents had been destroyed by fire, I believe, but people there recalled that the night she was born, her house burned down and she and her mother were carried out on a mattress.

"As I stood on the bridge (at Esdraelon) I got the idea for the verse and wrote it when I returned home."

Let Belle Butler Elliott's poem be a memorial to the entrepreneurs.

Esdraelon

I stood on the bridge at Esdraelon
And gazed at the river below -
The milldam has crumbled in ruins
Where waters now silently flow.
I looked at a house that was empty:
Within all was lifeless and still.
Silent the sound of the humming saws
That sang in the old water mill.
I thought of the folks who had left it -
The boys with their stubby feet bare,

The men and women who called it home,
And the girls with their braided hair.
Where are the Gillmors who built these mills?
Grass has o'er grown their sawdust spills.
Where are the men who tilled this earth,
Who wandered so far from this land of their birth?
How could they leave it?
These green-wooded rills...
There's beauty and peace in the
Heart o' these hills.
But time has stilled those restless feet,
On Forest Hill with markers neat.
Though east or west they chose to roam,
Esdraelon finally called them home.

Belle Butler Elliott

Bridge at Esdraelon, built in 1933

Wheat Mill

The gristmill at Esdraelon for buckwheat and oats was conveniently near. The wheat mill was at Bristol, about twelve miles from Knowlesville. Erma: "I remember a trip Grandpa made to Bristol. Early in the morning he hitched his team to his farm wagon bearing his wheat in bags. I went with him in the wagon as far as Glassville. He let me off at the corner of the road to Bristol. I walked to Aunt Ida and Uncle Bill McBrine's."

The mill, on the east edge of Bristol, sat on the bank of the Little Shikatehawk, a small tributary of the Saint John River. It was powered by a water wheel. A cog connected to a vertical shaft, about 30 feet up the bank of the stream conveyed power to the mill.

The mill had a series of owner/operators: Beecher Stockford, Juddie Giberson, his son-in-law, Staff Banks, and Fred Milbury. Mr. Banks brought a gasoline engine from Carlyle to run the mills.[26] Whoever was operating the mill in Alfred Corey's time wasn't long grinding his wheat into flour and bran. Erma said, "Grandpa was back in Glassville just after dinner." That trip was perhaps before 1910.

The mill continued into the 1930's. The writer remembers a spring trip, about 1935. My father, and my brother Wilfred, took a long sled load of bagged wheat. Stanley Whitehouse and I were allowed to enjoy that visit to a "large" town. Prince and Don were fast pacers. The route through Esdraelon and thence over the Black Brook Road, then new, didn't seem long. After we unloaded the wheat we hurried down town. We got a big bag of dulse for five cents. Then we met Stanley's sister, Edna, and Lewis Prosser. He was wearing a black band on his sleeve, because his mother had recently died. He was carrying their first born, Donald, a heavy load. Lewis said, "I wish he could stand."

Erma: Grandpa's crop of wheat produced enough flour

for Grandma to make our own bread, year round. The bran was a special treat for the pigs and cows. I remember especially, two cows: Blackie and Daisy. They gave us plenty of fresh milk in summer. Each had her own place in the milking yard where Grandpa brought them at milking time, morning and evening. From the cream my grandmother made butter. The farm produced nearly all our food. Grandpa planted a garden with enough potatoes for our own use, and also a variety of vegetables: carrots, beets, beans, turnips, and cabbage. Some summers he planted cucumber on newly cleared land across the Cold Stream.

Newly cleared land could produce a special quality of vegetables. Roy Hemphill described it: "I remember seeing my grandfather[27] plant potatoes between the roots and the stumps that were partly rotted and partly burned. The potatoes had a sweet flavour. To cultivate the new land he used a Newland harrow. The v-shaped frame had spike teeth. A spring in the frame allowed it to squeeze inward between stumps". Land clearing continued, now and then, for some years. Our father, during one of his visits home, cleared some more land of trees.

Grandpa had the foresight, early in his land-clearing years, to plant an apple orchard. Nearly every farm in the region had orchards with a wonderful variety of apples: Yellow Transparents and Crimson Beauties in August, New Brunswickers, Wealthies, Alexanders, plus some nameless varieties, maturing in the fall, and lasting through the winter. All were delicious whether crunched raw, cooked into applesauce, baked whole, or in pies. Farmhouse cellars had bins for storing winter apples. In Erma's childhood they also preserved apples by drying. The process required peeling, coring and stringing. Sometimes they had a group of neighbours come for an apple-stringing work bee, and social evening.

Farming in Grandpa and Grandma's time gave rewards and satisfactions; it took a lot of hard work, planting, weeding, hoeing, cultivating and harvesting. Erma: During my childhood

Grandpa often worked alone. From 1908-1912 my father worked at various jobs in the region: farming, butchering, logging and mail driving. Occasionally, when between jobs, he came home to visit and to help grandfather.

The anecdote with the Oliver plough[28] which occurred this era, illustrates one of those working visits at home. It also indicates that Grandpa progressed in methods of farming, e.g., by acquiring machinery and more horses. Farm life had its own values: a home and a source of food for the family; also property ownership and independence. Despite the benefits, the rewards, the progress and the satisfactions, however, it left some wants, especially more cash income. Hence, Grandpa continued to seek income from other sources.

Besides the seasonal jobs away from home, Lucretia and Alfred had an enterprise at home. They kept the Post Office in their house during the time of the Sir Wilfred Laurier Government, about 1900-1911. Enoch Estabrooks, or sometimes his son Claude, brought the mail from Rockland, Monday, Wednesday and Friday, by horse and wagon in summer; by sleigh in winter. He arrived about noon, and ate his lunch at Corey's. Later the mail came from Glassville in the evening. In the winter it came in the morning; on Tuesday, Thursday and Saturday.

The Post Office brought other benefits besides money from the Government. Sociability, always a characteristic of the Corey home, was enhanced by the Post Office. The arrival of the mail brought a neighbourhood social gathering. Many people in the community gathered at Corey's for the evening mail. Kenney boys; Phillips girls; Doucette girls; Edith Cook; Roy Carle; Whitehouses — Prince, Elwood, George H., George W.; and the Avery Boys: Cecil and Earle., "talking horse". The mailbag was emptied on the kitchen table. Eager onlookers watched for their own mail and their neighbours'. "I'll take that to them."[29]

Grandfather also had another government job — miles

from home. For three summers, 1909-1911, Alfred was employed as a fish warden. Will Hayward, Jr., a close relative, probably a brother or an uncle of Rev. Amos H. Hayward, came to Knowlesville, probably from Coldstream, hired Alfred and swore him in. He served on the South Branch of the Miramichi River. Focal points were the Governor's Table and the Forks of the North Branch and South Branch, below Juniper.

I remember the first time I saw the Governor's Table. My father took Claude, Warren and me trout fishing down the South Branch. He stopped his car on the edge of the stream where a big rock protruded from the water. As he cast his fly hook onto the water he said, "This is the Governor's Table. The Governor ate his lunch here one time." That was the summer of 1939, just after I returned from my first year of high school at Doaktown. Nobody told us then that our grandfather had served as warden there 30 years earlier, before the era of cars. Alfred didn't hesitate to walk back and forth to the Miramichi, from Knowlesville, though in 1911 he was 70 years old.

In the summer of 1910, Uncle Jud was the live-in substitute postmaster in Knowlesville. It was the year he brought his family home from Maine.

In the summer of 1911, while Grandpa was at the Miramichi, the Laurier Government lost to Borden, over the reciprocity issue. Father Ira, not wanting to let the new government take away the post office, because of political party affiliation wrote a letter resigning the position. The post office was soon transferred to James Hobbs. However, the Corey family retained another connection with the mail delivery through their daughter, Ida McBrine. After the McBrines moved to Glassville, Aunt Ida drove a horse from Glassville, bringing the mail to Knowlesville. She dropped the bag of mail at James Hobbs, keeping out Corey's mail to deliver to their house.

Pioneer farming must have left little leisure for Alfred. Yet he found time to give many free services to the community. He was one of two voluntary undertakers in the early Knowlesville community. The other was Henry Doucette, son of Rev. Cyril Doucette, the first pastor. When he was at home, Alfred often got called upon to serve as an undertaker. That was a community service, without pay. It was much less expensive to die in those days. One of the last calls Alfred got was to go with neighbours, to Skedaddle Ridge to bring the body of Jim Fisher, on a hand sled, to South Knowlesville and arrange his funeral.30

Alfred also served as an amateur veterinarian. Neighbours came for him when they had sick cows or horses. He diagnosed; he administered medicine. He also freely gave his service as a water-diviner.31

Highlands Baptist Church

Alfred's most sustained service and highest loyalty, it appears, were given to the Highlands Baptist Church. Beginning with the organizing meeting in January 1880, at the home of Alfred and Sarah Price, on the second farm north of Corey's,32 and continuing over 30 years, Alfred and Lucretia Corey faithfully attended and served that church. It grew out of two smaller groups. Rev. A.H. Hayward, who organized the Knowlesville and Glassville Baptist Church in January 1880, also organized a church in Northfield in October 1880. "At a meeting at Argyle, Nov. 18, 1885, the two churches were united and called the Aberdeen Baptist Church, .." At that point Alfred Corey was named clerk and Edward H. Smith and Robert McElhiney, deacons.33

Alfred Corey appears to have been a steady office-holder from the time of the combined congregations. "At a meeting of the Aberdeen Baptist Church held at Highlands, August 14th, 1886" Alfred Corey was one of three "brethren" appointed as trustees; the others were: Edward H. Smith, and Duncan McDermid. Alfred was also one of the "brethren appointed to the building committee."34 "During the year 1887 a house of worship was begun at Highlands, and in November of the same year was blown down when all ready for the clapboards."[35] "The House of God" was completed in autumn of 1891. It was dedicated on September 20, 1891, as "The Highlands Baptist Church"[36] It stood near the end of the road to Highlands from Knowlesville, in sight of the intersection of the road from Glassville to Juniper. On June 21, 1892, Alfred was still listed as trustee, along with Duncan McDermid, Robert McElhiney, Robert McIntosh and Fred D. Skinner.[37]

Alfred also kept the record book for several years. However, other handwriting appears in the book. In several cases Alfred's signature appears at the end of a set of minutes in another handwriting. Apparently he had some help in writing the reports of business meetings and recording other data, e.g., lists of members and officers.

An assistant clerk was identified by name only once, that is on p. 42. An entry on that page is signed C.W. Biggar, Assistant Clerk. Besides serving as clerk, trustee, and member of building committee, Alfred was appointed, together with Deacon R. McIntosh, to arrange place and date of ordaining council. In concurrence with the Windsor Church, they were planning to ordain Lic. E.P. Calder, in April 1899.

Also, Alfred was, on occasion, involved in the negotiation of aid which, at least some years, the church received from their Home Mission Board. At a business meeting of Aberdeen Baptist Church, April 16, 1899, with Pastor E.P. Calder as chairman, and Alfred Corey as clerk, it was voted that the church raise the amount of $125.00 for the ensuing year and ask the Maritime H.M. Board for assistance to the amount of $100.00.[38]

Having reviewed the history of Highlands Baptist Church and the membership of Lucretia and Alfred Corey in it, we are left with a question: Why did they drive their horse about three miles up hill to Highlands Church, whereas the Knowlesville Church was much nearer? Both churches were Baptist. The question presses us further when we recall that the

Coreys appear to have been a very gregarious people, welcoming neighbours into their home, offering their friendship, giving valuable services to their community, and entering enthusiastically into social activities in Knowlesville, e.g., the Lodge of Good Templars.[39]

Erma thought that Grandpa and Grandma chose the Highlands Church on some doctrinal basis. A consultation with Frederick C. Burnett, Upper Brighton, N.B., a recognized historian of the Baptist groups, and also of other denominations of that era, affirmed that there were "considerable differences" between the two churches. The Knowlesville church was known as the Free Christian Baptist Church. That is affirmed by the title: "F.C.B. General Conference", on lot 18 of the land grant map. It was the 100 acre lot granted by the Government to "the Free Christian Baptist General Conference of New Brunswick."[40] Mr. Burnett says the Highlands Church was "Regular Baptist." In doctrine they were Calvinist. The Knowlesville Church was Arminian. That is, they held the doctrine of Arminius, a Dutch Protestant theologian of the 16th century. He opposed the views of Calvin, especially on predestination.[41]

Mr. Burnett summarized:

"The articles of doctrine of the Knowlesville Church allowed for no predestination. They held that salvation is possible to all people, that Christ died for all, not just 'the elect'."

As F.C. Baptists, the Knowlesville Church held to the "general atonement". Also they believed in the possibility of falling from grace. The Knowlesville Church practised "open communion". With them the Lord's Supper was open to all Christians. In the Highlands Church only immersed people were invited to the Lord's Supper. Mr. Burnett said, further, "Most of the members of the Highlands Baptist Church had a

Presbyterian background. Some said regular Baptists were simply immersed Presbyterians." This perhaps helps explain the membership in the Highlands Church, of some of the Scottish folk, e.g., Mrs. Murdock McKenzie[42], and the Robert McIntosh family.

The Coreys, however, were not Presbyterian in background. Mr. Burnett asked me, "Where did the Coreys come from?" I said, New Canaan. He said, "The people there were almost solidly Regular Baptists." This probably explains Alfred's inclination toward Regular Baptists. Lucretia, however, is listed in the 1861 census as "Free Baptist".

Despite the differences in doctrine and practice between the two Baptist churches, they were remarkably alike in their relationships with Christians of other denominations. Both churches were ecumenical. The Highlands Baptist Church declared an open policy in a resolution that was passed on the eve of the dedication of their new House of Worship:

Glassville, Sept. 19, 1891
"At a business meeting today at the Highlands Baptist Church, the trustees came to the following resolution: Resolved that this house be open to any evangelical denomination for worship when not occupied by the Baptist."

Trustees	Alfred Corey
	Duncan McDermid
	Robert McIntosh
	Robert McElhinney
	Fred Skinner, Sec.

Mr. Burnett was not at all surprised about the resolution. The Regular Baptists were cordial toward other denominations. At the dedication service on September 20, 1891, Rev.

J.K. Bearisto, of the Glassville Presbyterian Church and Rev. Ben Jewett, a Regular Baptist, were recorded as "visiting ministers".

The Knowlesville Baptist Church was very friendly toward other denominations. They recognized, e.g., that some families in Knowlesville were Methodists: e.g., Averys, Hemphills, Brandscombes and Manuels. For some years a Methodist minister held regularly scheduled services in the Knowlesville Church.

Regular Baptists and Free Baptists

Though the Highlands Church and the Knowlesville Church had much in common, there were recognized differences between them, and not simply on the local level. Their doctrinal differences were represented in different organized structures. The Regular Baptists were organized in associations under their Maritime Baptist Convention which encompassed all their churches in New Brunswick and Nova Scotia. It dated back to 1846.

The Free Christian Baptists were organized in districts under conferences. There was a Conference for New Brunswick, and a Conference for Nova Scotia.[44] The doctrinal differences between the two Baptist groups probably account in considerable measure for the Corey's preference for the Highlands Church. However, there probably were other factors affecting that preference.

Involvement and Belonging

The writer has observed that people become most committed and gain most satisfaction in church life when and where they are able to find opportunity for involvement. Opportunity for charter membership in the church that was being newly organized in 1880, only about six years after the Coreys arrived in

Knowlesville, was perhaps a strong initial allurement. Perhaps another factor in church preference was a sense of identity. It appears that the Knowlesville families who became involved in the Highlands Baptist Church were, for the most part, families who came after the pioneer families. An exception is Maurice and Abigail Hobbs who are on the list of charter members.[45] The Hobbs were also members of the pioneer group that came from Nova Scotia to Knowlesville in 1861.

Alfred and Lucretia, as relatively late comers to Knowlesville, may have had a strong need for identity and belonging. That need must have been fulfilled as Alfred became extensively involved in the offices of the church and took a prominent part in the building of a new "House of Worship". Helping to sustain the church must have brought a continued satisfaction.

Why Didn't It Continue?

If the Highlands Church met the needs of the Corey family in that era it must also have met the needs of about 150 other people in the vicinity whose names are recorded on the membership lists between 1880 and 1912.[46] This leaves us with one more question: why, then, did the church not continue? That question is probably in large part answered by an event in Baptist history.

Baptist Union

In the years 1905 and 1906 a union took place between the Free Baptists and the regular Baptists of New Brunswick and Nova Scotia. The proposed union had able promoters in a process that, from beginning to conclusion, went on for nearly a quarter century. Prominent promoters among Free Christian Baptists in New Brunswick were two sons-in-law of Rev. Cyril Doucette: D. McLeod Vince and Rev. C.T. Philips.[47] Mr. Vince was a schoolteacher who also preached as a licentiate, and afterwards had a career in the militia. He was influential in the Conference.[48]

Voting for Union

In response to the Free Christian Baptist General Conference, the Knowlesville Church voted in favour of the Basis of Union. On October 23, 1904, at the close of the Sabbath morning sermon the vote was taken on Baptist Union as accepted by the General Conference convened at Tracy Station in the last part of September. Moved by Deacon R.H. Kenney that this Church accept the Basis of Union as per General Conference. The motion was seconded by Deacon Byron Ricker and unanimously carried.[49] Delegates from all over New Brunswick, probably travelling by train, by river steamer and by horse and carriage, had assembled in their general conference at Tracy Station, Sunbury Co. From September 17th to 20th, 1904.[50] The Knowlesville Church acted promptly following the conference sessions.

I find no record of a vote being taken in the Highlands congregation. However, Mr. Burnett says that the Regular Baptists probably did not vote by congregations.

The Regular Baptists took votes in their associations. In New Brunswick the Eastern Association took the lead in voting for union. The Western Association eventually followed, as did the associations in Nova Scotia. Following votes by their associations, the Regular Baptists, through their Maritime Baptist Convention, made their decision for union in 1905.

"The Free Christian Baptist General Conference of New Brunswick"[51] also voted for the union in 1905. The Free Baptists, having two conferences, one for New Brunswick and one for Nova Scotia, took their votes independently of each other. The Nova Scotia Conference didn't finalize their vote until 1906.[52]

United Baptists

The final decision for union took place at a gathering of Baptists in Saint John, N.B., near the beginning of the 20th century. The business meetings were held from October 7th to 9th in Waterloo St., a Free Christian Baptist Church. They held one service, open to the public, in Main St. Baptist Church — a larger building. It was the last Free Christian Baptist Conference meeting. The Conference disbanded and amalgamated with the Regular Baptists. On October 10, 1906, the combined Baptist groups formed "The United Baptist Convention of the Maritime Provinces of Canada"[53]

At another gathering in Saint John, near the end of the 20th century, a very high tribute was paid to the Union, by Rev. Dr. Philip G.A. Griffin-Alwood, then of Lawrencetown, N.S., and then president of the Baptist Historical Society of the Maritime Provinces. Speaking to the Genealogical Society in Saint John, on March 27, 1996, he attributed a high success to the Union, in terms of the number of Christian groups that came together as United Baptists. Besides the "Frees" and the "Regulars", there were many other groups and congregations of Baptists of varying names, and sizes, who became United Baptists. However, it must be recognized that not all divisions were healed. Not all Baptists of the two provinces became a part of the union.

When the union of Baptists in New Brunswick and Nova Scotia was consummated in 1906 both the church in Knowlesville and the church in Highlands were "United Baptist". Mr. Burnett said that the Knowlesville church came into the union as one of the stronger Free Baptist Churches of its area. The two ministers related to the first pastor of Knowlesville gained much recognition. Mr. Philips later became an officer in the United Baptist Convention. Also a D.D. was conferred on him, as is indicated on his gravestone in Upper

Woodstock.[54] The degree was probably from Acadia University.

D. McLeod Vince had already attained status among Free Baptists as is recorded in the 1906 yearbook of the United Baptists:

> "To the Assoc. of U.B.Churches of N.B.......
> "We recommend that all cash, stocks, bank deposits and other securities now in the hands of Col. D. McLeod Vince, as Treasurer of the Board of Managers of the late Free Baptist Conference, be transferred and delivered to him by this Assoc.in its corporate name, to be held by this Association in trust as provided in the Act incorporating this Association."

His status carried over into the new Convention. In the 1910 "Year Book of the United Baptists of the Maritimes", just inside the front cover, we find a picture of D. McLeod Vince, K.C., D.C.L. The caption says: "President Maritime Convention"

Highlands Church

It appears that little recognition was accorded the Highlands Church after the union. Mr. Burnett said that after the union there would not be much reason for Highland congregation to carry on. Were they perhaps losing their raison d'etre as they anticipated union?

In retrospect it appears that the best years of the Highland Church were over before the union. They must have had some very good years. The membership lists record a total of 128 names. These are in addition to the charter members of the two uniting churches, making a total of well over 150. Probably most of them became members in the quarter century between 1880 and 1905. That is an impressive number, compared to the population of the area in that time.

Perhaps the best years of the church were those of Rev. Amos H. Hayward, "his pastorate extending over a period of 14 years in all, there being a space of two years between his pastorates which was filled by Rev. H.J. Shaw." [55] The records have a long list of persons baptized by Mr. Hayward. Yearbooks of "The Baptist Convention of the Maritime Provinces" list A.H. Hayward in connection with other places: Hartland, Florenceville, Bristol. In 1892 he is listed as pastor of "Aberdeen", and with address Florenceville. Probably he had a circuit. In 1904 and 05 he is listed in Florenceville. In 1898 he is listed for both Hartland and Bristol. The Bristol report says: "We have a house of worship well under way..." A.H. Hayward and his brother, Judge Hayward were from Ashland. "A.H. Hayward travelled a lot and was influential. He was a good man, respectfully spoken of by people who were not Regular Baptists. His family were Free Christian Baptists. He is buried in Rockland."[56]

Whether the anticipation of union affected a waning of interest and activity among members of Highlands Church is in question. The records are not extensive for any period. However, from the turn of the century onwards there seems to have been few business meetings. There is no mention of a business meeting between 1899 and 1903. Both those meetings deal with engaging a pastor and requesting aid or assistance. Here is the brief record of the 1903 meeting:

> "Licentiate C. Frank Rideout accepted the pastorate of church July 1st, 1903. At business meeting, Sept. 9th, Pastor in the chair, it was voted to raise $100.00 and also to ask H.M. Board for assistance to the amount of $100.00. Alfred Corey, Clerk."

This is the last mention of a pastor, and next to the last record of a business meeting. The last meeting report says:

"At reg. conference, Oct. 1st, at Foreston it was voted to ask H.M. Board for a continuance of aid.
 C.W. Biggar, Asst. Clerk"

The year? This is written on the same page, 42, as the 1903 request for aid. Was it possibly the next year, 1904?
Meeting at Foreston may seem strange. Mr. Burnett explained that Baptists held conference meetings in different parts of the parish. Sometimes, to reduce travel they even held two meetings simultaneously in separate places. The story of Highland Baptist Church will conclude in the next chapter.

[1] See Chapters II and XV

[2] "Elegy Written in a Country Churchyard"

[3] Erma Corey Shaw. See also, The Story of Knowlesville, p. 107

[4] See The Story of Knowlesville, p. 111-113

[5] T.C.L. Ketchum, A Short History of Carleton County, New Brunswick, p. 67

[6] J.M. Corey, The Story of Knowlesville, p. 1

[7] A History of the Glassville Settlement, p. 137; also a letter to the writer from Belle Elliott, Manchester, Ct., Sept. 1996. See also the Gillmor genealogy.

[8] See Chapter I

[9] Roy Hemphill

[10] Annie Dyer, quoted by J.M. Corey, op.cit., p. 74

[11] Roy Hemphill

[12] Vella Scott, and Gillmor Genealogy

[13] Letter to the writer, Sept. 1996

[14] D.O.H. Map #26

[15] Glassville, op.cit., p. 138

[16] Vella Scott, Esdraelon

[17] A History of the Glassville Settlement, p. 138, 170; also see the A.H. Gillmor genealogy

[18] Roy Hemphill

[19] Data from Roy Hemphill, and Vella Scott; see also *A History of the Glassville Settlement*, p. 138.

[20] Roy Hemphill

[21] Vella Scott; also Gillmor genealogy

[22] Wright, G.E., and Filson, F.V., editors, Westminster Historical Atlas to the Bible: Philadelphia: The Westmister Press, 1946, p. 52,55.

[23] Erma Corey Shaw

[24] See *The Story of Knowlesville*, p. 33

[25] Elegy in a Country Churchyard, op.cit., p. 169

[26] Roy Hemphill

[27] John Hemphill, 1841-1930

[28] See Chapter XVI

[29] See, *The Story of Knowlesville*, p. 38 f.

[30] See *The Story of Knowlesville*, p. 39, and 69

[31] See story in Chapter X

[32] Prices lived on lot #30, later possessed by Ozias Carle. See <u>The Story of Knowlesville</u>, p.IV and 37.

[33] Records: loose notes p. 1f; also record book, p.15.

[34] Record Book, p.5

[35] Record Book, loose notes, p.2

[36] Record Book, p. 18

[37] <u>Ibid</u>, p.6

[38] <u>Ibid</u>, p. 35

[39] See Chapter I

[40] See <u>The Story of Knowlesville</u>, p. IV and p. 70

[41] Concise Oxford Dictionary (Oxford: The University Pres, 7th edition, 1982), p. 47.

[42] See <u>A History of the Glassville Settlement</u>, 1st edition, p. 88f.

[43] Highlands Church Record Book, p. 17

[44] Rev. William O'Grady, and F.C. Burnett

[45] The writer regrets that the Hobbs and also Edward H. and Mrs. Smith were accidentally omitted from the list on p. 79 of <u>The Story of Knowlesville.</u>

[46] See <u>The Story of Knowlesville</u> p. 79f.

[47] See <u>The Story of Knowlesville</u> p. 115, and lot 21 on L.G. Map

[48] Data from F.C. Burnett

[49] Knowlesville Church Record Book, p. 52.

[50] F.C. Burnett

[51] Thus the name is written on a surveyor's map. See <u>The Story of Knowlesville</u>, p. 70.

[52] Burnett and O'Grady

[53] Data from F.C. Burnett, and from Rev. Wm. O'Grady, Saint John

[54] F.C. Burnett

[55] Highlands Records, loose p.5.

[56] F.C. Burnett

CHAPTER IV

HOME-COMING

On the 31st of October, 1908, a rainy day, I looked out the kitchen window of my grandparents' home in Knowlesville and saw coming into our yard a horse and wagon carrying two men. The driver reined directly toward the barn. One of the men got out of the wagon and opened the big barn door. I said, "That is my Papa." My grandmother, whose eyesight was growing dim, replied incredulously, "That isn't your Papa." The other, Dave Harvey of Argyle, drove his horse and wagon onto the barn floor. I had last seen my father on the eve of his departure for Western Canada two and a half years earlier, in March 1906. What enabled me to be so sure that the passenger in the wagon was my father was a picture of him we had recently received in the mail. As soon as he had opened the barn door my father burst through the kitchen door and took me, his five and one-half year old daughter in his arms. This is my treasured memory of the happy homecoming of my father. He had arrived in Hartland by train the evening before. It happened that Dave Harvey was in Hartland on business. After a night in the Exchange Hotel they mounted Dave's wagon. He headed his horse toward Knowlesville.[1]

The day my father arrived Grampa brought a wagonload of sawdust from Crawford's Mill at Argyle to bank the house for winter. The next day, Nov. 1st, Grandpa hitched his team to his farm wagon and drove us all to Glassville. There we visited two families: Aunt Alma Miller's and Aunt Ida McBrine's. Thus we shared my father's happy homecoming with our close relatives.

His homecoming was the earliest I remember. During my childhood with my grandparents I saw the homecoming of several of my aunts and uncles after some years of sojourn in far away places. One homecoming was especially exciting; it included children my age. On a March day in 1910, as I was walking home from Knowlesville School, three of my cousins, Berta, Earle and Annie, came walking down the road to meet me. They took me by complete surprise. Annie, the spokesperson, introduced them all. Excitedly, I hurried home to meet three more cousins; Esther, Alfred and David. My uncle, Judson A. Corey and my Aunt Alice Corey and their six children had come from Auburn, Maine by train to Bristol where relatives met them. I had no expectation of their arrival, but I think my grandparents expected them.[2]

The move from Maine to Knowlesville in 1910 was, for Judson Albert Corey, déjà vu. He had made such a move in the 1870's with his parents and four siblings. They had lived in Houlton and Hogdon, near the border of New Brunswick. Judson and his younger sister, Ida, was born in Maine: Judson on August 1, 1870, and Ida on May 26, 1872. Sometime after the birth of Ida, May 26, 1872, the family returned to New Brunswick and began pioneer farming in Knowlesville. There Alfred's and Lucretia's children grew up. In 1910 Judson's children were moving, as he had as a child, from Maine to Knowlesville, N.B. Also for the two eldest children, the 1910 move was a repeat journey. The parents had brought them from Maine on an earlier visit. During that sojourn in Knowlesville, the third child, Annie, was born in May 1903 at the home of our Aunt Ida and Uncle Bill McBrine.

The surprise arrival of my cousins in March was the harbinger of an eventful summer for the children and the adults. That spring, my cousins and I had great times playing together. We went up into Charlie Branscombe's field which, was directly above our house, and at that time, below the main road. When summer came we went down to the Coldstream and made a dam. We also had a playhouse. My most memorable episode of that summer involved a kimono and a funeral. My cousins, i.e., the girls, brought with them from Maine, new kimonos. I wanted one too. Aunt Alice offered to make one for me. Aunt Alma sent the cloth from the Miller store in Glassville. I liked the kimono so much that I wore it even out-of-doors to play. One afternoon when I was wearing it at play by the roadside with David, then only two and a half, along came Aunt Alma Miller and Kate, driving their horse from Glassville. They were coming for the funeral of Mrs. Frazier at the Knowlesville Baptist Church. Aunt Alma stopped her horse and took David and me into her wagon. In the church yard Aunt Alma tied her horse, left Kate, David and me in the wagon, and entered the church for the funeral service. I left the wagon and slipped into the church. When Aunt Alma went up front to walk by the coffin, I traipsed behind her, bare-footed, and wearing my kimono.

That episode was near the end of David's status as the youngest of his family. On June 10th, his sister, Edna, was born at our grandparent's farmhouse in Knowlesville. My six cousins increased to seven. During the birthing period I was sent to Glassville for a visit with my Aunt Ida and Uncle Bill McBrine. My father was boarding with them and working in Glassville. When I returned to Knowlesville after three weeks, my grandparent's home was a little crowded. Two of the girls, Berta and Annie, slept with me upstairs. The days we all lived together ended all too soon. When Aunt Alice had recovered from childbirth she took the baby and all their children for a visit with her stepmother and two brothers, Will and Harold Howlett, at Lake Edward, Victoria County, N.B. She hadn't seen them for a long time.

Uncle Jud stayed at my grandparent's home all that summer. He milked the cows, tended the garden and kept the Post Office in place of my grandfather who was serving as Fish Warden at Miramichi Forks. It was my opportunity to form an attachment to my uncle. I ran errands for him and he was tolerant of my childish blunders. Once he called to me to bring salt for the cows. As I ran down the hill I shouted, "I's a-comin' Uncle Jud." Then I fell and spilled the salt.

Infantile Paralysis

A little later that summer, I had another fall. When I came downstairs one morning my foot was asleep. I started to run down the hill. I must have fainted away. I fell flat on the grassy field. My muscles had gone weak. They must have had to carry me in and put me to bed. I slept. When I awoke my grandmother and my Uncle Jud were standing over me, saying prayers. Both my arms and both my legs were paralyzed. I had been stricken with infantile paralysis. Grandma recognized the symptoms from having seen an earlier case. I was in bed for two weeks. Fern McBrine, my cousin, and Bessie Haines came to visit me. Grandpa was also there for a few days. He must have come home from the Miramichi for a weekend.

After an anxious time, much love and care, and prayer by my grandmother and my Uncle Jud, I recovered the full use of my body, except for my right foot. When I got out of bed I was like a baby learning to walk all over again, by pushing chairs. We were very grateful that our prayers for healing were answered for both arms and one leg. Uncle Jud didn't understand why my right foot was not healed.

I was very glad he was with us that summer, 1910. When the crippling disease struck me my appreciation of him grew. For me, there was nobody like Uncle Jud. I was not the only one who appreciated him. His three eldest sisters: Aunt Mina, Aunt Alma, and Aunt Ida, all living in the vicinity, were so glad to have him at home that summer that they came to the Corey homestead to celebrate his 40th birthday, August 1, 1910. They brought food, spread a cloth on the grass, and made a picnic. That was the first time I saw them all together.

A Ministry Begins

Before the end of that summer there was another reason for family gladness: Opportunity opened for Judson to begin his ministry in the church near and dear to them all, Highlands Baptist. For several years he had been preparing for a ministry. While working in Lewiston, Maine, he had engaged in studies and he had preached in a mission in Auburn. In 1907 he had been authorized to solemnize marriage in Maine. On May 23, 1910, soon after his homecoming, he was authorized by the Province of N.B. to solemnize marriage.

Judson's first church in New Brunswick was the one that had had its first meeting in Price's farmhouse in the neighbourhood of Alfred and Lucretia Corey. They had become charter members when it was organized in January 1880, under the name, Knowlesville and Glassville Baptist Church. The Corey family had been much involved in the church. Judson's three sisters living nearby: Mina, Alma and Ida were all listed on Alfred's clerical book, as were also three siblings farther away; Charles, Bertie and Laversa.

As we intimated in the last chapter, in 1910 Highlands Baptist Church was nearing the end of its history as a gathering congregation. Whether or not it was fully recognized, the church was in decline. Clues can be found in the meagre records. A reading of some of the year books still being preserved at the office in Saint John, of the United Baptist Convention of the Atlantic Provinces, indicates an apparent slackening of reporting to the Baptist Association and Convention. The church is variously listed as "Aberdeen" and "Highlands". The 1886 report shows 39 members; 1888 records 46 members; 1892 records 33 members, a "sitting" for 160, $200 raised for local purposes, $5.00 raised for "denominational", and $1,000, Value of House of Worship. In 1906 year book "Aberdeen" is on the list without statistics. The 1908 year book says, "no report, 1906,7,8,9." In 1910 and 1911

"Aberdeen" and "Highlands" are both listed without statistics, except 57 members. Alfred Corey is listed as clerk in most of those yearbooks.

Whether the Highlands Church had continued to have a pastor every summer up to 1910 the records do not indicate. It would be remarkable if they were able to have a pastor every summer, considering the situation of both Baptist denominations as Dr. George Levy described it:

One of the most obvious reasons for union was the overlapping of the pastorates of the two denominations with a consequent needless expenditure of money and effort in some areas, and the neglect of many others. There was nothing unusual in the report presented to the Baptist Convention in 1884 that fifty fields were pastorless and eighteen more would be when the ministerial students returned to their studies. The pressing need of funds to take care of increasing Home Mission interests, along with this "dearth of ministers" often created a very acute condition in the churches. At the same time poorly paid pastors, one from each of the main Baptist groups, might be found serving in practically the same area. There were very obvious ills in the existing situation, which ought somehow to be corrected. The advocates of union argued that the speediest and wisest way of correcting them would be for the two denominations to unite. This would overcome the wasteful duplication and extend the assistance some ministers were already rendering the needy churches in the communities near their pastorates.[3]

Erma said George Kierstead, a distant relative of Grandma Corey, was pastor the summer before her son became pastor. That would be in 1909. Erma said, "He came calling — walking to our house."

Though in 1910 the church was nearing its close, it must have been gratifying to Alfred and Lucretia after 30 years of faithful service to the church to see their son in the pulpit. As it turned out, he was the last minister to hold regular services at Highlands Baptist Church. However those last two summers of services at that church provided valuable experience to the son of the long-standing clerk. Highlands Baptist Church presented him the opportunity for a beginning as a minister of the gospel among people of New Brunswick. Perhaps in those last two summers of services the Highlands Church was fulfilling its mission. It had, in its brief life, met the needs of many people. Its influence would reach far. For J.A. Corey it was the beginning of a ministry that was to last the rest of his life.

The Doucette House Opens

About the time the Highlands Church opened to Judson A. Corey, a house also opened to his family: the Doucette house on lot #23, range 5, in E. Knowlesville. Though the vacancy was fortunate and opportune for the Corey family, it must have been a little sad for other families in Knowlesville.

Lots 23, 22 and 21 had been in the possession of the Doucette family since early in the Knowlesville settlement. Rev. Cyril Doucette and his son-in-law, D. McLeod Vince, had owned and occupied lots 22 and 21. Henry, oldest son of Rev. Cyril Doucette, the first pastor of Knowlesville Baptist Church, had owned lot 23. Jacob, nephew of Henry Doucette and grandson of Rev. Cyril Doucette, built the house on lot 23. Jacob, son of Leonard Doucette, married Dora Cook on June 20, 1906.[4]

In the summer of 1910 Jacob and Dora moved to Saskatchewan. Jacob's father, Len Doucette, had gone to Western Canada in 1909.

Perhaps family ties had kept Jacob and Dora in Knowlesville a year longer. Her parents, Charles and Ruth Cook, and her sister Edith, later to become wife of Claude Manuel, were still living in Knowlesville. Another sister, Ella, wife of Osbert Whitehouse, lived on the lot across the E. Knowlesville road from Jacob's house. The departure of Jacob left few of the Doucette family in Knowlesville. Only Henry and his son Caleb and family remained for a few more years.[5]

It seems strange now but Jacob bought from Alfred Corey a bay horse named Harry to add to the possessions he was shipping west by boxcar. Not many years later, dealers, e.g., Bill Burnham of Florenceville, were importing horses from the West.

The house was not long vacant. Near the end of the summer, 1910, Alice Corey and the children returned from Lake Edward, N.B. Erma was very glad to see them. Earl, the first to greet her, said, "You wait till Annie comes; she's got something for you." Soon the J.A. Corey family moved into the Doucette house. It was to be their home for the next three years.[6]

School, Moose, Music

The four eldest Corey children: Berta, Earle, Annie and Esther, attended school in Knowlesville.[7] On a school day of that year occurred the much-told tale of Uncle John and his imagined moose. On their way from school the children cut through the corner of woods below Osbert Whitehouse's. By coincidence, John and his son were in that woods and had sounded a moose call. Hearing the sound of tramping on the fallen leaves, John and his son climbed a tree. When the noise ceased, John hurried to the Corey home and described with uncontrollable excitement their escape from "a mighty big moose."[8]

The winter storms and severe cold forced the Highlands Baptist Church to close in winter. It functioned in spring, summer and fall. In late fall the walls of the Doucette house in E. Knowlesville began to reverberate with the sound of music. Esther Corey Smith remembered that the organ was brought each fall from the Highlands Baptist Church to their home in E. Knowlesville to protect it from the dampness of winter. Alice Corey still had a music book she had brought from England. With the help only of that book, Annie, just past seven when they moved into that house, began to develop her skills in music.

Another Homecoming

The year following the arrival of Judson A. Corey and family from Maine, the Knowlesville Corey family experienced another homecoming — this one by complete surprise to the whole family. It was like a drama: the time: a summer evening in 1911; the scene: the Corey Homestead in Knowlesville, where a crowd of neighbours are standing around waiting for their mail. Uncle Bill McBrine's horse made its accustomed stop in the Alfred Corey yard. In his mail wagon are two passengers: a young woman with a small boy. She walks up the steps to the veranda, carrying the boy. The young woman was Sadie, long absent daughter of Alfred and Lucretia.

Where did Sadie come from on that visit to Knowlesville? Someplace in New England. Like all her sisters, she had gone as a young woman, to work in a New England industry. Where? One work place was a cotton factory, probably in Massachusetts.

Somewhere in New England, she had met and married Ralph Fletcher. They had three boys: Waldo, Ned and Fred. Fred Fletcher, the youngest, born 1908, was the boy Sadie carried into his grandparent's home. Erma said, "At age three he was a heavy armful." Their eldest son Waldo, then a lad of about 18, was already a sailor. Sadie spoke of him sailing all over the world.

Despite her long absence — probably since the 1890's, Knowlesville was home to Sadie. She was the first member of Alfred's and Lucretia's family to be born in Knowlesville — on February 7, 1875. They named her Sarah Louise and affectionately called her Sadie.

For Erma, that homecoming was unforgettable. She dated it without hesitation: "Aunt Sadie came after I had polio, which was 1910, and just before the Post Office moved to

James Hobb's from Corey's, which was at the end of the Laurier term, summer of 1911."

Though she had travelled far and had been absent long, Sadie had not lost an apparently prevalent belief in retribution. Referring to Erma's having been stricken with polio, she asked, "Do you suppose that is because Ira used to mimic Ozias Carle?" If the Corey's were to be judged and held accountable for all their mimicking they would receive a long and harsh sentence.

Neither had Sadie's long absence freed her from accountability to her mother. Fairly early in Sadie's visit a very unhappy encounter occurred between daughter and mother. One afternoon Lucretia returned, very disturbed, from a visit with Mahalia Carle, a near neighbour. Apparently Mahalia had told Lucretia, "Your daughter is separated!" Had a report or rumour about Sadie's status leaked to Mahalia? Or had she picked up a rumour and then given it a trial run? Inevitably the intelligence would emerge. In this case the medium made the message most difficult to accept. In that day, for any family, separation/divorce was difficult enough to accept without hearing it from one who might have taken satisfaction in breaking the news. Lucretia came home in an irate mood and vented her extreme displeasure on Sadie. Despite that stormy encounter, Sadie stayed most of the summer, mainly at her parents, but also visiting her other relatives.

A Wider Ministry

The same summer that Sadie visited her family in Knowlesville her brother, Judson, enlarged his ministry to include the United Baptist Church in Knowlesville. In road distance the move was not far. Only about three miles separated the Highlands Church from the Knowlesville Church. From J.A. Corey's residence in East Knowlesville, the Knowlesville Church was even closer, only about one mile.

The theological distance between the two churches

apparently had been large enough to warrant building a separate church at Highlands. That distance, up to the time of the movement toward union, had been greater than the road distance. Dr. G.E. Levy succinctly described the theological differences that had existed between the two Baptist denominations before union:

> The Regular Baptists were the protagonists of God's unqualified election, of a limited atonement, and of close communion, while with equal zeal the Free Baptists preached the doctrine of a general atonement, defended the freedom of man's choice to accept or reject the merits of the atonement, and maintained their practice of open communion. But gradually the strong doctrinal dividing line between the two groups had weakened; the Regular Baptists had become less insistent on the points which had constituted the distinguishing marks of their denomination, and the Free Baptists had moved away somewhat from their original position of undiluted Arminianism. In 1884, at the time the first official conversations on union were mooted, it was said 'in both denominations are members not a few who hold Calvinistic and Arminian views. The difference is not essentially one of doctrine, although perhaps the majority of one denomination is what is termed Calvinistic, and the other Arminian...'[9]

As the doctrinal divisions had diminished in the two denominations, so apparently they had diminished on the local levels. That diminishing of differences appeared to diminish the distance between the Highlands Church and the Knowlesville Church to the point where one pastor could serve either or both churches. The move of J.A. Corey to the Knowlesville Church was not far, but was far-reaching. From that point on, many of the

Coreys attended and became involved in the Knowlesville Church.

Precisely when Rev. J.A. Corey's ministry to the Knowlesville Church began is not definite. Erma thought he was pastor of the Highlands Church only through the summer of 1911, which appears to have been about the time he assumed the Knowlesville circuit. Perhaps there was some overlapping. A note by H.N. Doucette, Clerk, under June 10, 1912, says: "Rev. Judson Corey has been Pastor since December.....[10]

Baptist Church, Knowlesville, built c. 1869

Thus December 1911 may be the official date of beginning of his ministry with the United Baptist Church of Knowlesville. However, he had earlier preaching invitations on the circuit.

An <u>Observer</u> report, May 1911, said, "Our Baptist minister, C.S. Young, is spending his vacation in P.E.I. His appointments are being filled by Rev. Judson Corey during his absence.[11] As a successor to C.S. Young, Judson Corey was following a pastor who had family connections with Rev. Cyril Doucette, who had founded the church in 1862. Mrs. C.S. Young was a daughter of Mary Doucette Lewin, and thus a granddaughter of Rev. Cyril Doucette.[12]

Judson A. Corey was prepared for a ministry with the United Baptists having been "ordained a minister of the Gospel in full fellowship with the.....Association of United Baptist Churches of N.B., on 14th of July, A.D. 1911, at Hartland..."[13]

Having grown up in the area, he was also conditioned for

the demands of circuit travel by horse and wagon or sleigh. Besides Knowlesville and Highlands his circuit included Windsor and Biggar Ridge. They were the two extreme points of the field. Initially, his itinerary could have included all four churches. However, if he served all four at one time it probably was for only a few months.

Serving the field that stretched from Windsor to Biggar Ridge was a sizeable task when travelling by horse, especially in winter. However, he probably did not have to cover the whole circuit on a Sunday, thanks to cordial relations and a spirit of cooperation among the denominations

Denominational Cooperation

The era in which Rev. J.A. Corey began his ministry appears to have been a time of much cooperation among the churches, especially Baptists, Methodists and Presbyterians. Erma Corey Shaw, who was born in 1903 and grew up in that era, said that in her youth in Knowlesville the Methodist minister came regularly. She recalled his schedule: E. Glassville in morning; Argyle in afternoon; Knowlesville in evening. However, that schedule probably applied no more frequently than every second Sunday, which would agree with the Knowlesville Church records. H.N. Doucette's minute of June 10, 1912, continues: "We have had preaching once in two weeks during the year by a Baptist minister, and the same by a Methodist minister."

We found no indication of a Methodist minister resident in the immediate area. Perhaps he travelled in from Hartland. F.C. Burnett says the Methodist minister preached in Matheson's Hall in Hartland. He also had services in Ashland and perhaps Coldstream.

A Union Meeting House

In Windsor the cooperation between Baptists and Methodists included the building of the house of worship. Erma stated, "Windsor was a Union Church — built as such." Mr. Burnett gave a brief history: The Free Christian Baptists and the Methodists both had congregations in Windsor. The Baptist Church was organized by George Orser in 1864. The congregations met in homes, schools, barns — wherever they could find adequate space. After some years the Windsor Church was built as a kind of a community church.

Baptist Church, Windsor

In that community denominational cooperation went right into the house of worship along with the lumber and nails. Erma also recalled, "The Presbyterian minister came there from Glassville." F.C. Burnett said, "The church was used regularly by the Methodists as well as by Presbyterians." He said further, "The United Church of Canada continued to hold services there about as late as the Baptists." That cooperation and spirit of sharing was also expressed in other ways. F.C. Burnett says the obituaries of the 1870's, 80's and 90's often report ministers of two, three, or four denominations, and even as many as ten ministers having part in a funeral service.

Identical Church Buildings

The cooperative spirit it seems applied also to the architecture of churches. Remarkable observations have been made about the architecture of the churches in Windsor, Mount Pleasant, and Knowlesville. The photos earlier in this chapter indicate clearly that the Windsor and the Knowlesville churches have the same architecture. Roy Hemphill says they are exactly the same in every way; they were built by the same carpenter, a man named Faulkner who lived near the Church of England in Hartland.

F.C. Burnett has also commented on the likeness of these churches. His observation includes also the Mount Pleasant Church. He says, "as built, those church buildings were very much alike." This is allowing for some later modifications. In Knowlesville, the gothic windows were not part of the original design. They were part of a series of improvements and additions the trustees carried out in 1911 and 1912. These included the steeple and the bell that Clarence LaPage brought from Hartland.[14]

Mr. Burnett has discovered some interesting data on pp.5 and 6 of the "minutes of the thirty-seventh General Conference of the Free Christian Baptists of New Brunswick held at Presque Isle, Carleton County, October 2nd, 4th, 5th, and 6th, 1869." They tell us: "The church at Knowlesville enjoyed a revival season during the fall under the missionary labours of Rev. T. Vanwart. He baptized eight, and the cause was generally strengthened. Brother Doucett has had the pastoral care of this church during the year. Two new meeting-houses are being built; one at Knowlesville, and the other at Cold Stream." Mr. Burnett explains that what was then called "Cold Stream", is now known as Mount Pleasant.

The date 1869 fits harmoniously with the few recorded dates we have for Knowlesville. The Baptist church in

Knowlesville was organized in 1862, only a year after the arrival of the first families.[15] The congregation was then meeting in a home. In 1867 a community mill was built on the Cold Stream at the border of the church lot.[16] Thus the mill was operating in time to saw the boards for the church. Roy Hemphill has observed that the boards in the church show the marks of the up-and-down saw of the water-driven mill.

How Churches Were Built

The church was probably built in stages. I remember Edmund Spinney sharing his recollections at the Knowlesville Sunday School. He described a platform with benches on it and said the sheep ran over it during the week. That must have been before the building was closed in. Mr. Spinney's recollection suggests that the church must have been a few years in construction. He was born in 1868. It would seem that he would have to be four or five years old to be able to remember. This suggests that in the early 1870's the church was still at an early stage of construction. This estimate agrees with Mr. Burnett's historical perspective: "1869 was the date these church buildings were started; I think it would be a few years before they were finished...The way some, perhaps most church buildings were built was that all involved who were able would cut logs in the winter and hew them square, haul the timber to the location, and let it season or dry. When it would dry they would frame it and set a day to raise the frame; the sills and floor joists would have been lain on the foundation first. The rafters would be put up when the frame was raised, and there seldom was any lack of volunteer labour to raise the frame...

"I once was up in the attic of our old meeting house in East Kemptville, N.S., begun in 1869; all the rafters, posts and timbers or beams for the ceiling were hand hewn by many different people; they were every size from 5 x 6 to 10 x 10 and from nearly perfect to very rough workmanship, according to the skill of the workers....Personally I saw two church buildings built or rebuilt, they used sawn timbers rather than hewn, but it took a lot of men to get the heavy timbers and rafters up in place."

Roy Hemphill cited the year 1873. That seemed to be a community tradition rather than a recorded date the Knowlesville Church was framed. But it fits harmoniously with other dates cited here. Mr. Burnett shared his historical perspective further: "...After the frame was up, the next thing was to board and shingle the roof and board in the sides and so on; it was quite common to hire carpenters to finish the inside and the outside...The last thing finished was nearly always the seats and inside walls."

We do not have a definite date for the building of the Windsor Church. Mr. Burnett says, "Windsor may have been started about the same time, but is not mentioned in the "minutes" because it was not strictly a Free Christian Baptist property as Knowlesville and Mount Pleasant were."[17] Mr. Burnett also tried to estimate the time of the building of the Windsor Church on the basis of its style. He observed that its fancy outside appearance and well-finished interior is a style later than the 1860's. Churches built in the 1860's were plain in style.

Argyle and Biggar Ridge

The church at Argyle was another example of denominational cooperation. "Though began by those settlers who were of the Methodist persuasion, the church was a "Union" church from the beginning; Baptists, Presbyterians and Anglicans sharing its pulpit on alternating Sundays with the Methodists."[18] Biggar Ridge also contemplated a "Union meeting house". At a community meeting in 1896 "it was decided that a Union meeting house similar to the one at Argyle would be built..." "John W. Biggar offered a portion of his farm for the purpose......Construction was

Baptist Church, Biggar Ridge, building begun, 1897

begun in the spring of 1897." However, the Union idea apparently was abandoned. "In 1899 John W. Biggar formally deeded the acre lot to the 'Free Baptist Church'...." In this community church building was begun before a church was organized. "....The first congregation was organized on July 9, 1904 at which time Edward Brooks was appointed deacon and Charles W. Biggar (Rowley) assistant clerk.[19]

Biggar Ridge and Highlands

The name Charles W. Biggar here clears up a puzzle for the writer. In the last entry in the Record Book of Highlands Baptist Church, apparently the same person signed his name, "C.W. Biggar, Asst. Clerk". He wrote and signed the minute of a conference meeting in Foreston. His report of the meeting says, "...it was voted to ask H.M. Board for a continuance of aid". Now we learn that Charles W. Biggar was Assistant Clerk of the Free Baptist Church in Biggar Ridge. Apparently there must have been some cooperation and sharing between Highlands Baptists and Biggar Ridge Baptists. They apparently had a common interest in aid from Home Mission Board, though the meeting was in 1904, two years before the completion of the union between "the Regulars" and "the Frees".

Perhaps there is a further reason for having a "Conference" meeting in Foreston. F.C. Burnett says that a Free Christian Baptist church was organized earlier in Foreston and was received into Conference in 1875. He also noted that George Orser organized a church in Foreston in that year. So there were organized groups of Baptists in Foreston nearly three decades before the church was organized in Biggar Ridge. Charles W. Biggar was later known as Charles Rowley. "He was raised...by John W. Biggar and was known as Charles Biggar until adulthood." Jack Biggar explained that Charles, at the time of his marriage, took back his original name, Rowley.[20] Charles inherited the John W. Biggar farm — the lot which ran from the church toward Juniper. It was later bought by Flemming and Gibson Co. and was known as the "Rowley Place". There they grew hay and oats for their horses.

A Circuit Pastor

In that part of Carleton County where Baptists were, at the time, the most numerous church group, my uncle, Rev. J.A. Corey carried a ministry over the Windsor/Knowlesville/Biggar Ridge circuit from 1911 to 1913.

Travelling that circuit in winter must have been a test of endurance, especially in January of 1912. The Observer of Hartland, N.B. reported: "The Knowlesville area was visited by two of the worst storms of recent years on the 9th and 15th of January, 1912." Between those storms on January 13th, Rev. J.A. Corey married his brother Ira to Nellie Brown Kenney at the pastor's residence in E. Knowlesville.[21] The Observer also reported: "In January, 1912, George Buchanan, an aged resident of Golden Ridge, when returning home from the mill at Esdraelon on Monday, lost his way in the storm and would have perished from the cold had not Elwood Shorey and Fred Hemphill gone in search of him and assisted him to the home of Mr. Hemphill where he spent the night."[22] Roy Hemphill further described Mr. Buchanan's brush with tragedy: The storm arose while Buchanan was at the grist mill. The miller at Esdraelon tried to persuade him not to try to go home. The storm increased to such fury that the road became invisible.

Horse and driver veered toward the woods. Roy narrated further: "Father and Elwood Shorey, a young fellow, put on snowshoes, took lanterns and located Buchanan at the edge of the woods. He was completely disoriented." They brought him to Hemphill's. They didn't try to bring the horse through the drifts that night. Instead, they led him to the shelter of a windfall further into the woods. They put a blanket on him and brought him hay and oats.[23]

Another winter episode — a delightful one — relates to Rev. J.A. Corey's circuit driving and the people's care and concern for him. One cold day, perhaps the same winter, Ed Carle, a neighbour, stopped at Alfred Corey's to warm his ears and to leave a scarf that Alice Corey had loaned him. Ed said, "I've come from Jud's place. I left him approximately $100.00 that we collected from the community for a harness for his horse. I didn't ask any of his relatives to contribute. We wanted it to come from the community."[24]

We can guess that the pastor's harness was breaking from age and much wear. If the sleigh got stuck in a deep drift and the horse gave a sudden lurch he could break a tug and/or other harness parts. The journey was cold enough without having to get out of the sleigh and wire up a harness. Ed Carle's grandparents, William H. and Amy Carle, like Alfred and Lucretia, came from New Canaan.[25]

In summer, travel over the circuit could be very pleasant. J.A. Corey's oldest son, Earle, recalled riding in the wagon with his father to Biggar Ridge on a Saturday afternoon. He wore his old shoes for trout fishing and forgot to take his Sunday shoes. He had to wear his fishing shoes to Biggar Ridge Baptist Church on Sunday morning. Erma, describing her uncle's schedule, said, "Usually he drove his horse to Biggar Ridge on Saturday evening." However he may not have gone to Biggar Ridge every week; when he did, his Sunday schedule started there.

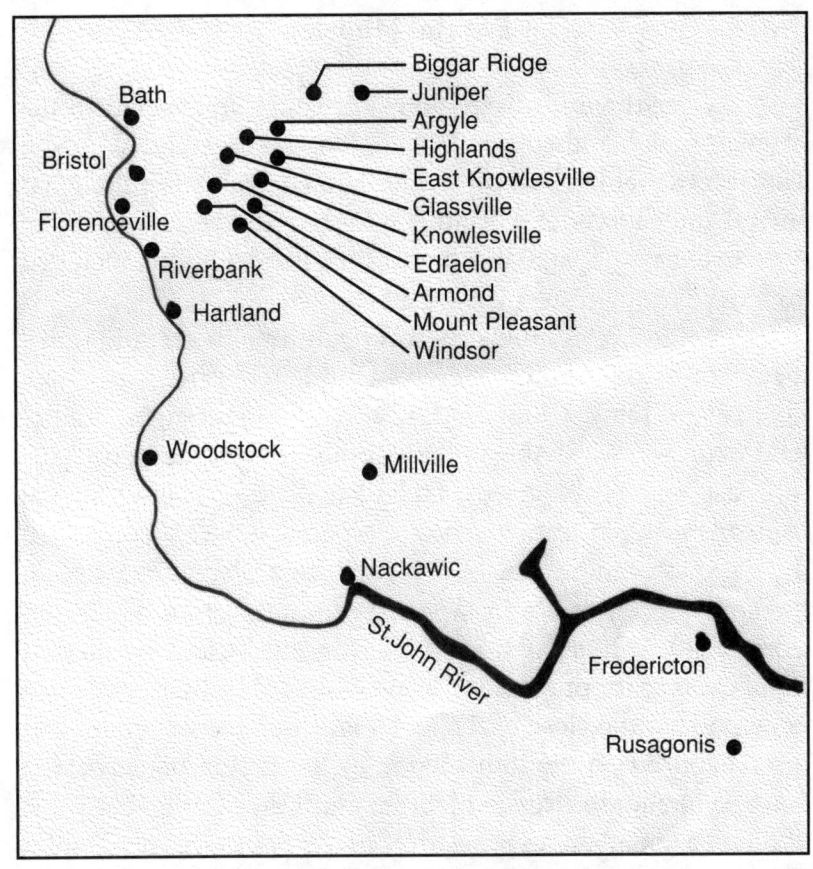

Rev. J.A. Corey's circuit, and nearby towns.

The sharing and co-operation in meeting houses and in scheduling worship services met a need. It was impossible for ministers on rural circuits to cover a whole circuit on one Sunday, especially in winter.

A Fruitful Ministry

Over three full years Rev. J.A. Corey ministered to the people of Highlands, Knowlesville, Biggar Ridge and Windsor. The record book of Knowlesville United Baptist Church has several indications of a fruitful ministry. To the church there were extensive repairs and improvements. Additions included gothic windows, a steeple, and a bell.[26]

J.A. Corey's ministry was fruitful also in additional members to the church. Received by letter were: Mrs. Wm. Phillips and John R. Keirstead. Also receiving the right hand of fellowship was Mrs. Abigail Branscombe. Sometime in the pastor's last year he baptized Mrs. Allen Boyd.[27] The additional baptisms resulted from a series of "special services" conducted by the pastor, Rev. J.A. Corey and Rev. Percy Fitzpatrick, Methodist.....". Dates were April 21st until 6th of May, 1913, Mr. Corey's last year as pastor. H.N. Doucette, Clerk, wrote, "A number arose for prayers and a few wishes to be baptized." Also he wrote, "At the close of the meetings three persons requested to be baptized on the 18th of May by the Pastor, namely: Mrs. Percy Whitehouse, Nessie McBrine and Edith Carle..."[28] Some of the new members were relatives of the pastor: his uncle John Kierstead, and John's daughter, Mary Boyd; also two nieces: Mrs. Percy Whitehouse, Clara; and Nessie McBrine; they were daughters of J.A. Corey's sister, Ida McBrine.

Leaving

In late summer, 1913, Rev. J.A. Corey responded to a call from the United Baptist Church at Rusagonis. Church Clerk, H.N. Doucette's entry for September 28, 1913, says:

> "Rev. J.A. Corey closed his labours with this church for the last three years. During the last year he has received

the amount of $70.00 on salary in cash, besides a number of useful articles. A few evenings before he left, a number of his congregation gathered at his home and presented him with a leather suitcase and his wife with a cabinet of silverware."[29]

Interestingly, $70.00 was less than the amount collected for the harness. However, Windsor and Biggar Ridge were also contributing to his salary.

When the family departed from Knowlesville there were eight children, the eldest was thirteen, the youngest age one. Six had come from Maine in 1910: Alberta, Earle, Annie, Esther, Alfred and David. Edna was born at the Corey homestead in Knowlesville in 1910. Mildred was born in the Doucette house in E. Knowlesville in 1912. Alice Corey, with the children, took the train from Bristol.

The pastor took a different route and mode of travel. He drove his mare all the way to Rusagonis, York County. Accompanying him on the route through Millville were two relatives: Ira Corey and Percy Whitehouse, each driving his own pair of horses, transporting the household goods on farm wagons. The journey took three days.[30] Erma, the narrator of that trek, felt a deep loss in the family's departure. She said, "I cried, and cried. However, the relationship remained warm and strong. We never became weaned away from Uncle Jud. He came every fall in the hunting season, sometimes accompanied by members of his family. How I looked forward to these annual visits!"

Annual Home-coming

J.A. Corey's annual visits to Knowlesville and region were also occasions for him to renew his relations with people on his former pastoral circuit. Two Knowlesville Church clerks recorded some of the years when he preached in Knowlesville:

1919: "three services"; 1920: "three sermons"; 1922: "two services"; 1923: "a service"; 1931: "two services". These services were all in the month of November, his month for a hunting vacation.[31] The Corey's were a home-coming family, and Knowlesville was a good place to come home to.

[1]See The Story of Knowlesville, p. 112f., also Chap. III of this book

[2]These home-coming stories were told by Erma Corey Shaw. Her stories continue.

[3]George Edward Levy, D.Th., The Baptists of the Maritime Provinces 1753-1946 (Saint John: Barnes-Hopkins, Ltd., 1946) p.268

[4]Annie Currie Dyer and Herbert Bradley, Supplement to History of Argyle..., p.1.

[5]See the Story of Knowlesville, p. 9ff., 35,115f.

[6]Ibid, p.116

[7]Ibid, p. 123

[8]Ibid. p.120f.

[9]George E. Levy, op.cit., p.269

[10]Knowlesville Church Record Book, p.63

[11]See The Story of Knowlesville, p.117

[12]Ibid, Doucette genealogy, p.213, also p.162

[13]Ibid., p.117

[14]The Story of Knowlesville, p.118

[15]The Story of Knowlesville, p.71

[16] Ibid., p.74

[17] These quotations are from F.C. Burnett's letter to the writer, dated March 31, 1998.

[18] Annie Currie Dyer, History of Argyle, p.18

[19] H.N. Bradley, History of Foreston.., p.55

[20] See H.N. Bradley, op.cit., p. 128, for more on the Biggar/Rowley name

[21] See The Story of Knowlesville, p. 119

[22] Ibid, p.105

[23] Conversation with Roy Hemphill, Nov. 5, 1996

[24] Erma Corey Shaw

[25] See The Story of Knowlesville, p.35; also a genealogy in the appendix, p.211.

[26] Knowlesville Church Records, p.62, 63, 64

[27] For a longer account, see The Story of Knowlesville, p.118

[28] Ibid, p.120; also Knowlesville Church records, p.54 and 64

[29] Ibid., p.64

[30] See The Storey of Knowlesville, p.121f

[31] Knowlesville Church record book, pp.68-75. See also The Story of Knowlesville, p.156f.

CHAPTER V

STONES AND STORIES

Diamond Stone, discovered by Ira Corey

This diamond-shaped stone is in the possession of John Corey, Florenceville, N.B. He is entrusted to keep it as a family treasure.

From ancient times stones have been placed as monuments of places and events to be long remembered. So it was with the people of Israel:

> When all the nations had finished passing over the Jordan, The Lord said to Joshua, "take twelve men from the people, from each tribe a man, and command them, 'Take twelve stones from here out of the midst of the

Jordan, from the very place where the priests' feet stood, and carry them over with you...'" Then Joshua called the twelve men...., whom he had appointed....; and Joshua said to them, 'Pass on before the ark of The Lord your God..., and take up each of you a stone upon his shoulder,...., that this may be a sign among you, when your children ask in time to come, 'What do these stones mean to you?' Then you shall tell them that the waters of the Jordan were cut off before the ark of the covenant of the Lord; when they passed over the Jordan....So these stones shall be to the people of Israel a memorial forever. And the men of Israel...took up twelve stones out of the midst of the Jordan...; and they carried them over....And Joshua set up twelve stones....in the places where the priests bearing the ark of the covenant had stood; and they are there to this day.
— Joshua 4: 1 - 9

The Story of Our Stone

The Coreys' diamond-shaped stone also evokes a question: What does this stone mean? Here's our story: This diamond shaped stone which appears to have been cut with a chisel, was discovered by Ira Corey on the Alfred Corey homestead in Knowlesville. Ira ploughed it out of the soil on the knoll south of the house, near the springhouse. That happened some time before he went to the Canadian West, which was in March 1906. Carved on the stone is "1907" and three sets of initials:

        H.J.P. - Heber J. Price
        R.F.P. - Roland F Price
        C.J.M. - Clarence James McBrine (called Claude)

The names for the initials were quickly recalled by Erma Corey Shaw. The date, 1907, is the summer the fellows carved their initials.

The Families Initialled on the Stone

In the late 1800's the Alfred and Sarah Price family lived in Knowlesville, on lot 30, the second lot north of Corey's. They were near neighbours. The Price family moved to Millinocket, Maine, about 1900. Heber and Roland were two of their six sons. Erma's explanation for the 1907 date is that Heber and Rollie returned to Knowlesville on a visit in 1907. Calculating from the ages listed on the 1871 census,[1] Heber and Rollie would have been about 45 and 43 in 1907 — no longer boys. Claude McBrine, born 1891, would have been only 16 in 1907. Though far apart in age, the three fellows apparently joined in initialling the stone at the home of Claude's grandparents, Alfred and Lucretia Corey. Claude was born in Knowlesville in 1891 and probably was still living there in summer of 1907. Or if the McBrine family had already moved to Glassville, which they did in 1907 or 1908,[2] then Claude was probably visiting his grandparents.

Members of the Price family would be welcome visitors at Corey's. Grandpa, having lived in Maine, liked to have news about families who had been their neighbours in Maine. He often inquired from visitors to Knowlesville about his former friends in Maine. This, Erma remembered well. How the stone became diamond shaped and how long it lay buried in the soil is hidden from history. But it has had an interesting history since Ira Corey ploughed it out of the soil and brought it into the Alfred Corey house where for many years it was used as a door stop.

When the Corey family moved from the Alfred Corey homestead in 1922 they left the stone. Thus it was there when Everette and Ethel Kenney bought the farm and moved in. Eventually the Everette Kenney family moved to the Roland Kenney house. Now we are into a story within a story.

The Alfred Corey House and Property

Early occupants of the house following the Kenneys' departure were Harold and Stella Jones and family. There followed a series of short-term occupants and owners of the property where our grandfather, Alfred Corey, lived and worked for half a century. The Coreys lived on lot 27 and also owned the adjacent lot 25. This property, it seems, was never registered in the name of Alfred Corey, but rather in the name of his youngest son, Ira Corey, as the land grant map shows. A deed describing a much later property transaction sheds some light on the question of why the land grant map shows "Ira Corey" and not "Alfred Corey" on lot 27. In part it says:

".....all land described in this deed was granted by the Crown to one George W. Boyer, and being the same land conveyed to Ira T. Corey, from Hiram Schriver and wife, under Deed bearing date the 27th day of June A.D. 1900, and registered in the Office of the Registrar of Deeds for the said County of Carleton in Book B#4 on pages 750 and 751 as number 42005.[3] Erma said Ira bought the Boyer lot #25. Perhaps in the same transaction he secured title to lot 27 where the Coreys had already been living for over a quarter century. In 1900 Ira was 23 years old. That was two years before his first marriage. The property transaction described in the above deed is the conveyance of the land from Claude and Edna Poitras to Otto J. Wallace, of R.R.3, Coldstream, on April 19, 1956. That deed was registered as No. 102052 on January 6, 1960, in Carleton Co. Registry Office.

It is difficult to give a precise account of the ownership transactions involving the Corey homestead and adjacent property; it seems that in some transactions the two lots were divided and sub-divided. In the 1950's Charles and Geneva Crabbe bought the property it seems mainly for the lumber. Kaye Foster recalled, "I remember Mum and Dad stopping at the Corey homestead to visit the Crabbes one Sunday evening. The above mentioned deed indicates that Charles Crabbe sold the back half of both lots to his son Wendell, on January 5, 1955. The next year Claude Poitras acquired the front half of both lots. His main interest, it appears, was to obtain the house. He moved the house away and located it on the road between Esdraelon and Glassville. From Mr. Poitras the front half of both lots was conveyed to Otto Wallace, a pulp dealer, Cloverdale. This is indicated on the above-mentioned deed. The next owner of the fronts of the two lots, i.e., two 50-acre portions comprising 100 acres, was Elmer Briggs, Bristol. He sold the land in smaller portions. One of the later owners is Douglas Fields, Juniper.

Where Was the Stone?

Considering all those changes to the property was there any hope that the stone would again be uncovered? Sometime while Ira Corey and family were living in Juniper and during one of the times the house was vacant before it was sadly towed away, Ira and his daughter, Erma, went to the site on a search for the stone. Though disappointed, Erma did not abandon hope.

One autumn evening in 1979 or 1980 the Knowlesville History Committee sat around a table at the Women's Institute Hall in Knowlesville, pooling memories for <u>The Story of Knowlesville</u>. Recollections were coming from far, both in distance and in time, especially by the two members with the longest memories, Roy Hemphill and Erma Shaw. Roy had interesting stories about Knowlesville people portaging to the Miramichi and the Nashwaak. Unexpectedly Erma's recollections leaped back to the stone. Taking a long shot, she asked Frederick Kenney about it. He went home. In half an hour he returned to the hall and presented the precious stone to Erma.

As the stone had been turned from the soil, so it turned up again from apparent oblivion. The Everett Kenney family had carefully guarded the stone for many years and had carried it from the Alfred Corey house to the Roland Kenney House. There it had lain forgotten in the cellarway for many years. Erma's joy in seeing her long-lost treasure could scarcely have been less than that of the man described by Jesus in His parable of the Kingdom — the man who found treasure hidden in a field. (Matt.13:44).

Keeper of the Stone

Erma left Knowlesville that evening carrying the stone. Thenceforth it was her treasure to be carefully guarded. As she approached her end of this life she planned for a home and guardian for the stone. On July 22, 1995, at the Corey Reunion in Knowlesville John Corey reported, "I have the stone at my house." In her last year Erma had instructed her son John Shaw that John Corey was to be the keeper of the stone. After Erma's passing in 1993, John Shaw delivered the stone to John Corey in Florenceville, N.B. Hearing the story, seeing Erma's delight when the long lost treasure returned, noting how she protected it and kept its story alive, and knowing how careful she was to entrust it for safe-keeping to her nephew — all that helped bring the stone to its status as a family treasure.

Twelve stones taken out of the Jordan River and set up in Gilgal, marked the crossing of the Jordan by the people of Israel and served to preserve the memory of the event. (Josh.4). One stone, ploughed out of the ground in Knowlesville has become a monument of events, experiences, customs, traditions, and ways of life in early 1900's. The Corey's diamond-shaped stone carries its own story of discovery, of being lost and rediscovered. It also brings to mind other stories — of growing up on a pioneer farm and going to a country school and church, of fun, adventures and predicaments that in retrospect are humorous and amusing. These stories, told by Erma the keeper of the stone and the preserver of oral history are windows into life in those times.

Our Stories

We know from Erma's earlier story, that infantile paralysis interrupted her life, fun and adventure at age seven. Here her story continues:

"I stayed home until I was nine. Then my grandfather drove me to and from school with old Bess — always in winter and lots of times in summer." At school she did not allow paralysis of one foot to stop her having fun, nor stop her schoolmates from having fun with her. They called her the grasshopper and described her movement on the playground: Two hops on one foot, one on the other, breaking into a run. She took it all in fun.

A New Baby and a Cake

One late summer day when I arrived home from school Uncle Bill McBrine was at our house waiting to babysit me. Grandpa must have been away from home. Uncle Bill and Aunt Ida had come from Glassville for a visit. Or maybe they had simply stopped on their mail route. Their visit was prompted by the arrival of a new baby. Mildred, the youngest child of Rev. Judson and Alice Corey was born Aug. 16, 1912 at the Doucette house in E. Knowlesville. Grandma and Aunt Ida McBrine drove a horse to E. Knowlesville to see the new baby.

In Grandmother's absence came one of my memorable escapades. I decided, "Here is my chance to make a molasses cake." I persisted despite Uncle Bill's warning, "You'd better not; your grandmother won't like it." Maggie McCammack had told me how to make a molasses cake. I stirred together the ingredients and put the pan in the oven. After a while I peeked. It was boiling like molasses candy. I decided to take it out. On lifting the baking pan I spilled the sloppy liquid all over the grate, the front of the stove and the floor. Then it came to me that I had forgotten one essential ingredient — the flour. That episode was in summer when Grandpa was not always free to come for me.

In winter he always planned to come to the school to bring me home.

Christmas at School

One day in the Christmas season when Grandpa arrived at the school we were singing "Jingle Bells". He left his horse standing and walked into the schoolroom. When his feet touched the floor they moved quickly into the rhythm of the song. The children were much amused as Grandpa tapped out the tune of "Jingle Bells" in a step dance.

Fun and faithfulness came together in Grandpa. Erma was proud of him and held lasting affection for him. She expressed her ongoing gratitude to Grandpa Corey for enabling her to attend Knowlesville School: "I owe my early education to my grandfather."

Under the Sleigh

Another incident illustrates both the faithfulness of Grandpa and Erma's ability to cope with mishap. At the time of this incident my cousin, Alberta Corey, was the teacher in Knowlesville School. She stayed with us.[4] One winter afternoon Berta and I started home, thinking that Grandpa wasn't coming. But he arrived just as we got started on the road home. He had to go on down to the school to get turned. As the mare walked by, I put out my hand to rub her side. One shaft of the sleigh went up my sleeve. By the time Grandpa got her stopped I was lying on my back in the snow and the runner of the sleigh was on me. I saw the mare's corked shoe as she lifted a front foot. I helped push the sleigh up as Grandpa and Berta lifted. My coat sleeve was badly torn.

Ford Frightens Bess

The time came when Erma was allowed to drive the mare. Grandpa would entrust her to few others. Erma described one episode with Bess. "Grandpa let Berta and me drive her to Cale Doucette's for an evening visit. We tied her to their hitching post behind their house. Then Elwood Whitehouse came roaring into the yard with his Model-T Ford. In that era of the early advent of cars, horses were terrified of them. The mare broke loose from the hitching post, from her harness, and from the wagon and trotted off home, wearing only her bridle. Elwood went nonchalantly into the Doucette house and visited. We had to walk home. The next day Grandpa had a big repair job to do on the harness. He never complained. Bess acted simply from freight. She had no disposition to give trouble. Erma managed her in other situations. For example, she led her by the bridle as she pulled the long rope that ran over pulleys to lift big fork loads of hay into the hayloft.

Highlands Baptist Church

Bess had a part in some of Erma's most cherished childhood experiences: One of my fondest memories is of the wagon ride with Grandpa and Grandma to the Highlands Baptist Church. The yellow fly net worn over the black mare, Bess, fascinated me. It covered even her ears. At the church I remember stepping onto the outside platform. One more step took us into the church. We sat with a sense of awe, not allowed to speak above a whisper. In the church I remember beautiful vases with bouquets of goldenrod. No flowers of today could be any more beautiful to me than were those goldenrods. On the pulpit was a blue velvet scarf. I've often thought of the atmosphere of that church: the sense of awe, reverence and quietness that pervaded it.

There must have been many people who experienced belonging and blessing in Highlands Baptist Church. Besides the estimated 150 members over three decades, there must have been others: adherents, and persons like Erma, too young to be members, who nonetheless found a spiritual foundation for life. The church's influence, over time and distance, has not ceased, though the house of worship has been long gone.

Where Did It Go

In 1934, when I spent the summer at my Grandmother's at Highlands, the building was still standing, vacant, as it had been for a score or more of years. Over the years there were inquiries about putting the building to other uses. Jim and Kate Hovey, e.g., when they were contemplating building their own home, came to our place to talk to Uncle Ira, a trustee, about the possibility of moving the building to Glassville and adapting it to a house, They abandoned the idea. In 1936 the church did go to Glassville, but for a use that could not have been predicted. Jesus said, "Foxes have holes..but the Son of Man has nowhere to lay his head." (Matthew 8:20) The foxes of the Lyon family in Glassville had a special status. They had pens made from the boards of Highlands Baptist Church.

The church's place in history and in geography is preserved by two enduring things: the written records and the cemetery. The Highlands records are brief but besides the clerk's book we discovered, in the records of United Baptist Church, Knowlesville, a letter:

GREETINGS

We, the undersigned Trustees and Officials of the
United Baptist People of Glassville and Highlands.
Tender our Greetings and Offerings to
The United Baptist Church at Knowlesville, N.B.
The Offering being the Interest we received from
Gordonsville United Baptist Church for one year

from November 1st, 1930 until November 1st, 1931.

    Signed: *[signatures:]*
Mrs. J. A. Majors
Mrs. Arthur McBrine
Iva T. Corey
Mrs. R. E. McBrine
C. A. W[—]
Mrs. Jas. G. Hovey Jr.,
D. P. Fitzgerald

    This letter, written by some of the Highlands Baptists who remained in 1932 was an encouragement to the Knowlesville Church who were experiencing an upsurge of interest and activity and were celebrating their 70th anniversary. It appears that the gift of $25.00 was used to help buy the materials for a horse shed that was being built in 1932. Cash was scarce in the 1930's.[5]

    Some records endure; so does the cemetery. The site of Highlands Baptist Church cannot be forgotten as long as the cemetery is preserved with its monuments to those who lie buried there. Regrettably, the cemetery was for many years neglected except for the grave plot of the Branscombe family. It has been carefully tended by Ivan Branscombe and family. In more recent years the grass cutting and maintenance work on the gravesite has been done by Ralph Boyd, a grandson of Charles and Sarah Branscombe. Ralph must have been named for an uncle who died in infancy. Ralph comes yearly in summer from Ottawa.

    We too have relations buried there: three children of our Aunt Mina and Uncle Eb McBrine. In August and September, 1996, I made three visits to that cemetery, in hope of finding markers for the graves of those children. The ground was

Edna Prosser at Highlands Cemetery

rough. The graves were hidden by trees and underbrush. I found no clue of the McBrine children's graves, but I located seven stones. Accompanying me on the second visit was my brother Keith. He found the Derrah stone. Our count was up to eight. On a third visit, with my brother Gordon, we found no more stones. Here are the family names on the stones we located: Branscombe, Chute, Dingee, Doherty, Derrah, McDermid, McKenzie, Scovil.

In The Story of Knowlesville (p.235f.), we have a longer list of names. That list was compiled by Myrtle Hemphill. As she explained afterwards, she recognized that some graves were never marked or else had only wooden markers. She found additional names by searching old newspapers and other records in the New Brunswick Archives, Fredericton. Thus she gave a valuable service to the community.

More recently an additional service has been rendered

to the community. In the late fall of 1996 I received a phone call from Myrtle Hemphill announcing a decision by the Knowlesville Women's Institute to provide the funds for materials, and some labour, for the restoration of the Highlands Cemetery. It was part of a larger community undertaking by the W.I. to restore gravesites. In summer of 1997, they restored the gravesite of the Frazier family on the Arthur Avery farm in Knowlesville.[6]

There seems to be an increasing appreciation of people who have gone before us, a sense of indebtedness to them, and hence an increasing recognition of the value of restoring and preserving gravesites. It seems that the sentiments of the 18th century poet, Thomas Gray, have been rekindled:

> "Perhaps in this neglected spot is laid
> Some heart once pregnant with celestial fire;
> Hands, that the rod of empire might have swayed,
> Or waked to ecstasy the living lyre."[7]

In Golden Ridge, on old farms that have returned to forest, two gravesites that were well nigh forgotten have been uncovered, freshly marked, and made accessible, in a project directed by Lorne Craig, E. Knowlesville. In Highlands it is as if the cemetery stones, like the cobblestones over which Jesus rode into Jerusalem, were ready to break their silence and cry out for recognition. During Jesus' "Triumphal Entry", when the Pharisees wanted the rejoicing voices of the disciples silenced, Jesus replied, "....if these were silent, the very stones would cry out." (Luke 19:40). Calls for restoration of the Highlands Cemetery were heard by members of the Women's Institute and volunteers who have kinfolk buried there. Volunteering to date are Myrtle Hemphill, her sister Edna, and Orland Budrow, and a son of Chesley Dingee; Arden, and his wife Ferne. They have cleared the underbrush, and cut the bush and some of the trees, leaving some for a park-like effect. They engaged Fred Burnett, a person with special skills in locating unmarked graves. By pushing a rod into the soil he determined grave boundaries, and marked each grave with a stake. On a return visit I beheld a changed scene — a pleasant place of quiet rest and reflection, surrounded by forest, grassland and potato and grain fields. The stones of Highlands Cemetery, now in full view, mark the site of Highlands Baptist Church and enable succeeding generations to remember that:

> "Beneath those rugged elms, that yew tree's shade
> Where heaves the turf in many a mouldering heap,
> Each in his narrow cell forever laid,
> The rude forefathers of the hamlet sleep."[8]

[1] See Chapter I

[2] See Chapter XII

[3] The writer has this deed, courtesy of Elmer Briggs, Bristol

[4] See The Story of Knowlesville, p. 131.

[5] See The Story of Knowlesville, p. 164.

[6] See The Observer, Hartland, Aug. 6, 1997, p.6B

[7] Thomas Gray, "Elegy Written in a Country Churchyard"

[8] Ibid

CHAPTER VI

THE LAST DECADE ON THE COREY HOMESTEAD

1912 - 1922

The decade began with a wedding on a very cold day.
Time: January 13, 1912;
Place: The Doucette House at E. Knowlesville;
Bride: Nellie Kathleen Brown Kenney;
Groom: Ira Thomas Corey;
Officiating Minister: Rev. Judson A. Corey;
Attending the Wedding: James and Hazel Brown, father and sister of the bride.

In the stormy January of 1912 Ira married his second wife, Nellie Brown Kenney. It was also Nellie's second marriage. Ira had been widowed since June 1904, after a two-year marriage with Emily Graham. Interestingly, Nellie Brown had been a pupil of Emily's at the East Glassville School in 1901.[1] Nellie had been widowed since 1910 after a two-year marriage with Arthur Kenney, son of Roland Kenney and Jane Phillips. After being widowed she had returned to the home of her parents, Mary and James Brown in Highlands.

Nellie and Ira had planned to have their wedding at the Brown farmhouse. When the day came it was so cold[2] they decided to spare the minister the drive to Highlands. Instead two sleighs carrying the bride and groom and Mr. Brown and Hazel went to E. Knowlesville.

After the wedding the couple returned to Nellie's parents for a reception in the evening. The next day, Sunday, they "appeared out" at two church services: E. Glassville and Argyle.

They began their life together at the Corey Homestead. For Ira that was a matter of making himself at home in the only permanent home he had known. For Nellie, returning to Knowlesville was a homecoming. She had lived in Knowlesville during her earlier marriage.

When Nellie moved, as a bride, into the Corey Homestead she came immediately into a place of work, caring for others, and entertainment. With her arrival there were six people in the farmhouse. Besides the two couples there was Ira's daughter, Erma, who had lived there since age one and was now approaching nine, and Nellie's son, Murray Kenney, approaching age three.

Belonging

It appears that Nellie soon established her place of belonging in the Corey family. Very early she became the entertainer. In June of her first summer in the homestead the Coreys entertained delegates to the Baptist District meetings. Among them were Jim Fisher and his son from Skedaddle Ridge. While the delegates attended the meetings at the church all day Saturday, Nellie, with help from Aunt Alma Miller, cooked dinner and supper. Erma estimated that delegates and relatives totalled about 25.

For Nellie and Ira it was a busy and eventful first year of marriage. In September of that year 1912 their first son, Wilfred was born. Grandpa, a life-long Liberal, named him after Sir Wilfred Laurier. Before the end of the year the Corey family had another occasion to celebrate, and Nellie had another and larger group of guests to entertain. Here is the account from "The Observer", Hartland:

50th Wedding Anniversary
        KNOWLESVILLE - Mr. and Mrs.

Alfred Corey of Knowlesville celebrated the 50th anniversary of their wedding Dec. 12. They have nine children, 35 grandchildren and two great grandchildren; of which five children, twenty grandchildren and two great grandchildren were present. A dainty supper was served after which Mr. and Mrs. Corey were presented with a gold watch chain and charm, a wedding ring, a purse of gold, also a number of other presents.

With some help from Ira's sisters, Nellie did a lot of baking in preparation for the celebration. It is little wonder, then, that Nellie soon endeared herself to the Corey family. When I was growing up I frequently heard Corey relatives affectionately address my mother as "Aunt Nellie." Most of them were near her age; some even younger.

World War I

The decade this chapter focuses on, 1912-22, encompassed the First World War. W.W.I. broke out in August 1914, only about two and a half years after Ira and Nellie were married. Many Knowlesville families were affected. Some young men were casualties of the war, including a near neighbour, Samuel Linder. Another near neighbour who lived on the road to Highlands, Ned Guthrie, and one of Nellie's brothers, Malcolm Brown of Highlands, served overseas. They returned safely.

Two other young men of neighbouring families, Roy Carle and George Guthrie, were expecting to go into military service. When informed that they were exempted and would not be leaving home as expected, they turned their energies to ploughing and harrowing for Ira Corey who was sick that spring with typhoid fever and was delayed in planting his crop. That was probably spring of 1915.[3]

One memory of W.W.I that Nellie long retained was a song, which seems to indicate some charitable work for people in Europe:

> All the folks at our house
> Are busy as can be,
> A-sewing for the Belgians
> Who live across the sea.
> Chorus: Gosh I wish I was a Belgian
> With all those clothes and a brand new shirt
> I'd be a regular gosh darn flirt.

She often sang that song, sometimes while doing the Monday morning laundry.

Three of the Corey children were born in those war years: John Robert, called Bob, was born April 23, 1914; Alice Marie, first daughter of the couple, was born Nov. 8, 1915; Norman Redlon was born October 16, 1917.

Two more boys were born at the Corey Homestead soon after the end of the war: Thomas Wallace, born October 16, 1919; Claude Eugene, born September 10, 1921.

A Growing Family on the Farm

While much was happening in the world, the children were growing up on the Alfred Corey homestead. Some anecdotes have been preserved from that era of Ira's family. Bob jealously guarded a claimed prerogative as the pea sheller. When Alice tried to help he told her, "No Allie, you can't shell peas, you have only little tiny eyes; I have great big eyes."

An unhappy episode happened in the hen house. Norman, a key participant, described it: Mama was cooking and very much wanted eggs. The hens didn't produce many eggs in winter but spring was approaching. She sent Alice and me to the hen house saying, "See if there are any eggs. If you don't find any, squeeze one out of them." We looked in all the nests — high and low. There were rows of nests nailed to the wall. There was also an extra nest setting on the floor — a large veneer tea box. Determined to fulfil our mother's need for eggs, and taking the "squeeze" instruction literally, we started catching hens and putting them in the tea box. Then we sat on them. After a while all movement and sound ceased. Dismayed, we returned to the house.

Erma found especially amusing Alice's report to her mother: "There's a dead hen down there. Yes, I think there's two of 'em." They had been smothered. It is an example of tragic results from failure to understand hyperbole. From that point of view it is instructive. In retrospect it is also amusing, despite the tragic outcome. Perhaps we could call it "tragic comedy".

It was common then for hens to stop laying eggs in the coldest months. The cows also dried up. Neighbours who managed to keep some milk flowing supplied others. Bob remembered going to Roy Carle's at the next farm to the north to bring home a kettle of milk. Not till years later did he relate his episode of falling on the ice and spilling the milk. He said, "They filled it again for me."

Supplementary Income

A growing family strained the income. Ira, as his father Alfred before him, engaged in seasonal work off the farm. In winter, Ira's extra work was often in the lumbering operations. From his early years he built himself a reputation as a foreman of crews and as a contractor. In later years he said, "The company used to run after me." Often he worked on contract, cutting by the thousand board feet. He took his team to the camp and hired a driver so he could oversee the crews. Thus he was often away from home in winter.

Some summers or parts of summers, were also spent in lumber enterprises away from the farm, but not in the woods. In at least two summers the family accompanied him, and thus had adventures away from home. The enterprises and residences of those two summers were well remembered:

Summer at Juniper

The summer of 1919 the family lived near Juniper. They left Knowlesville before school closed, probably right after the spring planting. That summer they stayed in a hunting and fishing camp of which Ira was a quarter owner. The other joint owners were Caleb Doucette, Tom Guthrie and George H. Whitehouse. Ira employed his team hauling deal to Juniper Station from Crawford Mill, Argyle. Probably he was on contract by the 1,000 board feet. Bob, who turned five that spring, remembered the wagon loaded very heavily, with sawn lumber piled very high. He thought father made two trips a day.

Summer at Crawford Mill

The next summer, 1920, the family lived at Crawford Mill, Argyle. Again, Ira employed his team hauling deal to Juniper Station. Nellie cooked for the mill crew, besides taking care of five children. All of the children except Erma went to the camp for the summer. They played with the children of Dave Harvey. Norman, feeling left out of the games, said, "I don't like them Harvey boys, do you Jean?" not knowing that Jean was their sister.

Erma stayed with her grandparents. She became a visitor and messenger between the family in Knowlesville and the family at Crawford Mill. She said, "Papa left an old grey mare at home for me to drive." She made her first trip to the mill alone, but on her return journey she had a passenger. Alice, then under age five, insisted on going back to Knowlesville with her. Alice protested against living at the camp, saying, "If you'd put some paper on the wall and a mat on the floor, it might look like a house." For the rest of the summer, Alice would go to the camp only for a visit. On one visit Papa asked her, "Do you help Erma?". "Yes, I wipe up every slop Erma makes." He said, "You must be a very busy kid." The family must have gone home to Knowlesville in time for school and for harvest.

Logging, Family and Growing Boys

That fall, 1920, Ira was back into lumber work. He built a logging camp on the Little Clearwater. There he had a crew working through the fall and winter. That fall's enterprise is documented by an extant letter written by Ira.[4]

For many years Ira moved back and forth between winter logging and summer farming. Usually he was able to be at home on the farm through the spring, summer and fall for planting, haying and harvesting.

During those years the elder boys were growing and developing skills. Mother described how Wilfred had learned to harness horses when he was so small that he had to climb up on the manger to put the collar on a horse. Soon he was competing with Grandpa for the reins.

At supper one evening there arose a question of who was going to drive the horses on the hay rake. Grandpa said, "Ira, I could rake that hay." Wilfred said, "'Spect you could do a wad." Unperturbed, Grandpa quietly asserted his competence: "I can do it." However, Wilfred got the reins.[5]

Grandpa, approaching 80, was still active and was still trying to maintain some part in the farm work. However, it seems he could accept competition from Wilfred, his pride and joy whom he claimed to have named.

Good Relations: Good Memories

The three generations and amalgamated family in the small farm house lived in remarkable harmony, as indicated by anecdotes and traditions which have been preserved and narrated. Grandpa and Grandma maintained a measure of independence. He kept his driving mare, Bess. Regularly he hitched her to the wagon or sleigh for a trip to Glassville. He would drive up to the door and, leaving Bess standing in the yard, he would walk into the kitchen and restlessly repeat, "The mare is getting anxious," until Lucretia was ready. That saying became one of Nellie's amusing and special memories of life on the Corey Homestead.

There were many good memories. One of Bob's boyhood memories was the excitement of catching trout in the Coldstream which ran across the property.

A Boy with Pneumonia

One of the most enduring memories was an experience of several weeks of intense anxiety near the end of that last decade on the Homestead. In the late winter or early spring of 1922 Norman, then age four and one half, was in a critical bout with typhoid pneumonia.

Four doctors became involved in the case: Dr. Somerville undertook surgery. With Norman lying on the kitchen table in the farm house in Knowlesville, he made an incision under the left shoulder blade and inserted a tube to drain the fluid from that lung. The surgery did not bring the relief that was hoped. Over following days two other doctors stopped their horses at the farm house. Dr. Cummins came from Bath. Later, Dr. Lorne MacIntosh came from Hartland.

There seemed to be little they could do.

Kate Hovey persisted in nagging the family and eventually persuaded them to call Dr. Belyea from Woodstock. Scrutinizing the surgery, he asked, "Who would do such a stupid trick as that?" His appraisal of the surgery was unhesitating and to the point: "I never saw such a botched job. The incision is in the wrong place." Holding up a tin cup he said to Ira, "If you wanted to drain that cup, would you drill a hole near the top, or at the bottom? The point of the demonstration was unmistakable and convincing. The incision should have been at the bottom of the lung. Dr. Belyea's pronouncement was indisputable: "That boy should go to the hospital but he would never live to get there. He should be operated on again to put the drain in the right place, but he would never survive the operation." In that critical stage of the illness, Dr. Belyea prescribed his best treatment in the circumstances — apparently the only treatment. He directed that Norman be placed on a slope with his head and chest at the lower end. This was to allow the fluid to drain from his lung.

Nursed to Recovery

To ensure that his instructions were followed and to give the boy every possible aid, Dr. Belyea brought Nurse Jones from Simonds to the Corey Homestead to give undivided attention to the critically ill boy. She stayed several weeks while Norman lay on the improvised bed, lingering between life and death. Mother long remembered the tension she lived under. As she re-lived it she sometimes described it: "I'd have to put my ear right down to his nose to discover whether he was breathing."

Signs of recovery seemed long in appearing. For days there were no signs. Then recovery began in the pussy willow season. As the pussy willows slowly emerged, so did Norman emerge from the critical illness. He remembers: "When I was recovering the pussy willows came. Nurse pasted them on a paper."

A Move is Initiated

About the time that Norman passed the critical stage of his illness and began the slow road to recovery, that spring of 1922, the Corey family began a new venture. It started with a sleigh ride to E. Knowlesville on a bright Sunday afternoon when the snow was receding. Ira took Nellie to see and explore the Hemphill Farm which had been vacant all winter — unoccupied since the 1921 harvest time. A chain of events that started with a tragic accident had transpired to bring about the abandonment of that farm by the Hemphills.

On February 19, 1921 William Wallace Hemphill, son of William Hemphill, became a casualty of the saw in the mill that was located on the east border of their farm. The mill was owned by Fred Currie, son-in-law of William Hemphill. In the tragic accident Wallace's leg was nearly severed at the ankle. Dr. Lorne MacIntosh came from Hartland to the mill site and amputated Wallace's leg at the ankle. Subsequently he went into shock and died next morning, at age 40.[6]

In the spring of 1921 Wallace's brother, Sam, came from Upper Woodstock and planted a crop for their father William. That was the last season the Hemphill family occupied their farm in E. Knowlesville. William died on September 12, 1921, at the age of 81. His widow, Jane Flemming, offered the farm for sale.

Ira's motive for the sleigh ride was not hidden. He wanted to buy the farm and was trying to interest Nellie in moving to East Knowlesville. Nellie's response was unhesitating, concise and negative: "Nothing would tempt me to move out there!" There was no disputing the appropriateness of Ira's proposed venture. The growing Corey family needed a larger house and a more productive farm. For Nellie it was a question of timing. It seems that Norman had not yet recovered to the point where she could feel fully at ease. Nellie needed a little more time to recover from the trying and anxious ordeal of that spring.

Considering the circumstances, the venture was remarkably swift in development from germination to realization — typical of Ira's ability to be deliberate. Ira bought the Hemphill Farm through a transaction with J.K. Flemming, brother of Jane: Ira, being involved in winter lumbering contracts with Flemming and Gibson, Ltd., the company put up the $5,000 mortgage — a large sum for that time. Thus in spring of 1922 Ira sold the property in Knowlesville and plans proceeded for the family to move to the William Hemphill farm in E. Knowlesville. When the family was about to move to East Knowlesville, Erma queried her father: "I thought Nellie didn't want to go?" He replied, "She feels alright now; she has Norman."

Norman's recovery from an overpowering infection in the days before antibiotics was indeed a cause for thanksgiving. About a decade and a half later Norman was in Dr. Belyea's office, in Woodstock, for a check-up. Coming upon the scar under his shoulder blade he asked, "What do we have here?" Thus Norman's case was brought back to him.

Leaving the Homestead

The above conversation between Ira and Erma was during her weekend visit from Armond where she was teaching that year and boarding with the Armond Henderson family. On the day of the move she was not home. Thus she may have been spared the emotional wrench of seeing the family move from the only home she had ever known. Over her long life Erma remembered the Homestead: "I can still remember the old log house, which by my time was being used for a pig pen." They had built a frame house about 1900. "I remember the two pine stumps on the knoll beyond the spring house. My father removed them after I was nearly grown up. A puncheon was set in the spring. Water came up through auger holes in the bottom. This was for family use. A pipe let water down to anther puncheon; the horses drank from it".

Alfred Corey at homestead in Knowlesville

Erma also had good memories of her life with her grandparents and much gratitude to them. She could not forget Grandpa's oft-repeated remarks: "When I came here, it was all green forest." Leaving the homestead they had pioneered must have been an emotional wrench for Grandma and Grandpa also, at ages 80 and 81, and in the 60th year of their marriage.

In that last decade at the old Homestead the family had doubled. When Nellie and Ira married, the number of people at the Homestead became six. In their decade together six children were born: Wilfred, Bob, Alice, Norman, Tom and Claude, a seven month baby at the time of the move to the Hemphill Farm. Twelve family members made that move: Alfred and Lucretia Corey; Ira and Nellie Corey; Nellie's son Murray Kenney; Ira's daughter Erma; and the six children born at the homestead. And we must add one more, nurse Jones accompanied them, bringing to thirteen the number making the move.

[1] History of Glassville Settlement, Appendix XVIII

[2] See Chapter IV

[3] See The Story of Knowlesville, p.127f.

[4] Ira's letter and more on Clearwater is in Chap. VII

[5] Remembered by Erma and Norman

[6] See The Story of Knowlesville, p. 136

CHAPTER VII

THE HEMPHILL FARM & GRANDPA'S LAST EIGHT YEARS

In April, 1922, while there was still enough snow for sledding, the Coreys loaded their household goods: furniture, cooking utensils and dishes; their farming tools and equipment, their hay and oats, onto sleds. They also moved livestock: cows, pigs and hens to the William Hemphill Farm, in E. Knowlesville.

Walter Whitehouse said at that 1991 Corey reunion, "I remember when the family moved." Afterwards he said, "I was only nine at the time. I was then living in Glassville and was with the Corey family for the day." Earlier, with his parents, Clara and Percy, and his elder siblings, he had lived on the Joe Still Whitehouse farm adjacent to the Hemphill Farm. Had they remained in E. Knowlesville they would have been the nearest neighbours of the Coreys.

That spring, 1922, Ira planted perhaps the smallest crop ever on that farm. No ploughing had been done the previous fall. Thus he had to both plough and harrow before planting; hence he seeded only a small acreage of oats.

Norman Recovering

While fields were being seeded Norman was completing his convalescence. He remembers that Nurse Jones accompanied the family to the Hemphill Farm. She slept in one of the four upstair bedrooms — the southwest room, overlooking the brook, the room later occupied by Erma and Alice. The new environment must have been favourable to Norman. He made a good recovery though the illness left him changed. Erma said, "Before he got sick he was a fat and roley poley boy. Afterwards he was long and skinny."

In the two places, Mrs. Jones was with the family for two months or more. She retained good memories of the Corey family. For some years she sent to the family letters, cards and snapshots, eg., one of herself standing between her two boys.

Norman and Grandmother

As soon as Norman was up and going he was given a task. Grandmother Lucretia was nearly blind. Norman said, "They used to get me to take her by the hand and conduct her to the outhouse and wait for her." That task, however, was of short duration. Grandmother's strength was failing when they moved to the Hemphill Farm.

However, she apparently remained quite active until near her last day. Later, Nellie related how she sat in a rocking chair in the yard of the farmhouse enjoying a June day and asked for roast beef. Nellie questioned whether she could digest it, but Ira insisted that his mother should have what she wanted. On June 17, 1922, Lucretia died. Funeral arrangements were simple and practical. Ira hitched a pair of horses to his sloven wagon. Murray Kenney, age 13, drove Grandpa to Glassville to select and bring home a coffin. Between planting and haying they conducted Grandma's funeral and laid her to rest in the cemetery of the United Baptist Church in Knowlesville.

Summer 1922

Haying occupied much of that summer. The small acreage in oats had left many fields in grass. The hay crop was so large they were not able to harvest it all. Fred MacKenzie long remembered looking across the woods in the late summer and seeing Ira Corey and Sandy Brown, hired hand, bring horses and mowers into the most easterly 20 acre field, then abandon it, judging the hay to be too mature to be worth cutting.

Fall 1922

Harvesting the oats must have been a relatively small job. Ira's biggest task that fall must have been pressing 47 tons of his hay.[1] This would have been in addition to the loose hay to be fed to the livestock at home. There were a few other farm tasks before winter logging: ploughing for next year's grain crop, and cutting some fire wood. By October, 1922, Ira had his logging crew on the Little Clearwater Brook, a little beyond Juniper, and to the south. Fortunately we have an interesting account of that fall's logging enterprise: a letter written by Ira himself to his daughter, Erma, who was teaching in Rusagonis that fall. He tells her a lot about his logging, his management of his crew, his camp and his regular visits home to pick up a load of hay to take to the camp. Ira's letter also tells us a lot about Corey relatives. As a preface to the letter we identify the persons mentioned: Jud McBrine, Ida Corey McBrine's eldest son; Dorothy, Jud's wife; Jud's sisters: Nellie Lindsay, Kathleen McBrine, Clara Whitehouse and Nessie Avery; Everette Kenney, purchaser of Corey Homestead; Amy, W.W.I bride, wife of James Kierstead; Cale = Caleb Doucette, Helen Brown, Nellie Corey's youngest sister; Lottie Whitehouse, Nellie's eldest sister, Elwood Whitehouse, Lottie's husband; Claude Corey, born September 1921, then the youngest of Ira's children.

Following is the letter written to Erma. It was treasured by her the rest of her life.

Knowlesville
Oct 29/22

My Dear Ernd
                It seems to
be quite a task for me
to settle down to write and
I came near getting away
again without writing. Only
that I had to stay home
to night and look up a horse
I got that bay one from
Elwood Whitehouse Luce got
hurt in the woods and they
had to shoot her; I gess
I am having some of the
luck that mother used to
wish on me. I came home
Friday Knight & Nellie and
I had to drive to Hartland
Sat to to fix up that deed
for Evert

Ira Corey's letter, p.1 of 6

Knowlesville
Oct 29/22

My Dear Erma

It seems to be quite a task for me to settledown to write, and I came near getting away again without writing. Only that I had to stay home to night and look up a horse. I got that bay one from Elwood Whitehouse. Luce got hurt in the woods, and they had to shoot her. I guess I am having some of the luck that Mother used to wish on me. I came home Friday night and Nellie and I had to drive to Hartland Sat. To fix up that deed for Evert.

It was a cold long drive, for Nellie at least. Helen stayed with the children. Murray was in the woods over Sunday with a load; he is coming home tomorrow. I have about 36 men in there now so the cooks are quite busy but are doing all right. I expect to go back in the morning. I would of went back today, only for getting a horse. Nellie Linsey and Kathleen is tending Central and Clara is down with Nessie helping to cook for Jud. I am working on the Little Clearwater in the camp I built two years ago, two miles beyond where Jud is working. He is in the same place he was last winter. Dorothy is often there with him, we pressed 47 tons of hay. I am hauling my own hay to the woods and Murray is supplying Jud with hay. Also hauling some for Fleming. He took in four loads last week. Pretty good for a kid. I suppose you heard about Bill Guthrie's foot going bad. They took him to the horse piddle and had his big toe taken off at the ball of the foot. The bone was infected. He is coming all right now. So you like Garrish pretty well do you? Well you will soon be done and hard to tell; you might get in a worse place next time. Job's comforter. Well that is the way of the world. We will have to be satisfied with our lot. I am getting about tired of the woods myself. Nellie says I will have to stay home after this winter; she says she would be willing to live on potatoes and pancakes. I could get them quite easy. I am afraid when the Eaton Catalogue came along, there would be a different cry. Oh no Cale isn't with me this year. I didn't send for him yet, nor he didn't ask for a job. I got four teams yarding. I am not sure about getting another one yet, they want me to cut 12,000,000. I would have to get the fifth team if I did. The cooks don't want me to get any more men; they have about all they can handle.

    Well I guess you have got the news in general about logging. I'm as bad as Kate Linder when I get started. I don't know much that is going on in the settlement as I am not home long enough, but I heard Lotty say today that Amy had an awful nice baby, and how good and nice looking it was; and how well she took care of it.

    The children are all well as ever. Claude can stand up alone in the middle of the floor and can take a step or two and push chairs. Well I hope you are getting along all right. I suppose I would write oftener if it wasn't for Nell writing, but I hear that way and saves me a lot of trouble writing. Well we got another dose of salve yesterday and Nellie went over the bunch again tonight and she is lying down having a sleep. How did you make out? Did you get it when you was home? Well, I will close for this time. Hoping this will find you well.

                                          As ever, your loving Dad Ira.

Farm Work, Fall of 1922

While Ira was spending winter months at Little Clearwater Brook, there was work on the farm: the care of the livestock and bringing firewood into the house for three stoves. Though Grandpa Alfred was then 81, nearer 82, and his eyesight was failing, he must have been doing all, or most, of the barn work.

The school records show: Murray, Wilfred, Bob and Alice on the E. Knowlesville school roll for the fall term.[2] Murray must have left school when the fall logging began. Ira's letter indicates that Murray was hauling hay to the camp.

Events of 1923: Birth, Holiday; Clearwater Again

In later years my father told me that he came home from that winter's logging just in time for my birth on April 16, 1923, almost exactly one year after the family's move to the E. Knowlesville farm. I was the first of my family to be born in that farmhouse. Going to hospital for childbirth was not even thought of then. Dr. Cummins, travelling from Bath by horse and sleigh, arrived in time.

Erma was teaching school at Windsor that year. Near the beginning of summer holidays she and Grandpa took the train from Woodstock to Hoyt Station to visit his son, Rev. Judson and family. It was a rare and brief holiday trip away from the farm for Alfred. In the fall of 1923 he must have been again doing the barn work. Ira was again logging on Little Clearwater. Murray, then age 14, was again driving one of Ira's teams, hauling hay and oats to the camp which stood where Clearwater Brook flows into the South Branch of the Miramichi.[3]

Winters at Home: 1924 - 1928

Beginning in the fall of 1924 and lasting for the next four years it appears that Ira took a surcease from winters in the lumber camps. Perhaps, only one winter late, he responded to Nellie's plea that he expressed in his letter of Oct. 29, 1922 asking him to stay home in winter. Recollections, though imprecise, give fairly clear indication that in those four winters he worked on his own woodlots.

In the fall of 1924 Nellie had the whole family at home. Irma was teaching in Knowlesville. That allowed her a special sport, driving a horse. About the time the Corey family moved to E. Knowlesville they acquired a fast trotter named Dick. In the fall of 1924 Erma was driving him to school in Knowlesville and stabling him in George W. Whitehouse's barn. It was the era when automobiles were coming in. Some horses were very frightened of them. Dick was not frightened by cars. He just didn't want to lose a contest to them in speed. Hence a story of a race.

One afternoon just as Erma headed Dick up the lane toward E. Knowlesville, Tommy Armstrong, on a visit from Saint John to his Brown relatives, pulled out of Elwood Whitehouse's and started up the lane behind Erma. She decided not to let him pass. Erma said, "Come on, Dick," and the race began. With a terrific burst of speed Dick climbed the lane, rounded the bends at the top of the Cook/Manuel farm and at Osbert Whitehouse's, and George H. Whitehouse's, passed the Joe Still Whitehouse place, and rounded the bend that brought them in sight of the Ira Corey farm. Keeping her lead, Erma trotted Dick across the field, down the hill and across the brook. As Tommy crossed the brook he shifted into second gear then low gear, and chugged laboriously up the pig pen hill. Without the slightest hesitation Dick trotted up the hill, ahead of the car. Erma met Tommy with a note of triumph as he parked his car and got out. When the snow came Erma changed from wagon to sleigh and continued driving Dick until Christmas. After New Year's she boarded with the George W. Whitehouse family.

Erma's younger siblings were in E. Knowlesville school. Wilfred was nearing the end of his school days, but apparently he was able to continue school for three of those four winters of logging on the Hemphill place. His name is on the school list for the year ending June 1927.[4] If he completed that term it probably was the last of his school days. June 1927 also marked the end of Erma's teaching — at least for her first time round. She was teaching in Simonds that year. On June 15 she married Allison M. Shaw. Simonds became her home.

Logging at Home

In the winter of 1927-28 Ira had a crew cutting logs on the east side of our farm, between Fall Brook and Malcolm MacKenzie's.[5] By the fall of 1927, Wilfred, just turned 15, was driving a pair of horses twitching the logs to the yards. Ira tended the yard and swamped the trails for the horses. George H. Whitehouse and Clarence LaPage pulled the crosscut saw.[6] The date of that winter enterprise, 1927-28, is verified by Warren. He recalls George H. Whitehouse reminiscing about it in the late 40's.

After New Year's, Ira's two teams, one driven by Wilfred Corey, the other by Olys Brown, hauled the logs to John Crawford's mill, Argyle. They made their own road. It ran up the brook on our farm toward Willis Branscombe's where it merged into the regular road, and followed it through the first swamp about as far as Billy Crawford's. From there they took a road that cut through the woods northeastward to Crawford's mill, east of Argyle.

There was a lively logging activity in the neighbourhood. Bill and Bob Guthrie cut logs on their lower place, afterwards owned and occupied by Bob and family. They cut a road through their woods and joined the road to the mill. Aubrey Lee worked with Bill and Bob. Charlie Branscombe, though handicapped by an amputated arm, cut logs on his place and hauled over the same road as Guthries. Osbert Whitehouse cut logs on the Weston place in E. Knowlesville. Archie Sewell drove Osbert's team hauling logs to the mill. Fred Currie and Jim Sewell hauled logs from Golden Ridge and connected with the road to the mill.[7]

That winter, part of the regular highway was abandoned. Traffic came across our farm on the sled road that ran right by our cow barn. Though I was only coming up to five the winter of 1928, I remember Verna LaPage riding in her sleigh, a tin mail box at her feet, and a buffalo robe over her knees, driving her black gelding, Rex, right through our barn yard.

That winter, 1928, Erma made her February sleigh journey from Simonds to E. Knowlesville and back. But the road I've just described was a trotting park, compared to sections of the road her horse travelled. Roads without logs and supplies being hauled could have deep snow.

School, Barn Work and Grandpa

There was no idleness in those years of winter logging. Alice, Norman, Tom and Claude were in school.[8] The boys were growing toward ability to assume more of the barn work. However, Grandpa continued working in the barn as long as he could. Norman remembers when he cleaned the cow stable every morning, even after his eyesight had become so poor that the tines of his manure fork were jabbing the cows' heels. Far into his old age, he worked about the farm, wearing his home-knitted wool cardigan with only the top two buttons fastened.

Grandpa was busy in all seasons, as long as he lived. In summer, he weeded and hoed the garden and thinned the turnips. He took the thinnings to the pigs, which recalls another story. One summer Uncle Jud and Aunt Alice persuaded Grandpa to visit them. He did, but only for a short stay. Soon he grew restless and was determined to take the train back home. Aunt Alice was long amused by this alibi: "I have to get back home to feed the pigs; Ira never could look after pigs."

His Own Room; His Own Turf; His Disposition

When feebleness slowed and eventually ended his part in the farm work, Grandpa still had his own chores to do. He managed his own room at the front of the house. There he had a tall cylinder stove in which he burned plenty of hardwood. He brought his wood on his hand sled from the outdoor woodpile to the front door. He kept plenty ahead for stormy days, including a variety of kindling wood, neatly sorted in boxes: birch bark, shavings and small splinters of softwood. I think he used the splinters also for lighting his pipe. If his fire went out, e.g., over night, he could quickly kindle it. At times he built very hot fires. Sometimes the stove was red hot.

He kept his hand sled with six inch high standards leaning against the house. One evening Annie Brown and Murray Kenney borrowed the sled. Sliding down the steep hill to the brook, it slewed sideways. One runner collapsed under the sled. "Grandpa was some mad."[9] He didn't fail to employ his ability to be assertive and claim his own territory, property and privacy. He needed that sled to bring his firewood.

That front bedroom was Grandpa's own territory. At times he would allow quite a group of us to visit in his room. He could be tolerant of our childish and adolescent behavior, up to a point. We didn't know how unsettling noisy boys could be to a man in his late 80's nor how much he must have needed quietness at times. He knew when it was time to claim his privacy and his territory. If we got too noisy, he simply lifted his cane and sent us all out of his room.

Ageing and Ailments

Grandpa had some afflictions and some discomforts. He had a skin condition he called eczema. He rubbed on Minard's liniment. Also he kept a mixture of kerosene oil and coarse salt in a pickle jar. In the bottle was a cotton swab on the end of a stick. He swabbed his legs, especially in winter. I think this was to stop the itchiness. Now, I wonder if he had psoriasis. Having had a touch of it myself, I know it can be itchy. Perhaps it is hereditary. He also had a hernia. He wore a truss by day and hung it on his bedpost at night. Probably that was prescribed by a doctor. Apparently surgery for that condition was not even considered in those days.

He endured another condition that perhaps was then considered to be expected in old age. Occasionally, when he was outside, perhaps at the woodpile, he would slump over, pass out, and lie still on his back. We said, "Grandpa is having one of his 'spells'." In a few moments he would get up and go again. It seems that people then didn't expect to have a doctor except for what they considered serious ailments.

Obviously there were times when he didn't feel well. Thus he should be commended for a pretty good disposition. He could be assertive. He could also be affectionate.

Generosity

Though never overly expressive in his affections, Grandpa could, in his own way, be warm, kindly and generous. At times he brought us liquorice; some in the shape of whistles, some in the shape of bent-stemmed pipes, complete with red decoration on top of the bowl, in imitation of fire.

I remember the cold and sunny winter day he returned from a visit to Miller's in Glassville and probably to Mina and

Ed McBrine's in E. Glassville. Bob had driven our fast-trotter, Dick, to Glassville to speed Grandpa home in the sleigh at the end of his visit. His return brought excitement to youngsters. He allowed us all in his room. He had brought from Glassville a bottle of raspberry wine, probably a gift from Kate Hovey. He gave each of us in turn a drink of his precious wine from his pint dipper, diluted with water from his pail that he kept on his stand. It was delicious.

Pleasure

Grandpa got pleasure from his pipe. Norman remembers that when his tobacco got low he walked to Glassville - seven miles by highway. He shortened the distance by walking through the woods from our farm to Bob Guthries, taking the Highlands Road to Dick Linder's, then taking a path through the woods to Robert Boyle's. Norman says Kate Miller Hovey gave him money for tobacco. Once when he arrived back at the farm he was very happy. He had a supply of eight or ten plugs of tobacco. Besides he still had money - nine nickels.

There came a time when the walk was too far. He had to get somebody to take him before his tobacco ran out. His son, Rev. Judson, during one of his visits by car, drove his father to Glassville. With amusement, Uncle Jud afterwards related that he picked up a large package of tobacco and asked his father, "How much of this would you like?" He replied, "I'll take the whole of it." That was, perhaps, his last supply. He had a few plugs left at the end of his life.

Era: Horses to Automobiles

A ride to Glassville by automobile probably never happened to Grandpa before he was past 80. Automobiles came at the end of Grandpa's life; they came at the beginning of mine. Grandpa's life drew to a close and mine began between two eras. The era of travel by horses was coming to an end. Travel by automobile was beginning.

My earliest memory of a trip by car farther than to Glassville for shopping was a visit to Erma Shaw's at Simonds, sometime after her marriage, 1927. It probably was while Grandpa was still living. We left after Sunday School at Knowlesville in the 4-90 Chevrolet with isinglass set in the side. At Hartland our excitement mounted as we entered the covered bridge over the Saint John River. The car travelled at the right speed for us to see the river through the spaces between the upright boards on the sidewalls of the longest covered bridge in the world. Viewing that river for the first time, my world expanded.

About that time Grandpa had what was probably the longest automobile ride of his life. In summer of 1928 he left the farm with Uncle Charles and Ivan. They had come in their little roadster to take him to their home on Campobello Island. Though I was only age five in 1928, I can still bring up on my memory screen a vivid picture of three generations of Coreys in that little one-seated car with the curtains open. Ivan was at the wheel. Uncle Charles was in the center of the seat. Grandpa sat by the passenger door. He had filled his pipe. Just as Ivan was about to let out the clutch, Grandpa struck his match up the outside of the door, leaving a conspicuous scratch. Never mind! It was always O.K. in his wagon! Apparently he had the ability to completely relax as he travelled. If asked, "Are you tired?" he would reply, "No, why would I be tired? I'm not doing anything."

It must have been soon after our trip to Simonds that I learned of a place called Florenceville. There, Bill Burnham sold horses that he transported in railway boxcars from Western Canada. One Saturday in early fall of 1928 Father drive his trotting horse, Dick, to Florenceville Norman recalls accompanying Father in the wagon. They trotted to Florenceville by noon. The dickering for a horse, and the selection, took quite a while. At length Father bought a big Clydesdale gelding.

They started for home, Norman driving Dick, Father sitting beside him holding the halter rope of the big western, walking at a good pace behind the wagon. They got only as far as the railway crossing in Florenceville before a catastrophe occurred. When the train blew its whistle, the western horse, probably frightened of trains after a long ride on a freight car from the prairies, jumped sideways. He pulled his halter rope out of Father's hands, and ran toward the tracks. Happily the train reached the crossing first. Father ran and grabbed the halter rope. It was long after dark when they reached E. Knowlesville. We were all in bed. As soon as we awoke on Sunday morning we ran to the horse barn. It was exciting to see that big bay Clydesdale with a wide, white face and white stocking legs. We named him Prince.

Logging Venture on Skedaddle Ridge

What prompted Father to buy the western horse was a contract with Heber Hatfield of Hartland to cut lumber on Skedaddle Ridge. Norman recalls that Mr. Hatfield come to our house to have the contract signed. Norman says, "I remember him sitting in a chair in the living room. They dickered. I think he stayed over night. At length they came to an agreement."

For yarding and later hauling the logs on sleds to the mill at S. Knowlesville, Ira wanted a heavy and able team. He mated Prince with a bay mare named Queen who had had a tendency to kick. He bought her from John Millie at Glassville. Bill McKenzie drove that team through the yarding season at MacIntosh Brook.

Engaging a cook gave us another ride in the 4-90 Chevrolet. On a Sunday afternoon in the early fall of 1928, Father drove to Mount Pleasant. Mother rode in front holding Keith, then under one year. In the back seat were Claude, Warren and I. At a farmhouse, Father talked to Bill Laskey. He was handicapped by the loss of a tear duct from one eye. He had suffered an accident when he opened an oven door. Flames from burning food hit him in the face. Apparently he cooked for Ira through the early fall until after the snow came. Then Charlie Cahill became the cook. Bob Corey remembered driving Dick with the sleigh to Crawford Mill to pick up Charlie and drive him to the Skedaddle Ridge camp. Why the change? It seems Charlie had agreed to come to Ira's camp at the completion of Crawford's logging. Bob, age 14, also made trips to Glassville for supplies: canned tomatoes, peas, etc. Norman then age 11, said, "We took them to the camp on Saturdays."

All the boys were excited when the men came out of the woods for the Christmas break and stabled the horses in our barn. Murray was driving Jim Hovey's team. For them, there were only two separate, single stalls on opposite sides of the horse barns. The saddle-backed bay mare whinnied pathetically for her mate when they were separated. That got to Murray. Old Dick had to change stalls so as to give the mare the stall beside her mate.

By Christmas, Wilfred, 16 that fall, was driving our pair of bays. During the "break" he allowed us, the younger brothers, to accompany him on the sled when he took supplies to the cook at the camp. I remember my first sight of the log structure. It was the first lumber camp I ever saw. When we arrived, Charlie the cook was in the yard splitting wood. He had brushed the snow off some upright blocks and placed handsful of barley on them. Curiously, we asked him about the barley. He sang a little song: "Oh I am Charlie and I've got barley, up the leg of my drawer." After a bit of teasing he said, "I put it there for the chick-a-dees."

Charlie Cahill had apparently agreed to stay at the camp over the Christmas break and keep a fire. He seriously failed his agreement, resulting in a catastrophe. When Father and his crew returned to the camp, after the holidays, they met a cold reception. Instead of a camp with fires burning and food prepared, there were ice filled containers, frozen food and bulged cooking utensils. Charlie had deserted the camp. It was said that he had "a fondness for the bottle". It was also said that he sometimes resorted to lemon and vanilla extracts, common flavouring supplies for cook rooms.[10] Mother had to go to that camp and cook for the crew of loggers for a few days or weeks, starting about New Year's. My sister, Alice, only 13 in November 1928, kept house at the farm.

Charlie returned and cooked for the crew the rest of the winter.[11] My father seemed not to hold anything against him. On trips to and from Juniper he sometimes stopped to see Charlie. Once he came home with a small New Testament in his vest pocket, compliments of the "New Testament Pocket League". Father was not unaware of possible pretences under which Charlie received a supply to dispense. It seems that everybody was very forgiving of Charlie.

I remember the cold winter day we brought Mother home in the long sled from the camp. When we came in sight of the farmhouse flames were coming out of the chimney. There was no panic. As soon as mother came into the house she got a pan of coarse salt and dropped it by the handful into the cylinder stove in the living room.

Grandpa was in his own room, apparently oblivious to the chimney fire. As he became less active he enjoyed the quietness of his room with a south window overlooking the brook and the highway, and a west window toward the sunset. He was in his sunset of life.

The last event I remember about the winter of logging on Skedaddle Ridge was the March homecoming of the men with horses and sleds laden with equipment. When the logs were all delivered to the mill the men packed up the equipment and abandoned the camp. On a pair of bob sleds, with a rough bottom of small logs stretched over the rockers, was a collection of equipment and tools: axes, crosscut saws, peaveys, chains, blankets and cooking utensils — plus one large item — a molasses puncheon that lay on its side on the sled for days. It had been drained and the head had been knocked out, exposing the inside of the big barrel. There was a residue of the thick sweet syrup that we could scrape with spoons from the barrel staves. We could consume a generous quantity of sweets.

Discovery and Learning; Pleasure and Pain

There is another recollection of that spring of 1929, however, that is in contrast to the discovery and excitement I've described. The school term began March 1st. I was coming up to six in April. All winter I anticipated the beginning of school in March. At Derrah's Store, Glassville, my mother had bought me a new slate and slate pencil. With expectation of venture and discovery, I went to the little white school house at the juncture of the Golden Ridge Road and the road to Argyle.

Seven decades have not erased the recollection of a cold and fearful atmosphere on that first morning. Half way through that long frightening morning, Eric MacDonald, the new teacher from Lakeville, ordered the whole room of students, of all eight grades, to stand in the aisles for exercises. The commands were in numbers: 1,2,3,4, which the initiated understood were to be translated into arm movements: upward, forward, sideways and downward. Embarrassed at not knowing what to do with such military-style commands I was seized with fright, lost control, and became even more embarrassed as I stood over a puddle. It leaked down through the cracks in the worn softwood floor. I sat in wet pants the rest of the long day and had to walk fast to keep them from freezing to me on my way home. Reflection makes me ask why youngsters who had run over the crust, or waded the snow, slid down hill, walked or snowshoed after milking cows, carrying pails, feeding calves, pigs and hens, should need such exercise.

The events of following days did not allay my fears.

There was little instruction for the arithmetic problems that the teacher put on my slate. For each incorrect sum he pulled my ear as far as it would stretch and then twisted it. Furthermore, I was ordered to stay at recess and "correct" all the sums. I sat there imprisoned and frightened until my brother Claude, 7 1/2, came and whispered, "Correct means to make them right."

However, there were happier times. The men had brought home from the camp a medium-sized black and white dog that had been trained by Charlie Cahill. On the command "Say your prayers", he would lay his head on the nearest surface, close his eyes and place his front paws at the side of his head. They had also brought a hand-crafted checker board and checkers. We all learned to play that game. We learned to make our own entertainment. I am still unable to comprehend what people mean when they talk about being bored. Growing up was an ongoing experience of learning, discovering many phenomena, and acquiring many skills. It was often exciting and pleasurable.

However, the excitement of discovery and the pleasure was sometimes mixed with pain. In my second year of school, spring term, 1930, our teacher, Louise Derrah from Glassville boarded with Corey's. After supper I struggled with my reader and got frustrated. On one page was: "lamb" and "plum", including a picture of each. Why the "b" on lamb? My mother, seeing my frustration said, "Louise will help you." That lesson concluded, I needed an outing. I went into the field on the west side of the house where the black mare, Nell, was grazing, with her pretty bay filly, named "Bird", at her side. The filly, only a few weeks old, swung quickly around and kicked me in the stomach with both her hind feet.

My mother comforted me, soothing my aching stomach, but that seemingly hostile move was harder to accept as I remembered the excitement her arrival had brought, only a month earlier. One morning when we came downstairs to the kitchen, our mother, between flips of buckwheat pancakes, had said, "There is a new colt in the barn." With unbounded excitement we ran to the box stall and saw the little filly already on its feet and reaching for its mother's nipples.

The pain that the innocent sometimes have inflicted on them doesn't always come from a hostile source. Offenders sometimes act out of fear. Claude experienced that in a much later incident. He was carrying a sap can of oats into a stall. Very surprisingly, the long-legged gelding kicked the bucket out of his hand. It was a reaction from fear. After that, any who entered that stall did so with caution.

My memory bank holds much of pleasure, little of pain. Perhaps euphoric recall has selected the pleasures to outweigh the pains, and hence the pains have largely faded. Among the pleasant memories that remain as a treasure are having a grandfather with us for at least part of our growing-up years.

Right to his end, Grandpa participated in family activities. Mother always sent one of us to call him to meals. He ate at the family table. At times of family Bible-reading and prayer, Mother always sent one of us to call him to join the circle. Grandpa's end came quietly and surprisingly, without any premonition. Or did we possibly miss some signs that his end was approaching, e.g., his unawareness of a chimney fire. He lived only one more winter after that.

On an August Saturday evening Father drove his 4-90 Chevrolet to Highlands, taking Mother to visit her father, James Brown, who had fallen through the roof of the shed between his two barns. He lay in bed suffering much pain from a broken back. I remember only mother holding me, age 7, on her lap on the way home. Such a comfort! From a mother whose affection had to be spread over so many of us. Next morning, Sunday, August 17, Mother was frying pancakes. Father must have been with the older boys milking the cows. Mother sent my elder brother, Claude, to call Grandpa to breakfast. Claude returned, puzzled: "Grandpa won't answer." As soon as Father came, Mother had him set down his pails of milk, then said, "You had better go and see why Grandpa isn't coming for breakfast."

Father discovered his father lying lifeless in bed. Without delay, Ira drove his 4-90 Chevrolet to East Glassville. He brought his sister Mina McBrine. Together they laid out their father's body. Ira told relatives, friends, and neighbors, "Father must have died very painlessly in his sleep. We found him in his usual position, on his right side with his hands between his knees." He emphasized his father's long life: 89 and six months. It seems that after the body was laid in the coffin and placed in the livingroom, Father and Mother again went to visit her father, our Grandfather Brown. That evening Fred and Agnes Hemphill came to visit. Bob explained our parents' absence and opened the coffin lid to show them Grandpa's peaceful face.

Only a few weeks earlier my father had taken Grandpa to the funeral of his long-time friend, John Hemphill, who had died on June 1st. Alfred Corey and John Hemphill were both born in 1841, and both died in 1930 at age 89. My father had an amusing story: Whenever Grandpa and John Hemphill met, Grandpa asked, "How old are you, John?" Once my father interjected: "When was the last time he asked you?" John replied, "The last time he saw me!"

Grandpa's funeral, near the end of haying season, brought the neighbors and many relatives — first to the farmhouse where the service began with prayers, before taking the body to the church by family hearse. One of his grandsons, Fred McBrine, drove the hearse — his truck. Jim Hovey and other relatives, wearing black arm bands, were the pallbearers. They lifted the coffin onto the truck and rode with it to Knowlesville United Baptist Church. There, according to Norman's recollection, our uncle, Rev. Judson A. Corey, conducted the funeral service. He also sang in a duet with Ira.

In the cemetery on the church grounds Alfred was buried beside Lucretia. There was another visit and task before Grandpa was left to rest. One evening Father drove his 4-90 Chevrolet to the cemetery. Claude and I rode with him. We collected the round-pointed shovels that had been left for the volunteers to cover the grave after the family members left the cemetery. Some years later, under the initiative of Kate Miller Hovey, a monument was erected in that cemetery for Lucretia and Alfred Corey.

[1] Erma

[2] The Story of Knowlesville, p.141

[3] Roy Hemphill remembered

[4] The Story of Knowlesville, p.145f.

[5] Norman Corey remembers

[6] Norman Corey remembers

[7] Recollections of Norman Corey

[8] The Story of Knowlesville, p.146

[9] Norman's story

[10] Currie and Bradley, History of Argyle..., p.82; also, recollections of Norman Corey

[11] See also The Story of Knowlesville, p.146

CHAPTER VIII

MINA McBRINE BRANCH OF THE COREY FAMILY

1865　Armina Corey McBrine　　1938
m. 1891
1867　Robert Edmund McBrine　　1936

Erma Corey Shaw:

As I was growing up in the home of my grandparents I learned the story of my Aunt Mina, as I learned about all my aunts and uncles. Wealthy Armina Corey was the second child of Alfred and Lucretia Corey. Their first child, also a daughter, died of cholera at age one year. Mina was born August 12, 1865, in Queens County, N.B. as were her sister Alma, and her brother Charles. With the Corey family, she sojourned in Maine and in Woodstock, N.B. before they began pioneer farming in Knowlesville, N.B., c. 1874. Mina was then about age nine.[1] Like all her siblings, Armina attended the Knowlesville School.[2] As a young single woman, also like her siblings, she worked in the U.S.A.[3] In 1891 Mina Corey married Robert Edmund McBrine. To the Coreys he became known as "Uncle Eb." They bought the former Lunnie Farm in East Glassville, which apparently comprised two 100-acre lots. Immediately after their marriage they moved into the farm house which was to be their home for the rest of their lives.

The farm was only about four miles north of Mina's parents' home in Knowlesville. While their children were growing up they often travelled the four miles to Grandma's and Grandpa's house in Knowlesville. In winter they came nearly every Sunday by team and longsled. I also remember the winter Uncle Eb stayed with us at the Corey Homestead. He was helping my father cut logs. He always had kindly words for me in the evening.[4]

Seven children were born to Mina and Eb McBrine. The four who grew up were:

> Alma Armina, b. Sept. 29, 1892; d. Sept. 4, 1979
> Glenna Lucretia, b. Feb. 9, 1894, d. Sept. 28, 1978
> Ferne Elzivetta, b. July 9, 1895, d. May 22, 1975
> Frederick Rice, b. Sept. 19, 1901, d. Jan. 17, 1983
> The three other children born to Mina and Eb died in infancy:
> A daughter, Claratta May McBrine, d. 1897; and
> A pair of twins, a daughter and a son, Delma Burns McBrine, Robert Edmund McBrine.

Apparently the twins lived about two years. Their dates are: 1899 - 1901.[5] The children were victims of cholera and pneumonia. They are buried in the cemetery of Highlands Baptist Church.

Mina Corey McBrine became a member of that church when it was called by its earlier name, Aberdeen Baptist. Her name is recorded on p. 15 of the record book kept by her father, Alfred Corey. It indicates that she was baptized by A.H. Hayward, May 23, 1886. On p. 25 of the same record book her name is recorded, "Mrs. Ed McBrine" on a membership list corrected to April 1899.

Erma:

"As a child I visited Aunt Mina and Uncle Eb a lot and always enjoyed being there. They had plenty of wood for winter comfort and they kept the house very neat. Mina did much farm work along with Eb. They had a team of horses: Darkie, pure black, and Chub, pure white. Chub was a brother of

Grandpa Corey's much favored Bess. Their dame was Polly. They kept four to six cows, had plenty of milk, and sold butter. They also kept sheep for a time. They took their wool to the carding machine at Bristol, where it was made into rolls. From the rolls Aunt Mina spun yarn with her spinning wheel. I remember her walking back and forth as she spun. She was the only person I ever saw spinning. From some of the spun yarn she knitted a set of underwear: shirt and drawers for Uncle Eb. Norman Corey said, "He wore them winter and summer." She also sewed nearly all their clothes.

"I have fond memories of the times I spent in the home of my Aunt Mina and Uncle Eb, in East Glassville. In the fall of 1909 I spent six weeks with them. Grandma Corey left me with them while she went on a trip, in company with Maude Miller. They visited Grandma's son Judson, and family in Lewiston, Maine; her daughter, Alberta, in Portland; and her son, Charles, and family on Campobello Island.

"Being age six in 1909 I began school in E. Glassville and attended for the six weeks I was at McBrines." The McBrine children must have been in the school with Erma. Alma, Glenna, Ferne and Fred, are all on the school register for year ending June 1910.[6]"

Erma's Year in E. Glassville, 1920-21

Eleven years after my beginning as a pupil in E. Glassville School I had my beginning as a teacher in the same school. I began my teaching career at the same school where I began as a pupil. That was in the fall of 1920. I was then 17 years old. Of course I boarded with Aunt Mina and Uncle Eb for that school year. Living with them was the more precious, knowing that my mother, Emily Graham, had also boarded with them when she taught in the E. Glassville school in 1901.[7]

Many other school teachers also boarded with Mina and

Ed McBrine next door to the school. One was Jennie Dickinson, from Debec, who taught in E. Glassville in 1915 and afterwards married Murray Lamont. Managing that school was indeed a remarkable undertaking for Erma. Some of the pupils

E. Glassville School

were related to her family. Some were almost as old as she was. When Erma was age 85 she still remembered most of her E. Glassville pupils: Annie, Helen, Elbridge and Archie Brown; Myrtle Haines; Donnie and Earl Lindsay. From the John Anderson family: Hudson and Jennie; from the Bob Anderson family; Jessie, Alta, Alex, Muriel and Don; Erma Lunnie; Helen Robinson; Gordon and Russell Spence; Evelyn Bromley; and George MacFarland - who built the fires in the mornings. The school list has additional names for the year 1920-21: Ruth Lindsay, Mary Ellen Whalen, and Edna Wilson.[8]

McBrine Family in 1920-21: Alma

In 1920 when Erma went to teach in E. Glassville, Aunt Mina's and Uncle Eb's eldest daughter, Alma, her husband, Clarence Robinson, and their first son, Morrill, were living on their own farm in E. Glassville. Alma Armina

Clarence, Morrill and Alma Robinson

McBrine and Clarence Gordon Robinson married on Sept. 15, 1915. Morrill was born August 5, 1916. Alma named her first-born son, Morrill, after a boy in hospital. "Before she was married, Mother worked as a practical nurse in Prescott Hospital in Woodstock. There she helped care for a little boy named Morrill. He caught her eye and won her affection." Thus Morrill explained his uncommon name when the writer visited him on July 6, 1996.

Glenna

Glenna: Where was Glenna in 1920-21? Erma did not, to the writer's recollection, mention Glenna's presence at McBrine's during the school year 1920-21. Other relatives, however, affirm that Glenna, then a 27 year old widow with a three year old son, Bobby, was at home with her mother and father in E. Glassville. In any case, Glenna's earlier move was to Saint John, perhaps near the beginning of W.W.I (1914-1918). There she met a young Saint John man, Joseph Thompson, a soldier in the Canadian Army. Glenna and Joseph were married about February 1917. Later that year Joseph was training in Val Cartier, Quebec. Glenna came home to her parents in E. Glassville.

In this photo of Joseph with the family at McBrine's he was on leave from Val Cartier. Apparently that was his embarkation leave.[9] Left to right, Joseph, Glenna wearing Joseph's uniform, Fred McBrine, Grandfather Alfred Corey, Mina, Grandmother Lucretia Corey, Ed McBrine, Ferne McBrine.[10] Joseph Thompson went overseas before the birth of his son, Robert, December 5, 1917, and hence never got to see the boy. Joseph was killed in action in France, September 30, 1918. In the preceding two years much had happened to the young couple, Glenna and Joseph: meeting, marriage, sailing overseas, birth of a son, and fatality in the war. "Glenna lived in E.

In this photo of Joseph with the family at McBrine's he was on leave from Val Cartier. Apparently that was his embarkation leave.
Left to right, Joseph, Glenna wearing Joseph's uniform, Fred McBrine, Grandfather Alfred Corey, Mina, Grandmother Lucretia Corey, Ed McBrine, Ferne McBrine.

Glassville with Grammy and Grampy McBrine until 1923 when Bob started to school."[11] Probably he started in September. He would have been age 6 in December 1923. The E. Glassville School list confirms his attendance in the year ending June 1924.[12]

About the time Bob started school, "Glenna went to New Hampshire to work for a widower," in a beautiful home. Bobby stayed with his grandparents, Mina and Eb McBrine. Glenna made trips from New Hampshire to visit her parents and her son in E. Glassville. Her visits were infrequent when Bob was little, so as not to disturb his attachment to his grandparents. As he got used to living with them, she came more

Joseph Thompson, Val Cartier, P.Q., 1917

often. He also made attachments to his cousins: Morrill, Edna, Eloise, and Claudine, and his school friends, Norman Spence and others.[13]

Ferne in 1920-21

Erma said, "Ferne was still living at home when I went there in 1920." the story of Ferne's marriage in Erma's first teaching year is a romance. Edna said, "Little did she know in 1920 that she would be a bride the next year, 1921 of a returning veteran of W.W.I. My mother, like many girls in her time, had occasionally been hired to do housework for other families, e.g., the Rogers family in Bristol. That was as far as she had been from home." In winter of 1921 Ferne went with her cousin, Edna McBrine, to Maine to work. Before Ferne left home a W.W.I veteran named Frank had become interested in her.

Frank Wheeler had enlisted early in W.W.I. His daughter, Edna, says that he sailed from Val Cartier, Quebec in 1914, and that by 1915 he was in the trenches in France with the Princess Patricia's Canadian Light Infantry. He was wounded at Vimy Ridge in 1917 and came home in 1918.[14]

Frank followed Ferne to Maine. Soon the young couple returned to New Brunswick together. From Bristol they came by mail team to Glassville. Ferne's brother, Fred McBrine, brought them from Glassville to her parents' home in E. Glassville. Ferne surprised her family. When she removed her glove she revealed her wedding ring. The couple had been married in Houlton, Maine, February 12, 1921.[15] Ferne Wheeler's first public appearance was at the Methodist Church at Argyle for the funeral of Wallace Hemphill who had died on February 20th, the day following an accident at Fred Currie's mill in E. Knowlesville. Ferne, a lover of music and also an organ player, joined her mother, Mina, and her cousin Erma Corey in the choir.[16]

Fred

Before Erma's school year in E. Glassville Fred had married Annie Lovely of Glassville in April, 1920. Like his sister Alma, Fred made his home in E. Glassville. The first home of Fred and Annie was the farmhouse next to McBrine's on the south side. It was the small farm where Bob and Mary Carr had lived - lot 70 on land grant map. The name, Carr, appears on the school list from 1904 through 1913. Names mentioned are: George, Herbert, Mary, Ada, Eliza. After Fred and Annie vacated the place, Barrian and Harriet McBrine Swim occupied it. Their children were: Verda, Ernest, Betty and Sheila.[17]

The children of Mina and Eb McBrine were marrying and leaving home. Perhaps it was an especially good time to have Erma with them, and to enjoy her company. One amusement for Uncle Eb in that winter of 1921 was seeing Erma learning to snowshoe. She recalled, "I sent to Eaton's for the snowshoes. On a Saturday I practised with them over the farm fields toward the woods. Uncle Eb said, 'I saw codfish tracks in the snow.'" In the comfort of the McBrine home in E. Glassville, Erma had her first experience in school teaching. Born May 23, 1903, she was only a month past 18 when she completed her first year.

McBrine Family 1921-1934

Erma's memories have portrayed to us the family of Mina Corey McBrine up to 1921. The following section will cover events and happenings between 1921 and 1934. For these years the writer is dependent largely on his own memories of family events, contacts and visits, plus input from a few other people whose memories precede his age of awareness. We will begin with recollections of visits and contacts between the Mina and Eb McBrine family and the Ira Corey family.

I remember Aunt Mina and Uncle Eb arriving in their buggy in time for noon dinner at the Corey farm in E. Knowlesville. They drove a horse across Bob Guthrie's fields, and through a narrow neck of woods to the west side of our farm. It must have been August. As they sat in the wagon saying goodbye Claudine, their granddaughter, was biting into a yellow transparent apple from our orchard. The black part at the bottom troubled her. Aunt Mina said, "That's the blossom end." They trotted their horse back home to turn over some hay to dry the under side while the sun was still shining. Visits flowed in both directions. On a summer Sunday evening Father drove his 4-90 Chevrolet to the McBrine home in E. Glassville. Accompanying him were mother and several of us, i.e., the younger children. I recollect discussion that evening about Fred and Annie moving into the McBrine house. Fred, already aspiring to carpenter work, was remodelling their woodshed into a kitchen and building a stairs to the upper level where he was making a bedroom. Annie came into the main house, sat on the oven door, and spoke enthusiastically about their new living space. She was happy that the work was near completion.

Glenna's Home Visits

In the 30's when there were not many cars and some who had them didn't register them every year, it was fascinating when a shiny car, bearing New Hampshire plates, appeared at the Corey farm in E. Knowlesville regularly for several summers.

Glenna McBrine Thompson

Glenna brought her parents to her Uncle Ira's and Aunt Nellie's for supper. Annually, Glenna drove her own car to visit her parents and her son Bobby who was attending school in E. Glassville. She also visited relatives in surrounding communities.

Claudine remembers riding to Woodstock with her to visit Nellie and Mary Lindsay. Claudine recollected further, "She always took us to Houlton. One trip was a disappointment. When we approached Houlton we saw flags all over. She had forgotten that it was Memorial Day - a holiday for stores."

Ferne

Most of the visits I remember were between E. Knowlesville and E. Glassville. However, I have one faint recollection of a visit to Frank and Ferne Wheeler's farm on North Ridge. Father was perhaps on a trip to or from Juniper; he drove his 4-90 Chevrolet up North Ridge and wheeled into their yard. I was too young to remember much but I can still visualize Ferne coming out onto the veranda and saying, "Hello, Uncle Ira." I also faintly remember a brief glimpse of the girls. Tom told us all their names. The year? Probably before the end of the 20's when much of the automobile travel stopped. Probably before 1929, the year I started school.

Ferne and Frank lived on the Harvey-McCain place, the former Ed Brooks farm on North Ridge, Carleton County.[18] Frank had acquired the farm through the Soldier's Settlement Board. H.N. Bradley stated that Frank bought it in 1923. Edna, their eldest daughter, dates the purchase in 1921.

When Ferne and Frank made the Brooks Farm on North Ridge their home they were both settling near their family homes: only a few miles from Ferne's home in E. Glassville; even nearer to Frank's home neighbourhood. Frank was born September 8, 1895, son of George Wheeler and Cassie Bell Wheeler. He grew up in the Asa Bell home in Foreston. His name is on the Biggar Ridge school lists between 1901 and 1907 and on the Foreston school lists for 1907 and 1908.[19]

East Glassville

I recall another visit to McBrine's in E. Glassville when I was nearing ten. My father had taken me with him in the sleigh on an errand to Glassville. On the homeward journey Father slowed the little bay mare from a trot to a walk as we approached Brown's Corner. There he pondered momentarily. Then he reined the mare northward, saying, "I guess we'll go and see Mina." We stabled the mare and had supper with Aunt Mina and Uncle Eb. Their grandson, Glenna's son, Bobby, then a teenager, was still living with them, but we didn't see him. Aunt Mina explained that Bobby and a neighbouring boy were having a venture in the woods. Edna remembers that Bobbie and Norman Spence had a little camp in the edge of the woods at the far side of a field. They forbade the girls to come near their place.

When we were taking leave, Father lingered a few moments talking to his sister, Mina. Uncle Eb lighted his kerosene lantern and started to the barn; I followed him. While he held the lantern, I entered the stall, slipped the mare's halter off, put her bridle on and snapped the reins. I was leading her out to the sleigh when Father arrived, saying, "You didn't do that, Jud?" Uncle Eb replied, "Yes he's got her ready to hitch; he did it all himself."

A year later that little bay mare took me to a longer visit: a half-year's sojourn to E. Glassville. My Grandmother Brown and my Uncle Archie had enticed me to come and stay with them at their Highlands farm and "do chores". On a trip to Glassville with the little bay mare Father dropped me at Brown's. I didn't know it was to be my last ride behind that mare. It was in April 1934. I was just reaching eleven., and a very shy boy.

Frightening Venture

I guess it was the adventure that lured me; and yet it was a frightening venture. The work didn't trouble me. Getting up at 6:00 a.m., milking cows, separating the milk, carrying skim milk to the calves, putting a finger into the mouth of a newborn calf to teach it to drink from a pail, feeding pigs and hens. That was not new to me. Having to get acquainted with a strange community and a new group of schoolmates — that was frightening.

The first steps in acquaintance, however, were easy and pleasant. Tom and Lucy Guthrie's youngsters: Velma, Olive and Claude, joined by Anna Marie Whalen, at Joe McDermid's, came right by Brown's. A few yards ahead, at the crossroads, we were joined by Marjorie and Leila Brown. We all carried leather book bags over our shoulders and lard-pail lunches in hand. We soon developed a camaraderie. The walk was interesting, perhaps the best part of the experience, i.e., the part that was accompanied by the warmest feelings.

The first two families we passed were my mother's relatives: Browns: Gibson, Phoebe, Alice and sometimes Winston Leavitt, on the corner; Malcolm, Lillian and Bonar across the swamp. With the help of my walking companions I soon knew all the families on the road: Haynes: Peter, Ellen, Billy and Myrtle up the hill on the left; and Swim: Barrian, Harriet, Ernest and Verda farther on the left. In the last house before the school was another family of my relatives: the Eb McBrine family — on the left.

Between the McBrine house and the E. Glassville School, but on the opposite side of the road, stood the sawmill. The hum of the saw and the whirr of the carriage permeated the air. Logs were piled in the mill yard, having been hauled there on sleds by local farmers before the snow melted. Initialled on their butt ends, they waited to be sawn into boards. The mill had been built by Fred McBrine and George McFarland, in part-

McBrine/McFarland Mill

nership, in 1932.[20] It was first driven by a motor from an old car that George had brought from Ontario.[21] The spring of 1934 was only the second season of sawing for the mill.

The first cutting was in the winter of 1933. It had met an urgent need. In January 1933 the Jim Brown house, at Brown's Corner, burned. Neighbours helped cut softwood logs and haul them to the new mill. In the coldest weather McBrine and McFarland, with help of many volunteers, milled their first logs into boards and 2 x 4's for Grandmother Brown's new house. Osbert Whitehouse was the carpenter. He was assisted by many volunteers.[22]

In the spring of 1934 I was living in that house, only a little more than a year old. Newness was all around me: Several new-born calves: A filly born in May, a sister to the one year old colt whose disposition I had to learn as I let him out to water and tied him again. In many ways the newness was fascinating. But the newness of community continued to intimidate me. Thus my venture into E. Glassville was fraught with mixed feelings.

In my ambivalent state there came to me the story of the little bay mare, Belle. On an errand in Glassville my father encountered Paul Stoddard who was driving the mail between Glassville and Juniper. He had a medium-sized, black workhorse named Bob, quite appropriate for pulling a load of mail bags and passengers. But the trotting mare was attractive. He could speed up his journey. My father needed another workhorse for the spring planting. A trade seemed to meet both needs. I was a little sad at the report of the little trotter having to pull a two-seated sleigh with about five passengers and heavy bags of mail. I identified with her. She carried a heavy load. I carried an anxiety of not being sure I belonged or could be fully accepted.

The big teenage boys apparently thought I didn't belong, and therefore that I was fair game for bullying. Probably it was too much to expect adolescents who seemed to be preoccupied with their own ambitions for a macho image, to have feelings for an eleven-year-old stranger in a strange place. To me, then, their treatment seemed utterly cruel. It was a foretaste of how cruel the world could be. For a time there seemed to me to be little hope of being accepted by the whole school. I struggled with the question of belonging. Did I belong? Could I belong?

Yes, acceptance began to dominate over rejection. As the snow melted and the streams and ponds swelled, some of us went at noon hour to the pond opposite MacFarland's. Eugene Stoddard invited the younger boys to help him with the catamaran he was making by nailing boards across bits of floating logs. A little later the polliwogs in the same pond were most fascinating. My mix of feelings began to change. Some measures of acceptance and belonging helped me to overcome some of my insecure feelings.

The McBrine Family in 1934

At length my intimidating venture into E. Glassville became somewhat of an opportunity for me to increase my acquaintance with my relatives. Among the pupils in the school were three of my McBrine cousins: Claudine McBrine, age 10 1/2, Harold Robinson 10, and Bobby Thompson, 16 1/2; living with his grandparents, Mina and Eb McBrine.

Fred

Fred McBrine, his wife Annie, and their two daughters, Claudine and Marion lived in one half of Eb and Mina McBrine's house. Marion, born the previous October was occasionally seen being wheeled in a carriage. What I didn't know that spring, 1934, was that only months earlier Fred had experienced a serious illness.

In 1933 his work was interrupted by a bout with cancer. This must have been soon after the completion of the first season of sawing in the new mill. A doctor in Woodstock removed a lump the size of a door knob from his thigh. Another developed in his groin, and was called "sarcoma cancer". Fred was then referred to Montreal. He and Annie, accompanied by Bill and Isabel Lamont, travelled by car. In Montreal Fred had the lump removed. Surgery was followed by deep x-ray treatment. Fred was advised that he could not hope to live to see their expected baby. That October Marion arrived and gladdened his heart. The doctor in Woodstock was subsequently surprised that the growth did not return.[23]

Alma Robinson and Family

In 1934 Alma and Clarence were farming in E. Glassville. They had two sons: Morrill, age 17 1/2, and Harold, age 10, one year younger than I. He talked to me often at the school. Morrill left the school in E. Glassville in March 1934, the month before I arrived there. Leaving school in spring to help with spring planting and other farm work had become for him a regular pattern: "After I was 13 or 14 I only attended school in winter. In the spring I drove a pair of horses on the harrow. I returned to school again after the fall work."[24] Spring of 1934 was his final exit. He did not return.

Ferne Wheeler and Family

In 1934 Frank and Ferne had four daughters: Edna, Eloise, Mary, and Nellie; and one son, Freddie. Their ages ranged from twelve to three years. That April, Edna, the eldest, came to her grandparents in E. Glassville for the Easter holidays. She remembers riding on the sled from N. Ridge with her father. He was driving his team to Glassville. He had told her, "I'll let you off at Brown's Corner. You'll have to walk up to McBrine's." She remembers, "I stopped at Lillian Brown's to get warm" Probably that was Good Friday. On the Saturday she and another girl, probably Claudine, waved to me from a long sled as they passed Grandmother Brown's enroute to Glassville. It was nice for a shy ll-year old boy to be noticed by pretty girls. Edna returned home on Easter Monday. Her instruction was to wait at Mrs. Brown's to keep warm till Paul Stoddard arrived with his mail sleigh. Recounting that visit awakened Edna's memories of other visits to her grandparents, and fun with her cousins: "In 1931, two weeks before the end of June, my teacher then, Elizabeth Logan,[25] let me take her bicycle to Grammy McBrine's and Alma's. I left on Friday morning and was there by noon. Bob and Claudine were just coming from school for lunch.

"In 1933, July or August, I was visiting Claudine. Her cousins Dana and Natalie Bishop were also visiting there. Bob drove us all to Woodstock to a movie. I think the car was Uncle Fred's. I saw Bob many times during our early teen years. He was a very affable young lad, but the biggest 'tease' to us girls, all in fun and laughter."[26]

It happened that the 1934 Easter visit to her grandparents was Edna's last while Bobbie Thompson was living there. Up to at least 1934 Glenna Thompson was still making her annual trips from New Hampshire for summer visits to her parents and her son Bobby who was living with them and attending the E. Glassville School. Edna says Bob left E. Glassville in the summer of 1934, or possibly 1935, and went to New Hampshire with his mother. This probable date of Bobby's departure from his grandparents' home agrees with school records. The last year his name appears on the E. Glassville School list is the year ending June 1934.[27] Perhaps after the end of that school year Glenna took Bobby with her to the U.S.A.

The Last Year of Eb McBrine

Little did anybody know when Bobby departed the E. Glassville farm how little time remained for his grandparents. I well remember a Sunday afternoon visit of Uncle Eb and Aunt Mina, perhaps their last, to the Corey farm in E. Knowlesville. During that visit Uncle Eb showed much pride in another of his grandsons, Freddie Wheeler, who at a very young age began to drive horses. With great delight he described the arrival on the Saturday morning of his grandson, Freddie Wheeler, driving his father Frank's pair of horses, hauling a load of logs to the McBrine/MacFarland mill on the McBrine farm. The incident can probably be dated in spring of 1936, at which time Freddie was age 10, and in which case he brought gladness to the heart of his grandfather in the last year of his life.

In July that year, 1936, only two years after the summer I sojourned in E. Glassville, my Uncle Eb McBrine died, at age 69. Bobby Thompson came with his mother from U.S.A. "The last time I saw Bobby", recollected Edna Wheeler Christman, "was at the funeral of our Grandfather McBrine." Born December 5, 1917, Bobby was 18 1/2 in 1936.

Claudine McBrine Whitehouse recalls the funeral service in the Knowlesville Baptist Church. Returning with her recollection of the event was her feeling of loss: "I thought I would die too; I cried many tears." The day was hot — both Claudine and Morrill recalled. The writer also remembers attending Uncle Eb McBrine's funeral. Many of the other relatives were also there, including Jimmie Miller. He came to Corey's for supper after the church service and the burial in the adjoining cemetery.

The Passing of Mina McBrine

Aunt Mina McBrine lived two more years. Her first grandson, Morrill Robinson, recalled filling one last request for her: "I got my first car in the spring of 1938 right after cropping. In June the new Union Church was being dedicated in Juniper. Grandma asked me to take her to the service. It was the only ride she had in my car."

Mina McBrine died in July 1938 at the Woodstock Hospital, age 73. Again, Claudine experienced a great loss because, "I loved her so much and she was so close to me." Living in a part of the same house, they were much involved. Claudine's sister, Marion Bell, tells us, "Claudine was very close to her Grandmother McBrine and was devastated when she passed away in 1938, after a brief illness. Claudine still has good memories of her grandmother taking her along, e.g., when Mack and Lillian Brown stopped for them on their way to church on Sundays. Also Claudine recalls accompanying her grandmother on a trip to Fredericton with Mack and Lillian for a Royal Visit.

Granddaughter Marion, under five when her grandmother departed, also expressed her good memories and her warm feelings: "I vaguely remember playing hide-and-seek with my friend, Myrtle (McFarland) Hemphill, and hiding under my grandmother's long skirt. I am very sorry that my grandmother and I didn't have longer to get to know each other, but I know how much she was loved and respected by all members of my family and I'm sure she must have been a remarkable lady.

Mina McBrine's funeral, like Eb's, was in the Knowlesville Baptist Church. Mina's brother, Rev. Judson A. Corey, with some family members came from Doaktown for the service. Mina was buried beside Eb McBrine in the Knowlesville Cemetery. The monument for Uncle Eb and Aunt Mina reads:

> Robert E. McBrine 1867 - 1936
> Mina W. wife 1866 - 1938

There is one error of one year. Mina was born in 1865.[28] George W. And Cecil Whitehouse left off haying and waited in the cemetery to fill in the grave. After greetings and farewells to the immediate family and other relatives, Rev. J.A. Corey and sons came to Ira Corey's. While Nellie Corey was cooking supper on the wood stove, the visitors patched a tire for Earle's car. A tire had gone flat on gravel road enroute. The repaired tire became their spare for their return journey. They declined to stay overnight as Earle's vacation was nearly ended and he was expecting to return soon to Massachusetts. Isn't it regrettable that we wait for funerals for some of our most memorable family gatherings?

The Descendants of Mina and Eb McBrine:

Glenna

Of their four children, three; Alma, Ferne and Fred married and lived in E. Glassville and vicinity. Glenna Thompson was the only one of the four who went far from home. Interestingly she seemed to be the best communicator. She kept up correspondence and visits. Her son, Bobby, also visited. Marion Bell remembers Bobby Thompson riding from New Hampshire to E.

Glassville on his motorcycle. A girlfriend, with a boy's style haircut, once rode with him. Perhaps it was service in the U.S. Army that brought an end to his visits.

Glenna's residence in New Hampshire continued at least into the 1950's. Marion Bell remembers Glenna coming from New Hampshire to Glassville to attend the funeral of Marion's mother, Annie McBrine, in June 1952. Glenna travelled alone in her own car. Marion said, "I went back with her to New Hampshire. She lived at West Campton, seven miles from Plymouth, N.H. I stayed two weeks. She took me on sight-seeing tours. It helped me to get over the loss of my mother."

Eventually Glenna moved to Florida. The date? Sometime after her 1952 visit to New Brunswick. She made more visits to New Brunswick, even from distant Florida. In a letter to Fred McBrine in 1975 she spoke of a visit "last year", i.e., 1974, and "nine years ago", i.e., in 1966. She stayed with Alma Robinson.

Why did Glenna move to Florida? Perhaps to be near her son Bobby. After his discharge from the U.S. Army, following W.W. II, Bobby Thompson had a garage and filling station in Key West, Florida. Bobby's cousin, Edna Christman, says that he lived with Glenna in Florida for a while — perhaps between marriages, Edna said, "he had two marriages". Also when each had his/her own residence, addresses indicate that they lived very near each other. Glenna maintained a close relationship with her son throughout his short life.

Robert E. Thompson suffered an untimely death

Robert Thompson, in U.S. Army

from throat cancer at age 53, on May 15, 1971. His obituary tells us that he lived at 460 Park Blvd., Pinellas Park, in St. Petersburg, Florida, and that his mother, Glenna Thompson, also lived at Pinellas Park. The family requested that in lieu of flowers, donations be made to the Cancer Society. His funeral was on May 18, 1971. Interment was in Barrancas National Cemetery, Pensacola, Florida. Listed as survivors, besides his mother were: two daughters, Mrs. Roberta Serrano, Chicago, and Mrs. Patricia Bell, Naples, Florida; a son, Michael Thompson, then in the U.S. Army, and two grandchildren.[29]

Correspondence

From Pinellas Park, Glenna kept up a steady correspondence with siblings and others the rest of her life. Several of those letters have been preserved by relatives. They give us interesting glimpses of Glenna's life in Florida after she was bereaved of her son. The earliest of Glenna's five extant letters was written to her sister, Ferne Wheeler, on December 13, 1973, when Glenna was age 79.[30]

Glenna said, "I have my new trailer, at last. Evelyn and Walter found it for me around two miles from the old spot, right on the Blvd...Webb's grocery is across the highway....where I have to do my shopping now.......My trailer is nice and bright and sunny. It's only 12 x 35 but that is large for me compared with my little old 8 x 28....It is heated by gas floor vents, so I don't have cold feet all the time, and don't have to dig ice out of the fridge any more. I have a lot of closet and cupboard space, more than in some houses....the drapes are pretty blue and white...."

In her delight over her new trailer she said to Ferne: "Wish I could have had it when you were here; you would have been more comfortable." Ferne visited Glenna in the spring of 1973, apparently in the smaller trailer. Ferne's daughter, Edna, spoke of the visit, saying, "Glenna moved on the trot. Mother couldn't keep up with her." Glenna's movements, however, appear to have enabled her to keep up very good relationships with a wide circle of friends and relatives: "This is a nice park....friendly....; I knew a few of them before I came in here, so I'm not lonesome. I've been over to the old park to see my friends three or four times, and they have been here......I get very tired but keep going. You know the man in the red trailer next to mine is in hospital about a mile from here, so I have walked up twice to see him. I don't think he will get better; seems to be his stomach; a lump that pains, so I wouldn't wonder if it would be malignant; poor old fellow. I must go again soon, but it is quite a walk, two miles round trip. I feel tired when I get home but I walk quite a lot. It's good exercise."

Despite waning strength, she showed remarkable ability to keep active: "I wanted to get a better card for you but the last time I went to the plaza I walked a lot. I had been to the old park, and the bank, got groceries..., had lunch at Eckerd's and got too tired to stand up and pick out cards, so I just grabbed a box of these." However, it seemed she was never too tired to be friendly. Glenna was delighted with visits to and from neighbors and friends. She seemed even more delighted with the visits of her relatives. She liked being able to entertain her grandson and family in her new living space: "Mike and his wife and little boy, two years old, were here on Sunday and had lunch with me. I have four chairs to sit on now, so we don't have to sit on the couch to eat. It's a lot easier to get a meal too."

Glenna was blessed also with other relatives then close enough for visits. She was especially fortunate at that time to have her second cousin, Walter Whitehouse, and his wife Evelyn, living nearby. She expressed much appreciation for their help."Evelyn and Walter gave me a lovely little stand with two drawers, walnut color, to set my TV on. It matches furniture in trailer.....Evelyn and Walter come and also take me to their home for evening meal. It always tastes so good. She is a good cook. Walter fixed my fan and several other things....."

Glenna's letter shows a sustained ability to keeping in touch with siblings, nieces, cousins and others: "I've got most of my cards written; still have to get Alma's and Fred's out....I wrote a letter to Erma and Kate and a note to Marie. I wrote to Claudia in Miami. She plans on coming up after Xmas, so Walter said. I also wrote Maddie and Clara." A remarkable correspondence! The next extant letter from Glenna was written to her brother Fred McBrine and wife Bernice. On June 5, 1975. It seems to portray a lessening of strength, but no lessening in determination to keep up relationships and communication with people near and far: "When I get my chores finished I make for the couch and lie down a while; then my friend....couple of trailers away comes in....Then we go over to Webb's Luncheonette, two or three times a week anyhow. We both hate to put on heat to get dinner. She is a friendly good person....."

Relationship with siblings appears to have become increasingly precious. One of the dreads of waning strength and health was loss of communication: "Poor Abby (Alma), I felt so bad to hear of the change in her......Poor old dear her eyes are so bad too....I have been looking for a letter from her and was thankful when I got yours. She was my old standby in letter writing and I will miss them so very much if she is unable to write any more....Write whenever you can....Don't ever think you're a poor letter writer. I'm getting that way and hating it more every day, but I love to hear from you; so I'll always answer as long as I am able."

Glenna feels secure with "a good pension" but says "with the passing away of so many, takes the joy out of life." She feels the loss of Fern, "also Jean Lamont and Faye Tracey". The passing of Ferne apparently touched Glenna deeply: "Life is so uncertain. The circle is broken and we do not know which one will be next. I seem to be quite fortunate at present. Get mighty tired at times but keep going when I feel like it....I rest a lot...." Glenna recognized the limitations of her energy. She said that

Walter and Evelyn Whitehouse invited her to travel with them on a trip north into Canada. As much as she wanted to see her family, she declined: "I don't believe I want to be on the road that long.....; I think I'm better off at home." She repeatedly expressed gratitude for their kindness: "Walter and Evelyn come often and Walter does so many things for me. They are both wonderful.......Bye now with my love to you and your family; Sister Glen (Nennie) P.S.: I love Teen (Claudine) and Mame (Marion, the preserver of this letter)."

The next extant letter from Glenna was written April 25, 1976, also to Fred and wife: "Dear Teddy and Bernice...." She mentions a letter from Alma, and is expecting another. Again she mentions the kindness of Walter and Evelyn who "were here yesterday. He is coming down on Saturday to put some of that solar X on my front windows....They plan on their vacation middle of August to some time in September and went me to go." She said, "I do want to see you all," but comments that she doesn't like travelling that far by car. However she is pleased with a recent health check: "blood sugar is good — this time only 96." Again she expresses concern for "poor old Abbey" (Alma), and says, "I'll write her before someone comes in, so bye now with my love to you and families."

The next extant letter from Glenna was written to Edna Wheeler Christman and family on January 22, 1978: "Dear Edna and family: Rec'd your lovely card just before Xmas; it was sweet of you to write a lovely letter with it...." The letter expresses again her high value on correspondence with her relatives, and how hard she was trying to keep it up, though it was becoming increasingly difficult: "......I wrote quite a lot of cards and letters and should have sent more but every year it's getting to be a bigger task. Sometimes I go for weeks and don't even write Alma. I have arthritis.....in my hands, mostly my thumb joints, and I can't....form the letters like I used to....they will probably get worse.....otherwise I'm not too bad off." Still she longed for letters: "I haven't had a letter from Alma or Fred since Christmas. Fred is also having a bad time with his hand, but I'm happy to hear that Alma is getting along so well. Fred said he expected them for Xmas dinner."

Glenna was also still appreciating good relations with her neighbors: "My neighbors run in a lot and I'm never lonesome. One woman who lives two trailers away comes every afternoon that she is home and she is home a lot. I usually have my rest right after I finish the dinner dishes.....; she has one too, then comes and chats till nearly suppertime; sometimes two or three at once, so I'm not alone too much. I get my work done in the forenoon as I never have a chance to do it in the afternoon."

She expresses delight in a visit from her grandson; "Bob's youngest child who lives in Naples......yesterday Mike and family came around 11 o'clock and brought the other Gramma with them. She is very nice and a Christian. Mike has a boy, 6 and a little girl, 14 months. ....Mike had to get back,.....had quite a drive. He is building a house and was expecting some materials......."

Glenna never ceased to appreciate the kindness of her cousins: "Walter and Evelyn come, usually on Fridays, and we go out to one of the malls, do a little shopping...have a nice dinner, and do grocery shopping on way home. They sure are a beautiful couple, and good to me. I was up to their house on Monday after Xmas. She had to work on Xmas day, so made a lovely dinner on Monday. Walter had to go to airport to meet sister Madeline, and Paul and Judy, youngest daughter. The Tampa airport was so congested that they didn't get home until after two o'clock. He had to change clothes, eat a hurried dinner and go to work at 3 o'clock. Evelyn and company brought me home in late afternoon......"

Glenna followed their happenings with interest and concern: "Walter works Sunday, 3 o'clock through Thursday; then Friday and Saturday off. They both go to work at 3:00 but don't always have same days off.....On Friday they take me out. I enjoy it so much...." "Evelyn Whitehouse is in Canada. Went a week ago. Her father passed away...She expects to be back on Wednesday...I do hope everything will be o.k. for her as I know Walter misses her so very much."

It happened that 1978 was Glenna's last year. Her closing of this letter was perhaps a premonition: "I really haven't felt good today...I had that virus after Xmas and it left me weak and I'm slipping each day, but I guess it's time. I have lived a ripe old age but I am very grateful that I can take care of myself like I do."

We have one more extant letter from Glenna. She wrote it on September 12, 1978, in the last month she lived: "Dear Teddy (Fred, her brother) and Bernice and family: I guess it has been a couple of months or more since I've written; just couldn't do much of anything. I've been sick all summer and no appetite and hardly able to do anything, and the night after Walter and Evelyn left I fell head first out of bed in my sleep and hurt my head on the side of my forehead and temple, and I have had headaches on that side off and on for six weeks. I keep thinking it will wear away but it doesn't. I can't seem to take anacin or aspirin, so Evelyn told me to try bufferin, and thank goodness that's ok. And then I had trouble with my eye. The pollen bothers every fall and it kept getting worse till it got infected and kept going down on my cheek, so Evelyn says,'You're going to the eye doctor'. So Walter took me for exam and he gave me a prescription for drops and ointment. His bill $35.00; prescription $10.39.

Walter and Evelyn are wonderfully kind and thoughtful — just couldn't do more....Evelyn's mother came back with them for the winter, I guess.....Walter goes by here on his way to work and Evelyn cooks lots of good dinners and Walter brings me meat, potatoes, and one or two other vegetables. She said I wasn't getting enough nourishment, and I guess I wasn't, as I got so weak I could hardly get around. I've got down to 103 lbs. but I feel a little stronger, but could feel a whole lot better and hope to before long.

Alma, Fred, Glenn, Ferne—McBrine siblings

"I had a nice long letter from Alma and was surprised to get it as it had been so long I didn't think she could see to write any more. She told me that you (Teddy) have been not too well this summer. I do hope you will feel better soon. Life is no good with aches and pains and distress. My hands are no good, getting stiffer all the time. I can't write good now. Walter and Evelyn wanted to see you but just couldn't, as their time was too short.....I would like to have seen you all but just too sick. P.S.: I'll write Dear Abby (Alma) soon. My love now to you all. Sister, Nenny."

Glenna died in Pinellas Park on September 28, 1978, at age 84. The foregoing letters by Glenna McBrine Thompson provide windows into her life and outlook. Without intending to, they indicate what a large part relationships, especially with kinfolk, have in the meaning and purpose of our lives.

Ferne

Ferne and Frank Wheeler lived on their farm on North Ridge most of their married life. There they brought up their four daughters and their son. Though his main work was farming and lumbering, Edna says her father had skills in carpentry as had his father, George H. Wheeler, and his grandfather, Richard Wheeler, who was also a schoolteacher. Edna said Frank made much improvement on the house, including the re-building of the stairs.

One of Frank's strong interests was his horses. Edna said he preferred Belgian horses, having observed them in Belgium during W.W.I. He bought Westerns from Bill Burnham, Florenceville. Frank took much pride in keeping his horses looking well. His daughter, Edna, said he brought the harness right into the kitchen on a winter evening, about once a month. He cleaned and oiled the leather and polished the brass.

Frank liked to keep his horses working, even if he had to hire a teamster to work his team in the lumber industry in winter. This sometimes involved the Corey family. One fall in the 30's Frank came to Knowlesville and enticed Wilfred Corey from temporary employment at Fred Hemphill's mill, to take Frank's team to yard logs for Flemming and Gibson Co. Freddie Wheeler remembers the event. He said, "They stopped at Corey's for clothes. Wilfred left his money with his mother to keep for him. Dad liked Wilfred a lot. He said, 'Wilfred will take care of the horses better than I could.'"

In the fall of 1939, the year W.W.II broke out, Ira Corey had crews cutting lumber for Flemming and Gibson Co. on the South Branch of the Miramichi. In January 1940 Frank brought his team to the South Branch to join in the "haul-off" of Ira's logs. Frank liked to compete in the large loads the teams were hauling.[31]

Military Service

Soon after that winter enterprise, it seems Frank felt again the lure of the military. On June 7, 1940, Frank "enlisted in the #7 Coy, Veterans Guard of Canada, Canadian Field Force, at Woodstock, N.B." Later, like Jim Hovey, and other W.W.I Veterans, Frank was doing guard duty at prison camps. Edna said he guarded at Trois Rivieres, Quebec. That round of military service for Frank was short. He was discharged on February 25, 1941, as "medically unfit".[32] It seems that old injuries from W.W.I re-surfaced.[33]

Two years after Frank's discharge from Veterans' Guard, Edna recalls visiting him in the Lancaster Hospital in 1943. She was then an enlisted member of the Women's Division of the R.C.A.F. She said, "I got 'compassionate leave', travelled to Saint John, and made him a surprise visit. When I walked into his hospital room he said, 'What are you doing here?'" Edna had enlisted on February 28, 1942: one year after her father was discharged from Veterans Guard.

It was while working in Civil Service in Ottawa that she got the idea to enlist. She and a girl friend went to the recruiting station together. She said, "The friend didn't pass, but I decided to still go through with my plan. I did office work in the R.C.A.F." The younger sisters also enlisted: Mary Wheeler enlisted in Bedford, N.S., on January 9, 1943. She had been working in Dartmouth. Eloise enlisted in Moncton, N.B. Their brother Freddie Wheeler entered the service in fall of 1943. He said, "In 1945 I had six months of 'farm leave'. I cut 120 cords of 16" fire wood on the Wheeler farm."

In the latter years of W.W.II, it seems that Frank Wheeler's problems with health increased. After reflecting in retrospect on her father's struggles for health, Edna came to think her father never fully recovered from his injuries in W.W.I. She said he carried effects, i.e., suffering and pain. The reading of Pierre Berton's, <u>Vimy</u>, prompted Edna to reflect on the ordeal and the trying experiences her father and other soldiers must have endured in the trench warfare of W.W.I. She recalled that he spoke of the Somme and the Battle of Vimy Ridge. After being wounded in battle, Frank was taken to a field hospital in France, and later to a hospital in England. The photo shows Frank and a companion in uniforms provided by the hospital in England, when the men had recovered enough to be able to take walks.

Frank apparently had returned to Canada by early 1918. His discharge certificate reads: "Private Frank D. Wheeler, Princess Patricia's Canadian Light Infantry, served with honour and was disabled in the Great War. Honourably discharged on April 5, 1918." Edna says she can understand Herbie Bradley's observation that though Frank was wounded in W.W.I he "was able to lead an active life as a farmer."[34] But she also says he carried on with far more difficulty than was evident.

She said he made many visits to the Veteran's Hospital in Lancaster during the 20's and 30's. Sometimes he was treated as an out-patient. Those times he stayed with his sister, Ida, who lived at 265 Duke St., Saint John W., in easy walking distance from the hospital. Such was Frank's confidence in the doctors of that hospital that he took his son Freddie to Saint John for a tonsillectomy — on the kitchen table in Ida's house.[35]

Family Moves

By 1945, it seems, Frank's health problems had increased to the point that he was determined to dispose of the N. Ridge farm. They sold it to Bill Harrington, a W.W. II veteran. About that time the Bell/Lee house in Foreston became vacant. It had been Frank's childhood home.

The historic and beautiful house had been owned by Asa K. Bell, Frank Wheeler's grandfather. On Mr. Bell's death in

1913, it passed to his daughter Cassie, and her second husband, Fred Lee. Cassie was Frank Wheeler's mother. Fred and Cassie Lee moved to Morna Heights, near Saint John, in 1946. Their son Joe Lee had moved there earlier. Thus Frank and Ferne Wheeler acquired the Bell/Lee house. After nearly a quarter century on their farm in N. Ridge they moved to Foreston in the early summer of 1946.[36]

By that time only the two youngest of the Wheeler family remained at or near home: Freddie, then age 20, and Nellie, 14 1/2. Freddie said, "I was discharged from the army in March 1946. I worked in Juniper in 1947." The three eldest: Edna, Eloise and Mary, were living in Ontario. They had all married while in the R.C.A.F.: Eloise, m. George Smith, August 28, 1943; Edna, m. Horace Christman, December 16, 1944; Mary, m. Charles Foster, June 29, 1944; Mary was discharged Jan. 5, 1945, at #3 Release Centre, Rockcliffe, Ontario; Edna was discharged February 28, 1945.[37]

The Wheeler family in Foreston were in the Bell/Lee house only a few months before Frank became seriously ill. My brother, Gordon, remembers accompanying our father, Ira Corey, when he visited Frank, then confined to bed, at the Lee house. Edna made two visits home in 1946. On her first visit, in June, she brought her baby, John, then nine months old. She said, "My father saw my son. I stayed one month before returning to Kitchener."

That fall Frank was taken to the Veterans' Hospital in Lancaster, then a separate city from Saint John. Ferne, expecting that Frank would have a long stay in Lancaster, moved into an apartment in the home of Frank's sister, Ida Odell, 265 Duke St. W. With her were Freddie and Nellie. Nellie enrolled in high school.

Edna recalled, "In November Mother phoned me in Ontario saying, 'come if you can!' For that visit my husband Horace and his mother kept our baby, John." The whole

Wheeler family gathered in Lancaster. On November 14th, 1946, Frank died in the Lancaster Hospital. His body was prepared at Brenan's Funeral Home, and then brought to Bristol.

Frank's funeral service was conducted by Rev. Arthur H. Holmes, Anglican Minister of the Parish of Aberdeen and Brighton. The service was in the Biggar Ridge Baptist Church. Pallbearers were members of the Florenceville branch of the Canadian Legion of which Frank was a member. Veterans of both World Wars were in attendance. Burial was on Bell land at the edge of the Biggar Ridge Cemetery.[38]

New Brunswick, Ontario and U.S.A.

Ferne kept the apartment in Lancaster until Nellie completed her school year in Saint John. Nellie's next high school year was in Juniper, N.B. Ferne stayed a short while in Foreston, then moved to Juniper. Subsequently she and Nellie went to live with Edna and family in Kitchener, where Nellie graduated from high school. Following graduation, Nellie and her mother returned to New Brunswick. Nellie enrolled in Nurses' Training in Woodstock, Hospital. On returning to New Brunswick Ferne again took up residence in Juniper. There she occupied two houses in succession. The first was the house that was subsequently occupied by Alice and Malcolm Mersereau, followed by Paul and Shirley Brooks. Her second home was near Kaye and Percy Field's. While in Juniper, Ferne often visited Nellie and Ira Corey.

While in Woodstock Nellie met Edward DeWitt, a veteran of the Canadian Army Campaign in Italy. They married on January 23, 1954, and subsequently moved to Massachusetts. On July 27, 1948, Freddie married Merna Field, daughter of Kay and Percy Field, Juniper. As a step in the direction of a permanent visa for working in U.S.A., Freddie and Merna moved to Maine and engaged in an enterprise. Subsequently they moved to Peabody, Mass., where they became neighbors of Nellie and Edward DeWitt. Before long they both had enterprises: Merna became a Real Estate Agent in Danvers, Mass; Freddie became a house builder and contractor.

Ferne's Last Years

Sometime after Nellie and Freddie moved to U.S.A., Ferne returned to Kitchener and enjoyed a few years with Edna and Horace Christman who then lived at 210 Heritage Drive. In 1974 Ferne became seriously ill. Edna said, "I took my mother to my doctor. She was diagnosed with kidney failure. She lived one year after that."

Ferne died at the Kitchener/Waterloo Hospital on May 22, 1975. She was the first of the four siblings to go. Obituary in the "Kitchener Waterloo Record", suggested donations to the Ontario Kidney Foundation or the Building Fund of Benton Street Baptist Church. Visiting was at Kilcollins Funeral Home, Bath, N.B., where Edna recalls being comforted by many Carleton Co. friends. Funeral service on May 26 was conducted by Rev. Philip Giberson. They buried Ferne beside Frank on land that was donated by Asa Bell adjoining the Biggar Ridge Cemetery. There the Wheeler monument reads: Frank David 1895 - 1946, Ferne 1895 - 1975. Markers indicate: Royal Canadian Legion and Odd Fellows

This may be the only memorial to the Wheelers in their home area. Their farm in N. Ridge is no longer readily identifiable. The buildings of all the farms on the Ridge have disappeared. The fences and many land marks have been removed. For a while the Flemming Lumber Co. planted crops on some of the farms. Now the whole ridge is one extensive farm — a potato farm owned and managed by McCain Foods Ltd., for the production of seed potatoes. Being a secluded area surrounded by woods, it is protected from spread of diseases.

The Descendants of Ferne and Frank

Except for one granddaughter in British Columbia, the offspring of Ferne and Frank Wheeler are living in Ontario and Massachusetts. There has been much communication and visiting between the Ontario Wheelers and the Massachusetts Wheelers. In a letter to Erma Shaw, April 21, 1983, Edna said, "The five of us Wheeler children and grandchildren (about 30 in all) are getting together in Danvers, Mass. The first week of July. (The first time we will have been together.) My husband and I may go on to New Brunswick to see Aunt Bernice and Morrill and Marjorie..." Edna subsequently reported that she and her husband had visits with Nellie and Freddie and their families.

The three eldest daughters, all now widowed, are living in Ontario.

Edna Christman is in St. Agatha. After the war, her husband, Horace Christman, began working as a millwright. He was also a pilot. His work required him to fly to the Canadian North and to Alaska to copper mines and other mines. Edna and Horace had two sons: John David b. Sept. 24, 1945, and Robert William, b. Dec. 9, 1957. Robert died by drowning, July 14, 1969. John David married Marlene Bitechy, Dec. 10, 1966. They have two children: John David ("J.D."), b. April 14, 1973, and Jennifer Ann, b. Nov. 2, 1976. They live in one half of a double house built for them and Edna and Horace. Horace died March 16, 1994. Edna, now living alone in her half of the house, is enjoying the proximity of her son and daughter-in-law. Edna has been very helpful in supplying data and photographs for this chapter.

Eloise Smith, formerly of Ottawa, now lives in Perth, Ontario. Her late husband, George Smith, was a major in the R.C.A.F. Some summers they spent his leave time in Juniper with Eloise's mother, Ferne Wheeler, and got to know some of their relatives, e.g., Gordon Corey. Gordon remembers that

The Wheelers: Nellie, Edna, Fred, Mary, Eloise, 1995

George pursued a hobby of prospecting. His partner in drilling and blasting was Edgar Boucher of Juniper.

George became disabled at the early age of 38. While in Europe on duty he suffered a stroke, leaving him paralysed on one side. He lived under care for several years until August 29, 1979. They had one daughter, Sharon Roberta, b. January 28, 1951. She married Ross Johnson, Nov. 22, 1974. They live in Victoria, British Columbia.

Mary Foster is living in Islington. Her late husband, Charles Foster was a musician and a professor of music at a Collegiate. He played in bands. He died June 19, 1995. They had two daughters: Barbara Joan Foster, b. July 14, 1948, and Judith Lea Foster, b. Sept. 4, 1955. Judith has one son, David Charles Foster, b. Jan. 4, 1985.

Ferne's and Frank's youngest daughter, Nellie, and her husband Eddie DeWitt, have been living and working in Massachusetts since the 1950's. They have two daughters:

Deborah Ann, b. Aug. 18, 1954, m. Kevin Cullen, Feb. 23, 1974; two daughters: Kristen Marie Cullen, b. Aug. 18, 1975, and Kelly Ann Cullen, b. Oct. 25, 1979. DeWitt's second daughter is Jodie Lynne, b. July 15, 1961, m. Michael Lemish, Dec. 16, 1987; their son: Connor Michael, b. April 12, 1992. Nellie's son is David Edward DeWitt, b. Aug. 19, 1962, m. Shelly Herlihy; they have two sons: Craig James, b. May 22, 1987, and Peter Joseph, b. May 15, 1989. Nellie is now retired from nursing at the Danvers City Hospital, and is enjoying a pension from the city. Eddie "did well as a carpenter". He retired five years ago following a heart attack. He continues to be active. In summer of 1998 he attended a reunion of his military unit in Fredericton.

Ferne's and Frank's one son, Frederick Joseph Wheeler, and his wife Merna Field, moved to Danvers, Mass., a little later than the DeWitts. In Danvers, Merna became a Real Estate Agent. Freddie soon became self-employed as a contractor with his own business, Wheeler Construction, Inc. They have one son, Robert Frederick, b. Sept. 14, 1952. He married Gail Baltoumas. Robert and Gail have two daughters: Stacy Ann, b. June 2, 1972; she married Sean Dunn, June 18, 1994. Second daughter of Robert and Gail is Jodi Lyn, b. May 6, 1978, the birthday of her grandmother, Merna. Robert Frederick Wheeler is operating Wheeler Construction Co., following Freddie's retirement.

Merna is also retired except that she still does some appraisal and mortgage work for a bank. Merna and Freddie visit New Brunswick frequently. In July, 1998, they attended the Corey reunion in Knowlesville. Freddie comes for hunting and fishing and visiting relatives. They have a home in Juniper, N.B. It became vacant in summer of 1998 when Merna's mother, Kay Field, died. Settling the estate has required many visits to Juniper.

Fred McBrine

Fred was a versatile person with many skills. His creativity and ingenuity is illustrated in an anecdote recalled by Bill Jordan and told by Myrtle Hemphill. Her grandfather, Billy George MacFarland, needed an artificial leg. Fred made a leg of wood and hinged it at the knee and ankle. Fred came to be described as talented and creative in carpentry. His versatility enabled him to work at farming, carpentry and milling. The mill built by Fred McBrine and George MacFarland acquired a heavy, four-cylinder motor from Flemming and Gibson, Juniper. It came from the log hauler the company had employed for a few winters in the 30's in transporting logs from Burnt Hill. Flemmings had bought the hauler from Sayer Lumber Co. who had employed it on the West Branch. It had been manufactured in Maine.[39]

Fred and George did not long retain the mill in E. Glassville. They sold it to Wallace Wiley, son of Ed Wiley. They located it on the Wiley farm in Divide. Wallace said, "We ran it with a truck motor." Wallace dates the move of the mill between 1936 and 1938. That was the time of the passing of Fred's parents. About that time it seems Fred was going through a period of transition. Near the beginning of W.W. II, Fred began to phase out his work on the farm.

Morrill Robinson recalled some of the moves Fred made toward terminating his farming and disposing of his equipment. Morrill said, "We got his horses. We bought his team, harness, long sled, bob sleds, and double wagon all at once. I think we got the horses in January 1940. We then had three teams to get our logs out. Fred said, 'I'll help you.' He worked for us the rest of the winter. That spring I planted his crop of grain." Fred's giving up farming was perhaps partly because he was spending a lot of time in carpentry. Perhaps it was also in preparation for leaving home for the army. However, he kept a few cows. Annie and Claudine took care of them while he was away, Marion recalls. Quite early in W.W.II, Fred enlisted in the Canadian Army. His daughter, Marion, thinks it was in 1941. It was about the same time that Bobby Thompson enlisted in the U.S. Army. Both in uniform, they met at the Canada/U.S. border. Neither dared cross over, Morrill recalled.

Fred enlisted in Woodstock and trained on the island with the Carleton and York Regiment. His daughter Marion, then about age eight, still remembers her excitement about waiting in Woodstock, watching a line of soldiers coming off the island, and eventually identifying her Dad. Later at Aldershot, N.S., when the regiment was about to embark for overseas, the word was spread that the Army needed carpenters. Some man reported that Fred could do that kind of work. From that point Fred was classified as a carpenter. In the winter of 1943 Fred's daughter, Claudine, was at the Business College in Fredericton. Claude and Jud Corey were in military training in Fredericton that winter. We occasionally met up with Claudine and her friends on the streets. She also became acquainted with Paul Foster who was at Normal School that winter. Later Claudine worked at Eaton's in Moncton for three years. She had occasional visits home via C.N. Rail through Juniper. She also worked for a year at Marcus Meed's Machine Shop, Bristol.

Fred McBrine, with Marion

In summer of 1943 the writer, then in advanced infantry

training at Camp Utopia, near Pennfield and St. George, N.B., discovered Fred at the same camp. He was a carpenter on the base. We visited a few evenings in the little hut that he occupied with a few other tradesmen. There he enjoyed his pipe after his day's work. His, "Hello Juddie" was a greeting from home for a boy far from home and having to make all new acquaintenances. Marion Bell remembers that her Dad mailed crates of blueberries home from Camp Utopia.

Changes at End of W.W.II

Soon after the end of W.W.II and Fred's discharge from the army, he sold the McBrine Farm in E. Glassville to Frank Pearson. Dennis thinks his father acquired the farm in 1945 and ploughed some fields that fall while the McBrine family was still occupying the house. In spring of 1946, Frank, being eager to plant a crop, borrowed a pair of horses from Lyon's. He ate his lunch in the barn. That spring and summer, 1946, Fred was building a house for his family in Glassville. It was located on a part of the Miller farm, at the edge of the Bristol Road, near the store built by Jim and Kate Hovey, and later owned by Tom and Marjorie Corey. The McBrine family moved to Glassville that summer, after a delay of a few weeks because Marion contracted scarlet fever. She said, "I was quarantined in the downstairs bedroom." It was a time of change for the whole family that year also. Claudine married Stanley Whitehouse. They too located in Glassville. After a short residence in an apartment over Derrah's store they built a house on the Centre Glassville Road, near the old Manse, by the brook. Marion's education was still in progress. She finished grade seven in East Glassville in 1946 before the move. The next year, 1947, she completed grade eight in Glassville, and began high school in Bristol that fall.

The building of the family home in Glassville, it seems, was the beginning of a house-building career for Fred. In 1950 he built a house in Florenceville for Douglas and Doreen

Thorne. It is the house now occupied by Kaye and Paul Foster. In 1951 he built Andrew McCain's house — still the residence of Marjorie McCain. It stands near the McCain Library. While Fred was building houses his daughter Marion was building a career in teaching. She began in W. Glassville at age 16, in fall of 1950. In the 1951-52 school year she was teaching in Knowlesville. It was an interesting experience but it turned out to be a time of interruptions — first in boarding places. She began at Claude Manuel's which lasted until housekeeper, Mrs. Estabrooks, had to go home. Marion then boarded with Marion and Bob Guthrie. It was a cold winter with heavy snowfalls. But Marion was well protected from the cold. After heavy snow falls Bob's pair of horses on a long sled transported her to school. She rode in comfort with blankets and a buffalo robe covering her and with hot bricks warming her feet.

Cold weather or heavy snow, however, did not prevent Marion from going home for a weekend. Home sickness energized her to wade snow to Highlands where she could meet a car to carry her home for a weekend. The extra holiday at the death of King George VI that winter was much appreciated.

A more serious interruption came in late winter. Marion's mother, Annie McBrine, became terminally ill. Marion was needed at home. She ended her teaching in Knowlesville on March 12th. Elizabeth DeMerchant took over the school. Marion went home to help care for her mother. Claudine was there too. Dorothy Lyon came to give needles. Annie died in the Glassville house at midnight May 31/June 1, 1952.

Then followed more family change. In September 1952 Marion went to Teachers' College in Fredericton. Left alone, Fred sold the house in Glassville and built a trailer but he did not leave Glassville immediately. Marion said, "In the fall of 1953 he was still living in Glassville. Perhaps it was about that time that Fred built a house in Centreville for Customs Officer, Morley Milbury."

Bristol Becomes Home to the Family

Soon, however, the whole family was to be located in Bristol. Claudine and Stanley moved there in 1953. Marion said, "I was teaching in Bristol. Later, Dad took his mobile home to Bristol, probably in spring of 1954." In 1957 Marion married Albert Bell who grew up in Bristol.

Fred's first job in Bristol was with Bristol Woodworking Factory. Hence he first set up his mobile home in the neighborhood of Bill Lamont and Harold MacDougall. In 1958 Fred was located on Stanley Whitehouse's property. Later, Fred set his mobile home on Curtis Hill, at top of Rogers St. In the later 50's and the 60's Fred engaged in a variety of jobs in building, carpentry and maintenance. For a while he worked with his son-in-law, Stanley Whitehouse, who was overseeing jobs for Edison MacFarlane. They built a school and the police barracks in St. George. Marion dates the St. George work in 1961. She recalls taking her daughter Kathy, then age three, to St. George that summer to stay with Claudine who kept Kathy while Marion attended Summer Session at Teachers' College in Fredericton. Marion's and Albert's younger daughter, Laurie, stayed with Albert's aunt in Bristol. At Fredericton Marion had a student companion, Monica Reeleder. Marion said, "We roomed together at summer school. We boarded with Monica's sister, Donna Dykeman." Marion was putting a big effort into reaching a licensing level then obtainable through summer school credits — a provision about to be dropped by a change in government regulations.

After the St. George contracts Stanley Whitehouse continued doing carpenter work until his untimely death on September 7, 1978. He would have been 55 on October 15th.

Fred's Late Years

In his later working years it seems that Fred McBrine found less strenuous work. A late job was tending and maintaining Syd Findlay's green house.

After being alone for 19 years, Fred married Bernice Bell, who then had her own house on Rogers St., in Bristol. Bernice was the widow of James Bell of Glassville. She was a person of long family acquaintenance. Fred and Bernice were married by Rev. Lawrence Bone of the Florenceville Pastoral Charge of the United Church, in 1976. Frederick Rice McBrine died January 17, 1983, after a bout with cancer. Bernice died October 29, 1988. She was buried October 31st in Bristol. A monument to Fred and Annie stands in the United Church Cemetery, Glassville. A footstone on Fred's grave, apparently placed by the Canadian Legion, indicates that Fred was a sergeant in the Carleton and York Regiment.

Descendants of Fred and Annie McBrine

Their two daughters, Claudine Whitehouse and Marion Bell, both now widowed, continue their residences in Bristol. Claudine's son, Robert Whitehouse now makes his home with her. Robert also took up carpentry. He alternates between carpenter work and seasonal work in farming. He works for Ronald Brown in Summerfield during potato harvest. In summer of 1996 he was putting a roof on the farm barn. Robert was married to Ida Nicholson of Beaconsfield. Their three children: Calvin, Carla and Christopher all live in nearby communities; the two sons live in Wicklow. Calvin married Shelly Lunn in 1991. They have a daughter, Christie, b. March 24, 1992 and a son Ty Calvin, b. Oct. 22, 1998. Christopher married Tracy Plant in 1996. Carla married Peter Carlisle, in 1991. They have two sons: Cole, b. 1994, and Luke, b. 1996. They live in Summerfield. Carla, a long time employee of the Motor Vehicle

Branch, has of late been dividing her time between the Bristol office and the Perth office. She has also been taking a computer course in Woodstock.

Claudine enjoys good health. She likes to drive her car, and often takes trips to Woodstock and to Maine. She also enjoys visits from her grandchildren.

Marion Bell was for several years a teacher in the Bristol Elementary School. Albert Bell worked for the Department of Highways. He also did part-time farming with his brother Charley. They raised prize beef cattle on the Bell homestead in Bristol. Albert's daughters, Kathy and Laurie, showed the cattle at fairs. After graduation from Northern Carleton High School both girls went to university in Halifax. Kathy graduated from Mount St. Vincent as a medical secretary, and Laurie from Dalhousie as a pharmacist. Kathy spent a year on the staff of the Community College in Woodstock, N.B. There she implemented a Medical Secretarial Course. Then she went to St. Thomas University, Fredericton, for a year in preparation for teaching in public school. She has been teaching ever since.

In 1983 Kathy married Ian Brown. His mother was Marjorie Ronalds of W. Glassville. They now live at Carleton Place, near Ottawa. Ian works for Northern Telecom. They have four children: Leah, Erica, Leslee and Andrew. While some of the children were at home Kathy taught half time. On Sept. 8, 1998, when the fourth child began school, Kathy returned to full time. Her specialty is elementary education. In 1995 she was teaching Kindergarten, and in 1996, Grade two. Laurie worked for Northern Carleton Pharmacy in Florenceville, N.B. While in that employment, in 1983; she married Ken Neal an employee of McCain Foods. Ken's employment with McCain's took them to Montreal. They lived in nearby Kirkland. Later he was transferred to a position in sales and marketing for Bunge Foods. With their two children: Kenneth Colin, b. 1985, and Ashley Alyson, b. 1988, they live in suburban St. Louis.

The Bell family was early bereaved of their father and

husband. 1989 was to be Albert's last year before retirement. However, in May 1989 he experienced discomfort in the night and was afterwards told he had a mild problem with his heart. October 31, 1989, he had by-pass surgery. After a winter at home he felt the urge to groom their cattle for spring showing. He was not able to complete that task. On March 16, 1990, Albert died of arrhythmia.

Marion has been retired since June 1988 from her teaching position in Bristol Elementary School. Periodically she visits her daughters and their families in Ottawa and St. Louis.

Alma

When Alma McBrine married Clarence Robinson in 1915 he already had his own farm in E Glassville. He had acquired it in 1913. He was only about a mile from where he grew up. His parents, Lindsay Robinson and Eliza Bell Lamont, lived "up over the hill" from Clarence's place, which was directly across the road from the McDougall place. In 1915 Clarence took his bride to the farm house which was to become home to him and Alma and their first born son for the rest of their lives. There, their two sons were born and grew up. Farming was a way of life for the family. The Robinson family occasionally visited Alma's Uncle Ira Corey and family in E. Knowlesville. I especially remember one visit.

A Ride with Joe's Horses

One Sunday afternoon in the early fall of 1935 there appeared on the west side of our farm a two-seated express wagon pulled by a pair of pretty sorrels that we recognized as Joe McDermid's team, Prince and Star. Joe had sold his farm at Highlands to his bordering neighbour, Tom Guthrie. Not knowing who he could trust to give his horses good care, Joe let them go to Lyon's fox farm. Clarence Robinson, hearing about the fate of the horses, traded an older pair of his horses for Joe's horses.

Morrill and his mother were enjoying a ride behind their newly acquired team. They had come across Bob Guthrie's farm and through a narrow strip of woods into our most westerly field. After supper, Morrill hitched the team and pulled the wagon in front of our verandah for Alma to mount. When she was seated in the wagon for the homeward journey she spoke enthusiastically of the horses. Just then my brother Bob climbed up to the spare seat to ride part way to Tom Guthrie's where he was working. Horses were nearing the end of their era as a means of travel on social visits and on trips to town, but they still played an important role in farming and in logging. Robinsons worked their horses in both those activities. Morrill recalled: "In 1936-37 we logged on Harold McDougall's land 'over the Hawk'." That was the winter following the death of Alma's father, Eb McBrine. Harold Robinson recalls that his grandmother,

Mack Brown, and Bill Lamont at "The Hawk"

Mina McBrine, "spent the winter with his mother and him when they looked after the cattle, while Clarence and Morrill worked in the woods, cutting logs." Harold's estimated date agrees with Morrill's: "The winter of 1937, just after our grandfather (Eb) passed away in July. He fondly remembers the delicious chocolate cake with chocolate cream icing which she used to make. It was the best cake he ever ate and no one seemed to know her recipe which was probably not found in any cookbook."[40]

Morrill reminisced further about their logging: "In the fall of 1938 we started on the old Robinson place. We cut for the next three winters. Some winters Dad and I stayed at the old Robinson house, a mile north of here. Mother and Harold stayed here and took care of the cattle. She cooked and sent the food up to us." Edna Wheeler recalled keeping house at the upper farm part of one winter. Morrill recollected further: "We had three men working for us. Later we had two local men, Chesley Dingee and Lee McBrine, helping us as we needed them. In the winter of 1940 Fred McBrine was helping us. That was just before he went into the army. We continued the logging until 1945."

Change in Occupation; Learning a Trade

When Morrill was about age 35 he began to make a marked change in occupation. "In the early summer of 1951", he said, "I went to work with Fred McBrine building a house for Andrew McCain", in Florenceville. That building job brought an unexpected end to Morrill's farming.

That spring, 1951, Morrill had planted two acres of potatoes. Harold had two acres also. Morrill tried to persuade Harold to buy his crop: "There they are, growing and fertilizer paid for. You can have them for $150.00." Harold didn't buy. Morrill continued: "I cultivated them in evenings. In the fall I dug them; I stored them all winter. In the spring I sold the 300 barrels for $9.00 a barrel. Out of the $2700 I bought a new Chevrolet Deluxe for $2400. Thus Morrill ended his farming on a success story. The price of potatoes was not always that good. He said, "I kept on carpentering. The Chevrolet Deluxe I bought in 1952 lasted me 10 years. Then I gave it to Dad, and bought a brand new Mercury."

Fred McBrine, having introduced Morrill to the trade, also helped him to begin working independently. "After Annie died in 1952", said, Morrill, "Fred stayed here a few days at Christmas time. We sat the kitchen wall back into the woodshed. We wanted him to build cupboards in the extra space. But Fred wanted to be able to use his power saw. Electric power was then being extended to rural communities. Fred said, "Call me when the power comes. I'll come and build cupboards". "Several times", said Morrill, "I asked him, 'When are you coming? Fred: 'In a few days.' Finally, Fred said, 'I'm busy; take my power saw and build the cupboards yourself.'" That initial set of cupboards established Morrill's reputation as a worker with wood, and opened up much work. Many visitors, on seeing the cupboards in the Robinson house, said, "Come and build me a set of cupboards!"

Morrill's first custom job was for George DeLong who had recently moved into the Barrian Swim house. Over the next few years Morrill left his handiwork in the houses of many families in nearby communities. He recalled: the double house at Dingee's, two sets; Walter Bramley's, Hilton McBrine's, Bonar Brown's, George McFarland's, Denis Pearson's, Reeleder's, Spence's, Guthrie's and Welch's. He estimated 50 sets. Relatives he remembered working for were Alice and Fred McKenzie, in E. Knowlesville, two or three times. Besides kitchen cupboards he finished bedrooms upstairs. Morrill also recounted his work for Roy Hemphill in Knowlesville: "I first worked for Roy in fall of 1955. He came here asking for me. We were in Bangor — Dad, Mother and I, visiting Hazel True, Dad's sister. When we returned, Harold said, "Roy was looking for you." I worked for three days, fixing up the old mill, and doing a little repair on the house. Then Roy said, "I'm all done building."

The following winter, 1956, the Hemphill mill burned. Roy spent two weeks pondering whether to rebuild. Then he wanted me to put a line shaft in his garage so he could make bowling pins. I was working for Allen McBrine on his potato house. I said, "You see Allen; if he says it's o.k., I'll come." Allen agreed. I took three days off from Allen's work. We set up Roy's machine for making pins. In the summer of 1956, we built Roy's new mill. In 1959 we built a cattle barn. I also put up other buildings in the mill complex." Roy's building had by no means ended."Beginning in summer of 1966 we built the new house for Roy and Pauline, on the Gilmor Road." Morrill's brother, Harold, had a part, at least in laying the foundation. "We had a little problem with the dormers. Roy took me to Woodstock to see Alan Lamont, Dad's cousin. He drew some diagrams and explained. I built three dormers. In February the house was finished. They moved in. I worked at Hemphill's 11 summers."

Harold Robinson continued at the East Glassville school, at least seasonally, until he was 16. On the school list his name appears for the year ending June 1940. As with Morrill, his first work was on the family farm. Later he changed occupations. In a sense, however, Harold lived all his life on the family farm. When he married he made his home on a lot cut off the front of the Clarence Robinson farm. On April 12, 1949, Harold married a local girl, Marie DeLong. Her father, George DeLong, moved from Glassville to the Barrian Swim house in E. Glassville when Marie was nearly grown up. The first home of Harold and Marie was the former Bob Lunnie house. They moved it from a farm north of Robinson's onto the Robinson lot. They added much to it and made it a comfortable and attractive home.

In his later work Harold has demonstrated versatility. At times he worked with Morrill in house building. He also

Harold, Alma, Clarence and Morrill Robinson

learned to install furnaces. Still early in life, he became employed by the Department of Highways, and eventually became foreman.

Harold and Marie have one son, Clarence Harold Robinson, b. Nov. 28, 1965. Morrill liked to take the boy on outings, e.g., Halloween in the neighborhood.

Wedding Anniversary: Alma and Clarence

The year their grandson was born, Alma and Clarence Robinson celebrated their 50th wedding anniversary, on Sept. 15, 1965. Celebrating with them were Ferne Wheeler, bridesmaid, and Harold McDougall, best man. Clarence lived almost four and one half years after that, until March 23, 1970. He died at the Bath Hospital, less than a month short of age 77. Alma lived until Sept. 24, 1979, just past her 87th birthday.

Harold McDougal, Clarence and Alma Robinson, Ferne Wheeler

Marriage

Morrill was not long alone. On January 26, 1980, at Florenceville, N.B., he married Marjorie Lyon, widow of Dean Lyon. As a schoolmate of Morrill in E. Glassville, he knew her as Marjorie Brown, daughter of Minnie and Norman Brown. Marjorie and Morrill enjoyed two very good years together before Marjorie was diagnosed with cancer. Morrill then phased out his carpentry work so he could spend his time with her. His last job was in his own neighborhood, putting panelling on Hilton McBrine's house. Morrill said, "I took the job with the agreement that I could work two hours in the morning, and two hours in the afternoon, or when I feel like it." Marjorie lived until October 24, 1985. They had five valuable years together.

Retirement

Morrill did not resume carpenter work after he was widowed. In 1989 Harold retired from his position as Road Commissioner with New Brunswick Department of Highways. But he didn't stop working. His versatility in work led to various jobs for neighborhood people. One task Harold had in 1996 and '97 was driving

Marjorie and Morrill Robinson

his brother on errands and doctors' appointments. The writer visited Morrill three times in 1996: July, August and September, and in March 1997 in the farmhouse where he was born and lived his entire life. On my first visit, July 6th, accompanied by Margaret, I found him comfortably seated in his living room and not moving far from his chair. He explained: "One January day I went on errands to Florenceville and Bath, moving as usual and standing in line at the bank. I was o.k. until I returned to my own driveway and reached for the door handle. Then I felt a sharp pain in my back." Since January 1996 he had been confined to home except when Harold drove him on an errand. A deteriorated vertebrae restricted his movements — as it turned out, for the rest of his life. His attitude was good. He appeared to have accepted his limitations, and to be enjoying the comfort of all the modern conveniences he had put into the house when he was an active carpenter: an improved kitchen and a bathroom close by. Also he was appreciating daily visits. One homemaker comes five days a week. Two others attended his needs on weekends. On my second visit, August 30th, Morrill reported a week-long visit from his cousin, Mary Wheeler Foster, her daughter Barbara Foster, and grandson David Charles Foster, then age 11. They took the boy to Hartland. He wanted to see the Hugh John Flemming Bridge. He had written his name on it on an earlier visit. Morrill spoke appreciatively of Beryl, the home maker who cleaned the house meticulously, in preparation for Mary's arrival. Also between my visits, Morrill's many good friends and neighbors had gathered for his 80th birthday on August 5th. Roy Hemphill told me, "I went early so I could talk to him before the crowd gathered."

The last of my summer series of visits to Morrill was on September 4th. My brother Keith accompanied me. We stopped at the Highlands Baptist Cemetery on a search for the graves of the infant children of Mina and Eb McBrine. Then we visited Morrill. During those 1996 visits Morrill related to me the interesting stories of his life that are included earlier in this chapter. He recounted the only times he had been away from his community overnight: visits with Marjorie to her daughters, and Senior Citizen tours. His interests remained high. He spoke of the Robinson reunion, which has been meeting yearly since 1993 in the Glassville Rec. Hall. He also planned to meet with Lamont relatives in September, 1996. On March 19, 1997, when the snow was ploughed to high banks on both sides of the E. Glassville Road, I made what turned out to be my list visit to Morrill. He came immediately from his bedroom when I called to him. We talked, but some of his earlier enthusiasm for sharing stories had waned. Earlier in the winter he had been in the Bath Hospital. Also, that winter he had acquired the support of a "life line". A press on his button could bring his brother, Harold or Bonnar Brown, or another neighbor. We had a quiet goodbye: "The Lord bless thee and keep thee....." "Thank you."

In April Morrill had to summon Harold to take him again to the Bath Hospital. His cousin, Marion Bell visited him there and also earlier at home. He died in hospital May 18, 1997. His funeral was conducted at the Kilcollins Funeral Home, Bath, by Pastor Olive Ann Archibald of the Glassville/Argyle/Juniper pastoral charge. He is buried beside Alma and Clarence in the Glassville United Church Cemetery. Twice in 1997, July 30, and November 22, I visited Harold and Marie Robinson. He told me of Morrill's call to him for help and his arrangements to take him to hospital. He said to me, "Morrill enjoyed your visits." He also expressed appreciation for Marion Bell's visits to Morrill in hospital. Harold is the only descendant of Mina and Eb McBrine remaining in E. Glassville. Now he is the eldest resident of E. Glassville. Like Morrill, he has lived his entire life there.

The Robinson houses are surrounded in summer by growing crops of grain and potatoes. The farmland was rented, later sold, to Bonar Brown, a cousin of the writer and a relative of the Robinsons through Lamonts. Since Morrill's passing his house has been sold to a son of Dennis Pearson.

Harold and Marie's son, Clarence Harold Robinson, married Peggy Norris, of Glassville, in August 1992. Cousin, Marion Bell, said, "I taught both Clarence and Peggy in the Bristol School. At the 1994 Robinson Reunion, Clarence and Peggy were recognized as the most recently married couple. They have one daughter, Brianna Rachael, b. June 12, 1995. They live in Fredericton, N.B. where Clarence is employed by the City as an engineering technician.

---

[1] See Chapter I

[2] The Story of Knowlesville, p.89

[3] See Chapter II

[4] Erma's recollections

[5] See The Story of Knowlesville, p. 235f. The list of "Persons Buried in Highlands Cemetery" was drawn up by Myrtle Hemphill, @ 1984. In addition to names on monuments, she searched names from Woodstock Sentinel and other records.

[6] See A History of Glassville Settlement, Appendix, p.xx.

[7] Ibid., p. xviii

[8] Ibid., p.xxi

[9] Photo and data from Edna Christman

[10] Photo from Marion Bell

[11] Edna Christman. Her source of this and other data: "It was told to me by my mother during my teen years."

[12] A History of the Glassville Settlement, appendix, p. xxi

[13] Edna Christman

[14] Edna and Erma

[15] Erma

[16] See The Story of Knowlesville, p.136

[17] A History of Glassville, Appendix, p.xix and p.xxiii

[18] H.N. Bradley, op.cit. P.97, 135

[19] Ibid p.154 and 141

[20] Roy Hemphill; diary record

[21] Myrtle Hemphill, Sept. 1996

[22] See The Story of Knowlesville, p. 153

[23] Marion Bell, in Sept. 1996

[24] Conversation with Morrill, July 1996

[25] See H.N. Bradley, History of Foreston..., p.144

[26] Letter to the writer, September 1996

[27] A History of the Glassville Settlement, Appendix, p. XXII

[28] See The Story of Knowlesville, p.233

[29] Edna K. Christman sent the obituary and shared other data by letters and phone. See also "Corey Courier", 1973

[30] Edna shared this letter also.

[31] See The Story of Knowlesville, p.179

[32] Discharge Certificate

[33] Edna Christman

[34] See H.N. Bradley, op.cit., p.97

[35] Letter and conversations with Edna Christman, Sept. 1996, and later

[36] See H.N. Bradley, op.cit., p.97 f., 119.

[37] Ibid, p.135

[38] See Neil Bradley, op.cit, p.48, for explanation of cemetery land

[39] Roy Hemphill.

[40] Story from Morrill and Harold Robinson.

CHAPTER IX

MILLER FAMILY
1867 Alma Corey Miller 1915
1862 Robert James Miller 1937

On August 14th, 1889 Alma Lizette Corey of Knowlesville and Robert James Miller of Glassville were united in marriage by Rev. J.K. Bearisto, pastor of the Presbyterian Church in Glassville.[1] Mrs. Jane Bearisto witnessed the marriage.

Alma Lizette Corey was the second surviving child of Alfred and Lucretia Corey. Alma grew up in Knowlesville. She was born in Cornhill, N.B., in her mother's native County, Kings, in the year of the Confederation of Canada, 1867, on January 12th. That was before the family began to move farther afield to seek work. When, after those sojourns, the Corey family arrived in Knowlesville to make a permanent home, Alma was probably about age seven[2]. Robert James Miller was the last child of Hugh and Jane Miller. He was born in 1862, the year following the Miller family's move to Glassville.

Alma Corey and Robert James Miller both had venturesome parents who had immigrated into Carleton County after living and working in other parts of New Brunswick. The story of the Corey family's pioneering venture to Knowlesville is told in Chapter I. Here, at the beginning of this chapter, we must tell the story of the origins of the Miller family and their pioneering venture into Glassville.

James Miller's father, Hugh Miller, born in 1830, came from Bellshill, near Glasgow, Scotland, to Saint John, N.B., in 1853. Hugh was accompanied by his brother, Robert, born 1834.[3] Hugh's great granddaughter, June Covey, has the Bible that Hugh purchased when he arrived in Saint John. It is dated 1852. "Hugh may have made an earlier trip" to Saint John in

213

1852.[4] Hugh, born 1830, and his brother Robert, born 1834, having worked in the Glasgow foundries "found work in the foundries of Saint John as moulders."[5]

It appears that through the foundry trade Hugh found not only employment but also a wife, Jane Pender. Her "father established Pender's Foundries", another Saint John business.[6] The Pender family lived in New Jerusalem, then a pioneer farming settlement in Queens Co., N.B. Its center was about eight miles west of Hampstead,[7] a village on the Saint John River, south of Gagetown. To the west of New Jerusalem was Petersville, an Irish pioneer settlement.

"In 1856 Hugh Miller married Jane Pender" who was born June 24, 1821. Hugh and Jane were married by Rev. Wm. Alves June 6, 1856.[8] The couple also settled in New Jerusalem ... at least for a time.[9]

The Pender family was also Scottish. "James Pender[10] with his wife Margaret Reid, came from Scotland in 1817 to New Jerusalem, ...with seven children." Jane is listed as the 9th child, born presumably in New Jerusalem. The Pender land area, i.e., grant, plus acreage they obtained later, totalled about 600 acres.

The Pender family appear to have had a strong creative and entrepreneurial bent. James Pender "was a stone mason". He "understood the process of dyking and through a series of swamps and brooks created three ponds with water gates and dams and built the first Pender watermill.[11] A further note tells us: "On....Pender's Brook was a mill operated as a grist mill by Pender's, McKee and Adamson." With modern equipment added, the mill operated "as a grist mill, saw mill and carding mill" and continued through the life of the community.[12] James Pender's sons apparently continued and expanded Pender enterprises. Son "James started or founded the Pender's Nail Works in Saint John.

Some brothers left Canada. Will and John went to

Australia where they also started a Nail Works."[13] However, some Penders long remained in New Jerusalem and vicinity. There they left a strong legacy, including their name on their neighbourhood. For example, James Pender left his name on the maps, e.g., Pender's Brook and Pender's Road. The community has since been obscured by Camp Gagetown military area.

The marriage of Jane Pender and Hugh Miller seems to have brought together two families of remarkable courage and venture. We shall see that there was ambition and entrepreneurial bent in the Miller family as in the Pender family.

Hugh and Jane Miller lived in her family's community, New Jerusalem, or other parts of Queens County, N.B., from the time of their marriage in 1856 until after their first four children were born. During that time he must have continued communication with his family, as he had done from the time of his arrival in Saint John. His sister, Agnes, and perhaps also his brother John, joined Hugh and Robert in Saint John, between 1853 and 1855.

In 1857, Hugh's father, John Miller, Sr., died in Scotland at the age of 71. "Apparently through Hugh's urging and financing, his mother and younger brothers came out to New Brunswick to reunite the family." Then there were five Miller brothers in New Brunswick: Hugh, Robert, John, David and Alexander. Their sister Agnes married William Love in 1855.[14]

About 1860 the Miller family began a move northward to Glassville in Carleton Co. "It is likely that Hugh, at least, spent part of that year in Glassville." "Apparently Hugh was the driving force behind the move to Glassville. He must have been aware of the survey of lands in the area in the late 1850's," and 60's. "Four 100-acre lots were reserved, side by side, in the centre of what became the village, but with one additional lot nearby......By May 1861 three of the Miller brothers, Robert, John and David with mother Agnes along with sister Agnes Love and her husband William and children, apparently came to

Glassville and......started clearing land and building cabins....."

Hugh apparently stayed at least part of the summer with Jane in Queens Co. It was a sad and trying summer for them. A son born July 23, 1861, died two weeks later. A daughter Margaret, age three, died October 27, 1861. Despite that sad experience, however, Hugh and Jane apparently continued with their plans to move northward.

It appears that before the end of 1861 the Miller family, including Hugh and Jane and two children, John, four and one half, and a daughter, Agnes, 21 months, had established residence in Glassville, where they were one of the earliest pioneer families. Also settling in Glassville was Jane's sister, Matilda Young. She was the mother of John Young Jr. In the year following the settlement of Hugh and Jane Miller in Glassville their fifth and last child, Robert James Miller, was born on July 12, 1862.[15]

Hugh Miller, Entrepreneur

Hugh soon began business activities. "He was appointed the first postmaster in March 1864.....He opened a general store from one of his two log cabins..." Their first new frame house was built about 1868..... "He constructed the new large store about 1875, with a spacious upper floor called Miller's Hall...." [16] Besides being an entrepreneur, Hugh Miller was also a community leader. He was one of the first elders of the Presbyterian Church. He was treasurer of the Aberdeen Agricultural Society.

An indication of Hugh Miller's business acumen and early progress to the point of having money to lend, is found in a legal document now in the possession of Marilyn Hicks,[17] and carefully preserved in plastic, the document describes a monetary transaction between Hugh Miller and Alfred Corey of Knowlesville. It tells us that on December 10, 1877, Alfred

Corey borrowed $100.00 from Hugh Miller, to be paid in one year. The terms of the loan are described in detail.

"As security of payment" Alfred's livestock and other farm assets were listed: 1 horse, chestnut color, age 8 years, previously owned by Noble Branscombe; 2 cows, age 8 and 12 years, light red color with white faces; 2 heifer calves, with white markings; 1 steer calf; hay on the premises. These assets could be sold by auction or private sale should the $100.00 not be paid. It was signed by Alfred Corey with a red seal, and witnessed by H.H. Hobbs. A payment of $5.50, cash, on October 7, 1879, is recorded at the bottom of the document. Interestingly, 1877 was the year that Alfred's son, Ira, was born, and 1879 was the year his second last child, Alberta, was born. Thus there were involvements between Corey and Miller families long before the marriage of Alma Corey and Robert James Miller, in 1889.

Alma and James Living in Glassville

We speculate that when Jim and Alma married they lived at the Hugh Miller home, and that their first two children were born there: Maude, 1890, and James, Jr. (Jimmie) 1892.

In 1893 Jim and Alma Miller acquired a separate house in Glassville. It had a notable history. Built by Jimmy Good about 1876, it was occupied by him for about 10 years. After Jimmie's departure from Glassville the house was occupied by James Hovey, Sr. Later occupants were: Michael Welch and wife Jennie Love, and Robert O'Dell and wife. James and Alma Miller lived in the house from 1893-1907[18]. During those years the latter three of their five children were born: Will, Kate and Wilma. Also the Klondike Gold Rush occurred. James Miller was in the Klondike, probably in late 1898 and early 1899. Family tradition says he returned home to Glassville because a baby was expected. Their third child and second son, Will, was born March 21, 1899; he was called the "Klondike nugget". Erma Corey Shaw recounted one memorable visit to the Good house. "On Nov. 1, 1908, the day after my father's home-coming to Knowlesville, he, my grandparents, and I visited his two sisters, Ida McBrine and Alma Miller and their families in Glassville. By that time Aunt Ida and Uncle Bill McBrine and family were living in the Jimmie Good house. Uncle Jim and Aunt Alma Miller had vacated it perhaps a year earlier." From the Good house they moved back to the Hugh Miller homestead. Erma was able to attach essentially accurate dates to these family residences and moves because of their occurrence in relation to the home-coming in 1908 of her father, Ira Corey, from his two and one half year sojourn in Western Canada.[19]

After that visit of the Coreys, the McBrine family had one more winter in the Good house. In May, 1909, the Glassville History says, "Jim and Alma sold their house,"i.e., the Good house, "to D. Perry Fitzgerald."[20] Perry and his wife Ella, daughter of Matilda Ann Gilmor and Alexander Scott, spent the rest of their lives there. Ella Fitzgerald died there in 1942, and Perry in 1956. The house, currently owned and occupied by Weldon Lee, has proved very durable. The moves of Ida and Bill McBrine and family are narrated in Chapter XII.

During most of that era Jim Miller's work must have been at the Hugh Miller place where there was a store, post office and boarding house, and two farms. Hugh's elder son "John (Jack) took over operation of the store in 1894. He also became postmaster...". It seems that Jim assisted his brother Jack in the operation of the store and the post office. Together they farmed the Miller properties and managed the various Miller enterprises.

While Alma and Jim were living in the Good house both his parents died. "Jane Pender Miller died in 1900 at age 78." Hugh Miller died in 1905 in Scotland, whence he had returned for a visit. Jack and his wife Emmeline Philips, were still living at the Miller homestead when Jim and Alma returned there in 1907. Jack and Emmeline had no children.[21] To the Miller house Jim and Alma brought their five children:

> Agnes Maude, July 5, 1890;
> James Hugh (Jimmy), Sept. 20, 1892;
> William John McAlpine, Mar. 21, 1899;
> Alma Kathleen, Sept. 4, 1900;
> Wilma Jean Lucretia, b. Feb. 13, 1907.

Agnes Maude and
James Hugh Miller c. 1899

William John and
Alma Kathleen Miller c. 1905

Lambs

Jack Miller also had another business, at least seasonally, in partnership with George Allan. Prof. Robert Love recalled that they gathered sheep — probably lambs. He said, "they drove them to a farm at Beaver Brook owned by my father. As a kid I helped drive them; it was fun. When the flock reached about 200 they drove them to Bristol to be carried live, by train, to Saint John." The business Prof. Love described was during his boyhood in Glassville. He said, "My mother stayed in Glassville until 1918 and then moved to Devon." How long Jack and Emmeline Miller remained at the Miller house is a question. Eventually they moved to Bristol or Bath and there operated a hotel or boarding house. At length, Jim and Alma became the operators of the Miller store in Glassville, and the boarding house.

Millers: Jack, Emiline, Alma, William, R. James, Kathleen, Agnes Bell, Wilma Jean, c. 1913

Erma's recollections

In my earliest memories of my Aunt Alma and Uncle Jim Miller they were living in the Hugh Miller home and keeping a store and boarding house. Their children, four of them older than I, were growing up in the Miller home in Glassville while I was growing up with my grandparents, Alfred and Lucretia Corey in Knowlesville. We visited Glassville frequently. Weekly, when the weather was favorable, Grandpa hitched his faithful mare, Bess. Grandma and I climbed into the wagon or sleigh and rode to Glassville for a visit at the Miller home, and for grocery shopping at the Miller store. During one of my visits at Miller's my cousins gave me an exciting report: "Nine cars came in that Bristol Road today!" From the back door of the Miller home they could look out on the Bristol road. It was the era when cars were just beginning to appear and to replace horses. Jimmie Miller later recorded: "The first automobile owned in Glassville was in 1905. Later it was sold to William Burnham of E. Florenceville."[22]

Erma recollected further:

The Millers also made visits to Knowlesville. I especially remember one visit in summer of 1910. Aunt Alma and her daughter, Kate, drove their horse from Glassville to attend the funeral of Mrs. Frazier in the Knowlesville Baptist Church. That was the time I followed her into the church wearing my kimono. I was seven that summer — the age Aunt Alma was when she came with the Corey family to Knowlesville. Perhaps Aunt Alma identified with me at that age in doing for me the kindness of sending a piece of cloth from the Miller Store in Glassville earlier that summer or spring for Aunt Alice to make the kimono for me. It was a kindness which must have resulted in an embarrassment. When she went up front to walk by the coffin I traipsed behind her, bare-footed and wearing my kimono.[23]

Miller's, A Busy Place

Perhaps a funeral was one of the rare occasions when Aunt Alma could be away from Glassville on a workday. Store keeping then involved extensive bookkeeping and accounting. Many customers ran charge accounts. Among them was Ira Corey. A statement of his account, dated January 1913, a year after his second marriage, is an interesting sample of an account with "James Miller, Glassville, N.B."[24]

"Ira Corey"
2 lb. Tobacco	1.30
3 Gloves	.30
2 Gal. Molasses	.90
10 lb. Tea	<u>3.00</u>
	$5.50

Hugh Miller house and store, Glassville, c. 1888

The account ledger was also a bit of a diary. A note at the bottom of the page says: Fine day, quite warm, very little snow – wagon to Bristol, sleds out Foreston.

Besides operating the store, Jim and Alma Miller maintained a boarding house and a stage barn. Some of Alma's boarders were long term. One of them was the village blacksmith, Murray LaMont, for about a year before he married.[25] The boarding house and stage barn together provided overnight accommodations for men and horses. The Miller place was a regular resting place for workmen travelling to and from the mills and lumber camps: loggers, scalers, foremen, contractors, and suppliers. Glassville was on the direct route between Bristol and Foreston and the Mirimachi. In the first decade of the 1900's probably they also catered to travellers connected with the building of the railroad through Juniper. Alma provided dinners and suppers to the travellers.[26]

A Growing Family and Much Caring

While Alma and Jim Miller were engaged in that demanding work they were rearing five children. One case of illness was well remembered. Will, at about age 10, was seized with appendicitis. Though medical care had severe limits in those days, it could make immediate, life-saving response to emergencies. Will had surgery on the dining room table of the Miller home. Aunt Mina McBrine held the kerosene lamp for the doctor. The incident occurred while Claude McBrine lay critically ill in the Welch house.[27]. Though there was much work and many to care for at the Miller place in Glassville, Alma did not forget her parents. Erma said, "Aunt Alma and Uncle Jim were very generous to my grandparents in their old age, often donating food." There was no pension in those days. Neither did Alma forget her church. Alma was a member of Highlands Baptist Church. The record book kept by her father,

Alfred Corey, does not indicate when she became a member. On a membership list dated June 1, 1904, she is listed: "Mrs. James Miller, residence, Glassville". Her son, Jimmie, shared recollections of her doing much work in support of the Highlands Church. The church was dedicated on September 20, 1891, exactly one year before Jimmie's birth.

Education: Jimmie

Neither did they forget education for their growing family. It appears that Jimmie at age 19, in the fall of 1911, started his studies at University of New Brunswick, Fredericton. He must have received sufficient preparation in the Glassville School, where he is first registered for the year ending June 30, 1899. It appears that he went directly from his last year in the Glassville School, ending June 1911 to U.N.B. that fall where he enrolled in the Department of Engineering.

A letter he wrote to his father, dated September 22, 1912, speaks of beginning his second year: "Dear Papa: I've settled down again and started courses. I'm taking another subject..and some forestry...." He mentioned initiation, stomach cramps, cholera and a "bad cold". He asked about crops: potatoes and oats. He listed articles he wanted sent to him: his suit, a fountain pen, cuff buttons, and French books from the cupboard; he added, "I'm short of money."

An earlier letter from Jimmie, dated January 9, 1912, reports a visit he made to a family relative, Wilfred Kierstead, in Fredericton. The letter said he was "asking about fowls", which, it seems, he had expected from Glassville and did not receive.[28]

Maude Miller

The oldest of the family, Maude, was a great believer in the value of education. She must have obtained all she could in the Glassville School. Her name is on the Glassville School records, beginning in the year ending June 1898 and continuing into the year ending June 1909. In later years Maude expressed to her family a feeling of not having had an equal opportunity. While Jimmie was enrolled in engineering at University of N.B., Fredericton, she felt compelled to stay home and care for her mother, Alma, who, it seems, was beginning to suffer ill health. It seems that Maude found it difficult to accept not being able to leave home to pursue further education.

However, Maude did have a couple of sojourns away from home. She went to Boston and began training in nursing, but didn't like it. She also went to British Columbia to visit her Aunt Agnes Miller Bell who was married to Dr. Dudley Bell. They had lived in Yukon Territory, and later in Vancouver[29]. Agnes must have welcomed a relative and visitor from home. Family tradition says Agnes was in a very unhappy marriage. The story is that Dudley Bell asked Agnes' father, Hugh Miller, for a loan to help him complete medical school. Hugh responded, "I'll lend you the money if you'll marry my daughter, Agnes."

To Agnes Maude, the eldest daughter of James and Alma Miller, romance came in a much happier way. Unexpectedly, an admirer came to Glassville. An invitation card, still extant, bears, "Miss Maud Miller", in handwriting at the top. The printed card reads: "The pleasure of your company is requested at an Informal Dance given by the Engineering Staff of Residencies 13 and 14, Friday Evening, February 19th, 1909 at McIntosh's Hall, Glassville, N.B. Committee: A.B. Blanchard, C.L. Foss, Gillmor Brown; Chaperones: Mrs. John McIntosh, Mrs. William McIntosh, Mrs. Gillmor Brown.[30] One of the members of the engineering staff was Charles Allen MacNearney, known as Mack. It appears that Maude and Mack met at the dance.

Mack was employed with the company that was building the railroad through Juniper area. It was the line that would run between Moncton and Edmundston. At that time, according to H.N. Bradley, the railroad was called the Grand Trunk Pacific line. Afterwards it became part of the Canadian National Railway.

> "The name (Canadian National Railways) was first used when the Government of Canada took over CNOR in 1918....Management of the existing Canadian Government Railways was entrusted to this...board later in the year. In 1920, the operation of the G.T.P.R. added a yet further responsibility for...the temporary board. The act constituting the Canadian National Railway Co. was passed in 1919 but only proclaimed in January 1923, when the final step was taken of bringing into this congerie of lines the GTR itself."[31]

Thus the line between Moncton and Edmundston was built and operating before the Canadian National Railway was constituted. "The first train from Edmundston to Moncton would pass through the wilderness on November 29, 1911."[32]

Where were Residencies 13 and 14? H.N. Bradley describes them as near the railroad and easily accessible from Beaufort.[33] The engineers, who socialized with local people, must have rented McIntosh's Hall in Glassville for the dance.

Maude's parents were not favorably impressed with Mack. They opposed their daughter marrying "a tramp". The couple almost eloped. They went to Rusagonis, N.B. Maude's uncle, the Rev. Judson A. Corey, was the Baptist minister there between 1913-1918. Maude Miller and Charles Allen MacNearney were married on June 3, 1914, presumably by her uncle. The couple went to Nova Scotia to live.

It was not long before Mack proved to be magnanimous. It seems that Maude's mother, Alma, again became ill, and Maude went back home to Glassville to care for her. Mack said, "Stay as long as you need to." It must have been a difficult time for the whole family. Maude's and Mack's first child was stillborn in Glassville. It was buried on a Miller grave.[34]

Alma Miller's Illness and Death

Erma Corey, then about age 12, recalled a visit at the Miller home during Alma's illness: "I went upstairs to see her. She said to me; 'Erma be sure to read your Bible; don't forget to read your Bible.'" Erma long remembered and treasured those words from her Aunt Alma, and she did indeed read her Bible all her life.

Alma died, August 20, 1915, at the early age of 48. The cause of her death seems not to have been definitely established. Erma said, "I remember that she complained of difficulty in swallowing." Two of Alma's daughters, it seems, deduced signs of cancer. Kate thought: uterine cancer; Maude, it seems, spoke of breast lumps accompanying menopause.[35]

The Family at Alma's Departure

Alma Miller left a young family. Maude, the eldest, was the only one married. Jimmie's whereabouts then we haven't traced. About the only definite record we have found of Jimmie in that era is that he served in the Canadian Army for at least part of W.W.I. We have no date of his enlistment. He did not complete a degree at U.N.B., but we do not know when he left the university or where he went from there. Since it was near beginning of W.W.I. perhaps his next step was enlistment.

Will, though only age 16, apparently had completed his studies at the Glassville School a few weeks before his mother died. The last entry of his name on the Glassville School lists is for the year ending June 30, 1915. It seems he helped keep house as long as he was home. Marjorie Lamont Martinson, second cousin, remembers helping him wash the dishes at the Miller home.

Two Daughters at Home: Kate and Wilma

Kate, two weeks under age 15 when her mother died, apparently was able to return to school for one more year. Her name is on the Glassville School list for the year ending June 30, 1916. However, it seems the task of keeping the home soon fell to her. While her siblings were embarking on marriage or education or going far away for jobs, Alma Kathleen (Kate) remained in Glassville and kept the Miller home for her father, Robert James, and her younger sister, Wilma.

Wilma Jean, born February 13, 1907, was only in her 9th year when her mother died. She apparently had two years of school while her mother was living. Her name first appears on the Glassville School list for the year ending June 30, 1914. How long Wilma remained at home in Glassville is not certain. Variously listed as Wilma and Jean, she continues on the Glassville School list into 1924. Marjorie Lamont Martinson remembers Wilma as a fun-loving teenager, sometimes slipping out after bedtime to have fun with the youngsters in the village.

Scattering of the James Robert Miller Family

The two sons:

In World War I, James Hugh Miller served in the Canadian Army, including some time overseas. He apparently remained in Britain after the end of hostilities, at least into spring of 1919. A printed identification card for J.H. Miller at Kinmel Park, which seems to be in Britain, is dated 26/04/19. Marilyn Hicks has the card and June Covey has a photograph of their uncle in uniform.

The younger brother, William John McAlpine Pender Miller, early in life embarked on an academic career, beginning with school teaching in New Brunswick, in the Coldstream area. One of his pupils was Marion Page. Afterwrds they were

James Hugh Miller, W.W.I

both enrolled at Acadia University. Marion, later Mrs. Roy Smith, told this story to June Hovey who was her boarder in Hartland. Will took a year out from his studies at Acadia and went to Saskatchewan to teach and to earn some money. In the Acadia University Alumni Directory 1989, p.285, Will is listed: Miller, John M., under "Class of 1922". After he graduated he worked in Chicago.

The year Will graduated from Acadia, 1922, Jimmie embarked on an adventure to the West — a sojourn that was to last for ll years. He left Glassville with trunks and with money given to him by his father. He sojourned in both Western Canada and Western U.S.A. Erma Corey received from him a package of dried figs "from sunny California". The neat container with strings and little red wheels served for years for her brother, Bob Corey, to keep his drawings in. Marilyn Hicks said that her Uncle Jim, when he spent his latter winters with them, often reminisced about the grapes and other fruit of California.

Change

The Miller family was scattering. A new era was breaking in Glassville, as everywhere. The automobile was replacing horses for travel, though horses were still much needed on the farms and in logging. Telephone lines were extending over the county. "It was reported in 1904 that the Michael Welch telephone station was at the residence of T.N. Belyea in Bristol."[36] Soon the line was extended to Glassville where the first telephone was in the Miller home.[37] Despite the changes, apparently the Miller place continued for some years to serve as a boarding place, and to provide over-night accommodations and a stopping place for people who travelled on many kinds of errands. Roy Hemphill recalled a group of seven men with two pairs of horses stopping in Knowlesville for directions to Tamarack Hill. He said, "Father went with them on his saddle horse to conduct them to the hill back of Skedaddle Ridge. They located a concrete block with a vertical copper bolt set in it. The block had a plaque with inscription in code". The installations on Tamarack Hill were part of a W.W.I. system connected with two other hills: Canterbury Hill in New Brunswick, and Mars Hill in Maine. Each hill was equipped with mirrors for sending signals at night in 1917 and 18. The party of seven men were boarding at Miller's in Glassville and stabling their horses there.

Roy Hemphill with Miller clock

Kate

James Alexander Hovey, after W.W.I

Kate differed from her siblings in being the stay-at-home one, yet she had a point of identification with her elder sister. As with her sister Maude, romance came to Kate in Glassville. Soon after end of W.W.I. a young overseas veteran, Jim Hovey, Jr., came to Glassville as an apprentice blacksmith. Jim apprenticed with Murray Lamont, also a W.W.I. veteran, the owner of the blacksmith shop at the corner of the road to Juniper, earlier owned by Murray's uncle, David H. Lamont. Jim's father, James Hovey, Sr. had worked on the Miller farm in 1885 and 1886. The Hovey family afterwards lived in Divide.

Maude MacNearney encouraged Kate to marry Jim.[38] Wedding arrangements began with a journey to Hoyt, N.B., where the bride's uncle, Rev. J.A. Corey, was pastor. Erma Corey, Kate's cousin, said, "They took me with them." Marilyn thinks Erma was a chaperone. It was probably required, then, even for couples on way to be married. On June 6, 1923, in the Baptist Parsonage at Hoyt, N.B., Alma Kathleen Miller became the bride of James Hovey, Jr., of Divide. Erma said, I stood up with them. I had taken a day off from my school at Windsor, N.B."The day following the wedding, Uncle Jud took me to Fredericton Jct. to board the train back to Hartland or Bristol. After the ceremony Kate and Jim went on a honeymoon trip to

Saint John and later to Nova Scotia. They visited Kate's sister, Maude, and family". In Glassville, Jim and Kate lived with her father, Robert James Miller, until January 1925 when they went to Boston. Jim worked as a mechanic. Kate worked in a hat factory. Not liking their Boston situation, they left for Glassville before the end of 1925.

James A. Hovey and Kathleen Miller, wedding in Rusagonis, 1923

Hoveys Return to Glassville

In Glassville the Hoveys returned to the Miller home and to blacksmithing. Ere long — Marilyn Hicks says not before 1926 — Jim built his own blacksmith shop, on land granted by Robert James Miller. Kate became the house keeper and the family anchor. There was plenty of accommodation and a warm welcome when Kate's siblings came for visits. Much of that time the only Miller present was Kate's father, Robert James. Wilma Jean, it seems, was there part of the time. She perhaps finished school soon after Kate married. Wilma Jean last appears on the Glassville School list in 1924. She must have gone to university soon thereafter.

My earliest recollection of Wilma Jean was a family visit at the Miller home. My mother, father and some of the youngest of my family members were invited to Sunday dinner. It was perhaps about 1929. I was six that year. Few of my memories reach farther back than then. Also that is the year when Wilma graduated from Acadia University. After dinner Wilma took us outside for recreation. I can still bring upon my memory screen an image of the pretty redhead saddling and riding her horse. The Millers had smart and beautiful horses — Marjorie Martinson remembers. I think the trotter, Rowdy, was long kept for Wilma.

Over the next few years of my childhood and youth there was much contact between the Miller/Hovey family and the Corey family. Some occasions remain in vivid memory. The summer I was ten, on the invitation of Kate to come and help pick strawberries, I was at Hovey's for two weeks. Between trips with the Ford car to other farms — even as far as Bob Guthries' — in search of wild strawberries, there was time to scout around the village and make acquaintenance with Weldon and Gerald Lee and Glen Lyon and others. There was also time for an occasional stop at Jim Hovey's blacksmith shop — perhaps the most interesting gathering place in the village.

Forge, Anvil, Hammer and Horseshoes

Many other times also I was privileged to both visit the Miller/Hovey home and observe that shop. The Corey boys all had turns going to the shop when a pair of horses needed shoes. Often we had noon meal at Kate's house.

It was most fascinating to watch horses being shod. There was skill in every phase of the job: beginning with handling horses and winning their cooperation in allowing a foot to be lifted, the worn shoe torn from the hoof, the hoof trimmed with cutters and smoothed with a rasp. Then the new shoe had to be tried for size and shape, heated red hot in the forge, the toe calk welded on, and the ends of the shoe bent down for heal calks. Still hot, the shoe was placed on the hoof for fitting. It might have to be carried by tongs back to the anvil for a few more hammer strokes to bend it to the shape of the hoof. Some

Jim Hovey, left, in Blacksmith shop, Glassville

big, strong horses put up resistance. My father said, "Jim is strong." He also knew how to handle horses. Usually he could persuade them to cooperate. Jim shod horses for farmers from miles around. Often several pairs of horses were waiting to be shod. Manzer Boyd told of waiting all day at the shop but he didn't mind, though he had to drive his horses all the way back to Golden Ridge in the evening. He said, "I had taken the day for it."

The blacksmith shop served many needs. Jim was versatile. Besides shoeing horses Jim did much iron and woodwork for the farmers. He built wagon wheels; also longsleds and bobsleds for hauling logs. For Ira Corey, in the winter of 1931-32, Jim built a complete "double hitch". It was a slender hardwood pole equipped with neckyoke and wiffletrees. It was designed for hitching two horses to a sleigh. When the thirties had slowed lumbering, Ira had delight in driving a pair of trotters on errands to Glassville and Juniper. Jim also built sturdy handsleds. Eric MacNearney in Nova Scotia said, "We still have sleds that he made."

Visits

The Miller home in Glassville long continued to be a stopping place for the Ira Corey family on errands to Glassville. Visits flowed in the opposite direction also. There was many a visit to the Ira Corey farm in E. Knowlesville, especially in summer. Those visits did much to maintain enjoyable family relationships.

Some visits are especially memorable, e.g., the spring afternoon Father was driving the little bay mare home from the Knowlesville Sunday School with quite a group of us in the wagon. The Hovey family in their Model "A" Ford overtook us and stopped. Kate, who had been quite accustomed to driving a horse, suddenly had an impulse to have the reins in her hands again. "Uncle Ira can I drive her home?" We all crammed into the car. Kate and their girls clamoured into the wagon. At the farm Jim sat on the front step and focussed his eyes on the road, saying, "She should soon be coming around the bend" — i.e., at the corner of the Joe Still Whitehouse farm and the Osbert Whitehouse farm. When they came trotting toward our barnyard he was as delighted as they were.

Kate's father, our Uncle Jim, often accompanied the Hoveys. A delightful story teller, he intrigued us, as youngsters, with Irish tales of fairies. Keith Corey still remembers: "Those little fairies that come from Ireland." Uncle Jim Miller's relationship with the Corey family began in my grandparents' time. He had endeared himself to the Corey family from the beginning of his involvement with Alma Corey. His mother-in-law, Lucretia Corey, long remembered and often repeated; "Jim Miller drew the plans for this house," i.e., the frame house in Knowlesville that was built about the year 1900.

Though widowed, Uncle Jim's relationship with the Coreys continued the rest of his life. A yearly hunting safari over 42 years helped keep him involved with the Corey family. In the hunting party, besides Jim's brothers-in-law, Rev. Judson

A.Corey and Ira Corey, were others from Knowlesville: Fred Hemphill, James Hobbs, and Clarence LaPage; also Wilmot Osborne from Campobello Island. As long as he felt able to trek the woods and sleep in a tent or an abandoned lumber camp, Uncle Jim was in the party.

A Second Jim Miller Appears

Until I was ten years old, I didn't know that our Uncle Jim Miller had a son who was also called Jim. He was James Hugh Miller, the elder son of Robert James Miller. I vividly remember the first time I saw the younger Jim. It was in April 1933 at the Ira Corey farmhouse in East Knowlesville. When we arrived home from school one April afternoon there sat the cousin whose homecoming was being celebrated after an absence of 11 years. Accompanying him were his sister, Kate Hovey, and two of her girls. They had driven old Rowdy over roads slushy with melting snow, and with pools of water hidden under the snow in low places. On their return journey the sleigh plunged into a water pool, soaking Kate's feet with ice-cold water. She borrowed dry wool socks from Hazel Whitehouse.

After the snow had disappeared, Jimmie was driving a car to farms in Glassville, Knowlesville and vicinity, buying milk cows and heifers to stock a dairy farm in Nova Scotia. I remember his buying young heifers from my father in East Knowlesville.

Venture Into Nova Scotia

James Miller, Sr., apparently in a move to help his home-coming son to establish a business, invested in a farm at Windsor Junction, N.S., near the home of his eldest daughter, Maude Miller MacNearney, and family. The plan was to market milk and perhaps beef in Nova Scotia, probably Halifax.

I also remember Jimmie coming to Corey's on a Saturday morning in May and taking me with him to the Miller farm. The large herd of freshened cows that Jimmie had gathered from area farms were then at the peak of their milk flow and producing such a large volume of milk that Kate was having a struggle to churn the large quantity of rich cream and work it into butter. I whirled the bail churn for her. I still remember the evening scene as the herd was brought from the pasture into the barn. Jim Hovey closed his blacksmith shop early and joined Jimmie Miller and Fred MacKenzie, hired man, in the milking task.

When, after a few weeks Jimmie had completed purchasing and assembling a large herd of cattle, he had them transported to Juniper Station and herded on to C.N.R. box cars to travel by rail to Windsor Junction.

Jimmie took Wilfred Corey with him as a farm helper. Wilfred must have worked horses there. He remarked afterwards, "In Nova Scotia they run the tugs all the way to the wiffle tree". The MacNearney home was a few minutes walk from the farm. Lynn MacNearney Fiske, then only seven, remembers her grandfather, James Miller, and her Uncle Jim, living with them. She said, "Uncle Jim gave us money for penny candy."

The venture had less than a happy ending. Before the end of the summer Jimmie sent for his Uncle Ira Corey to come to Nova Scotia to help him. Norman Corey recalls: "Bob, age 19, and I, age 16, had to finish our haying" — with help from younger boys. What did father do in Nova Scotia? I remember his speaking about helping peddle meat. After a few weeks, Father and Wilfred returned by train to Juniper Station.

How long did the beef and dairy farm continue? Certainly longer than that summer. Lynn Fiske remembers seeing beef carcasses hanging in the barn after the cold weather came. Before long, both James Millers were back in Glassville. The Nova Scotia farm remained vacant. Eric MacNearney recalls a letter to his father from his Grampy Miller. He referred to the farm as "that sink hole", and talked about disposing of it.

New Ventures

Within a year or little more both Jim Millers entered new vetures:

In the spring of 1934 James Miller, Sr., took their car and went on a trip, not telling anybody where he was going. In a few days he surprised the family by returning with a bride. What family members didn't discover for several days, or even weeks, was that he was also driving a brand new car. It was of the same make, model and color as the car he had driven from home. At length the story leaked out:

He had had an accident on a level crossing at Blissville, between Fredericton Junction and Hoyt. The car had stalled on the railroad crossing and failed to start again. After a momentary attempt to push the car off the crossing, James and his bride walked to safety, leaving the car to the fate of the train.

The bride was Adelaid Lyon, a native of New Jerusalem, who had retired there after working in U.S.A. She was a relative of Jane Pender Miller who was also a native of New Jerusalem. The couple were married by James' brother-in-law, the Rev. J.A. Corey, then ministering at Keswick Ridge. After the accident he was summoned to pick up the couple. They stayed with the Coreys at the parsonage at Keswick Ridge until they got the new Ford car.[39]

An Enlarged Family

The Miller homestead had again become a busy, well-peopled place. There were two James Millers, Jim and Kate Hovey and three daughters: Jean, Kathleen and June. Adelaid brought the number to eight people living in one household. Kate called Adelaid "Aunt Ad"; we all did.

Two Houses

It would have been most remarkable if that many people of such diverse ages could have continued without stress in relations. Tensions arose, prompting the Hoveys to look for their own living quarters. In 1935 they moved to an apartment behind Derrah's store. Ere long, however, they had their own new house. Kate's father, after consultation with son, Will Miller by letter, had a good-sized building lot staked off from Miller property as a building lot for Kate and Jim, just south of Jim's blacksmith shop. There, in the summer of 1936, they had a new house built. The builders were Osbert Whitehouse and Jack MacKenzie of Knowlesville. The Hoveys moved into the new house just two weeks before the birth of their fourth daughter, Carolyn, on November 27th, 1936.

Jimmie Miller

After his return from the Nova Scotia venture, the younger James Miller, affectionately known as Jimmie, began farming. He kept some milk cows and raised some cattle for beef. Soon he ventured into a meat retail business. He butchered livestock, his own, plus some he bought from other farmers. He carried the meat on white sheets in the 1934 Ford, rear cushion removed, to the farmhouses throughout Glassville and its neighboring communities. Fresh meat at the door was welcome. There were no refrigerators in those days. His route reached at least as far as North Ridge. Edna Wheeler remembers his stops at their house. He didn't fail to stop in E. Knowlesville and select a good big roast for his Uncle Ira and family. Often his Aunt Nellie invited both Jimmie and Ted for dinner or supper. Ted Welch, who had suffered a stroke and loss of speech, travelled with Jimmie and dispensed the candy to all the youngsters.

Jimmie also raised some grain and some potatoes. At

least one year he ventured into raising potatoes in a field he had rented on a neighbor's farm. Hence a story:

Pigs, Potatoes and a Night Journey

One brisk autumn morning in the fall of 1936 my brother Tom and I left E. Knowlesville bound for Glassville, driving Prince and Don. On the sloven wagon we carried live pigs boarded and boxed in. Our father must have transacted the sale of some pigs to Jimmie. Besides delivering the pigs, it seems there was another errand, probably having the horses shod at Jim Hovey's shop. Our errands were complete at noon.

We had noon dinner at Miller's. At that time — after the move of the Hoveys — only three people were living at Miller's: Uncle Jim, Aunt Ad and Jimmie. Over the dinner that Aunt Ad had cooked for us, Jimmie asked us if we would stay the afternoon and pick potatoes for him. He had a crop at Welch's. Lewis was digging them. Tom drove our horses to Welch's and stabled them. Jimmie took me in his car. We picked potatoes until dark. Then he took us back to Miller's for supper.

Over the supper Jimmie made another proposal. Tom would stay the rest of the week and continue picking potatoes. He milked the cows while Jimmie drove me again to Welch's where they helped me, a boy of 13, hitch the horses for a dark journey to E. Knowlesville. As I mounted the wagon Jimmie handed me a dollar bill — pretty good, I thought; standard then for a full day of work. Next day Lew Welch observed, "He was looking pretty wild when he left here," as Tom quoted to me afterwards.

I knew the route well; so did Prince and Don: northeast, past Tom Guthrie's and Joe McDermid's, now lonely and deserted; south at Brown's corner; past Norman and Minnie Brown's and Bill and Babe Guthrie's and Dick and Kate Linder's. Then across Bob Guthrie's farm and into a strip of our woods on a narrow winding wagon road, that was even darker than the route thus far, because overhanging branches blocked the moonlight. The horses ducked their heads nonchalantly, knowing that crossing two more fields would bring them to their own stable. They were as glad as I to be home.

The Passing of Robert James Miller

That visit to the Miller home in Glassville is the last I can remember while Uncle Jim Miller was living. Less than a year later, on September 29, 1937[40], James Miller, Sr., died at that home. His youngest daughter, Wilma, had come home to visit him a few weeks ealier. She took time away from his bedside one evening for a brief visit, with Jimmie, to the Corey family in E. Knowlesville. I also remember seeing her at Kate's new house following the funeral service at the Miller home, conducted by Rev. L.D. MacDonald, the minister of Glassville United Church, 1936-39.[41] The Rev. J.A. Corey, invited to speak at the funeral, gave high tribute to his brother-in-law.

Adelaid made her tribute, quietly, after the service: "We had three good years together." She remained at the Miller home, keeping house for Jimmie and serving meals to his hired casual workers, though she had not been accustomed to housekeeping or much practiced in cooking.

Adelaid was, however, practised in cordiality. As a maiden lady, she had been an attendant to a wealthy lady who lived in the Carolinas in winter, and in Lowell, Mass., in summer.[42] Adelaide and Jimmie maintained traditional Miller hospitality. Ira Corey remarked about the welcomes he received. Other members of his family attested to her cordiality on visits to Glassville. Wilfred returned from a visit reporting, "Aunt Ad gave me a nice glass of cidar." Gordon remembers being treated to big molasses cookies.

For a time Jimmie carried on this weekly delivery of meat in summer. He also ventured into raising hogs for meat market. When potato price was low he fed potatoes, cooked in 5-gallon pails by steam piped by hose from Jim Hovey's steam boiler. The war years brought many changes to Jimmie's occupations and even more changes to the Hovey family.

Shortly before the outbreak of W.W.II Jim Hovey built a grocery store between his blacksmith shop and their house. June remembers the opening Saturday evening when the shelves remained empty because the supplies had failed to arrive. They sold homemade icecream and gasoline. It was Kate's business. Soon the management fell entirely to her. On June 18, 1940, Jim enlisted at Woodstock, N.B. for service in "Veterans Guard of Canada".

For a brief time Jim served at a prison camp at Ripples, N.B., which was "under the care of The Canadian Provost Corps and The Veterans Guard of Canada." The story of Canada's wartime prison camps is told by Ted Jones in two volumes published nearly half a century later. On June 19, 1940, Prime Minister William Lyon MacKenzie King announced in the House of Commons that at the request of the British government Canada had "agreed to receive here interned aliens from the United Kingdom, also German prisoners from the United Kingdom...." "Twenty-six major Canadian internment camps were to be in operation by the end of World War Two; they were to house 40,000 German prisoners and civilian internees transferred from England.....Along with our own enemy aliens, who reached a total of 1,500. The new arrivals moved back and forth across Canada, spending long periods of time in the various camps."

In Volume One he describes "The European refugees who fled from Nazi oppression, only to be arrested in England, shipped across the ocean, and imprisoned in the wilderness of a New Brunswick forest. Ironically, upon their release, many remained in North America to become prominent citizens." Jones' first volume describes the only such camp that was built and operated in the Maritime Provinces. "It was near

Fredericton, New Brunswick, opening on two different occasions and....housing a variety of prisoners: Internees and Refugees.....from August 1940, to June, 1941; enemy merchant seamen, German and Italian civil internees..., from July, 1941, to September 1945." Jones speaks of "the challenge of administering a barbed-wire community in the fly-infested backwoods of New Brunswick..."

Jones tells us further: "Among the inmates of the Fredericton camp during the Second War, there were some of the most intelligent, talented, provocative, and notorious men of their time, many whose names today are representative of their chosen careers. Those who felt that they were unjustly interned expressed no wish to remain anonymous...." They are proud to have their stories unfold..."[43] Jones tells the stories of all the former inmates he could locate.

On June 14, 1941, Jim was discharged from the Veterans Guard as "medically unfit by existing standards". Briefly he resumed blacksmithing, with a modification. If no forge work was needed, he sometimes travelled to farms. I remember him bringing his tools in his car to shoe horses at the Corey farm.

Scotland and Glassville in War Years

On November 6, 1941, Jim re-enlisted at Woodstock for active service. He served with The Canadian Forestry Corps near Aberdeen, Scotland. He volunteered to serve in France but was told that at 48 he was too old. While Jim Hovey was overseas, Kate ran the store. Her brother, Jimmie Miller, operated the Miller farm. He had over 100 pigs, plus poultry, cows and horses. He also cut wood in winter. Despite all that work he was always in the store in the evenings to help Kate feel more secure when the men who drank a bit much came for gas. He waited till Kate had closed and was in the house safely. He also got up many nights to help Kate get gas for people who were stranded. The store alone was a full-time job. Other tasks and events added to the burden. Kate hurried through morning chores in time to drive the elder girls to Bristol High School. Sickness added to the burden. In the winter of 1943-44 Marilyn was very ill with a kidney infection and pneumonia. Dorothy Lyon, nurse, and the doctor took the 5-year old girl to hospital.

An accident added a very great burden. Jimmie fell from the haymow injuring his neck. Kate took him by train to the Montreal Neurological Hospital. They travelled in the mail car, Jimmie on a stretcher and Kate staying by his side. While Jimmie stayed some weeks in Montreal, Kate returned to tend the family, the store and the farm. Feeding several pens of pigs was task enough. The burden increased when she fell in the cow barn, dislocating her shoulder, and breaking an arm. Cast on arm, she tended the store. Neighbors had to help with the barn chores. At length Jimmie, recovered, returned home and resumed his farming.

Considering all the burdens and struggles, is it any wonder that Kate was asking to have her husband brought home on compassionate grounds? Jim Hovey returned from Scotland in fall of 1944. On November 29th he was discharged on compassionate grounds to return to civilian life.

Blacksmith Shop and Store in Flames

After three years of idleness the sound of hammer on anvil again made music in the village. Jim re-opened his blacksmith shop soon after his return from Scotland. As earlier, horses came for shoes. Work increased, Jim hired Henry White to work for him. He also installed new equipment. He bought a new acetylene welder using some of his War Veteran's Allowance. For another year the shop served the farmers and woods workers. On a December day, shortly before Christmas,

1945, a tragic fire broke out in Jim's blacksmith shop, at the noon hour, while the workers were out. Henry had gone for lunch. Jim was in Woodstock on business. Kate was in bed with a cold. June: "I was keeping store. I ran for Uncle Jim." Kathleen left Bristol High School and rode the fire truck to Glassville.[44] Marilyn, a grade-one pupil in Glassville School: "Jen Lamont, teacher, let us go because we were so upset. I stood on the platform of Derrah's Store, very frightened. Evelyn Watters took me to Bromley's, the house of the telephone office."

The sudden and terrible conflagration consumed the shop, all the equipment and a pair of horses belonging to George Brooks, brother-in-law of Henry White. That was not all. The store also burned, and with it the family Christmas gifts that Kate had gathered — all except June's new skates, which had been taken to the house to be tried for size.

The house, with furniture removed from the living room, and shelves erected, soon provided space for a temporary store. Thus store keeping soon resumed. Indeed it was so soon that a potential fire was found smouldering in a pair of melton-cloth pants. A spark from the store fire had lodged in them and had been carried into the house with goods rescued from the store. The fire was soon squelched.

I remember my first visit to Glassville and Hovey's after the drastic change in "old Scotia's grandeur." Only a heap of debris marked the spot where the blacksmith shop had stood for 20 yeas. At the house customers came and went through the front door. It must have been in February 1946. I had returned from England at end of January 1946. Jim had been home for more than a year, and had spent a year working in his shop. Now, instead of hammering red hot iron and nailing shoes on horses' hoofs, he was sitting in the kitchen, appearing like a person of leisure — a most unusual sight. He helped in the store as Kate needed a heavy box lifted. In the evening we shared stories. The customers thinned; at length Kate turned off

Hovey properties: house built 1936, later possessed by C. and A. Corey; store built 1946, later possessed by T. and M. Corey

the front lights and sat with us.

Jim's leisure, however, ended when winter ended. In the spring, recognizing that his blacksmithing had ended with the fire, he turned his energies and skills to other enterprises. By summer 1946 he had built a new store south of their house, and installed a gasoline tank. Ere long, a service station, with gasoline and lubrication facilities, arose on the corner lot, which the Hoveys had sold to Irving Oil Co. It was at the intersection of the Bristol Road. Jim became the manager.

Hoveys' Last Decade in Glassville

Much was happening in the Hovey family in their last decade in Glassville. Jean graduated from Bristol High School in 1944. She taught school in East Glassville, September to February, before entering nursing training at Victoria Public

Hospital in Fredericton in 1945. I remember seeing her briefly at the front desk when I was in Fredericton awaiting discharge in March 1946.

Kathleen and June were then rooming in Bristol and attending high school. I remember a trip with Jim in an army truck to pick up the girls on a Friday afternoon. Jim had bought the truck to carry supplies for their store. Later he taught Kathleen to drive it and even to change a tire. She then drove it daily to Bristol High School and picked up other students in Gordonsville.

Kathleen graduated from Bristol High School in 1946. On February 10, 1947, she enrolled in Nurse's Training at Victoria Public Hospital, Fredericton. She and Jean were there together for one year.

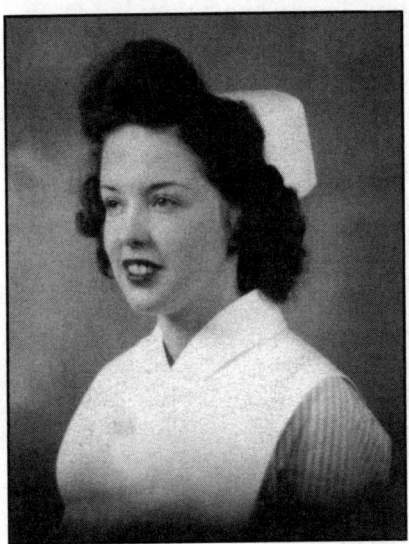

Alma Jean Hovey, Fredericton, 1948

Jean graduated from Nurses' Training in 1948 and went to work in Juniper as the Red Cross Nurse. On December 26, 1949, she was married to Basil Flemming at the United Church Manse in Juniper. June Hovey and Bobby Flemming stood up with them.

June took grade 9 in Bristol, grade 10 in Juniper, and returned to Bristol for grade 11 and graduation. For the 1948-49 school year she went to Nova Scotia. She lived with her Aunt Maude and Uncle Charles MacNearney at Windsor Junction and commuted by train to Queen Elizabeth High School, Halifax, where she achieved grade 12 and senior matriculation.

With the three eldest daughters well on their way to

education and careers, and Jim and Kate, both having worked very hard, they decided to give themselves a holiday. In the summer of 1949 Jim and Kate Hovey and their two youngest, Carolyn and Marilyn, embarked on a trip to the West Coast, by car and travel trailer. June said, "I returned from Nova Scotia to Glassville in June. I kept the family store for the summer while my folks were away. Agnes McIntosh stayed with me and helped me." At Marion, Ohio, they decided that their time was too short to reach the coast and back. They turned homeward. They stopped in Montreal to see Kathleen, then in training at the Children's Hospital. She had a letter from home. It told them of Aunt Ad Miller in the Bath Hospital. She had suffered a fall and a broken hip. Kate took her to their new home and cared for her. They carried trays to her in their spare room upstairs. June Covey remembers, "Dad carried her downstairs, on Christmas Day. She then insisted on staying downstairs with the family." They set up a bed for her in the living room. They helped her to resume walking. After that strenuous year the Hoveys sold both the store and the house to Tom and Marjorie Corey and prepared to move to Fredericton. Adelaid's niece, Hazel Lyon came to Glassville and took her to her home in Wirral, near New Jerusalem.

On May 1, 1950, Kate and Jim and Marilyn, youngest daughter, and Aunt Ad left for Fredericton. They took Fred McBrine with them to build cupboards and do other carpenter work on the house they had bought at 853 George Street. Some family members extended their stay in Glassville. June stayed with Tom and Marjorie to help in the store until after their son, Roger, was born, May 25, 1950. Carolyn, completing grade 8 and preparing to write high school entrance exams, also stayed with Coreys until the end of the spring term. Then Marilyn returned to write her June exams at Glassville. She stayed with Dolly Lyon.

The colonial-style Hovey house was soon sold to Tom's brother, Claude and Alice Corey. Tom and Marjorie decided they didn't need the house. They built a dwelling on the back of the store. Thus relatives of Millers and Hoveys occupied both store and house. But only one person was left in Glassville, named Miller — Hugh's grandson, James Hugh.

Adelaide Miller lived about two years after she left Glassville. After a short time with the Hoveys in Fredericton, her niece, Hazel Lyon took her to her home in Wirral, near New Jerusalem. June Covey remembers: "News of her death came in a shocking way to me. I was working for the Telegraph Journal in Saint John. As I was measuring space for classified items, the obituary of Adelaide Miller came across my desk. I phoned Mum; nobody had told her."

Hoveys in Fredericton

Among their roomers and boarders were several relatives: Kathleen and Shirley Corey, and their friend, Audrey Manuel, who were attending 1950 summer session at Teaches' College; also Alice and Margaret Shaw; John Shaw at U.N.B; Keith Corey, working in Tourism Office; Gordon Corey, working in Dominion Store. Boarders who were attending Teachers' College and U.N.B. came from Carleton County, from Quebec, Ontario, and other countries. Carolyn and Marilyn Hovey, two youngest daughters, had the convenience of attending Fredericton High School. Carolyn graduated in 1954. Thus Kate Hovey's hopes for her daughters were moving toward fulfilment. Feeling that she had been deprived of the opportunity for education, Kate was very insistent on education for her daughters. Some of their peers were quitting. In Fredericton and area Jim Hovey soon turned his versatile skills to new jobs; construction work at Camp Gagetown and Fundy National Park — both then being developed. Soon he was employed by Alfred Horsnell, in Fredericton, at first at their machine shop on King St. They sent him to Montreal for training in spring-making and repair. Then they opened a shop, City Spring Works,

Jim and Kate Hovey, 853 George St., Fredericton, 1955

across the river, on Gibson St. They installed springs in big trucks. Roy Hemphill spoke of stopping there for a friendly visit with Jim. During that employment, Jim did a renovation on their three-story home in his spare time. He converted it into smaller apartments.

City Spring Works was Jim's last employment. At work he had a spell, and then sat down for a rest. At home, later, he showed signs of not feeling well. Marilyn said, "I was home on holiday from nursing. Mother had taken the two Bearisto sisters to a strawberry festival. Dad was asking, "Where is your mother?" Next morning while preparing to go to work he suffered a severe heart attack. In hospital, two daughters, Jean and Kathleen, nursed him. Liver damages from wartime, hitherto not evident, now emerged with grave consequences. While overseas during the war he had had jaundice. It became evident

Bill and Marilyn Hicks, Len and Kathleen Wade,
Ron and Carolyn Rowe, Jerry and June Covey;
May 1, 2000, 50th anniversary of Hoveys' move to George St.

that he had also had hepatitis. The doctors had trouble controlling bleeding through the kidneys. Through his critical illness Jim sustained hope and interest. His son-in-law, Jerry, had accompanied him on hunting and fishing trips, and had admired Jim's ingenious ways of putting skids across a stream and driving his jeep over them. Jerry said, "On our last visit to him he said, 'Get the equipment ready, Jerry, for a fishing trip.'" On the tenth day a blood clot developed. He died on July 26, 1959, at age 63.

Family Gathering in Carleton Co.

Kate lived 20 years after being widowed. On April 27, 1963 she married Raleigh Britton. Both having folks and friends in Carleton Co., they bought a house in Simonds. That summer residence was a great asset to family relations. In the summer of 1967 Maude MacNearney stayed with Kate in Simonds. Erma Shaw enjoyed having her cousins in her neighbourhood. Kate appreciated neighburs. Once she fell from a ladder while trying to catch a bat. An injured leg resulted in phlebitis.

Jimmie Miller benefitted too, by the gathering of family members at Simonds. On one occasion when Jimmie was in Bath Hospital, his sister, Maude MacNearney and her daughter, Lynn, came from Nova Scotia and stayed at Kate's house. Perhaps it was the summer he fell off a load of hay, and his Uncle Ira Corey came out of retirement and helped on the Miller farm with haying and feeding the pigs. Lynn Fiske recalls a visit with her children and her mother at Kate's, and a visit to Jimmie in hospital. One afternoon Lynn instructed her son Jock to baby sit his two younger sisters. As they prepared to leave, Jock said, "Tell me again where is that place where you are going to take a bath."

Jimmie - The Last Miller in Glassville

Jimmie Miller kept the Miller property for more than a quarter of a century after his closest relatives departed Glassville. As his energy waned, his farming was reduced to gardening. For a time in the '50's he kept the Post Office in the front of the house.

Jimmie was fortunate in care and attention from his relatives. In his later years he spent winters with his sister and his nieces, beginning with Kate and Jim Hovey in Fredericton. He spent the winter with Kathleen Wade and family in Ottawa. June Covey said, "He visited us in Grand Falls and St. Stephen." Bill Hicks said, "When we lived in Woodstock he began spending some of the cold season with us." Marilyn said, "Initially it might only be a month. From 1975 on he spent winters with us in Fredericton." For two years he had a bedroom, "then a bed in the family room. He loved children and took much interest in them. Peter, then developing his reading skills, read to his Uncle Jim articles from the World Books. Jim delighted in sharing his fresh knowledge over the dinner table."

Each spring he returned to Glassville. Marjorie Martinson said he was always glad to get back. It seemed that Jimmie and the house had a built-in durability. In his notebook he describes the house that Hugh Miller built in 1868. It had "shaved shingles on the north side which lasted seventy-five years. Not one board needed replacing."

He continued to garden. He planted far more vegetables than he could use and gave them to neighbours. He liked the children too. From the neighbourhood they came to be played with. In a game they especially liked, he held a youngster by the feet, head downward, and shook him. As he shook he scattered coins on the grass with the illusion of shaking them from the youngster. One boy said, "Shake hell out of me, Jimmie, I need a quarter awful bad." Marjorie describes Jimmie as very considerate and eager to return favours. If she sent a dish, he brought a small piece of antique: a little chair, table, or a mustard barrel. When her father, D.H. Lamont, died Jimmie attended the service at the house. "Aren't you coming to the church?" "No, somebody should stay with your mother."

James Hugh Miller died January 14, 1979 at the

James Hugh Miller, Glassville, 1970's

Chalmers Hospital in Fredericton. Marilyn Hicks said his last illness began at Christmas. Three nieces, Marilyn, Carolyn and June arranged his funeral at the funeral home in Florenceville, N.B. Another niece, Lynn Fiske, Halifax, also attended. The service included the hymn, "In the Garden". Jimmie's body was placed in the vault in Glassville. A foot stone on the Miller plot in the Glassville United Church Cemetery reads:

    Gnr.   James H. Miller
1893 - 1979[45]
CGA, C.E.F.

Kate died the same year as her brother James - 1979, September 28th. In her last five years she was confined to her home on George St., on account of failing health. Finally, she became an invalid. Her funeral, at Brunswick St. Baptist Church, was attended by friends and relatives from Glassville and other parts of Carleton Co. Keith and Gordon Corey were among the pallbearers.

Subsequently, Raleigh returned to Hartland and resided with his sister, Florence Britton.

MacNearney Family 1914 - 1944

Maude and Charles Allen MacNearney - Mack - lived in Nova Scotia from the beginning of their marriage, in 1914, about two months prior to the outbreak of W.W.I. During that war they lived in Halifax. Their first surviving child, Robert Edwin, born in 1916, came near to being a casualty of the Halifax Explosion, December 1917. That morning, after his bath, his mother put him in his carriage with the hood up. As she bent over to pick him up a window blew inward onto the carriage, at 9:05 a.m. When he went to school he discovered that some of his classmates had bad scars. The MacNearney's first daughter, Janet Elizabeth, was also born in Halifax, June 8, 1918. Another boy, Hugh, born 1920, died as an infant of an

Agnes Maud Miller McNearney

infection from circumcision. From Halifax the MacNearney family moved to Windsor Junction. There their later children were born; there the family grew up. It was from that era that my family in New Brunswick began to become acquainted with them through their summer visits to the Millers and Hoveys in Glassville. Maude also drove her car to E. Knowlesville, bringing some of her children to visit her Uncle Ira Corey and family. Her family interest was evident; e.g. a family photograph given to us. Also, she spoke of stopping on Kierstead Mountain, N.B., inquiring about Kierstead relatives, as she motored to or from Nova Scotia.

Mack worked for the Nova Scotia Department of Highways, eventually becoming Chief Engineer for Halifax and Hants Counties. He occasionally accompanied Maude and children. Once I saw him when I was visiting at Erma Shaw's, in Simonds, N.B. They came to noon lunch. It must have been about 1937, when I was 14. It seems to have been the occasion marked by a snap shot that Lynn Fiske presented to me in July 1998 at Knowlesville. I am standing among a group of children. I think probably Mack took the photo.

We grew up expecting visits by the MacNearneys to New Brunswick, but never expected to be visiting them in Nova Scotia. That opportunity came to me unexpectedly in June 1944. Surprisingly, the train I was riding stopped at Windsor

Top.
The Fiske family.
Back: John and Jock.
Front: Patricia, Lynn, Julie, Sharon, Joan. 1974.

Left.
The McNearney family.
Back: Eric, James, Allison, Anne.
Front: Douglas, Kaylan, James and Jessica.

Junction, a name familiar to me. It occurred to me, "This is where the MacNearneys live." I was part of a small contingent of Canadian soldiers who, the day before, had boarded a train in Montreal bound for Halifax where we would board a troop-carrying ship, the New Amsterdam, sailing to Britain. When we were told we had a wait of a few hours, I said to my friend, George Isford, from Winnipeg, "I have relatives here, will you come with me and try to find them?" The station agent gave us precise directions to their house. "Walk a half mile that direction....."

A Story: MacNearney Hospitality

There was a friendly atmosphere about the MacNearney house. Paula, in her 16th year, smiled at us from a hammock where she was relaxing and recovering from a stomach pain. In a superb way, Maude's hospitality that warm June afternoon met the needs of two young soldiers who had spent two days and a night on the train. How would you like a swim, while I prepare some food? Eric, then in his 14th year, found us bathing trunks, then conducted us over a path across a field to a lake with a clean sandy beach, and fresh, clear, clean water of pleasant temperature. "I still remember that," Eric said to me in January 1999. Back at the house, delicious refreshments over friendly conversation crowned the gladdening experience and left us in a high mood as we walked back to the station. George was exuberant about the refreshing experience we had enjoyed — while the others wearily whiled away the time, waiting for the train for Halifax. George wrote home about it.

My brother, Claude, also stopped at MacNearney's during his soldiering days. Lynn still remembers seeing him coming along the railroad tracks carrying a bag of fiddleheads from New Brunswick. Anticipating Claude's travel in Nova Scotia, Kate Hovey had asked him to deliver the fiddleheads.

The MacNearney Family in 1944

I remember seeing only Eric, Paula and Lynn. The older siblings had earlier begun scattering from home. The year before my visit, the MacNearney family had been bereaved of their second son, John Douglas. In 1943 he was a casualty of the war in Europe, at age 21.

Early in W.W.II, after a year as a student at Acadia University, John Douglas, at age 19, left university and enlisted in the RCAF. He trained in Western Canada. After only one visit at home — his embarkation leave — he went overseas in 1942.

On March 27, 1943, John Douglas MacNearney, Pilot, and his navigator, an Englishman, were dispatched in a Mosquito aircraft from Portreath, England, bound for Gibraltar. They were reported missing. John's sister, Lynn, said, "Mum wrote to the parents of the navigator, who replied that the two young men were shot down." Apparently all that was officially reported was that the plane went missing between England and Gibraltar. Dougas' parents, for a while, clung to hopes that their son would show up.

Eric, Douglas's younger brother, has sought to learn all he could about his brother. Eric describes a Mosquito as a fighter-bomber, with a powerful engine that made a high-pitched sound. It was also used for photoreconnaissance. Searching for more about his brother's experience, Eric sent to Ottawa and obtained Douglas's records from the archives. He discovered: "My wife's father, Dr. Angus Edward Murray, had examined my brother when he enlisted in the RCAF in Halifax.[46] The MacNearney's eldest daughter, Janet Elizabeth, born June 8, 1918, also enlisted in World War II and served overseas as a nursing sister. There she met George Wallace, a Canadian serviceman. The second daughter, Alice Elaine, b. January 5, 1925, was perhaps in training in 1944. She became a nurse and later worked at the Kentville Sanitarium. Robert Edwin, eldest of the

MacNearney family, was married before the beginning of W.W.II. On May 18, 1939, Edwin married Kathleen S.L. Vaughan. Their son, Derek Archibald, was born February 11, 1940; and their daughter, Nancy Louise, was born June 6, 1942; and Beverley Kathleen, born August 31, 1948.

Acadia: A Meeting Ground

My next encounter with MacNearneys was at Acadia University, in Wolfville, N.S. When I arrived there in September, 1946, I felt like a stranger in a strange place. Soon I met on the campus two pretty girls hurrying to class with books in hand. I recognized them as the girls I had seen at Windsor Junction in June 1944: Lynn and Paula. I was proud to be related to them.

At the end of my first Acadia year, in May 1947, I again had a train wait at Windsor Junction. I again visited Maude and Mack MacNearney. She spoke of a community movement to erect a monument to the local service men and women. There was still hurt from the loss of their son, John Douglas. Later, I saw Maude and Mack on the Acadia campus. It must have been at Lynn's graduation in 1948. Acadia University seems to have been a common ground for several of the Miller family. Will and Wilma Miller both graduated from Acadia.

Will Miller

Will Miller, after a short sojourn in Chicago, U.S.A., following graduation from Acadia University in Nova Scotia in 1922, became a professor of psychology and English at University of New York, in New York City. When Lynn Fiske recounted that phase of Will's life it brought to my memory a Sunday afternoon visit he made to the Corey farm in E. Knowlesville. The visit was early in W.W.II, probably 1940. He seemed to take a special interest in me, perhaps because I was a high school student. "What do you do?", I asked. "I teach English..." In retrospect, his inquiring mind was evident then. He questioned some things that other people accepted without question, e.g., he observed, "The German people are a very great and accomplished people..." — most understandable now; questioned at the time. That was before the USA was involved in W.W.II.

William John Miller, Acadia University

Will liked to visit his family and friends in Glassville and relatives in surrounding communities. He sometimes came in an open convertible with a rumble seat. June Covey remembers being given a ride to Centre Glassville in the convertible with streamers flying. She recalled, "We had to sit on our knees in the back. He was then friendly and outgoing with a bright and happy disposition." Edna Wheeler Christman also recalled him in his convertible breezing into their house in N. Ridge. She said, "He threw his arms around my mother", — his cousin, Ferne McBrine.

In the same sporty style Will drove to Nova Scotia to visit the MacNearneys. Lynn Fiske said, "Often he came in his convertible with a rumble seat, sporting plus fours, and wearing an ascot bandana around his neck.

Lynn also shared her awareness of her Uncle Will's interest in Socialism, and hence his vulnerability to injustice during the anti-communist era in U.S.A. While in New York, Will became a victim of Joseph McCarthy's communist witch hunt. My earliest awareness of McCarthyism, that I can now recollect, came in 1953. I was a graduate student at Andover Newton Theological School, in Newton Centre, Mass. A travelling lecturer from England, visiting the campus, said to students and faculty, "Can't you do something to stop McCarthy?" Little did I know, then, what a threat he was, much less that his hunt would victimize a cousin of mine. Later I learned how horrifying was McCarthy's witch hunt. Canadians were among his victims. One jumped to his death from a high storey building in California. Many responsible, respected people had their careers destroyed, as a result of probing inquiries by McCarthy into earlier activities and associations. Among McCarthy's victims was Will Miller. In Chicago, decades earlier, he had attended a meeting of a communist study group. Many students, in years before communism was outlawed in U.S.A., explored such groups, out of intellectual curiosity. That experience was tragic for Will Miller. He lost his position at New York University, and subsequently had a nervous breakdown. He never worked in university again. For a time he was in hospital.

After his career in teaching at University of New York, Will was able to find other employment for his remarkable skill and knowledge. His residence at 155 East 52nd Street in New York, near the United Nations, positioned him to make a living by tutoring in English to foreign diplomats at the UN. He taught the language of social graces and of the banking system. He also taught English to the Japanese students at the Japanese Embassy.[47] Fortunately, Will was able, in later life, to recover some of his bright outlook, and the friendly disposition some people still remember, e.g., his second cousin, Marjorie Lamont Martinson, of Glassville. She remembers his visits with pleasure. Also she carried on a correspondence with him for years. She said he was fond of everything Japanese, e.g., gardens, flowers and calendars. His letters carried recipes.

Lynn Fiske also spoke of recipes that her Uncle Will sent with his Christmas cards. They featured, e.g., peppers, garlic

William John Miller, P.E.I

and caraway. He liked to cook, especially spicy foods. Lynn also recalled with pleasure, "He visited us on holiday on P.E.I. between 1975-80. He loved seafood. On a flat we dug clams, quahogs, and oysters. We sat on the deck and ate them. He took some back with him to U.S.A."

Will liked to visit his relatives. He also welcomed visitors in New York. Among them were Niece Lynn, and John Fiske; also nieces Gail and Linda, daughters of Wilma Jean Williams. Relatives and friends who knew Will in depth appreciated him and came to understand his struggles and hurts, which were probably too painful to share with many people.

With St. Francis we could pray: "O Divine Master, grant that I may not so much seek to be...understood, as to understand....". Some said Will's trouble came from too much education, which perhaps brings him into comparison with St. Paul, to whom Festus said, "Your great learning is turning you mad." (Acts 26:24). One area of Will's learning was in the psychology of Carl Jung. Will left his collection of Jung's books to the Vaughan Library of Acadia University.

Will Miller died September 5, 1985. His niece Gail Williams Pfister, wrote, "I was the administratrix of John McAlpine Miller's estate, (my mother's brother Will) and as such worked hard but was pleased....to be in touch with all my first cousins on my mother's side." Cousins who travelled to New York to help Gail settle Will's estate and vacate his apartment were: Kathleen Wade and Carolyn Rowe, daughters of Kate Hovey from New Brunswick; and Janet Wallace, daughter of Maude MacNearney, from Boston. Gail's sister, Linda VanWart, was then living in South America. Carolyn said, "It was sad."

Will must have always considered Glassville his home. His ashes were brought to the Miller family plot in the United Church Cemetery in Glassville. Eric MacNearney spoke of being in Glassville for the burial, in company with other family members. He remembers the hills. Will's name: William John McAlpine Miller, is lettered on the family monument (1899 - 1985).

Wilma Jean Miller Williams

Wilma Jean Miller left Glassville at an early age to attend university in Nova Scotia — first in Halifax and then in Wolfville. Her daughter, Gail Pfister, has narrated that phase of her life:

"She first attended Dalhousie for one year and lived with her sister Agnes Maude MacNearney in Windsor Junction, N.S. She transferred to Acadia University and graduated with a BA in Drama and English degree in 1929." In Acadia University Alumni Directory, 1989, p.287, she is listed, Jean Wilma Miller. She later attended university in Seattle, Washington, where she met Randy Williams.

Wilma Jean Miller, Acadia University

Gail continues her mother's biography: "On September 26, 1933, she married my father, Randall Smallwood Williams

Jr. in New York, where she was teaching. He was born in Tacoma, Washington on September 26, 1907. He graduated from Harvard Business School, with an MBA in 1930. They had two children: myself, né Gail Williams, born May 6, 1936 in Seattle, Washington; and my sister, né Linda Williams, born January 6, 1943 in Washington, D.C. As children of an economist who was a Foreign Service Officer for our growing up years we were raised in various countries: Iran, 1944-1949, Egypt, 1950-1953, Italy, 1953-1959. I attended Marymount University in Rome, Italy 1955-57. I graduated from Oberlin College with a BA in Economics in 1957. I have Masters Degrees from Fairleigh Dickenson University and New York University in History and Economics respectively. I have taught economics at the University level at many locations for the past 25 years."

Gail continues her own biography: "I married John Stowell Williams in New York City on August 23, 1958. He also graduated from Oberlin College with a BA in 1957. He graduated from Cornell Law School in 1960. We have two children: Eric Randall Williams, born September 30, 1959 in Ithaca, New York; and Lori Jean Williams, born October 5, 1961. I divorced their father in July, 1979.

My son, Eric Randall Williams married Donna Cummings in Scranton, PA., on December 2, 1984. They have three children: Gabriel Williams, born March 20, 1980 in Olympia, Washington, Randall Williams, born April 13, 1982 in Washington, DC, and Jennifer Williams, born January 2, 1987 in Scranton, PA. They divorced May 25, 1996. My son is graduated from Scranton University, with a BA in Communications, June, 1993. My daughter, Lori Jean Williams graduated from Oberlin College with a BA in Physics and Mathematics in 1982. She graduated from the University of Michigan with a Phd. in Mathematics in 1992. She is not married.

Currently I am married to Major General Cloyd H. Pfister (ret.) who also graduated from Oberlin College with a BA in 1957. He has an MA from American University in International Affairs. We married on April 24, 1982. I have thus acquired four step-children: Gabriela, Catherine, Michael, and Romy." Gail and Mike Pfister reside in Alexandria, Va., a suburb of Washington, D.C.

Linda Williams, second daughter of Wilma Jean Miller Williams, was born January 6, 1943 in Washington, D.C. Linda Williams married Donald T. VanWart, December 28, 1963. Issue: Donald "Van" VanWart, born November 19, 1964; Tara VanWart, born December 11, 1967; Justin VanWart, born January 28, 1971. Donald "Van" VanWart married Jennifer Goehl, June 19, 1988. Issue: Austin VanWart born March 21, 1995; Jake VanWart born March 21, 1995; Paige VanWart born June 2, 1997. Tara VanWart married Michener Chandlee, August 13, 1994. Issue: Chiara Bell Chandlee, born September 11, 1996. Justin VanWart married Daniela Christ, March 15, 1997.[48]

Donald T. VanWart was a banker working with the World Bank. His work kept him and his family travelling around the world. Finally, in recent years they moved from Paris to New York City.[49]

Descendants of Maude Miller and Charles MacNearney

Robert Edwin MacNearney, eldest son of Maude and Charles, had a career with National Cash Register. For a time Edwin and Kathleen lived on Prince Edward Island. Early in life Edwin developed a brain tumour. N.C.R. used him very well. He had surgery in Montreal to remove the tumour. In two operations they took what they could. It grew back. Edwin died in 1958 at age 42.

Edwin's father, Charles, died later the same year, 1958, on December 21st, at age 72. Maude lived until October 20, 1972.

Edwin and Kathleen had a son, Derek Archibald, b. February 11, 1940, a daughter, Nancy Louise, b. June 6, 1942,

Kathleen MacNearney, widow of Edwin,
their children and grandchildren, P.E.I. 1999

and a daughter, Beverley Kathleen, b. August 31, 1948. Derek married Pearl MacDonald. They have three children: Ian, Craig and Jennifer, and four grandchildren: Alexander, Heather, Jessica and James. Nancy Louise married Arch Moore. They have two sons, Gregory and Peter. Beverley married Frederick (Rick) Rutledge. They have two children, Leah Elizabeth, b. December 9, 1975, and Kyle Robert, b. October 20, 1984 (adp.) They all live in Nova Scotia.

Janet

Janet Elizabeth MacNearney married George Wallace in 1945. Both had been in military service overseas. They married after they returned to Canada. They went to Ontario, his home province, where he became a teacher of Science and Math. By 1950 George was working for the John Hancock Life Insurance

Co., in Botson, and the family was living in suburban Wellesley, Mass. Janet's brother, Eric MacNearney, visited them there about 1951. They took him to a ball game at Fenway Park.

Janet and George had four children: John Douglas, married Catherine White in Kelona, B.C. in 1992, Jill Allyne, born 1949, married Robert Millar in 1976, their two children are Silas and Farley; Meredith Leigh, born January 4, 1951; Shelagh Jean, married Kees Ooderkerk; their daughter, Alana Christine, born April, 1988. Meredith died of a brain tumour in 1976. They buried her ashes in Windsor Jct., N.S.

Jan MacNearney Wallace, son Douglas, daughter Jill, P.E.I. 1999

Janet now lives in Glocester, Mass. As an octogenarian she enjoys very good health. Her sister, Lynn, said she comes every summer and visits us at Chester, and other relatives in the Halifax area. All her family live in Massachusetts and Maine except Douglas, in British Columbia.

Alice

Janet's sister, Alice Elaine, also lives in British Columbia. She married Edward Mitton, January 13, 1951. They live in Nanaimo. They have three children: Thomas Courtney, born May 5, 1952; Peter Alan, born November 17, 1953; and Jennifer Anne, b. August 5, 1955, married Caprian Libera. They have a daughter Nell Emmeline, born April 30, 1995. All of Alice's family live in British Columbia.

Paula

Paula, youngest of the MacNearney sisters, also lives in British Columbia. Much earlier, Paula and Alice came together by happenstance in Kentville, N.S., during Paula's student years. Paula's last year at Acadia was interrupted by illness. She became a patient at Nova Scotia Sanatorium in Kentville. Alice MacNearney was, at that time, employed as a nurse at the San.

After a year at the San, Paula returned to Acadia and graduated with B.S.N. in 1951. At Acadia, Paula met Gerald A. Fry, son of the Anglican rector in Wolfville, N.S. Gerald received from Acadia, B.A., 1950, and B.Ed., 1951. Paula and Gerald were married in Wolfville.

They have three children: Charles Allan, Janice Elaine, and Leanne. Paula and Gerald live in retirement at 21472 Cherry Ave., Maple Ridge, B.C. All of their children, and their grandchildren: Katherine, John, Troy, Heather, Emmalyn and Kathleen, live in the Vancouver area of B.C.

Lynn

Lynn MacNearney, third daughter of Maude and Mack, graduated from Acadia University in 1948. At Acadia Lynn met John R. Fiske, an engineering student, from Clarence, N.S. John had been a student at Acadia in 1943-44 in the #2 Canadian Army University Course. In 1947 he obtained from Acadia a diploma in Engineering. He went on to Nova Scotia Tech to complete engineering studies.

In 1949 John obtained his degree in Civil Engineering from the Technical University of N.S. He has engaged in a variety of work and enterprises. One of his earliest positions was with Fraser Brace Terminal Construction, a contractor for The Corps of Army Engineers who were building the Dew Line across the North. This work was in Saint John, N.B. where the Fiske family lived from 1952-54. Later, John worked for

Donald O. Turnbull whose father invented the variable pitch propeller.

In 1957 John graduated from the Bureau of Highway Traffic, Yale University. In Nova Scotia he has worked for the Department of Transportation as a construction engineer, and also as a Provincial Traffic Engineer. In 1960 he began general construction and formed the firm of Stevens and Fiske Construction. He has participated as a contractor/developer on major projects in the commercial, residential and historic restoration fields.

John also has been active in many professional, community and provincial organizations: National Capital Commission, N.S. College of Art and Design, Scholarship Fund Raising Drive, Heritage Canada Foundation, Construction Association of N.S., Halifax Industrial Commission, Technical University of N.S. as Governor, Lloyds of London as an Underwriting Member, Halifax Board of Trade, Association of

Alice Mitton, Jan Wallace, Lynn Fiske, Eric MacNearney, P.E.I., 1999

Professional Engineers of N.S., and Heritage Trust of Nova Scotia.[50]

Lynn and John have one son, four daughters, and seven grandchildren, all living in Nova Scotia.

Son, John Sutherland Fiske, whom they call Jock, is also a graduate of Acadia: B.B.A., 1979; C.A.S., 1983. Jock works with his father as a manager: real estate, an apartment building, a motel in Cape Breton, and land development at Fall River. Jock married Katherine I. Hall, September 1983. They have two sons: Jonathan MacNearney Fiske, born March 21, 1987, and Kevin Hall Fiske, born September 15, 1990.

Daughters of Lynn and John Fiske are: Patricia Jane, born June 24, 1949; Juliana, born May 1951; Sharon Lynn, born July 6, 1957; and Joan Marie, born October 20, 1959. Juliana married G. Redding, 1979. They have two sons: Jason Fiske Redding, born July 5, 1980; and Tyler Fiske Redding, born October 8, 1982; Joan Marie married John Garden, 1982. They have three children: Katie Lynn Garden, born June 12, 1984, and twins, Kyle John Fiske Garden, and Brett Corey Fiske Garden, born July 6, 1985. Since 1959 John and Lynn have lived on Royal Pine Ave., Halifax. They also have a summer home at Chester, N.S. where they are visited by relatives: their own offspring, Lynn's sister, Janet and Wilma Jean's daughters. A Cape Islander boat brought from Cape Breton named, "The Hebridean", provides recreation and helps to entertain. Lynn and John spend winters in Florida.

Eric Corey MacNearney

Youngest of Maude and Charles MacNearney's family, born December 1, 1930, has been an adventurer and enterpriser. "After high school," he said, "I went to sea on an Imperial Oil tanker, in 1948-49. After that I went to Acadia". From Acadia University Eric received a certificate in Applied Science in

1952. This gained him entrance to Nova Scotia School of Technology and hence a degree in Engineering. He also did graduate study at Yale University, New Haven, Conn. Eric married Anne Isobel Murray who is also an Acadia graduate, BAS, 1956.

One of Eric's early work adventures was with Shell Oil Co. in Alberta. An assignment with Shell took him into Texas and New Mexico. In Hobbs, New Mexico, he had a surprising experience when he took his dog to a veterinarian named George Spanko. Conversation revealed that George was one of the Americans who had joined the RCAF, in 1944, trained in Moose Jaw, Saskatchewan, and flew Mosquito aircraft during W.W.II. "Did you know my brother, Douglas?", Eric asked, "No, but my wife would know him. She organized the dances on the base", said George. He called in his wife who immediately recognized Douglas in the photo Eric showed her. She said, "I knew him well."

Eric's employment in the West included work for two other companies: Colorado Oil and Gas, and Canadian Export Gas. Then it was time to come home.

"The Return of the Native"

In 1962 Eric and family returned to Nova Scotia. He developed a business, Truefoam Ltd. with a plant and office in Dartmouth, N.S. They manufacture insulation, including styrofoam boxes for keeping fish cold in transit.

In the early 70's Eric moved his family to Windsor Jct, where he had grown up. He inherited the family home, which is within easy commuting distance from Eric's office in Dartmouth. There is also a sizeable acreage of land which Eric and his siblings inherited together. It comprises the "Miller Farm", a name which has historical roots. A local family named Miller had owned it before James Miller, Sr. and Charles MacNearney bought it. Maybe it could still be called a farm.

Eric and Anne keep a pair of horses. To the property where Jimmie Miller had undertaken to establish a dairy farm, Charles MacNearney adjoined additional acreage. Much of that acreage is now included in a development which the family has named the "Charleswood Subdivision". Eric has developed it with streets and water. He manages it for the family. They want to open it; they are waiting for churches and schools.

Eric's main business is manufacturing which he has expanded to two additional locations. In Fredericton, N.B. he has a 50,000 sq.ft. Plant that produces about half building insulation and half fish boxes. Salmon farmers buy the boxes. The plant and office is at the corner of Doak Road and Vanier Highway. Travelling north, it is just before the Corey Feed Mill.

Eric's third manufacturing plant is at Bishop's Falls, Nfld. It is managed by his son, David, a biologist. That business is called Newfoundland Styro, Inc.

Eric's business has taken him on travel to Germany, Yugoslavia, Iran, El Salvador and Cuba. He has managed to avoid times of hostilities. He goes often to Boston.

In 1985 he attended a convention in Las Vegas, Nevada. It was an opportunity for a little exploration and for a family visit to a cousin. They travelled into Arizona, passed through Phoenix, and with a rented car, got to a military town near the border of Mexico. Eric said, "We visited my cousin Gail Williams Pfister, and her husband Mike. He was then still an officer in the U.S. Army, stationed at Fort Huachuca, Arizona." Gail's husband is Major General Cloyd H. Pfister.

MacNearney Family

Eric and Anne have two daughters and a son: Christine, David, and Alison. Each has four children, making twelve grandchildren.

Elder daughter, Paula Christine MacNearney, is a graduate of Acadia with a B.Sc., 1978. She was a classmate of her second cousin, Kathryn Rowe who was Valedictorian. Christine is class president. Christine has an M.D. from Dalhousie University. She is married to Paul Christensen, also an M.D. Christine has a general practice in Bathurst, N.B. She works an intensive week in Bathurst, then comes home to P.E.I. for a week. Earlier, she was a family physician in Chatham, N.B.

Paul is an anaesthetist practising in hospitals on P.E.I. and in Moncton, N.B. Paul's father served in army in W.W.II while his brother worked the family farm. The brother was killed in a farm accident. Paul's father came home on compassionate leave and later rejoined the service in the RCAF. Christine and Paul have four children. All have Danish names: Lica, Kaj, Lars and Thora. They live at Long River, RR1, Kensington, P.E.I.

David MacNearney is a biologist with a B.Sc. from Acadia, 1982. He married Kathleen Telfer, also a biologist, with a BSCH from Acadia, 1984. Kathleen was the owner/operator of the Greenhouse Co-operative at St. Peters, N.S. David was Managing Director of Salmonid Propagation Assoc., Coop Ltd., St. Peters Fish Hatchery. Later, he was aquaculture biologist, with Extension Services of N.S. Department of Fisheries, Halifax. David and Kathleen and their four children: Robin, Douglas, Donald and Ellen live in Bishop's Falls, Newfoundland.

Alison Kim MacNearney graduated from Acadia with a BCS in 1983. She married David Kalyan, also a graduate of Acadia, B.Sc. 1991. Earlier they lived near her mother and dad on Charleswood Dr., Windsor Jct., N.S. They now live in Fort McMurray, Alberta. David works in the Tar Sands. Their children are: Jessica, Andrew, James and John Robert (J.R.)

Descendants of Kate and Jim Hovey
Jean Hovey Flemming

After graduating an R.N. from Victoria Public Hospital, Fredericton, N.B., in 1948 Jean worked for a time for that hospital. One of her early assignments was caring for a patient named Miss Ingraham. Jean went with her to her home near Davidson Lake. Jean stayed with her for about two weeks, doing housekeeping, preparing meals and sleeping on a horsehair-stuffed couch in the patient's room. The couch was an antique, afterwards acquired by King's Landing.

Later in 1948 Jean became the Red Cross Nurse in Juniper, N.B. In Juniper, Jean met Basil Flemming, son of Sprague and Maude Flemming. Jean and Basil were married on December 26, 1949.

In Juniper and area Jean is remembered as a compassionate and caring person. A special act of kindness Jean is remembered for is caring for a newborn baby of the family of the United Church Minister, Rev. Harold O'Brien, who served on the Glassville/Argyle/Juniper pastoral charge 1951-55. Mrs. O'Brien came home from hospital very ill with an infection acquired at childbirth. She was subsequently treated at the Lahey Clinic with a drug that left her deaf. Jean, whose second daughter, Pamela, was then very small, took the O'Brien baby home and cared for it until Mrs. O'Brien could care for it herself.

Shirley Corey Brooks recalls Jean's kindness to our mother when she had ceased to do the variety of baking she had in her younger years. Jean shared her Christmas baking with her Aunt Nellie who was also welcomed into her home in Juniper.

Jean and Basil had three children: Carol Joy, born September 22, 1950; Douglas Leslie, born January 29, 1953; and Pamela Jean, born March 25, 1954. Douglas died at age eight months, on October 27, 1953. He is buried in the Miller plot in the Glassville Cemetery.

Jean and Basil Flemming, Jim and Kathleen Hovey, Marilyn, Carolyn & June Hovey, Joy and Pamela Flemming, Sprague and Maude Flemming, grandson Brown

Jean continued her nursing position in Juniper until early 1956, when the family moved to Woodstock. She did some nursing in hospitals: Woodstock and Bath. In Fredericton, Jean, along with her sister, Kathleen, was special nurse to her father, Jim Hovey, in his last illness. Jean arrived in uniform from Woodstock about the time the ambulance brought her Dad to the hospital.

In Woodstock, Basil Flemming pursued his insurance business until January 1960, when the family moved to Saint John where Basil became manager of Dominion Life Insurance, a position he held until January 1970. Subsequently he worked for Royal Trust.

In Saint John, Jean worked for a time as a nurse at the Dr. Roberts Hospital School. In the City she continued her caring thoughtfulness for people. In their home she kept Connie Flemming's daughter, Carolyn, then a small child. She visited Kay and Jimmer Thompson's son in hospital, also Bob Lyon from Glassville, who was in a city hospital.

Family memories of Jean indicate that she was very much a giving person. Her sister, Kathleen, said, "Everyone of us were taught to help people." Jean liked to be involved with people in church and community. In Saint John West she put her talents to work, e.g., in organizing the annual bazaar at St. Mark's United Church. She also joined a bridge club.

In the latter years of her Saint John residence, Jean suffered ill health. Her family was very helpful. Her mother, Kate Hovey, made visits and helped with the children and the housekeeping. June and Gerry Covey were living in Saint John part of the same time period. They brought Jean to their home for visits.

Jean's early death, under age 40, at home in Saint John, on October 17, 1967, came as a shock to the family. Sister June said, "We had been transferred to Fredericton just before she died." Jean Hovey Flemming was buried in the United Church Cemetery in Glassville. There her monument stands.

Jean's sisters remember her as a kind and gentle person. June said, "She gave her life for everybody else; she didn't think about herself." Marilyn Hicks recalls some of Jean's acts of kindness and some of their family visits: "She made my wedding dress from white velvet, which was very difficult to sew", Marilyn said. "They visited us when we lived in Bathurst. She taught me a lot about housekeeping; she sent me recipes."

Marilyn has a special memory of a family visit when Jean was feeling well. Marilyn and Bill, with their first child, were staying in a cottage at Davidson's Lake. Bill was working on the Trans Canada Highway near the Moonlight Inn. Jean and Basil came up from Saint John for the weekend. That was in 1966.

The two daughters of Jean and Basil Flemming live in

the Saint John area. Joy Flemming married, in 1979, James McAvity Crosby, President and owner of Crosby Molasses Co., Saint John. They live in Rothesay with their four children: James Flemming Crosby, born September 19, 1981, is a 1999 graduate of Rothesay Collegiate School. Being a prefect, he lived on campus. He plans to attend Queens University, Kingston, Ontario, beginning in September, 1999. Courtney Jean, born October 25, 1983, and Frederick William, born August 13, 1985, are both students at Rothesay Collegiate School. Cecilia Joyce, born July 1, 1988, is a student in public school, Rothesay.

Pamela Jean Flemming lives on Kennebecasis Drive, Saint John. She was married to Stephen Ritchie. They have two daughters: Michelle and Sara. Michelle Lee Ritchie, born November 17, 1974, is living in Vancouver, B.C. She received a degree from University of B.C. in May 1999. She is working for Canada Trust. Sara Renee Jean Ritchie, born September 19, 1978, is living with her mother, Pamela Flemming.[51]

Descendants of Kathleen Miller, at home of Carol Joy Crosby, Rothesay, Oct. '97

Emily Kathleen (Kay Hovey) Wade

Kay, second daughter of Alma Kathleen (Kate Miller) and James Hovey, was born on Thursday, January 31, 1929, in Glassville, Carleton Co., N.B. Kay attended: Glassville Elementary School, 1934-1942; Bristol High School, 1944-1946. She enrolled in nurses training at the Victoria Public Hospital, Fredericton, on February 10, 1947, and graduated February 10, 1950.

Kay married Leonard Wade, a UNB graduate, in class 1950. The wedding was in Brunswick Street Baptist Church, Fredericton, on November 25, 1950. The service was conducted by Rev. Judson A. Corey (a great-uncle to the bride).

Kathleen Hovey in Nurses Training, Fredericton, 1949

Len served overseas for three years during W.W.II. He later had a military career from 1951-1972 which was followed by 11 years employment with the Federal Government. During this period the family lived in Quebec, Ontario, Manitoba, Saskatchewan and Biloxi, Mississippi. During their 20 year stay in Ottawa, Kay worked as a nurse at the National Defence Medical Centre.

Kay and Len have four children: Daughter Debra Lynn, was born in Montreal on October 23, 1952. She graduated from Ottawa University with a B.N. She married Rudy Drijher, born August 3, 1950. They have three children: Cailin Elizabeth, born October 18, 1984; Daniel James, born November 27,

1986; and Lukas William, born April 4, 1988. They live in Ontario. Daughter, Deanna Lee was born in Montreal on May 14, 1954. She attended Carleton University for three years in science and economics. She married John Kennedy. They have three children: Robert Andrew, born January 30, 1980; Lisa Kathleen, born February 17, 1983; and Adam Hamish, born May 21, 1984. Son, James Hovey was born in Fredericton on June 13, 1956. He graduated from Carleton University, Ottawa, with a B.Mech. Engineering. Jim has one son: Daniel Aaron, born May 20, 1989. Jim was married to Maria Marquis, July 26, 1999. Daughter, Cheryl Joyce was born in London, Ontario on August 24, 1960. She attained a diploma in photography from Algonquin College of Ottawa. Cheryl and Gary Weeks, live in London, England. They have three daughters: Alysha Rae Maya Wade, born September 8, 1995; Amber Jasmine Wade,

Kathleen Hovey and Leonard Wade

Deborah and Rudy Drijher; Cailin, Daniel and Luke

born June 10, 1997 and Alannah Cora, born January 14, 1999.

Kay and Len, following his retirement in 1983, moved to New Brunswick and located in Harvey Station. Currently, they reside in their cottage on Harvey Lake during the summer and in Largo, Florida in the winter. In May 1999, before returning to New Brunswick, Kay and Len travelled from Florida to Texas to visit their son, James Hovey Wade, in his new home. Jim's company had transferred him from Ontario to Texas that month.

June Hovey Covey

June Yvonne Hovey, born November 23, 1931, in Glassville, has happy memories of growing up there and attending the one-room school. She remembers her teachers: Jessie Elliot, Marion Gilchrist, Gertha Hornbrook, Jean Edler, Madeline Tedford, Clara Welch MacPhail, Gwlithyn Gray and Joyce McIntosh. June says, "They were enjoyable days."

June and her sisters came home at noon to dinner. There were often visitors at the table. Their mother and father always fed the people who were in the store and the blacksmith shop when dinner time arrived. June recalls many happy times with family and friends at picnics, family reunions and church and school concerts.

Another "happy memory" June recalls is visiting her Uncle Ira and Aunt Nellie Corey in E. Knowlesville. "Sister Kathleen and I walked to Knowlesville. At Bob and Marion Guthrie's we borrowed two pairs of snowshoes and hiked over the fields and through the woods to the Corey farm during the Easter Holidays."

June attended high school in Bristol, Juniper and Halifax.

After the Hovey family moved to Fredericton in 1950, June had work at Zellers and attended Fredericton Business College. She worked for the Potato Marketing Board in

Hartland, N.B. Later, in Saint John, she worked at Telegraph Journal Office and at Schofield Paper.

On March 7, 1953, at the Brunswick St. Baptist Church, Fredericton, N.B. June Hovey was married to Gerald A. Covey, a native of Dartmouth, N.S. and a member of the R.C.M.P. The wedding was performed by Rev. Dr. W.H. Elgee. Other participants were: Matron of Honor: sister, Kathleen Wade; Bride's Maid: Carolyn Hovey. Guest book was circulated by Marilyn Hovey.

The R.C.M.P. assigned Gerry to many postings: Woodstock, McAdam, Grand Falls and St. Stephen, N.B., then Ottawa, Ontario, and then a return to New Brunswick at Saint John; and finally to Fredericton Headquarters where he retired in February 1973 at the rank of Staff Sgt. Major — the first such rank in the Province of New Brunswick.

June and Gerry have a daughter, Heather Lynn, born February 18, 1958; and two sons: Stephen Earl, born September 3, 1961; and Gregory Mark, born April 16, 1969.

Heather married Michael O'Donnell. They have two boys; Michael, born June 5, 1984, and Nicholas, born July 16, 1985. They live in Saint John East.

Stephen Earl married Celine LaFond. They have two girls, Alexandra, born May 11, 1991, and Justine, born May 14, 1993. Stephen Covey is in the R.C.M.P. He has served in Regina, Baie Comeau, Montreal and Ottawa. On July 17, 1999 he was transferred to Italy for a four-year posting. He has a B.A. degree and is proficient in English, French and Spanish. In preparation for foreign service, he is studying Italian and completing the requirements for an M.A. degree, including a thesis. He received his commission before going to Italy. June and Gerry went to Ontario for a family visit before the departure for Italy.

Gregory is a welder, now working in Red Deer, Alberta, having learned the trade in Woodstock, N.B., and having taken another course in Saint John, N.B. Gregory's one son, Eric, died

Michael and Nicholas O'Donnell, children of Heather Covey

Justin and Alexandria Covey, children of Stephen Covey

at three days of age.

At retirement in 1973, Gerry and June purchased a farm at Dumfries, N.B., with purebred Shorthorn breeding cattle. In July 1979 they sold the farm and moved into a new home they had built across the road.

For 27 years June carried on a ceramics business. She started at the farm and continued at the new house. She also taught ceramics lessons, having "students from far and wide". In her last five years of business she also taught tole painting. June retired from her business when they started wintering in Florida.

June and Jerry spend their summers in the new house on the road to Davidson Lake. There visitors can enjoy traditional Miller and Hovey hospitality. June has not forgotten Glassville: "I still enjoy taking our family back to Glassville to attend funerals, church suppers, to renew old acquaintenances and see the rolling hills of home."

Carolyn Hovey Rowe

Carolyn Adell Hovey was born in Glassville, November 27, 1936, in the new house the family had moved into that

June and Gerald Covey, Prince William, N.B.

month. Carolyn completed grade eight in the Glassville school in June 1950, and then joined the family in Fredericton where they had moved that spring. In 1954 Carolyn graduated from Fredericton High School. Briefly she attended U.N.B. She received an MRS degree before changing to secretarial training.

On September 16, 1955, Carolyn married Ronald James Rowe of Gatineau, Quebec. Ron attended U.N.B., 1952-57. He graduated with a B.Sc.,C.E. Both Carolyn and Ron developed businesses: Carolyn in ceramics; Ronald in construction. Carolyn and Ron have three children: Robert, Kathryn and Randall.

Robert James Rowe, born September 16, 1956, is a graduate of University of New Brunswick with a degree in Civil Engineering. He also has an M.A. in Public Health from Minnesota. He is employed by the Nova Scotia Department of Health as a Public Health Engineer. His work involves both engineering and sanitation. He oversees environmental protection and deals with river and water pollution, septic tanks, trailer park sanitations, sewage treatment plants, and fertilizer plants. He has received several engineering awards, e.g., for supervising control of a fertilizer plant fire near Canning, N.S. His attempts over the years to deal with ocean pollution from Halifax sewage has met with resistance, but is now being recognized.

Robert married Carolyn Rand. They have four children: Matthew, born October 9, 1980; Daniel born March 23, 1982; Jonathan, born August 23, 1984; and Andrew, born December 5, 1986.

Kathryn Jane Rowe, born August 18, 1957, graduated from Acadia University with a B.B.A., in 1978. In residence at Acadia, she roomed with her second cousin, Christine MacNearney, daughter of Eric and Anne MacNearney. The two cousins graduated with honors. Kathryn was the Valedictorian of her class, Christine was the Class President. Carolyn, recalling the moving experience, said, "Anne looked at me and said, 'Aren't you proud?'"

In 1979, one year after her graduation, Kathryn married Leo Deveau on the day of his graduation from Acadia with a B.A. Leo was the Cap and Gown speaker for his class. They were married in the chapel of Acadia.

After graduation the Deveaus lived in Halifax, then Fredericton. In 1983 they moved back to Wolfville. In 1987 Kathryn set up her shop where she does picture framing, photography, photo restoration and art sales. She has a full service business at "The Perfect Corner", at 9 Chestnut St., Wolfville, N.S.

Leo Deveau was the owner of Leo J. Deveau and Associates, in Wolfville. In the 1998-99 academic year Leo was a student at Dalhousie University, Halifax, studying for an M.A. degree in Information Science, a new form of Library Science. He is employed with a computer company.

Kateryn and Leo have two daughters: Leah, born March 31, 1983 and Danielle, born November 6, 1985. The

Carolyn and Ron Rowe, hosts, Kathleen, June and Marilyn; Joy and Jim Crosby, and families; Mactaquac, Thanksgiving, 2000

Carolyn & Ron Rowe; daughter Kathy, son, Randy; their families, P.E.I. 1999

writer talked to Kathryn in Wolfville in May 1999, just three days after they celebrated their 20th wedding anniversary.

Randall Jeffrey Rowe, born October 8, 1960, is a graduate of Fredericton High School. He has his own business, "Atlantic Sprouts", of Harvey Station, N.B. He grows bean sprouts, alfalfa and other products for the Atlantic region. His mother says he was self taught. Randy married Denise Joyce Currie. They have two children: Jill Elizabeth, born June 19, 1985; and Kate Denise, born January 27, 1987.

Carolyn and Ron Rowe have eight grandchildren. Ron has retired from his construction business. Carolyn is semi-retired from her ceramics business. They spend their winters at their own place in Estero, Florida. In early spring they return to Mactaquac, eager to start their green house plants for their garden, and go picking fiddleheads with Marilyn and Bill Hicks. In summer of 1999 Ron's parents, 86 and 88, came from Ontario and are living in a senior complex in Fredericton.

Marilyn Hovey Hicks

Marilyn Miller Hovey was born in the new house in Glassville, on December 11, 1939. She attended Glassville School until May 1, 1950 when the family moved to Fredericton. After graduating from Fredericton High School in 1957 she began training in Victoria Public Hospital, Fredericton. In 1960 she graduated as a registered nurse. In 1962 she graduated from Dalhousie University with a diploma in Public Health Nursing.

In October 19, 1963, Marilyn married William R. Hicks, of Sackville, N.B. Marilyn's sisters, June and Carolyn, and also Bill's younger sister stood up with them. Bill, a civil engineer, was employed by New Brunswick Department of Highways. They lived in Bathurst, Fredericton and Woodstock, and then returned to Fredericton. Marilyn and Bill have four children: James, Janet, Peter and Sharon.

Marilyn and Bill Hicks; Jamie, Janet, Peter and Sharon, 1989

James Anderson Hicks, born February 20, 1966, works as a civil engineering technologist for the Province of New Brunswick. On July 11, 1992, he married Krista McElman. They have a daughter Katie Taylor, born August 22, 1996.

Janet Miller Hicks, born September 9, 1967, is a police officer for the City of Fredericton. On February 20, 1993, she married Benjamin Edward Smith. They have one daughter, Cameron Miller, born March 5, 1996; and twin boys: Benjamin William, and Clayton James, born March 8, 1998.

Peter Raymond William Hicks, born August 4, 1968, is a graduate of U.N.B. with a B.A. He works for "Learn Stream" computer company. We have the benefit of his computer work in the Miller genealogy. On October 23, 1993, Peter married Krista Ann Reid.

Sharon Elizabeth Hicks, born June 24, 1971, is a graduate of U.N.B. with a Bachelor of Business Administration (B.B.A.). She

Cameron Smith, Katie Hicks, Grace Simpson, Ben and Clay Smith, twins, Sterling Simpson, Dec. 1999

Descendants of Maude and Kathleen Miller, at Stanley Bridge, P.E.I., Sept. 1999

is employed with Sunbury Transport Co. On September 25, 1991, she married Drew Lawrence Simpson. They have a daughter, Grace Marilyn, born November 12, 1997, and a son, Sterling Gladwyn, born June 4, 1999.

Marilyn and Bill Hicks are living in their Fredericton home on Mansfield Circle year round. Though Bill retired as Director of Highway Construction in 1992, they have not been lured south. They enjoy their six grandchildren who all live in the Fredericton area. In summer the children are attracted by the swimming pool. The Hicks home is decorated by many antiques from the Miller home and store in Glassville. There are treasures to show visitors; account ledgers with hand written names, items purchased and prices. There are also mementoes from the Klondike. Marilyn and Bill have been most hospitable to the writer of this family history and have been the source of much data on the Miller and Hovey history.

Conclusion

Descendants of Alma Corey Miller, and Robert James Miller had a cousins' reunion on Labor Day Weekend 1999 at the summer resort of Dr. Christine MacNearney and Dr. Paul Christensen.

[1] See Chaper I

[2] See Chaper I

[3] See A History of the Glassville Settlement, pp. 29f.,36

[4] Glassville, op.cit., pp.29f.,36

[5] Glassville, op.cit., pp. 29f.,36

[6] Glassville, op.cit.,pp.29f.,36

[7] Annie E. Elder, The History of New Jerusalem, Fredericton, Ubsdell Printing Ltd.,

c.1953 Private edition

[8] Recorded in Family Bible in the possession of June Covey

[9] Glassville, op.cit., p.30

[10] Elder, op.cit., p.77f.

[11] Elder, op.cit., p.77f.

[12] Ibid., p.1

[13] Ibid., p.78

[14] Glassville, op.cit.,p.29f.

[15] Ibid., p.30

[16] Ibid.,p.32

[17] Marilyn Hicks is great granddaughter of both Hugh Miller and Alfred Corey

[18] Jimmie Miller's notebook

[19] See Chapter IV

[20] Glassville Settlement, p.36; see also p.123ff.

[21] Glassville Settlement, p.36; see also p.123ff.

[22] James Miller, Jr., notebook, p.8

[23] See Chapter IV

[24] The Miller ledger is in the possession of Marilyn Miller Hicks,

[25] Erma Corey Shaw

[26] Ibid

[27] Erma Corey Shaw; also see Chap. XII

[28] Letters are in possession of Marilyn Hicks

[29] See <u>Glassville, op.cit.</u> p.36

[30] Lynn Fiske, Halifax, N.S. has the card

[31] Robert F. Legget, <u>Railways of Canada</u>, c.1973, p.133

[32] H.N. Bradley, <u>History of Foreston...</u>, p.58

[33] <u>Ibid</u>., p.61

[34] Lynn Fiske

[35] Marilyn Hicks and Lynn Fiske

[36] <u>The Story of Knowlesville</u>, p.105

[37] Erma Corey Shaw's recollections

[38] Erma Corey Shaw

[39] Edna Corey at Corey Reunion at Knowlesville, July 22, 1995

[40] Date is recorded in a Bible now in possession of June Covey

[41] Glassville History, p.74

[42] From June Covey

[43] Ted Jones, <u>Both Sides of the Wire</u>, Vol. One, "The Fredericton Internment Camp," (Fredericton: New Ireland Press, c.1988), the prologue and back cover.

[44] Notes and oral recollections from June Covey

[45] His d.o.b. should read 1892

[46] John Douglas MacNearney is listed in the book: <u>Commonwealth Air Training Plan Museum</u>, Inc., published by McGill Field, Brandon, Manitoba, p.455.

[47] Conversation with Lynn Fiske, Halifax, N.S.

[48] From Gail Pfister, July 1997

[49] From Lynn Fiske, June 1997

[50] From resumes of candidates for Board of Governors of Acadia University, printed by Assoc. Alumni of Acadia, 1985.

[51] Data from Basil Flemming and from genealogy

CHAPTER X

CHARLES HADDON SPURGEON COREY
b. July 26, 1868, d. August 24, 1945
Married in 1891
ELIZABETH THURBER
b. March 1, 1875, d. May 4, 1959

Charles Corey was born on July 26, 1868, in Queens County, N.B., in the vicinity of Canaan Forks, Coles Island and Havelock. He was the first son of Alfred and Lucretia Corey. They named him Charles Haddon Spurgeon Corey, after the Baptist preacher who was then at the height of his oratorical powers in his pulpit in the Tabernacle, in London.

There were interesting points of comparison in the two Charles, especially in their childhood and youth. Both Charles Spurgeon and Charles Corey were country boys. Neither showed any great promise at birth. Charles Spurgeon, born at Kelvedon, Essex, England, June 19, 1834, has been described as a "homely, coarse-looking, crude Essex County boy."[1] Charles Corey was so frail at birth that his mother carried him on a pillow; he was so small that she could slide her wedding ring right over his hand and up to his elbow.[2] Both Charles moved early from their places of birth. Spurgeon's early moves were to Colchester, Maidstone and Cambridge. When Charles Corey was no more than two years old he moved with his parents and two elder sisters, Mina and Alma, to Maine.

Probably Charles did not remember much about their sojourn in Maine. When he was only about five or six, the family returned to New Brunswick. By that time Charles had three sisters and one brother. At the Corey homestead in Knowlesville, the family celebrated Charles' birthday by enjoying their earliest batch of green beans from their garden. That became a tradition.³ Charles, like all his siblings, attended the Knowlesville School. The list of pupils for 1878 includes: COREY; Charles H.S., age 10.⁴

Like Spurgeon, Charles Corey, early in his life, became a church member. In the record book kept by his father, Alfred, who was the clerk of Aberdeen Baptist Church, Highlands, Charles' name still stands on two lists of "Non Resident Members", pp. 31 and 41. He is listed: Charles Corey, Campobello, Char. Co. Also Charles became a charter member, at age 18, of Pride of Aberdeen Lodge, at its organizational meeting, held in Free Christian Baptist Church, Knowlesville, on October 1, 1886. It was a "Lodge of Good Templars". On March 12, 1887, Charles was one of the participants chosen for a debate that took place on March 19, 1887, at a weekly meeting of the Lodge.⁵

To Maine and Return

Early in life Charles followed the custom of many young New Brunswick workers, including Coreys, in going to New England to work in industries. In Lewiston, Maine, he met Elizabeth Thurber, a young girl from Campobello Island. They were married on November 10, 1891, in Lewiston.⁶ Sometime between 1891 and 1896 Charles returned to Knowlesville with his young wife. There, their first child, Ivan, was born on February 29, 1896.⁷

To Campobello Island

Apparently after only a short stay in Knowlesville, the couple and first child went to Campobello Island. For Elizabeth it was a return to her birthplace. There, in the neighbourhood of her people they found work and a livelihood. Early in the family's residence on Campobello, Charles and Elizabeth Corey became the keepers of Head Harbour Lighthouse, and the adjoining fog alarm, called "The Whistle".[8] The lighthouse provided both employment and a residence.

On September 28, 1996, almost a century after Charles and Elizabeth took residence there, their grandson Gerald Corey took Margaret and the writer to see that lighthouse. From Wilson's Beach we travelled to the end of the pavement, then over a short strip of dirt road, and a short causeway. Where traffic ended we had a good view of the lighthouse. An iron ladder runs down a cliff face on the edge of Campobello. On the far side of a narrow channel of water, stairs run up another cliff to the lighthouse.

On the island two more children were born to Elizabeth and Charles:

> Edith Lucretia Corey, July 8, 1898, and
> Noel Charles Corey, May 11, 1900.

The family's residence at the lighthouse extended into the children's school years. Gerald told us, "My father, Noel, crossed that channel daily to go to and from school." Charlie Corey and Ivan, Jr., confirmed that their father, Ivan, also went to school from the lighthouse. Travel to and from the main island required climbing down and up stairs, and crossing the channel by boat at high tide, or on foot when tide was out. On August 30, 1997, I

Elizabeth, Ivan, Charles, back;
Edith, and Noel, front

Jud, Gordon and Margaret Corey at Quoddy Head Lighthouse, 1997

again stood looking across chasms toward that lighthouse. With me were my brother Gordon, his wife, Esta, and my wife, Margaret. Several persons gazed out to sea watching for whales to surface. In the chasm below, a woman, shoes in hand, accompanied by her children, crossed the channel. From the other side she reported, "It's cold but not deep."

In 1910 Charles and Elizabeth bought a property on North Road. It included a house and enough land for a good-sized garden and a small hay field. Buying a property probably indicated intention to make the island their permanent home. Charles' mother, Lucretia, seemed to find it difficult to understand how he could be content in Campobello. Repeatedly she remarked, "Charles ought to come off that island!"[9] Indications are that he made himself very much at home there. He entered into the life of the community. He became director of the choir of North Road Baptist Church. The North Road house was to be their home for the rest of their lives, and endure beyond their time. There, their children and one family of their grandchildren, were to grow up.

However, Charles did not forget his native home. He made occasional visits to Knowlesville, though travel was difficult in those days. Charles' niece, Erma Corey, recollected; "The first time I saw Uncle Charles was in Knowlesville. I remember him coming up there on a visit in winter. While he was there a young man named Norval Crawford, of Argyle, died. Uncle Charles and his mother — my grandmother — drove by horse and sleigh to the funeral in the Methodist Church at Argyle. I think it was on that same winter visit that he brought home a partridge that he had shot in the near woods."

From Knowlesville we expect that Charles took farm skills he had learned from his parents. He employed them on their island property where they grew their own vegetables, kept cows and produced their own milk and butter. In summer their cows, along with those of the neighbours, grazed the common pasture on the hillside. For winter feed Charles cut hay on neighbourhood fields. They also kept pigs and laying hens. Farming, however, was not the main occupation. For a good part of his life, it appears, Charles' major work was fishing. He had his own weir.[10]

Seasonal Employments

Besides fishing, Charles Corey found additional seasonal work. Being versatile, he engaged in various jobs as opportunity presented, e.g., pipefitting. He worked in Maine with his son Ivan and others. Lalia has a photograph of the men carrying long pipes on their shoulders. She thinks it may have been as early as the late teens or early 1920's.

In Maine, Charles also picked potatoes some seasons. His son Ivan, and Cecil Thurber joined with him.[11] In the fall of 1921, potato picking in Maine became the occasion of a visit to their relatives across the border in New Brunswick. Erma remembered vividly: "Ivan, and I think also Noel, accompanied Uncle Charles. They came to Aunt Mina McBrine's for a visit. Papa went up to E. Glassville and brought them to my grandparents' home in Knowlesville. They stayed over the weekend. At the Knowlesville Baptist Church I learned what a beautiful singer Uncle Charles was. In the choir, his love of music and song was evident. Also I can still visualize Ivan and where he was sitting in the church."

Visits to Campobello

"The following summer," Erma continued, "my cousin, Glenna Thompson, and I, visited Uncle Charles and family on Campobello Island. In July 1922, we travelled by train to Saint John. There we stayed over the weekend at the home of Johnny McBrine, an uncle of Eb McBrine, Glenna's father. At Saint John we boarded a boat for Campobello.

"Staying with Uncle Charles and family, we got acquainted with their way of life: gardening; keeping pigs, hens and cows; and Aunt Lizzie making butter and selling some of it to the tourists. Uncle Charles' major activity, however, at that time, was fishing. He had his own weir. He and his son Ivan took Glenna and me out in their boat when they went to put new stakes in their weir.

"They wanted to take me also to Head Harbour Lighthouse. It held special interest for me; I had lived there for a few weeks when I was a child near one year of age. My mother was ill and my father had brought her and me there for convalescence at the home of Aunt Elizabeth and Uncle Charles. My mother died there in June 1904.

"During my 1922 visit Aunt Elizabeth shared with me her memory of my mother in 1904. She described to me how her strength was waning to the point where she found it very difficult to bathe me — then a one-year-old baby. Aunt Elizabeth asked her, "Would you like me to bathe her?" "Yes," my mother replied, "Alice was doing it for me", i.e., when they were living in Lewiston, earlier.

"I didn't get to visit that lighthouse during my 1922 visit to Campobello Island. They decided that it would be too far for me to walk beyond the point they could reach by boat. However, Glenna and I visited another interesting place. We walked to the home of Aunt Elizabeth's two maiden sisters: Agnes and Ella Thurber. We spent a day with them by the sea shore."

Seventy-four years after Erma's visit, the writer visited the island and learned family history connected with the Thurber house. Aunt Elizabeth grew up in that house and probably was born there. It was the home of Sylvanus (d. Sept. 27, 1923), and Edith A. (d. Nov. 21, 1922) Thurber. Their daughters were: Eulalia, Elizabeth (Lizzie Corey) Agnes, Ella, Clara Estella, Georgetta and Addie.[12] Estella was a traveller. She was reported in Australia in 1922 when her mother died, and in 1923 when her father died, and apparently was still there in 1928 when Edith Corey was married.[13] Later Estella worked in the U.S.A. for years and came home to Campobello on visits.

The Charles Corey Family in 1922

By the time of the visit of Erma and Glenna in 1922, the three children of Elizabeth and Charles Corey had all reached their twenties. However, the family then recalled a few anecdotes of the childhood and youth of Ivan and Elizabeth. These stories Erma remembered.

Ivan was eight years old before he had a birthday. Born on February 29th, 1896, the normal expectation would have been for another leap year in four years. It was omitted in 1900. Hence he had to wait until 1904 to mark his birthday on February 29th. Perhaps this explains an apparent tendency to seek a little extra fun, which sometimes took the form of playing pranks, e.g., setting the dog on the cat.

Edith, though not the youngest of the family, was called "Babe". As a child she showed great talent in singing, which the family recognized, providing soprano lessons.[14] Also early in life, Edith's health was interrupted by an unfortunate accident. When sliding down hill on the snow she ran into a wire fence and hurt her shoulder. The hurt lasted a long time and took her to several chiropractic treatments.[15]

Erma's visit to Campobello Island in 1922 gave her a very positive image of Uncle Charles' family that she retained for the rest of her life. She especially remembered the singing: "The Corey men had rich bass voices. Edith also was a very good singer." The family enjoyed much pleasure from singing. Neighbors and relatives joined in the singing and the pleasure at home gatherings.

It appears that Erma's visit to Campobello was well timed; the whole family was still at home. The next summer, 1923, Ivan and Noel went to Saskatchewan on a harvest excursion. While they were there their grandfather, Sylvanus Thurber, died. His obituary lists the two grandsons in Liberty, Sask. It seems that the family was about to enter a new phase: children maturing, marrying, some leaving home. A girl who grew up in the family left the home, it appears, about the time the grandchildren began to arrive.

Alice

Charles and Elizabeth Corey brought up a girl named Alice. She was with them from age 7 to age 17. That was in the years 1917 to 1927. Lalia had two photos: in one Alice is in the center; nearby are Aunt Estelle Thurber and Edith Corey. In the second picture Elizabeth is sitting in a lawn chair at North Road. Alice is sitting on an arm of the chair. At an early age Alice married Walter Mitchell and lived on North Road. They had two sons and a daughter. Alice had a second marriage and lived in Waterville, Maine. Alice returned to see her foster mother, Elizabeth, about five years before she died.[16]

The Second Generation Matures

Ivan Corey married Elsie M. Daggett, on January 2, 1926. There was a custom that the eldest son stayed home. Hence Charles and Elizabeth made room in their home for Elsie and Ivan, and the grandchildren as they arrived. The first baby was born on September 12, 1926, two months prematurely. She weighed only two pounds. "The doctor said to my grandmother, 'She is worth saving. Bathe her in olive oil.' They carried her on a pillow. They gave her the name of Charles' eldest sister, Mina. She grew to be strong and healthy."[17]

Coreys: Alfred, seated; Charles, behind chair; Ivan, holding baby, Charlie; daughter, Mina, in front

Ivan's first son, Charles Daggett Corey, was born May 7, 1928. He was called Charlie. The summer of his birth was marked by a visit of his great grandfather, Alfred Corey, to Campobello.

Alfred Corey, Water Divining

In his home area, Carleton Co., N.B., people over an extensive neighborhood called upon Alfred for water divining.

He used as divining rod a forked green stick, sometimes apple. He walked over the ground holding his forked green stick just above the ground. Where the stick dipped, he said, "Dig right there!" Thus he indicated to many people the exact spot to dig a well.

People on Campobello needed Alfred with his water divining skill to locate wells for them. Ivan Corey, accompanied by his father, Charles, drove his one-seated roadster to E. Knowlesville to pick up Grandpa Alfred.[18] On the island he located sites for wells. The photo, probably taken on a Sunday, and preserved by Lalia Morehouse, marks the 1928 visit.

About a decade after Alfred's visit to the island my Uncle Jud told me of Grandpa's gratis service. In a rocky part of the North Road community about fourteen families in one neighborhood had been carrying water from one well. When they dug where he indicated, each family got its own well.[19] Uncle Jud told me further, "People in his home county had learned from experience not to try to change the location even by a few feet, for convenience of location. Some called him back: 'We didn't strike water.' 'You didn't dig where I showed you."

Edith: Marriage and Family

That same year, 1928, on November 8, Charles' and Elizabeth's only daughter, Edith Lucretia Corey, married Edgar Allen Mitchell. They were married by Edith's uncle, Rev. J.A. Corey, who was then pastor at Keswick Ridge. The wedding was in North Road Baptist Church "under an attractive arch of autumn leaves and berries, made by friends of the bride." Her "gown and veil were a gift from an aunt whose home is in Australia." Accompanying the bride and groom were Miss Vivian Mitchell, sister of Edgar, and Noel Corey, brother of Edith. Organist was Miss Florence Thurber. There were 200 guests, many beautiful presents, and a buffet lunch at the home

Edith Corey and Edgar Mitchell, m. Campobello, 1928

of the bride and groom.[20]

The Mitchell house was an easy walk from Corey's home, just around a bend in the shore line. Edgar Allen Mitchell's father was also named Edgar Mitchell. His mother was an American, Mercy Emerys from Eastport, Maine.

Edgar Jr. had a career in drafting before his marriage. He worked for Hood Rubber in Boston, manufacturers of tires. Also he worked for American Engineering Corporation, on the Quoddy Dam Project. The money ran out and the dam was never completed, but part of it can still be seen between Eastport and Lubec. That work was before Edgar was married at age 31. He could have continued working for the engineering company, but he was eager to go fishing.[21]

Edith and Edgar had three sons:
David Harold b. 1929
Noel b. Sept. 28, 1933
Robert b. Dec. 1935

Noel: Work, Marriage, Sojourns

That same year, 1928, the youngest of the Corey family, Noel, completed a study course and became a qualified electrician, though there was then no electric power on Campobello

Island - not until nearly 20 years later. While still living at home he took a correspondence course in electrical wiring. In this study he had to persevere against the supposed better judgement of both his father and his elder brother, Ivan. They maintained that it made no sense at all, and that he would find no possible use for an electrical trade on the island. Noel looked farther ahead. Meantime, like his father and elder brother, Noel engaged in seasonal fishing. In later life he told his son Gerald that the job he most enjoyed in his whole life was tending the weir for several years.

Noel did find work at his trade for some time in late 20's and early 30's in Bangor, Maine. Thus, early in life, he showed a tendency to venture farther afield. During his Bangor sojourn, he tried another venture. He bought a package of cigarettes. It seemed to be the thing to do at the time. He smoked half of one, then threw it and the rest of the package in the Penobscot River, as he was crossing the bridge.

In 1934 Noel married Bessie Frances Calder of Campobello. At the beginning of their marriage they went on a venture to Baltimore, Md., where they worked on an estate. While there they purchased a Model A Ford Roadster. Their journey toward home in that car proved troublesome and costly, with repeated breakdowns and engine work. At a border town, anticipating that negotiating the car through customs would be problematical, they decided to try to store it. While Noel was inquiring about storage, a passer-by, attracted by the car's shiny appearance, asked, "Will you sell that car?" "Yes, said Bessie, for fifteen dollars." It was a surprise to Noel, but a relief to both.

On returning to Campobello from Baltimore in 1935, Noel and Bessie Corey were especially fortunate in housing. Noel's Aunt Estelle Thurber invited them to live in her house.Thus Charles' and Elizabeth's family were together again on Campobello.

The Corey Family in Charles Last Decade

Ivan lived almost his entire life on Campobello. There their six children were born and grew up:
Mina, b. September 12, 1926
Charlie, b. May 7, 1928
Inez, b. February 14, 1930, d. October 3, 1938
Melvin , b. May 15, 1931
Lalia, b. August 10, 1932
Ivan Alfred, b. July 6, 1936

Road Commissioner

By the time Ivan's children were growing up, Charles Corey had found new employment. Ivan's eldest son, Charles Daggett Corey, the babe in arms at the time of his great-grandfather Alfred's 1928 visit to Campobello, said, "By my time my grandfather had given up fishing. He was then Road Commissioner." Charlie's brother, Ivan, said, "I believe my grandfather was Road Commissioner when I was born in 1936." Ivan, Jr. thinks his grandfather was overseer of the building of the new road that connects to the bridge to Lubec. It is now called Friar's Beach Road. Ivan said, "My father was working with his truck on that road."

The probable date of the beginning of Charles Corey's position as Road Commissioner was 1935, near the beginning of Allison Dysart's government. Being also minister of public works, Premier Dysart "launched a number of road and bridge building projects to create employment."[22] Interestingly, Charles' brother, Ira, was terminated from the position of Road Commissioner for Parish of Aberdeen in Carleton County, at about the same time, i.e., when Dysart's Liberals succeeded L.P.D. Tilley's Conservatives. Alfred Corey, father of Charles and Ira, was a known Liberal. It appears Ira supported the

Conservative Party from the time he began contracting for Flemming and Gibson Co., in the J.K. Flemming era.

Ivan: Work and Travel

Ivan had a trade that was perhaps mostly free from political factors. Early in his life, it appears, he began to learn pipefitting. His daughter, Lalia, had a group photo of seven men in Maine, all pipefitters. She has identified her father Ivan, and her grandfather Charles. He is holding a long, large-diameter pipe on his shoulder. She has estimated the date as 1914. Between pipefitting jobs and seasonal fishing, it seems that Ivan engaged in various activities.

I remember the November afternoon in 1936 when he arrived in our farmyard in E. Knowlesville. He was the passenger in a truck that pulled into Ira Corey's farmyard. We, the boys, told him where to place the truck to load firewood we had for sale. "We didn't come for wood," he said. Then my mother said, "Hello, Ivan." "Hello, Aunt Nellie," he replied. I had seen Ivan only once before — in 1928, when he drove his roadster to E. Knowlesville to pick up Grandfather Alfred for water divining. I was then only age five.

The driver in 1936 was Russell Calder who wanted to buy livestock for beef. My father and Tom came home at dark from their logging contract at McCrossin Field, between Golden Ridge and Skedaddle Ridge. The visitors spent the evening with us in the farm house. At bedtime Mr. Calder asked my father, "What time do you leave for work?"

Next morning Mr. Calder arose before daylight and rode on the two-wheeled wagon with father, part way to his logging site. Mr. Calder returned, walking, to the farm and told us that he was taking a heifer on his truck. On the ride he had persuaded my father to sell him one of the fat heifers that Warren, age 11, and I, age 13, had driven the previous day from summer pasture at Bob Guthrie's. Not until 1997 did I learn, from

Charlie Corey, that Russell Calder had a store and a van and that in summer he peddled meat and groceries on the island. He lived only until end of 1938.

Family Visits

The next fall, 1937, Uncle Charles made a visit to Carleton Co. How he travelled from the island and who accompanied him is obscure. He was at the Ira Corey farm in E. Knowlesville when we arrived home from school. Who brought him? Perhaps Kate Hovey. His visit was timed to coincide with the arrival of Uncle Jud for his annual hunting expedition. In summer of 1938 Campobello Coreys made another visit to Carleton Co. Accompanying Ivan in his Ajax car were Elsie, children: Mina, Charlie and Lalia, and grandparents, Charles and Elizabeth. Lalia remembers that they stayed at Kate and Jim Hovey's in Glassville, that Kate wore round glasses, that there was a washtub and washboard in the house and that Mina Corey and Jean Hovey, being the same age, chummed together. Lalia also recalls a line-up at the bathroom. Fortunate were they to have one of the few bathrooms in the area. It was a feature of

L. to r. Nellie and Ira Corey, Ida McBrine, Charles and Elizabeth Corey

the new house the Hoveys had built in 1936. There was a cistern in the basement that stored rainwater, and a pump to force it upstairs.

Lalia has good memories of the visit but recalls that the family later regretted that they hadn't taken their middle daughter, Inez, with them to Glassville. On October 3, 1938, Inez died of diphtheria, at age eight. In 1993 Mina commented that Ivan was deeply troubled by Inez' early death, and that he took a long time to become reconciled to the tragedy of her choking to death of the dread disease.

Not long before the outbreak of WWII in 1939 Coreys of Carleton Co. visited Coreys of Campobello. Ira Corey drove his 1938 Ford. Wilfred took a turn at the wheel. Also on the trip were Aunt Ida McBrine and Nellie Corey and son Gordon, then age five. He still remembers a guessing contest and some banter about the size of Uncle Charles' pig. Nellie asked Gordon his estimate of the size. He made a non-controversial reply. "It's just as big as Charlie said it was." In a telephone conversation, March 1993, from New York State, Mina Corey recalled taking the visitors in a dory across the harbour to Wilson's Beach to visit Berta and Mayford Anthony. She carried Gordon from the wharf up the ladder. Father came home with great praise for Aunt Lizzie's hospitality, especially her percolated coffee, served with condensed milk.

Noel

Visits and sustained communication between the families of Charles and Ira Corey led to an unusual work venture for Noel Corey who, it seems, was unemployed in fall of 1939. Just after WWII broke out that fall, Ira expanded his logging. Under a contract with Flemming and Gibson, Ira had a large crew and several pairs of horses cutting and yarding logs on the South Branch of the Miramichi. After a letter from Charles, Noel's father, to Ira Corey in fall of 1939, Noel came up to E.

Knowlesville area and worked a few months for his Uncle Ira. He described Noel as a strong worker. Before he learned the skill and advantage of using a peeve he lifted logs straight up.

Some evenings in the lumber camp Noel enjoyed his favourite escape, reading mystery stories by the light of oil lamp. One evening as he lay on his bunk reading, just when he was carried into the most mysterious experience, somebody turned out the oil lamps, leaving him lost in a strange world. Lights went out at 9:00 p.m. in lumber camps. Work began at daybreak. Noel's venture into lumbering in mainland New Brunswick lasted until the crew suspended work for Christmas.

Return to Trade

Soon after that venture in logging, Noel found opportunity to return to his trade. World War II brought demands for electricians. He worked at Saint John Shipyard and Dry Dock, and also at Indian Town, building mine sweepers. Bessie and the boys continued residence on Campobello in the Thurber house which carried much family history. Randall said, "I was born there, as was my father," forty years earlier. We guess Noel's mother came there for childbirth during their lighthouse era. All three sons of Bessie and Noel were born during the era of living in the Thurber house:

Gerald Grant Corey, b. January 28, 1936,
in Lubec Maine;
Noel Randall Corey, b. April 18, 1940, on Campobello;
Harry Douglas Corey, b. June 3, 1946, in St. Stephen,
at the Chipman Memorial Hospital.

Ivan

During the war a work opportunity came also to Ivan and his father, Charles. A new school was being built on Campobello in 1943-44. With the assistance of his father, Ivan did the plumbing and installed all the pipes. Lalia remembers getting rides to school in the family car that winter in preference to riding in the bus. That job was perhaps nearly Charles' last employment.

Charles and Elizabeth Corey, N. Road, Campobello, c. 1941

The Passing of Charles H.S. Corey

Charles Corey was a diabetic for twenty-two years. His grandson, Ivan, who lives with the same condition, described it: "My grandfather started taking insulin in 1923, only a year after the discovery of insulin. In the early days of treating the condition there was no way of measuring the amount of sugar in the blood. Hence it was not uncommon to experience a reaction from taking too much insulin." Another grandson, Noel Mitchell, also remembers that Charles sometimes misjudged the amount of insulin to inject by needle, and got too much. Noel also remembers some of the struggles his grandfather had, e.g., carrying a forkful of hay on his shoulder, falling under it, rolling it off him, swallowing some of Elizabeth's coffee, then responding, "I'm fine!" as if nothing had happened. In later falls, Noel said, "he got damaged with cuts."

Despite that strain on his health, Charles lived past age 77 — thanks to the devoted care of Elizabeth. "My grandmother", Noel said, "took good care of Grandfather. She took him by the arm when he needed support; she read to him; she watched his diet." In the end, it appears that the diabetes hastened Charles' death. The final episode of his life is told by his youngest granddaughter, Lalia Morehouse.

"One Saturday in the cranberry season Grandfather went to the common pasture to pick cranberries. He was delayed. Elizabeth went searching for him, carrying coffee and sugar. He was suffering a coma. She revived him and brought him home. The following Friday he announced: 'I'm going back to pick some more cranberries.' My grandmother, sensing danger, opposed his going and tried to dissuade him. Taking cranberry prongs and a flour bag, he left the house, saying, 'I'll be back in two hours, at 2:00 p.m.'"

When he didn't return at the expected time his son, Ivan, and grandson, Charlie, went looking for him. Charlie described the pastureland: as partly wooded, with a dozen cow paths running through it. He said, "The man who found him was not even looking for him." It was Raymond Calder. He also had a pasture in the same area, and happened to be in the neighborhood at the same time. Ray reported having seen Charles on top a hill, "walking in circles."

Lalia concluded: "A nurse came on the scene. She helped get my grandfather into a car. They brought him back home and walked him into the hosue. He should have been carried. They put him on the couch. He opened his eyelids and looked at me. My grandmother asked him, 'Do you want more coffee? Squeeze my hand: one time for 'yes'; two times for 'no'. He raised his head and said, 'yes', then he was gone before she got back with the coffee. Meanwhile my father and Charlie were searching for him." Charlie said, "He had died before we got back."

On August 24, 1945, Charles H.S.Corey died at age 77

years and one month. Grandson, Gerald Corey, said, "My grandmother was devastated on the death of the man she called 'Charl', with whom she had shared life and to whom she had given her devotion for 54 years, i.e., since she was age 16". However, she had no cause for regrets.

Ira and Nellie Corey had recently moved from the farm in E. Knowlesville to Juniper. They drove to Campobello for Charles' funeral, taking with them Ida McBrine, a sister of Charles and Ira. Gordon Corey remembered going to the farm to stay until his parents returned.

Charles and Elizabeth Corey had 12 grandchildren. All of them were born on Campobello Island, or neighboring Lubec, Maine. Only one, Harry Corey, was born after the death of his grandfather. Most of them grew up on the island. Those who talked to the writer seemed to be unanimous in affirming that Elizabeth's devotion to Charles was unwavering.

Eldest granddaughter, Mina, recalled Elizabeth's statement on their 50th anniversary: "After 50 years we are still in love." Their relationship was strong and enduring. Mina also described how Elizabeth helped to manage Charles' diabetes. She cooked special foods for him, and monitored his diet. Also, Mina described how she applied a sympathetic psychology. When he pouted in a corner she indulged him in a bit of pampering: "What is wrong with Charles now?" It took only minutes for her to extract from him what was bothering him. Noel Mitchell said, "She had a pretty good disposition."

Charles as he is Remembered by his Grandchildren

"My grandfather was a hard worker", said grandson, Charlie, with a note of affection. Despite hard work Charles Corey had an ongoing recreation. He was a great lover of music. Winnie Mitchell said, "He had music in his sole (soul)." His foot kept time to the music. He played several instruments. Granddaughter, Lalia, said, "I remember my grandfather playing the Jew's Harp, and violin, and several times I saw him play an organ." Granddaughter Mina remembers, "At Christmas we got together for a sing. Grandfather played the organ. Lalia also played the organ sometimes.

Mina says, "Grandfather stood out as a devout Christian. One way his devotion was expressed was in his role as choir director in North Road Baptist Church for many years. Besides being very musical, he was also a very good conciliator. With a note of triumph, he reported to Grandmother after rehearsal, 'I managed to resolve that spat.'" David Mitchell has vivid recollections of singing in the choir of North Road Baptist Church when Charles, tenor, was directing, and when family members Edith, soprano, and Noel, bass, were also singing. Charles' Christian devotion was also observed in his continued reading of his Bible despite his failing eyesight. Gerald and Randall remember their grandfather in his later years as he sat with Bible and magnifying glass.

Gerald and Randall also have recollections of Grandfather's farming and gardening. When they were growing up Charles had two memorable cows, named Jude and Molly. Gerald remembers his grandfather chasing a heifer around the barn. Lalia says that earlier he had three milking cows. Ivan Jr., says he also had a horse he called "Old Fred", who pulled the hay mower. Without a horse Ivan pulled the mower with his truck.

Gerald and Randall also remember their grandfather, Charles, as a person of great humor, which came out spontaneously, as he went about his daily chores. They vividly remember the incident in which son-in-law Edgar Mitchell approached Charles as he sat milking a cow. Expecting sympathy over stolen vegetables, Edgar asked, "Bubba, what would you say about a man who would come into another man's garden and steal the biggest pumpkin in his patch?" "I'd say", replied Charles, "that he had pretty good judgment."

Grandson Melvin, it appears, inherited some of the humor. Melvin related a story about his grandfather when he was in his 70's, making his first attempt to drive a car. Ivan, the usual driver, was in Saint John. Grandfather backed the car from the barn, and with Grandmother beside him and Melvin in the back seat he began his practice driving. While Grandmother screamed about scraping picket fences, Melvin made a mental recording of a hilarious story.

With determination Charles Corey did learn to drive a car. Noel Mitchell remembers his grandfather driving a car to Mayford Anthony's house, carrying choir members packed in like sardines. Noel also has memories of Charles' choir rehearsals and Charles' perseverance, despite his failing eyesight and his difficulty in keeping on the right line, and seeing the words. Elizabeth lived nearly 14 years after being bereft of Charles. Grandson Charlie said she had pretty good health up to her last year. She was bedridden probably for a year, and by that time she was nearly blind. Elizabeth died at home on Campobello on May 4, 1959, at age 84 and two months. Charles and Elizabeth are buried in the North Road Cemetery. Their names, together with the names of two of Elizabeth's sisters, are recorded on a gravestone:

Clare Estelle Thurber	1882 - 1955
Agnes Lois Thurber	1877 - 1941
Charles Hadden Corey	1868 - 1945
Elizabeth May Corey	1875 - —

Edith and Edgar Mitchell

Edith Mitchell, only daughter of Charles and Elizabeth Corey, lived her entire life on Campobello. Edgar was often out on the water, fishing. He had a succession of several large boats. Edith was busy with the care of the children and the house; and she did not always enjoy good health. Apparently she never fully recovered from her sliding-accident injury. Her nephews, Gerald and Randall Corey say she had a lot of trouble with her shoulder and she couldn't raise her arm very high.

Despite busyness and handicaps, however, she took time to cultivate her talent in singing and music. Her talents are well remembered by her son Noel: "My mother was a singer; she had voice training and piano lessons. She had a piano to practise lessons. Also she passed papers on high opera singing. An accomplished singer, she sang in the choir of North Road Baptist Church.[23] Sometimes she sang in duets with her brother Noel Corey and later with his son Gerald.

Edith saw her youngest son, Robert, go directly from high school to Bible School about 1953. Cancer claimed Edith's life at age 64, on November 22, 1962, only three and one half years after her mother's passing. Nephews, Gerald and Randall still retain a high regard for Edith: "Aunt Babe was a lovely person; very kind." Edith's husband Edgar Mitchell lived until September 30, 1977, three days before age 80.

The Children of Edith and Edgar Mitchell

Noel Mitchell

On Noel's birthday, September 28, 1996, Margaret Corey and the writer visited Noel and family at the Edgar Mitchell house on North Road, Campobello. Noel reviewed some family history: his grandparents, Charles and Elizabeth Corey; his parents, Edith and Edgar Mitchell; and his brothers, David and Robert Mitchell. Noel shared some family experience in fishing: a trawler in summer; a seining boat in winter; sardine weirs in-shore.

Noel also described an accident and injury he suffered, at age 17, when helping pour a concrete foundation for a new house. He was walking a plank and carrying two 12-quart buckets of cement mix. The plank broke; Noel crashed onto a wheelbarrow and suffered crushing injuries. Noel also suffers from epilepsy. He thinks it stems from injury in the fall.

Subsequently Noel regained enough strength to work in fishing industry. For a time he worked in-shore, tending the weir, and taking the fish from the nets. He also worked for a time on the big family trawler. He told us about trading the small boat for a bigger boat, i.e., a "dragger", 65 ft.long, with some help from the government loan board. That was in 1958. Noel's brother, David, later added to the description: "I was the captain of the large fishing boat, a dragger. It had a crew of four: Edgar Mitchell, father, Stanley Mitchell, uncle, David Mitchell, son, Noel Mitchell, son. They named the boat "Norwin", from David's daughter Norma, and his wife, Winnifred, also a native of Campobello Island.

Noel was a shareholder in the "Norwin". He worked aboard the boat when he was able. Describing his experience on the big fishing boat, Noel said, "I was the 'ice man', I cleaned and iced the fish. They had to be freshly cleaned for inspection at Beaver Harbour, N.B." They pulled aboard large catches, 10,000 lbs. and upwards. David said their largest catch was 96,000 lbs. in three six-hour outings.

During that time David was contemplating the Christian ministry. In 1949 he had gone to Providence, R.I. He said, "It didn't work out." He returned to Campobello and resumed fishing for 21 years more, making 24 years in total. During that time he married Winnifred Fitzsimmons. In 1970 David and family left Campobello Island to enter the Bible School at Victoria, N.B.

Noel Mitchell, middle son of Edith and Edgar, born September 28, 1933, remained on Campobello later than any of his family. It appears that the injury he suffered in his fall, and the epilepsy, have handicapped him. However, he undertook some enterprises: He had a business in applying undercoating to cars. He had a ramp in his yard to elevate cars for applications. People brought their cars before the winter and salt season. Noel was not able to do undercoating in cold weather. The cold aggravated his epilepsy. Also, for a time, Noel had a grocery store situated next to their house.

Noel Mitchell's Family

Noel married Marie Ginsen, daughter of Nellie Colwell and stepdaughter of Rev. Eldon Colwell, one-time Baptist minister on Campobello. They have two sons and a daughter:
Samuel Mitchell, born June 30, 1971
Suzanne Marie Mitchell, born June 6, 1975
Andrew Allen Mitchell, born January 9, 1982

At the time of our 1996 visit Suzanne was a fourth-year student at Atlantic Baptist University, Moncton. She had graduated from Campobello High School with the highest standing in her class in several subjects. She received several scholarships. In 1996 the two sons were at home with Noel and Marie. Samuel, since graduating from high school, had been working with his father.

Andrew was in grade 8, and doing very well in school, despite living with a severe condition of diabetes, which he has had since he was one and a half years of age. Andrew has experienced a very difficult ordeal with diabetes. Lacking insulin, he has needed injections most of his life. Blood sugar has been difficult to regulate, requiring frequent tests. Blood sugar has been affected by emotional frustrations, and other complications, including excessive amounts of pain control drugs. He had been in St. Stephen Hospital. On July 1996 he was in such critical condition that he had to be taken to the I.W.K. hospital for children in Halifax. His mother, Marie, accompanied him. They found a kidney stone and a blocked and enlarged bowel. The pain which had come from that condition had been treated with excessive amount of pain drugs. As a further complication, he had become addicted to the excessive quantities of drugs.

Andrew's parents subsequently acted on the counsel of a doctor in Saint John. "If he has a flair-up, bring him straight here to the Regional Hospital". He had two admissions to the Regional Hospital in fall of 1996. His condition was aggravated by a blow he received at school resulting in temporary blurred eyesight. He returned home but had to be readmitted. I visited him there twice in December, during his second fall admission. Andrew is a very interesting person to visit. Obviously he was making very good relations with hospital personnel. Also he expressed insight into his condition. He said, "After I'm in hospital a while my condition clears up." He expects to have to be in hospital periodically, especially while he is still growing. His sugar level, and hence the amount of insulin needed, changes with growth. He was being taught emotional control.

In the next year Andrew had more admissions to hospital in Saint John. On one admission a doctor said, "If he had been half an hour later arriving here he wouldn't be living. You'll have to move nearer to a hospital or he'll be dead."

In November 1997 Noel's family made an urgent move from Campobello. They went first to the home of Marie's brother, Matthew Colwell, in Fredericton. In March 1998 they moved to an apartment in Marysville. Their next move was to a motel in the summer of 1998 while they were negotiating the sale of their house on Campobello and the purchase of a house in Lincoln. This necessitated the storage of some of their belongings. Marie said, "My brother and his wife helped us find a place close to a hospital."

In September 1998 the family moved into a white house at 1864 Lincoln Road. Andrew contemplated resuming school but couldn't stay out of hospital on account of low sugars. The move was fortunate in proximity to hospital, and also for work opportunities. In 1999 Andrew began working as a carpenter's assistant. He hopes to enroll in a school of carpentry. Since February 1999 Samuel has been employed in restaurant and motel work. Both boys are happy with their new location.

Noel, however, has been less fortunate. He was admitted to hospital in Fredericton after the move. He stopped driving. He suffers from arthritis, fluid in joints, and swelling. Nearly two years later he still only drives "when he feels up to it."

Suzanne graduated from Atlantic Baptist University in

spring of 1997. She went to work immediately at Sears Department Store in Moncton. In 1999 she is in a new position with "a Christian company". After training with a sewing machine she has been making decals. She still works part time for Sears. She is working hard to repay her student loan.

Noel and family were the last of the Edith and Edgar Mitchell family to leave Campobello. David and Robert Mitchell, the eldest and youngest sons of Edith and Edgar left Campobello Island much earlier, both to pursue education for the Christian ministry.

Robert

Robert went directly from high school, about 1953, to New Brunswick Bible Institute, Hartland, N.B. Following graduation in 1957 Robert married Adrienne Brown of Wilson's Beach, N.B. They went to the United Baptist field at Cross Creek, N.B. There Robert gained experience in the pastorate before entering mission work. He expected to go on a mission to France. Instead, he went to Quebec, ministered for 12 years, and planted a church in Verdun. Robert then moved to the headquarters of his mission: Bible Christian Union, in Hamilton, Ontario. He became Canadian Secretary for the mission.

In later years Robert returned to pastorates: Toronto, Halifax and Lindsay, Ontario. His work now is "Grace Ministries." They meet in the gymnasium of the Elementary School in Lindsay. They also have a Christian Camp. Adrienne Mitchell has a woman's ministry. She belongs to the Women's Conference of Associated Gospel Churches. She has spoken at conferences: Miramichi, N.B., Muskoka, Ontario, Maine and Florida. Robert and Adrienne have four children: Brent, Philip, Colleen and Peter. All are graduates of N.B.B.I. Two sons: Brent and Philip have been missionaries in Senegal, West Africa. They learn language readily.

Brent is "a born linguist." He married Debbie Brawn

Debbie, Brent, Chris, Matthew and Sharon Mitchell

from Hainesville. They have three children. In 1999 the family is on furlough in Canada. Brent is visiting his supporting churches. Debbie is in college studying business. Christopher, 19, is a student at Royal Military College, Kingston, Ontario. The question of return to Senegal depends on arrangements for education for Sharon, 16, and Matthew, 13. The mission school in Senegal closed.

David Mitchell

David graduated from N.B.B.I. in 1973. They went immediately to Melvern Square Baptist Church, near Kingston, N.S. for a pastorate of five and one half years. Succeeding pastorates were at: Sawyerville, ...Hatfield Point, N.B., Colebrook, New Hampshire, and Belleville, N.B. On July 20, 1991 David, accompanied by his brother Robert, attended the Corey reunion in Knowlesville. David and Winnie were then completing their ministry to Belleville Community Chapel in N.B. and were preparing to move.

In the fall of 1991 they went to Clark's Harbour, Cape Sable Island, N.S., where he became pastor of New Testament Baptist Church. In June 1997 the Mitchells moved from Cape Sable Island to their new home in Waterville, N.B., in sight of Waterville United Baptist Church. They also have a camp on Indian Brook Lake, near Millville, N.B.

In semi-retirement, David has undertaken ":Fishers of Men Ministries". It engages ministers with experience in fishing, and seeks to establish ministries in fishing ports. Its head office is in Bon Secour, Alabama. A travelling representative is Rev. Wayne Mund, "the fisherman". On May 29, 1997, David was appointed Canadian Director for Fishers of Men Ministries. He expects to be travelling to fishing ports. He has been to Newfoundland.

David is now having to nurture his health, which includes managing diabetes. In the summer of 1999 David and Winnie had an accident on the Maine Turnpike on their return journey from teaching missions at a church camp in Maine. Both suffered pain and discomfort for some days. In the fall of 1999 David is seeing a specialist in Fredericton who has diagnosed collagen disease, said to be in the same family as fibromyalgia. David thought he had arthritis. Some drugs he tried worked havoc with his blood sugar.

David and Winnie have a daughter and two sons: Stephen and Gordon. Their daughter, Norma Gail MacKenzie, studied in Vancouver, B.C. at International Asia Pacific University. She majored in computer programming and earned an M.B.A. degree in International Marketing. She said, "I can run international companies". In a telephone conversation in 1997 she spoke of back trouble from an extra disc on her spine. She said she was then on disability from work. In fall of 1999 she is taking another computer course by correspondence. She wants to start her own business from her home in Downsview, Ontario.

Stephen Mitchell is a carpenter living in Port Williams,

N.S., and working for a building company. In spring of 1997, when David and Winnie were moving into their home, he came to Waterville, N.B., finished the siding on an addition, and also did some inside finish work. Stephen has two daughters: Haley and Abbey. Gordon Mitchell lives in Lisbon Falls, Maine, and works the 4:00 p.m. to midnight shift at the shipyard in Bath, Me. He also owns a body shop where he works mornings. His wife was a medical secretary at Maine Medical Centre, Lewiston. They have two children: Megan and Dean.

Ivan and Elsie Corey: Closing Years

Charles' elder son, Ivan, lived only a few months after his sister, Edith Mitchell. He suffered severely with lung cancer. "It went all through his body," said his son Ivan; and "despite the pain, he worked. In 1962, his last year, he tended his herring weirs. He kept at plumbing too." He spent his last illness in the West Side Community Hospital, the former D.V.A. Hospital in Saint John West — a place well known to the writer, having been a patient, a visitor and a neighbor.

In the spring of 1943 I was brought there from Camp Utopia, and spent three weeks recovering from mumps. We had a grand view of the Reversing Falls. After W.W.II I visited my brother, Claude, in that hospital. He was recovering from tuberculosis, contracted in his war experience. Ivan Jr. recalls a visit to his father in the hospital combined with an invitation from relatives then living in Saint John West. Ivan Jr. said, "Mel and I had supper with Jean and Basil Flemming."

On February 28, 1963, his 67th birthday, Ivan died in the hospital, that no longer stands. The buildings were torn down in 1994. Since 1986 I have lived in walking distance from the site. Ivan's funeral on Campobello was attended by Corey relatives from Carleton County: Nellie Corey, Claude and Alice Corey, Shirley and Paul Brooks, and Erma Shaw. In a letter dated May 14, 1972, Mina Corey tells Erma: "I think I met you at the time of my father's funeral..."

Elsie, wife of Ivan, lived ten years beyond him. She kept the Corey homestead on Campobello in summer. There, my mother, Nellie Corey, visited her in 1965, the year following the death of my brother Claude. Mother asked Alice Corey, Claude's widow, to take her to Campobello. "I'd like to see the relatives there once more," she said. Alice knew the Campobello Coreys. They had visited her and Claude at the Hovey house in Glassville — after his three-year convalescence in Saint John. Lalia Morehouse remembers the visit. She says Uncle Ira was, at the time, staying with Claude and Alice. Also they had visited Campobello, taking time out of Alice's visits to her mother, Mrs. Jones, in St. Stephen. The 1965 visit was my first to the island, and my only visit before 1996. I was invited to go, along with three boys: Frederic, David and Gregory Corey. We stayed at Mayford Anthony's. Nellie Corey stayed with Elsie, where she felt much at home. They had become good friends. Mayford motored to North Road to see his Aunt Nellie.

In her late years Elsie spent winters with her daughter, Mina, in the U.S.A. at Sleighton Farm School in the Philadelphia area, later in Paterson, New Jersey, and finally in the parsonage of the Waverly-Fleetville Baptist Churches, in Pennsylvania, where Mina became pastor in February 1972. In a letter to Erma Shaw, dated May 14, 1972, Mina wrote: "my mother and I are very happily located in Waverly. We have a nice large parsonage....My mother has quite a problem with angina, so I do not expect she will be able to attend the picnic." It was then being planned for Hartland, in August 1972.

In May 1973, Elsie became ill. Mina and Melvin decided to bring her back to her home area. They were accompanied by a nurse. The trip took 13 hours with three drivers taking turns at the wheel. They took Elsie to St. Stephen Hospital, in New Brunswick, where she was a patient from Wednesday to Sunday. Then they moved her to a nursing home in Lubec, Maine. Campobello didn't have one then. Elsie died June 13,

1973, in Lubec, three weeks after she returned from Pennsylvania.24

There is a family monument in the cemetery on North Road, Campobello. It is a gravestone with very legible letters:

COREY
February 29, 1896 Ivan   February 28, 1963
    his wife
August 12, 1898 Elsie M.   June 13, 1973
February 14, 1930 Inez   October 3, 1938
September 12, 1926 Mina E   ———

Descendants of Ivan and Elsie Corey

Their six children grew up in the home of their grandparents, Charles and Elizabeth Corey.

Mina Corey, born September 12, 1926

After graduating from the new school on Campobello in June 1944, Mina spent two years working in an office in Saint John, N.B. During that time she "became aware of a very clear call from God to prepare for full time Christian service." She graduated from Gordon College, Boston, Mass, worked two more years "in the business world", then entered Eastern Baptist Seminary, Philadelphia. From that school she received two degrees: Bachelor of Divinity and Master of Religious Education. In September 1957, Mina became Institutional Chaplain at Sleighton Farm School, in

Mina, high-school graduation.

the Philadelphia area. During that ministry she was ordained at the Brandywine Baptist Church in Chadds Ford, Pa., on May 28, 1962. She also received additional training in the area of hospital chaplincy. After serving twelve years in the Institutional Chaplaincy , Mina accepted a call to be the Minister of Education and Youth at the Broadway Baptist Church in Paterson, N.J. From there she went to Waverly, Pa. On February 27, 1972, Rev. Mina E. Corey was installed as pastor of the Waverly-Fleetville Baptist Churches. Her brother, Rev. Melvin R. Corey, then pastor of First Pentecostal Church, Williamsport, Pa., gave the installation prayer. Mina has also served in New Jersey and New York.

In recent years she has been serving as an interim pastor with the American Baptist Churches, U.S.A. They arranged the interims. Her brother, Ivan, said, "I visited her in 1990. She has stored her belongings in Williamsport, Pa., apparently with the intention to return there in retirement." In November, 1991, she wrote from S. Williamsport, Pa. Since then she has returned to serving churches in New York State. She concluded one ministry in January 1993. In February 1993 she went to a church at Castorland, near Watertown, N.Y., where she had earlier served as an interim pastor. The congregation invited her back. On March 12, 1997, Lalia reported that Mina had returned to Williamsport to rest for six months. On July 30, 1997, David Mitchell said, "Mina is re-evaluating her ministry, and deciding what to do. Perhaps more interim ministry."

Charles Daggett Corey

Ivan's eldest son, Charles, born May 7, 1928, is called Charlie to distinguish him from his grandfather. Charlie is living on the same plot of land where his grandparents, Charles and Elizabeth Corey, lived most of their married life. Charlie married Lillian Chute. He said, "Uncle Jud married us in July 1951, at the home of her brother, Edwin Chute." He lived "in the valley, by the breakwater".

The young couple's first dwelling was Aunt Stella's house. Charlie said, "My wife and I lived there three and a half years after we got married..." Later they built their own home within 50 feet of the home of his parents and grandparents, on the same plot of land. At that time Charlie's father, Ivan, his mother, Elsie, and his grandmother, Elizabeth, were still living in the old house. It has since been demolished.

Charlie has engaged in fishing. In the 90's Charlie, in partnership with his son, Carl, and his brother Ivan, had an enterprise in salmon farming at Welshpool. In February 1993 Charlie underwent heart by-pass surgery in the Saint John Regional Hospital.

Besides their son Carl, born 1961, Charlie and Lillian have a daughter, Inez, born 1952. Inez is married to Theodore Olson. They live in Lubec, Maine. They have two children: Jason, born July 7, 1971, and Trevor, born August 27, 1976. Trevor is in the U.S. Air Force.

Melvin

Second son of Ivan, Melvin Robert Corey, was born May 15, 1931. After a short stint at fishing, he left the island early in his life to prepare for a ministry. On March 11, 1953, Melvin was granted his first license to preach by the United Pentecostal Church, Fredericton, N.B. He has had a mixed career: a singing and preaching ministry and a painting trade. Mel Corey's letterhead from Freeburg, Penna.; publicized his "Country Gospeltime" radio program: "Sing Unto the Lord", described as "the very best in country gospel music". It was broadcast from WSEW, Selinsgrove, Pa. In later years Melvin's main work, while his health permitted, was in contract painting, interior and exterior.

Melvin has had serious problems with his health. A heart condition resulted in six-way bypass surgery in 1991. He has suffered from diabetes, which has made healing difficult. Leg injuries from his ladder rungs left sores that resisted healing. He has also had sores on his feet. For a time he was in a wheel chair to give his foot a rest. When he arrived in Knowlesville in July 1993 for the Corey reunion, he had one foot in a cast.

At that gathering he noted the 40th anniversary of his first license. He mentioned Pastor Jacques. Melvin also spoke of 25 years in radio ministry and 32 years in contract painting.

For some years Melvin has made his home in Williamsport, Pa. He has had some sojourns in other areas, which have continued into recent years. On July 30, 1997 David Mitchell reported, "Mel is again in California." He was reported back in Williamsport in October 1997.

Melvin Robert Corey was married to Alma Hooper. They had three children: Debbie, Angela and Melvin. Melvin, Sr. died August 9, 2001.

Debbie, born March 8, 1957, married Alan Jones. Their children are: Corey, born May 21, 1986, and Jeremy, born October 18, 1991. The family lives in South Carolina.

Angela, born January 8, 1962, married Rich Osgood. They live in Williamsport, Pa.

Melvin Jr., born October 27, 1964, married Hope Eisenhauer. Their children are: Heather, born November 8, 1983; Trisha born May 1, 1986, and Travis, born June 13, 1990. The family lives in Lewisport, Pa.

Lalia Morehouse

Youngest daughter of Ivan and Elsie Corey, Lalia Marie Corey, was born August 10, 1932. She graduated from Campobello High School. On October 1, 1949, Lalia married Fred Morehouse.

Fred is a veteran of W.W.II with extensive experience on continental Europe, starting in Italy. He spoke of fighting at the

Senna Dykes, then crossing to the west side of Italy. He said, "We left Fort Leghorn in March 1945. In a five-day move we passed through Italy, France and Belgium, and into Germany." His unit arrived in Holland in April, 1945, while fighting was continuing there.

Lalia and Fred have lived on Campobello Island, at Lincoln and at Zealand. In 1968 they built a new house on Claudie Road, Lower Douglas, near Nashwaaksis, N.B. Erma Shaw spoke of going there with Kate Britton to visit them soon after they moved into their new house.

The writer has visited Lalia and Fred several times on Claudie Road. She has been very helpful in supplying data about the Charles Corey family for this history. She has also lent photos for the book. Lalia is an ardent photographer and collector of photographs. She has volumes of family photos, orderly mounted in albums. Lalia and Fred have five children, now all adults: Connie, Eunice, Ira, Mina and Owen.

Connie Goodine

Connie, born August 7, 1952, is married to Larry Goodine, who was from Fredericton. They live in Calgary. For some years Larry has worked for the city of Calgary in electrical inspection. Connie is a legal secretary. Beginning in December 1992, she worked for a firm that writes tax laws. She has since returned to working as a legal secretary.

Connie will be remembered for making a video of the 1991 program in Knowlesville wherein Jud Corey played the role of his grandfather, Alfred E. Corey. When Connie needed more tape to complete the coverage of the program, she was assisted by John Shaw. Connie and Larry have three children: Kerry, born August 6, 1980; Jared, born January 12, 1987; and Rebecca, born November 15, 1989.

Eunice

Eunice Gill, born July 31, 1956, lives and works in Fredericton, having moved there from Lincoln, N.B. She worked as manager of Mr. Photo at King's Place, and later in photo finishing for Wal-Mart at Regent Mall. She has one boy, Jason, born May 29, 1984.

Ira

Ira, born January 25, 1965 first son of Lalia and Fred, is named for his grandfather Morehouse, and his great-great uncle, Ira Corey. Ira Morehouse has worked for City Transit, Fredericton. Now he is self-employed. His enterprises are: Perma Shine, and playing in a Fredericton area band. He is the lead guitarist. In music Ira is following the pattern of great grandfather, Charles Corey, who played in a band in his early life. I have heard Ira practise at the home of his parents in Lower Douglas. He makes his electric guitar sound like a piano. He lives at Lincoln, N.B.

Mina

Mina, born July 17, 1966, third daughter of Lalia and Fred, lives on Vancouver Island, B.C. She also worked for a photographer. Her job was putting make-up on customers in the studio. She gave up the job when her baby, Mitchell Skidnuk, was born December 4, 1993.

Owen

Owen, born November, 1969, second son and youngest of Lalia's family, lives in Hawkley, on the western outskirts of Toronto. He delivers heavy cylinders of liquid air, by truck. Earlier he delivered seat covers for automobiles.

Ivan Alfred Corey

Ivan Alfred Corey, born July 6, 1936, on Campobello Island, is the youngest of the family of Ivan Grant Corey. After completing high school on the island, he began preparing for a career in teaching.

In 1957, at time of the death of his great uncle, Ira Corey, Ivan was a student at Teacher's College, Fredericton. He clearly recalls that his father joined him in Fredericton, having rode with the school principal from Campobello to Fredericton. Relatives — Kate and Jim Hovey, perhaps? took them to Carleton County to the funeral. Ivan, Jr. remembers that while he was living in Fredericton he visited Kate and Jim Hovey on George St. He says Jimmie Miller was there too. Another relative Ivan met during his short teaching career in New Brunswick was Shirley Corey Brooks.

Most of Ivan's teaching career was in Maine. In 1959 he went to Washington State Teachers College at Machias, — now University of Maine, at Machias. While there he met Beverley Porter. In summer of 1960 he worked on road construction connecting with the bridge then being built to Lubec. Ivan's first teaching in Maine was at Calais. While teaching there he attended evening classes at University of Maine in Orono, for eight semesters, in the late 60's and early 70's. He travelled the airline route from Calais. Five dollars worth of gas took him to Orono and back.

Beverley was also teaching. She taught in Lubec, Maine, while living on Campobello. That was before 1962 when the bridge linked the island to Maine. She crossed in a punt. Later she taught in Charlotte, Maine; still later in Calais.

On November 11, 1961, Ivan Corey and Beverley Porter were married. Beverley was born in Massachusetts, the daughter of Albert Victor Porter and Muriel Frances Alexander. They were island people. Beverley told the writer, "The Rev. Judson A. Corey married my father and mother in 1919, at Wilson's

Beach, perhaps in the parsonage." The Alexanders maintained a house on the island which Ivan and Beverley now occupy.

In 1971, after a few years of teaching in Calais, Ivan became, at age 35, a Superintendent of Schools, a position he held for 15 or 16 years. During that career he met two second cousins, also superintendents in Maine. One was Joe McBrine, son of Jud McBrine who lived in Haynesville, Maine. The other was William MacDonnell, whose folks lived in New York City, and later in Houlton, Me.

In 1986 Ivan gave up his position as superintendent. He and Beverley retired to the Alexander home on the island. Ivan joined with his brother Charlie in acquaculture. In 1993 Ivan and Beverley returned to Maine. He was principal of a school in Calais for one year. Then they sold their house at Red Beach, eight miles outside Calais.

It was time to return to Campobello to stay. Ivan said, "We came in spring of 1994." It was also time to nurture his health. In August 1994 he had heart by-pass surgery. He is also diabetic. He said, "I'm type two. I started taking the pill in 1991". He appears to be well informed about the history of the disease in the family, about his own condition, and to be managing his health very well.

On Campobello, Ivan Corey resumed working in salmon farming with his brother Charlie, Charlie's son Carl, and two other partners: Neil Calder and son Roger. When the writer and Margaret visited Ivan and Beverley on Saturday afternoon, September 28, 1996, Ivan was watching the clock. He said, "I have to leave in 20 minutes to go and feed the salmon." He explained, "We feed seven days a week. All the partners take their turns feeding on Saturdays and Sundays." Nevertheless he took time to review some of his career and some family history.

Ivan and Beverley have one son Scott Corey, born July 27, 1964. His wife, Susan, is a U.S. Marine Officer. They have three children. Ivan told us, "In July (1996) we met our latest grandchild." She was born in Japan. Susan has been on duty in

Japan. The family lived there for three years. In summer of 1996 Susan was on duty at a naval station in Cutler, Maine, where the family was then living.

On Sunday afternoon we returned for a more leisurely visit. Then we met Scott and the three bright winsome children under his care:

    Joslyn   born April 16, 1990;
    Ivan Alfred   born April 1, 1992;
    Brianne   born June 19, 1995, in Japan.

The mother was on duty.

On August 31, 1997 we stopped again briefly, at Ivan Corey's. We met the Marine Officer, Scott's wife, a friendly, outgoing person. Scott was there also; he was on leave. He had taken a job servicing oilrigs in the Gulf of Mexico. He has travelled far with the Merchant Navy.

We also visited Charlie Corey and Noel Mitchell's family. That weekend several Corey relatives visited on the island: Gordon and Esta Corey, Jud and Margaret Corey, Gerald and Betty Corey and Clair and Mildred Shirley. Lalia Morehouse and daughter Connie had been there the previous week.

In 1997 Ivan seemed more at ease. That spring the Coreys and their partners had sold their salmon farm to Connors Brothers. Ivan had bought a pleasure boat in Nova Scotia. His cousin, Gerald Corey had gone to Nova Scotia with him to bring it by trailer.

Noel Corey: Work, Family Residence and Moves

During most of the years of W.W.II Noel was employed in Saint John, while Bessie and their boys continued to live on Campobello. In the years following the war Noel's pursuit of work kept him on the move. There was a brief period, however, when he was able to work on Campobello and live at home.

In 1948 electric power came to Campobello Island. Then the island people saw the pay-off of Noel's foresight in learning his trade. He got a lot of work wiring houses, at about $75.00 per house. E'er long, pursuit of work put him on the move again. He worked on electrical contracting jobs in Ontario; he had several sojourns there. He also worked in Nova Scotia.

Family residence continued in the Thurber house. It was very pleasant in summer but cold in winter. Gerald remembers having to dress by the wood stove in winter. Part of the time some of Noel's maiden aunts lived there also. Randall said, "Agnes Thurber died when I was a baby, 1941." Aunt Stell moved back from the States in 1948. The Thurber house came to be known as Aunt Stell's house. She outlived the other maiden sisters, and hence was the final owner of the house." Noel Corey's family remained in the Thurber house until 1950. Then the Calder homestead, the home of Eddie Calder, Bessie Corey's grandfather, opened to the Corey family.

More than a decade of pursuing work away from home while the family continued living on Campobello, and concern about the future for his sons, prompted Noel to move from the island. The place where he found work most often was Saint John. The family had lived there with him at intervals. In 1953, he and Bessie and their boys made a permanent move to Saint John. That year Noel worked at Irving Pulp and Paper Mill at Reversing Falls doing electrical wiring on a construction job. Later he worked on Simonds High School.

The move to Saint John did not immediately bring permanent residence. The family lived in a number of neighborhoods; on the West Side, and in the North End, including Douglas Avenue. Five years after Noel's family began residence in Saint John, eldest son, Gerald, found a bride. On July 5, 1958, he married Betty London who grew up in the North End of Saint John. Betty and her mother-in-law, Bessie, became the discoverers of a permanent house for the Coreys. In the spring of 1963 Bessie and Betty, on an exploration, discovered a new house that was being built in Red Head, in East Saint John.

There the Noel Corey family settled. However, Bessy's time in that house was tragically cut short.

The Corey families moved to Red Head in 1963. In 1966 Gerald and Betty moved to Rochester, N.H. While they were living in Rochester Gerald's mother, Bessie, suffered a fatal accident.

On June 6, 1967, Bessie and Noel were on their way to Rochester to visit Gerald and Betty and Cheryl. On the Maine Turnpike, near Biddeford, a tire blew. Noel reported afterwards that his car went completely out of his control. Bessie and Noel were both taken to hospital in Biddeford. Bessie was unconscious. She died there on June 11th, never having regained consciousness. Her funeral was in Saint John, N.B. Noel could not attend the funeral. He was in hospital for several more days in Biddeford. Niece, Lalia Morehouse, has very kind memories of Bessie. She said, "Bessie was almost a mother to me. She kept me a lot."

The loss of Bessie at the early age of 57 was very difficult for Noel. He said to his son Gerald, "Come home!" Gerald, recalling it long afterwards, said, "We couldn't respond immediately. We had bought furniture. Customs required a full year of ownership before we could enter it in Canada." In 1967 Gerald, Betty and Cheryl brought their mobile home back to New Brunswick, at Quispamsis. Gerald worked for McAvity Crane.

In 1968 Noel Corey married Marian Bernice Allingham, a cousin of Bessie, and an acquaintance of early years on Campobello. She was born at Welshpool. Marian was the widow of Michael Flynn of Boston, Mass. who died of cancer. Marian worked as a seamstress for a dry cleaning company in Cambridge, Mass. After being widowed, Marian moved to Bangor and cooked in a residence for college girls. Cooking was an art she had practised on Campobello for summer residents. From Bangor, Marian came to Saint John and cooked for Mrs. Steed. Through a mutual acquaintance at Calvary Temple, Noel

Corey and Marian revived an old romance. Gerald and Betty returned to U.S.A. Gerald worked as a machinist in the Woodland Mill, in Maine. It produced newsprint and crafts. In 1972 Gerald and family were back in New Brunswick, and before long, living in Red Head.

Though Noel remarried about a year after being widowed, the question remained whether he recovered from the loss of Bessie. Gerald said his father continued working past retirement age, right up to age 73, the last year of his life. That year he spent several weeks in St. Joseph's Hospital, Saint John, where he died October 26, 1973.

The Sons and Grandchildren of Noel and Bessie Corey

Until the spring of 1999 all three sons of Noel and Bessie were living in the Red Head neighborhood of East Saint John — had been for several years. Each had his own house.

Gerald and Randall have trades. Both had some experience working with their father, Noel, in electrical wiring. Gerald began to learn the trade, but didn't like running wires. Randall continued apprenticing with his father and qualified for the trade. Gerald switched to the machinist trade. Beginning in 1976 the two brothers worked for Irving Oil Refinery in Saint John - Gerald as a machinist; Randall as an electrician

Gerald and Betty Corey

Through reading <u>The Story of Knowlesville</u>, Betty discovered that, like Gerald, she also has roots in Carleton County, N.B. She said, "My grandfather came from there and my father was born in Bristol, N.B." At a Corey Reunion in Knowlesville Betty made another discovery: John Long, who delivered her ceramic supplies for the ceramics business she had in Red Head, is a relative. He is the grandson of Erma Corey Shaw.

Gerald's deeper roots are on Campobello Island. He and

Betty have long maintained a summer place there, have made frequent visits, and have enjoyed boating. In the spring of 1998 Gerald inherited a house on the island that had long been in his mother's family. The house was built in 1912 and belonged to Gerald's grandparents, Harry and Agnes Calder.

The last Calder family members to occupy the house were an unmarried daughter and son of Harry and Agnes. They lived there 18 years together. The daughter, Lillian Calder, died in 1993. The son, Gerald Calder, lived five years longer, until April 1998 when he died in the Regional Hospital in Saint John, after spending his last winter with his nephew Gerald Corey, and Betty Corey in East Saint John. In the summer of 1998 Gerald and Betty spent vacation time renovating the Calder house on the island.

In the spring of 1999 Gerald Corey took retirement from Irving Oil Refinery; he and Betty sold their house in Red Head and moved to Campobello. Gerald's brother, Harry, helped him move several truck and van loads of household belongings to the Calder house on the island. In summer of 1999 Gerald was renovating: restoring the dining room, and preparing for an addition, for another bedroom and a second bathroom. The footing was poured late in summer. The house is located on North Road, three houses north of Deer Island Ferry terminal. Gerald's cousin, Ivan Corey, lives five houses north of the ferry terminal. Gerald says relatives are welcome. The teapot will be on.

Gerald and Betty Corey have a daughter: Cheryl Ann, born June 30, 1964, and a son Blair Grant, born August 30, 1972.

Beginning in 1987 Cheryl lived, worked, and attended university in Ontario. In September, 1996, she married Chris Gerardi. Gerald and Betty attended the wedding in Kitchener, Ontario. Cheryl and Chris have a son, Dakoda, born November 9, 1998.

In April 1998 Chris suffered a paralyzing accident in a

race on a dirt bike. For a year and a half he has been confined to hospital in London, Ontario, undergoing rehabilitation. He has had an expensive pacemaker installed to enable him to breathe. He expects to be coming home for one day, November 9th, the baby's birthday. A month later he expects to be able to stay at home.

Cheryl and the baby are living in a new house in Waterloo, Ontario, made possible by a generous businessman who wrote a cheque for $65,000. The man and his son were present at the bike race. The same benefactor also paid the balance remaining on the cost of the pacemaker after government grants. Three times a week Cheryl has been making the 120 km journey from Waterloo to Kitchener to visit Chris. Cheryl and the baby visited Gerald and Betty on Campobello in early summer 1999. In August Gerald and Betty visited Cheryl in the new house in Waterloo.

Blair Grant Corey is living and working in Saint John. He is making his home in the North End. He and Dawn Porter have a son, Brandon, born November 23, 1998. Blair also has a daughter, Haley Elizabeth, born 1995. Haley visited Betty and Gerald on Campobello, summer 1999.

Randall Corey

In 1958 Randall graduated from Saint John Vocational School with a trade and ready for apprenticeship. He apprenticed with his Dad. Then he worked as an electrician on construction jobs for nine years. On July 27, 1963, the year Noel and family moved to Red Head, Randall married Judy Cooke. They lived on Belmont St. E. before joining the other Corey families in Red Head. Since 1979 they have been in their permanent home on Red Head Road.

In 1966 Randall went to work for N.B. Power. Since 1976 Randall has been employed with Irving Oil Refinery in E. Saint John in the electrical field. Judy has been teaching school.

She keeps a genealogical table of all the descendants of Charles and Elizabeth Corey.

Randall and Judy had three sons:
Mark Randall Corey, b. July 31, 1967, d. July 31, 1967
Dean Douglas Corey, b. January 3, 1970, and
Dwight Charles Corey, b. October 19, 1973.

Both sons are educated for professions. Dean prepared for teaching with two degrees: B.A. and B.Ed. He completed the last part of his course work at Machias, Me. After volunteer, substitute, and half-time teaching in Saint John area schools, Dean is now a full time employee of District 8 School Board. His middle school teaching position is at Fundy Shores School, Maces Bay, N.B. Dwight Charles Corey has a business degree from UNBSJ.

Both sons are now married. Dwight married Angelisa Belyea, September 12, 1997. They have a daughter: Clarissa Sabrina Victoria, born May 8, 1998 and a son, Aston Joshua, born November 30, 2001. Dean married Michelle Rose Grant of South Bay, Saint John, on July 17, 1999. They are living in Saint John.

Harry Douglas Corey and Family

Harry, the youngest of Noel Corey's sons, was born June 3, 1946, in St. Stephen Hospital. Except for a few months in Woodbridge, Ontario, when his father was on a job there, Harry lived on Campobello Island until 1953 when the family moved to Saint John.

On June 29, 1968, Harry married Beverley Schnare of Halifax. They met in the senior choir at Calvary Temple. Harry and family live in the house that Noel and Bessie bought in 1963, in Red Head. Harry describes his father's generosity to him. When Harry married, Noel said, "You can have this house; you take over the mortgage payments and it'll be yours. My other two sons already have houses. This will help you get a start." Noel made that offer even though he was marrying his second wife that same year. He decided to go to an apartment rather than have the up-keep of a house.

Harry runs a life and liability insurance business out of his own house. He began as an agent for North American Life. About five years ago he became a broker. He deals mainly with Industrial Alliance; he also places insurance with Hartford Life and Royal Life. Harry is happy being a broker. He says, "I now work for people rather than for a company. I enjoy helping people." In his helping role he identifies with his father. Harry was happy to find that people on Campobello had good memories of his father and his Uncle Ivan. He recalled, "In 1992 I went to Campobello to promote insurance." He said, in many houses he was told stories: "Your father wired this house; or, your uncle did the plumbing in this house."

Harry likes discovering relatives and having contacts with them. At a meeting of insurance agents in Fredericton in 1999, he discovered Kathy Corey. Also in 1999 Harry's cousin Melvin Corey phoned from USA to get re-acquainted and to trade comments on country music, Wilf Carter and Hank Snow; and on gospel songs. Near the same time Lalia Morehouse phoned and subsequently sent four photos "of me, my Mom and Dad, and my brothers."

Beverley Corey is employed by Olsten Health Services. She cares for sick and elderly people in their homes. Harry and Beverley had three children:

Christa Beverley Francis, b. March 16, 1971;
d. June 24, 1983;
Daniel Douglas, b. August 13, 1975;
Kimberlee Dawn, b. August 30, 1979.
Christa died of bone cancer at age 12.

Daniel Douglas Corey graduated from Simonds High School with "high honours" in June 1993. He was the valedictorian of his class. He studied two years at UNBSJ. In 1995 he transferred to Dalhousie University, Halifax, and studied pharmacy. In 1999 he graduated from Dalhousie with a degree in pharmacy. He worked a few weeks in St. Stephen in a Superstore Pharmacy. Then an opportunity opened for him near home. He is now a fully licensed pharmacist at Shoppers Drug Mart, Parkway Mall, E. Saint John. On October 7, 2000 Daniel married Karen Joleen Elliott, from Grand Manan, N.B. They have a daughter, Abigail Kristine. They live in Millidgeville.

Kimberlee Dawn Corey graduated from St. Vincent's High School in Saint John in June 1997. She took one year in the faculty of arts at UNBSJ. In fall of 1998 she switched to Business Technology at New Brunswick Community College, Grandview Ave., East Saint John, not far from home. In September 1999 she started her second year in the business course at NBCC. In 2001-02 she took the one-year course at University of Cape Breton to obtain a business degree. Her ambition is to enter a marketing field, perhaps with a business of her own. She is a hockey enthusiast, and especially enjoys the games of Saint John Flames.

The sons, daughters-in-law, and grandchildren of Noel were very kind to his widow, Marian Allingham. She lived more than 20 years after being widowed from Noel. Judy and Randall Corey and their boys visited Marian. Betty and Gerald also visited her. From Red Head she went to an apartment on Rockland Road.

Marian was fortunate in having a nephew, Arthur Ingersoll. He and his wife, Lois, befriended Marion, giving much help. Later she lived in an apartment in their house. In 1980 they had to vacate that property for the new road to the new hospital. Marian then went to an apartment in Stephenson Tower, Millidge Ave. Lois and Art took her to the Wesleyan Church, nearby.

After 12 or 13 years in Stephenson Tower apartment, Marian suffered a fall. She was found by Lois on a Sunday morning. Lois went with her in the ambulance to St. Joseph's Hospital. It was her first hospital admission in her life. Permanent damage from the fall prevented her returning to her apartment. Lois and Art helped her find Burns Special Care Home, at Forest Hills, E. Saint John. There she made her home until she suffered congestive heart failure and was taken again to St. Joseph's Hospital, where she "died very peacefully." Lois and Art were her companions until her end, on April 1, 1994.[25]

We have told the story of Charles and Elizabeth Corey and their descendants. One hundred years after his birth, Charles' birthday was marked by the first organized summer gathering of the descendants of Alfred and Lucretia Corey. The gathering was on July 26, 1968, at the Women's Institute Hall, Simonds, N.B. On September 28, 1996, at his home on Campobello, Ivan Alfred Corey recalled the gathering, and attendance by members of the Charles Ivan branch. Ivan, Jr. enumerated:

Mel with three children, Charlie with two, Lalia with all her children, and himself with son, Scott. All but Mina. Though not annual, the gathering continues.

[1]Gladstone, W.E., editor, Orations of British Orators, revised edition, Vol. II, p.392

[2]Erma Corey Shaw

[3]Ibid

[4]The Story of Knowlesville, p.89

[5]Record Book, p.7 and 48-50, kept by Harry W. Machum, and Charles H. Gayton, secretaries

[6]See Chap. II

[7]Charlie Corey, Ivan Corey, Jr., and Lalia Morehouse all remember many family references to the birth of their father in Knowlesville

[8] Erma Corey Shaw and Ivan Corey, Jr.

[9] Erma Corey Shaw

[10] Erma Corey Shaw, Charlie Corey, and Lalia Morehouse

[11] Gerald and Randall Corey and Lalia Morehouse

[12] Obituaries of Sylvanus and Edith Thurber

[13] Newspaper report of wedding

[14] Lalia Morehouse

[15] Gerald Corey

[16] Lalia Morehouse and Gerald Corey

[17] Lalia Morehouse

[18] See Chapter VII

[19] See The Story of Knowlesville, p.39

[20] Newspaper report of wedding

[21] From David Mitchell; he said his father was an excellent draftsman

[22] Arthur T. Doyle, The Premiers of New Brunswick, (Fredericton: Brunswick Press, 1983) p.61f.

[23] Conversation with the writer during a visit on Noel's birthday, September 28, 1996. Affirmed by Lalia

[24] Lalia Morehouse

[25] From conversations with Judy and Betty Corey and Lois Ingersoll, October 1997

CHAPTER XI

1870 JUDSON ALBERT COREY 1952
m.c. 1899, in Lewiston, Maine
1874 Eliza Alice Howlett 1955

Judson A. Corey, fourth child, and second son of Alfred and Lucretia Corey, was born in Maine, August 1, 1870, during the family's brief sojourn there. When the family returned to New Brunswick, about 1874, Judson was next to the youngest of the children, then numbering five. Their first home in New Brunswick was a log cabin, probably erected the summer they arrived.[1]

The Knowlesville school records show that Judson was enrolled as a pupil by 1878.[2] The only other references to Judson's childhood and youth we found are in the minutes of "Pride of Aberdeen Lodge"[3], a "Lodge of Good Templars", which was organized at a meeting in the Baptist Church in Knowlesville, on October 1, 1886. Judson's father, mother and three of his siblings: Charles, Alma and Ida were charter members.

The name, Judson Corey, appears many times in the secretary's minutes of the weekly meetings, especially in connection with debates and entertainment. He is first mentioned as a participant for the affirmative in a debate: "Resolved that there is more true enjoyment in pursuit than in possession." That was on December 4, 1886, when he was age 16. On December 11, 1886 he volunteered, with other members, "to entertain the Lodge at its next meeting."[4] On March 12, 1887 he gave a reading: "Mule and Bees."[5] On March 19, he was leading the affirmative in the debate: "Resolved that the mechanic is of more benefit to the country than the farmer."[6] James Hobbs was leader of the negative. At the same meeting Judson was appointed with his sister, Ida, and others, "as Literary Committee to entertain Lodge at our next meeting."[7]

This interesting minute book, giving glimpses of Judson A. Corey in his teens, seems to show signs of social leadership and good humour. The humorous stories he later told for entertainment also give us a few glimpses into his youth and seem to indicate an early developing ability to see the humour in many situations.

One story he told was about a man bringing his bride home to his farmhouse. He stopped his horse in front of the door, ran into the house, found an old coat and told his bride, "You can sew buttons on this while I'm unharnessing and stabling the horse." How did that story leak out? "I companioned with their son. One rainy day we were playing upstairs. The parents fell into a quarrel. She reminded him of that incident, unaware that the story was coming up through the ceiling."

Early Work

Through memories shared incidentally, we also have a few glimpses into Judson A. Corey's early work experiences. I recall a scene in the yard of the Miller home in Glassville on the afternoon of the funeral of Judson's brother-in-law, R. James Miller, at the beginning of October 1937. Waiting in the yard after the funeral was a Glassville area resident. He told my father, "I want to see Jud Corey." When the Rev. J.A. Corey emerged from the house he and the waiting man had a friendly greeting and a brief review of their camaraderie on river drives, years earlier — probably in Maine, but perhaps in New Brunswick. Later the writer heard J.A. Corey speak about working on the Penobscot River in lumbering and log driving. It even came up in a sermon.

Marriage and Family

In the 1890's it appears that Judson's pursuit of work in Maine brought him to Lewiston where he met and married Alice Howlett. Apparently they remained in Lewiston a few years. Sometime after the birth of their first two children — Alberta, 1900, and Earle, 1902 — Judson and Alice Corey returned to New Brunswick. Annie Ruth was born in Knowlesville, May 5, 1903, at the home of Judson's sister, Ida, and her husband Bill McBrine.

Erma Corey Shaw said, "Annie's birth was just before Uncle Jud took the family to Auburn where he could attend night school, in preparation for ministry." Thus the family embarked on a second sojourn in Maine with a specific purpose. The family lived in Auburn. Judson Corey worked in Lewiston. By day he worked as a cobbler. In the evening he attended classes. Eventually he also became the preacher for a Mission in Auburn. More of the story of J.A.Corey's life and work in Maine, and also of a brother and sister there at the same time is told in Chapter II. The story of Judson's return with his family to Knowlesville in 1910 is told in Chapter IV.

Successive pastorates were at:
Knowlesville and circuit 1910-13
Rusagonis, 1913-1918
Wilson's Beach, Campobello, 1918-1921
Hoyt Station 1921-1925

Keswick Ridge/Mactaquac 1925-35

In the autumn of 1925 the Rev. and Mrs. Judson A. Corey, accompanied by their three youngest children: David, Edna and Mildred, arrived in Keswick Ridge, N.B. They came from Hoyt Station in a 4-90 Chevrolet car. One of the first persons the Corey family met in Keswick Ridge was Harold Smith. He had bought a general store there in January 1925. The key to the Baptist Parsonage had been left at the store. Harold said, "They drove into the yard; I gave them the key." Thus began an acquaintance that would, e'er long, bring Harold into the Corey family. He recalled the curiosity and delight expressed by the youth of the Village when they gathered round the new family, especially the girls, when they observed that the minister's daughters were allowed to wear make-up — at least face powder.

Esther, the daughter Harold was to become interested in, did not arrive until later. She and her three elder siblings, Alberta, Earle and Annie, were all teaching school in other communities. They all came to live at the parsonage at the end of the school year — at least for the summer.

Scattering of Judson and Alice Corey's Children

By the time Judson and Alice Corey arrived in Keswick Ridge in 1925 their elder children were employed and the scattering process had begun. Soon the daughters began to marry — two in 1926. The eldest, Alberta, married Mayford Anthony on Campobello. Second daughter, Annie, married Albert Haines, in Presque Isle, Maine. The following summer, 1927, third daughter, Esther, married Harold Smith. Erma Shaw reported, "Esther was at my wedding on June 14, 1927." She accompanied her father, Rev. J.A. Corey, to Knowlesville where he married Erma to Allie Shaw, in the Baptist Church. Three weeks later, July 6, he married Esther to Harold Smith.

The wedding of Esther Corey and Harold Smith under an archway of flowers on the veranda of the Baptist parsonage at Keswick Ridge, drew many relatives of both families. For the rest of their life Esther and Harold retained a little booklet printed by Judson Press, containing part of the wedding service and the signatures of many guests. Clearly discernible in the picture, though the scale is small, are Ira and Nellie Corey and Kate and Jim Hovey. Jim is holding in his arms their first daughter, Jean, born December 14, 1926. Signatures in the booklet include: James Miller, Mr. and

Mrs. James A. Hovey, Mr. and Mrs. Ira T. Corey, Mrs. Albert Haines, Alfred Corey, David W. Corey, Edna Corey, Mildred Corey. Also there are four persons named Howlett: B.; E.A.; and two with first names illegible — relatives of Alice Corey.

Besides the three eldest daughters, the eldest son, Earle, also married within two years of the family's move to Keswick Ridge. Before his marriage Earle ventured in several work experiences.

In company with a group from Campobello, including Mayford Anthony and a Newman boy, Earle went on a harvest excursion to Western Canada. The boys made amusement of Earle's eagerness to reach the grain fields of the prairies. They said that at times he ran ahead of the train.[8] The farm Earle worked on must have been in Alberta. He told the writer about meeting Wilmot Ricker and family at church and of being invited to supper at their house. Earle knew that Rickers had moved to Alberta from Knowlesville.Earle's Uncle Ira Corey had accompanied that family to the West in 1906, and worked for them for a summer.

Earle taught school briefly. Not liking teaching, he worked in a sawmill. He also tried a fish business for one summer. He acquired a Model T. Ford pick-up. He bought fish on Campobello Island, and sold them in the country surrounding Fredericton. The business was short-lived; he had difficulty making the payments on his truck.

Still early in life, Earle went to Massachusetts. Having been born in Lewiston, Maine, it was not difficult to migrate to U.S.A. seeking work. But he didn't look for a wife in Massachusetts; he already had a girlfriend, Lois Morgan of Nasonworth, before he went to Western Canada on the Harvest Excursion. Years later she recalled receiving a letter from the West in which he described his treatment of a finger he had injured in New Brunswick before leaving. Apparently soon after becoming established permanently in Massachusetts Earle returned to New Brunswick for his bride. His father, Rev. J.A.

Corey married Earle and Lois at Nasonworth, on September 21, 1926.

The Ministry at Keswick Ridge and Mactaquac

With three daughters and a son — half their family — married and establishing their own homes, Judson and Alice Corey pursued the work of their new parish, while the second half of their family pursued education and moved toward independence.

Rev. J.A. Corey had three churches on his circuit. The Mactaquac church was about a mile and a half from the parsonage at Keswick Ridge. There was a smaller congregation at Scotch Settlement. There was also another fairly large congregation on the west side of the Saint John River at Kingsclear. In winter he drove his horse and sleigh across the river on the ice. In summer he took his car across the river on a ferry. The ferry landing was about two miles from the Keswick Ridge parsonage.

Horse and sleigh was the only means of travel on country roads in winter. Nobody then expected that the wind-swept roads, often blocked by drifts, would ever be kept open in winter for travel by automobile. The Baptist minister was not alone on the roads. His neighbour and good friend, Dr. Robertson, had five horses. He kept them stabled at farms along this route.[9] The roads, often heavy with falling and drifting snow, could exhaust a horse. He had a system somewhat comparable to the earlier English stagecoach practice of changing horses at intervals along the route. Thus he could speed to families who called him from all over the district.

The mailman, Wilfred Jewett, also had several horses stabled at farms along his route. Thus he delivered mail on daylong treks over the snow-covered roads. Also he collected and dispatched mail in the Village of Keswick Ridge. He picked up a bag of mail from the Post Office in Harold Smith's store, delivered it to the Railroad Station, and brought another bag from the Station to the Post Office. Jewett's delivery route extended ten miles up the river, then made a circle around Scotch Lake.

J.A. Corey had a good horse, which took him to his Sunday services and on a lot of parish visits in winter. His faithful horse served him in other ways also. One spring a neighbour, a farmer, made a generous offer: "There's a field you can plant in potatoes." The minister's horse and Harold Smith's horse were harnessed as a team to the plow, harrow and other implements. Thus they planted and harvested a good crop of potatoes and beans.

In his later years at Keswick Ridge the Reverend J.A. Corey was in need of a replacement horse. His brother, Ira Corey, in E. Knowlesville had an ageing driving horse named Dick. In his younger days he had a reputation for speed. He was still good for a trot. Ira got Clarence LaPage to transport old Dick on his truck down through Millville to Keswick Ridge on a cold December day before much snow had accumulated. Covered with blankets and banked with bales of hay and bags of oats, old Dick rode in comfort.

In winter when the snow brought cars to a standstill, old Dick took the pastor to their churches on Sundays and to pastoral visits through the week. Often Alice Corey accompanied him. She appreciated one special comfort. When the pastor prepared to harness the horse he removed his blanket, nicely warmed by body heat, folded it, and placed it in the bottom of the sleigh. It formed a comfortable, warm pad to keep their feet warm for the journey. She told an amusing story about old Dick. Sometimes he started a journey with a limp. She would say, "Oh dear, Jud, I don't like to drive behind a lame horse." When they arrived at a fork in the road, if he reined into the road that led to the church of the shortest distance, old Dick suddenly stopped his limp. He had the luxury of summer holidays in pasture. Keswick Ridge was old Dick's final home. He was also Pastor Corey's last horse. Winter road plowing came about the time old Dick went to his rest.

While Pastor and Alice Corey carried on their ministry at Keswick Ridge/Mactaquac, their four youngest children were finding their places in the world. In the late 20's and early 30's the two younger sons, Alfred and David, also went through a period of search and struggle. Both became students at U.N.B., Fredericton. Alfred, arriving in Fredericton earlier, boarded with Mrs. Forbes. After Esther and Harold Smith moved to Fredericton, Alfred and David boarded with them.

Summer work, if available at all, was strenuous. One summer they rode bicycles door to door, selling silk stockings. Another summer they worked at sandblasting and painting on the Reversing Falls Bridge in Saint John. After two years at U.N.B. David sought regular employment. For a short while he worked as a salesman for Ted Burton, a chicken rancher on Regent Street, near Prospect. Alfred continued his studies at U.N.B.

The year 1933 brought a turning point to several members of the Corey family. David went to the U.S.A. for permanent employment. His brother-in-law, Harold Smith, recalled: "I was ill at home in Fredericton. David came to see me. He said, 'I've made up my mind to go to Gardner.' Soon, like his brother, Earle, he was employed with Heywood Wakefield." That same year Alfred graduated with a B.Sc. from U.N.B., Mildred went to Acadia University, and Rev. J.A. Corey was elected President of United Baptist Convention of the Maritime Provinces for one year, 1933-34. Edna worked at F.W. Woolworth's in Fredericton. She boarded with her sister Esther, and Harold Smith.

After U.N.B. Alfred experienced a brief period of uncertainty, apparently with a brief time at home. I remember one year he came to E. Knowlesville with his father for the annual hunt. Work was scarce in the 30's. Alfred's mother said the only job he ever refused was a half-day's threshing, for 25 cents because the dust gave him breathing trouble. At length he received a fellowship from the Fraser Lumber Co. to study at McGill University, Montreal.[10]

Move to Doaktown

For the Corey's, change and scattering was accelerating. In 1935 Rev. Judson and Alice Corey terminated their ten-year ministry at Keswick Ridge/Mactaquac and moved to Doaktown, on the Miramichi. That year Mildred graduated from Acadia University with a DHE. She lived briefly with her parents in Doaktown and worked briefly as a hairdresser in Newcastle.

It was in Doaktown that the writer was intimately involved with his Uncle Jud and Aunt Alice, and through them began high school. In the spring of 1938 he completed grade 8 at Knowlesville School and wrote high school entrance examinations at Hartland. A new teacher, Alice Rideout, came to E. Knowlesville, a school that traditionally covered grades 1-8. She agreed with my parents that she would help me with grade nine. Through the fall, into November, she helped me with French and other subjects.

Uncle Jud and Aunt Alice had told my mother and father that they would like to see me attend high school. My mother had sent some of her butter money to Eaton's mail order store in Moncton for a new suit for me to wear to church. When the annual hunting safari brought our uncle and aunt to East Knowlesville they were ready to take me back with them to Doaktown.

Near the end of their visit at the farm a very heavy snowfall came and blocked our road to all wheel traffic. The minister's car had to be pulled. My father had only one team - a pair of colts that hadn't gone to his lumber camp. Two neighbours, Ralph Boyd and Carvell MacKenzie brought teams. The three pairs of horses pulled the Hudson car - Aunt and Uncle in the front seat, I in the back - to Argyle, ploughing through deep snow.

At Argyle we connected with the ploughed road. That afternoon we travelled only as far as Glassville, where Jimmie Milller and Aunt Ad made us comfortable for the night. The morning was so extremely cold that the Hudson car didn't start until early noon, and then only with a tow by one of Jimmie's horses. On hard-packed snow we reached Fredericton before dark. After a hospitable supper and overnight at Esther and Harold Smith's we crossed the Saint John River and travelled toward the Miramichi. It was near dark when we reached Doaktown on a snow-covered road.

Before that venture into the unknown I had been as far as Woodstock. I was encountering a strange new world. On my first morning in Doaktown, Uncle Jud escorted me across the highway from the Baptist parsonage, past the Baptist church, across the South Road to the school. He introduced me to Ralph Howe, the high school teacher, who was also principal of the school. He directed me to a seat among the grade nine pupils. Through the long morning Mr. Howe moved from grade to grade. At length he came to our section and assigned questions: What beliefs did Voltair and Rouseau hold? The class was in a different section of Myers History from where I had been studying. After three weeks of classes and my reading of the French Revolution in the section of Myers they had studied all fall, I encountered a week of exams. Then I took the train to Juniper for a holiday at home.

Over two winters I observed a pastor, 68 years old in 1938, ministering to about six congregations — three each Sunday — morning, afternoon and evenings. I sometimes travelled with him down river to Blissfield, or up river to Ludlow. Some small communities gathered on a weeknight. In two or three communities he had "prayer meetings" though not all of them every week. One stormy Thursday night I accompanied him to Hazelton, and stood on the bumper or pushed to help him get to his prayer meeting. One village he reached by train, thus avoiding drifting snow.

Despite a demanding schedule the pastor managed to have some evenings at home. A little radio that Annie and Albert Haines had brought from Maine brought not only news, but also amusement, e.g., "The Green Hornet." On an occasional afternoon they could take time to laugh together over the "Eb and Zeb" program.

Rev. Judson A. Corey and Alice Corey, Baptist Parsonage, Doaktown.

Salmon

All through my first winter in Doaktown the boys at school talked about the black salmon run. When the ice ran down the river American sports fishermen came. Outfitting and guiding was a spring business. Rev. J.A. Corey didn't need a guide. He knew where the pools were and he was well equipped. In his study room he kept a supply of feathers of many colours, and deer tails, and a little vice to hold the hook while he arrayed it with feathers and hair, held in place by thread and shellac. When he cast one of his home-made flies over a salmon pool he could relax from his cares. It perhaps helped him to keep vigorous into his late 70's. In the spring of 1939 he outfitted me with rod, line, reel, and flies. I caught my first salmon by standing on the railroad bridge and letting my line float down stream.

In June I learned another skill — swimming. On the lower side of the traffic bridge, an abutment made a pool without current. There the boys swam. Bob Murray held me by the ribs till I could do a few strokes. I went home to the farm for the summer.

In August WWII broke out. That fall of 1939 few were directly affected by the war. It was a calm, a year before the "Battle of Britain".

In October 1939, Uncle loaned me a .22 calibre rifle. After school and on Saturdays I followed a path up the brook into the woods. I was rewarded with several partridge to bring home. That fall Mildred left her position in Eastport, Maine and came to Doaktown for her last visit before marriage. We picked her up at Esther and Harold Smith's in Fredericton.

Jud Corey, Miramichi River, Doaktown

Family relations were very valuable to Judson and Alice Corey. She corresponded regularly with all their children: Presque Isle, Gardner, Wilson's Beach, Fredericton and Campbellton. Also there were visits. Edna came on "the Hooper" from Fredericton for an occasional long weekend. Once she brought Jean Smith with her. Most of the other siblings came for summer vacation visits.

Leaving Doaktown

I left Doaktown at end of June 1940, expecting to return. In September an opportunity opened for me nearer home, at Carleton County Grammer School, Woodstock, N.B. In 1942 my uncle and aunt also left Doaktown and moved to Rusagonis. His memory lingered in Doaktown and not only among his own parishioners. He was well known to the fishermen on the river — and remembered. When I was in Doaktown for a high school reunion in 1971 one of the "locals" told me a story. One morning when the pastor hadn't landed a salmon, the "local" said, "Some of us had some grilse, I said, 'Would you like a fish, Mr. Corey?' He replied, 'Let me stand back a little; throw it to me; then I can go home and tell my wife I caught it.'" Alice Corey was remembered too. A Doaktown mother came to Miramichi Lake, years later, and told my sister Kathleen Foster: "When I had a sick child or any problem, I talked to Mrs. Corey." The mother who had reared eight children had invaluable counsel to give.

Rusagonis

The move to Rusagonis in the middle of W.W.II was a return to a community they had left at the end of W.W.I. The Corey's grandson, Earle Smith, provides a window into that phase of their life and ministry. He expressed affection, admiration and appreciation of them:

"My grandmother and grandfather Corey have had a special place in my life. Many of my happiest memories have been of times spent in their home. After they had moved to Rusagonis I would drive out from Fredericton on my bicycle on as many weekends as I could.

"My grandmother Corey was a sweet, even-tempered, calm and quiet lady whom I remember with great fondness. One thing that stands out in my mind is being alone with her and being able to talk with her about various things of interest to me as a teenager. She was a self-effacing person, who didn't push herself forward, but she was there, and it was a joy to have her there and to be with her. She was one of those most admirable persons, a quiet, Godly lady.

"I admired and respected my grandfather greatly as a man and especially as a man of God and servant of the Lord Jesus Christ. An illustration of the kind of man he was is an incident that happened when he was in his mid-upper seventies. I was at Rusagonis shortly after it happened and was told of it by my grandmother. He had been out hunting alone when he stepped on a rotten log and fell, cracking several ribs. He returned to his car, kept one arm behind him gripping his other elbow for support, and drove home. That evening he conducted prayer meeting, and only after that did he go to the doctor, who taped him up."

A Hunter, a Box and Stories

Earle Smith's reference to his grandfather's hunting in the Rusagonis area brings us to a facet of J.A. Corey that is waiting to be presented. Earle's story represents Mr. Corey's late life when his hunting outings were much reduced. I have memories of his earlier three-week holidays in hunting season.

Every October or early November, when I was growing up on our farm in E. Knowlesville, we expected him. Upon arrival from school on an autumn afternoon we would find an old wooden box setting on the kitchen floor. It had arrived at the farmhouse every autumn as long as we could remember. It meant our uncle had arrived. By whatever travel, his own car, or by C.P.R. train to Hartland, he brought the box that bore marks of travel over rough roads and much banging about in old lumber camps. Sometimes the box was the only indicator of his arrival. Where is he? we asked our mother. What follows is a composite story with elements from more than one season. The events varied a little year to year.

Where was he? Eager for sight of a deer, he had changed all his travel attire, donned his breeches, his moccasins and his red hunting jacket. He had picked up his prized rifle and gone on a scout to the far fields and the near woods. Before dark, and before our mother finished frying the buckwheat/buttermilk pancakes, he would appear in the kitchen.

Meanwhile, the box evoked excitement, but not from curiosity about the contents. We knew that it contained food supplies for about three weeks: baked goods — bread, doughnuts, molasses cake and cookies, date squares and pies — all home made. Also, sugar, molasses, cocoa, tea, coffee, and condensed milk. We expected also that the old box held treats for us, but we had learned to curb our excitement. At the right moment the cover of the box would swing up on its strong iron hinges, but not by our timing.

Our excitement sprang from many-faceted symbolism of the box. It symbolized the very special person to whom it belonged. Our Uncle was not only a hunter, he was a raconteur. Like the householder in the parable, he brought out of his treasure things old and new — in his case, stories.

While our mother prepared supper we hurried with the chores that came with the short days. We rounded up the turkeys from the fields. As soon as the hens went to roost, we chained the door against coons. We fed the cows and the horses and bedded them with clean straw. Right after supper we milked the cows, separated the milk, fed the calves and pigs. We expected a delightful evening. The hunting party's nightly entertainer would, tonight, be our entertainer; mother's kitchen stove would be the campfire. The stories began:

A traveller stopped in an isolated community and asked a friendly resident, "Are there any deer around here?" "Oh yes", came the enthusiastic reply, "Plenty of them." "Do you ever shoot one?" Eager to brag, the resident responded, "One, I've shot 14 of them already this fall." Solemnly, the visitor interjected: "Do you know to whom you are speaking?" "No, I can't say as I do." "I'll tell you", continued the visitor, "You are talking to the chief game warden of this county." Unhesitatingly, the apparently witless resident rejoined, "Do you know who you are talking to?" "No, I can't say as I do", replied the visitor. "Well, I'll tell you", asserted the happy-go-lucky resident, "You're talking to the biggest liar in this county."

Our beloved storyteller also told some old favourites: Uncle John and his son climbing a tree to escape a moose because they heard rustling in the leaves. Uncle John loading his two-wheeled ox cart with mill slabs tipped toward the rear, till the oxen were lifted off their feet. Another time the oxen were pulling the wagon up Hartley Brook Hill; the attachment broke; the wagon went crashing down the hill. Uncle John ran after the oxen shouting over his shoulder to the little boy, "Stop that wagon". It mattered not that we had heard them before. It was not a surprise ending or a punch line that was eagerly awaited. It was the drama, the mimicking, the voice inflections and the characterization that we enjoyed so much that we never grew weary of the stories. Pity the deprived persons who have only TV to entertain them.

After the stories the storyteller flipped up the cover of the box. Behold the generous supply of baked goods, lovingly prepared for the hunting party by our Aunt Alice, the refined lady who was born in London, England and had marvellously adapted to life in New Brunswick. Gracious person that she was, she did not forget us, though she also had a large family to feed and care for at home. Uncle passed around a box of brown sugar fudge with walnuts. It was delicious. On a later evening there would be divinity fudge, made from white sugar.

Spiritual Prelude

The old wooden box symbolised also the approach of the annual safari when a party of men would assemble at our farm to begin their trek into the deep forest. But "though on pleasure he was bent", the minister didn't forget spiritual matters. The good people of his former circuit — Biggar Ridge to Windsor — still expected from him during his visits a spiritual uplift. Before retreating to the woods he would give Sunday services. This merited an evening of rehearsal of hymns and a duet he and my father would sing. Hazel Whitehouse, from a nearby farm, pumped the foot pedal and played our organ at a lively clip. The music and the voices reverberated through the wall from the living room to the kitchen, where we sat round the table with our books.

On Sunday morning Father drove his 4-90 Chevrolet to Biggar Ridge. In the afternoon, the minister retreated to his room for rest and meditation, preparing to meet the community that would gather in expectation at the Knowlesville Church. Meanwhile Father went stealthily to the horse barn and undertook a task we had never before known him to do on a Sunday. He nailed a shoe on Prince, his fast pacing Western horse. This was in preparation for an early Monday morning departure to the deep woods. It was also an indication of a high place on the scale of values for "The Hunt". It could supersede Sabbath rules.

The Departure

Our farmhouse became the rendezvous for the party. Uncle Jim Miller came Sunday evening. Early Monday morning Fred Hemphill came, bringing the Venerable Mr. Osborne from Campobello Island. Clarence LaPage and James Hobbs also came from Knowlesville.

The wagon was loaded. For the horses: a bundle of hay and a bag of oats. For the men: Uncle's box, luggage of other party members, and a folded tarpaulin tent that had been stored at Hemphill's for many seasons. Roy Hemphill said it was brought to Knowlesville by the first settlers about 1861. Also a stove. That left room only for the teamster, Wilfred Corey. The hunters scouted ahead and behind, carrying their rifles. They would get turns at intervals for a rest on the wagon, especially on level stretches.

They headed toward the Nashwaak, via Golden Ridge

and the South Branch. The route and the driver varied year to year. Sometimes it seems they went via S. Knowlesville and Skedaddle Ridge. Roy Hemphill was sometimes the driver. He still remembers enjoying the trip, including the noon stop at Doughboy Lake. He said they ate their lunch at the wardens' shack at the mouth of the lake.

As soon as the horses finished eating they resumed the trek. Before dark they must reach the Nashwaak River, build a shelter for the horses: a lean-to against a row of trees covered with spruce bows. Also they must pitch the tent, set up the stove, kindle a fire and start water heating. Fatigue from the long trek made them ready to bed down early. Stories and antics could wait for a leisurely evening.

Early in the morning the horses were eating oats and hay in preparation for the return journey. After a hearty breakfast the driver set out on his lonely return journey. On the second evening there was deer steak for supper. It never failed that at least one member of the party shot a deer on the first day. Evening entertainment began.

Humor pervaded the entire holiday. One morning when the party was about to fan out in various directions, Fred Hemphill was rubbing his neck with oil of wintergreen. His doctor had prescribed it for a cold. J.A. Corey, always ready to insert wit into a situation, said, "Let me have a bit of that!" As he applied it to the lapel of his jacket, curiosity mounted in the others. "What is that for?" asked Uncle Jim Miller. Mr. Corey explained, "When a deer smells that it will stop right in its tracks." Jim said, "Let me have some too." He applied the sweet scent to his jacket lapel. That day Jim shot a deer — his first ever. Of course he was convinced of the effectiveness of oil of wintergreen. Isn't it true that many claimed cause/effect relationships are built on no firmer foundation.

The Return

About the end of the second week a pair of horses — Hemphill's or Corey's — arrived at the camp to bring the party home with their equipment and their game. Norman Corey also recalls a trip — perhaps via Skedaddle Ridge. "Arnold Hemphill and I went for them. I went to Hemphill's on the eve of the trip and stayed overnight. We left early in the morning. It took all day to reach the camp on the Nashwaak. There was a nice shelter for the horses. We stayed one day, then brought the party home." Some years there was a snowfall while the party was in the woods. I remember the season the party brought their game home on a longsled: several deer and a moose.

The annual safaris of the hunting party continued 42 years. Roy Hemphill remembers the recollection of his father, Fred, who was a continuous member of the hunting party. He said, in the 42 years Rev. J.A. Corey missed only two seasons: one because of a quarantine for diphtheria at Rusagonis or Hoyt, and one when he was recovering his health on Campobello. Over the years the hunting areas and the equipment changed. The party members became fewer. The last time I saw my Uncle Jud in a hunting connection was in fall of 1942. He and son Alfred were staying at my father's logging camp on the South Branch of the Miramichi. Keith and I walked to the camp to see him on a Sunday.

Rusagonis - Closing Years

The next time I saw Uncle and Aunt was March 1946, right after I completed the discharge procedure at the military base in Fredericton. I went by train to visit them. At the station I met Betty Anthony, their granddaughter from Campobello. She was a student at the secretarial course at Fredericton High School. She often visited her grandparents on weekends. We rode together to Waasis Station, where the pastor was waiting to take us to the parsonage at Rusagonis.

Alice Corey, the gracious lady who gave us a warm welcome, received special honour later that year. In August, during the annual assembly of the United Baptist Convention in Wolfville, Acadia University, in a special convocation, conferred upon Alice Corey an honorary Master of Arts degree. Her M.A. was in recognition of her ministry through the Women's Missionary Society and in children's mission bands, and in many other facets of the ministry of a Home Mission pastor. The honour was also in recognition of the contributions to ministry of many other pastors' wives.

In the fall of 1948, when Judson Corey was 78 and Alice Corey was 74, they "retired from full pastoral work." On the evening of October 4th they were given a community surprise party in the Orange Hall at Rusagonis. "It was crowded to the doors by a gathering of 200 people", representing the four churches of the pastorate: Rusagonis, Nasonworth, Waasis and Lincoln. There were also representatives from a former pastorate at Hoyt and Patterson Settlement. An envelope of money was presented from each of the six churches.[11]

From Rusagonis they went to Wilson's Beach, Campobello Island, to make their home with their eldest daughter, Alberta, and Mayford Anthony. This was another return home. They had ministered in Wilson's Beach, 1918-21. It was also a return to some of the farm chores of his youth, e.g., gardening. His grandson, Ross Anthony, then age 10, said, "He took over my barn work. He milked the cow and raised a healthy calf. One morning he felt devastated when the cow kicked over the milk. He volunteered to forego for a week his milk drinking with meals — a life-long enjoyment. The family wouldn't hear of it.

Two things the Rev. J.A. Corey had difficulty giving up: his annual hunting safaris, and his ministry. He had one more hunting safari after he retired to Campobello. Gordon Corey described a trip up the Teague Brook about 1950 — probably the last. Only three members of the party then remained: Judson and Ira Corey and Fred Hemphill. Gordon transported passengers and equipment in a jeep borrowed from Flemming and Gibson Co., Juniper. He described their camping site: a tent equipped with a stove to keep them warm and to cook their food. A stovepipe came through a hole with a metal collar in a tent wall. Ross Anthony says his grandfather shot a deer and brought it home to Campobello.

On the island he ministered in the Baptist churches, between resident pastors. A letter to Shirley Corey from Aunt Alice mentioned that he baptized 14 people at Wilson's Beach on August 28, 1949. Also he did interim preaching in the Baptist churches at St. Andrews, Woodstock, and Hartland. Pearl Boyd, living at Peel, near Hartland, entertained him for supper.

He never gave up ministry, though his strength waned. Aunt Alice told me, after she was widowed, "I tried to persuade him to give up preaching, to save his strength. He felt he must continue." Finally he suffered from an enlarged prostate. His devoted wife tried to persuade him to have surgery. He was dissuaded by other cases of men who didn't recover. He continued preaching to the end. Ross Anthony said, "He conducted the funeral service for Grampy Anthony only about a week before his own death", in the St. Stephen Hospital on November 22, 1952.

His funeral was in the United Baptist church, Wilson's Beach. Burial was in the nearby cemetery. Ira and Nellie Corey and many other relatives attended. She wrote, "They laid him to rest in a very peaceful spot." These lines from R.L. Stevenson's epitaph might be appropriate for J.A. Corey.

"Here he lies where he longed to be;
Home is the sailor, home from sea,
And the hunter home from the hill."

In February 2000 Theresa Haines mailed me clippings. Among them was my tribute written in 1952 for the Maritime Baptist:

"The writer can speak out of intimate acquaintance with

Rev. J. A. Corey in home and family life. From earliest boyhood I remember his much looked-forward-to visits to my home. More than can ever be measured, the deep respect he commanded has had, and will have, an abiding influence upon my own family and I am sure also upon many others. The writer speaks also as one who spent one full school year and part of another in his home and learned to appreciate the wholesomeness and Christian character of his home life.

To his wife we extend our sympathy and an equal measure of respect. She has set a high standard for a pastor's wife."

Judson M. Corey

The following tribute, also published in 'The Maritime Baptist", was by the minister of George St. United Baptist Church, Fredericton:

"Rev. J.A. Corey will live in the memory of his many friends. Especially will his fellow-labourers in the Christian ministry remember him as a loyal comrade, whose presence brought zest to either a formal gathering or a chance meeting.

"The larger wisdom of his years did not hinder his gift for putting himself on a ground of perfect equality with his younger associates. He was ever mentally alert and eager for a good discussion. One would come away from such conversations refreshed and mentally stimulated. He had the happy faculty of brightening any conversation with the witty anecdote and as a storyteller his name has become something of a legend.

"A real lover of the out-of-doors, it was more than just a hunting trip or a fishing expedition when he struck out with his friends for a day in the woods or to cast his home-made feathered lures upon some shaded salmon water. Few men can hope to have such a record of long and faithful service as Judson A. Corey. His utter naturalness and genial disposition endeared him to the hearts of the people to whom he ministered. Devoting himself to the work of the rural ministry, he has left a high standard for all who will follow. In spite of his many and varied interests, home life took full place in his affections and loyalties, and the thoughts of his many friends are with the members of his family."

Rev. Austin MacPherson

Alice Corey was a very caring person. Shirley Brooks still has a letter written to her on August 29, 1949, telling her of two girls from Wilson's Beach she would meet at Teachers' College, Fredericton. Alice's children were also very caring of her. After she was widowed she spent winters in Gardner, Mass., with Earle and Lois Corey, and enjoying the company of David, Edna and Mildred, all on the same street. I too enjoyed one last visit from her in May 1955. Earle and Lois and Mildred brought her on a Sunday morning to Bow, N.H. My father, Ira Corey, was visiting with us too. That was the last time I saw her. She died on September 18, 1955. Her funeral was in the United Baptist Church, Wilson's Beach.

In Wilson's Beach, past the Baptist Church, past Canada Post, then turn right on a shore road that leads to the cemetery, there stands the Corey monument and beside it the monument of their daughter and husband:

COREY
Rev. Judson A. Corey
1870 - 1952
Alice E. His wife
1874 - 1955
"Asleep in Jesus"

ANTHONY
Mayford E. Anthony
1899 - 1978
Alberta L. his wife
1900 - 1964
"Blessed are the dead which die in the Lord."

The Children and Grandchildren of Judson A. Corey and Alice Howlett:

Alberta Corey Anthony

Alberta Lois Corey, first of eight children, was born December 20, 1900, in Lewiston, Maine. In 1910 she came with the family to Knowlesville. In 1913 the family left Knowlesville for Rusagonis. In 1918 Alberta returned to Knowlesville as the teacher of The Knowlesville School.[12] That year the family moved to Campobello Island. There the Rev. J.A. Corey was ministering to people suffering influenza epidemic following the end of W.W.I. Because of fears of the epidemic the Knowlesville School was closed for four weeks or more. Alberta had been living with her cousin Erma and their grandparents Alfred and Lucretia Corey in Knowlesville. During most of the school closing Alberta stayed with another cousin, Kate Miller in Glassville.[13]

In June 1923 Alberta was still, or perhaps again, teaching in Carleton County. That was the summer she invited Erma and Grandpa Corey to come to visit her family at Hoyt.

In the 1925-26 school year Berta was teaching on Campobello Island. There she met her husband, Mayford Anthony, who was born on the island in October 1899. Bernice Martin, sister of Mayford, said, "I was in her grade two class. They got married at Easter that year." Mayford's regular work was fishing. He had a summer job in a baby carriage factory in

Massachusetts in a town near Leominster. His son Burdell thinks he stayed in Massachusetts only one summer because he couldn't stay away from Campobello long. He was always anxious to get out on the water, especially in the winter season.

The home of Alberta and Mayford on Campobello was a welcoming place. Edna Corey said that Berta "always welcomed all who came to visit her", which included more than her immediate family. Alice Corey, cousin, when she married Fred MacKenzie in July 1936, spent about a week with Berta and Mayford. Fred went out with Mayford in his fishing boat. They raved about the delicious flavour of fresh seafood. They brought home clams. Edna described her sister Berta as "...a quiet person who was a very good influence over the rest of us."

For several years Berta suffered from ill health without knowing the cause. Ross said, "She was ill a lot during my time in high school. She kept doing her house work until about her last year when she was forced to spend much time in bed." Once dialysis brought her back from a coma for about a week. This became a clue to kidney ailment. But not until the autopsy after her death did they determine that she suffered from polycystic kidneys. Alberta died on November 9, 1964.

In the United Baptist Church at Wilson's Beach the Bible stand is a memorial to Alberta Anthony. The communion table is a memorial to her father Rev. J.A. Corey.

Mayford Anthony experienced loneliness after he was widowed. Burdell said, "he often phoned us in Saint John: 'Are you coming down for the weekend?'" Burdell and Doreen did spend holiday time with Mayford. They were spending a week there in the summer of 1965 when we took my mother to the island for a visit.[14] They gave us a cordial welcome. I remember the fresh fish for dinners.

On October 9, 1966 Mayford married Florence Small, a widow on Grand Manan. They lived on Grand Manan in summer. She dreaded winter boat trips to the mainland; hence they lived on Campobello in winter. In their late years Florence had to be in a nursing home part of the time, but was home a lot with Mayford caring for him. Mayford died suddenly at a supper and entertainment in the Baptist Church at Seal Cove. After reading one of his poems he fell out of his chair with heart failure on the Saturday evening before Thanksgiving, October 1978. Florence returned to the nursing home.[15]

Alberta and Mayford Anthony's children are:

Elizabeth (Betty) b. August 24, 1927;
Burdel, b. May 17, 1930;
Ross, b. March 22, 1938

Betty

On finishing her secretarial course in Fredericton in 1946, Betty went on to work there. Her first job was in the law office of H.H. Gunter. Later she worked for an insurance company. In 1955 Betty married Donald Bilensky of Fredericton. They had a business — Bilensky Insurance, which they sold when they retired. They still live in Fredericton. In winters they have gone to Florida, California and British Columbia. They have a daughter, Karen, born March 6, 1956, and a son Brian, born August 22, 1959. Karen married Daniel Long. They have two sons: Jeffrey, born January 11, 1982, and Gregory, born October 23, 1983. Jeffrey graduated from high school in 1999 and went to work.

Brian Bilensky married Eleanor Scott. Brian is also in the insurance business. After working in Ontario he is back in Fredericton. With an office in his home, he works for Pafco and travels over New Brunswick. Brian and Eleanor have two sons: Christopher, born 1992, and Mitchell, born 1993.

Burdell Anthony

Burdell graduated from Campobello Island Consolidated School in 1947. He spent the academic year 1947-48 at Saint John Vocational School in a course in automotive mechanics. On graduation he began work with Battery and Electric (now Autotec), a garage on Duke St., Saint John, a position which lasted 47 years. He retired in July 1995. Burdel married Doreen Hunter. They have two daughters and a son: Judith, born May 6, 1953, Barbara, born May 18, 1957, and Mark, born February 22, 1960.

Judith Anthony married William McCain. They have two sons: Jeffrey McCain, born May 8, 1975; and Russell McCain, born August 12, 1978. Judith was working for the Royal Bank before "down sizing". Then she went to work for a call center.

Barbara Anthony married Fred Dickinson. An engineer, he did computer work for about five years. Now he works at an office on Dever Road Saint John W., for two Irving interests: Irving Paper and J.D. Irving. Barbara works in the office of Fernhill Cemetery. They have two sons: Anthony Dickinson (Tony) born January 29, 1980, and Adam born August 23, 1984. Tony is a student at Atlantic Baptist University, Moncton, N.B.

Mark Anthony married Mary-Jean Bettle. They have a son, Darren, born October 6, 1982, and a daughter, Darlene, born February 1986. Mark has been working at the refinery of Lantic Sugar for about 16 years.

Ross Anthony

Ross graduated from Campobello Island Consolidated School in 1956. In 1956/57 he was in the motor mechanics course of Saint John Vocational School. From 1957-1964 he worked with his brother, Burdell, at Battery and Electric, on Duke St. On July 20, 1964 he became a member of The City of

Saint John Police Department, a position he held until February 1994. Toward the end of his 30-year career on the force he "experienced low stamina, and felt beat out at work." Eventually his condition was diagnosed as polycystic kidneys, the same condition his mother had suffered. In 1994 he had a kidney transplant, and about that time took early retirement.

Then followed a series of surgeries and treatments: removal of his second kidney, another transplant, functioning for a time on one transplant, and eventually functioning without any kidneys, and being sustained by dialysis. He also had a hernia operation, and treatment for eye cataract, a side effect of his treatments. He has had 13 surgeries since 1993.

Ross has experienced about three different types of dialysis. Until the winter of 2000 he was applying a home process four times a day. Then he moved to a new dialysis that he undergoes while sleeping. Anticipating possibility of another transplant, Ross is now in an instruction group at Saint John Regional Hospital.

Ross married Jean-Anne Fawcette. They have two children: Brenda Jean, born August 26, 1962; and Stephen Ross, born May 2, 1965.

Brenda married Douglas Colquhoun. Douglas worked for Autotech, and later for Irving Oil Refinery, Saint John. Currently he is on disability from environmental illness. He is able to keep house for the family in Quispamsis, while Brenda works for Shoppers Drug Mart. Brenda and Douglas have two children: Sharis Colquhoun, born May 20, 1987, and Alex Colhoun, born September 13, 1989.

Stephen Ross married Leslie Braid. They have two sons: Owen Ross Anthony, born February 16, 1994, and Nathan Stephen, born October 8, 1996. They live on Champlain Drive. The polycystic kidney ailment has now reached the fourth generation - from Alberta to Ross to Stephen to Owen. Stephen has high blood pressure, a symptom, and Owen is showing signs of a cyst.

Earle Corey

While he was single, Earle Corey went to Massachusetts seeking work. His son, Eugene, remembers his speaking about rooming with two other single fellows. Harold Smith recalled that their brother-in-law, Mayford Anthony, helped Earle make contacts in Massachusetts. Earle found temporary employment in a paint factory in South Gardner. Soon he began employment in Gardner in the office of furniture manufacturer, Heywood Wakefield, a position that advanced to sales manager and lasted the rest of his working years.

Gardner proved to be a home and gathering point for Coreys. The children of Earle and Lois were born and grew up there: Eugene, July 4, 1928, and Wilma, February 15, 1931. Three of Earle's siblings: David, Edna, and Mildred, also came there to live and work. Earle retired in 1969. Harold Smith retired the same year. Earle and Lois and Harold and Esther Smith celebrated with a motor trip across Canada. They visited the Butchart Gardens on Vancouver Island. They returned via U.S.A.

Earle was among the strongest supporters of the Corey Reunion. He was prominent among the attendants at our first gathering at Simonds, N.B., July 26, 1968. He brought with him Lois, their daughter Wilma, Lois' sister-in-law, Mrs. Morgan, and Esther and Harold Smith. In a letter to Erma Shaw, March 13, 1976, Earle said, "My main thought is to see as many of our kinfolks as possible..."

In the same letter he described a very active retirement: He papered walls and made and repaired furniture. He said, "We had a new rink open a year ago and I have skated two to four times most weeks." He also spoke of trout fishing with Dave "on the numerous brooks in the area." In a later letter, August 10, 1976, Earle said he had made eleven fishing trips to Quebec with friends. Earle spoke of frequent visits from Eugene and Wilma and their families. "We see them frequently; they live only about 60 miles in opposite directions from here."

Rev. J.A. Corey, Eugene and Earle Corey, at Corey Farm, E. Knowlesville

In September 1976 Earle and Lois celebrated the 50th anniversary of their wedding. Among the relatives who gathered at the Baptist church in Gardner were Doreen and Burdell Anthony and Esther and Harold Smith from Saint John, and Sally Haynes from Framingham. Ross Anthony said, "Jean and I visited Earle and Lois later; we took our '78 Malibu."

Earle remained active all his life, though in his last few years, "his heart was not good." On his last day he went to the Baptist Church in Gardner. In the afternoon he went for a walk with Lois. Then he suffered pain and was taken to the hospital in Gardner where he died of a heart attack, July 3, 1983.

Lois lived another nine years. After she was widowed she went to live with daughter Wilma and her husband Charles Kusch, in Saugus, Mass. They built an extension on their house for her.[16] Lois continued annual visits to the Corey relatives and her Morgan relatives in New Brunswick. Edna brought her. The last time I saw her was in the fall of 1991 in Saint John at home of Ross and Jean Anthony. Lois died July 13, 1992 — also in Gardner Hospital. She had gone to Gardner to visit Edna Corey.

Children and Grandchildren of Earle and Lois Corey

Wilma

Wilma was a secretary. One place she worked was the office of the Methodist Conference in Boston. Wilma was married to Charles Kusch who died August 3, 1994. She continued to make her home in Saugus, Mass. She has also continued to make annual visits to New Brunswick, often staying with Jean and Ross Anthony in Saint John. In 1999 she travelled with a couple who were going to Moncton for visits.

In May 1999, after being alone for five years, Wilma had a happy meeting with a high school boyfriend, Robert Eddy, at a high school reunion in Gardner. He has been living in Florida. She also has been making annual winter visits to Florida. Recognizing Robert's loneliness, being an only child with few relatives, Wilma went to Florida early enough to spend Christmas with Robert. Through the winter they have planned their wedding and chose the date of March 10, 2000 for their wedding day.[17]

Eugene Corey

Eugene married Marilyn Bennett, a daughter of a Baptist minister in Gardner. Eugene Corey worked in Springfield and lived in E. Longmeadow, Mass. After retiring at the end of 1991, he and Marilyn moved over the city line to Springfield and into a larger house. They have also enjoyed a summer cottage at Old Orchard Beach, Maine. On July 20, 1984, Eugene, in company with his mother, Lois, and other family members, attended the Corey Reunion at Knowlesville.

Eugene and Marilyn have a son, Steven Corey, born August 3, 1953, and a daughter, Arlene Corey, born September 30, 1955. Steven graduated from Carleton College, Northfield, Minnesota, in 1974. He works as a computer programmer. He lives in New Haven, Conn. Arlene is a physical therapist, working with handicapped children in schools. She lives in Seymour, Conn.[18]

Annie Corey Haines

Annie Ruth Corey, second daughter of Rev. Judson A. and Alice Corey, was born May 25, 1903, in Knowlesville, N.B. Soon she went to Maine with the family and lived there until the spring of 1910, when the family returned to Knowlesville. Between ages 7 and 10 Annie lived with the family in E. Knowlesville. There, she showed signs of a precocious child: At age seven she had learned to bake bread and knit and at age eight, she knitted socks for her brother, Earle, then nine.[19]

There also Annie began learning music, using the music book her mother had brought from England, and playing on the church organ which was sheltered in their house in winter.[20] Sister Edna said, "Annie developed a remarkable ability to play music by ear. She could hear a piece of music and sit down and play it. She had much natural talent. Though she had only two or three lessons, she played for her father in services he conducted in country churches and school houses at some points on his circuit."

Annie, at age 19, and her sister Esther, at age 17, were students at Provincial Normal School, Fredericton, N.B. A letter dated July 5, 1922 from their grandfather, Harry Howlett, in Andover, N.B., indicates that the girls were then writing exams, probably at graduation time. The grandfather also expressed intention to visit the family in Hoyt, N.B., a month later.

"Annie …began ….her teaching career in a one-room school house in Lower Haynesville, N.B. That is where she met her future husband, Albert Wilfred Haines. They were married in Presque Isle, Maine, on June 23, 1926 at the State Street Baptist Church by the Reverend James B. Ranger. They set up housekeeping in various rooms at boarding houses and apartments. Annie was talented in nearly every hand work discipline: knitting, sewing, crocheting, embroidery and tatting. I was told by Aunt Lois Corey that wherever they lived, Annie decorated with her handiwork with bright curtains, tablecloths, her crocheted doilies and her handiwork. Her plants, African violets and various blooming plants, also were prominent. She was also an expert wallpaperer. She liked decorating her home. She was a superb housekeeper. She was a very good cook. Her oatmeal brown bread and home baked beans were outstanding, as well as her desserts (especially her doughnuts). Her preserves were wonderful and varied. I always told her that she could preserve an old shoe and it would be delicious.

"Albert found work in various jobs. For some time he worked in a lumber mill in various positions: cutting, sawing, distributing, and producing mill-worked items for building companies. After he left that company, he went to work as an office manager for Sunshine Biscuit Company in Presque Isle. When that office was closed, he continued working at Sunshine as a salesman and distributor of the various products in Aroostook County stores. He retired from that position in the early sixties after he suffered a heart attack.[21]

"Annie was a very talented seamstress and had a large clientele in Presque Isle. From simple hems to alterations for both men and women (most of these clients were either large or of unusual sizes that necessitated complex dressmaking or alterations). She sewed all her own clothes, even coats, because she was so petite and tiny (4 feet 11 inches and 82 pounds), she couldn't purchase clothes for her size except in the children's department. Although her clothing was suitable for a mature woman, they were extremely stylish and she embellished basic patterns that could be found in major fashion magazines as if she had been a "professional". She also undertook any job such as reupholstering and Albert always worked with her on those large jobs."

Annie and Albert had two sons: Albert Beverly Haines, born December 2, 1928, and Keith Wilfred Haines, born August 13, 1932.

"Annie and Albert lived a happy life together for many years. Albert enjoyed fishing, hunting, photography and all things out of doors. They enjoyed rides in the country, picnicking and visits with family and friends." Edna Corey recalls an autumn ride with Annie and Albert into Northern Maine to see the leaves in colour. Albert stopped at some stores to see some people he had not seen since his retirement. He was welcomed warmly with a hug and a, "Glad to see my good friend."

"A devoted couple, they celebrated their 50th anniversary June 23, 1976. All of Annie's siblings and families, except Berta who was no longer living, attended the celebration," in a local hotel. Other relatives attending were Jud Corey and Kaye and Paul Foster.

"During these years, they were active members of the Star City Senior Citizens Club. They enjoyed the companionship of their weekly pot luck dinners, meetings, and various field trips. Albert served in many activities and offices. Annie contributed also, but more memorable was her accompaniment on the piano for their opening rituals.

"In the early 1980's, Annie began showing signs of dementia. Albert devotedly cared for her until his sudden death of a massive heart attack on January 17, 1985. His last words were about his concern for her. At his death, it had already been arranged for her to move into the Presque Isle Nursing Home. We were all comforted to know that so many of the caretakers had known her for many years. She was a favourite of most of the folks there. Our favourite anecdote was described by the director of recreational activities. Late in her life she was no longer able to formulate words so conversation was impossible. Every Sunday night a group of singers would entertain the residents. They sang old popular songs, hymns, etc. Even though she could no longer speak, she sang along with the group in her sweet alto voice. The staff members who cared for her were constantly amazed by that phenomenon." She had many visits from her sons and her siblings, also other relatives, but in a later stage was unable to recognize her family members."

Annie and Albert were regular attendants at the Corey Reunion. Their last registered visit was on July 18, 1981 at Knowlesville. Her brother, Alfred Corey, had arranged to bring them. On July 11, 1987, daughter-in-law Theresa wrote, "If she were well, she would be there, you can be sure and we are sorry that she is unable to travel and be aware of her surroundings." In letters for "The Corey Courier", on June 11, 1987, and on June 20, 1989, Theresa Haines requested that news of Annie be conveyed to Erma: "Annie had a special fondness for Erma and Annie always loved her so much..." The two cousins were born two days apart in May 1903, and had kept in close relationship all their lives. Determined to have a visit with Annie, Erma Shaw had her son John drive her to Presque Isle. Erma came away very distressed because Annie didn't recognize her.

Annie "died on May 7, 1990. Her funeral service was held at the Bethany Baptist Church in Presque Isle, presided by

Reverend Albert Q. Coffee. She was a charter member of the church and sang in the choir for many years. She also was an active member of the "Up and Coming Club" that performed various charity work for local and foreign missions. She was buried at Fairmount Cemetery next to Albert, her beloved partner for the greater part of her life."

Sons and Grandchildren

Albert Beverly Haines "excelled in school and after high school he enlisted in the U.S. Army and served in Italy for a year. After his discharge, he attended the University of Maine in Orono and earned a degree in Engineering Physics in 1952. Because he was in the ROTC program in college, after graduation he served with the rank of 1st Lieutenant for two more years in the U.S. Army Signal Corps. After discharge from that service he began employment as an engineer at the Westinghouse Electric Corporation in Baltimore, Maryland.

"In November 1959 Albert married Theresa Spinelli Hurtley, a widow with two little girls. In a few years he adopted them and they are Jane Haines Ingold, born May 20, 1955 and Sandra Haines Hetrick, born October 30, 1957. Their grandchildren are Sarah Jane Hetrick, born January 1, 1982; Rebecca Claire Ingold, born November 1, 1983; Matthew Corey Ingold, born October 7, 1987; and Benjamin Albert Haines, born May 19, 1990.

"Mathew Corey Ingold is to "be a recipient" of a rocker that was made by his great great Grandpa Corey for his great grandmother, Annie Haines. The great great grandfather was Rev. Judson A. Corey.

"Albert retired May 1991 and he and Theresa live in their home in Columbia, Maryland that they purchased in 1960 shortly after they were married. Albert enjoys fishing, hunting and golf besides many other interests and activities."

Keith Haines "Also was a good student and like his

brother, he enlisted in the U.S. Army; He served in Japan. After discharge, he attended the University of Maine in Orono. He earned a degree in Chemical Engineering in 1957. After graduation he began working for the Dupont Company until he retired. After his retirement he worked as a consulting engineer in various locations, both in and out of the country.

"While he lived in Chicago, he met Nancy Johnson. She had a little boy named Mark. Keith and Nancy were married on August 12, 1961. Keith later adopted Mark and in the spring of 1965, they adopted a baby girl named Deborah who was born in February, 1965. In October 1965 their son David was born and in September 1967 their son Matthew was born. Keith and Nancy were divorced in 1974.

"Keith married Peggy Bryan who was the mother of three grown children who have their own families now. They all remain a close family. Keith and Peggy live in a home they had built in Trout Run, Pennsylvania. He enjoys golf, fishing and playing tournament bridge. Peggy enjoys her part time job in a collectibles and antiques shop."[22]

Edna Corey said that both Albert and Keith, in their travels, often stopped in Gardner for welcoming visits with their aunts, uncles and cousins.

Esther Corey Smith

Esther Lucretia Corey was born in Auburn, Maine, February 10, 1905. In the spring of 1910 the family returned to her father's home community, Knowlesville, N.B. Esther lived in New Brunswick the rest of her life. She attended the Provincial Normal School in preparation for teaching. It appears she graduated in 1922.

Soon after her marriage to Harold W. Smith, in Keswick Ridge, July 6, 1927, Esther was working in his store. Besides owning a general store in Keswick Ridge, Harold was engaged in lumbering in winter. Esther and one of Harold's sisters ran the store. Harold was still lumbering when their son, Earle, was born, March 21, 1929. Harold said, "Dad finished the lumbering that day." That fall, Harold and Esther and baby Earle moved to Fredericton. There they rented in winter; they continued to live in Keswick Ridge in summer. Jean also was born at Keswick Ridge, in the Baptist Parsonage, July 21, 1933.

In Fredericton Harold worked for Beatty Brothers, a dealer in appliances. In January 1942 they transferred Harold to Moncton. The family moved into a house there in May. They rented some rooms to wartime military training personnel. In 1943 Smiths moved back to Fredericton. Earle was delighted to return to Fredericton High School. Harold worked briefly for an insurance company. His next move was to Saint John to work for Wartime Prices and Trade Board. In 1944 the family, except Earle, moved to Saint John. Earle stayed with his Smith grandparents in Fredericton so he could complete high school there.

The Smith family lived on Mount Pleasant Ave. in E. Saint John. In 1946 my father and I stayed overnight with them there. We were visiting my brother, Claude, then a patient in the East Saint John Sanatorium. Later I stayed overnight with them when I stopped to visit Claude on my way home from Acadia.

In the years following the war, Harold Smith had a series of jobs in Saint John: Credit Manager with Calp's, Accountant/Treasurer for Star Motors, and Accountant in the E. Saint John Hospital. Also he spoke of a travelling job that took him as far as the North Shore. Referring to his father's work as an accountant, Earle said, "It was a source of satisfaction to him to know that he was well respected as a man who did his work well."

The family lived for a while in Lancaster. Returning to E. Saint John, they located on Park Hill Drive. There they had a comfortable place with space for a garden. The house also had a rental apartment. In that neighborhood Harold and Esther were among the initiators and builders of a new church, Forest Hills United Baptist, organized in 1964. Harold was the treasurer.

In retirement, which began for Harold in 1969, he and Esther planned with foresight. When their apartment became vacant they moved into it and rented the house. They sold the furniture they no longer had room for and parted with many household articles in yard sales. Was it a difficult experience? "No. We advertised and posted the signs. Periodically we put out the signs again. People came and bought more readily than we expected. Visiting grandchildren had fun selling articles."

In 1983 the Smiths sold their house in East Saint John and moved into a third floor apartment in Loch Lomond Villa. Address: 219 Ellerdale. There also they maintained hospitality. I visited, sometimes accompanied by my son Christopher. There we met with Mildred and Clair Shirley. My sister Kaye Foster and Paul also visited. From Massachusetts came Edna, Earle and Lois Corey.

Hanging on the wall of their living room was a painting of the cottage in Papua New Guinea where their daughter Jean Smith was translating the New Testament into the Mian language. Jean recalled: "In 1987 I returned to Canada and began working as Atlantic regional representative for Wycliffe. At the same time it was good to be able to help my parents out as they were getting older and beginning to need some help. As my mother began to fail I carried on with my responsibilities in a limited capacity."

Esther spent her last ten months in the infirmary of the Villa. Harold and Jean visited her frequently. Also Earle and Ruth "were happy to visit Earle's parents several times" in 1993. Again in December they arrived from Ontario for Esther's last few days. Esther died December 31, 1993. Ruth and Earle stayed with his father for a month.

Subsequently Harold and Jean moved to Regency Towers in E. Saint John. Still they maintained hospitality. In the fall of 1994 when Christopher and Suphaphon Corey were about to leave again for Thailand, Jean invited us to the Smith apartment for supper. Harold reminisced far back to the days of his lumbering. It was our last visit. When I returned home one afternoon Margaret gave me a telephone message: "Your favourite man has gone." Harold died March 17, 1995 four days short of age 93. The funerals of both Esther and Harold were held at Forest Hills Baptist Church, East Saint John: Esther's in January 1994, and Harold's in March 1995. Interment is in Fernhill Cemetery. Margaret and Jud had supper with Jean and Earle at the apartment before Earle returned to Ontario. It was an opportunity to gather more stories for this chapter.

Harold and Esther, by son Earle

I think that my father and mother were extraordinarily ordinary. They went about their work quietly and diligently without fanfare or show. They were not demonstrative but they loved their children, and we knew that they loved us. Above all, overshadowing and controlling their lives was the Lord Jesus whom they trusted with a quiet and consistent faith. My parents were active and faithful in their church as long as health and age permitted. They were steady, dependable, unassuming, and could be counted on to do to the best of their ability anything they were asked to do. They liked people and had many friends. In their last few years when they were not able to get out too often, they had faithful friends who regularly visited them. They enjoyed those visits greatly.

Earle W. Smith: autobiography/resume

"I was converted in 1947 at age 18. I was student pastor in Grand Falls and Ortonville, 1948-50. I graduated from London Bible Institute and Theological Seminary in 1953. I was pastor of Fundamental Baptist Church in Central Bedeque, P.E.I. from September 1953 to December 1954 when I went home with tuberculosis."

During 17 months of his illness Earle was a patient in

the Sanatorium in E. Saint John. He had two faithful visitors: his mother, Esther, and his friend Ruth King. He and Ruth had met at London Bible Institute. She had grown up in Queenstown, Ontario. In Saint John, Ruth worked as a V.O.N. nurse. Earle and Ruth were married in Lancaster Bible Church, December 15, 1956.

Earle served as pastor of: Temple Baptist Church, Chance Harbour, Calvary Baptist Church, Maces Bay, and Bethel Baptist Church, Little Lepreau, N.B. from January 1957 to June 1958; Independent Baptist Church, Clark's Harbour, N.S., from June 1958 to August 1965; First Baptist Church, Georgetown, P.E.I. 1965 until March 1970; Fundamental Baptist Church in Summerside, P.E.I. until December 1974. Calvary Baptist Church, Cornwall, Ontario, 1975 up to the present - 2000. Also, in Cornwall, Earle taught Systematic Theology for 13 years at Seaway Baptist Bible Institute, and Ruth taught Christian education subjects.

In a letter dated August 16, 1993, Ruth expressed thanks for the "Corey Courier". "Information from this will help us tell our children of their roots. We have also learned of a few distant cousins that we might be able to look up. Recently Earle conducted a funeral. During the reception he met a Corey relative from near Ottawa...His name is Larry Whitehouse, from Greely, Ontario.....My parents came from England in 1928, so I'm not so blessed with Canadian relatives as Earle is." Ruth died June 18, 1994 from melanoma which went to her lungs.

Earle and Ruth Smith had four children: Thomas Wayne, b. October 20, 1957; Allan Robert, b. February 17, 1959; Nancy Louise, b. April 24, 1961; Colleen Esther, still-born, September 9, 1964.

Wayne Smith has been working for the Darling Nuclear Power Station. He married Brenda Fram, August 4, 1979. They have three children, Ryan Benjamin, b. October 10, 1982; Darren Richard, b. May 22, 1986; and Corey Daniel, b. January 25, 1989. They live in Peterborough, Ontario.

Allan Smith works at Stebbins Engineering, Watertown, N.Y., as a computer programmer. Allan married Lori Rae Seifert, b. November 29, 1962. They have three children: Joshua, b. November 6, 1989; Benjamin Allan b. May 5, 1993; and Miriam Esther, b. October 1999.

Nancy Smith married Jonathan Underwood, July 17, 1982. Their children are: Jill, b. April 10, 1983; Christopher, b. March 10, 1986; Kaylyn, b. November 15, 1988; Joseph Nathan, b. June 4, 1992; and Lia, b. September 1996. They live in Cornwall, Ontario.

Jean Smith: Resume/Autobiography

Nurses training at Saint John General Hospital; graduated 1954; London Bible Institute, Ontario; graduated 1957. "That year, 1957, I returned to Saint John where I joined the staff of the operating theatre in the General Hospital. The summers of 1960 and 1961 I took the linguistic training offered by the Summer Institute of Linguistics on the campus of the University of Oklahoma, Norman, Oklahoma. During the second summer I joined Wycliffe Bible Translators. January 1962 I attended the field training camp for WBT in Southern Mexico.

February 1963 I went to Papua New Guinea to work on Bible Translation. While waiting for a partner to work with I filled various job roles but mostly worked in the store as bookkeeper. In 1969 I joined Pam Eston to begin working on the Mian language in the Sandaun province of PNG. Mian was an unwritten language so our first task was to reduce the language to a written form, learn the language, teach the people to read and write that written language and translate scriptures for the people. In 1987 we had completed the New Testament, with the help of many Mian people, the two main ones being Daning and Kasening. We also helped establish a pre-school program, teaching the younger children to read and write in their own language. That program is still going."

Following the death of her father, Jean remained in Saint John for a year. "In 1996 I came to Toronto to work in the Eastern Regional Office in Applications and New Member Services, helping others to begin the task of Bible translation. Having had Christian grandparents and parents has been the basis for all that I have been able to accomplish. I appreciate the godly heritage I have had. My parents are the ones who started me on this road, prayed for me, encouraged me and supported me in many and various ways. Certainly they had a major role to play in the translation of the Mian New Testament." Jean is living in Etobicoke, Ontario.

Carolyn Smith Rempel: Autobiography/Resume

Carolyn, b. October 22, 1940:
I was raised in a Christian home in Saint John, New Brunswick. At 10 years of age, I accepted the Lord through the ministry of a Baptist pastor. My formative years were spent in a Baptist Church. During my teen years I attended Lancaster Bible Church (AGC) in Saint John. Through Youth for Christ rallies, Christian films and the influence of my church, the Lord gave me a burden for foreign missions. Education: New Brunswick Teachers College; Fredericton, Diploma; Ontario Bible College - B.R.E.

Carolyn married Neil Rempel August 3, 1963. Neil, b. January 30, 1939. Education: Tyndale College (London College of Bible and Missions) B.Th.; Wilfred Laurier University - B.A.; Trinity Evangelical Divinity School - Grad Studies; Briercrest Biblical Seminary - Grad Studies.

Ministry: "For 15 years, 1968 - 1983, we served as church planters and field administrators with Greater Europe Mission in Austria." The Rempels established a fellowship in Wiener Neustadt, and worked 13 years. Now it is an organized church, ".....meeting in a rental building that has been renovated to meet their needs. We are grateful to the Lord that He enabled us to lay the groundwork for that ministry."

Currently, Neil serves as Director for Greater Europe Mission in Canada and continues to represent the mission in the Maritimes, Manitoba and Saskatchewan. His basic responsibilities include the overall administration of the mission, recruitment and processing of applicants for summer, short and long term ministries. As well as making about 20 campus visits every year, Neil ministers in numerous churches. Hobbies: home renovations, stamp collecting, reading, horticulture. Carolyn accompanies Neil on some of the speaking engagements, but is mainly involved in Calvary Baptist Church here in Oshawa as Director of Women's Ministries. Once a week, Carolyn volunteers as a counsellor at the Pregnancy Help Centre. She also volunteers at the Greater Europe Mission office.

Children and Grandchildren of Carolyn and Neil Rempel

Carolyn Smith and Neil Rempel have three children: Mark, b. April 3, 1967; Michelle, b. October 5, 1969; and Monika, b. March 17, 1971.

Mark is married to Laura Perreault.

Education: Mark: studied diesel mechanics at Red River Community College. Laura studied education at University of Manitoba for two years.

Mark is a realtor in Winnipeg. Laura is a Mary Kay consultant.

Hobbies/activities: Mark: golf, billiards, watching TV sports, auto mechanics. Laura: crafts

Michelle is married to Brad Warkentin
Education: Graduate of Providence College (Biblical Studies major)

Hobbies/activities: Handcrafts, reading, listening to music.

Brad is an inner-city missionary with Living Bible Explorers in Winnipeg.

Children: Samuel, b. 1997; Nathaniel, b. 1998

Monika is married to Tim Hooper.

Education: Monika studied at the University of Winnipeg majoring in German and Biology for Secondary Education

Tim: Graduate of Providence College

Tim and Monika have served in pastoral ministries in New Brunswick and Winnipeg and for the past year have operated an outreach cafe in Winnipeg.

Hobbies/activities: Monika: Knitting, spending time with friends, listening to music. Tim: restoring VW beetle.

Children: Michael, b.1994, Madison, b.1995, Alexander, b. February 2000

Alfred Joshua Corey, D.Sc.

After receiving his doctorate degree from McGill University about 1937, Alfred immediately went to work as a chemist for the Fraser Pulp and Paper Company in Altholville,[23] on the edge of Chaleur Bay in the north of New Brunswick.

Alfred married Dorothy Burpee of Fredericton. They lived in Campbellton. Their two children were born there: Jon, Nov. 17, 1938; Sally, July 20, 1940.

In the early fall of 1939, Rev. Judson and Alice Corey had occasion to visit Campbellton. The Miramichi North Shore United Baptist Association held their fall meetings there. They stayed with their son Alfred, and Dorothy, and their latest grandson, Jon. The trip was soon after I had returned to Doaktown to begin grade 10. They arranged for me to have meals at Dickinson's, and for Harland Dickinson to stay at night with me.

On one visit Alfred took his father on a tour of the mill. My uncle brought back samples of nylon and other products from the pulp mill. He delighted to show them.

I saw Alfred in Montreal in autumn of 1943. I was privileged to be spending an academic year at McGill University in the program called Canadian Army University Course. He was in Montreal presenting a paper on Fraser's chemical process for making various products from wood pulp. He was staying at a hotel in walking distance from Douglas Hall where my C.A.U.C. group was being housed. He left a message at the desk for me. I visited him at his hotel that evening. He gave me a copy of his paper — somewhat heavy reading for me then. It was much easier to talk about the hunting expedition he had enjoyed a few weeks earlier with his father, my father, and others on the South Branch of the Miramichi.

Near Sally's fifth birthday, July 1945, the family moved to Edmundston. As the truck was being unloaded neighborhood children gathered to play. Dorothy invited them to a party for Sally. Alfred worked at the Fraser mill on the bank of the Saint John River, there forming the border with Maine - and not far from the Quebec border.

Alfred lived a "well rounded" life, as Sally described him. He liked hunting and fishing. He took Jon and Sally on partridge hunts. Jon said, "he liked to fish both trout and salmon; he beat me." Jon has good memories of many outings. Alfred also liked badminton, curling and golf. He hurried to the golf course after work, sometimes persuading Dorothy to go with him.

Jon and Sally Corey both attended Horton Academy, Wolfville, N.S., from 1954 to 1957. Jon is listed under class of 1956, and Sally Ann class of 1957. Sally Ann Haynes is also listed in 1995 Directory.[24]

Alfred Jon married Sylvia Blackburn of Nova Scotia. Sally married Richard L. Haynes. Their children are: Jon Edward Haynes, b. March 29, 1965; Lynda Patrice Haynes, b. July 30, 1969; and James Richard Haynes, b. May 27, 1971.

Dorothy Burpee Corey lived to see Sally's three children, but missed seeing Brenda Corey, Jon's daughter. Dorothy Burpee Corey died October 1971 in Edmundston. Her daughter-in-law, Sylvia, said, "I was three months pregnant then."

After being widowed Alfred lived nearly 20 years.

Among his activities were visits to his family. In 1974 he spent a month with Sally's family in Framingham, Mass., helping with their children while she was in hospital. Before returning home to Edmundston he visited his siblings in Gardner.[25]

On May 10, 1981, Alfred wrote to Erma: "I will be going down to the Halifax area to see my son and family around the end of June...." He planned to be back before the Corey gathering in Knowlesville, July 18th. On May 17, 1985, Alfred mailed to Erma the charts he drew of the descendants of Judson and Alice Corey. They were a big help toward the genealogy printed later by Neil Rempel. On July 20th he was at the Corey gathering in Knowlesville. He attended again July 18, 1987 - his last recorded visit.

Alfred remained active until the year he was 80. That year, 1986, he went with Sally, her son and daughter and two of their friends on a trip to Switzerland. He was enjoying the trip, especially the Alps, until they reached 6,000 ft. above sea level. Then one night he came to Sally's room saying, "I can't breathe." She found a doctor who spoke English well. In hospital he was diagnosed with fluid around his heart, and with need of bed rest 24 hours a day. Sally was compelled to return home with her party. Alfred remained three weeks in hospital.

Alfred enjoyed quite a lot of activity after that, but Sally said he never fully recovered his strength. She and Jon kept in touch with him. She was with him when he underwent cataract surgery in Fredericton. She went for two weeks and stayed with him seven. She said, "I loved being around my Dad."

In a late illness Alfred was in hospital in Edmundston; he stopped eating, mistrusting the hospital. Exercising ingenuity, Sally phoned his best friend: "Go and get a fresh package of his favourite cookies and some ice cream...take them to the hospital. He'll eat." He did, and he recovered.

Eventually Sally and Jon, on a visit with their Dad in Edmundston, found him "unable to care for himself." They helped him arrange to sell his house. They divided the family valuables. Alfred went with Jon to Nova Scotia. He lived almost two years with Jon and Sylvia in Hammonds Plains. He enjoyed some outings, e.g., the tatoos and buskers. A portable chair made him comfortable, after short walks.

Alfred died in Victoria General Hospital, Halifax, March 19, 1991, at age 84. His funeral was at Rockingham United Church, Bedford. The burial site of Alfred and Dorothy is in Edmundston. Jon described his Dad as a "great father", Sally said, "he was an excellent father".

Alfred's and Dorothy's Children and Grandchildren

Jon's work - installation of telephone offices, took him to Nova Scotia. He said, "I married here and I stayed here." Alfred Jon Corey is now retired from 34 years of telephone work: 12 1/2 with Northern Telecom and 21 1/2 with M.T. & T. He now works for a small private company two days a week. Sylvia is working part time in "Market Research". She makes many visits to stores. Their daughter, Brenda, has plans to be married to Lonnie Dauphine on May 6, 2000 in Halifax.

Sally Ann Haynes

After Horton Academy, Sally attended Mount Allison University two years. Then she was at Chandler School for Women in Boston. She specialized in legal secretarial work.

She worked in "American Medical Response" until she had a heart attack about 1995. Dick called 911. She reached hospital in Boston before the attack. She did not return to that work. She says now that she is away from the stress, she "feels great.".

Sally and Richard Haynes live in Framingham, Mass. Richard is a tax accountant. He says his family and Albert Haines' family have a connection. They are planning a Haynes family gathering. Sally and Richard's two sons and daughter are all married.

Jon Edward Haynes married Mauree Zocchi. Their children are: Anna, b. September 11, 1995, and Alexander Corey, b. March 1998. Lynda (Patty) married David Ersoff in December 1997. They have a daughter: Morgan Alexandra, born February 10, 1999. She has made a good recovery from open-heart surgery at five months. They live in Lousiana. James Richard Haynes married Melissa Conmay in August 1997.

The families of Jon Corey and Sally Haynes have kept up visits. Sally said, "Jon came for the weddings of all three of my children." Sally and Dick and all their children and spouses are planning to be in Nova Scotia for the wedding, May 6, 2000, of Brenda Corey, daughter of Sylvia and Jon.

David Winburn Corey

David Corey was born in Auburn, Maine, June 30, 1908. The family returned to Knowlesville in spring of 1910, before he was two. Other places he lived in New Brunswick were: Rusagonis, Campobello Island, Hoyt Station and Keswick Ridge.

When David went to Gardner, Mass. in 1933 he began work with Heywood Wakefield, furniture manufacturers. The job developed to a secure position in the shipping department. In Gardner, David also found a bride: Verna M. Stevens. They had a daughter, Ellen M. Corey, born November 7, 1936, and a son, Neil D. Corey, born July 1, 1946. For years David and family lived on Lincoln St. in Gardner close to his siblings: Earle and Edna Corey and Mildred Johnston.

Ellen Corey Lau and family

Ellen Corey married Thomas J. Lau, M.D. They had three children: Thomas J. Lau, Jr., born November 19, 1961,

David M. Lau, born March 16, 1963, and Eric Corey Lau, born January 20, 1975. Early in Dr. Lau's medical practice, and when their first two children were small the family went to several countries of special need: to Africa with the Peace Corps, to Malaysia, to Brazil with the Hope Ship, and to Costa Rica.

In July 1970 the family suffered a sad tragedy while they were visiting friends in Lexington, Mass. Their first son, Thomas J. Lau, Jr., then under nine, darted out from the swimming pool and was struck by a car. The family was about to go to a new position at the University of Connecticut.

In 1973 the Lau family were having an eventful summer. Their sailboat was hit by lightening which burned the interior. They took it to New Jersey for repair, then returned to New England. On August 4, 1973, Ellen, Dr. Tom Lau, and their son David, were among several members of the Rev. J.A. Corey branch who attended the Corey Reunion at Hartland. Also attending were Ellen's father and mother, David and Verna Corey, Earle and Lois Corey, Alfred Corey, Harold and Esther Smith; Albert and Annie Haines, and Keith Haines with children, Deborah, David and Matthew. Ellen expressed much elation about meeting so many relatives. In the guest book they registered, "enroute to Florida".

Neil D. Corey married Patricia Coleman. They have two sons: Matthew N. Corey, born August 26, 1973, and Joshua Thomas Corey, born February 20, 1981. They live in Worcester, Mass. Neil is a database administrator.

David and Verna - Late Years

On July 23, 1983, David Corey again attended the Corey Reunion at Hartland. Also attending from his branch were: Edna and Alfred Corey, Annie and Albert Haines, Mildred and Clair Shirley, Doreen and Burdell Anthony, and Harold and Esther Smith.

Throughout a long lifetime David retained memories of

early Corey visits in New Brunswick. At the 1995 Corey Reunion in Knowlesville Edna Corey recollected: "David still remembers a trout fry at the Ira Corey farm in E. Knowlesville." Their mother, Alice Corey, was frying trout. My mother, Nellie Corey, was frying pancakes. David, with many others, sat at the long dining room table eating trout.

Into his 90th year David sang in the choir of the Baptist Church in Gardner. In his last spring he suffered a malignant tumour in a lung. After hospital care he came home with an oxygen tube in his nose, and under hospice care, and with the loving care of his family. His daughter-in-law Patricia was there. His daughter, Ellen Lau, came from Florida and stayed two weeks beside her Dad. David died on June 12, 1998, 18 days short of 90 years.

Following the funeral, Ellen recalled, "I spent the rest of the summer helping mother". They disposed of the furniture and the house on Oak St. Verna went to an "assisted living" place in Gardner. After a year, Ellen said she couldn't manage by herself. She suffered a cracked rib.

In January, 2000, Neil reported in a telephone conversation that his mother had been in Worcester since September 1999. She lived with Neil and Patricia for a time and when managing her medicines became too difficult, she went to a rest home in Worcester. Neil and Patricia visit Verna every day. Also they have driven to Gardner to bring Neil's Aunt Edna to visit his mother.

Ellen and Dr. Lau and family have lived in Florida many years. Dr. Lau became a pathologist. Ellen taught drama and world history at Gainsville High School for 20 years. They have been coming from Florida every summer to visit her family in Massachusetts.

Grandchildren of David and Verna Corey

David Matthew Lau, on graduation from Furman University in S. Carolina, had rank of captain in the R.O.T.C. He spent four years in the U.S. Army. David married Heide Handspeiker, a first grade teacher, on July 6, 1985. They have a son Brett, born October 4, 1991. They live in Palm Harbour, Florida. David works for Bayer, Biologics Division. Eric Corey Lau is a graduate of Louisiana State University where he met Jennifer Irene Robin, of Lafaette, La. Eric and Jennifer were married January 2, 1999. They are both in graduate school in 2000 at Michigan State University. David is working for a doctorate in saxophone performance. Jennifer is finishing a masters in flute in May 2000. Matthew N. Corey is a fire fighter for the City of Worcester. He married Christina in May 1999. Josua Thomas Corey is a student at Marist College, Poughkeepsie, N.Y.

Mildred Corey Johnston Shirley

Mildred Corey was born August 16, 1912, in the house that had been occupied by Rev. Cyril Doucette, the first pastor of Knowlesville, with his family. From 1910 - 13 Rev. J.A. Corey and Alice Corey lived there. Mildred was the eighth and last of their children and the only one born there. She lived at Rusagonis, Wilson's Beach, Hoyt, Keswick Ridge, and Doaktown — places where her father ministered.

After graduating from Acadia in 1935[26] she lived briefly with her parents at Doaktown and worked in a hairdressing shop in Newcastle. In Doaktown she made a life-long friend, Ruth Brown, who later married Rev. Armand Steeves. Their families kept up visits.

Later, Mildred worked in a beauty parlour in East Port, Maine. There she met John Johnston, an officer in the U.S. Coast Guards. She had planned to come home to be married by her father, but the 1939 war had restricted U.S. military personnel from travelling to Canada.[27] Mildred came to Doaktown for a three-week visit. Then she went to Gardner, Mass, to the home of her brother Earle Corey, and Lois, then living on Maple St. Mildred and John were married there in late fall, 1939.

They made Gardner their home — first on Bancroft St. Mildred and John had one daughter, Elaine Johnston, born May 11, 1943. Elaine remembers that when she was five and a half they moved to Lincoln St. There, in partnership with Earle and Lois, they bought a double tenement house. Elaine also remembers her father coming home weekends.[28]

After 30 years in U.S. Coast Guards, John Johnston retired as Chief Petty Officer. Living in Gardner, he and a partner started a small business selling auto equipment in Fitchburg.

For 15 years Mildred Johnston worked for Gardner's weekly newspaper, proof-reading type. Elaine said, "She started that job when I started college - to help pay expenses." Mildred received a pension and benefits.

John Johnston died of a heart attack at home, May 4, 1964. The writer, then living in Boston, attended the funeral and read a scripture portion at the Baptist Church in Gardner. Relatives gathered in the home on Lincoln St. There I met Sally Haynes, daughter of Alfred Corey.

On August 15, 1970, Mildred married Clair E. Shirley. Clair's resume: born, August 6, 1923, Old Town, Maine; graduated from Old Town High, 1941; USNR, 1943-1946; graduated University of Maine, 1951; Scout Executive B.S.A., 25 years; Personal Financial Planner, American Express, 13 years; received M.A. from Liberty University, Lynchburg, Va., 1992.

Clair and Mildred attended three of her class reunions at Acadia: 50th, in 1985; 55th in 1990, and 60th in 1995. They also attended the Corey Reunion gatherings very enthusiastically. In her late years Mildred's condition, healthwise, was similar to the condition of her sister, Annie Haines, in her late years, as we have described it earlier in this chapter. In 1989 Mildred suffered congestive heart failure, and in 1994, shock. Clair cared for her with much devotion, lifting her in and out of his car and taking her to gatherings in a wheelchair. Thus he continued to bring her to the reunions at Knowlesville. On Labour Day weekend, 1997, he brought her to Wilson's Beach, Campobello Is. I sat with them at the Baptist Church on the Sunday morning.

The following winter Mildred was in a nursing home in Gardner, Clair having cared for her as long as he could at home. He visited her every day. In that time he read five books to her. Mildred died June 2, 1998.

On July 18, 1998, Clair attended the Corey Reunion, bringing Edna. Later he wrote: "I returned to my roots in Maine on November 28, 1998. I purchased a new home here on Pushaw Lake", near Stillwater.

Daughter and Grandchildren

Elaine, daughter of Mildred and John Johnston, was married to Charles Schindler. They had two children: Charles E. Schindler, born February 25, 1974, and Christina E. Schindler, born August 28, 1976.

On June 28, 1981, Elaine married John Billiard, a widower with a daughter and three sons. John sold his home to his son Tom and built a new home for him and Elaine on Arndt Road, Easton, Pa.

On July 18, 1987 John, Elaine, Christina and Charles attended the Corey Reunion at Knowlesville, in company with Clair and Mildred Shirley. Elaine is proud to be descended from the Coreys — people whom family tradition tells her were of strong character and firm resolve.

Elaine Johnston Billiard is employed by Mallinckrodt/Baker Chemicals. They produce lab grade chemicals. Her job is in "Demand Forecasting." John Billiard retired in 1997.

Elaine's Children

Charles E. Schindler graduated from Ursinus College, Collegeville, PA., in 1996. He is employed by Pentamation Computer Programs.

Christina E. Schindler graduated from Alfred University, Alfred, N.Y. in 1998. She is employed by "Stage Bill", a lap top publisher in Kennedy Center for Performing Arts, Washington, D.C.

Edna Violet Corey

Edna was born in Knowlesville, N.B., June 11, 1910, the seventh child of Rev. Judson A. Corey and Alice Howlett. Earlier that spring the parents and Edna's six elder siblings had come from Auburn, Maine.[29]

After the family moved to Keswick Ridge in 1925, Edna worked at F.W. Woolworth in Fredericton. She lived with her sister, Esther Smith, and family. Eventually, Edna took a secretarial course.

In 1942 she went to Gardner, Mass., where three of her siblings: Earle, David and Mildred, were living. Edna worked in the office of Massachusetts Electric, a branch of New England Electric Co., in Gardner. She lived with Mildred and family, and later with Earle and Lois. The two families lived in a double tenement house. When, in late years, that house was sold Edna went to an apartment in Gardner.

Edna is now the sole survivor of eight siblings. In Gardner she has no relatives but family members keep in touch with her. Some come to Gardner to see her. Jean and Earle Smith, e.g., have travelled from Ontario several times to visit her at Thanksgiving. Before Christmas 1999 Edna's niece,

Elaine, and John Billiard came from Pennsylvania and took Edna to their home and brought her back after the holiday.

Edna has been an enthusiastic attendant at the Corey Union, and has contributed much to keeping family memories alive.

She clarified the story of the rockers and cedar chests. Her father made at least one for each of his daughters. For Alberta he made several chairs for their porch. Burdell and Ross Anthony and Betty Bilensky still have some. Also for each daughter J.A. Corey made a cedar chest. Edna still has hers. The others have been bequeathed to oncoming generations.

In her 90th year, Edna's health is strong, and her medical needs are few. She had a slight shock, which affected her left hand slightly. She described a blocked artery. The doctors dilated it and inserted a metal tube to keep it open. She says she can now walk much easier and can climb to the second floor without difficulty.

In 1998 Edna gave up her car, but still travels. Clair Shirley brought her to the Corey Reunion in Knowlesville, July 18, 1998. In Gardner, friends have been driving her. Beverly Black picks her up for church. Ethel Kendall, the widow of Earle's friend, has driven her to Worcester to visit Verna. Edna is much appreciated by the family. Niece, Ellen Lau, said, "If we want to know about other members of the family we ask Aunt Edna." Nephew, Ross Anthony, described her as "one lovely lady."

---

[1]See Chap. I

[2]See The Story of Knowlesville, p. 89

[3]The writer has the beautifully hand-written record book in his possession. The name frequently appearing as secretary is Harry W. Machum. Several other names appear as secretary or assistants: Kate R. Wheaton, James M. Hobbs, Chas. H. Gayton

[4] Record book, p.26;

[5] Ibid., p.48

[6] Ibid., p.48f.

[7] Ibid., p.50

[8] Burdell Anthony

[9] Harold Smith

[10] Harold Smith and Sally Haynes

[11] Newspaper clipping

[12] See The Story of Knowlesville, p.131.

[13] Erma Corey Shaw

[14] See Chapter X

[15] Burdel Anthony and Betty Bilensky

[16] Edna Corey

[17] Edna Corey and Ross Anthony

[18] Telephone conversation with Eugene, January 8, 2000

[19] Theresa Haines, daughter-in-law

[20] See Chapter IV

[21] Theresa Haines

[22] Quotations in this biography of Annie Corey Haines not otherwise indicated, are from Theresa Haines

[23] Harold Smith and Sally Haynes

[24] Acadia University Alumni Directory, 1989, p.350; 1995, p.68, and p.140

[25] "Corey Courier", 1974, p.2

[26] Acadia Univ. Alumni Directory, 1989, p.231; 1995, p.304

[27] Edna Corey

[28] Telephone conversation with Elaine Johnston Billiard, March 21, 2000

[29] See Chapter IV

CHAPTER XII

McBRINE FAMILY

1872 IDA COREY McBRINE 1953
m. 1890
1865 WILLIAM GEORGE McBRINE 1921

In my earliest memories of my Aunt Ida McBrine and family, they were living on the second farm lot from Grandpa Corey's, going south.[1] McBrine's house was only a short walk from the home of my grandparents. The farmhouse in Knowlesville was the first home of Ida Corey and William George McBrine. They were married in November 1890, by Rev. J.K. Bearisto, the Presbyterian minister in Glassville. Bill moved from Glassville. Ida had only to move to the next farm. Both families — McBrines and Coreys — were relatively new immigrants to Carleton County. William McBrine was a son of Christopher McBrine and Mary Burns. "Christopher......was born in Ireland. He came to New Brunswick about 1855 and settled in Golden Grove area of Saint John County." Christopher McBrine, in company with three other young Irishmen: George Reid, Robert Boyle and Robert Montgomery, came to Glassville soon after the new settlement was opened.[2]

Ida Mae Corey was born in Maine, May 26, 1872. When her parents, my grandparents, Alfred and Lucretia Corey, left Maine and brought their first five children to Knowlesville, Ida was the baby of the family, probably about age two. Thus the estimated date of the move to Knowlesville is 1874. It is certain that the move was before the birth of Ida's next sibling, Sadie, on February 7th, 1875.

A year after Ida Corey married William McBrine her sister, Mina Corey, married William's brother Robert Edmund McBrine. He was called Eb. Two Corey sisters married two

McBrine brothers. The names of both William and Robert Edmund McBrine are on the Glassville School list from 1872 through 1878. The names of their three brothers; Frederick, Archibald and Arthur, are listed. They had three sisters.

We have only brief glimpses of Ida while growing up on the Corey homestead in Knowlesville. My father had an amusing anecdote about his sister. A window was broken at the Corey house. The youngsters formed a habit of running to that window and sticking their heads out to see who was coming on the road. After the glass was replaced, Ida, on hearing the sound of horses and wagon on the road ran to the window and put her head right through the glass.

Thanks to the records of three local organizations we have a few citations of Ida in her early years. Knowlesville School records tell us that she was enrolled at least as late as 1887; thus she attended at least into her 15th year.[3]

The record book of Pride of Aberdeen Lodge lists Ida Corey as a charter member on October 1, 1886. On December 11, 1886, "Ida Corey L.H.S." is recorded as a "pro tem" officer. Also she is listed, along with her brother Judson, and others, as a volunteer to entertain the Lodge at its next meeting. On February 12, 1887, Ida is listed on the affirmative side of a debate: "Resolved that there is more beauty in art than in nature." On February 19, 1887, Ida was named to the pro tem office: R.H.S. On February 26, 1887, Ida is listed on the affirmative side for the debate: "Resolved that there is more happiness or pleasure in married than in single life." On March 5, 1887, Ida is again named to a committee to entertain. At the next meeting, March 12th, she recited: "Touch not the Glass." That evening she was named on the negative side for a debate: "Resolved that the Mechanic is of more benefit to the country than the Farmer." On March 19, 1887, Ida was appointed to the "Literary Committee to entertain at our next meeting."

The record book of Highlands Baptist Church, of which

Ida's father was clerk, states: "Ida Corey, baptized by Herman Shaw" (p.15 f.). On the membership lists for 1899, and 1904 she is listed: Mrs. William McBrine, (pp. 25 and 36).

Children

While Ida and Bill McBrine were living on the farm in Knowlesville their first eight children were born: Clara and Claude, twins, 1891; Jud, 1894; Nessie, 1896; Ellen, 1899; Vola 1902; Kathleen, 1904; and George, 1907.

More recollections from Erma: "My grandparents often took me to Aunt Ida's and Uncle Bill's house for an evening visit. I liked the McBrine's house, and I liked the whole family. When I was too sleepy to walk home my grandfather carried me piggyback. I also went in daytime to visit the family in the frame house that was a little larger than the Corey house."[4] "I liked to play with the McBrine girls, my cousins, especially Nellie, Vola and Kathleen, who were near my age. But our time together in Knowlesville was all too short. Sometime after the birth of George, 1907, the family moved to Glassville. That was before I started school. I missed them a lot. I continued to visit them, but not so often."

Erma's story of her father's home coming in fall of 1908, and their visit to Glassville, confirms that the McBrine family was in Glassville by 1908.[5] The Glassville school register lists Nellie and Nessie McBrine for the school year ending June 1909.[6]

Residences in Glassville

In Glassville the McBrine family first lived in the house owned by Ida's sister and brother-in-law, Alma, and Jim Miller, before it was sold to Perry Fitzgerald, in May 1909. "People were asking, 'Where will the McBrine's go now?' I, at age six, said,

'What about the Dr. Welch place?' They moved into the Welch house probably about the time the Miller house was sold."

About ten years earlier, Dr. Edwin Welch had moved to the U.S.A. and left vacant the house he had built on the east side of the village of Glassville, on the road toward Highlands. The house had an attached apothecary.[7] Erma added, "Quite a few bottles of drugs were left there when the doctor vacated. I remember my father, Ira Corey, coming in for Benzene to use as a cleaning fluid."

A Funeral and a Birth

The first year the McBrines lived in the Welch house they suffered a sad loss. Their eldest son, Claude, died there at age 18 after a long illness that had confined him to bed. Erma, age six in 1909, remembered: "A phone message came from Miller's in Glassville, to G.W.Whitehouse's in Knowlesville to inform Claude's grandparents of his death. I remember King Avery coming to our house carrying the message from Whitehouse's, near the school, to Grandpa and Grandma Corey. In those days messages were carried by school boys.

"On the suggestion of Grandpa Corey, Rev. J.D. Wetmore from Florenceville, was engaged to conduct the funeral. It began with prayers at the Welch house. At the conclusion of that part of the funeral, Uncle Bill lifted Aunt Ida by the shoulders to help her from her chair. She went into labour about the time the family and friends left the house. I think Aunt Alma stayed with Aunt Ida.

"I can still visualize the funeral procession from Glassville to Knowlesville for the service in the Baptist Church. Just behind the sled, bearing the coffin, was Uncle Bill, Nessie, Nellie, Vola and Jud, travelling by team and sled. Next were Clara and Percy Whitehouse, travelling in their own one-horse sleigh. Clara was then already married and living in E.

Knowlesville. Grandpa said, 'Let them go next.' He reined his mare in behind Percy's sleigh." There was mourning and pain and new life in the McBrine family on the same day. Their youngest daughter, Lucretia, was born in the Welch house on the day of her brother Claude's funeral, on November 16, 1909.

Two more children were born in the Welch house: Leland, 1912, and Lorne 1916, bringing to eleven the children born to Ida and William McBrine. Ten lived to mature ages.

More of Erma's Recollections

"My visits with my cousins, the McBrine girls, in Glassville, became more frequent, I spent many a happy hour with them. In summer we played with dishes. During one of my winter visits Nessie was keeping house in the absence of Aunt Ida who was on a visit at Spence's. That day our joyful play was interrupted when a group of men appeared on the road. We could see them coming by Ted Welch's. Nessie, inciting much fear, huddled us all into hiding, saying, 'The Dagoes are coming.' They were Italian workers walking from the C.N. Railway at Juniper.

"In the summer of Haley's Comet, 1910, I was at McBrine's for three weeks. My father, Ira Corey, was there too, boarding with Aunt Ida and Uncle Bill. One evening she said, 'Ira, Haley's Comet is out tonight.'"

Meat, Mail and Mischief, by Erma

"That summer, my father, Ira, and Jud McBrine, then only about 16, were running a slaughter house in the neighborhood of the Welch house. They used an abandoned house at the top of the hill near the swamp and on the opposite side of the road from the site of the later dance hall. They peddled the meat from a wagon. That summer my father also worked for Uncle Bill McBrine as a part-time mail driver between Glassville and Bristol. He also carried passengers to and from the train.

"Mail driving was a kind of a family enterprise for the McBrine's, and a part of their livelihood, for a few years. Ida McBrine managed two mail routes out of Glassville. One went to Ketchum Ridge, on Tuesday, Thursday and Saturday. Occasionally, Viola drove the horse and delivered on that route.

"The second route was to Knowlesville, on Monday, Wednesday and Friday. Aunt Ida dropped the mailbags at James Hobbs' Post Office, but delivered the Corey's mail to their house. Thus she kept up visits with her parents. Sometimes Uncle Bill, when not busy with other work, brought the mail to Knowlesville. One mail day when he left his horse standing in Grandpa's yard I narrowly escaped a crash. I hopped into the wagon, took the reins, started the horse, and almost upset the wagon."

Other family members took turns delivering mail to Knowlesville. Nessie's daughter, Betty Gray, and daughter Kim Morrison, cited recollections by Nessie and Nellie of their driving a horse through Esdraelon and delivering mail to Knowlesville. Apparently Bill McBrine also had turns delivering to Ketchum Ridge. Here is a story told by John Lyon who grew up in Ketchum Ridge — "Our mail was delivered by horse and buggy or sleigh by Mr. William McBrine....One Christmas day he drove into our yard with a parcel from Eaton's. He told my mother he had overlooked it the day before and thought it might be something she had got for Christmas and the children would be disappointed if this wasn't delivered."[8]

A Property in Glassville

Glassville was the abode of Ida and Bill McBrine and family for several years — several houses. After three years in the Dr. Welch house, Ida and Bill bought the house and property that had belonged to John Home, a minister of the Church of Scotland, who had emigrated from Aberdeen in 1865. He had "served as minister in Woodstock". He "spent the last decade of his life as a farmer in Glassville and also as a schoolmaster....". He taught in Glassville: 1883 and 1894, and in various schools in the parish of Aberdeen, e.g., Beaufort in 1896 and Biggar Ridge in 1897. He was also a "correspondent for the Woodstock papers."9 Mr. Home died in 1898 at age 69.

The McBrines bought the property from the widow, Mary C. Home, for $1,000. The deed, dated July 4, 1912, was drawn up by Alexander G. Lindsay, J.P. of Carleton Co. The McBrines did not long retain the property. A deed, dated May 24, 1916, shows that "William G. McBrine and wife" sold the Home property to D. Perry Fitzgerald, merchant. The deed was registered on January 2, 1917 by Donald Munro. The property, situated next to the former school, now Glassville Recreational Hall, is now possessed and occupied by Elsie MacIntosh, daughter of Bill McIntosh. She also possesses the deeds.

The Love Hotel and its Neighborhood

Another place where the McBrine family lived in Glassville was the Love Hotel. It is quite probable that they went there directly from the Home place. They must have made their home in the hotel for five or six years.

Norman Corey recalled a boyhood visit with some of our relatives in that neighborhood. He said, "I went to Glasville with my father. When we arrived at the Miller place, Kate Hovey pointed across the field to the Bristol Road and said, 'Right over there are two boys — your relatives. You can play with them.' Near the old cheese factory I found Leland and Lorne."

Walter Whitehouse recalled the old telephone office on that end of the Bristol Road. He reminisced further, "John Hood had a blacksmith shop and barn. He lived in a little shack back of the barn." The telephone office was over the blacksmith shop. Walter said, "Mother, (then Clara Whitehouse) ran the telephone office. My grandmother (Ida McBrine) was then in the Love Hotel." It appears there was still some business at the Love Hotel when the McBrine family moved into it. Erma Corey Shaw said, "They kept travellers overnight and served meals". However, the business was waning before the McBrine's time there. "The hotel business continued to thrive at least through the first decade of the twentieth century and particularly during the construction of the railroad through Juniper. Afterward, however, with railway access from that end, Glassville and the hotel trade suffered. The hotel deteriorated, eventually was rented, and finally destroyed by fire on February 24, 1922."[10]

Perhaps business at the hotel was then seasonal. In any case the McBrine's were on a job in Juniper while the family was still living at the hotel. Erma said, "Aunt Ida was cooking in Juniper." Apparently Uncle Bill was helping her. It happened that it was his last job.

The Early Death of Bill McBrine

Erma said, "Uncle Bill died there in June 1921. It was when I was about to finish my first teaching year at E. Glassville. I was home in Knowlesville that Saturday. My father made a trip to Highlands that day with his team and wagon to deliver a butchered veal. He received a message, probably via his mother-in-law, Mary Brown, that his brother-in-law, Bill McBrine, had died in Juniper. Word spread via those who had phones."

Bill McBrine died at the early age of 56. His funeral was from the hotel to the Presbyterian Church in Glassville. His stone stands in the northeast corner of the adjacent cemetery:

McBrine
1865 William G. McBrine 1921

A Bereaved Family

Erma said, "The family continued living at the hotel for a time." It was a short time. Marjorie Martinson said, "There was nobody living in the hotel at the time of the fire in 1922." The family had moved out before that time.

Ida McBrine, widowed at age 49, had to be the breadwinner, at least for the youngest family members; George, 14; Lucretia, 12; Leland, 8; and Lorne, not yet 5. However Ida was versatile in work: mail driving, cook. Also she served as a mid wife. One of her patients was Bessie, wife of Arthur MacIntosh, in the early 20's.[11] Most of the elder family members, however, were no longer dependent on a parent. The three eldest daughters were married.

Clara married Percy Whitehouse while the McBrine family was still living in Knowlesville. The McBrine family moved to Glassville, about 1908. Later Clara and Percy and children also moved to Glassville.

Nessie was married to Cecil Avery, son of Alice Day and Arthur K. Avery, of Knowlesville. Their first child, Dorothy, was born in 1921. Nellie was married to Harry Lindsay. Their first child, Mary, was also born in 1921. Vola McBrine married Archie Barker, September 13, 1922.

Eldest son, Jud McBrine, married Dorothy Bedell, in 1920. She was

Claudia Whitehouse, baby; Clara, mother, standing; Ida McBrine, grandmother, seated, l.; Lucretia Corey, g-grandmother, seated, r

from Maine, but had relatives in New Brunswick — the Wiley family. In Glassville they lived in the house built for Presbyterian ministers. When there was not a resident minister, the house was rented. It came to be called the "old manse."[12]

Jud was an early entrepreneur as indicated by a letter written by his Uncle Ira Corey, on October 29, 1922 to his daughter, Erma.[13] Ira had a logging crew on the Little Clearwater that fall. In his letter Ira recorded that Jud McBrine also had a camp and a crew on Little Clearwater. He added: "Dorothy is often there with him." Ira tells us further that Jud "is in the same place he was last winter." Thus he had begun a logging enterprise at least as early as fall of 1921. In summary, Ira's letter provides us a window into the work situations of five McBrine siblings. He tells us, Clara and Nessie are cooking for Jud, and "Nellie Lindsay and Kathleen are tending Central", i.e., the telephone exchange in Glassville.

Another position which Jud McBrine had while still a very young man was "road commissioner". Roy Hemphill recalls seeing him driving a beautiful horse through Knowlesville and stopping to supervise a crew of road workers. One project Roy especially remembers: the road between Hobbs' and Carence LaPage's had veered around a swampy area. Jud had his crew haul a whole rock pile from a field and fill in the swamp. Thus they straightened the road. Evidently, Jud McBrine, early in life, moved into entrepreneurial and administrative positions usually occupied by older men.

McBrines Leaving Glassville

Despite his ability as an entrepreneur Jud and Dorothy did not long remain in Glassville or vicinity. They moved to Maine whence Dorothy had come — probably by 1924. Marjorie Martinson said the manse was needed for a resident minister by 1924. In the early 20's most of the Ida and Bill McBrine family were leaving Glasssville.

Nessie and Cecil Avery went to Jacksonville and Woodstock area, where Cecil farmed with his brother Earle. Nessie must have continued some employment after marriage. Following the winter of cooking for her brother, Jud McBrine, on Little Clearwater she spent a winter in a lumber camp on the Nashwaak River, run by Cecil's father, Arthur Avery, of Knowlesville. Cecil was also at the camp. He was the bookkeeper. Their first two children, Dorothy, age two, and Alice in her first year, were with them in the camp that winter, 1923-25.

The camp correspondent rated Nessie's cooking very highly: "We are sumptuously fed by Mrs. Cecil Avery assisted by Robert Rideout. Our menu would shame the Mount Royal."[14] Rideout long remembered the experience. About three decades later, on a Hartland street, he remarked to Warren Corey, "I cooked for Nessie." He also kept the memory alive with Betty Gray by frequently recounting the winter Dorothy and Alice were toddler and baby at the camp.

Ida

It appears that Ida McBrine also made an early departure from Glassville. Pearl Buchanan McBrine recalls a story told to her by Ida and Nellie. Pearl recounted, "Ida took some of her youngest children and went to Skowhegan, Maine, and stayed with Jud McBrine and family there." It would probably be between 1924 and 1926, the estimated time of Jud's sojourn in Skowhegan. This story might explain why Leland and Lorne are not on the Glassville school list in 1924. Leland, however, in his reminiscences did not mention Skowhegan. Apparently they returned to Glassville. Leland and Lorne again appear on the school list.

Leland's name last appears on the Glassville school list for the year ending June 1926. Perhaps he left then permanently. Though he apparently left when in his early teens Leland long retained good memories of Glassville.

Memories of Glassville and Area

In October 1999, Leland McBrine recalled some of his boyhood experiences and ventures. He spoke of staying with Jud and Dorothy when he was a very young boy at the old manse and at a lumber camp. He said, "Dorothy kept me there and taught me my letters. He still appreciated the kindness of Dorothy and Jud.

About the logging scene, Leland flashed up random images with hazy chronology: "The old Gray house" turned into a bunk house, with bunks in several rooms and across a whole wall; Jimmie Sharp keeping the fires burning; salmon eggs brought on the train for a hatchery; building a bridge across the S. Branch for hauling logs; icing roads; lumber piled along the railroad tracks; horses and men opening a road after a snow storm; teams of horses trekking to Glassville at end of hauling season.

In Glassville Leland learned to ride. "A man who was ploughing for Millers on their lower farm allowed me to ride one of the horses to the barn at the end of the work day. Next I was allowed to ride Miller's saddle horse into the cow pasture. I filled the saddlebags with rocks. When I rode out to bring in the cows I threw rocks at the bull. He got very angry but the horse could outrun him." This anecdote from Leland's youth in Glassville may be a foreshadowing of his later venture and daring on the high buildings. Also it may have been the beginning of his great fondness for horses, and his later hobby with racehorses.

Clara and Family in Glassville

By the mid-twenties, it appears there were few of the family of Bill and Ida McBrine left in Glassville. Perhaps the last to leave was Clara and family.

There is still one person in Glassville who retains and cherishes vivid and happy memories of companionship and long-valued friendship with several members of the McBrine family, especially those who remained latest in Glassville. That Glassville resident is Marjorie Martinson, daughter of Maggie and David Lamont. Marjorie especially remembers Clara and her family. She said, "Clara lived above John Hood's shop. She kept the telephone office in her house for years". Helping Nessie cook for Jud on Little Clearwater in fall of 1922 was perhaps a temporary change of work and scenery, for Clara.

Marjorie remembers Clara's children as they were growing up in Glassville in her time: Claudia, Clarence, Walter, Madeline and Kathleen, and also Clara's youngest sister, "Cretia". She also recognized special qualities in Jud. Marjorie said, "They were all smart, especially Cretia and Claudia. They could go to the store, get a piece of cloth and go home and quickly whip up anything, without even a pattern. Claudia, Cretia and I were friends — bosom pals — though both were older than I."

Though Claudia left Glassville at a very early age, Marjorie described warm friendship and long-cherished relationship with her. Marjorie recollected further: "Cretia and I wrote the Normal School entrance exams together in 1926." Soon thereafter Lucretia left Glassville. Marjorie thinks Lucretia left in 1926, about a year after Claudia left.

The McBrines, on leaving Glassville, scattered somewhat. Soon, however, many of them regrouped in one place: New York City.

McBrines Migrating to New York City

A construction boom in New York City in the 20's lured workers. First of the McBrine connection to make the venture were Nellie and Harry Lindsay; then Kathleen and Percy Williams. John Lindsay, of Halifax, son of Harry Lindsay, says much of the work in New York City starting in the 20's was in, on, or connected with the earliest high rise buildings.

John said, "My father worked on Radio City and on the Chrysler Building and the George Washington Bridge. He and his crew put the spire on the Empire State Building." John added, "Any of the family who went to New York for work got jobs through my father. He was in the union, and a foreman." Percy Whitehouse and Cecil Avery were early migrants to New York. Percy's sister, Delma Whitehouse, kept house for Percy and Cecil in their early time there. Clara went to New York on visits but never took up residence there.[15] Claudia Whitehouse also joined the relatives in New York, quite early. The last year her name appears on the Glassville School list is 1925. When Lucretia McBrine left Glassville, about 1926, she also went to New York.

After some time on the farm in Jacksonville, Nessie joined Cecil in New York. We have only clues to indicate when the Avery family came together in New York. Their third daughter, Betty, said, "I was born in Woodstock," in 1928. Cecil Avery, Jr., fourth child and only son, was born in Brooklyn, New York, in 1933.

By the time the writer was gathering this history only one of the McBrine siblings was living and able to narrate the New York venture - Leland, next to the youngest of the family. When did you go to New York? "I was big enough to work when I went there." He thinks he was about age 15, which would be in 1927. This would agree with the possibility of leaving Glassville in 1926, and allow for some time in Maine, before going to New York to work — a brave venture for a boy. His story:

"I was staying with Jud and Dorothy McBrine in Haynesville, Maine. I received a message from one of my sisters in New York, instructing me to take a train to Boston. There I was to change to another station. ' Follow the crowd to the second station.' Nellie met me at that station. From there we took the train to New York."

In New York, Leland said, "Harry Lindsay got the job for

me." Leland described his first job. "I was fixing, straightening and re-threading bolts and nuts and connectors. After we repaired them we took them up," i.e. to where steel beams were being put in place. Then he progressed to the stage where, "I was putting them in and tightening them."

"Then an old Italian fellow said to me, 'you're wasting your time here; come with me.' We became friends; I loved him. We rode up on the load; we were roped together. I learned to ride beams and run across them. The beams were hooked in the middle and had a guide line to balance them. We unhooked the beam, then stood on the sling and rode it down. A man swung on the beam; he put a bolt in each side. The beams were bolted and riveted by machine. The big rivets were heated before going in."

John Lindsay, Leland's nephew, said, "He had a fall. One time he was swinging on a beam. The men got him down. They had to pry his hands loose — he was gripping it so tightly". Leland reminisced further about the high buildings: "Radio City — a music hall — was the first. I was on it for a long time. It had three floors under the street - Lexington Ave. Wall St., where the money people are, is a giant. The buildings were getting taller and taller. Every building of height — I was on it. I was paid $15.40 an hour for an 8-hour day; double time for overtime, including Saturday. Some days I worked till dark. I stayed on the Iron Works quite a while."

Ida McBrine and Family in New York

At length, Ida McBrine also went to New York, probably taking her youngest, Lorne, with her. Kaye Thompson says the year was perhaps 1927. Leland said, "My sisters brought my dear mother to New York, i.e., to Brooklyn. She stayed with Cretia." Whatever the initial living arrangements, Ida became the housekeeper for Leland and Lorne. Clara's daughter, Kaye, had a visit of several months with her grandmother, Ida, during that time. Kaye said, "I was very fond of my grandmother. I went with Lucretia who had come to New Brunswick on a visit, in 1929. I went to school there. I stayed until my mother came the next spring, with Aunt Vola and Uncle Arch Barker. I came home with them in Uncle Arch's car."

McBrines Leaving New York; Some Staying

Dr. Edward Williams, son of Kathleen and Percy, said, "I was born in New York in 1929." He shared some memories: "Dad worked as a mechanic in a big garage in New York." Dr. Williams also remembers his Uncle Harry Lindsay: "He took me to the circuses."

Betty Avery Gray remembers living with her family in Brooklyn, N.Y. "In an apartment in a brown stone house." She also remembers her first school. "It had a big iron fence."

Leland McBrine got married in New York, he said, "to a lovely lady - the sweetest thing that ever lived." Her name was Marion Lindquist; she was born in Brooklyn, N.Y. Leland: "When I stopped working in New York, Marion and I came to Maine. We lived there for a while. Then Marion and I came home," i.e., to New Brunswick. "Archie Barker had a service station in Lakeville. He wanted me to run the gas station."

John Lindsay: "When I was eight we left New York, and came to Woodstock, N.B. That was in 1934." Making the

Leland and Marion Brine

move were: mother, Nellie, and children: Mary, born 1921; John, born 1926 in Brooklyn; and Harold born 1929 in Brooklyn.

Betty Avery Gray: "We left there in 1936, when I was eight." In that move were mother, Nessie, and children: Dorothy, born 1921; Alice born 1923; Betty, born 1928; and Cecil born 1933. They also returned to New Brunswick - first to a temporary house in Foreston.

Dr. Edward Williams, son of Kathleen and Percy Williams: "We left New York in 1937 and moved to Maine. Dad had much experience as a mechanic. He had worked for Archie Barker before going to New York. Dad wanted to own a garage. Jud and Dorothy McBrine were living in Hynesville. He said, "There are two for sale: one in Haynesville; one in Linneus. Dad bought the latter."

Harry Lindsay remained in New York and continued with his trade as an ironworker. Cecil Avery, Sr., also remained in New York.

Percy Whitehouse remained in New York, apparently through his working years. His daughter Claudia, remained and married in New York in 1928. They lived nearby. Percy's only sister, Delma Whitehouse, in her later years, lived in Concord, N.H. She had a house in an attractive residential part of the city. In 1955 I took my father, Ira Corey, to visit her. He was visiting me at Bow, N.H., bordering on Concord. In his late years Percy came to Concord, N.H. and lived with Delma. She cared for him in his last illness. He died in Concord and is buried there.[16]

Lucretia McBrine married Edward MacDonnell in New York and remained there long after her siblings had left.

McBrine: Six Daughters; Four sons

We have carried the story of Ida and Bill McBrine and family through the time of their scattering to Maine and New

Nessie, Clara and Ellen, McBrine sisters

York and over New Brunswick. Now we tell the story of each of the 10 siblings, the closing years of their mother, and brief stories of the children and grandchildren. The 10 McBrines:

Clara	1891-1992
Jud	1894-1974
Nessie	1896-1986
Ellen (Nellie)	1899-1984
Vola	1902-
Kathleen	1904-2001
George	1907-1972
Lucretia	1909-1990

Leland   1912-
Lorne   1916-1963

Clara

Clara Jennie, daughter of Ida Corey and William G. McBrine, was born in Knowlesville, N.B., December 3, 1891. She and her twin brother, Clarence, are listed in Knowlesville school records for 1898 and 99.[17]

Clara was married to Percy Whitehouse, probably before the McBrine family left Knowlesville about 1908. For a few years Clara and Percy lived with his parents, Jerusha and Joseph Stillman Whitehouse in E. Knowlesville.

Clara Whitehouse and her sister, Nessie McBrine, were baptized on May 18, 1913, by their uncle, Rev. J.A. Corey, then pastor of the Knowlesville United Baptist Church. The names of the two sisters are on the list of members of Knowlesville United Baptist Church, reported in June 1913.[18]

Clara and family were still living in E. Knowlesville in the fall of 1913. In October Percy Whitehouse helped move Rev. J.A. Corey to Rusagonis. Sometime between 1913 and 1917 the family moved to Glassville. Claudia and Clarence appear on the Glassville school list for year ending June 1917.

Clara Whitehouse continued to live in Glassville, perhaps longer than any of her siblings. However, her family also was much affected by the McBrine family's migration to New York. Both Percy and their daughter Claudia were among those who went to New York for work.

Some time after the McBrine family had scattered from Glassville, Clara moved with her younger children to Jacksonville. They lived briefly with Nessie Avery on the farm, before taking residence in Woodstock. Marjorie Martinson, a lifetime friend of Clara and family, remembers visiting her on Broadway. Daughter, Madeline, remembers Broadway School.

In 1931 Clara married Weldon Flemming of Juniper. The writer, then age 8, remembers the autumn day his father, Ira Corey, returned to the farm in E. Knowlesville from Juniper where he regularly delivered butter. He gave a glowing report of discovering that Clara was living in Juniper. She had given him a warm welcome in her new home.

In Juniper, Clara Flemming soon became a part of the community. She is credited with being instrumental in the building by Flemming and Gibson Co. of the Union Church in Juniper, which was dedicated in June 1938 for use by the Anglican, Baptist and United Church congregations. A photo portraying the Juniper Church choir of that era includes the beaming face of Clara Flemming in the front row.[19]

Her alto voice was often heard in duets — Madeline said, with their Uncla Ira, with Tom Pat and others. Madeline also recalled her mother working on church suppers: cooking chickens or turkeys. Mary recalled her mother "making up trays of food for basket socials. She said "She was an excellent cook." Marion Spence said, "She was most generous. She gave to everything and anyone in need." She saw a need for additional furniture in the principal's apartment when Larry and Ruth Dow's first baby arrived.[20]

Madeline recalled also her mother visiting the sick. "She went late one night to a sick child at Juniper Station." With her community work she continued to be a mother to her grown children. Madeline said, "We all idolized her." Kaye said, "She was a great mother."

There was much communication and transaction between the Ira Corey family and Clara and Weldon Flemming and family. Ira Corey had been involved in winter logging contracts with Flemming and Gibson Co. from the time of J.K. Flemming, who was Premier of New Brunswick from 1911-1914. Ira's contracting reached into the 1940's. Several of Ira's sons also worked for the company. In September 1941 Weldon asked me to go to Burnt Hill to a job as clerk and scaler at Charlie Crabbe's camp. The following fall he came to the farm to pick me up and send me to a camp across the North Branch, and later to a camp up Tague Brook.

In 1945 Ira, Nellie and their three youngest: Kathleen, Shirley and Gordon, moved to Juniper. Gordon Corey became an employee of Flemming and Gibson at about age 14. He recalls the morning Weldon was looking for a truck driver. He turned to Gordon, still only 14: "What.....are you waiting for; get in that truck and go with it."

My father, Ira Corey, in his retirement years in Juniper, was employed on various jobs: counting logs being unloaded, and caring for horses and cows. About that time the company built a new barn. Ira billed the hay and oats to the lumber camps. He fed the work horses and groomed and exercised Weldon's race horses. He milked the two cows and distributed the milk to the homes of Weldon and Hugh John Flemming and Sam Billings.[21]

Kaye and Shirley Corey, arriving in Juniper in their early teens, recall Clara's kindnesses to them. Many people, members of their large family and others, visited Clara and Weldon. They found a cordial and hospitable home. "You didn't have to be in the house very long to see that the relationship between Clara and Weldon was a love affair", said Shirley Brooks.

It seems that Weldon Flemming's responsibility increased in his later life. In 1953 he "replaced consummate millman Sam Billings as president" of Flemming & Gibson. Weldon's responsibility also involved carrying a business partnership with Sam Bell's mill at Stickney. That relationship had been growing since the war years. Then "the Stickney mill had been filling planed lumber orders from Flemming and Gibson....."[22] In 1945 Sam Billings and the Hon. Hugh John Flemming became partners in S.W. Bell Ltd.

Near the end of his working years Weldon Flemming

and his company suffered a heavy loss. "In January (1964) the Juniper mill was destroyed by fire ...Weldon Flemming.....,was forced to retire due to ill health within a few months of the fire."[23] But retirement for Weldon did not hold long enjoyment.

Weldon Flemming was one of two well-known Carleton County men to suffer an untimely death and leave "a vacuum" in industry. ".....Sam Bell died unexpectedly in 1968. .....Sam Bell's untimely death left a vacuum in the Stickney saw mill's operations as well as in Juniper, because since 1964, the Flemming and Bell operations had become more closely allied than ever."[24]

After a heart attack Weldon and Clara enjoyed some family visits, e.g., with Mary in Florida, and Madeline in Oromocto. Weldon spent some time in hospital in both Fredericton and Woodstock. In his last illness he was in the home of Walter and Evelyn Whitehouse in Victoria Corner. Evelyn was his nurse. He appreciated her care very much. In March 1967 Weldon suffered a second heart attack and died at their house.[25]

Mary Flemming remembers her father as "a kind, loving, giving person who didn't want to see anybody in need." She recalls travelling with him to Stickney to do business with Sam Bell at his mill, and to Florenceville to buy horses from Bill Burnham. She said, "I did not mind long waits sitting in the car because I loved being with Dad. I adored him. I often think, if only we could have had him longer".[26]

After being widowed Clara was able to continue some family visits: e.g. she spent part of the winter of 1973 with son Walter Whitehouse and Evelyn, in Florida, and the winter of 1976 with daughter, Madeline Oliver in Oromocto.

In 1980 Clara suffered a major heart attack and several strokes. She was in hospital in Woodstock for six weeks. There her daughters Ruth and Mary gave her therapy. Clara recovered somewhat from paralysis, but required care the rest of her life.

Mary cared for her mother at her home in Juniper for nearly 13 years. "She knew people until her last two years, even then she sometimes recognized people; she always knew me."

Clara's 100th birthday was celebrated December 3, 1991. Helping to celebrate were her daughter Claudia Lundberg and four more generations of daughters. Clara lived until August 28, 1992. Her funeral was held in the United Church of Canada, Juniper. In the United Church Cemetery, Glassville, stands the monument:

```
         FLEMMING
1895   Weldon      1967
1891   Clara       1991
```

Claudia Whitehouse Lundberg

Claudia was born January 8, 1909 or 1910 in E. Knowlesville, N.B. She attended school in Glassville, N.B. approximately from 1916 to 1925. At an early age she joined the McBrine relatives in New York. Her sister Madeline said Claudia was only age 17 when she left Glassville. In New York she met John (Jack) Lundberg who was born in Lexington, Mass., in 1907. An ironworker, he worked on high buildings in New York City: Empire State, Chrysler and many more. Claudia and Jack were married August 2, 1928. Their first two daughters were born in Brooklyn: Barbara, September 19, 1929, and Clair June 28, 1932.

For a short interval Claudia and Jack lived in New Brunswick. When her brother Walter Whitehouse began managing the farm at Victoria Corner, N.B. Jack worked on the farm and Claudia kept house. Their two youngest daughters were born in Woodstock: Jacqueline in 1936, and Joan in 1937. After about two years they returned to U.S.A., first in Portland, Me., then in Boston, where Jack had two sisters. Eventually they returned to New York City where Jack worked until 1972.

Claudia kept up visits with family. She retained an affection for her Aunt Delma Whitehouse. In Delma's last illness Claudia came to Concord, N.H., and took care of her.[27] Claudia also visited her mother, Clara, in Juniper, and others in New Brunswick.

Children and Grandchildren of Claudia and Jack

Barbara Shirley Lundberg married William Barrington of Mass., in 1948. Their children are Jean, Robert and James Barrington. Claire Joyce Lundberg married John W. Johnstone Jr., of New York in 1956. Their children are: Thomas, James and Robert Johnstone. Jacqueline Ann Lundberg maried Walter Innes of Kansas, in 1958. Their children are: Paula and Douglas, born in Orange,Texas, and Judith and Carol, born in Elizabeth, N.J. Joan Lorraine Lundberg married Joseph Koller in Woodside, N.Y., in 1962. Their children are: Joan, Deborah, and John Koller. Claudia and Jack have 13 grandchildren, 25 great grandchildren and 2 great-great grandchildren. Their

Jack, 94, and Claudia, 91

names are in the genealogy. In retirement Claudia and Jack moved to Florida. After suffering losses in a hurricane in 1995 they moved to Watertown, Wisconsin. In year 2000 — both in their 90's — they are living in a nursing home. They are still communicating with relatives. Bobby and Margaret Flemming reported making a tape of a TV interview. Jack was describing work on the Empire State Building.[28]

Clarence William Whitehouse

Clarence, son of Clara McBrine and Percy Whitehouse was born in E. Knowlesville, July 12, 1911. The Glassville school lists him as a pupil for years ending June, 1917 through 1924. Most of his working years were with the Flemming and Gibson Co., Juniper. In 1932 he was a clerk in the company store — recalled Vella Scott who was teaching in Juniper that year.

Clarence was in the Canadian Army during WWII. In the fall of 1941, I remember seeing him at Burnt Hill. He was spending part of his "leave" on a hunting outing. He and his brother Walter stayed at Charlie Crabbe's camp. Clarence served in the Postal Corps in Italy for four years.

After the war Clarence resumed work with Flemming and Gibson. He became Woodlands Manager with responsibility for supplying logs to the mill — a position delegated to him by Weldon Flemming. Eventually Clarence became Vice-President of Flemming and Gibson.

Clarence married Grace Cummings, an office employee of Flemming and Gibson. She was the daughter of David and Cora Cummings of Juniper. Clarence and Grace had two daughters: Jan Elizabeth, born March 4, 1950; and Jill Elaine, born May 18, 1957. They lived in the former Claude Fitzgerald house in Juniper.

In the winter of 1981 Clarence suffered a fractured hip and pelvis bone in a fall from his roof, when removing snow. In the early 80's Clarence and Grace moved from Juniper to Fredericton. There Jill attended U.N.B. In his retirement years Clarence unfortunately suffered from two heart attacks. He lived to see his daughter, Jill, graduate from U.N.B. He died of cancer in the Dr. Everett Chalmers Hospital, Fredericton, July 17, 1988.

Grace Cummings Whitehouse lived eleven years in Fredericton after being widowed. In her last year she suffered a lengthy illness in the Dr. E. Chalmers Hospital. Madeline Oliver visited her often. Grace died December 27, 1999 at the hospital.

Grace's burial in Glassville was in June 2000. In attendance were daughters Jan and Jill, Walter and Evelyn Whitehouse, Madeline Oliver, Kaye and Jimmer Thompson, Ruth Shute and Robert and Margaret Flemming. Marjorie Martinson, with the assistance of her sister Marion Spence, gave the group a warm reception with tea at her house in Glassville.

In the United Church Cemetery, Glassville, stands their stone:

> Whitehouse, Clarence W. 1911-88
> Grace Cummings 1922-99

It is adjacent to the monument of Clara and Weldon Flemming. Daughter Jan Good, said of Clarence and Grace, "They were wonderful people and excellent parents. Both lived full lives; a joy."

Children and Grandchildren of Clarence and Grace

Jan Whitehouse married Charles Good. They have two sons: Nicholas, born 1980; and Aaron James, born April 15, 1992. Jan has a kidney condition which necessitates dialysis. Charles Good works with Coughlin Transport. They live in Fredericton. Nicholas is a student at U.N.B.

Jill Whitehouse was called to the bar during a ceremony of the Court of Appeal, Fredericton, N.B. in June 1989.[29]

That year Jill married Raymond T. French, also a lawyer. They live in Saint John.

For eight years Jill worked for CBC in research and as a news producer, sometimes appearing on local TV programmes. She commuted to Fredericton. In September 2000 she began a new position as a director for a communications company, which involves travel. She has an office in Saint John.[30]

Jill and Raymond have two sons: William French born 1995; and Ian French born 1996. The family lived in a historic house on Orange St. and now lives on Mt. Pleasant Ave., Saint John.[31]

Walter Whitehouse

Walter was born March 24, 1913, when the family lived on the Joseph Stillman Whitehouse farm in E. Knowlesville. The school register indicates that he attended school in Glassville in the school years ending June, 1919 through 1924. His sister Claudia, and brother Clarence, are on the same lists.

Marjorie Martinson remembers Walter as a boy in Glassville. She illustrates his uninhibited, outgoing nature: One morning he went into Arthur McIntosh's store; Arthur was in the stock room. Walter shouted, "Arthur, I'm going berrying, I want to buy a kettle". Walter carried his geniality into youth and early adulthood. When he became a teamster in Juniper, the neighbourhood boys gathered at the barn when he went to tend the horses. He sang songs for them.[32]

Walter's work with horses shifted in the late 30's to a farm at Victoria Corner that Weldon Flemming purchased from the estate of the Hartland physician, Dr. MacIntosh. Horses used in logging in winter were sent from Juniper to the farm in spring. Walter was the manager of the farm that was equipped with modern machinery. Among the helpers were three Corey brothers: Wilfred, Bob and Tom, in successive summers.

Walter married Evelyn Briggs, R.N., an employee of

L.P.D. Fisher Memorial Hospital, Woodstock. They have a son, Larry, born June 29, 1944; and a daughter, Judy, born June 30, 1947. In the late 1960's, when their children were in university, Walter experienced ill health with a heart condition. He and Evelyn left the farm and went to Florida. After a winter there they returned to New Brunswick, obtained visas, and went to live in Florida. There Evelyn wrote papers and obtained nursing credentials. Walter became a maintenance man for an apartment building, and later for a big mall.

In Florida, Walter and Evelyn lived near enough to Glenna Thompson, Walter's cousin, then living in Pinellas Park, to visit her often, bring her to their house for visits and dinners, take her shopping, and do many errands and maintenance tasks for her. They renewed a long-standing, close relationship between Glenna and Clara's family. Madeline Oliver said that Glenna had stayed for a time with Clara in Woodstock, and that in Florida, Clara and Weldon Flemming also visited Glenna. In her extant letters, dated from 1973 through 1978, Glenna expresses frequent praise for Walter and Evelyn for their kindness to her.[33]

After a decade or more in Florida, Walter and Evelyn returned to New Brunswick. In the summer of 1980 they built a new house on a lot cut from the Briggs farm where Evelyn grew up and where her brother still lived. It is at Weston, N.B., near the border of Maine, and not far from Woodstock.

On October 17, 1994 the writer, accompanied by Margaret, visited Walter and Evelyn at Weston. It happened that their son Larry and his wife Ruby were visiting. Walter and Larry were putting a new cover on the well. Larry took time to tell us about his profession. Larry is a research scientist. He works for Health Canada Research in the Drugs Directorate. He said "I run a research lab in the area of biotechnology, examining the safety of products coming or soon to come on the market. Our mandate is to protect Canadian health with respect to drugs on the market, or soon to be introduced." Walter and Evelyn mentioned that Larry's work involves research in D.N.A. His travels might take him to British Columbia, London, or Switzerland.

Larry and Ruby in 1995

Larry Whitehouse married Ruby Sutherland, from Newcastle, N.B. They have two children: Aaron born 1974, and Michael born February 1976. In 1995 Aaron was in a science programme in University of Ottawa, and Michael was graduating from Grade 13. They live in Greely, near Ottawa, Ontario. Both Larry and his sister, Judy, studied at Dalhousie University: pharmacology and medicine. Larry was in Halifax; 1973-1984.

Judy remained in Halifax. Judy is a radiologist; she does research in breast cancer. She was recently in the news as an authority in nuclear medicine. Her work also involves travelling. Dr. Judy Whitehouse married Dr. William Caines from Newfoundland. She became Dr. Judy Whitehouse-Caines. They have three children: Ian born 1978; Megan, born 1983; and Colin born 1987. They live in Halifax. In October 1992 Judy was working at the Camp Hill Medical Centre, Halifax, researching needle biopsies as an alternative to surgery in distinguishing malignant from benign lesions in the breast.[34]

Dr. L.W. Caines' first degree was a B.A. from King's College, 1955. A Rhodes Scholar, he graduated from Balliol College, Oxford University in 1958. He graduated in medicine from Dalhousie University in 1966. He also studied in New York, Winnipeg, and Scotland. His speciality was plastic and reconstructive surgery. He became the Director of the Plastic Surgery Residency Program of Dalhousie University.[35]

Dr. Caines' distinguished career ended in 1996 when he was diagnosed with cancer. He chose not to have hospital care and treatment. He stayed at their Halifax home with the care of nurses round the clock.[36] He died on June 17, 1997.

Dr. Cains lived to see their son Ian Whitehouse-Caines become a distinguished graduate of Halifax Grammar School, and gain the rank of 10th in Canada in the University of Waterloo Mathematics competition. He participated in a group of 60 top Canadian math scholars. He scored exceedingly high in Princeton University SAT tests. He was one of only 30 students chosen to write the Winter Training Examination to compete for the most prestigious high school mathematics competition in the world — the International Mathematical Olympiad, scheduled for Argentina in 1997.[37] In their retirement Walter and Evelyn have been able to keep in touch with their children and grandchildren. They have made trips to Halifax to visit Judy and family and to Ottawa region to visit Larry and family. In late years their leisure has been interrupted with medical appointments and treatments for Walter. In the winter of 2000, accompanied by his sister Madeline Oliver, Evelyn and Walter travelled to Saint John for radiation treatments at Regional Hospital. He has had the advantage of much counsel from both his daughter and his son. He has retained a good measure of health and strength.

Madeline Whitehouse Oliver

Madeline Whitehouse was born in 1919 in Glassville, N.B. She lived briefly in Jacksonville. She remembers going to school there one day. Not being allowed to sit with Walter, she didn't go back. She began at Broadway School, Woodstock, at age eight. After school in Juniper she returned to Woodstock for high school. She also worked in Woodstock for the Bank of Nova Scotia.

In the winter of 1946, when the writer returned from Europe, Madeline had returned to her family in Juniper and was making plans for her marriage to Paul Oliver. He had served overseas as a druggist in the Canadian Medical Corps, and had returned to his home in Woodstock in 1945. Madeline and Paul were married by Rev. William C. Amey at the Union Church in Juniper in March 1946. The reception was at the home of Clara and Weldon Flemming.

Madeline and Paul lived in Woodstock where he was employed with Newnham and Slipp. Later they lived in Grand Falls. In 1958 Paul acquired his own pharmacy in Oromocto. Beginning in 1980 he operated it under the Shoppers Drug Mart name.

Madeline and Paul had six children: Sally Joy Ann, b. June 8, 1947, Mary Jane, b. December 6, 1948, Paula Kae, b. December 10, 1949, Michael James, b. August 4, 1953, Ruth Ann, b. November 9, 1956, and Judith Elaine, b. August 8, 1963. Madeline and Paul helped them all with education. Madeline said, "At one time I had four children at U.N.B."

Their son Michael graduated from Dalhousie University, became a pharmacist and worked with Paul in the Oromocto store. In 1985 Paul suffered a heart attack. Then Michael took over the pharmacy. Paul and Madeline moved to Fredericton where they lived seven years before his death, May 24, 1994, at age 76.

Children and Grandchildren of Madeline and Paul

Sally Joy Ann received a degree from U.N.B., Fredericton. She married Blair Kindervater. They have been living in Australia since 1981.

Mary Jane received a degree in nursing from U.N.B. She was a nurse in Saint John. She is now doing home visitation nursing in Fredericton. One of her patients is Madeline's Aunt Vola Barker. Mary Jane married Michael Philips. They have three children: James Alexander, a graduate of U.N.B. in Forestry; John Anthony, a student at U.N.B.; and Sarah, a high school student. The family lives in Fredericton.

Paula Kae also became a nurse. She studied at a college in Alberta; also at U.N.B. where she received a degree in nursing. She married, first, Peter Anderson. They had two daughters: Emily and Melissa. Michael died 1987 of A.L.S., when Melissa was age one. Paula Kae m. second, Richard Wilson. They live in Woodstock, where Paula Kae is still nursing. They have a cottage at Skiff Lake.

Michael Oliver married Gail McCready who grew up in St. Stephen and lived in Fredericton. After their marriage they lived in Oromocto. After his father died Michael sold the Oromocto store and moved his family to Bridgewater, N.S. They have three children: Joshua, a student at Acadia University in 2000; Luke; and Stephen.

Ruth Ann married David Beardsmore. They have four children: David, Jeremy, Jennifer Ann and Harley. They live in Edmonton.

Judith Elaine attended U.N.B., at Fredericton. In 1986 she married David Winters of Oromocto. He was a graduate of U.N.B., and was continuing studies in the Royal Canadian Navy. They lived in Dartmouth. They had two children: Jeffery, b. 1987; and Brandon, b. 1990. Judith and David divorced.

Judith and Terry Rose have a son, Corey Rose, born 1998. They live in Dartmouth, N.S. Judith is a taxi driver. Judith remembers attending a family reunion at Betty and Walter Gray's house in Jacksontown, N.B. Judith said, "I go home to see Mum three or four times a year."

From 1995 to winter of 2000 Madeline lived in an apartment in North Fredericton, then moved to an apartment on George St. In the summer of 2000 she was recovering from hip replacement surgery. She is much in touch with her children and grandchildren, and also her siblings, nieces and nephews. She has been very helpful in putting the writer in touch with other members of the McBrine family, and in helping gather data.

Kathleen Whitehouse Thompson

Following her sojourn in New York in 1929-30 Kaye attended school in Woodstock. In 1931 she moved with the family to Juniper. From the Juniper school she returned to Woodstock and graduated from Carleton Co. Grammer School.

Kaye began her university education at Mount Allison University, Sackville, N.B., where she earned a diploma in Secretarial. "She continued her studies in Dalhousie University in Halifax, N.S., where she earned a Bachelor of Science degree. In 1948, Kaye completed a research assignment at the Harvard School of Medicine in Boston."[38]

That year, 1948, Kaye married B. Jerome Thompson (Jimmer), a graduate of U.N.B. in Forestry. They have been living in Juniper since Jimmer came there to work for Flemming and Gibson Co. in the early 50's. Kaye and Jimmer have five children: Robert, b. 1951; Jerome, b. 1953; Megan, b. 1954, Andrew, b. 1956, and Paul, b. 1958.

In 1977 Jerome Thompson joined the new company - Juniper Lumber, as Vice President, responsible for sales, and as a member of the executive. He became Vice President of Operations and later, V.P. of Corporate Affairs. A hobby and recreation for Jimmer is keeping riding horses. He and Kaye have entertained other equine enthusiasts at their home in Juniper.[39]

Children and Grandchildren of Kaye and Jimmer

Robert, as a small boy became a delightful companion of his great great Uncle Ira Corey who then worked around the Flemming barn. Ira often talked about how smart Bobbie was. While still a small boy he suffered damage from a severe case of encephalitis. Up to then a brilliant child, he was left handicapped. Robbie is now a resident of "Community Living" in

Woodstock. He has his own room. In 2000 he had a part time job at Canadian Tire Corp. He comes home to Juniper for a weekend about once a month.

Jerome, Jr., called Joe, is also handicapped. He is living at home in Juniper. He does many helpful tasks: feeding the horses, cutting the lawn and shovelling snow. He is much appreciated by the older folks in Juniper. Joe lives with Kaye and Jimmer in the former Hugh John Flemming house in Juniper.

Megan Thompson married Charles Kelley in 1981. He was then living and working in Juniper. They have two sons: Christian, b. 1983, and Ethan, b. 1986. They live in Bristol. Charles has his own company: C.R. Kelley and Sons. He does trucking and forestry work. Currently he is working for H.J. Crabbe and sons. In summer of 2000 he was logging on Grand Manan Island, N.B. Megan is teaching in Carleton North High School in Bristol.

Andrew married Sharon Viel of Juniper, in 1980. They have two sons: Scott born 1980, and Isaac, born 1982. Scott is living at home. His communication is limited by autism. He reads and takes much interest in his computer. Kaye said, "Andrew and Sharon have devoted their lives to Scott. They are determined to keep him at home." Isaac graduated from Woodstock High School in June 2000. That summer he went to Ottawa for a summer course in radio. His plan was to pursue the subject at Community College, Woodstock.

Andrew Thompson is a graduate of the Forestry School of U.N.B. He has done forestry cruising. Now he has his own computer consulting company. As a computer programmer he worked three days a week for Glassville Logging Co., in the Juniper office. Andrew, Sharon and sons live in Woodstock.

Paul Thompson was living in Boston and working with an investment company, Equity Trading Inc. In fall of 2000 he returned to New Brunswick to a job in Woodstock.

Ruth Flemming Shute

Ruth Flemming, born January 8, 1923, lived in Juniper from 1931 through her early school years. Her high school studies were at Mount Allison School for Girls. She also graduated from Carleton Co. Vocational School, Woodstock, N.B., and she had two years at Mount Allison University, Sackville, N.B.

Ruth's work experience in Juniper included serving as postmaster during W.W.II, keeping a clothing store up over the general store, and working in the Flemming and Gibson office. Her memories of Juniper include visits of Ira Corey in home of Clara and Weldon. She said, "I loved Uncle Ira." She entertained him with singing, playing the piano, and playing the role of an opera singer, dressed in an evening gown.

Ruth married Wesley Fawcett of Sackville, N.B. Later she married Noble Coleman. The relationship was very brief because of illness. Noble had recently lost his former wife to cancer. Noble also became a victim of cancer only months after he married Ruth. Noble left a daughter, Lomie Coleman. Ruth became a supporter and mother to Lomie and has maintained the relationship.

After being widowed, Ruth established a woman's shop in Fredericton — a proud accomplishment. However, she found the business demanding in that it required buying clothing almost a year in advance. Hence she undertook a nursing career. She went to Toronto and obtained an R.N. at age 48. She practiced nursing in the old Victoria Hospital in Fredericton.

Then, Ruth said, "I married Frank Shute." Frank was a versatile man: jeweller, pilot, fancier of springer spaniels. They made a home on the shore of Mactaquac Head Pond.[40] Ruth: "After he retired and I retired from nursing, we spent winters in Florida."

Frank liked Lomie very much. At the time of Frank's last illness, Lomie, by that time an M.D., came to be with him.

Frank Shute died March 13, 1999. Ruth said, "He was the great love of my life. I was sick at the time with a breathing problem. Lomie thought I was going too. She got me into hospital. We couldn't have the funeral then. Lomie said, 'I can't go home.' She stayed with me." Ruth explained that her illness turned out to be influenza, complicated by diabetes. They held a memorial service for Frank on March 26 at Christ Church Cathedral, Fredericton.

Ruth has been in Woodstock, N.B., since October 1999. She said, "I was sick when I came here. My daughter came again; she got me into hospital. They drained fluid from my lungs. I didn't move into my house until after Christmas. I am feeling better now. My daughter was here to see me again" — in June 2000. They went to P.E.I. and stopped again on their way back to Ontario.[41]

Dr. Lomie Coleman is married to Dr. Colin MacPherson. They are practising medicine in Pembroke, Ontario, near Ottawa. They have two sons: Graeme, b. 1992, and Stuart b. 1995. Ruth lives near the library and the Post Office in Woodstock.

Robert Flemming

Robert Flemming, born 1925, graduated from Juniper High School. At Acadia University he was a member of the Royal Officer Training Corps in 1943. In Juniper Robert became sawmill manager for Flemming and Gibson Co., a position he held until 1967.[42]

Then Robert and family moved to Fredericton and worked for Barker Equipment. After that company was sold, Robert had a business selling machinery across the Saint John River at Lower St. Mary's.

Robert married Margaret Ann McMullin September 2, 1953. They have two daughters: Cathy, b. November 7, 1955 and Jennifer, b. May 25, 1958.

Cathy married Andrew Atkinson in 1979. They have three children: Julie, b. 1981; Emily, b. 1984; and David, b. 1986.

Jennifer married Lorne Davis in 1989. They have two children: Alyson, b. 1990, and Sean, b. 1991. They live in N. Carolina.

Mary Flemming

Mary, born 1933, daughter of Clara and Weldon Flemming, graduated from Netherwood School, Rothesay, N.B. in 1951. She married John Chesley, son of Dr. Arthur Chesley, Saint John, N.B. They had three daughters, all born in Saint John: Shawn, 1955; Cari, 1957; and Zoé, 1959. The family lived briefly in Halifax and Truro, N.S., and in Montreal — about 12 years. Mary moved to Florida, then returned to Canada at Fredericton.

Shawn graduated from Dalhousie University, Halifax. Shawn Chesley married Scott Morrison. They had two daughters: Lindsey b. May 18, 1982 and Keltie, b. January 21, 1984. They lived in North Vancouver, B.C. and in Calgary, Alberta. Shawn worked in real estate in Vancouver. Shawn brought Lindsey and Keltie to be christened by Rev. Willard Picketts who had been pastor of the Glassville/Juniper charge, 1934-36. Then he had christened Mary. Later, in Truro, N.S., he had christened Shawn.

Lindsay Morrison is a student at Dalhousie University, Halifax. Keltie, in her second year at Trinity School, Port Hope, Ontario, is doing grades 12 and 13 in one year. Shawn lives in Toronto.

Cari Chesley graduated from U.N.B., Fredericton, and also from Mt. St. Vincent, Halifax. Cari met Bill van Lingen in Calgary. They were married in Rothesay, N.B. June 4, 1983. They returned to Calgary, but soon moved to New Brunswick, then to Halifax. Cari and Bill have a daughter, Zoé Brittany Reid van Lingen, born 1994. They brought her to Juniper, N.B., for her baptism in June 1994 by Rev. Chris van Buskirk, Anglican. They now live in Halifax.

Zoé Chesley graduated from St. Thomas University, Fredericton. Zoé married Bruce Frame of Maine. They have one son; Andrew Weldon Flemming Frame, born 1992. Now divorced, Zoé, with Andrew, lives in Woodstock.

In 1994 Mary sold the house in Juniper and bought a house in Woodstock. Her daughter Zoé and grandson, Andrew live with her.

Family of Judson LeRoy McBrine, Sr. and Dorothy Bedell McBrine

Jud and Dorothy McBrine lived in Glassville, N.B. until after the birth of their first two children: Judson, Jr., 1922, and Winnifred, February 24, 1924. From Glassville the family moved to Skowhegan, Maine. There are recollections: Roy Hemphill remembered his father, Fred, going from Knowlesville to Lakeville and buying a flat record gramophone with a high cabinet. Jud McBrine had left it with his sister, Vola Barker, when he went to Skowhegan.

The purpose of going to Skowhegan was to learn bricklaying and masonry. There two more children were born to Jud and Dorothy: Clarice, February 8, 1926; and William, 1928. He died at eight months of age. The family's next move was to Haynesville, Me., Dorothy's home town. Her mother and sister still lived there then.

The McBrines in Haynesville

In Haynesville Jud bought a small farm. Farming, however, was not his main occupation. Jud McBrine was a versatile man; he had many skills, e.g. carpentry. His brother, Leland, who had a stay with Jud and Dorothy before going to New York to work said Jud built cabinets in kitchens. He worked with a local house builder. In Haynesville three more children were born to Dorothy and Jud McBrine: Joseph, November 24, 1932, Judith, April 22, 1934, and Mary Jane, December 13, 1937.

World War II took three of the McBrine family away from home. The eldest, Judson, Jr., served in the U.S. Army in Europe. Winnifred and Clarice worked in a shipyard in S. Portland, Me. Clarice said, "I was a welder." She recalled further, "I came home in 1944 to return to high school. I finished my last year in 1945." W.W.II was almost ended when the McBrine family had to bear the sad news of the loss of the firstborn of the family. Judson McBrine, Jr. was killed in Germany in May 1945, three days before the end of the war.

Son Joe came to be a helper to his father. He said, "I tended him on chimney building. He built his own wood-burning furnace with a square brick containment. He was an excellent carpenter and mason. He also worked in the woods at times. Joe's recollections confirm the many facets of the work of Jud and Dorothy McBrine. He said, "They had a store and a Post Office. Mother kept the Post Office. Dad did the books." Daughter, Judy, said, "He was also the town manager. During his term of office he taught himself to type. He knew history and geography." He developed all those skills though he only reached grade five in a New Brunswick school. Joe recalled also, "They kept animals enough for family purposes." Nephew, Dr. Edward Williams, recalled going with him in his truck on a trip to New Brunswick to bring back a cow or calf.

There were frequently visitors from New Brunswick. Judy recalled her grandmother, Ida McBrine's visits: "She stayed with us a lot. She made rhubarb pudding in season". Judy also remembers her grandmother taking her suitcase to the road as she did in Juniper. There she sat on it, waiting for a family member to come for her. She would return to the house when one of the family played the piano.

The McBines lived in about four successive properties in Haynesville. Usually they had a little farm land, and plenty of garden space. A place the McBrines had before 1955 had a house with dormers, a large barn, and another building, perhaps the store, with an Esso sign in front.

About 1955 Jud and Dorothy McBrine sold that property and gave up the Post Office. For a few years they lived in a rented house on Route #9 — called Nine Road.

In 1955 the family celebrated the 35th anniversary of the wedding of Jud and Dorothy McBrine. Judy said, "It was at the home of Aunt Mary Hatch (Dorothy's sister) at the former Bedell place. Pearl McBrine's photo shows the couple cutting a large cake.

Jud and Dorothy McBrine and two daughters

About 1960 the McBrine family bought a property with a large house at the intersection of Route 2 and the road to Danforth. It is near the bridge over the Mattawamkeag River. It is the property where daughter Judy Oliver lives now, with all the up-to-date conveniences. At the new location Jud and Dorothy again came to be the keepers of the Post Office. They also expanded their enterprises. "When a new bridge was being built across the river," Joe said, "Mother started cooking chicken; She prepared food for the bridge workers." Clarice said, "Mother had a large counter with stools." Joe summed it up: "They had a Post Office, a store and a restaurant, all in the same building." Paul Brooks remembers stopping there for lunch when he travelled in Maine on trucking errands for Flemming and Gibson.

The writer had a memorable visit at that McBrine place

at the time of the death of my brother, Claude Corey, in January 1964. I travelled from Conway, Mass. to Glassville, N.B. My two elder children, Frederic and Carolyn Corey, were with me. We stopped at Haynesville. The next day, Sunday, Judy drove Dorothy and Jud to Glassville to visit the bereaved Corey family.

Dorothy McBrine died in September 1973. Jud McBrine died August 29, 1974 at age 80, "at his residence at Haynesville." Funeral service was at the Haynesville Baptist church, where he was a member. Interment is in the Riverside Cemetery, Haynesville.[43]

Children and Grandchildren of Jud and Dorothy McBrine

Winifred, second child of Jud and Dorothy, married in 1945, Weldon Winchester. He had three children: Donald, Judy and Joan. Winnifred married second, Lloyd Carr, in 1964. Winnifred also had a restaurant for several years. After Dorothy and Jud McBrine gave up the Post Office it moved to Winnifred's house in the same neighbourhood. She kept it. Winnifred died 1995. Lloyd Carr still lives in Haynesville.

Clarice, second daughter, also lives in Haynesville. She married, in 1946, Ralph Shorey. Seven children were born to them in Haynesville: Michael, June 10, 1946; Roberta, September 25, 1947; Ralph, April 5, 1949; Colby, April 4, 1950; Sharon, August 31, 1952; Judith, August 2, 1956; and Melody August 3, 1957. Ralph Shorey died November 26, 1957.

Clarice married, in 1961, Raymond Irish. They have two children; Scott Irish, born June 16, 1961 and Raymond Irish, Jr., born June 25, 1966. Clarice and Raymond live in Haynesville, about a mile from where Judy and Donald Oliver live.

Children and Grandchildren of Clarice and Ralph Shorey

Michael Shorey m. Jackie Spinney. They have one son, Timothy, born October 26, 1968. They live near Judy Oliver, in Haynesville. Roberta Shorey m.1, Victor Hartley. They had one daughter; Lauren, born June 26, 1967; and two sons; Victor, born June 11, 1969; and Ted, born August 5, 1971. Roberta m.2, Carl Clark. Roberta lives in Florida and works in a nursing home. Ralph Shorey, m. Judy Sylvester. They have three children: Jason, born September 7, 1973; Tonya, born 1978; and Terri, born 1980. Colby Shorey, m. Pamela. Their children are: Melanie, born August 20, 1972; Hollie, born December 1978; Ryan, born August 19, 1981. Colby d. in 1987, at age 37, the victim of a shooting in a friend's house in Colby's own neighborhood. Sharon Shorey m. Gary Dixon. They have two children; Tanya, born June 11, 1972, m. Rick Poulen; and Gary, Jr., born December 19, 1975, m. Jen. Sharon is an R.N., working in Waterville. The family lives in Clinton, Me. Judy Shorey m. David Ireland. They have three children; Shawna, born November 13, 1976; Jeremy, born January 14, 1979; and Bridgette, born July 9, 1981. Shawna m. Nathan McNally, January 2001. Nathan is in Air Force in North Dakota. Melody Lee Shorey, born August 3, 1957, became the victim of an accident on the highway soon after she began Grade 5, in September, 1967. She and a friend were walking at the edge of Highway #2. An express truck avoided a car and trailer, and struck and killed the two girls.

Children of Clarice and Raymond Irish

Scott Irish is in U.S. Army in Germany. He m. Nam. Raymond Irish, Jr. is a carpenter working with house builders. He m. Anne; they have two children: Jonathan, born March 5, 1997 and Bethany, born February 3, 2000. They live in Shalton, near Worcester, Mass.

Joseph Franklin McBrine, Sr.

Marie and Joe McBrine

Joseph McBrine, only surviving son of Judson and Dorothy McBrine, was born November 24, 1932. Early in life he began a career in teaching. On August 15, 1953, he m. Marie King, also a teacher. Their first home was a trailer. Places where Joseph and Marie have lived and served in Maine include: Haynesville, Hogdon, Presque Isle, Lincoln, Auburn and Bangor. Joseph also taught for a while in a private school. Early in his career Joseph became a Superintendent of Schools. He retired from that position once, and later was induced to return to it. He is now in the office of superintendent at Eastport. He has four town meetings to report to. Marie retired from teaching in 1999. They live in Machias.

Joseph and Marie have five children, all married, and all but one living in Maine: Mark, born October 13, 1961; Lauren, born March 5, 1963; Judson, born December 8, 1965; Joseph, born October 21, 1969; and Jonathan, born September 19, 1971.

Mark Judson McBrine, m. Linda Cox, April 2, 1983. They have six children: Andrew, born December 4, 1989; Stephen, born December 23, 1990; Micah, born December 3, 1993; Sarah, born September 16, 1995; Rebecca, born September 16, 1996; and Rachel, born November 18, 1997. Mark is managing Ramada Inn in Bangor. He also has a farm, which started as a hobby and has become a lot of work. He is much involved in his church.

Lauren Jo McBrine, m. Christopher Sprague, July 1, 1989. They have two daughters: Hannah, born June 27, 1996; and Lydia, born June 24, 2000. Lauren is a teacher.

Judson Leroy McBrine III, m. Paula Norton, August 4, 1990. They have a son Jacob, born December 12, 1998. Judson is Headmaster of Washington Academy, a private school in E. Machias.

Joseph Franklin McBrine, Jr. m. Lorilee Look, March 18, 1995. They have two children; Vincent Emery, born February 17, 1983, and Olivia, born January 23, 1997. Joseph is a game warden.

Laren, Judson and Joseph, Jr. all live near their parents, i.e., in Machias and Jonesboro.

Jonathan King McBrine is in U.S. military service, stationed in Texas. He m. Becky Washburn, August 14, 1993. They have a son Daniel, born June 7, 2000. They were able to join the family in Machias for Thanksgiving in 2000.

Judith A. McBrine, born April 22, 1934, in Haynesville, Me. Graduated from Houlton High School in 1951. She became a teacher and physical education instructor. On December 30, 1955. Judy m. Donald Oliver, also a teacher. Donald became a principal in Hodgdon. Judy's last position was at the Houlton High School. For several years they lived on the same street as Dr. Edward Williams in Houlton. Judy and Donald have two sons: Joel, born June 5, 1957; and Matthew, born January 12, 1969.

Judith McBrine, h.s. graduation

Judy and Donald, in retirement from teaching since early 90's, are living where her mother and father last lived. She said, "My Dad willed it to me." At the beginning of their retirement Judy and Donald bought a wood lot. Donald cut trees with a chain saw. Judy pulled together the logs with a skidder. The enterprise lasted eight winters.

Judy has had, for some years, an enterprise on the farm. She plants vegetables in spring and sells them in Houlton in summer. On July 25, 2000, the writer and his sister, Kaye Foster, visited Judy at her vegetable market in Houlton where customers were coming steadily. In lulls in the traffic, Judy gave us information about the McBrine descendants.

On January 17, 2001, the writer and his sister, Shirley Brooks, visited Judy and Donald Oliver at their house in Haynesville, where the McBrines and some descendants have been residents for nearly three quarters of a century. Conversation touched on Hodgdon which Donald said is only about three miles from the New Brunswick border. They were surprised to learn that Alfred and Lucretia Corey and their first five children lived in Maine and that Ida was born there, probably in Hodgdon. Joining us at Judy's house was her sister, Clarice Irish, with birthday book in hand. We gathered more data on the descendants of Jud and Dorothy McBrine.

Sons of Judy and Donald Oliver

Joel Oliver graduated in Forestry from University of Maine, Orono. He lives on a farm near Hodgdon. Joel married Lynn Wilson, a teacher. They have two children; Britta Jo, and Dylon Wilson. Matthew Oliver is a school principal in Danforth. He married Lee-Rae Jordon. She is teaching in Bangor.

Mary Jane McBrine, born December 13, 1937, youngest of the children of Jud and Dorothy McBrine, became a schoolteacher. She married, first, James Miller. They had four children; James, born September 24, 1959; Richard, born January

11, 1961; Karen, born July 25, 1962; and Seth, born December 5, 1964. James Miller, Jr. was struck and killed by a truck, at age 12. James Miller, Sr. died September 24, 1972.

Richard Miller m. Lisa; they have two children, Molly and Christopher. Karen is a teacher in Caribou. She has one daughter, Jasmine, born 1989. Seth Miller is a student in a medical school in Texas, in the graduating class of May 2001. Mary Jane married second, John Chick in 1999. They live in Caribou, Me.

Many of the descendants of Jud and Dorothy McBrine are still living in Maine.

Nessie

Nessie Alberta, daughter of Ida Corey and William McBrine, was born in Knowlesville on July 23, 1896. With the McBrine family she moved to Glassville about 1908. After the move she apparently made visits to the community of her childhood while her sister, Clara, was still living in East Knowlesville. Perhaps it was during such a visit that the two sisters were baptized and became members of Knowlesville United Baptist Church.

Only a few miles from the neighbourhood where Nessie grew up, is Foreston, a historic stopping place on the South Branch of the Miramichi. There, in the Staten house, Nessie, with her children; Dorothy, Alice, Betty and Cecil, Jr. found a home in the summer of 1936 when they returned to New Brunswick from New York. Madeline Oliver says, "Aunt Nessie had an earlier summer stay in Foreston to escape the heat of New York City, and to do physical therapy on Dorothy," following infantile paralysis.

Living in Juniper 1936 - 1947

Betty recalled, "Before school opening we were in Juniper. In September 1936, I entered grade three in Juniper

School. My brother Cecil was a beginner. Grandmother Ida McBrine laced his boots while he ate breakfast."

Ida, Nessie's mother, lived with them during much of the family's residence in the house later occupied by Mrs. Frances Crabbe. Ida did some of the housework and prepared meals while Nessie was at work. Nessie had two enterprises: a restaurant where she fed both the night crew and the morning crew from the Flemming and Gibson Mill — later opened to the public; also a dress shop/clothing store.[44]

In the Juniper School the four Avery siblings received a major part of their education. Dorothy graduated from Juniper High School in 1940. From Juniper she went to Acadia University, Wolfville, N.S. From Acadia she received a B.A. in English in 1944.[45] Betty's educational pursuits took her also to the Acadia campus. The year after Dorothy graduated from Acadia, Betty graduated from Horton Academy, i.e., in 1945, in June, the month following the end of W.W.II. After Horton Academy, Betty attended Bob Jones University in Tennessee for one half-year. After Acadia, Dorothy taught English at Juniper High School, while her family was still living there.[46]

Nessie's house in Juniper was a friendly place. I recall a family gathering there in the summer of 1946, when Lucretia and Edward MacDonnell were visiting in Juniper from New York. In a recent conversation Betty Gray recalled, "I played the piano. You and Edward sang hymns." Others sang too. I was living with my parents in Juniper that summer, working in the office of Flemming and Gibson, before entering Acadia University, Wolfville, N.S. In late 1946 Nessie married Guy McLaughlin, a mechanic employed by Flemming and Gibson Co.

Scattering from Juniper

In 1947 Nessie and Guy moved to Hartland. On the Sommerville side of the Saint John River, they built a big house

Ida McBrine and family at White Swan Inn

with an apartment upstairs. Nessie's mother, Ida McBrine, lived there with them. On the ground floor of the house they built a restaurant named, "The White Swan Inn". Besides serving meals they catered, e.g., to wedding receptions. The mother of a groom described Nessie as a "charming hostess."

Beginning before 1947 both Dorothy and Alice Avery were employed at the CFNB radio station in Fredericton. Dorothy worked in the record room; Alice was a receptionist. They boarded at Nellie's, before Pearl Buchanan went there in January 1947.[47]

In Fredericton, Alice met Murray E. Cook, an R.C.A.F. Veteran who had returned to Canada in 1946, and enrolled in the forestry course at U.N.B. In 1947 they were married in Juniper by Rev. William C. Amey, United Church Minister on the Juniper/Glassville Charge, 1943-48. Murray had summer employment with Price Brothers Pulp and Paper Company of Chicoutimi, Quebec.

About 1948, Betty Avery returned to Brooklyn, N.Y. where she had begun school. She said, "I lived with Aunt

Crissie and Uncle Mack", i.e., Lucretia and Edward McDonnell. "Dorothy was there part of that time also. I worked in New York City for six years." Her job was with Cannon Towels. "While I was living in Brooklyn," Betty recollected, "Aunt Bert came to live with Lucretia and Mack. She was there about two years before I left."[48]

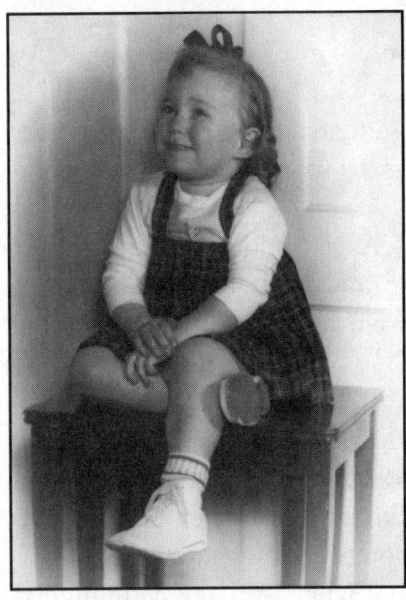
Jane Cook

In May 1949 Murray Eaton Cook graduated from U.N.B., Fredericton. With Alice and their daughter Jayne, born 1948, Murray returned to Chicoutimi to employment as forestry engineer with Price Brothers. In November 1949 Murray Cook, with a companion, set out in an aluminum canoe on the Shipshaw River to estimate the amount of pulpwood in the river.

The two men failed to return at the expected time. The company sent out a search party. "Those who searched for Murray were all personal friends and keen to go in the hope of finding him safe and sound...." On Saturday, November 12, Murray's body was found. It was believed that he and his companion had drowned on Wednesday, November 9. Those who had worked with Murray said he was a strong swimmer. Some of them believed that he drowned in an effort to save his companion who was not so strong a swimmer.

Rev. C.W. Cook, Murray's father, received a letter from J.R. Walton, representing Price Brothers Pulp and Paper Co. He explained circumstances surrounding the drowning. The above quotation is from the letter. He described Murray as "one of our best and most promising forest engineers..." He said, further, "Murray was an exceedingly fine young man and it was indeed a pleasure to see what a happy family he, his wife, and little daughter made.....He was exceedingly popular and respected by all who came in contact with him." Mr. Walton expressed his "heartfelt sympathy."

Murray Cook was the only son of Rev. and Mrs. C.W. Cook, Baptist minister in Berwick, N.S. Murray's life of only 26 years was distinguished. He graduated in Arts from Acadia Univerity in 1943, before he was 20 years of age. He served as a pilot with R.C.A.F. overseas.

Johnny McBrine drove Alice's mother and brother, Nessie and Cecil, to Chicoutimi and brought Alice and little Jayne to Fredericton, and on to Nova Scotia for the funeral at Berwick United Baptist Church.[49]

The funeral was conducted by Rev. Austin D. MacPherson, then pastor of Middleton United Baptist Church and formerly pastor of George St. Baptist Church, Fredericton. He described Murray as "a constant and dear friend during college days". He brought also a note of tribute from George St. Baptist church and Sunday School where Murray had taught a class of boys.

Dr. F.W. Patterson, president emeritus of Acadia University, in his address, expressed the "promise that nothing shall separate us from the love of God." Also participating in the service were Dr. Frank Eaton, Canning, and Rev. W.C. Amey, then United Church minister at Red Bank, N.B. Participants at the grave side service: Rev. H.C. Olsen, pastor of Wolfville Baptist Church; Dr.Patterson; and Dr. C.B. Lumsden, representing the Canadian Legion, and Acadia University.[50]

The writer was at the sad graveside gathering, along with other students of Acadia University. We had been told that Rev. and Mrs. Cook of the Berwick Baptist Church had suffered the sad loss of their son. At the graveside the father said, "He was out on a river in a canoe counting logs."

Alice and Jane Cook took residence in Fredericton. There she had a sibling reunion. Betty Avery said, "Dorothy left New York before I did; she returned to New Brunswick and lived for a time with Alice. Their brother Cecil Avery, Jr. was also with them for a time, while a student at U.N.B. Alice set up an eating place and served meals to students. E'er long the three siblings dispersed.

Going Away; Coming Home; Marrying

Alice and William Craig

Alice Cook married a U.N.B. student, William A. Craig, (Bud) from St. Andrews, N.B. Right after their marriage they went to Alberta. Pearl McBrine said, "They stayed with us over night. We took them next morning to the airport." A card written by Alice on May 26, 1952 in Calgary said, "Wonderful trip! Jane was very good. Going to Edmonton tonight....kisses for David; all our love, Alice, Jane and Bud." It was addressed to Mr. & Mrs. J.W. McBrine, York St., Fredericton, N.B. William Craig (Bud), a geologist and a geophysicist, worked for an oil company. Apparently Vola and Archie Barker visited Alice. A card posted in Edmonton, September 20, 1954, also to Pearl and John McBrine, says, "Alice has a very nice home, all on one floor.....Love, Vola".

Cecil Avery went to Ontario to work for a finance company.

Dorothy Avery married Perley Seeley, brother of Arnold, in 1952. Perley was a C.P.R. engineer. They lived at Edmundston, N.B.

In 1953 their grandmother, Ida McBrine, died at the White Swan Inn, Hartland.

In 1954 Betty returned to Hartland. On December 31, 1954 she married Walter Gray, son of Fred Gray, Somerville. Betty said, "Cecil came from Ontario for my wedding."

Walter was in business in partnership with Arnold Seeley. They had the garage at the end of the bridge in Hartland. Soon the business expanded. Gray and Seeley became agents for Massey Harris. Later they dissolved the partnership: Arnold Seeley kept the garage; Walter sold Massey Harris machinery on Rockland Road. Walter also became an agent for Esso furnace oil and farm gasoline.

On May 17, 1958, Cecil Rhodes Avery married Margaret Anne MacAffrey in the Presbyterian Church, Madoc, Ontario. Walter Gray was groomsman. Cecil's mother, Nessie McLaughlin and his sister Dorothy Seeley were also present. Following a wedding trip to Niagara Falls and New York State, the couple planned to reside at Sault St. Marie, Ontario.[51]

A Gray Trip

"We took a five-week trip to the West in the summer of 1967", recounted Betty Gray. She and Walter were accompanied by their four children:
Kimberley, b. December 1, 1955
Jeffrey, b. March 21, 1957
Robert, b. May 11, 1959
Timothy, b. October 1, 1962

Betty narrated, "We stopped in Calgary. We saw the Calgary Stampede. We travelled the Fraser Valley; we saw the Fraser Canyon. We stopped at a camp site on the way to

Vancouver. Large, tall trees hid the sky. We also stopped in Hope, B.C. On Vancouver Island, at Nanaimo, we met up with Bobby and Margaret Flemming. They were on a trip to Victoria".

Back on the mainland they saw more interesting places: "Moon Mountain Dam that was then being built on the Peace River. They were taking gravel from a glacier for the dam. We travelled north toward Dawson Creek to visit my sister Alice Craig and family. They were staying temporarily in Dawson Creek on a work assignment. Also the Klondike Days were being celebrated there".

Alice and William Craig had three children: William, Jr. b. 1952; Michael, b. 1955; and Carol b. 1957. "When we arrived in Dawson Creek, Carol Craig, age 10 was in a burn unit in Edmonton, their home city. The day before we arrived, Carol had suffered a burning accident in a tree house. We visited Carol in the Edmonton Hospital. Then we had to start home. Our time was running out. Carol died while we were enroute home. We travelled 10,000 miles." It was a wonderful trip, but touched by tragedy and sadness.

The end of the trip was near the end of an era. In the next two years there was much change in Nessie's family. Her husband, Guy McLaughlin, died March 9, 1969, at Lancaster Hospital. That spring Nessie sold The White Swan Inn.

A Venture

In June 1969 Betty and Walter Gray, with their four children then ages 13 to 6, moved from Hartland to Ontario. Betty said "Mother (Nessie) went with us." Betty described the business venture: "We bought a trailer park in partnership with my brother Cecil. We also had trailer sales in Oshawa. We lived in Brooklin — a suburb". For Betty it was from Brooklyn to Brooklin. They did not long retain the enterprise. "There were too many by-laws. In 1971 we sold it and returned to New

Brunswick in April — glad to be back."

The Gray's made their home in Woodstock. After another year or so with Gray's, Nessie married Rev. Dr. Harold Carpenter, a retired Baptist minister who had had part of his ministry in Maine. After a lengthy illness he passed away September 8, 1974 at Carleton Hospital, Woodstock. He is buried in Waterville Baptist Cemetery beside his first wife. There their monument stands:

    Rev. Harold Carpenter 1905-1974;

    wife Evelyn   1905-1972

Winnifred Mitchell, who viewed the monument in her neighbourhood, spoke of meeting Carpenters' son in Maine. He was a visiting preacher in the Rockport area.

Nessie returned to living with Betty at Woodstock and later at Jacksontown, where the Gray's located in 1980. Betty cared for her mother until a stroke necessitated care at Central Carleton Nursing Home, Hartland. Nessie died there, November 12, 1986, at age 90. She is buried in Greenwood Cemetery, Hartland, beside Beulah Gray, mother of Walter Gray.

Nessie's Children and Grandchildren

Though the family was scattered widely over Canada, they bridged the miles and cared for one another.

Cecil Avery, b. 1933, remained in Ontario the rest of his life. By his first wife, Margaret MacAffrey, he had a son Jeffrey, born 1957. By his second wife, Linda Hotchkiss, he had a son, Joshua, born 1974.

Cecil suffered from cancer and became terminally ill before age 50. In 1982 Betty and Dorothy made their farewell visit to their brother Cecil in hospital in Durham, south of Owen Sound. Betty's memory: "We arrived in the afternoon. Dorothy's son, Donald, who was working in the area, took us to the hospital in Durham to see Cecil. He was heavily sedated. Linda spoke to him: 'Dorothy and Betty are here.' He looked at us and said, 'Hi'. He died that night," December 31, 1982.

Dorothy Avery, born 1921, suffered polio at age 11 which left her without the use of her left arm. Also one lung lacked full development. With courage and determination she pursued education and taught school.

Dorothy and Perley Seeley had three sons: Peter, born 1953; Donald, born 1955; and David, born 1958. When David was age seven or eight Dorothy returned to university, this time to U.N.B.; she obtained a B.Ed. In Edmundston, N.B., Dorothy taught English as a second language. She completed 17 years of teaching before retiring at about age 64 or 65.

David remembers his mother as a strong and determined person. "People told her she wouldn't be able to go to university; she wouldn't be able to get married and have children. After she received her education degree she got a car, had it equipped for one-arm driving, obtained her license, and drove herself to school. Dad was often on the train. Mother was also an artist. Her paintings hang on many walls."

In the winter and spring of 1989 Dorothy was in intensive care in Chalmers Hospital, Fredericton, following surgery for two hip replacements. Her illness was complicated by lung problems stemming from polio. She was on a machine for a while. After hoping to be able to return home, she was transferred to the Edmundston Hospital where she died in the spring of 1989.[52]

Perley Seeley was born in Minto, N.B. His family moved to Hartland. Perley worked for Hatfield Industries. He worked for the railway for 37 years. He became a locomotive engineer. He drove trains into Quebec as far as Montreal; also the Day Liner to Moncton, N.B. A well respected leader, he became president of his union. Perley died in Edmundston, August 6, 1992.[53]

Sons and Grandchildren of Dorothy and Perley Seeley

Peter Seeley, born September 19, 1953, is the one son who remained in Edmundston. He lives on the homestead. He is a millwright working for Fraser, Inc. at their pulp and paper mill. He married Suzanne Migneault. They have two sons: Jason, born 1977; and Michael, born 1980.

Donald Seeley, born March 19, 1955, is living in Surrey, B.C. He works for University of B.C. in the computer department. Donald married Laurie, from British Columbia. They met in Toronto. They have a daughter, Jennifer, born 1985; and a son Matthew, born October 1988.

David Leigh Seeley, born 1958, grew up in Edmundston, N.B. There he attended a Pentecostal Sunday School, and in his youth attended the United Church of Canada. David has two degrees from University of New Brunswick: B.Ed., 1980; and B.B.A., 1985. From Acadia Divinity School he has M. Div., 1988.[54] He was ordained by the United Baptist Convention of the Atlantic Provinces in 1989. His first pastorate was in Shelburne United Baptist Church, on south shore of Nova Scotia. His 10-year pastorate was a historic record for the church

David married Lori Banks of Shag Harbour, N.S. They have two daughters: Sarah, born 1994, and Christina, born 1997. In June 1998 the Seeley family moved to Prince Edward Island. David is pastor of Hazelbrook and Alexandra United Baptist churches. They live on MacEachern Road, near Charlottetown. Lori Seeley, R.N., is a casual nurse in Queen Elizabeth Hospital, Charlottetown. They have a summer home at Shag Harbour. Since October 2000 David has been enrolled in the Doctor of Ministry Degree Program of Acadia Divinity College.[55]

Alice Avery Cook Craig

In April 1988 Alice Craig came home to New Brunswick, after living for 33 years in Edmonton, Alberta. Her homecoming followed bereavement, and then a disabling illness.

Less than a decade after her daughter, Carol, died in Edmonton, Alberta, from a burning accident, Alice suffered the loss of her younger son, Michael Craig, born 1955. In the spring of 1976 Michael, a university student, took a summer job on an oilrig in Alberta, intending to return to university in September for his final year. Early that summer he suffered a fatal blow on the head by a boom.

While living in Edmonton, Alberta, Alice had an unfortunate illness called Gillian-Barré Syndrome, caused by an allergic reaction, which affects nerve endings. In the early stage of the disease she was totally paralyzed. She was in hospital for several months. Her sister, Betty Gray, said, "Mother and I visited her; we drove to Edmonton. We were gone three weeks. In recovery she progressed to use of crutches. Fortunately she regained much of her muscle use, but nerve endings didn't grow back. Also she still has weak muscles in one foot which has left her lame.

When the writer saw Alice in Woodstock in spring of 1991 she was riding a little electric scooter on the sidewalk. We had taken Erma Shaw on an errand to Woodstock. We stopped to visit Alice to pick up some written data for the "Corey Courier". While I was looking for Alice's apartment, Erma saw her scoot by. The scooter, obtained with the assistance of Dr. MacLaughlin of Woodstock, has given Alice much increased mobility. In Woodstock Alice is among relatives. Her sister, Betty Gray, and family often take her on outings. Two cousins, Ruth Shute and Mary Flemming, live nearby.

Alice's Children and Grandchildren

Alice's daughter, Jane Cooke, married Wayne Silsby, an engineer. He worked in Newfoundland for a Montreal engineering company. The family lived in Ottawa. When their children were in university, Jane and Wayne had a working tour in Tehran, Iran. In 1999 they were in Western Canada. Their Children:

Marc, born 1974 is a graduate of Carleton University, Ottawa, In 1999 he was working for a computer company in Ottawa.

Erin was a student at Queens University, Kingston, Ontario, working for a master's degree in engineering.

Gregory, after studying at Queens was an engineer working in Africa.

Alice's son William Craig, (Billy) born 1952, married Elizabeth. They have two children: Taylor, born 1988; and Tashia, born 1991. They live on Vancouver Island.[56]

Betty and Walter Gray and family

In 1980 Betty and Walter Gray moved from Woodstock to Jacksontown. Betty's mother, Nessie, came with them. Betty said, "I was working for Dr. Sutherland, dentist, in Woodstock when we moved here." She continued until her mother needed care at home.

The Gray's property in Jacksontown has a large farmhouse and barn. It is situated on a hill overlooking a prosperous farming community, on the west side of the Trans Canada Highway north of Woodstock. The Grays have modernized the house and added comforts, yet it has retained the character of a farmhouse. The table in the kitchen is very convenient for writing notes on family stories and for tea and cake. A delightful atmosphere.

The barn was very suitable for Walter's next enterprise — aquaculture. At first they reared salmon in ten large tanks of fibreglass. Betty said, "We dug three wells and struck a good water supply." They also made fibreglass tanks for sale, which has continued.

Their aquaculture is now located at Northampton, a few miles below Woodstock, on the opposite side of the Saint John River. Travelling down river from Grafton, look at the river side of the highway. There is a large building housing tanks of small salmon. Also there are several large round tanks setting in the open. They are home to 1,000's of salmon of several sizes. Screens exclude the birds.

On October 26, 1999, Walter gave me a tour and a comprehensive interpretation of the acquaculture. He explained, e.g., "Fresh water flows into the tanks from wells on the river bank. There is very little variation in temperature of the water in the tanks from summer to winter."

The thriving business, called Gray Aqua Farms, is raising approximately two million smolts per season. They are all inoculated to control disease. The enterprise employs 20 plus persons, including the Gray's one daughter and three sons.

Kimberly said, "I look after the hatchery in hatching season. It is a seven month seasonal job." Her husband, Bruce Morrison, also works at the Aqua Farm. Their house is on the grounds of the Jacksontown property.

Jeffrey, who was a teacher in Rothesay, is now putting his knowledge of biology to work at the farm. He and his family live at Woodstock.

Robert, a civil engineer, designed the site of the farm. He and his family live at Jacksonville. Timothy, after studying at University of Maine, is the resident business manager of the farm in Northampton. "He does the head work and the paper work."

In the fall of 1999 the Grays were developing a new water company called Neva Springs. They have drilled wells in the bank above the Aqua Farm, which have the capacity for 8000 gallons/minute. A building for a bottling plant was in progress. They were expecting the automated bottling machinery to arrive from Italy.

Children and Grandchildren of Betty and Walter

Kimberly Gray married Bruce Morrison in 1976. They have two daughters: Neallie, born 1977, and Whitney, born 1982. Neallie is graduating from Atlantic Baptist University, Moncton, with a major in psychology. Eager to go to work in the family business, in 1999 she became Director of Public Relations for Neva Springs. She finished her university courses by correspondence.

Whitney went on a venture in the summer of 1999 with "Teen Mania Ministries" of Garden Valley, Texas. After training in Texas, Whitney was one of 137 youth who flew to Bolivia. They were based in Sucré. They put on a play in a ladies' prison in Cochabamba. Whitney graduated from Woodstock High School in 2000. She is now in a course in communications at Atlantic Baptist University.

Jeffrey Gray and Corinne MacLean, married August 1991, at United Baptist Church, Woodstock, have four children: MacKenzie, born 1992; Isaac, born 1994; Keegan, born 1997; and Hunter, born 1998.

Robert Gray and Nancy Bradley, married in 1987, have two children: Matthew, born 1991; and Joshua, born 1992.

Timothy Gray and Michelle Polchies, married June 1991, have three children: Alexandra, born 1992; Samuel, born 1994, and Benjamin, born 1996.[57]

Betty Gray has been the main storyteller for the Nessie branch of Ida McBrine's family. She has shared their ventures, their accomplishments, their tragedies, their triumphs and their joys.

Nellie McBrine and the Lindsay Family

Ellen Arlene McBrine, b. November 8, 1899, was called Nellie or Nell. She is in the school register in Glassville, N.B. for years 1908 to 1914. Apparently she continued some employment after her marriage to Harry Lindsay of Woodstock, and after the birth of their daughter, Mary, February 3, 1921. In the fall of 1922 Nellie was helping "tend Central," i.e., the telephone exchange in Glassville.[58] It appears that Nellie and Harry Lindsay were the first of the McBrine connection to migrate to New York City for the construction work. In Brooklyn two more children were born to Nellie and Harry: John, June 2, 1926, and Harold, January 26, 1929. Soon after Nellie Lindsay, and Mary, John and Harold, returned to New Brunswick in 1934, John began a visit of several weeks with the family of his great uncle, Ira Corey, on their farm in E. Knowlesville. John recalls his Uncle Ira taking him trout fishing in a local brook, perhaps the Coldstream, in Knowlesville. They cut alders for fishing rods and strung their trout on forked branches of alders. John also remembers that Warren and Keith Corey, nearest his age, introduced him to a special fun — grabbing a calf by the tail and having it pull a boy across a field. Warren also remembers the sport.

Horses also represented an adventure for John. I remember the first time I saw him. It was on a Sunday afternoon visit to the Corey farm from the farm of my Grandmother Brown, where I was staying that summer. When I went to the horse barn, as visitors often did, it was evident that John had become quite familiar with the horses. He warned me: "Don't go near that horse; he kicks like the Deuce." Soon, on that Sunday afternoon, John had coaxed Claude to hitch old Nell to the driving wagon and let him drive across fields. After much persuasion and minimizing, Claude consented to allow John to touch the mare lightly with a whip.

At noon hour he would try to persuade my father to let him take out a workhorse. "This is their time to eat." "Well dinner is over now." He thought a horse ought to be able to chew his oats and hay as quickly as he could consume his dinner. In retrospect it seems that at age eight John was demonstrating a bent for venture and experiment. He poured milk into the outlet pipe in the water puncheon in the woodshed and then ran down to the horse puncheon to see it come through.

That summer, 1934, Nellie and her children were housed temporarily in the Staten House, Foreston. It was the house that Nessie Avery and children also used temporarily in 1936. Nellie and her children were in Woodstock for school opening, September 1934.

I also remember Harold Lindsay a few years later, visiting us at the Corey farm. His mother and a member of Clara's family brought him. I think I was 15, at which time Harold would be only nine. We rode bicycles to Golden Ridge. The last two miles we walked to the S. Branch of the Miramichi. We brought home two stringers heavy with trout. Father remarked on the enormity of our catch — so late in the season — near school opening. Then there was no limit on the day's catch.

At age nine Harold had no difficulty peddling a bicycle over rough gravelled road. It must have been later that he suffered from rheumatic fever which left him with an enlarged heart, filling two-thirds of his chest.[59]

Woodstock

John recalls from Woodstock days a feat of swimming the Saint John River. When John and a friend named Arnie had swam the whole width of the river, Harold was half-way across. John swam back to meet him and accompany him over. Arnie and Harold walked home over the bridge, while John re-swam the river.

When I was a high school student in Woodstock, 1940-41, I occasionally made small purchases at the Selrite store from Mary Lindsay, a clerk. John quit Woodstock High School in Grade 11 and joined the Canadian Army. In the early forties, it appears, the Lindsays were leaving Woodstock. Mary went to U.S.A. and Nellie and Harold moved to Fredericton. At Camp Petawawa in Ontario, John had a buddy who had been in mining in South Africa. He advised John: "Go to university." "He had quite an influence on my life." After discharge from the army in 1946, John took a DVA course for six weeks in which he reviewed high school and covered what he had missed. Thus he prepared for university. He chose Dalhousie because it had a mining engineering department.

Iron Workers

That summer before his first university year, John said, "I was an iron worker in New York." He worked with his father who had returned to New York after wartime work in the South.

During WW II Harry Lindsay had been seconded from Bethleham Steel and sent to Oak Ridge, Tenn. There he worked on the plant where they were making the atom bomb. Workers made the radioactive materials, not knowing what they were producing. Harry lived in Lenore City, Tenn. Harry Lindsay's iron work took him onto nearly all the high buildings in New York, New Jersey and area. Some reached 70 or 80 stories, e.g., the World Trade Centre. He worked primarily in New York City, mostly for Bethlehem Steel; he also worked for American Bridge. John also mentioned Fairless Works, a steel mill in Pennsylvania.

John said, "My father had Mohawk Indians from Montreal, working for him. Indian gangs who worked on high buildings liked working with Dad — a Canadian. I worked in a gang of all Indians except me and the bellman. The highest I worked was fourteen or fifteen stories."

John Lindsay experienced and learned a lot about construction of high buildings. He described derricks for hoisting heavy steel beams. He said sometimes there were two or three derricks working up through the centre of a building. There was keen competition between the derrick gangs. The crew that finished earlier received bonuses. There were also "raising gangs". They climbed up and hooked beams and connected them with bolts. John said, "My first partner was an Indian lad." John also described a plank gang — doing more dangerous work. Planks, 3 x 12, and 20-24 feet long, were spread over a floor. The gangs picked out the planks and brought them out to piles. John can tell us lots more stories about work on high buildings.

Living at MacDonnell's in Brooklyn

In the summer of 1946 John and his sister Mary had a hospitable living accommodation at the apartment of Lucretia and Edward MacDonnell. The MacDonnells went to New Brunswick. It was the summer I saw them at Nessie's in Juniper. Lucretia and their children, Bill, then ten and Donna then three, made an extended visit with relatives in New Brunswick. After two weeks Mack returned to New York and to work. John and Mary had an interesting time with their Uncle Mack, an ardent member of Sixth Avenue Baptist Church.

Mary had been living with the MacDonnells and working in New York during the war years. In 1946 Mary was courting Byron Hand — by long distance between New York and New Jersey — it seems. Earlier when visiting her Aunt Kaye Williams in Linneus, Mary had met Byron. Linneus, Maine, was his home town. Later he went to New Jersey where he had relatives. Late in 1946 Mary Lindsay and Byron Hand were married. They lived in New Jersey, eventually Rahway. Pearl McBrine said, "They had a lovely home there."

John Lindsay returned the second summer to work on the high buildings. He was a bit hesitant about running across the planks until he got the nerve again. After his second summer, John said, "I got married; then I didn't want to go anymore." In 1948 he married Marjorie Langin. The summer of 1948 he found a much less venturesome job with Nova Scotia Department of Highways, as "assistant resident engineer." He ran the transit.

Harold Lindsay

While John was in university his brother Harold was maturing at home. Even with an enlarged heart he became a chef — "a very good chef", John said. He was employed at the Beaverbrook Hotel in Fredericton. While John was still a student at Dalhousie University Harold visited him and Marjorie. In Halifax Harold went to a doctor who afterwards told John, "He was the sickest man I ever saw walking around."

At the time of Harold's last illness Pearl McBrine was at the apartment he and his mother kept in Fredericton. Pearl had boarded there. After she and Johnnie McBrine were married they lived at Nellie's a while. Pearl recalls: "One day when I came home from work I could hear Harold breathing. I called Dr. Bob Chalmers, only recently back from the war. He said, "Take him to the hospital right now." We walked across the intersection to the Victoria Public Hospital. Nellie was then on a visit with Mary in New Jersey. Johnnie phoned her. She arrived in a day or two. When she visited Harold at the hospital the doctor assured her that he would be alright. Johnnie said to Nellie, "Let's go for a ride." Back at her apartment, we received a phone call. Harold had died.

Harold's life was short 1929-1950. Rheumatic fever had left a damaged heart. The family, including Harold's father, Harry Lindsay, gathered at United Baptist Church, Woodstock for the funeral. Harold was buried in the cemetery on Houlton

Road. Nellie Lindsay sold her furniture and moved to New Jersey.

John W. Lindsay

The year his brother Harold died John's son, John W. Lindsay, Jr. was born. John Sr. was then nearing completion of study at Dalhousie University.

John's first job after Dalhousie was in Northern Quebec. He worked for an aluminum company who were building a dam on the Peribonca River. Housing was at Alma, far from the work site. John's day, including travel, was from 5:00 a.m. to 7:00 p.m. The situation for Marjorie, with their first baby, was also difficult. They stayed through the summer and fall.

John's next job was in Newfoundland working on U.S. military bases — 1953-57. At Mercy Hospital, St. John's, Nfld., on October 31, 1954, their daughter, Deborah Anne, was born.

John: "In 1959 I started my own company — Lindsay Construction. My first job was in Goose Bay." There he maintained an office and took on other construction work in Newfoundland and Labrador and also in Greenland and Iceland, for the U.S. military, over a period of 14 years.

John Lindsay also had another enterprise in Newfoundland: "A friend of mine, John Beck, had worked in Newfoundland with me. I became a partner with him in Beck Construction. We were in a variety of enterprises: real estate, shipyard construction, steel business, culverts, etc. After John Beck died, we bought the company from his widow and joined it with "Lindsay Enterprises".

Mother, Nellie

Though managing several enterprises, John Lindsay took time for his mother, Nellie, and his sister, Mary. From New Jersey, Nellie returned to New Brunswick to help her sister

Nellie Lindsay, holding David McBrine, Fredericton, 1957

Nessie at the White Swan Inn. In Hartland Nellie met and married Howard E. Adams, senior funeral director of New Brunswick, a leading citizen of Hartland for more than half a century, and a choir leader of Hartland United Baptist Church for ten years. H.E. Adams died in March 1959. Among the pallbearers were Nellie's brother John McBrine, and her brother-in-law Weldon Flemming.[60]

After being widowed, Nellie married William D. McLeod, a produce broker in Hartland. At his warehouses on the railway siding, he bought potatoes from the local farmers and shipped them in railway cars. He was one of the last of the potato brokers.[61]

After Nellie was widowed John had a new house built for her in Hartland. I remember making a Sunday evening visit in that home in summer of 1973. It happened that several of the McBrine relatives, Walter Whitehouse and others, were enjoying Nellie's hospitality.

Nellie maintained an active life. She was employed for some years with the Hartland Clothing Co. She was an active member of the United Baptist Church, including their Philathea Class; she was also a member of Hartland Women's Institute.[62] Through 1976 she was a regular attendant at the Corey Reunion. Her activity continued, it appears, until about the last six years of her life.

"Nellie McBrine McLeod is a patient in Halifax General Hospital......After surgery, she visited her son John Lindsay, in Halifax, but developed blood clots and has had to be returned to hospital...."[63] John recalled that after an operation in Halifax, Nellie had a stroke and was never again ambulatory. Mary Hand wanted her mother to come to New Jersey. John arranged for her to go by plane.

Being away from home proved to be difficult for Nellie, especially without medical coverage in U.S.A. "Nellie McLeod returned to her home in Hartland in the spring of 1980". John recalled: "Mother and Mary flew up to Presque Isle". Mary stayed with her mother in their Hartland house and, with the help of a nurse, cared for her.

From the time of her return to Hartland in 1980, Nellie had a special comfort — a travelling van provided by her son. John had it equipped in Halifax with a cable lift to pull the wheel chair up a ramp and snap it securely. With the help of the nurse, Mary could wheel Nellie onto the van and take her for rides, shopping trips, and visits to relatives.[64] They went to Linneus and Houlton to visit Nellie's sisters, Kaye and Lucretia, who sometimes travelled with them. They visited Vola Barker in Fredericton. They travelled to Halifax several times. John said, "They went everywhere; they put 100,000 kms. on the van." The writer remembers seeing Nellie and Mary with the van in Knowlesville at the Corey Reunion. They, and Jeffrey Greenig of New Jersey, are in the record book for July 18, 1981.

The Family of Mary and Byron Hand

Mary and Byron had four children: Jill, born 1947; Judy, born 1952; Jayne, born 1957; and Byron, born 1961. By 1980 the three daughters were married in the U.S.A. A year or two after Mary went to Hartland to take care of her mother,

Byron E. Hand, Sr. died suddenly — perhaps of heart failure — in Rahway, N.J.

Mary brought her youngest, Byron, Jr. from New Jersey to Hartland. He became a student at nearby New Brunswick Bible Institute, Victoria Corner. There he met two third cousins: Colleen Mitchell and Paul Long; all are descendants of Alfred and Lucretia Corey.[65] Byron graduated from N.B.B.I. in 1983. In May 1984 Byron received a Bachelor of Arts degree in Pastoral Studies from Washington Bible College, Lauham, Maryland.[66]

Byron's grandmother lived until after two of his graduations. A month after Byron's B.A. degree Nellie McBrine McLeod died at her home in Hartland, June 10, 1984. Her monument stands beside that of her parents, William and Ida McBrine, in the U.C. Cemetery in Glassville, N.B.

A year later, on June 22, 1985, Byron H. Hand and Jacqueline Ward were married in People's Church, Somerville, N.B.[67] In the spring of 1988 Byron graduated with Master of Divinity degree from London Baptist Seminary, London, Ontario. Mary attended Byron's graduation. Byron H. Hand was ordained May 26, 1989, in Hyde Park, Ontario, where he was pastor.[68]

Mary Lindsay Hand

Mary Hand inherited the Hartland house by a will which John had arranged with their mother. During her residence in Hartland Mary was blessed with visits from her children and grandchildren. In August 1991 Mary had all her children visiting her: Jill Moran, with son Billy; Judy and Dr. Robert Light and their four children; Jayne Babij, then with three children; and Byron and Jacqueline Hand and Christina.[69]

In her last few years Mary Hand suffered from cancer. Her brother John said it went undetected while she was treated for other ailments. Eventually she had surgery in Halifax. There she was cared for by John and Marjorie. Mary stayed with them between treatment sessions and admissions. At one stage of her recovery Mary stayed with her Aunt Vola Barker in Fredericton. John said after treatment she had two good summers and was able to visit her children in U.S.A.

Mary Elizabeth Hand died December 5, 1992, in the Victoria General Hospital, Halifax, N.S.[70] Her funeral was at United Baptist Church, Hartland, December 9, conducted by Rev. Robert McNutt. Besides John Lindsay and family, relatives attending included: Kay Williams, her son Dr. Edward Williams, Vola Barker, Leland McBrine, Evelyn and Walter Whitehouse, Shirley Brooks, Kaye Foster, and Alice Long. Interment was in Woodstock Rural Cemetery. Relatives and friends gathered at the home of Betty and Walter Gray, Jacksontown.

Memorial

"In Memory of Mary E. (née Lindsay) Hand", Feb. 3, 1921 to Dec. 5, 1992, her brother, John W. Lindsay, on July 6, 1993, mailed to the writer of this history a cheque — a generous donation — with the note: "This contribution is for assistance in publishing 'Stories of the Coreys'."

Mary Lindsay Hand, with children

Children and Grandchildren of Mary and Byron Hand

Jill Hand married 1, Robert Greenig; they had one son, Jeffrey, born 1973. Jill married 2, William Moran; they had one son William, born 1982. Jill is a nurse living in New Jersey.

Judy Hand married Robert Light, 1977; they have four children: Courtney, born 1980; Jeremy, born 1984; MacKenzie, born 1986; and Peter, born May 22, 1988. Robert is a professor teaching in Erie, Pa.

Jayne Hand married Rev. Joseph Babij, 1980; they have four children: Rebecca, born 1983; Naomi, born 1984, Joshua, born 1986; and Elizabeth, born 1996. Joseph is an American Baptist minister in E. Millstone, N.J.

Rev. Byron H. Hand and family now live in Moline, Ill. He is a pastor there.[71]

John W. Lindsay

John Lindsay's business enterprises and affiliations have been many and varied. He said, "We had the shipyard in Halifax for seven or eight years. We sold it to Irvings". John mentioned another company: "Atlantic Industries", at Dorchester Cape, N.B. He also mentioned a business in computer software.

John also has had many affiliations, e.g., the "Notice of Annual General Meeting" of M.T. & T. for April 30, 1991, lists "John William Lindsay of J.W. Lindsay Enterprises, Ltd., Real Estate Management, Halifax, N.S.", as a "Director since 1989". A footnote says, "Mr. Lindsay, ...is also the Chairman of Maritime Life Assurance Company, Chairman and Chief Executive Officer of Purdy's Wharf Development Limited, a Director of Canada Trust, and a Director of a number of companies in the Atlantic Region."

One of John's latest undertakings is environmental waste disposal. "We just did a job in Bosnia. We finished the tests; we might have to go back to Europe." John W. Lindsay, at 75, is still going strong. "You must be getting tired?" "No." "You go to Florida for the winter?" "No, I get bored in the South, and I like to be home. We'll go to Arizona for two or three weeks in January."

Children and Grandchildren of John and Marjorie Lindsay

John William Lindsay, Jr.: One of his earliest work experiences was in Japan. Employed by Osaka Y.M.C.A. from fall of 1969 to September 1970, John had a variety of work experiences. He worked with people who were involved in Expo '70 Osaka, including those who wanted to practice English. He taught some English. He wrote guides for those who were doing sailing instruction in English.

John W. Lindsay, Jr. is now a real estate and development manager. He manages commercial properties for Eastport Developers and for Halifax Commercial Park and Leaseholds.[72] His Dad said, "He manages some of my stuff also."

John W. Lindsay, Jr. married 1, Beth Carman. They had three children: Jason, born 1981; Lauren, born 1984; and Alexander, born 1987. John married 2, Ann Campbell. The children are with John and Ann.

Jason is a student at Dalhousie University, Halifax. Lauren is in grade 11, and Alexander is in grade eight. John W. Lindsay, Sr. said earlier, "The children of Judy Whitehouse Caines are in school with my grandchildren".

Deborah Ann Lindsay married Luca Rotta-Loria in 1981. Luca's family is Italian, but he was born in Cairo. His parents also were born in Egypt. Luca has his own computer software business. He distributes across Canada. Deborah and Luca have two sons: Andreas, born 1983, and Nicolas, born 1991. They live in Toronto.

Andreas, now in Ontario grade 13, is hoping to come to

Dalhousie University in 2001. Nicolas is in grade four. John and Marjorie have the prospect of three grandchildren in Dalhousie University in 2001.

Vola McBrine Barker

Vola Rideout McBrine, fourth daughter of Ida and William McBrine, was born in Knowlesville, N.B., March 19, 1902. At about age six Vola moved with her family to Glassville. Her name first appears on the Glassville School list for year ending June 1910. Among her schoolmates were cousins: Alice and Christine McBrine and Kathleen and William Miller. Vola's name last appears on the list for the year ending June 1919. However, she must have been a pupil only for the fall term of 1918. In the term ending June 1919 she was, at age 17, the teacher in the E. Knowlesville school.[73] That was before Ira Corey and family moved to E. Knowlesville.

In 1922 Vola McBrine married Archie Barker. They had one son, Billy, born February 13, 1924, in Hartland.[74] They lived in Lakeville, N.B., where Archie had a garage and service station. "In 1926 he was the first agent for Chrysler in Carleton County."

In 1935 Archie Barker ran for the New Brunswick Legislature under Allison Dysart who became premier that year.[75] Barker missed becoming an M.L.A. by only 32 votes.[76] However, Archie Barker became involved with the provincial government as an importer and supplier of heavy equipment for road building, snow ploughing and also mining. Archie's brother-in-law, Leland McBrine, recollected being called to run the garage in Lakeville. The Barker family moved to Fredericton. Leland said, "Billy was quite a big boy then."

It seems that the business Archie Barker undertook in Fredericton was under different names at different times. His obituary says, "Mr. Barker was a founding partner of Eastern

Equipment in 1941..." Another name was "Creighton and Barker Equipment." That business was on King St. The partner was Fred Creighton. An early employee was Leland McBrine. He said, "Archie phoned me and asked me to come to Fredericton to work. I became an operator, demonstrator and instructor in use and maintenance of equipment". He described the business: "We brought machines from U.S.A. by railroad carloads; Michigans, crushing plants, shovels, back-hoes and mining outfits, i.e., big underground machines for Minto."

Leland also described road-building machines. "We brought in the first new grader and sold it to the government. It was a caterpillar, a six-wheel drive. We could put four rear wheels on the road and the front wheels in the ditch. We also brought in a loader with a 30-yard bucket. It had sharp prongs in front for digging in ledge. We could push that to the bottom of a rock. That machine was bought by a contractor — Forbes and Sloat. They did a lot of road building on the T.C.H. and also a piece of road below Oromocto.

We sold many machines to the government for building roads in summer and plowing snow in winter. "We sold machinery.....heavy equipment, over the province, all the way to Edmundston. We also imported and sold Oliver equipment; tractors and other farm machinery."

At the end of W.W.II Archie Barker's son, Billy, began to work with Creighton and Barker. Billy Barker had served overseas with the R.C.A.F. Also Leland's brother, Johnnie McBrine, who had served overseas with the Canadian Forestry Corps, began working for the company in late August or early September 1945.

In 1946 Archie Barker founded a new company: "Barker Equipment". After a brief location in S. Devon, Barker Equipment moved to Woodstock Road, Fredericton, into a new building that Archie had built. The photo, thanks to Pearl McBrine, shows Oliver Tractors on display at Fredericton Exhibition in early 1950's. In front of the tractors are: Charlie

Staff of Barker Equipment

Harper, Bruce Urquhart, Archie Barker, Johnnie and Leland McBrine, unknown, and Billy Barker.

Johnnie McBrine was listed as "Parts Manager". He brought other skills to the company. Pearl says, he learned a lot about operating heavy equipment when he was overseas with the engineers and foresters. Paul Brooks, who worked for Flemming and Gibson in Juniper, recalls Johnnie's demonstration of the first grader that Flemming Co. bought from Barker Equipment. Paul said, "He ran it with ease and skill. He could make it do whatever he wanted." Johnnie worked with Barker Equipment until early 1950's when he started his own business,

"Bearings and Equipment".

In later years a nephew of Vola Barker, Robert Flemming, moved from Juniper to Fredericton and worked with Barker Equipment.

Residences and Vacations

Archie and Vola Barker lived on successive streets in Fredericton: Argyle, Smythe, Charlotte and finally at Elmcroft Place.[77] Vola drove her own car in the city. Driving was perhaps an extension of a skill she had learned when growing up in Glassville. Then she drove horses delivering mail.

Vola had a camp at Grand Lake, near Minto. Family photos indicate that many relatives gathered there in summer. Archie had a hunting and fishing camp on Magaguadavic Lake.

Vola and Archie took many trips. Postcards mailed to Mr. & Mrs. John McBrine indicate some of the places visited: Edmonton, 1954; Daytona Beach, Texas and Tennessee 1956. They rented a Winnabago and toured southern states. A card from Kingston, Jamaica indicates a boat trip.

Billy Barker and Family

Billy had part of his education at the Vocational School in Woodstock. After returning from overseas Billy married Janet Moore (Jennie) of Woodstock. They adopted two children: Philip Wm. Barker, b. October 23, 1949, and Judith Louise Barker, b. March 14, 1953. One place they lived was on Smythe Street up the hill from the intersection of King's College Rd. where Leland McBrine lived. The last place Billy lived in Fredericton was Hawthorne Terrace, off Smythe St.

Billy Barker suffered ill health early in life. In the summer of 1976 he underwent heart surgery in Boston. Jennie said, "Something went awry after the by-pass surgery. He was only

52." On November 12, 1976 he died suddenly of a heart attack in Hollywood, Florida. His funeral was in Fredericton at Brunswick St. Baptist Church. Burial is in Rural Cemetery Extension, Woodstock Rd.[78]

Barker Equipment and Archie Barker

Billy Barker was president of Barker Equipment. Two years after he died the company was sold to Bob Wallace from Sussex......in 1978. Archie Barker was then president and chairman of the board.

Archie Barker, the founder of Barker Equipment, died December 22, 1982. His funeral was at Brunswick St. Baptist Church, conducted by Rev. Fred Smith. Burial was in Rural Cemetery Extension.[79]

Vola Barker

Vola has continued residence at Elmcroft Place. In relatively recent years she was still attending Brunswick St. Baptist Church, Fredericton. Marilyn Hicks, a relative, has spoken with her there. In more recent years Vola has been confined to her home. On the phone in September 1997, she told me, "I haven't been going anywhere."

Madeline Oliver has been accompanying her daughter, Mary Jane Phillips, nurse, on her regular visits to give Vola a needle. Madeline said, "Aunt Vola has not been up to having visitors except for caregivers and a few close relatives. She has had a lady living with her, and others helping by day. She is somewhat deaf and nearly blind." On February 19, 2000 Madeline said, "She talked about Claude, her brother who died at age 18, and her father. Vola's nephew, Dr. Edward Williams, visited her in the spring of 2000. On March 19, 2001, she was age 99.

Jennie Barker and Family

Jennie Barker lives in New Maryland, N.B. In a phone conversation April 23, 2001 she shared with the writer her interests in her children. Her son Philip Barker, married Shirley Gilliland of Gagetown. They have two daughters: Marjorie, born 1981, and Meghan, born 1985. Meghan is in high school in New Maryland. The family lives on Sunset Drive. Marjorie lives at Keswick Ridge. She has one daughter, Katelin, born 2000.

Jennie's daughter, Judith Louise Barker, married Dwight Lewis. In 1976 they were living in Salisbury. They had one daughter, Kelly Louise Lewis. Judy returned to Fredericton in 1978. After divorce she took back her maiden name. Her daughter Kelly, from age six, also went by name Barker.

Kelly is married to Andrew Take. They are now in Cambridge, England. Andrew is on a three-year scholarship at Cambridge University. He is about to receive a PhD. in engineering.

Judy Barker now lives near Burtts Corner. Her place is on the road to Stanley, N.B. She said, "I love it here". In recent years Judy has looked up both her birth parents. She says, "I was close to my adoptive Dad." She hesitated for some years to look for her birth father. When she did, she was excited to trace her connections with the Gibbons and Atwell families of N. Ireland. She has been to Ontario for visits. Judy is intensely interested in her involvements, e.g., a Pentecostal Church at Douglas, and her work. She is Executive Director of Fredericton Crisis Pregnancy Centre. Judy is very eager to learn about relatives.

Kathleen and Percy Williams and Sons

Kathleen McBrine was born in Knowlesville, N.B., January 30, 1904. When she was about four the family moved to Glassville, N.B. The name, Kathleen McBrine, is on the Glassville school list for the school years ending June, 1912 through 1919. Among her school mates were: Allan, Alice,

Christine, Edgar, Edna, Florence, Frank, George, Gordon, Harriet, Harry, Lucretia, Nellie, Nessie and Vola McBrine, and Kathleen, William and Wilma Miller.

Kathleen McBrine married Percy Williams of Williamstown, N.B. They lived in Lakeville. Percy worked for a time at Archie Barker's garage. Kathleen and Percy Williams were among the first of the McBrine relatives to go to New York in the building boom of the 1920's. Their first born son, Edward, said, "I was born in New York in 1929." A second son, Robert, was also born there, in 1930. He lived only until 1932. Percy and Kaye brought the baby boy to New Brunswick for burial. In recent years Edward has been making inquiries and trying to locate the grave in Long Settlement.

In 1937 Percy Williams left his job as a mechanic in a large garage in New York City. The family moved from Brooklyn, N.Y. to Linneus, Maine. There Percy bought and maintained a garage and service station. In Linneus another son, William, was born in 1941.

Both Edward and Bill cherish very pleasurable youthful experiences with their cousins of the McBrine connection in New Brunswick. Edward said, "We loved Clara and Weldon Flemming, but we liked Fredericton more than Juniper. So we visited more in Fredericton." Bill Williams also recalls visits of his cousins, Bill and Donna MacDonnell. They liked to come to Maine for summer holidays. It appears there was much visiting among the McBrine cousins, siblings and in-laws. The Williams were very cordial.

Walter Gray recalls that when Percy Williams was present, "conversation often followed Percy's keen interest in cars. He knew many makes and models." There was mechanical ability in the Williams family. Percy's brother, Flight Engineer Ron R. Williams of Long Settlement N.B. was described as an "expert mechanic". He received special recognition as a member of the Royal Air Force Transport Command. He prepared Prime Minister Churchill's bomber, and also accompanied him on trips e.g., a "Cairo-Moscow" trip, August 1942, and a Casablanca trip. Williams was "commended in the King's Birthday Honors List, for valuable service in the air."[80]

Percy Williams was very eager to help his son Edward. When he was a student at Bowdoin College in Maine, Pearl and Johnnie McBrine sometimes went to Linneus and kept the service station so Percy and Kaye could go to Bowdoin to visit Edward.

At Bowdoin College Edward was a James Bowdoin scholar, "the highest award given in that college." For medical school Edward returned to New York City. There he attended Cornell University. In his last year Edward was awarded a medical study grant from the State of Maine. He was president of his fraternity, and also presiding senior of his class — the highest honor given at Cornell. He was one of three out of his class chosen to take a course in surgery at Bellevue Hospital.

Dr. Edward Williams' internship was with the U.S. military. He served two years in the Air Force in the midwest before setting up practice in Houlton, Maine, in 1958.[81] Edward married Nadine Tidd in 1953. They have a daughter, Sheryl born 1956; and a son Jonathan, born 1958.

Eddie Williams

Later Years of Percy and Kaye Williams

Dr. Edward said, "Dad kept working in his garage in Linneus, Maine, as long as he lived. He died in 1976". Kay continued residence in Linneus for ten years longer. On January 21, 1983, Kay was honored by the Town of Linneus for 45 years of community service in town, school and church. Master of ceremonies was her pastor, Rev. John Ruth. Kaye's two sons, Dr. Edward Williams, Houlton, and Bill Williams, Holden, Maine, were present. Approximately 200 people gathered.[82]

In 1986 Kaye Williams moved to Houlton. There her sister Lucretia lived with her before she went to a nursing home. In June 1991 Kaye suffered a broken hip. She spent part of her convalescence with her sister Vola Barker, Fredericton.[83] In 1996 Kaye entered a nursing home in Houlton. In 2000 Dr. Edward Williams spoke of visiting her there regularly. On January 30, 2001, they observed her birthday; she was 97. The doctor said, "She has no pain; she sleeps most of the time." On March 3, 2001, Kaye Williams died.[84]

Edward Williams and Family

Sheryl and Jonathan Williams, 1961

Dr. Williams retired from medical practice in 1996. They have a home in Houlton and a summer place on E. Grand Lake. In mid-March they go to California for four weeks. Their daughter, Sheryl, and their son Jonathan and families live nearby.

Sheryl married Michael Martin. They have three children: Lindsay, born 1985, Kelsey, born 1988, and Taylor, born 1990. Sheryl is a registered nurse.

Jonathan married Nancy Fitzpatrick. They have one son Geof, born 1987 March. Jonathan is a pharmicist in Houlton.

Bill Williams

Bill Williams' career has been in music. For years he owned Knapp's Music Store in Bangor, Maine, having bought it from Mr. Knapp. It was a "full line" store, selling printed music and musical instruments: organs, pianos, guitar. They also kept a service truck "on the road". They serviced and rebuilt pianos and organs. Bill has recently sold the store. He now works for the new owner. The store retains the Knapp name. Bill has performed in musical productions, e.g., with a Gilbert and Sullivan Society. His group performed at Buxton, England, near Sheffield, at their first International Festival, about 1995. They won first prize for their production.

Bill Williams married Joanie Flitz in 1996. They lived in Holden, Maine, until recently, when they moved to Jennifer St. in Bangor. Bill expresses a fondness for family and a sense of tradition. He holds to the value of families keeping in touch. He reads the "Corey Courier" with much interest. [85]

1907 George McBrine 1972

George Corey McBrine, second son of Ida and William McBrine, was the baby of the family — about age one — when the family moved from Knowlesville in 1908. His name first appears on the Glassville School list for the year ending June 1914. Among his schoolmates were cousins: Alice, Allan, Christine, Edgar, Edna, Florence, Frank, Gordon and Harriet McBrine; and Kathleen, William and Wilma Miller. George's name last appeared on the list for 1920.

George McBrine married first, Flossie Williams, a sister of Percy Williams, of Williamstown, N.B. They had one son,

Richard, born March 17, 1927. They went to New York City where many of the McBrine relatives were working in the building boom of the 1920's. George became a mechanic, his brother Leland said. In New York, George and Flossie separated. George met and married Ruth Ross who was from Cape Breton.

Later George and Ruth came to Juniper, N.B. George worked for Flemming and Gibson. The first time I saw George he was running a bulldozer. We had come to Juniper to pick blueberries. We stopped at the mill. My father said, "There's George McBrine." It seems that Richard (Dick) also joined the family in Juniper. George and Ruth had two sons: John Ross McBrine, born December 26, 1935, and Kenneth Wayne McBrine, born August 14, 1939. In the late 30's, George worked with Jim and Bill Lewis on the log hauler that pulled about ten sets of sleds. George also worked on snowploughs, Warren Corey recalled. The memory of George and Ruth is kept in Juniper by their beautiful wedding photo that Kaye Thompson displays in her living room.

Ruth and George McBrine

From Juniper George joined the Canadian Army along with Jim Petre, Buster Kelly and others. George went overseas with the Forestry Corps. Following the war George and Ruth lived at North East Margaree, Cape Breton, N.S., where Ruth's forebears had possessed property since about 1800.

Cape Breton

Ruth Ross was a descendant of Harriet LeJeune who was born in France in about 1741. Her second husband was killed in the siege of Louisberg in 1758. At Little Narrows, Cape Breton, Harriet married James Ross. They had two sons and two daughters. They moved to North East Margaree about 1800. There Harriet was the first white woman resident. Harriet Ross "nursed the sick of the area, even during a smallpox epidemic, and often travelled miles through the woods on horse or on foot to act as a midwife." She continued her care well past her 100th year. She died at N.E. Margaree, Inverness Co., N.S. in May 1860.[86]

At N.E. Margaree stood Ross House, a beautiful large house with a veranda across the front, and shuttered windows, including a bay window. In September 1953 Pearl, David and Johnnie McBrine visited George, Ruth, John and Kenneth at that house. Johnnie and Pearl took Ruth and Kenneth with

Ross House, Cape Breton

them round the Cabot Trail. John was perhaps in school or working. George was running a road-grading machine at Cheticamp. Seasonally, George worked on highway construction as a heavy equipment operator.

The property of George and Ruth included a small farm. Photos show David McBrine fascinated with a handsome large workhorse and with a flock of sheep. George raised lambs. George and Ruth also entertained sportsmen, fishermen in spring and summer, and hunters in autumn. George was a guide.[87]

George, holding David McBrine, at Cheticamp, C.B.

Sons and Grandchildren

Dick McBrine, with his bride Marion Spring, made an overnight stop in Fredericton with Pearl and Johnnie. A photo shows Dick and Marion holding David McBrine, about age two, in front of 652 York St. They are holding Pearl's English bulldog on a leash. They were enroute to Cape Breton on their honeymoon. It appears that their visit to

Dick and Marion McBrine

Cape Breton was the same fall as the visit of Pearl and Johnnie. Photos show Marion, George and Ruth in front of Ross House, also Dick and Marion on the Cabot Trail.

Richard and Marion had four children: Deborah Mae Louella McBrine, born October 26, 1954; Richard (Ricky) McBrine, born November 1955; Kenneth Wayne McBrine, born December 1957; and Robert McBrine. Dick was "A good family man". They lived in Ontario where Dick "maintained a good job; he was a 32nd degree Mason."[88] Pearl said, "Dick worked with Ontario Hydro." She also recalled, "We visited Dick and family when we were on a trip to Ontario in 1955. Later, when David McBrine was in Mississauga with A.E.C.L. he used to talk with Dick who worked in Toronto, but lived near Barrie. His address in 1978 was RR2, Stroud, Ontario. L0L 2M0.

John Lindsay also

Marion, George and Ruth McBrine, at Ross House, 1953

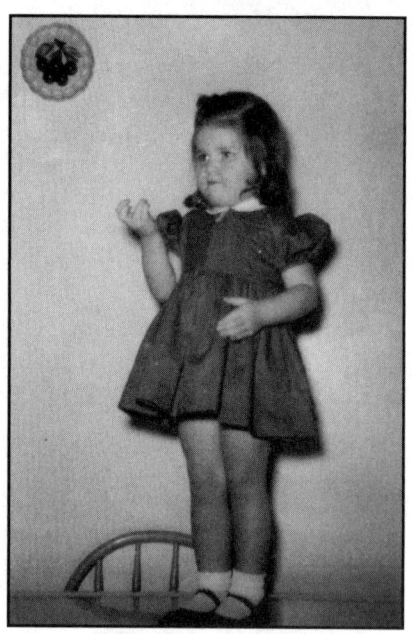

Debbie McBrine, 1956

reported Dick's meeting with relatives: "He brought his daughter, Debbie, to the wedding of Donna MacDonnell in New Jersey in 1968. We all stayed at Mary's", his sister, then also living in New Jersey.

John Lindsay also reported encountering Dick's half brother, Kenneth McBrine. "Kenneth worked for a time in Halifax. He was in sales and promotion, and soon went to another job. The last I knew, Kenneth was executive director of the milk bureau in Ottawa." From their 1953 visit Pearl remembers John McBrine as "a very sweet boy."

Closing Years

In his last few years - late 1960's and early 1970's - it appears that George increased his communication with his relatives. In summer of 1968 he wrote to Tom Corey and enclosed a contribution to "The Corey Courier." In May 1970 George wrote a note to Erma Shaw for the "Courier". He disclosed that they had sold their farm in Cape Breton and were packing to move. Perhaps they had left the "Ross House" the year before. In September 1969 my family and I were touring Cape Breton on the occasion of bringing our daughter, Carolyn, to Acadia University, from New York State. On the Cabot Trail we stopped and saw them. Their place then was on the edge of a stream.

George's note of May 1970 also told Erma that in the late fall of 1969 he and Ruth had made a nine-week visit to New Brunswick, Maine and Ontario. The note also reported that after returning to Cape Breton both George and Ruth had to be hospitalized, Ruth in December 1969, and George in spring of 1970 for over a month [89]. Medical needs sometimes took George McBrine to Camp Hill, the veterans' hospital in Halifax. A grand niece, Judy Whitehouse, then a medical intern, was assigned to George. He said, "You're not a doctor; you're just a little girl." Judy's brother, Larry Whitehouse, also studying medicine in

Ken, Dick, George and John McBrine at N.E. Margaree

Halifax, visited George in Camp Hill Hospital.[90]

In potato digging time, 1970, when Erma Shaw was keeping her grandchildren while her daughter, Alice Long, worked on the potato harvester, George stopped at Long's home, near Hartland. Erma was glad to see her cousin and long remembered the visit. Probably it was the last time she saw him.

George's last illness was in Camp Hill Hospital, Halifax. Ruth travelled from Cape Breton regularly to visit him. Marjorie and John Lindsay welcomed her in their home, in walking distance from the hospital. Marjorie said, "We picked her up evenings". They also visited George. On March 13, 1972 George Corey McBrine died at Camp Hill Hospital. George and Ruth McBrine are buried in N.E. Margaree.[91]

Sometime in the mid-nineties, Dick and Kenneth McBrine motored from Ontario to Cape Breton to sell the property there and settle the estate. They made a hurried stop at a lunch place in Fredericton. Dick phoned Pearl McBrine from there.

1909 Lucretia McBrine 1990

Lucretia McBrine, youngest daughter of Ida and Bill McBrine, was born in Glassville on November 16, 1909. Her name is on the Glassville school list for the school years ending June 1916 through 1926, except for 1922. In 1926 she wrote the Normal School Entrance Exams. Marjorie Lamont, a close friend who wrote the exams with Lucretia, says that soon after the exams Lucretia joined other members of her family in New York. Marjorie said, "We carried on a correspondence, and I saw her when she came to Glassville to visit Clara. Marjorie still has a post card and a photo of Lucretia in a boat off Coney Island."

Lucretia married Edward P. MacDonnell, a postal worker in New York. She remained in New York though all her siblings who had lived and worked there had left by the end of the 1930's. Many of the relatives came to the MacDonnell's apartment in Brooklyn to visit. Pearl McBrine recalls being with a whole carload of people who spent a night with the MacDonnells - sleeping on sofas and on floors. Their apartment was noted for hospitality. Some relatives boarded with the MacDonnells or lived in the apartment while working in the city: Betty and Dorothy Avery, and Mary and John Lindsay.

One story of hospitality was lauded by many relatives. Lucretia's Aunt Bert Redlon, after years without contact with any of her family, came to the MacDonnell's apartment and spent her last few years.[92]

Though Lucretia and family were separated in distance from her siblings and their families they kept up much relationship. They made yearly visits with relatives in Maine and New Brunswick. During Mack's summer holidays the family came north. They visited the Williams family in Linneus, Maine; and the McBrine and Barker families in Fredericton, N.B. They also came to Juniper. In the summer of 1946, the writer remembers that Lucretia and Mack were staying with Nessie and family in Juniper and visiting Clara and family.

Lucretia and Edward MacDonnell had a son, William, born November 14, 1936 in Brooklyn, and a daughter Donna, born in Fredericton, N.B., July 25, 1943. Both grew up in New York. Donna said, "I was born while my mother was visiting Vola Barker in Fredericton." Bill MacDonnell was fond of his cousins: e.g., Bill Williams in Lianeus, and Ronald McBrine in Fredericton.

Maine

Bill MacDonnell liked Maine so much that he elected to begin his teaching career there — in a one-room school, in 1963. Joe McBrine was his superintendent. Lucretia continued to reside in New York until after Mack died in August 1965. In November 1965 Lucretia and Donna moved to Houlton, Me. Donna, a nurse, worked in the hospital. Having difficulty adjusting to small town Houlton, Lucretia and Donna moved to New Jersey in fall of 1967.[93]

Kaye Williams' son, Dr. Edward Williams, said, "After Dad died, Lucretia returned to Maine and lived with my mother in Linneus. The two sisters were very close. Lucretia also visited with Vola Barker in Fredericton. For a time she was hospitalized in Fredericton. She was back and forth between Fredericton and Maine." Bill MacDonnell said, "Even after my mother began to develop Alzheimers, Kaye cared for her." Judy Oliver said, "Kaye loved her to death." In the 1980's, in the later stages of Alzheimers, Lucretia was in the care of a nursing home in Houlton. She died on July 4, 1990.

Son and Daughter of Lucretia and Mack

Margarete and Bill MacDonnell, New York

Bill MacDonnell's school career culminated in the office of superintendent in Maine School Administration District 29, a position he held for twenty years, 1977-97. He was one of three second cousins in the position of superintendent in Maine.[94]

Bill MacDonnell married Margarete Martin. They have a son, Richard, born 1962, and a daughter, Liesl, born 1969.

Donna MacDonnell married Donald Bachman. They have an adopted son, Jonathan, born 1980. They live in Concord, N.C.

Grandchildren of Bill and Margarete

Richard MacDonnell married Laurie Jo Harvey. They have two sons: Seth, born June 1994; and Nathanael, born April 11, 1999. They live in Florida.

Liesl MacDonnell married Robert Lilly. He had two sons: Jarrod, born 1980, and Gavin, born 1984. Twin Girls: Madison and Annabelle (Maddie and Annie) were born to Liesl and Robert September 15, 1999. Since 1998 Bill and Margarete have had a home in Saco, Maine. Thus they could be near their daughter Liesl and family over the period of childbirth.

Dr. E. Williams, who reported the above news, kept in close touch with his cousin Bill, and Margarete. He said, "We spent two days with them in September 2000. Bill has Parkinson's but it has made little change in his condition. He is still alert and active, e.g., in his church.

In December 2000 Bill and Margarete began a drive southward. After spending Christmas with Bill's sister, Donna Bachman and family, in North Carolina, they continued their drive to Florida. Their plan was to start back to their home in Saco at the end of April 2001, and stop at Donna's in North Carolina. Bill and Donna have been helpful in phone conversations.

Leland McBrine

Leland was born in Glassville, N.B. on October 12, 1912. He was eight years and eight months old when his father, Bill McBrine, died. The anecdotes earlier in this chapter of Leland's youth in Glassville and area suggest that he early learned to be resourceful and venturesome. They also express special appreciation of his eldest brother Jud McBrine and his wife Dorothy.

Leland's return to New Brunswick from New York and Maine, as mentioned earlier, was on the invitation of his brother-in-law, Archie Barker, to operate his service station in Lakeville. Leland said, "I built a house in Lakeville. I operated the garage there for quite a while.

"Then Archie Barker called me and asked me to come to Fredericton and work in the business he was establishing. He sent me to U.S.A. to take courses at every factory where we bought machinery. I spent two weeks at each factory. I learned the mechanics of each piece of equipment and how to operate it. I earned many diplomas."

"Back home in Fredericton, we put on demonstrations. Then I travelled all over the province and demonstrated and instructed. I taught all the drivers how to operate the machines. But unfortunately they didn't know how to service that new equipment. Later I received trouble calls from all over the province. Sometimes I travelled all day and all night.......in times of winter storms."

Leland related a vivid memory of one winter trouble call: "Gil Titus, engineer for northern part of the province, kept the plows working day and night, clearing snow. They pushed the plows with Walter trucks with huge diesel engines. They had fuel injection going through the top to the pistons. When men took the injectors out to clean them they left no clearance. They screwed them down so tight they ruined some. Gil Titus had them bring the trucks into the big garage to check them. He called me. I had to come all the way from Miramichi, through St. Quentin, to Edmundston. I told them what to do and what not to do in service to the engines. I was with Gil all that day and into the next day. Then I returned to Fredericton and slept for a day or two."

This story of his work with Barker Equipment, Leland told on an October day in 1999, at his comfortble bungalow on King's College Road, Fredericton. There also he had employed his skill with heavy equipment. One of the earliest to build on that block, he used a company machine to dig for drainage and for the foundation.

Family

Leland McBrine has been widowed since 1985, from Marion Victoria Lindquist. She died on December 2, at the Dr. E. Chalmers Hospital, after a ten year illness with cancer. Marion was a member of Brunswick St. Baptist Church. Her funeral was conducted by Rev. Fred Smith. Interment was in Forest Hill Cemetery.

Marion and Leland McBrine had a son Ronald William, born April 28, 1936, and a daughter Linda, born September 14, 1942.

Family must have been important to Leland and Marion. At Christmas time 1947 Leland drove from New York to Florida, 1,432 miles in 32 hours without sleep, when Marion's sister, Helen, died.[95]

On walls of Leland's bungalow hung framed photographs of seven racing horses he had owned and raced. They prompted one more story on that October day, 1999, about his hobby — horse racing. His fondness for horses that started at Millers' farm in Glassville, had not been displaced by ascending multi-story buildings, nor by occupation with powerful machinery.

On February 10, 2000, we again viewed the photos; Leland expanded his story: "I raced six horses, mostly in the evenings at Exhibition Park, Fredericton. I also raced at Woodstock, Houlton, Bangor and Saint John. I had seven horses going; one belonged to another man; I drove him. They took him to a veterinary

Ronald McBrine, age 11

Linda McBrine, age 5

in Bangor to be treated for a lameness." With a note of triumph he concluded, "I brought him in at the head of the race." It was also a good conclusion to my last visit in that house.

My October and February visits were fortunate in timing. In retrospect I am very glad to have elicited Leland's stories while his memory was still good. At Easter 2000 a telephone conversation with Ronald informed me that Leland had been in Chalmers Hospital for a month and had been diagnosed with Alzheimer disease. Ronald had brought him to his home for the holiday weekend. Subsequently I had telephone conversations with Leland.

Ronald and Jeanette McBrine

Ronald McBrine received a B.A. from U.N.B. in 1959. That summer he was sending post cards from Europe. One from London, and one from Frankfurt, Germany, were addressed to Mr. and Mrs. John McBrine, York St., Fredericton. In November 1960 he sent a card from Ottawa where he had begun studies in journalism at Carleton University.

From Carleton University Ronald received a Bachelor of Journalism degree. At their convocation on May 26, 1961, Ronald also received the Kenneth R. Wilson Memorial Award for journalism. Ronald returned to U.N.B. and received an M.A. He also did graduate study at Syracuse University, working toward a Ph.D. in communication.

At U.N.B. Ronald held a position for several years as assistant to Dr. Colin B. MacKay, and subsequently to other presidents. Ronald was also Director of Public Relations and Development.[96]

In 1964 Ronald married Jeanette Stubbard who was born in England in 1944. Her father was there, in the Canadian Forces. In 1945 Jean, at age 2, came to Nova Scotia with her mother — a war bride — from Britain, on the Queen Mary.

They lived on Cape Breton, near New Waterford. In the early 50's Jean's father rejoined the Canadian Forces. Jean, with her sister and brother, grew up on military bases, including Base Gagetown, N.B. From Oromocto, where Jean attended high school, she went to U.N.B. to work. There she met Ronald McBrine.

In 1982 Ronald was ordained a deacon in the Anglican Church. On May 25, 1983, he was ordained priest. He served the parish of New Maryland. The family lived in the rectory at Nasonworth.

On May 31, 1998 Ronald retired from the Anglican ministry. The family moved to their new home on Woodbine Lane in Upper Kingsclear. From T.C.H. exit onto Mazerolle Settlement Road.

Jean has had her own interests and her own career. When the McBrines lived at Douglas, N.B., 1970-81, she joined with three other women of that area and formed a group known as Century Crafts. Jean's specialty was making period dolls, with costumes of the early 1800's. Ronald sculpted the doll heads.[97] Since 1989 Jean McBrine has been working for the Canadian Mental Health Association. She is Executive Director for the Fredericton/Oromocto Region.

Children of Jean and Ronald McBrine

Jean and Ronald McBrine have two sons and two daughters:

Sean Michael McBrine, born 1966, was named for Johnnie McBrine. Sean works for SMT bus company in Fredericton. He lives in the city.

Shelly Victoria, born 1969, is a teacher. She is married to Todd Way, also a teacher. In August 2000 they went to Newfoundland where Todd is a student in medicine at Memorial University. His grandparents and an uncle live in Newfoundland.

Matthew McBrine, born 1972, has been a student and football player at Bishop's University, Lennoxville, P.Q. He is now coordinator of alumni affairs for the university, and still does some football coaching. Matthew is engaged to be married to Nancy Richard of Quebec in July 2001.

Patricia Corey McBrine, born 1974, is a graduate of U.N.B. She is currently at Queens University, Kingston, Ontario, studying mediaeval literature, and preparing to teach English in university. In 2001 she plans to go to University of Toronto to achieve a Master's degree.

Linda McBrine Adkins

Linda McBrine was a student at Teachers' College, Fredericton in 1961.[98] She taught school and later worked in retail. Linda married Brian Adkins. They live in Fort Worth, Texas. They have a daughter, Gretchen, born October 13, 1970. Gretchen is married to Tomazo (Tom) Leone. They live in Virginia.

In summer of 2000 Linda, Brian and Gretchen visited Leland and also Ronald and family in Fredericton and area. I met Linda and Gretchen at Kings College Road. By that time the family had anxiety about Leland and difficulty in helping him to manage. They decided that he could not safely manage alone at his own house.

Much of Linda's visit was spent helping make arrangements for Leland to enter a special care home. Before she returned to Texas, near the end of September, she and Ronald had found a home for Leland. He was then diagnosed with Alzheimers with dementia. He is at Reta's Retreat Special Care Home, 21 Christopher Dr., Burton, N.B. Visitors are welcome.[99]

1916 Lorne (Johnnie) McBrine 1963

The youngest of the children of Ida and William McBrine was born in Glassville, February 8, 1916. They named him Lorne William McBrine. This name appears on the Glassville School list in the years ending June 1923, 1925, 1926, and 1927.

By 1927 many of the McBrine family had gone to New York to work. It appears that Ida McBrine, widowed in 1921, left Glassville in 1927, taking Lorne, then age 11, with her to join the family members in New York. The boy's certificate from the Board of Education of the City of New York reads: "Lorne W. McBrine has satisfactorily completed the course of study for elementary schools, has earned the approbation of the principal and teachers, and is entitled to pursue any high school course in the City of New York." Pearl Buchanan McBrine, who possesses the certificate dated February 5, 1932, says Johnnie attended high school in New York. She said "He was quick to learn and had a retentive memory."

Though the boy is registered as "Lorne" both in Glassville and in New York, early in life he came to be called "Johnnie". It was perhaps an affectionate nickname started by his brother, George, and adopted by their mother.

In New York, Johnnie married Dorothy Garvie in 1935. They had a daughter, Patricia, born March 1938. It appears that by 1938 Johnnie began moving toward "home". He made a visit with Kaye and Percy Williams in Linneus, Me. While Dorothy and Patricia remained in U.S.A., Johnnie returned to New Brunswick. He was visiting in Centreville and Lakeville in 1938 and 1939. His visits included a hunting camp.

Early in W.W.II, Johnnie enlisted in the Canadian Army, at Woodstock, N.B. He went overseas with the Engineers, probably by early 1941. His brother George McBrine went to Scotland with the Forestry Corps. George claimed his younger brother to join with him in Forestry. Pearl McBrine has a fold-

Johnnie and David McBrine, 1952

Debbie, Johnnie and David McBrine, Niagara Falls, 1955

out "service photo" by Pirbright, Surrey, of No. 4 Company, Canadian Forestry Corps, Canadian Army Overseas. The number of men in the company is estimated close to 200. George and Johnnie spent about four years at Aberdeen. They came home together on the same boat. Johnnie used to say it was four years, four months and four days from time of his embarkation from Halifax until his return there in 1945.

By that time Creighton and Barker were in business in Fredericton. Johnnie went to work for them. For a time he stayed with his brother, Leland, and Marion, then living on Westmorland St.

In Fredericton, Johnnie met Pearl Buchannan. She grew up in Centreville, N.B. Her mother, Evelyn Tedford, was from Windsor. Pearl said, "I came to Fredericton in 1945 and began teaching in the Business College. In January 1947, I began boarding with Nell." Through Nellie Lindsay,

Johnnie's sister, Pearl and Johnnie met. "We married in 1949, and in 1950 we began building a house on York St." While the house was being built they lived with Nellie and Harold.

Pearl and Johnnie had one son, David John McBrine, born March 28, 1951, in Fredericton. When David was growing up they took car trips, e.g., to New York and Maine. "Johnnie loved to go to Skowhegan. He liked Jean's restaurant. While he went to the horse races, David and I enjoyed the pool."

Interests and Business

Johnnie McBrine participated extensively in the Dale Carnegie Course. On the roster for class #3, he was listed: McBrine, Lorne W. "John", Parts Manager, Barker Equipment Co. On the same list is Barker, Wm. W. "Bill", 125 Argyle St. Business: Salesman, Barker Equipment Co. Johnnie's certificate, dated May 28, 1953, says, "Lorne W. McBrine has successfully completed the Dale Carnegie Course in developing courage and confidence, effective speaking, leadership training, and human relations." Marion and Leland McBrine are photographed at the Carnegie Party. On a subsequent roster Johnnie is listed as a "Director". This position as an instructor he held for three courses.

In the early 50's Johnnie McBrine left employment with Barker Equipment and started his own business: "Bearings and Equipment", near the railway station on Aberdeen St. Extension, Fredericton. Pearl said, "He had a little gold mine there." In January 1963 Johnnie sold the business.

Suffering with heart, lung and liver ailments, he died May 31, 1963. His funeral was held in George St. Baptist Church, Fredericton. The church was packed. Johnnie is buried beside his mother and father in the United Church Cemetery in Glassville. The McBrine monument was erected in the 1950's, apparently after the death of Ida in 1953. The members of the family of Ida and William jointly purchased the stone and had

it lettered. Johnnie's foot stone reads:
L.W. (John) McBrine
1916 - 1963

Johnnie, it seemed, came often to the affections of his mother, Ida McBrine, especially in her closing years. Members of the Ira Corey family with whom she stayed at intervals in Juniper still recall that she packed her suitcase frequently and waited, saying, "Johnnie is coming for me." The fantasy, long retained, need not be surprising. Pearl says that Johnnie and Leland would do anything for their mother. If she wanted to go to Hartland to visit her daughter Nessie, or even to Haynesville Me., to see her son, Jud McBrine, and family, they would drive her there for an evening.

Pearl Buchanan McBrine

Pearl's education in business gave her the special skills to work as an "engrossing clerk" for the New Brunswick Legislature. She held that position through nine sessions of the Legislature in the 50's. In later years Pearl was employed with Fredericton businesses; e.g., accounting for a construction company, an electrical company and an insurance company.

In Fredericton, about 1995, Pearl had a visit from Patricia Wusterbarth, née McBrine. Patricia was then married to David Wusterbarth. They were living In Meridan, Conn. Patricia said that on a trip to Montreal they "took a detour to Fredericton". Patsy gave the names of her children by another marriage: Debbie, Robert and Denise. Patsy also said her mother had married again. Thus Patsy had half brothers and sisters. Pearl McBrine continued to live on York St. until 1997.

David McBrine and Family

David was educated in technology at N.B.I.T., Moncton. He had two years in mechanical engineering. He wrote his thesis on "Aluminum Welding". He has been employed by N.B. Power Commission. Beginning as Fitter I, he has held several positions. At Newcastle Creek Power Plant he received his Industrial and Mechanical License, interprovincial. He was Grand Lake and area co-ordinator for three years.

The Commission sent him to Mississagua, Ontario, for training with Atomic Energy of Canada. He had two years of training at the A.E.C.L. Laboratory at Sheridan Park. At Point Lepreau Power Plant he has worked in engineering and construction of the Reactor Building; as Commissioning Assistant; currently he is working as a Senior Fuel Handling Specialist, as a foreman/supervisor.

David and his wife, Deborah Lynn Niles, live on Campbell Road, across the Nerepis River from Westfield, N.B. They have a daughter Christa Lynn, born February 22, 1973, and a son Jonathan David, born July 19, 1977. David's mother, Pearl, is living nearby at Grand Bay. She sold her house in Fredericton and bought a house in Grand Bay in 1997. Since the move, Pearl has suffered a restriction in eyesight and is unable to drive her car.

Christa Lynn McBrine married John Frederick MacKay. Their two children are: Amber Carolyn MacKay, born May 8, 1991; and Devin Allan Donald MacKay, born September 14, 1995. John died November 19, 1997, of a rare blood disease, at age 24. Christa has had a range of education and training: Business College, a year in French School and a five-week course in French Immersion at Chicoutimi, Quebec. She has worked as a Vacation Counsellor for Tourism, and at a call centre. Maintaining employment has been difficult because of the need for day care, or night babysitting. Also Christa has had to give extra care to her daughter, Amber, who has both diabetes and rheumatoid arthritis. Amber has had several admissions to hospital, including the I.W.K., Halifax. Christa lives at Ketepec. Amber and Devin attend the French Immersion School in Millidgeville.

Jonathan David McBrine, born July 19, 1977 married Melissa St. Pierre, born May 24, 1977. They live in Saint John. Jonathan has inclination toward mathematics and mechanics. He has a welder's ticket.

Debbie McBrine keeps herself available to accompany Christa and Amber to hospital, and to take Pearl to appointments. She arranges her part-time job at Zellers with a flexible schedule.

[1] It was the former Wm. M. Connell farm, on lot 23, range 3. See map p.IV, in The Story of Knowlesville

[2] A History of the Glassville Settlement, p.185 f.

[3] See The Story of Knowlesville, p.89

[4] See Chapters IV and IX

[5] See Chapters IV and IX

[6] A History of the Glassville Settlement, p. XLIV

[7] A History of the Glassville Settlement, p.142 ff.

[8] "The Observer", in the 1980's, when J. Lyon lived in Lakeville

[9] H.N. Bradley, History of Foreston p.42; also, A History of the Glassville.....p. XLf.

[10] A History of the Glassville Settlement, Vol.2, p.158

[11] Marjorie Martinson, sister of Bessie

[12] Marjorie Martinson

[13] See Chapter VII

[14] The Story of Knowlesville, p.141 and 190

[15] Madeline Oliver

[16] Kathleen Thompson

[17] The Story of Knowlesville, p.91

[18] Ibid., p.120. Also record book of Knowlesville Baptist Church, p.64f.

[19] "Timber Times", a publication of Juniper Lumber Co., Special Edition, "Our Roots Time Capsule."

[20] Kaye Foster

[21] Gordon Corey

[22] Dawn Bell Logan, By the Sound of the Mill Whistle; Carleton County Historical Society; c.1999, pp.105

[23] Ibid, p.145

[24] Ibid, p.145

[25] Madeline Oliver, in telephone conversation; Aug. 12, 2000

[26] Telephone conversation, Nov. 6, 2000

[27] Kay Thompson and Madeline Oliver

[28] Madeline Oliver

[29] "The Daily Gleaner", Fredericton, June 29, 1989

[30] Telephone conversation with R.T. French, Nov. 8, 2000

[31] "Up and Around", Saint John, April 24, 1997, p.3

[32] Norman Corey

[33] See Chapter VIII

[34] "The Observer", Hartland, N.B.

[35] "The Bugle", Woodstock, N.B., July 23, 1997, p.3

[36] Madeline Oliver

[37] "The Observer", Hartland; and The Bugle, Woodstock

[38] "Timber Times", a publication of Juniper Lumber Co., March 1998, p.9

[39] The Observer

[40] Ralph Hay, "In Retrospect", <u>The Gleaner</u>, Fredericton

[41] Telephone conversation with Ruth, June 28, 2000

[42] "Timber Times", a publication of Juniper Lumber Co., Issue 2, March 1998, p.8

[43] Obituary, clipped by Pearl McBrine

[44] Betty Gray

[45] Acadia University Alumni Directory, 1989, p.193; 1995, p.381.

[46] Betty Gray and Gordon Corey

[47] Pearl McBrine

[48] See Chap. XIV on Alberta Corey Redlon, b. 1879, daughter of Alfred and Lucretia Corey

[49] Pearl McBrine

[50] Sources, in addition to Mr. Walton's letter, are newspaper accounts clipped by Pearl McBrine

[51] The Observer, Hartland, N.B., June 26, 1958

[52] "Corey Courier", 1989, p.2; and Betty Gray

[53] David Seeley

[54] Acadia University Alumni Directory, 1989, p.229; 1995, p.300

[55] "A.D.C. Today", Vol.22, No.1, p.3, in The Atlantic Baptist, March 2001.

[56] Betty Gray

[57] Kimberly Morrison

[58] See Ira Corey's letter in Chap. VII

[59] John Lindsay

[60] "The Observer", Hartland, obituary

[61] Paul D. Foster, Florenceville, N.B.

[62] "The Observer", Hartland, obituary

[63] Corey Courier, 1978, p.4

[64] "The Corey Courier", 1981, p.1; 1983, p.2

[65] "The Corey Courier", March 1987, p.2

[66] Clippings from Pearl McBrine

[67] "The Corey Courier", 1987, p.2

[68] "The Corey Courier", 1989, p.3

[69] Newspaper clippings from Pearl McBrine

[70] "The Corey Courier", 1993, p.5

[71] John Lindsay

[72] Telephone conversation with John Jr., April 7, 2001.

[73] The Story of Knowlesville, p.143

[74] Obituary

[75] A.T. Doyle, <u>The Premiers of New Brunswick</u>, p.60f.

[76] Paul D. Foster

[77] Pearl McBrine

[78] Obituary, "The Fredericton Gleaner"

[79] Obituary, "The Fredericton Gleaner"

[80] "The Observer", Hartland, N.B., June, 1943

[81] Family notes from Pearl McBrine

[82] "The Corey Courier", March 1983, p.1

[83] Corey Courier Supplement, July 1991, p.1

[84] Donna Bachman, telephone conversation, March 7, 2001

[85] Telephone conversation, March 1, 2000.

[86] Newspaper clipping, possessed by Pearl McBrine

[87] Pearl McBrine

[88] John Lindsay

[89] "The Corey Courier", June 1970, p.1

[90] Walter Whitehouse

[91] John and Marjorie Lindsay

[92] See Chapter XIV

[93] Dr. Edward Williams, Bill MacDonnell, and Donna Bachman.

[94] See Chapter X

[95] Pearl McBrine's notes

[96] The Daily Gleaner, Fredericton

[97] The Daily Gleaner, Fredericton, Sept. 14, 1975, p.13.

[98] The Daily Gleaner, Dec. 21, 1961

[99] Telephone conversations with Jean and Ronald McBrine

CHAPTER XIII

1875
SARAH LOUISE COREY FLETCHER
19??

Sarah Corey, affectionately called Sadie, was born February 7, 1875 in Knowlesville, N.B. – the first of the children of Alfred and Lucretia Corey to be born there. After her surprise visit to her parents in Knowlesville in the summer of 1911,[1] Sadie Fletcher came to New Brunswick on several subsequent visits: Once she brought her second and third sons, Ned and Fred. Once she came to Glassville for a Christmas holiday with her sister, Alma Miller and family.

Where did Sadie make her home? Massachusetts was most often indicated. Her son Fred was born in Somerville.[2] For a while at least she lived in or near Boston, close enough to shop at Jordan Marsh's. During one of her visits to Knowlesville, Norman Corey, born 1917, and then about three or four, asked her, "Where did you get that pretty dress?" Pleased that Norman noticed her dress, she replied, "In Jordon Marsh's Store". On her 1911 visit she had not gone to church, feeling that her shoes were not good enough.[3]

Another Surprise Visit

For many years there was no news of Sadie's family. Then in the spring of 1938 her youngest son, Fred Fletcher, made a visit to Knowlesville that was as surprising as the visit he had made with his mother in 1911. Fred arrived at Ira Corey's farm in East Knowlesville when the gravel road was still soft, with winter frost coming out of the ground. His car got stuck in the mud at the lower entrance to the farm. We looked across the wide field and saw a stranger walking toward the farm buildings. As he climbed the steep hill from the brook he encountered my father dipping a pail of water from the horse puncheon. He greeted my father: "I used to be your uncle." Papa appreciated the humor. The ensuing conversation soon revealed that Father was having a happy reunion with a long-lost nephew.

Fred explained that he was living in New Hampshire and that he had come on a business trip to Houlton, Maine. While he was close, he decided to look up his long-lost relatives in New Brunswick. A pull by a pair of our horses got Fred's car over the muddy stretch of road. He brought it up over the hill to the farmyard and his overnight case into the farmhouse.

After the cows were milked and the milk separated, the family gathered in the farm kitchen. Visitors were always welcome at the farm; the visit of a relative was delightful. With undivided attention we sat and listened to the stories of a cousin we had never before seen. Fred's reminiscences made it apparent that as a youngster he had spent considerable time with Grandpa and Gramma Corey at the old homestead in Knowlesville. Apparently as a boy his behavior had not endeared him to his grandfather. When he was helping throw firewood he accidentally hit Grandpa on the head with a stick. He recalled another escapade of having exasperated Grandpa to the point of his chasing Fred and shouting to him, "You critter." Fred said, "I was left wondering what a critter was," but he didn't miss its derogatory connotation.

At the time of Fred's 1938 visit his mother Sadie was no longer living. If he told us the year of her death, none of us remembered it. Fred's father may have been still living. My father asked Fred, "Do you know where your father is, or if he is still alive?" With strong emotion, Fred replied, "I don't know where he is and I don't care. He never was good to my mother."

Fred told us about his business. His calling card indicated "chemicals". He had a paint store in Milford, New

Hampshire. While he sat on a rocking chair he reeled off about half his fishing line and gave it to my father for a salmon line. He said, "I occasionally fish on a lake, but I never have that much line out."

The next morning Fred's Uncle Ira, always an early riser, as soon as he had fed the horses, went down to the brook, rod in hand, to try for a trout for Fred's breakfast. It was too early; the brook was still in spring flood. However he enjoyed oatmeal, fried pancakes, and eggs. He endeared himself to his Aunt Nellie as well as his Uncle Ira, to the extent that before he left he had worked out a plan to return in hunting season.

When Fred returned in November 1938 Father had a lumber camp at the McCrossin Field, Skedaddle Ridge. Fred stayed alternately at the camp and at our farmhouse, as did his uncle, tending his crews and coming home. At the farmhouse Fred raved about his Aunt Nellie's cooking, and especially about the soda biscuits fresh out of the oven on a winter evening. He entertained us with stories and jokes: "Hey, pass that lasses." "You ain't got no education. You should say molasses!" "How can I say molasses when I ain't had none yet?"

During Fred's extended visit another of his uncles, Rev. J.A. Corey also arrived at the farmhouse for part of his hunting holiday. While both guests were at the farmhouse a very heavy snowfall stopped all wheel traffic. However, it did not shut us off from the outside world. A new radio brought us news and forecasts. Fred had brought it to us from U.S.A. – complete with batteries – our first. He also brought gifts for the youngsters, e.g., fountain pens. Father took Fred into our woods. They routed a deer but the deep snow didn't impede its escape. Fred, quite a heavy man, came home exhausted from wading, and fell onto the couch.

That November was the beginning of the end of my life on the farm. When Uncle Jud and Aunt Alice left for Doaktown they took me with them. The three of us sat in their Hudson car, pulled by three pairs of horses.[4] Fred, dressed in his heavy boots and wool breeches, waded snow, fascinated by the manoeuvring of horses, sleds and chains, and tried to help.

When I came home at Christmas they told me that Fred didn't leave until he got a deer to carry on his car back to New Hampshire. Warren and Keith Corey harnessed a pair of colts and brought the deer to the farmyard.

When the writer lived in New Hampshire, 1953-56, he often saw in the Concord press reports of Fred Fletcher's speeches in the Capitol. "He was elected to the House of Representatives in 1949 and was elected to the State Senate in 1953." In April 1954 my brother, Tom Corey, with Marjorie and Roger, brought my father and mother, Ira and Nellie Corey, to Bow, N.H. During their visit with us they motored to Milford, N.H. Fred and Mary gave them a cordial welcome and dinner on April 12. That visit was probably the last meeting of Fred with his Uncle Ira. When my father died in March, 1957, Fred sent flowers. The card read, "To Ira Corey, a very fine man."

Subsequently Fred came to New Brunswick and visited his Aunt Nellie at Juniper, bringing gifts. She accompanied him on calls to Clara Flemming and Paul and Shirley Brooks. Paul dates that visit in 1960 or 61. He recalls that Fred's Cadillac was so low that he had to avoid straddling the high points in their driveway. Fred kept in touch with his Aunt Nellie with cards and letters.

Fred expressed his family sentiments in a letter:

Frederic H. Fletcher

> 11 Mount Vernon Street, Milford, New Hampshire 03055
> July 21, 1970
> Dear Erma,
>
> I have missed so many of our family reunions in

the past that having to miss the 1970 reunion makes me feel particularly nostalgic. Business obligations have filled my calendar to overflowing. The company now has seven stores, the paint factory, and we now also own and operate a paper mill. The entire operation keeps me on the go constantly and requires my undivided attention.

This year's copy of the Corey Courier carried my thoughts to my childhood days and of the fond memories they hold for me. My – but that seems so long ago!

I do hope that I can come to New Brunswick soon...You will find enclosed a check for $20.00 for the fund. Please give my kindest regards to everyone and especially to cousin Rev. Judson Corey.

> Kind Regards, Fred

On at least one trip to revisit scenes of his childhood Fred stayed in the area a few days and renewed old friendships, e.g., with Jimmie Miller and Murray Lamont in Glassville.

On June 2, 1977, Fred, with Mary, made a surprise visit to his cousin Erma Corey Shaw at Simonds, N.B. Erma compared the visit to the surprise visit his mother made in 1911, bringing Fred at age three. On June 4th, Saturday, Fred and Mary returned to Erma's when I was there for the weekend. Kaye Foster generously prepared a full-course dinner, including rhubarb pie. Fred and Mary drove Erma and me to Florenceville. We all enjoyed a lively conversation with Kaye and Paul in their dining room.

The following year, on August 5, 1978, Fred and Mary Fletcher attended the Corey reunion, in Knowlesville. At the reminiscing in the church he expressed the feeling that there should be more appreciation of Grandma Corey, i.e., Lucretia. That evening Kaye and Paul Foster entertained Fred and Mary and other attendants of the reunion. On the patio, Fred, with Geoffrey Foster, engaged in a lively conversation on Republican politics, continuing until 2:00 a.m.

Regrettably we did not have the pleasure of the attendance of Fred and Mary at another reunion, as they had planned. Instead Mary sent the following letter:

Milford, N.H.   July 18, 1983

> Dear Erma,
> Fred and I had planned to come to Hartland for the family reunion on July 23. But Fred died on June twelfth. I am enclosing newspaper clippings which I found to be a very nice tribute to Fred.
>
> As Always,
> Mary

The Passing of Fred Fletcher

Frederic H. Fletcher died Sunday evening June 12, 1983, at the Mary Hitchcock Hospital in Hanover, N.H. Calling hours were on Tuesday and Wednesday evenings. Memorials were suggested for Shriners' Burn Centre, Boston. Fred was a 32nd degree Mason. Private funeral services were held, June 16, on what would have been his 75th birthday.

Thanks to Mary Fletcher for several articles from New Hampshire newspapers. They not only express the high esteem that people of his community held for Fred; they also tell us far more than we had known about the extent of his business and political life.

Apparently Fred did not enjoy the best of health. In 1968 during the closing weeks of his campaign for Republican nomination for governor he was stricken with a severe case of appendicitis. In later years he participated in some of his town's business from home. The vice-chairman of selectmen said, "Fred...said he couldn't get around very well physically, but he did a lot just sitting home and advising." Fred was a Director of the N.H. Diabetes Association. He worked politically for benefits for patients. At the time of his death "he had been in the hospital for observation, and had been expected home in a few days."

Political Involvement

Besides serving in his State Legislature, the Senate and the Executive Council, Fred Fletcher worked for the Republican Party at several levels; Hillsborough County, chairman; candidate for nomination for governor of N.H., 1968; delegate to the Republican National Convention in 1980. Fred served the town of Milford as a selectman for many years. In his late years he again became chairman of the Board of Selectmen. In that position, which he held the rest of his life, he found a police chief, dealt with the crisis of a contaminated town well, and solved the problem of their sewage treatment plant.

Business

Fred made many business ventures: he raised potatoes; he started a cordwood project; he operated the Windsor Embassy Chemical Co.; he made and sold duplicator supplies and rubber stamps; he studied the manufacture of paint and for many years supplied much of the highway paint used in New Hampshire; he established a chain of factory outlet stores, selling paint, wallpaper and related supplies. He bought a paper mill in Henniker, and was involved in real estate transactions. He was president of Fletcher Paint Works in Milford and of the Contoocook Valley Paper Co. in Henniker.

Family

Besides his wife, Mary B. Fletcher, Fred had two daughters, Victoria Fletcher of Milford and Brenda Brooks of Hennicker, and a son, Richard W. Fletcher of Milford, and four grandchildren.[5] On one visit to New Brunswick, Fred Fletcher shared with Erma Corey Shaw some brief data about his brother Ned. Ned Fletcher had owned rental houses in New Hampshire. In a heavy rain and flood Ned suffered the loss of several of his houses. Soon thereafter Ned died of a heart attack. It seems that the two brothers had a bent for business. This is one of the few bits that were disclosed, or at least preserved, about the Fletcher family.

[1] See Chapter IV

[2] Obituary

[3] Erma Corey Shaw

[4] See Chapters XI and XIX

[5] The Union Leader, New Hampshire's Daily Newspaper, June 14, 1983; The Telegraph, Nashua, N.H., June 14, 1983; and The Milford Cabinet and Wilton Journal, June 16 and 30, 1983.

CHAPTER XIV

1879
ALBERTA JERUSHA COREY 1955

Alberta Jerusha Corey, next to the youngest of the children of Alfred and Lucretia Corey, was born in Knowlesville on March 11, 1879. Like all her siblings, she attended the Knowlesville School. She is listed as "Bertie", age 12, in 1891.[1] She is also listed in the Record Book that her father, who was clerk, kept for the Highlands Baptist Church. Her name appears in three entries: Bertie Corey, 1895, member by baptism (p.10); Bertie Corey, Portland, Maine, (p.31); and Mrs. F.W. Redlon (Bertie Corey), p.41.

Recollections of Erma Corey Shaw, niece: Like all her sisters, Alberta went to New England early in life to find work in a factory. Alberta married, probably in Maine, Francis Winburn Redlon, a dentist. They lived at 78 Danforth Street, Portland, Maine. Together, they made a few visits to Knowlesville and area. At the end of one visit Alberta's brother, Ira Corey, was taking them to Glassville, the first lap of their journey to the train at Bristol. They stopped for dinner at the home of Alberta's sister, Mina McBrine, in E. Glassville. While they were there, Alfred Corey's mare, Bess, came trotting up the road. Erma was in the wagon with her grandfather. On first sight the party was alarmed, but as the wagon drew closer they said, "Erma is laughing; there can't be any trouble." Grandpa and Erma were bringing some clothes Bert and Francis had left in the bedroom at Corey's.

We did not see Bert and Francis Redlon very many more times. They came home to New Brunswick for the funeral of Alberta's sister, Alma Miller, in August 1915. From about that time it appears, there was a period when relatives in New Brunswick were not hearing from Aunt Bert. However, she was not forgotten. Norman Corey, born 1917, was named Redlon – middle name. She was remembered in U.S.A. also. Her sister, Laversa Garns, named a daughter, Alberta, born 1919, after her. Also Bert must have had some contact with some of the family of Ida McBrine when they were living in Brooklyn and working in New York City in the late 20/s and early 30/s. Clara Flemming used to say to my sisters, Kathleen and Shirley, "You look so much like your Aunt Bert. She was the most beautiful woman who ever walked down 5th Avenue." There is also a story that Aunt Bert wanted to adopt Lucretia McBrine when she was a young girl.

One communication from Aunt Bert was especially remembered. She wrote a letter to her brother, the Rev. Judson A. Corey disclosing that she and Francis had separated. That apparently was after a period of silence. Judson shared the news with other family members – his sister Mina McBrine for one. Mina's daughter, Glenna, carried the news to Campobello Island. Erma Shaw recalled that during the visit she and Glenna Thompson made to Campobello, Glenna took their Uncle Charles aside and disclosed to him, quietly, the news of Bert's separation. That was in 1922. Gradually, it seems, the family learned of the status that Aunt Bert found difficult to disclose. Uncle Jud wrote a response to Bert, reassuring her of love, care and acceptance.

Sadly, Aunt Bert dropped all communication. For many years she did not communicate with any member of the family, even to inform them of her whereabouts. Could it be that despite the prompt, reassuring reply from her brother Jud, she could not be confident that her family could accept either her separated status, or her as a separated person? It appears that she retained a troubled feeling. For one thing, she must have known that her sister Sadie had encountered a very strong disapproval from her mother when she learned, indirectly, about Sadie's separation.[2] The few incidental remarks that the writer has heard dropped by a few family members have left the impression that Aunt Bert found the experience very hurtful, and perhaps never became reconciled to it. However, the story has a happy ending.

The Curtain Opens in Brooklyn, N.Y.

The silence broke about 1952 when Lucretia MacDonnell received a phone call: "Your aunt is in hospital, quite ill." Betty Gray, then Betty Avery, was living with the MacDonnells and working in New York City. She recalls: "On a Sunday afternoon Lucretia, Mack, and I went to the hospital. We found her quite ill. She had had a colostomy. She recovered and came and lived with Lucretia and Mack."

Lucretia's daughter, Donna Bachman, adds to the story: "Aunt Bert had cancer – thus the colostomy. She was quite ill when she came to our apartment. I was then nine or ten. My brother, Bill, was about to leave home for college. Our cousin, Eddie Williams, was in medical college in New York. He saw her on visits. Aunt Bert was a cultured and a remarkably refined and elegant lady. She had a smart and sharp look. She was impressive with her hair in an upsweep. While she was with us she regained her strength. Her health became quite good. Betty added, "After her health improved she did some housework and she upholstered a chair.

Donna recalled that Aunt Bert shared with the family some bits about her earlier life. When she was married she had lived quite comfortably – for a while – in Waldoboro, Me. After separation she worked as a companion to a lady. Betty also recalled some personal experiences that Aunt Bert shared. After separation Francis wrote her a letter wanting her back. She did not respond. Betty also said that the hospital got in touch with Francis. He paid some of her hospital costs. At MacDonnell's, Aunt Bert enjoyed visits from "a close friend – a lovely, sweet lady named Jess." Donna said, "Our pastor came in and talked with her."

A Happy Reunion

In Brooklyn Aunt Bert had a very happy and dramatic reunion with her sister-in-law, Alice Corey, widow of Rev. Judson A. Corey. This story was told by Earle Corey, Alice's son, of Gardner,

Mass. While Alice was visiting her children in Gardner they took her to New York to see her long-absent sister-in-law. Making the motor trip were Earle, wife Lois, Earle's sister Mildred, and her husband Johnnie Johnston. "At the bottom of the stairway to the apartment," Earle recalled, "Johnnie and I offered to join our hands to make a seat and carry Mother up the stairs. She was in too big a hurry; when she reached the top she was almost running." Donna added, "There were three flights of stairs; the apartment was on the 4th floor." Lois remarked, "I never before saw two people so glad to see each other."

Earle Corey recalled the visit years later – May 30, 1973, in a letter to Erma. Referring to family of Aunt Ida McBrine, he said, "I always liked the family and I think Lucretia is a lovely person. We spent a few hours at her home in Brooklyn and Mother and Aunt Bert met that day after about 40 years and they were both so excited."

The happy reunion was near the end of life for both. Aunt Bert died in April or May 1955; Aunt Alice Corey died September 1955. Donna Bachman remembers that Aunt Bert was taken away from New York. Betty Gray remembers that she was brought home to New Brunswick for burial. We have not found any record of burial site.

[1] The Story of Knowlesville, P.89

[2] See Chapter IV

CHAPTER XV

1882 Laversa Corey 1969
m. Luther Garns 1880 – 1956

At noon one day in haying season 1936 a car bearing Maryland plates drove into Ira Corey's farmyard in E. Knowlesville. The car carried seven persons: four adults, one teenager, and two children. Only one of the passengers was known to Ira's family: our Aunt Ida McBrine. She had piloted the driver to Ira's farm. Even he knew only one other of the passengers – his and Ida's sister Laversa Garns. The others were: her son Edward Garns, the driver; his wife, Hazel, their two sons, David, age 11, and John, one; and Laversa's youngest daughter, Bernice, approaching 14. They had traveled from Hagerstown, Maryland [1]— a long trip in the days before super highways were even thought of, and some roads were not even paved. That day, however, they came only about five miles from E. Glassville, the home of Aunt Mina and Uncle Eb McBrine. The visitors brought excitement and surprise. We were meeting an aunt, age 54, the mother of nine grown children, and we hadn't even known that our father had a sister named Laversa.

Laversa Ella Corey, youngest child of Alfred and Lucretia Corey, was born in Knowlesville, July 1, 1882. She attended the one-room Knowlesville School, at least until she was age 15. Her name and those of her eight siblings appears in the school census for 1897. Their recorded dates run from 1878 to 1897.[2] Laversa Corey is also recorded in "Aberdeen Baptist Church membership list, corrected to Apr. 1899". The list is on p. 25 of the clerk's book, kept by Laversa's father, Alfred Corey, who was clerk for several years. She also appears as Mrs. Luther Garns on the list of non-resident members, p.41.

Laversa followed the pattern of all her siblings in going

to U.S.A. to work. Erma said, "She was the last of Alfred and Lucretia Corey's children to leave home. She was gone by 1903," – but not before summer of 1902. She attended the wedding of Ira Corey and Emily Graham at Maple Ridge, N.B., on July 16, 1902.[3] Laversa's first journey from home was relatively short. She told the writer, "I first went to Houlton, Maine. After working there a while, I went to Lewiston, Maine, where my brother Judson A. Corey was living."[4] Laversa's move from Houlton to Lewiston could not have been before the early summer of 1903. That was when Judson and family returned to Maine from Knowlesville. They left Knowlesville soon after the birth of their third child, Annie, which was on May 25th in Knowlesville. Hence by the time Laversa arrived in Lewiston, Judson and family were on their second sojourn in Maine.[5]

A Romance

Laversa lived in Auburn and "worked at various occupations:" a boarding house in Auburn; a bakery making chocolate goodies, a shoe factory assisting with the books. In Auburn. Laversa and her brother, Judson regularly attended a gospel mission. A young man with dark, curly hair began to attend the mission also. His name was Luther Garns. At length, "Jud, Laversa and Luther became casually acquainted..." One evening Luther noticed that Jud was by himself. Laversa "had been detained at home." Luther approached Jud and said, "I see your wife did not get here tonight." Jud answered, "She's not my wife, she's my sister." Jud's wife, Alice, was probably at home taking care of their three children.

Luther was delighted to find that Laversa was single. "At the next service Luther lost no time in getting better acquainted with Laversa." After months of courtship their friendship was culminated, "with a lovely wedding ceremony in the little Gospel Mission in Auburn, on December 14, 1903.[6]

That year Laversa and Judson were joined by a brother,

Ira Corey. Thus there were three units of the Corey family living in Auburn/Lewiston: Ira and Emily and daughter Erma, under 1 year; Judson and Alice and Alberta, Earle and Annie; and Laversa and Luther Garns. The two brothers and families were living together. Laversa and Luther had their own place. They visited one another and met in church. These living arrangements are indicated in a letter written by Emily Graham Corey in Auburn, Maine, to Lucretia Corey in Knowlesville, about 1904.[7] In the spring of 1904 Ira left Maine with his first wife, Emily, and their one-year old daughter, Erma, and moved to Campobello, N.B.

What a remarkable homecoming the 1936 visit was for Laversa, the youngest of the Corey family, and for Ira, her youngest brother. More than three decades had elapsed since they had said, "Goodbye", in Auburn, Maine. In the 32-year interval much had changed: Family members had deceased: Ira's wife, Emily, in 1904; their sister, Alma Miller, in 1915; their mother, in 1922, and their father in 1930, at Ira's farm in E. Knowlesville. There Laversa found Ira with his second wife, Nellie, and their twelve children, none of whom Laversa had met.

The only one of Ira's family who had ever seen Aunt Laversa was Erma. She recalled: "I remember one visit that Laversa made to Knowlesville. She came from Delaware bringing her first-born, Edward, then age three. I was then four, which dates the visit in summer of 1907. Edward and I played together, e.g., with my blocks that had faces of animals. Grandpa Corey remarked about Edward's ability to mimic all those animals." That 1907 visit was at Grandpa's old homestead in Knowlesville. Ira missed seeing her then. He was in Western Canada.

A Long-Neglected Relationship

In 1936, how did Ira know where to begin a re-acquaintance with his long-absent sister? There seemed to be no awkward moment. Father had no anxiety about their reception. He knew that Mother had a warm welcome for people – anybody who happened in, even at mealtime. Being accustomed to cooking for a large family, there was always plenty, even in the thirties. That day we had plenty of new potatoes, dug that morning, and green beans and perhaps peas, picked that morning. Probably there was also pie, perhaps rhubarb, the season's earliest, or perhaps raspberry.

Father treated his long-absent sister like any welcome visitor. After dinner he took the visitors to the horse barn and proudly showed them the horses, including a new bay team he had bought only about a month earlier. Aunt Laversa asked, "Do you leave the harness on them?" "Only over the noon hour", Father replied. She said, "I used to handle horses. Now, I'd be scared to go near one."

It was an opportunity for family acquaintance. Some of Ira's boys who were working away from home came on the weekend. By listening, we learned about Aunt Laversa's family. She had seven daughters. Only the youngest, Bernice, accompanied her. Bernice didn't go far from her mother, or from the farmhouse. We tried to help her learn a little nature lore that life in a big city didn't provide. I tried to strike up bits of conversation with her. Holding in the palm of my hand an empty shell, open side down, I said, "this is what a turkey egg looks like." She reached for it, and finding it surprisingly light, exclaimed, "Oh, I thought I had broken it!" David roamed and romped over the farm with the boys.

During their stay at our farm the family from Hagerstown visited other relatives – e.g., Kate Hovey and family at Glassville; Clara Flemming and family at Juniper – piloted by Ira who also replenished Edward's motor oil from a five-gallon pail he kept on the farm. The rainy day they went to visit Erma Corey Shaw and family at Simonds, Hazel stayed at our farmhouse and washed a big batch of diapers. We strung rope in the woodshed to hang them on. I think she had to hang them outside the next fine day.

The visit of a week or more was highlighted by a Sunday-evening service at the Knowlesville United Baptist Church. Father arranged for Edward to preach. He spent Sunday afternoon in the bedroom and emerged with an interesting sermon laced with stories.

Family Roots

Laversa Corey and Luther Garns both grew up in country places with one-room schools. Luther Walt Garns was born near Lemasters, Pennsylvania, on Nov. 8, 1880. He was the son of Malinda Walt and Henry Garns.[8] "Henry Garns was a descendant of the sturdy stock of German immigrants who immigrated to Pennsylvania from the Rhine Valley of Germany with his four sons. He was a weaver and continued in that craft for a while after getting settled in the State of Pennsylvania."[9] When his children were still school age, Henry Garns, a cobbler by trade, moved his family into Lemasters where he was more accessible to his customers. In that village they were still in country surroundings. They kept a cow. Grew vegetables and gathered wild fruit.

At age 17 Luther Garns was teaching school in his home community. While still very young his "desire for adventure....search for knowledge" and "desire for spiritual things" took him north. At Northfield, Massachusetts, Evangelist D.L. Moody "had established a school for the teaching of God's Word." He had a girls' school in Northfield and a boys" school across the river at Mt. Hermon. Luther Garns attended the boys' school in 1899. At Northfield he also attended conferences where Ira Sankey,[10] F.B. Myer, C.I. Scofield, R.A. Torrey, A.B. Simpson, and other well-known religious leaders, sang and preached.

While living in the north, Luther enjoyed travelling, e.g., to see the beaches of Maine, the mountains of New

England and the magnificence of Niagara Falls. His travels brought him, at length to Auburn, Maine where he settled and worked.

Meeting in Auburn

"Luther found lodging at a lovely little boarding house at Auburn during the same time that Laversa Corey was working there but....they never remember of even catching a glimpse of each other while the two of them were in such close proximity....."[11] Instead we have the story of Laversa and Luther meeting in the mission church.

While they were living in Auburn, Me., their first child, Edward, was born on August 31, 1904. "Luther and Laversa moved to various locations during the ensuing years, depending on Luther's occupation...." At length Luther became employed by Hollingsworth Wheel Co. in Hagerstown, Md. His main occupation there was woodworking.

Building a House in Hagerstown

The family, then with their first six children, were living in the country about five miles outside Hagerstown. Luther was travelling to and from work on a bicycle. He decided to use his skill in woodwork to build a family house. A friend in the Brethren Church loaned him money interest free. Luther bought city lots in Hagerstown. First he erected a one-room building, 14 foot square, for living quarters while he was building the house. He worked evenings and went to his family in the country over Sunday. "On Monday morning he came to work in Hagerstown at the factory."

After the family moved into their new home three more children were born. Eagerly they watched as utilities and upgrades came to their neighborhood: electric line to replace oil lamps; phone wires, beginning for the affluent; paved streets with curbs. Finally, a sewer and bathroom replaced the "old outhouse."[12] At 1025 Rose Hill Ave., Hagerstown, Md., nine Garns children grew up.

The Nine and their Children

Luther and Laversa Garns had two sons, followed by seven daughters:

James Edward Garns, b. August 31, 1904, became a pastor. "He pioneered several churches in Virginia; also he pastored several larger churches in Virginia, N. Carolina, Maryland and Pennsylvania." Edward married Hazel Slye. They had three sons: David, John and James. David preached intermittently. He became a building contractor. Jimmy became a safety police in Florida.

Paul Henry Garns, b. October 18, 1907, enlisted in U.S. Army while very young. He married Mary Dixon. They had one son, Jack. Paul "again joined the U.S. Army during W.W.II. He served in Europe" as an aeroplane technician, and was injured. He became an assessor. His last position was city assessor in Denver, Colorado. He died July 29, 1959. He is buried in Boonsboro, Md.

Malinda Lucretia Gail Garns, b. August 19, 1909, taught public school until retirement. She married Gerald Bast. They had one son, Douglas. Gerald had a furniture store; when he died in 1987 he left it to Douglas. They lived in Boonsboro, Md. which is near a Civil War battlefield, Antietam. Douglas, a student of history, became a guide to groups coming to tour the battlefield. He also had a museum with artefacts of the war. He also bought and sold antiques.

Ruth Elizabeth Garns, b. October 7, 1911, married Harry Mowen. In July 1957, during my visit to Hagerstown, Aunt Laversa took me to visit Harry and Ruth on a farm outside the city. The delicious supper included succotash – a first for me.

In his later years Harry "worked in a store where he sold farm equipment. When he retired they moved to Hagerstown where they enjoyed visits from their two children and also grandchildren, who lived nearby. Ruth continued to live there after being widowed. Ruth and Harry had a son, Harry Luther, and a daughter, Harriet Laversa Mowen. Harry Luther Mowen served in the U.S. Army, and later became a correctional officer, with the rank of major, in a prison south of Hagerstown. Harriet owns a furniture store in Hagerstown.

Miriam Edith Garns, born March 21, 1913, worked "as a home missionary, planting and establishing churches in the rural sections of Maryland, Virginia and nearby states." She has been recognized by the church council for 50 years of service as an ordained minister.

After her father, Luther Garns, died September 3, 1956, Miriam returned home to take care of her mother, Laversa. Miriam worked in her local church. After her mother died, October 22, 1969, Miriam kept the house that her father built on Rose Hill Ave. There she welcomed visits from the family. In 1986 she visited the Holy Land.[13]

Esther Laversa Garns, b. January 22, 1915, married Obie Harrup, a minister of The Assemblies of God. Positions he held were: Pastor of their church at Alexandria, Va.; secretary-treasurer of the Potomac District of the Assemblies; president, for five years, of Valley Forge Christian College – for students wanting to enter ministry. Many years Esther and Obie served in the ministry together. They have one daughter, Mary Catherine, and three sons: Obie, Jr., James Lowell, and Paul Alfred. All three sons are in the ministry.

Mary Catherine Garns, born August 3, 1917, received her R.N. from Washington Co. Hospital, Hagerstown, and was employed on their nursing staff for a few years. She attended Eastern Bible Institute at Valley Forge, Pa., where she met

Robert Krempels, also a Bible student. Both had musical ability. Robert taught music at the college. After they married they ministered together in preaching and music.

One place they ministered was in Winnipeg, Manitoba. In May 1997, writing from Hagerstown, Robert spoke of an imminent "return to Winnipeg for the 90th anniversary of a church which I served as assistant pastor and minister of music for eight years." They were, at that time, also in the process of selling their home and buying 'a single-floor dwelling'. He said, although we are semi-retired, I am still active in ministries at our local church and elsewhere."

Mary and Robert have three children: Douglas, born April 3, 1947, David, born November 18, 1949, and Deborah, born July 31, 1960, and three grandchildren: David, Craig and Lynnea Krempels.

Kaye and Paul Foster, on their way home from Florida in April 1996, had a rendezvous outside Hagerstown with Mary and Bob Krempels, after their Sunday morning church service. The two couples went to the Garns home where they again met with Miriam and Gail. Bob, remembered for his courtesy, conducted the Fosters out to the highway to Pennsylvania.

Alberta Maude Garns, b. July 24, 1919, married Jacob Hershman. They were living in Hagerstown, on the same street as Aunt Laversa when I visited in 1957. He took me on a tour of the city, including a large new high school. Education was his interest, which he continued into receiving a doctorate. He taught in high schools in Maryland, and in State College, Pa. His last position was with the Department of Education in Washington. Alberta and Jacob were very hospitable. On Monday, as I was preparing to leave, they made a quick trip to the shopping area and brought me a miniature grain-grinding mill, representing the Hutterites of their area. That souvenir is still displayed on our mantelshelf. Albert and Jacob extended their hospitality on other occasions.

Their children: Joan, born 1944, married Bob Rhoden, Supt. Of the Assembly of God Churches in the Potamic District; John, born 1948, became pastor of a large church in Richmond, Va.; Luci Ann, born 1953, married Richard Poole, a teacher. They have three children in Pennsylvania. In 1997 Jacob, at age 84, a widower, was residing in a rest home in Virginia.

Bernice Louise Garns, born November 11, 1922, married Andrew McDearmid. They both attended Eastern Bible Institute in Valley Forge, Pa. For 25 years they were missionaries in India. At time of Laversa's death they were in Bangalore. They retired in Norfolk, Va. In 1997 Miriam was finishing a book describing the McDearmid's ministry in India. Bernice and Andrew have two daughters: Carol and Andrea. They had a son, Richard, who died in youth. Andrea married "a navy man"; they live in Norfolk. Carol and her husband, both having grown up in India and become attached to the people, returned to minister there.

Keeping Family Connections

Laversa's visits to family in New Brunswick in 1907 and 1936 were not her only homecomings. In summer of 1954 family members brought her to Juniper, N.B. where Ira and Nellie Corey then lived. Clara Flemming provided hospitality. When the visitors started back to Maryland, trailer in tow, Ira accompanied them as far as Bob and Maude Corey's at Richmond Corner. Enroute they visited Erma Shaw in Simonds, and Nessie McLaughlin at the White Swan Inn, Hartland. I did not see Aunt Laversa and company then. My father told me about it when I arrived on vacation from New Hampshire.

The 1954 visit was the last time Laversa saw her brother Ira. In March 1957 Laversa attended Ira Corey's funeral. Again her son Edward Garns brought her by car. Accompanying them were Edward's wife and two of his sisters – perhaps Esther

Daughters of Laversa and Luther Garns:
l. to r. Gail, Ruth, Miriam, Alberta, Mary, Bernice and Esther

and Alberta. They arrived on Sunday afternoon, March 17th at the home of Maude and Bob Corey at Richmond Corner, N.B., on the Houlton Road, just in time for prayers at the house.

The procession moved to Knowlesville for the funeral service in Knowlesville United Baptist Church. From there the procession moved northward, passing the site of the Alfred Corey homestead, over a narrow road enclosed with very high snow banks on both sides – the accumulation of the winter's ploughing. A few yards past the site of Highland Baptist Church the procession turned left onto the Glassville/Juniper paved road. At the committal service in the U.C. Cemetery, Glassville, Edward and the writer said prayers. Relatives gathered at the home of Claude and Alice Corey in Glassville.

Aunt Laversa and company accepted the invitation of Clara and Weldon Flemming in Juniper for hospitality. On Monday evening relatives gathered there for social time, games and refreshments.

The writer returned to Port Hope, Ontario, with the resolve to seize an opportunity to visit Aunt Laversa and family in Maryland. In July of the following summer, 1957, the "Protestant Community", a group I had joined at Andover Newton Theological School, was having its summer gathering at Kirkridge, near Bangor, Pa. Leaving Kirkridge on afternoon of Friday, July 26, I motored to Hagerstown. Aunt Laversa and Miriam welcomed me at 1025 Rose Hill Ave. On Saturday morning Jacob Hershman gave me a tour. Late that afternoon Aunt Laversa piloted me to the farm home of her daughter Ruth and son-in-law Harry Mowen. On Sunday we went with Jacob and Alberta Hershman to an outdoor gathering of the churches of their faith at a park on the edge of the Potomac River.

In summer of 1963, enroute from Wisconsin with my family, we stopped in Hagerstown. Family members took us to Antietam, a battlefield of the Civil War in the 1860's. Later we made a stop at Gettysburg. We were invited to spend the weekend at Edward's in Virginia. Aunt Laversa accompanied us to show us the house.

On Sunday morning we travelled 35 miles to Edward's church. He asked me to preach. He celebrated communion. On Sunday evening we went to Obie Harrup's church at Alexandria, Va., on the edge of Washington, D.C. He was on vacation. Edward was the guest preacher. On Monday morning we travelled north through Baltimore and back to Massachusetts. Aunt Laversa stayed for a visit.

On another stop in Hagerstown, as planned, we found a note on the Garns' door: "Please go to Hershman's at Hancock." They were getting organized after a move. They made us their guests at a motel. We had breakfast with them. On still another trip they entertained us over a Sunday at Lancaster, Pa. After church and dinner they took us for a tour of a nearby Amish community. Fred Corey remembers Jacob's description of an accident, a year earlier. In the impact, the key penetrated his knee.

Aunt Laversa, in her late years, enjoyed visits from several of her Corey relatives: Aunt Ida McBrine, Mildred and Clair Shirley, and Eleanor Shaw. In October 1969 Melvin Corey in Williamsport, Pa. phoned me in Averill Park, N.Y., to tell me that Laversa Garns had died on October 22nd. Her husband, Luther, had predeceased her on September 3, 1956. They are buried in Boonsboro, Md.

Communication continued. On June 27, 1971, Miriam wrote to Erma Shaw: "Thanks for your note and the ....'Corey Couriers'. I gave copies to Ruth and Gail." On July 13, 1972, Miriam wrote to Erma: "I received a letter from Aunt Nellie....I would like to hear from you too.....I do want to stay in touch with Mama's people....I heard Mama mention all your names many times...I'm still at the home place and employed by my local pastor,......assisting....the church." Visits of relatives at 1025 Rose Hill Ave. also continued. Mildred and Claire Shirley stopped enroute from Florida.

On March 12, 1984, Paul and Kaye Foster, enroute to Florida, visited the Garns cousins in Maryland. By phone arrangement Gail Bast met them at routes 70 and 81. Gail conducted them to 1025 Rose Hill Ave., Hagerstown. Soon Ruth and Harry Mowen and Miriam arrived. They shared much family updating. Gail took them to Boonsboro for lunch and tour of the museum kept by her son Douglas Bast. They had tea at Gail's apartment. Fosters returned to Hagerstown for overnight at Miriam's. They awoke to four inches of snow – unusual there. Paul scraped Miriam's car and helped her on her way to her church office by 9:00 a.m.

Fosters, continuing their journey to Florida, stopped at Gail's in Boonsboro for breakfast. There was more exchange of family news. Gail spoke proudly of her sister Bernice, then living in Texas, after missionary service in India. The enthusiastic sharing extended into lunch before the Fosters resumed their travel south to their next stop with Eleanor Shaw at Winston Salem, N.C.

That 1984 visit to Aunt Laversa's family in Maryland prompted a return visit the same year. Miriam Garns and Gail Bast flew to Presque Isle, Me., on August 23rd, Thursday. Paul and Kaye Foster met them and brought them to their house in Florenceville, N.B. After supper that evening they visited Erma Shaw. On Friday, Kaye gave Gail and Miriam a tour. They picked up Erma. They stopped at Nellie McLeod's house in Hartland and met cousins: Mary Hand, Vola Barker and Lucretia MacDonnell. In Knowlesville, they visited the church, the grave of Alfred and Lucretia Corey, the former schoolhouse, and the site of the Alfred Corey home. Miriam gathered some boards and rocks.

They visited Clara Flemming at Juniper. On Saturday evening there was a picnic at Erma's. Several of the Ira Corey family came to meet the sisters from Maryland. On Sunday morning Geoffrey Foster took Miriam to Simonds to meet Erma at her church. Early Monday, Paul and Kaye returned Miriam and Gail to Presque Isle.

In 1985, at their request, I sent "<u>The Story of Knowlesville</u>" for Gail and Miriam. On October 19, 1985, Gail wrote enclosing a cheque for five more books – one for each of their sisters for Christmas.

Gail's letter said: "I've already read a good part of your genealogy of my mother's people and the place where she and all of you were born and raised. It was wonderful to have visited there and met such lovely people. Miriam and I still talk of Erma, Kaye, Paul and you and all.....Give Kaye, Paul, and Erma our love and all others which are the family tie that we met."

[1] See also "The Story of Knowlesville", P.174

[2] See "The Story of Knowlesville", P.89

[3] Ibid, P.107.

[4] Conversation during my 1957 visit

[5] See Chapter II

[6] Miriam Garns, The Garns Family Roots, 1987, P.42 f.

[7] See Chapter II

[8] Miriam Garns, op.cit., P1.

[9] Ibid., P.11 f.

[10] Ira Corey was named for him

[11] Miriam Garns, op.cit., p.40 f.

[12] From notes written by Miriam Garns

[13] "The Corey Courier", 1987, p.4

Ira and son Gordon Corey, with Belgian horse "Duke of Aroostook"

CHAPTER XVI

1877 IRA THOMAS COREY 1957

"What was your father like?" That question was put to me point blank by Malinda Bellefeuille at their home in Beaver Dam, N.S., on September 19, 1995. Her question was innocent – a genuine desire to know more about her family. To me the question was overwhelming. It brought me to silence. How could I tell her or anybody else, what kind of a person my father was? He was a complex person.

It is not without significance that the person asking me the question is Erma's granddaughter. She didn't know that Erma had declined to describe her father. In February, 1993, I had stopped at Alice Long's, Somerville, N.B. to see Erma and glean some more family stories from her. I said to her, "I think you should write the chapter on our father." Her response took me by complete surprise: "My sake alive! No! I couldn't do that! I never knew my father." Such a response would not have surprised me nearly as much if it had come from almost any other of my siblings. Erma, having been for over eight years, Ira's only child, I thought she might have experienced more intimacy. Her response was in contrast to her ready disposition to describe a close and affectionate relationship with Grandpa and Grandma Corey. This is understandable; they brought her up.

Interestingly on the same occasion Erma went on to describe one intimate moment, treasured perhaps because it was rare: "Sometimes I wished my father would give me more attention. One happy episode I cherish. I was playing in a field one day when my father was ploughing with three horses on an Oliver Plough. He stopped his horses and asked me if I'd like a ride. He took me up onto the seat with him. I felt wonderful. It was a rare opportunity to be close to him". The situation Erma described was on Grandfather Alfred's homestead. Most of that time Father was away from home working on various jobs. Sometimes between jobs he came home and helped Grandpa. Another example of one of those rare moments was told to me by Warren. He was transporting the hunting party to their campsite toward the Nashwaak. They encountered a tree across the road. Father stayed with Warren to help clear the road. Uncle Jud Corey and Fred Hemphill walked ahead to the camp. Darkness overcame Warren and Father. They made a tent of blankets. "Don't touch the blanket; then the rain won't come through it." They had a memorable evening together.

We cherished the few moments of warmth and appreciation we experienced with Father. It seems they were rare for all of us. Shirley described the experience for us: He seemed not to have the ability to express affection, at least not readily or often. Yet Shirley too recalled an occasion of warmth and appreciation:

"He took us, i.e., Mom and the younger children to the woollen mill in Woodstock. Mom chose a selection of yarns including some coloured skeins to knit sweaters for us. Soon after that, Dad came home with plaid cloth with colours well suited to go with our sweaters. This was for Mom to make skirts for Kaye and me. He was a good provider."

Intimate moments are cherished, but the rarity, or even lack of them, is not a reason to fail to appreciate the relationship we experience. The disposition among the siblings now is to recall more and more good qualities in our father and to appreciate him for them. Close emotional sharing is not the only measure of a parental relationship. Furthermore, there is the question, How do we come to know a person? Any person? Dr. Tournier maintained that we never can know the kind of person anybody is, or was, simply by having another person describe that person to us. He cited the case of a young man who never did get to know his father until he took a train journey with him. Up to that time his image of his father was as his mother had described him.

Our mother did sometimes subdue our behaviour by

telling us what our father might do when he arrived home. It probably did have a little influence on our images of our father, but we also knew that Mother needed all the help she could get in managing a large family. However, our father eventually responded to what he perceived to be Mother's tendency. He said, "The children came to dread me." He announced a new posture in relation to the last three children: Kaye, Shirley and Gordon. He told people: "I said to Nellie, these three are your responsibility. You bring them up your way." He carried it even further; he sometimes told people, "These three are Nellie's responsibility". The implication seemed to be: judge for yourself how they've turned out.

Back to Malinda's question: After reflection I now know that I cannot, by direct description, tell anybody the kind of person my father was. What I can do is recall some of the activities and events of our growing up years. The recollections, stories and anecdotes about father at home, on farm and in the community, may serve as windows into the personality of Ira Corey and convey an appreciation of his qualities. We'll include some of his own stories.

I'm now thankful for Malinda's question. Though it brought me to a nonplus, it's ultimate effect was to bring me out of a quandary about what to say, and into a disposition to pick up my pen and let my father's biography flow.

Recollections of Home

One of my earliest memories is of a Christmas morning when the whole family was conducted in a most orderly manner. After the milk was brought from the barn and separated, we ate breakfast, as usual, round the dining room table. We carried our plates and dishes through the living room to the kitchen. Then we returned to the living room and sat waiting to hear our names. Father stood at the shapely tree, picked up the wrapped gifts, one at a time, and called the name on the tag.

This anecdote may illustrate an orderliness and discipline that father maintained in the family.

An important part of the orderliness centred in and around the dining room and table. I remember when there was no direct route between dining room and kitchen. Each family member carried his chinaware and cutlery to the kitchen. Visitors remarked on what a well-organized family we were. One rainy June day when we came home from school, Osbert Whitehouse was at work with saw, hammer and chisel, cutting a doorway through the wall between the kitchen and dining room. This direct passage made it much easier for Mother to set the table for meals. Soon we needed a larger dining room table. Uncle Jud, handy with saw and hammer, took a few hours from his hunting vacation to attach an extension to the table. With the oilcloth covering the whole unit, it looked like one long table.

Meal time was conducted in a very orderly manner. Conversation was minimized. We developed a quiet system and thoughtful attitude. Look around. Do you see someone's pancake without molasses? Pass him the jug. To avoid breaking the quiet atmosphere with, "Pass the...." we signalled to one another when we wanted a dish passed. If conversation became loud, or if more than one person spoke at a time, Father simply tapped the table with the handle of his knife, saying, "Let the victuals (vit-'l) stop your mouth." The unhesitating asking by Ed and Doug Olmstead for more cabbage, etc., stood out when they stayed for supper.

The quiet atmosphere paid off. We learned to listen. When guests were at the table – fairly frequent in summer – we did not miss a word of the stories. David Pinsky, e.g., the buyer of junk, told us of working his way from Montreal in a wagon pulled by one horse, and of shipping his purchases from various rail stations to Montreal – "90¢ a hundred, freight".

At that dining room table there were also amusing incidents. One July morning a Mr. Adams from Glassville arrived at our farmyard. He had fed all his oats and needed enough to carry his horses through haying into harvest. Knowing that Ira Corey always had oats he came with bags. "Put your mare in the barn. Give her some oats while we bag oats and load your wagon. Come in to dinner!" At the table Mr. Adams turned down the meat and several other foods that were passed. "I can only chew soft food," he said. After several refusals, Father broke the formality: "Why don't you get teeth?" "I haven't got many more years to chew", was the reply. None of us laughed at the time but we had amusement long afterwards.

Discipline, Freedom and Authority

Orderliness and discipline were integral to family and farm life. Discipline, however, was mitigated by a very large measure of freedom and opportunity for exploration and creativity. For example, we had access to the machine shed where there was a workbench and tools: hammers, saws, files, axes, brace and bit, and augers; and supplies: nails, bolts, screws and paints. In that shop we made our own play equipment. Our play was creative, imaginative, learn-by-doing experience. In imitation of the farming and logging equipment, we made our own play equipment, adapted by season.

Rarely, a little discipline was interjected into the freedom, exploration and accountability. I remember one incident: Claude and I were in the machine shed on a rainy summer morning using the tools at the workbench. When the rain increased we dropped our tools and prepared to make a run to the house to avoid being drenched. The door had to be fastened with a wooden pin. I was having difficulty inserting the pin into the hasp. Claude was coaching me to hurry up. In frustration I threw the pin and hit Claude in the face. Our father appeared suddenly on the scene, perhaps from the horse barn. He grabbed the nearest tool, a 2 ft. x 1 ft. steel square, and gave us each a slap on the bottom. Quarrels were especially difficult for him to tolerate.

"Nuff sed"; no argument. A little reminder like that lasted a long while. Our father had no difficulty in disciplining us, though we were a large family; his words were usually all that was needed.

Father expected us to learn quickly and even to have skills without being taught. Perhaps that was one reason why there was such a large measure of freedom, e.g. in use of tools. He seemed not to understand why we didn't simply know how to go at a job and do it. He would sometimes grab a peeve or other tool right out of a boy's hands, saying, "You don't know how to do that!" There was some instruction. Sometimes he said, "I'll show you." Some skills we learned by watching him as he went at many jobs, hammer and tongs. There was also instruction — older sibling to younger. Tom said to me, "Don't bring your axe straight down to cut a bush; it can hit a rock." Fortunately we were not slow learners. We learned by watching and by doing, and we learned to be resourceful.

Father's voice had power. At a fair in Maine where a stallion he had trained on our farm was among the horses on exhibition, father entered the barn where the horse stood resting one leg. He spoke his name, "Darkie", and the horse immediately came to the alert on all four legs. Even horses recognized Father's commanding voice and charismatic personality. Father liked to tell a story about Prince and Don. The boys had hooked them onto a big log. Father came along: "What's the matter?" "It's too much for them; they can't haul it." Father's clinching line: "I just picked up the reins; they walked away with it."

He spoke with authority. Norman, cooking for his logging crews on Tague Brook, reported that one crew member came late to the cookhouse for an evening snack, waking the early-rising cook. Father was waiting in the cookhouse when the fellow came, yelling, "Open the door or I'll come through it." Surprised by Father's reply, "You'll have to come through me," he quickly disappeared.

Father's voice projected authority; it also projected far.

Warren vividly recalls the day Arthur Jordan, from Golden Ridge, was passing our farm enroute to the gristmill at Esdraelon. Our farmhouse was in the middle of a block of 4-100 acre lots. Hence it was at least 1/4 mile from the highway. Father called across the fields to Arthur, "Bring me a bag of buckwheat bran from the mill." Arthur could only wave in reply. Our sister Erma must have inherited Father's voice projection. People across the St. John River reported hearing her calling her family to dinner. However, Father didn't depend on projecting voice messages over the extensive farm. With ingenuity he hung a rim of a car wheel from the lilac bushes. Near noon he beat on the rim with an iron rod. Not only did Wilfred or Bob hear it in a far field, Vernon Whitehouse heard it in a far field of Osbert's farm. The rim and rod was called the gong.

Father could be authoritative; he could be resourceful; he could also be deliberate. In the early 30's he dug up all the lead pipe that brought our water from the spring on the hill to the house. To reduce the digging with pick and shovel, he had Wilfred, with a pair of horses, plough some of the soil from above the pipe. That action was motivated by the speculation that Olys Hughes' illness might have come from lead poisoning. We were well aware of Father's ability to take deliberate action. When any of us had a loose primary tooth we protected it as long as we could. We applied ground cloves to cavities to stop aches. When we complained of an ache he fastened his pliers onto the tooth and pulled it out.

Calm in Critical Circumstances

Visualize the family sitting in the kitchen while the thunder crashed loudly and the lightening flashed through the windows. Mother and the youngsters were very frightened. Father sat quietly coaching all of us to be calm. He seemed not to understand our fear. This calmness, coupled with ability to take command of situations, is illustrated in one of his own stories from his lumber camp experience, belonging apparently to the period before he became a foreman and contractor with his own crew. It is a story of a bleeding horse. The teamsters must have been on rotation for turn at the yards and on the logging roads. Thus he arrived late at the camp one evening and found that another teamster had suffered an accident to one of his horses. She was bleeding from a cut on her rump. Father went to supper. The troubled teamster came into the cookhouse pleading "Oh Irey, please come out and help. I can't afford to lose that mare." Undisturbed, he replied, "I'll come out as soon as I finish my supper." Nonchalantly he ate his supper then walked out to the hovel where some men were standing helplessly watching, while others were applying flour to try to stop the bleeding. They had tied burlap to the harness to try to hold the flour on the bleeding area. They had used almost a 100-weight of flour. Still she was bleeding. Father concluded, "I just reached into the cut and pinched the blood vessels. The bleeding stopped immediately."

Surgery

We could call this a kind of surgery, however he learned it. He castrated calves and pigs at home and for other farmers. For pigs he kept a straight razor over a beam in the pigpen. He dipped it in creolin. A boy sat on a bench gathering a little pig's four legs in his hands, and holding him immobile. Father sprinkled creolin on the incision. The surgery didn't seem to phase the little friskers. Immediately they returned to the mother's udder. In another week, healed and grown noticeably, they were weaned. Other farmers came and got some of them.

Another kind of surgery that was employed – happily infrequently – was bleeding. Probably it was based more on superstition than from any established benefit. We had a mare that had suffered a deep cut in a hind leg. It swelled periodically. Father thought that bleeding might help her. But he didn't undertake it himself.

He engaged John Hood, a former blacksmith, then doing some veterinary service, to come to our farm. He took up the mare's swollen leg and cut into her foot with a hoof-paring knife, until he fetched blood. When he had drained about half a pail and replaced the shoe over a piece of leather from a boot top to prevent infection, he said, "No need to tantalize her any more."

We watched Father doctor farm animals; we experienced his doctoring on ourselves. One evening Wilfred stopped his horses in front of the veranda, and asked Claude to throw the hand potato digger out of the wagon. When he swung, it scraped the back of Wilfred's head. Father applied iodine, an antiseptic that was always kept in supply for treatment of bleeding wounds and cuts. He seemed to know intuitively what to do for any injury, little or big, and be able to respond calmly.

The summer I was nine I had an accident that brought my father's home doctoring quickly into action. I had planted Morning Glories. The vines climbed up a veranda post. One morning I climbed up the post to help some stray vines wind around the post. On the way down the inner edge of my right hand caught a jagged nail. In panic, I let go of the post. The nail, still into my hand, ripped a big tear the full length of my hand. It bled profusely. Mother called Father from some farm job. He commanded everybody to be quiet, called for a basin of water and his blue vitriol crystals from the horse barn.

On other occasions we had been fascinated to see the crystals dissolve and turn water to a purplish blue, when Father put them in a pail of water as an antiseptic for a cut on a horse's foot or leg. For several days, at noon, Father removed the bandage, soaked my hand in the blue vitriol, and re-wrapped it with strips of white cloth that Mother tore from old garments. No infection developed. The ugly, jagged tear healed; only a scar remained.

Gordon suffered a severe cut when he was about 10. Playfully, he was exploring the machine shed where Father stored his logging equipment, including a big collection of double-bitted axes, standing on the floor. Gordon tripped. Putting out his hands to stop his fall, a finger hit an axe blade. Gordon said "I almost cut off one of my fingers." He severed a cord. Mother screamed. Shirley made a Marathon run to a far field where Father was turning his buckwheat for drying. Out of breath, she reported the accident. Again Father calmly bound up the finger, stopping the bleeding. Gordon said, "he poured on about half a bottle of iodine which hurt worse than the cut."

Ability to meet emergency needs was a striking trait of our father. The nearest M.D. was 15 miles away at Bristol, and often only travel by horse was available, and sometimes winter storms and snowdrifts blocked the road. When medical attention was deemed necessary we travelled to Bristol, e.g., when Claude awoke one night with a severe pain in his abdomen. We pondered the possible cause. Claude and I were cutting logs that week for Bob Guthrie. But he had no apparent injury. Could it possibly be appendicitis? Deciding to go for an examination, Father started the car at 3:00 a.m. Warren and I accompanied him. At Bristol we awoke the doctor. He probed Claude's abdomen, decided there was nothing critical, and prescribed paregoric.

In the summer of 1936, Shirley at age four, was struck by a horse. It was the accident that brought us the most intense anxiety. She was walking nonchalantly across the yard toward the granary, her eyes trained into the frosting dish that she was scraping with a spoon. Tom led the new pair of bay horses out of the barn and let them go to the puncheon to drink. The mare walked briskly with her head high, unaware of low objects. She simply walked right over the little girl, knocking her down. Apparently a foot or leg struck Shirley on the head. She fell unconscious. Mother ran and picked her up and carried her to the veranda. While she sat holding her, her eyes rolled back. We all feared the injury was fatal. Father called for cold water. He sprinkled it on her face and forehead. He said, "She's alright." She began to breathe, but remained unconscious. Did Father know about the danger of brain damage? Or did he simply have an intuition about stimulating breathing?

Fortunately the 1928 Chevrolet was in the machine shed, though Wilfred was a part owner. He was working for Flemmings at Juniper. Mother held the four-year old girl on her lap as they drove to Bristol. A doctor there advised them to take her to Woodstock Hospital. Mother reported afterwards that the heavy shower and wind swayed the car on the old river road to Woodstock. Encouragingly Shirley began to move a little. Father came home that evening reporting a concussion, and a broken collar bone.

    Mother remained in Woodstock, staying nights with Aunt Mary and Uncle Bob Carr, and taking a taxi each day to the hospital. A kindly visiting lady rocked Shirley to sleep each evening. In about a week they brought Shirley home with tape around her collarbone, and carrying a new doll. After about a week of sitting in a rocking chair with her doll, she was back to normal play.

Man of Justice

    The man who was unhesitating in home treatment was also unhesitating in the face of injustice. Keith said, "Father always stood for what was right." Advocacy for victims of injustice pervaded his personality and value system. Neither could he tolerate anybody putting anything over on him, as this story illustrates:

    During his sojourn in Western Canada, when a young man, apparently one employer, failed, or refused to pay him. In Vancouver, where it seemed some loggers stayed during the spring break-up, he took his case to court. He described the scene: Two lawyers argued his case. One was a very effective speaker. The other periodically wrote a note and pushed it in front of his partner. Finally the judge pronounced, "Pay the man the money!" Father concluded, "The boys almost carried me back to the hotel."

    Father's travels and experience in Western Canada came

out bit-by-bit in little anecdotes as we sat around the kitchen on Sundays or stormy days. Thus he gave us glimpses of his earlier ventures. Before marriage he went on harvest excursions to Western Canada. Later, after being bereaved of his first wife, he went with the Ricker family from Knowlesville to Alliance, Alberta. From the Ricker's farm, Ira must have gone to other farms and ranches on the prairies.

His fondness for horses permeated his stories. Visitors and people on errands on the prairies always came on horseback. Distances between farms were too far to walk. His most dramatic story was about his attempt to ride a bucking bronco. It seems that somewhere on the prairie he worked on a ranch. One day the ranchman managed to bridle and saddle a wild horse and Ira volunteered to try to break him. The ranchman held the horse by the bridle while my father attempted to mount him. He put one foot in the stirrup but before he could swing up into the saddle the horse took off leaving the bridle in the other man's hand. Fortunately Ira's foot pulled out of the stirrup so he was not dragged very far.

He seemed to like the prairies. He spoke of the government provision whereby settlers could stake claims, and after three years of continuous residence, gain title to a section of farmland. The problem, he said, was that there was no way of earning any income during the winter. Perhaps for that reason he pursued other work, e.g., log driving on the Red River.

From the prairies, Ira went to British Columbia. Considering his fondness for horses, it is not surprising that he drove a six-horse team twitching huge logs. He mentioned several places in British Columbia that he visited in his work and travels: Peachland and Summerland in the Okanagan Valley; Arrowhead, Enderby, Kootenay, Revelstoke and Vancouver. His daughter, Erma, treasured for years cards they received from some of those places.[1]

Returning to New Brunswick he brought on the train a

big trunk made of rough boards. Gordon still has it and also his .32 Special hunting rifle. Two pairs of boxing gloves lasted for years – used by his own boys and borrowed by others, e.g. Archie Brown and Reid Boyle.

Father also told us about his early experience in the lumber industry in New Brunswick, e.g., the spring drive. He described to us the rigours of driving logs down the icy rivers during the spring freshets. The men slept in a tent with their feet toward the fire, drying their socks overnight. They were soon wet again in the morning.

Bringing Experience to Community

At length Father brought his varied experiences in lumbering, farming and road work into community life. His leadership abilities extended from logging crews to road commissioner to Sunday School. A very important part of our upbringing and our community life was Sunday School in the Knowlesville Baptist Church. Father was often the superintendent.

Through the 30's Sunday School was a weekly event to look forward to – a welcome relief from farm chores and weeding hoe crops. Our little bay driving mare, Belle, could take quite a group of us, wedged in the wagon like sardines. But she didn't like to be tied. She broke loose from the horse shed one Sunday morning, broke her harness and broke out of the shaves. Vernon and Lorne Whitehouse, passing by, freed her from the one strap still holding. She stood facing the door when we emerged after the closing hymn and benediction.

In Glassville Father bought a new, heavier rope. A stander-by said, "That ought to hold her Ira." She didn't break it, but she halfway pulled over Cecil Whitehouse's ramp for draining motor oil. Some stories, not funny at the time, but amusing in retrospect, relate to our Sunday School attendance. A much publicized episode occurred one Sunday morning when Murray Kenney, visiting from Maine, took his car to

Cecil's for a consultation. Murray, always very accommodating to the younger boys, allowed them to ride in his rumbleseat. Then he forgot the time until Father arrived by horse and buggy, announcing that it was time for Sunday School. The boys didn't like going bare-footed and wearing their work clothes. Murray offered to take them back to the farm to change to church clothes. Father insisted that it was time for Sunday School and the boys should immediately cross the road to the church – barefoot and work clothes. It was a matter of priorities. I was at Grandmother Brown's that summer; the story soon reached there – carried by Elwood Whitehouse.

Amusement aside, Sunday School was a valuable learning experience, with dedicated people leading and teaching. Edmund Spinney taught the adult class, also called the Bible Class. He was a thorough scholar of the Bible. He studied diligently the O.T. history. He told Father that he worked on the lesson all week. Some of our teachers were Cassie Avery, Blanch Whitehouse and Agnes Hemphill. Through the rest of his life Warren Corey carried a valuable, positive reinforcement. Agnes Hemphill told our mother, "Warren is a very good reader." Leadership was also contributed by Perry Fitzgerald, Glassville. As a representative of the Maritime Religious Education Council, he promoted Sunday Schools all over the Parish of Aberdeen. He made visits to Knowlesville Sunday School. He especially liked to be present for the spring opening.

Sunday School was very enjoyable in spring, summer and fall. When they tried to carry on in severe winter weather we sometimes had to leave the class assembly in the pews and warm our feet around a big cylinder stove. Experience eventually brought the stated wisdom that morale and attendance was better if they closed for the coldest months, Christmas through March, and resumed in Spring.

Sunday School was notable in that lay people carried it on and learned to participate. Often the only ordained ministry was in the summer months. For me the most memorable session of Sunday School was the rainy Sunday afternoon when the attendance was so small that they decided not to have Sunday School, at least not the usual session. They did, nonetheless, without intending it or knowing it. We sat on the bench between the firewood bin and the cylinder stove on the south side of the church. There Ira Corey and Fred Hemphill recalled to each other a mutual pact they had made, some years earlier, to reactivate the Sunday School that had lapsed, apparently for lack of leadership.

The setting of that pact was a river – a branch of the Miramichi or the Nashwaak. As they stood waist deep in the river, casting their flies for salmon, they discussed the lamentable situation of the community of Knowlesville without a Sunday School. The pact, as I remember it, was made when Fred Hemphill said to Ira Corey, "If you will take the lead in re-opening the Sunday School, I'll be there every Sunday with my family." Subsequently Fred Hemphill also took his turn as superintendent.

At Roy Hemphill's funeral in the Knowlesille Baptist Church, on January 15, 2001, Murray Whitehouse told a strikingly similar story. He recalled that when he was conducting supply services at the Mount Pleasant Baptist Church, Pauline and Roy Hemphill arrived one Sunday. They told him about their need for a Sunday School. Apparently it had again lapsed. "Will you come and help us organize it again? We think it will take about three Sundays." Murray said, "I came for three Sundays and stayed twelve years."

All such stories are to be treasured. Thank heaven television had not been invented when we were growing up! We learned the value of story, to listen for stories, to search out stories and also to pursue our own interests in creative ways. At home Father reinforced the value of stories – Bible stories. Right after breakfast we assembled in the kitchen. As long as Grandfather Alfred lived he was called to sit in the circle. Father took his Bible from the high shelf on the south wall. He had, I think, no system of selecting passages. Rather he started a book and continued. But I think when he got into some of the more difficult parts, e.g., the wars between the people of Israel and the Hittites and other neighbouring peoples, he turned to the New Testament.

I especially remember the dramatic stories: creation, exodus from Egypt, Abraham's dramatic encounter with the heavenly messengers visiting his tent. The pronunciation was sometimes a little distorted, e.g., "Peradventure", in the King James version, was rendered "pre-da-venture." The dramatic story, nonetheless, became fixed in my memory. There it remained until, years later, insight was added to the story. Abraham's impassioned pleading with the heavenly messenger to spare Sodom and Gomorrah; his downward bidding from 50, to 45, to 40, to 30, to 20, to 10 of righteous people in the doomed city, conveyed the age-old wisdom that even a very small minority of good people could redeem a city from corruption.

Father also brought home some of the songs. His rich tenor voice that rose distinctly in the Baptist Church, in the choir, in the congregation and in the Sunday School, often broke into song at home, e.g.:

Jud Corey with father, Ira Corey

"Is there any one can help us,
One who understands our hearts;
Who in loving grace imparts
Just the very, very blessing that we need?
Yes there's One, only One;
The blessed, blessed Jesus, he's the One."

[1] The Story of Knowlesville, p.112f.

CHAPTER XVII

GROWING UP ON THE EAST KNOWLESVILLE FARM

In August 1930 the children of Ira and Nellie Corey were bereaved of both their grandfathers. Alfred Corey died August 17; James Brown died a week later. Their passing marked, in a way, the end of an era of relative prosperity and the beginning of the era called "the great depression", and "hard times". Perhaps the grandparents were spared some anxiety.

We had little awareness, much less comprehension, of what was happening in the world beyond us, e.g., the Stock Markets of New York, that were later said to have brought the crash. My only recollection of any inkling that an event in the larger world might affect us was a report that Father brought home from a visit to Fred Currie's. Lizzie Currie had told him that she had written an order to Eaton's, but had decided not to mail it. Newspaper articles perhaps convinced her to hold on to her money. E'er long, changes in far-away markets and economy came to be felt even in Knowlesville.

A change for us was that Father's logging enterprises came to a stand still. Because of a slowing of the lumber industry in the early 30's Father was home for a few winters. But I recall no fretting about "hard times". We experienced little change in livelihood. We had built no expectations of added conveniences; much loss of luxury.

Now we shall share with our readers what it was like growing up on the farm in that era. We shall describe activities and narrate events, anecdotes, episodes and learning experiences within a seasonal framework. I begin with winter where the "change" was most noticeable.

Winter

As we have narrated in Chapter VII, Father had spent several winters logging: contracting for Flemmings, with crews in Miramichi and Nashwaak areas. Also some winters cutting logs from his own wood lots and hauling them on sleds by teams to a mill. My recollection is that in early 30's our family made creative use of a change of pace with less pressure.

They cut hardwood for firewood, planning for some to sell to truckers who came to the farm in fall; some spruce to be sawed into boards at Hemphill's Mill for repair to the farm buildings, and some cedar to be sawed into shingles at Lewis Carle's mill at Esdraelon. Looking forward to summer and the enjoyment of ice cream, they cut ice on Argyle Lake. An old granary with a leaky roof on one of the Hemphill lots accommodated a sawdust bin for burying the ice.

There was a little more time for pleasure, e.g., a little play with horses. Father broke the little bay filly that Murray Kenney had brought to the farm. He mated her with our old driving horse, Dick, losing his speed with age. Father had Jim Hovey, blacksmith in Glassville, make a slender hardwood pole, complete with neck yoke and wiffletrees. This he attached to his sleigh, and thus revived the "double-hitch".

I remember a ride to Glassville and back in that sleigh behind that pair of trotters, in February 1932. I sat between Father and Wilfred, the driver, comfortable under the buffalo robe that covered our knees. My errand was to get a new scribbler and pencil at Derrah's store in preparation for beginning school March 1.......that spring in Knowlesville.

The errands done, the pair trotted most of the way to Brown's corner, slowed to a walk up Highlands Hill, began an easy downgrade trot at Norman Brown's, continued past Bill Guthrie's, Dick Linder's, Bob Guthrie's, the Ozias Carle place, then deserted, over the Roy Carle Bridge, past Charles Branscombe's perched on the hill, Everette Kenney's on the old

Corey homestead, past George Guthrie's, and Mrs. Roland Kenney's. Wilfred reined the trotters to a brisk walk as we turned up the lane between George W. Whitehouse's on our right, and Claude Manuel's on our left. When they rounded the turn they broke into a trot again, past Osbert Whitehouse's, George H. Whitehouse's and the deserted J.S. Whitehouse place, recently vacated by Alfred LaPage. Our barn looked good to old Dick; the three-year-old mare was still going eagerly.

The word got out about Father breaking colts. Billy Crawford had an unbroken filly. Mina wrote a note to Ira asking him to break it. He took a week to respond. When he went for the filly he saw her being led behind Ed Scott's sleigh. He had bought her.

Our mother's wish to have Father home in winter[1] was fulfilled for a while. However, he didn't spend that many winters at home. From about 1933 to 1935 he was working winters in Juniper, usually with a pair of horses, sometimes hauling deal from the mill to the railway. On a cold January morning in 1935 Father and some of the elder boys left home. That evening the kitchen chimney sent up flames. Fortunately the roof was covered with snow. Nonchalantly, Mother put coarse salt in the stove.

In the fall of 1935 Father resumed logging at Skedaddle Ridge. He had no time for the double-hitch, but he kept the black-painted pole and accessories. When the E. Knowlesville farm was sold he returned it to Glassville and stored it under Claude Corey's porch.

In winter Mother continued to market butter in Juniper. She stored the pound blocks in the woodshed; they froze as hard as bricks. We did not need a refrigerator. With heavy brown paper from Eaton parcels she wrapped the blocks in bundles of about 10, tied with Eaton cord, and addressed to customers in Juniper. We carried them to the mailbox. We also received frozen bundles in our mailbox. Wilmot Osborne sent from Campobello, codfish spread out flat, resembling small snowshoes.

The boys, in play, imitated winter logging. We made miniature bobsleds. A one-inch board, on edge, made a runner. Small chains or pieces of binder twine crossed, attached the front sled to the rear. A rack sat on top for miniature logs. We made whiffle trees to attach to the front sled. Eaton cord made loop traces. The two boys playing the horses stood inside the loops. We loaded the sleds with alders we had cut into logs. Each boy got his turn as the teamster.

For indoor entertainment we had a gramophone with cylindrical records, giving us songs and humour. For a change we carried a potato basket of records to MacKenzie's and traded for theirs. There was also a bit of picture entertainment, brought by Ivan Branscombe. He snowshoed to our farmhouse carrying his magic lantern with batteries. Mother hung a bed sheet on the wall. He projected pictures onto it – an early foretaste of movies. Throughout the winter we enjoyed snowshoeing and sliding.

In March we returned to school in E. Knowlesville. There were advantages to the one-room school. We learned from pupils in grades ahead of us. I still remember Paul Brandscombe reading aloud the story of John McIntosh, a homesteader in Ontario, discovering the seedling apple tree that produced the McIntosh apple. The story includes Alan McIntosh's learning grafting, budding and pruning.[2]

The winter/spring school term progressed through a wide range of weather. In March we hiked over the crust and also had long slides on our handsleds, at recess and noon. In a few weeks the winter broke. The days became warmer; the hard-packed snow on the roads softened; the horses' feet punched through it. Teams with sleds waited for better travelling. In that season, one year, a strange event happened in E. Knowlesville, the full meaning of which didn't strike me until years later.

Baskets of Learning

It happened at noon hour on a day we had come home for lunch. Usually, we carried lunch to school. That season, perhaps excited by the signs of spring, for a few days we took to hiking across the fields and over the brooks to have lunch at home. One day we arrived early at the farmhouse and had a few moments to sit on the veranda. We looked in the distance and saw a very strange phenomenon moving on the road. Because the sled runner tracks had softened with approaching spring there was little travel with horses. That day there was only one movement – that strange phenomenon. We puzzled. If anybody then had talked about space travel we might have said, it's a creature from another planet.

After a few moments of puzzling, my father said, "Oh, its two Indians walking side by side – one in each sled track; they are carrying baskets." At closer range we could see the baskets roped together and suspended from their shoulders. I was frightened. My fear, heightening as they drew nearer, eventually burst into a question to my father: "What are you going to do, get your gun and shoot them?" He quickly pooh poohed that idea, apparently having no clue of where I got it from, i.e., the school history book that described the English and the French settlers in encounters with the various tribes of Native people. One teacher spoke of the Iroquois being especially ferocious and warlike. There were pictures in the history books of scalping.

In that moment filled with fear and suspense, Father stepped from the veranda into the house. Now he kept his rifle on a set of deer antlers over a door in the kitchen. There were no laws then about safety. When he came back to the veranda he had in hand only one small object – his wallet. He greeted the visitors in a friendly way and bought several baskets from them. We had plenty of uses for them on the farm.

What was far more valuable than the baskets, in that day's experience for a boy of about eight, was the beginning of an enlarged perspective on race relations, and of a transformed view of history.

Spring

Spring was a time of new life. Any morning the boys might find a newborn calf. They announced it when they brought in the milk to be separated. Soon the younger boys were pulling on breeches and gum rubbers and going to the barn in the cold, early morning to see the colourings and markings of the new-borns.

Spring was also lambing time. In the early morning, in the sheep shed, Father might find a pair of twins or even triplets that had arrived in the night. Sometimes they were chilled and unable to stand and reach the udder. Father would pick them up in a potato basket, lined with a burlap sack, and carry them into the kitchen. Behind the wood-burning stove they revived, took a few drags of milk from a bottle, got the energy to stand, and then were returned to the barn to start nursing at the udder. Soon the precocious little creatures were frolicking about the barnyard.

Maple Syrup

In the spring of 1931 maple syrup-making on our farm expanded, thanks to an inheritance from Grandfather Brown. James Brown had a maple grove of 100 acres or more. He was equipped with several hundred sap cans and spiles, and an evaporator, housed in a log hut in his woods. For years he had maintained a large maple sugar enterprise. After Grandpa Brown's death Grandma Brown divided sugaring equipment between her family members. The Corey family received about 300 sap cans and spiles. Thus we became well equipped for making maple syrup.

In late March or early April signs of new life drew us to

the maple grove north of the house, and the four-acre field. Warm sunny days following frosty nights sent the sweet sap rushing from the roots up the trunks of the trees. Walking on the crust or on snowshoes, we drilled into the maple trees with brace and bit. In large trees we drilled two or three holes. We hammered a cast iron spile into each hole. As soon as we hung the bucket on the hook, on the spile, the sap began playing a merry tune as it dropped in rapid, steady rhythm into the metal bucket. We soon learned what trees had the sweetest sap. A swig while gathering gave us quick energy.

Gathering was a family enterprise. I remember the day Wilfred had the bay horses harnessed and hitched to the longsled when we came hurrying across the fields from school. Keith, who was not yet of school age, had just come from the henhouse, having gathered the eggs in his cap. We all climbed into the long sled. As the horses followed the circle cut through the woods the boys fanned out on both sides, lifted the cans from the hooks on the spiles, carried them to the sled, poured the sap into two big molasses puncheons, re-hung the cans and brought more full cans. When we had come full circle we were at the boiling place. There two large cast iron pots hung on a cross bar chained to two trees. A third pot hung from a crane, bolted to a tree. There Wilfred parked the sled loaded with sap. Back at the house at suppertime, Keith removed his cap. It still contained two eggs.

In the early morning Father dipped sap from puncheons to pots and kindled a fire under the pots. Hardwood sawed and split from dead trees kept the sap boiling all day. As evaporation reduced the volume of sap, more was dipped from the puncheons. Before nightfall the sap was condensed to very sweet syrup in the one pot that hung on a crane. While hot, the syrup flowed readily through a cloth to strain out the bits of bark and debris.

The sweet aroma of maple also permeated our kitchen. On the stove Mother refined it further. She skimmed off a few more bits of debris that came to the surface in white foam. The golden, sweet maple syrup poured over the pancakes she fried on a black griddle made an unforgettably delicious flavour. Mother, in her closing years expressed nostalgia when she rode past the Brown farm. She'd say, "I'd like to go into that woods and see if the evaporator is still there."

More New Arrivals

In April or May a litter of pigs arrived. Father had to watch the new-born till they were able to move quickly. When the mother sow prostrated herself to present her two rows of nipples to her brood of sucklings she could awkwardly role over onto one of the little pigs and smother it. At three weeks they could be weaned. Neighbours came, caught some of them by their hind legs, put them in burlap sacks and tossed them in their wagons. They quickly learned to drink dairy milk from a low trough.

Planting Time

In early May the last traces of snow disappeared from the fields. The soil dried enough to be harrowed. My brothers, beginning with Murray and Wilfred all had turns driving two pairs of horses over the ploughed fields. After the harrow, came the seeder drill, putting seed oats, grass seed and fertilizer into the tilled soil.

While the fields were being harrowed, my father might be cutting potato seeds. He sat on a plank stretched over two barrels. The plank had a knife set into it, blade toward him. He seized the potato in both hands and pushed it against the knife, watching carefully to see that each section had an "eye". Those seed sections were poured into the holding tank of the potato planter that was pulled by a pair of horses. That tank let down seeds into a turning horizontal wheel with sections for seeds.

Father rode the rear seat, making sure that each section of the turning cog contained a seed. One time his finger got caught in the moving cog and painfully jammed. With a finger cot over it, he continued to work.

Planting concluded with buckwheat. In the churchyard men asked each other, "Have you planted your buckwheat yet?" It was the last grain to be sown; it matured early.

If there was ever a dull time, it was not in spring. After spring freshets the brook that ran through our farm lowered to normal level. Then trout would come for our earthworm-baited hooks. It was exciting to see speckled, yellow-bellied trout swarming in a pool. Sometimes we had to step back behind a tree, then drop in the hook. The tug of a trout on the line sent a tingle of excitement through a boy's whole body.

Spring was also the season for whistles. We made our own from sections of sapling about 3/4" in diameter. We tapped the round cross section of the sapling with the back of a jack knife to loosen the bark. A twist brought the bark off, cylinder-shaped. We whittled away half the peeled wood, notched a blow hole and an air escape hole. Then we slid the bark back on to the sapling. We blew our whistles all the way to school. There, we dropped them in a pail of water to keep them from shrinking out of shape.

Grandpa didn't hesitate to lend his black-handled jack-knife, important to him for cutting his plug tobacco. I still have many scars from cuts on my left hand. Through trial, error and much freedom, we learned to be creative. We never expected anybody to provide entertainment for us. There was no use saying, "there is nothing to do." We knew that if we did not find something to do it was because we were either too lazy or too lacking in imagination.

Summer

Near school closing wild strawberries ripened in fields that had not been ploughed for a few years. Their aroma and flavour were delightful. Later in the season picking became tedious. Shirley and Kaye still remember how Warren, weary of the task, devised a trick. He presented a heaped container, then sat down to rest. When the top layer was taken off, behold a bowl of leaves.

The biggest family task of summer was haying, beginning in mid-July. The horses mowed all morning. At noon they came from the field and drank gallons of spring water from the molasses puncheon. We all had turns riding the rake in the afternoons. It was fun tripping it at windrows. Cocking the hay from windrows was harder. Pitching the cocks up on to the hayrack was the hardest field job. In truth, our father did most of that; we built the loads. That required skill to distribute it evenly so it would not fall off.

When we arrived at a barn with a load, the boys would run into the woodshed for water piped from the spring on the hill. We were prone to linger, enjoying the thirst-quenching refreshment and unrivalled taste. Eager to get the hay off the wagon into the mow, Father would shout, "Now let's play ball" – about the only ball game we ever got to play. It did require teamwork, and coordination of workers: several in the mow, one on the load, one driving the horses – the only fun job when unloading hay.

The horses pulled a rope that ran through several pulleys and hoisted the hay into the mow. In the horse barn a miniature railway track ran inside the peak of the roof. The hay fork – distinguished from a pitch fork – was let down on a rope to the load on the wagon parked in front of the barn. The fork was punched down into the hay. Then a prong at the bottom was pulled into a horizontal position by means of a lever at the top. Thus the fork grabbed a large bundle of hay. When the horses pulled the rope through the pulleys, they hoisted the forkful of hay up to the gable end of the barn. When the fork was tripped it dropped the hay in a heap. With pitch forks the fellows in the mow distributed it evenly.

While the haying was in progress there were other tasks in July, e.g., tending the garden and weeding and thinning a big patch of turnips. It could be tedious. It was more like fun when Warren and I hitched old Nell to a one-horse cultivator. One of us drove her; the other steered the cultivator. Thus we loosened the soil and eradicated the weeds between the rows. Turnips grew fast. After a few weedings only the cultivator was needed.

A change of tasks was a relief. At about 10:30 Mother called us to go to the field and dig cobblers. In a pail, with water, we whirled them round and round with a broom handle. The soil and the skins came off. Oh that I might recapture the flavour of those clean, white potatoes which went straight from the soil to the pot. Served with string beans and peas fresh from the garden, the dinners were delicious.

About once a week, in summer, Mother had us churn the cream into butter. It was not fun, but I remember a pleasure connected with it —riding with Father to Juniper on pay-day. I sat beside him as he trotted the little bay mare carrying the butter for delivery to customers: Gallops, Turnbulls and many others. He seemed to know every family in Juniper. I especially remember calling on Mrs. J.K. Flemming, then a widow, at her neat house on the bank of the S. Branch. She took from her icebox a bottle, and poured me a sparkling glass – my first taste of carbonated drink. The mare, a bit sweaty, had us back at the farm before the family had finished noon dinner.

"Goings and Comings"

There was pleasure, and sometimes excitement, in every "going": to Glassville for tea, sugar, spices, bananas, and to have horses shod; to Esdraelon to have Eddy Speakman mash oats or grind buckwheat, and to trade buckwheat meal with Jimmie Bell for molasses and other commodities, and to trade rabbits for chocolate bars, or to sell a calf hide.

We also liked "comings". Our house was nearly 1/4 mile from the highway, situated in the middle of four 100-acre lots. If we saw a vehicle on the gravel road we eagerly hoped it would turn into our driveway. Some of the "comers" were buyers and peddlers. Old David Pinsky drove one horse pulling a heavy wagon. He bought materials that otherwise had no monetary value: e.g., rags and horsehair. He tried to motivate us to prepare for his next visit: "If a horse dies, go and cut the hair from its tail and mane." As we currycombed the horses we accumulated, on a shelf, balls of hair. They waited till he returned. The Brown brothers: Sam, Saul and Harry came by truck to buy livestock: cattle, lambs, pigs. Jimmie Miller came weekly with freshly butchered meat. He was as much a visitor as a peddler. He often stayed for dinner.

We often had Sunday visitors. Some awaited our arrival from morning Sunday School: perhaps Annie and Jack Allan. Afternoon and supper visitors: perhaps Norman and Minnie Brown, Malcolm and Lillian Brown, Clarence and Alma Robinson, Jim and Kate Hovey. Olys and Wilma Brown might come in the fall by longsled. All brought children or youth. Mother welcomed visitors with meals. We youngsters often had to wait for a second sitting; we still liked visitors.

"Goings" and "comings" excited us. But we were never dependent on anybody for amusement. We made our own, e.g., little wagons. The binding sticks from cedar shingle bundles made the axles. Cutting with a saw, and whittling with a jackknife, we rounded both ends of the stick, then slid a horsepower wheel on each end. A nail through the stick/axle kept the wheel on. A bolt through the front axle allowed it to swing. Boards or a box made the top. We attached a pole for pulling, steering and holding down hill.

We also made stilts. We cut young saplings 8' or 10'

long and about 3" diameter at bottom. A short piece of 2 x 4 shaped and nailed to the pole, made the foot hold. The idea came from the geography textbook. It described Scandinavians using stilts in swampy or flooded areas. We built a dam on the brook using stones and sods. The water wasn't deep enough for a swim, but allowed a good dip on a hot day.

Argyle Picnic

A widely-known and long-lasting summer event in that era was the Argyle Picnic. The site was a little west of Argyle Corner, on the north side of the road. There was a little clearing in the woods, with grass. Near the end of haying, families came from all the surrounding communities by horse and carriage, by team and farm wagon, and by car and truck. The time of transition allowed shifting back and forth from horses to horseless carriages.

Warren remembers an early year when Wilfred drove a team of our horses. Enroute he picked up Mina Crawford and Melvina Boyd. Probably our parents came by horse and buggy. I remember Murray Kenney, driving his curtained car jammed with Coreys and MacKenzies. I remember sitting on Lawrence MacKenzie's knees on the back seat. One year Warren and I walked until we were overtaken by Malcolm MacKenzie, Sr., with his sorrel mare. He and his younger boys filled the seat. Warren and I were invited to stand on the rear axle. At the picnic ground horses were tied to the trees and stood switching flies all afternoon.

I also remember riding on trucks. From Knowlesville, King Avery drove his truck, bringing Nellie, Jack, Ronald and Dawn and Bessie and Ellery Wasson, and others. Clarence LaPage also drove his truck bringing Eva, Cora, Elmer, Myrtle and Velma. Together King Avery and Clarence LaPage gave rides to people all along the route from Armond to Argyle.

From S. Knowlesville came Addison, Lois, Viola and

Tressa Spinney; George, Grace, Marion, Lorne and Frank Simms; Ernest, Parazanda, Annie, Archie, Ethel, Elbina Cora and Ruby Sewell; and George, Irilla, Edna, Jack, Harold, Irene and Olga Lawson. From E. Knowlesville came the families of Osbert Whitehouse and George H. Whitehouse, Alfred LaPage, while they lived there, Coreys, Curries, MacKenzies, Willis Brandscombe's and Attle Boyd. From Golden Ridge came Manzer and Ralph Boyd and Billy Campbell. From E. Glassville came Bob Anderson and family; Billy George and Gertrude McFarland; Fred and Annie McBrine, and Annie's sister Mrs. Bishop, and Floyd. From Divide came the families of Alex Lindsay, James Hovey, Ed White and others. From Juniper came the Cummings twins. From Foreston/Argyle came Harveys, the Olys Hughes family and the Charlie Crawford family.

There were many volunteers: Vince Lunnie hauled the water in molasses puncheons on a sloven wagon. All afternoon Alex Lindsay kept a fire under big black farm boiling pots. He also kept the bean pots around the fire. At the canteen Manzer Boyd scooped ice cream at 5¢ a cone, dipped lemonade from butter crocks and sold chocolate bars.

The girls and boys, after spending their limited allowances at the canteen, roamed around getting acquainted and waiting for the supper and the races. The older folks enjoyed sitting and exchanging news – a much-needed social experience.

At suppertime every family put food on the tables: potato salads, fresh bread and rolls, cake, cookies and pie. Frank Hughes announced, "I want some of Nellie Corey's beans." Alex Lindsay, with a pitcher in each hand, went from table to table shouting, "Hot tea; cold water." It was a delicious feast.

Supper over, the crowd assembled for the races on the gravel road. There was little traffic; a car could easily be heard approaching. Alex Currie won the youth and young men's race year after year. Though he did not appear athletic he had unbeatable speed. Albert Hovey was his closest competitor.[3]

Near the end of the picnic's long history an unfortunate dispute arose at Argyle in planning for the annual supper. On our way home that picnic day, Father drove into Hughes' yard, intending a brief errand. Though we were hurrying home to milk the cows Mrs. Hughes insisted on telling her version of a disagreement that had risen in the discussion and planning for that year's picnic. She had advocated a paid supper to raise money for the Argyle Church. She emphasized, "We would have worked our fingernails off." Ed White reportedly had maintained adamantly that the long tradition of a free supper should not be broken. That apparent inability to compromise was perhaps a strong factor in the demise of the picnic. I don't remember that there was another one. The outbreak of W.W.II followed soon thereafter.

The picnic, which was believed to have started in 1899,[4] and was maintained over nearly forty years, had contributed much to the social life of the parish of Aberdeen.

Autumn

Ripening apples and grain were signs of approaching autumn. Every day, starting in mid-August, we checked the Transparent apples. About that time the oats were beginning to turn yellow.

Soon it was time to harvest them with the binder – a fascinating machine pulled by three horses. A rotating set of wooden slats pushed the standing stalks of grain toward the cutter. The cut stalks fell onto a canvass conveyor. Iron arms portioned enough stalks for a sheaf. An inside mechanism wrapped a string around it, tied it and cut it. A steady stream of sheaves dropped onto a carrier. At intervals my father tripped the carrier and dropped the sheaves onto the ground in windrows.

My brothers and I had our turns at stooking. Four sheaves standing head to head make a stook. Sometimes, as a stooker grabbed a sheaf in each hand, a bumblebee or hornet jabbed a finger with his stinger. Soil, moistened with saliva, drew out some of the poison and eased the sting.

After a few days of drying we pitched the sheaves onto wagons. We hauled some loads directly to the threshing machine. We began replenishing the granary. Also we then began a straw stack below the cow barn, for the cows to munch in winter during their daily outings. One winter our big boar hog burrowed into the stack and slept cosily. Norman coaxed him out in the morning with a basket of pulped turnips and mashed oats.

Most of the oats in sheaves we pitched into a big mow in the barn. They could be threshed in fall and winter, as they were needed for horses, cows, pigs, hens, turkeys, or for hauling to lumber camps.

As a boy I saw the transition from horsepower to gasoline engine, for running the threshing machine. I remember Harry in the horsepower. In other work he might lag, or even occasionally kick, but when he walked onto that lag and it rolled downward, he could only climb steadily upward. At noon he was led, subdued, to his stall for oats and hay.

Ploughing, Digging, Picking, Pressing

After grain harvest came fall ploughing in preparation for next spring's planting. Two pairs of horses, working steadily for three or four weeks, ploughed 40 or 50 acres. Meantime the maple leaves had become beautiful – red and yellow and golden.

Not so beautiful was a potato field on a frosty morning. In those days they waited for the frost to kill the plants. The horses exerted strong muscle pulling the digger. We endured the back-bending task of picking up the potatoes in baskets and pouring them into barrels. Never mind! Potato digging was a short season.

More pleasant was bringing bushels of apples – red, yellow, green – Alexanders, Fameuse, Wealthys, Wolf Rivers – from orchard to bins in the cellar. Meantime Mother baked New Brunswickers and pickled or jellied, crab apples.

Another fall task was pressing hay into bundles that could be transported to the Juniper mill or to lumber camps beyond. The press, a heavy machine that looked like a low set wagon with steel wheels, was hired from George Allan, Centre Glassville. On top was a sliding steel cover. It opened and closed by a big arm, which was activated by a long pole.

A pair of horses hitched to the end of the pole swung it back and forth over about 180°. When the sliding cover was open one man pitched in hay, tramped it, and got out quickly before the steel plate could close on his legs when the horses pulled the pole back in the other direction. Horses did such work several more years before being replaced by motors. Horses worked in logging still longer.

Pork

When the weather was cold enough to keep meat, several boys and men took part in butchering a pig. We boiled water in a big black pot. One fall Tom scalded a leg when carrying two pails of that steaming water to the scalding barrel that leaned at a 30° angle against the threshold of the pig pen. Two men dipped the slaughtered pig into that scalding water long enough to soften the bristles. Then they pulled him out onto a clean board. Then, one working from each side, with sharpened knives, they scraped off the bristles, leaving a clean, white skin. Then he was pulled up by rope over a pulley, head down. From that position it was easy to complete the butchering. We had fried liver for supper. Hams and front quarters hung from the joists in the woodshed.

Christmas

Whatever the work in progress, on the farm, woodlot, or farther away in the lumber camps, all activity stopped or changed pace as Christmas season approached. Teams of horses from the logging camps were travelling homeward. Besides celebrating Christmas it was a time for practical jobs. The horses were taken to blacksmith shops to have shoes refitted for the rest of the winter. If the pork and/or beef was running low it was time for butchering.

It was a season of exciting anticipation. One year Bob, wearing a fur coat, played Santa Claus, as an early warning to the younger boys to shape up. We did!

Christmas was a feast day. Right after breakfast Mother put into the roaster the biggest and best rooster from the summer flock. Chicken with gravy, mashed potatoes, carrots, bottled beans, and homemade pickles made a delicious plate. Then there was apple and mince pie.

In my earliest recollections we had small candles mounted in metal holders that clipped onto the boughs of the Christmas tree. Bob lit them one Christmas evening and watched them carefully.

I've described a family farm, for a few who will feel nostalgia, and for many others who can know that disappearing way of life only by description.

"We Lived Here"

Where a house pointed a chimney to the sky,
Where barns sheltered horses, cows, sheep,
And a family worked hard for their keep;
Now only trees greet all passers-by.

Where horses neighed, cows mooed, sheep said bah,
Dogs barked, roosters crowed, bulls roared,
Gobblers gobbled, pigs squealed and cats purred;
Now only trees stand dumb and blah.

Where orchards displayed white, pink, red, green,
And a blaze of colours could be seen
In clover, potato, carrot, beet and bean;
Now only pine trees stand, evergreen.

Where men planted and harvested with honest toil,
Where hay, oats and barley rewarded their labour,
And buckwheat and potatoes filled their table;
Now pine trees lay claim to the soil.

Here Ira pressed many bales of hay,
And Murray hauled them to the camp,
And Nellie made their breakfast by lamp;
Here now trees stand idle night and day.

Here Nellie cooked, morning, noon and night,
Here she stirred buckwheat and buttermilk,
Here she washed the separator after milk;
Now pine trees only stand, day and night.

Here Ira sharpened a scythe and shod a horse
Wilfred and Bob worked horses mowing hay,
And Norman raked; they filled the bay;
Now transplanted trees know no remorse.

Here Nellie gave life to Jud, Warren, Keith,
Anna Kathleen, Shirley and Gordon Neil,
And watched them crawl, creep and cut teeth;
Now trees hide all they worked to bequeath.

Alice MacKenzie, Kathleen and Shirley Corey, sisters

Here Tom made snowshoes; built a camp;
Claude, Jud, Warren, Keith milked cows,
Weeded turnips, steered cultivator and ploughs;
Now pine trees claim to be champ.

From here Erma drove a trotter to school;
Here Alice learned to cook and sew,
And dress Kaye and Shirley with a bow;
Now only trees stand, idle and cool.

Here Kathleen and Shirley slid down hills,
Waded the brook; cast a baited hook,
And from their mother learned to cook;
Now trees know nought but to drop spills.

Here a family worked at many an occupation:
Ploughed, harrowed, planted, harvested, threshed,
Pressed, cut, sawed; many cogs meshed;
Now imported trees obliterate all habitation.

[1] Letter in Chapter VII

[2] See Marsha Boulton, "The Original Big Mac", in Just a Minute, Glimpses of Our Great Canadian Heritage, p.186f.

[3] Norman Corey, whose memory reaches further back than that of the writer, recalled names of families and participants. Obviously we have missed some.

[4] A.C. Dyer and H. Bradley, History of Argyle..., P.56

Nellie and Ira Corey,
East Knowlesville farm

Marjorie and Norman Corey

CHAPTER XVIII

IRA T. COREY BRANCH OF THE DESCENDANTS OF ALFRED AND LUCRETIA COREY

1877 Ira Thomas Corey 1957
m. January 13, 1912
1891 Nellie Brown Kenney 1977

To this marriage Nellie brought a son, Murray Kenney; and Ira brought a daughter, Erma Corey.

Nellie Kathleen Brown

In 1908 Nellie Brown, daughter of Mary and James Brown, Highlands, N.B. married Arthur Kenney, son of Jane and Roland Kenney, Knowlesville, N.B. Nellie and Arthur had one son, Murray Arthur Kenney, born May 10, 1909. Arthur Kenney died of an illness they called "TB of the intestines", in 1910 at age 23. His monument, erected by Murray and Nellie, stands in the Knowlesville Church Cemetery. Nellie, with her young son, returned to home of her parents in Highlands. Years later I heard her say, "My Father came right down for me and said, 'your home is still here.'"[1]

1909 Murray Arthur Kenney 1979

Murray attended school in Knowlesville and East Knowlesville. He began doing farm work with horses while very young. At age 13 and 14 he was hauling hay to Juniper and Little Clearwater.[2] Before age 20 he worked for neighbouring farmers and for Jim Hovey in Glassville.

About 1930 Murray, along with Fred McKenzie, Ernest Whitehouse, and other men of Knowlesville and area, went to Michigan for summer employment in the construction boom. They returned to New Brunswick for winter work.

Murray's next move was to Maine, while he had "papers" for employment in U.S.A. In the early 30's he began working for farmers in Maine: a Parlin family in Easton; Littleton also comes to mind; later, Ned Porter. Murray always kept in touch with us at the Corey farmhouse in E. Knowlesville. Mother wrote to him frequently during longer absences, e.g., in winter. One winter he worked in a logging crew near Machias.

In summer he visited us about every second weekend. Early he acquired a car and managed to keep it running through the 30's. I remember going to the horse barn on a Sunday morning. Murray and a companion visitor, Sedge Kierstead, or maybe Arthur, were putting on shirts and ties. They had bedded in some of Ira's lumber camp blankets in a stack of hay in the storage area of the horse barn. They had arrived late on Saturday evening after we all had gone to bed. Other siblings came home from nearer jobs. The beds were all taken.

We were always very glad to see Murray. We delighted to have a ride in the rumble seat of his 1931 Chevrolet coupe. We also delighted when he played his mouth organ and sang songs, some of them of hobos, out of work:

"May I sleep in your barn tonight Mister?";
"Get off, Get off, you railroad bum";
"Away up in the Big Rock Candy Mountains."

Warren Corey guesses Murray may have learned the songs from gramophone records.

Murray brought interest and excitement in various ways: e.g., being very fond of horses, he brought two from Maine, an unbroken stallion and a mare, to the Corey farm. Even after marriage, Murray managed to continue involvement in our enterprises. One winter he put together a pair of his

Murray A. Kenney

horses and worked in Ira Corey's logging crew on the S. Branch of the Miramichi.

In fall of 1938 Murray Kenney married Myrtle Haynes, daughter of Peter and Mary Ellen Haynes, East Glassville. Myrtle kept house one winter at the Corey farm for Warren, Keith and Kathleen. Warren and Keith amused Myrtle's daughter, Mary, then under two. They gave her rides on a handsled pulled by a year-old colt. Warren played horse and rider with Mary before bedtime. Nellie Corey cooked at the S. Branch camp. Shirley and Gordon were there also.

As soon as she could get immigration papers Myrtle joined Murray in Maine. They acquired a farm at Ludlow. Myrtle helped milk and manage a large herd of dairy cows. There they brought up six daughters and a son:

Mary, born 1939, now living in Ludlow;
Gladys, born 1941, also living in Ludlow;
Claude born 1942, now living in Houlton;
Sharon, born 1944, now living in Ludlow;
Gwendolyn, born 1947, now living in Arizona;
Sandra, born 1948, now living in New Limerick, Me.;
Barbara, born 1950, also living in New Limerick, Me.

Gary Corey remembers spending "48's" with Kenneys so he could bring back work clothes and other commodities for Bob and Maude. Gary recalls Murray, on trips to Woodstock; stopping at Richmond Corner for dinner. He also visited Everette Kenney.

In their later years Murray and Myrtle sold their farm and moved to a place on Ludlow Road, with a small barn and bit of pasture for a cow and a race horse. Murray died May, 1979; Myrtle died August 12, 1989. At Murray's passing Claude said, "I never knew two people to work so hard as my father and mother". Their descendants and spouses are listed in the accompanying genealogy. Data was gathered by Mary Grant and her granddaughter, Chantelle.

We are keeping in touch. On August 14, 1999, Mary and Avon Grant entertained a gathering of Kenneys and Coreys in Ludlow. It was planned when Norman Corey from Burlington, and Warren Corey from Port Alberni, were visiting.

Nellie Corey

Nellie Corey spent most of her lifetime caring for family. Her first decade of marriage to Ira Corey was spent at the Corey Homestead in Knowlesville. There their first six children were born: Wilfred, Robert, Alice, Norman, Thomas and Claude. (See Chapter VI) Six additional children were born at the E. Knowlesville farm: Judson, Warren, Keith, Kathleen, Shirley and Gordon. In addition to the 12 children of Nellie and Ira there was her son, Murray, and Ira's daughter, Erma. Though they were not often all home together, still they all came under Nellie's care.

Besides the care of a large family she had the management of the farmhouse and her part of the farm economy. Her day's work began early. While many hands were milking and separating, our mother, often single handed, was frying buckwheat pancakes and sliced pork, stirring oatmeal, and perhaps baking apples in the oven, while at the same time caring for small children.

After breakfast every day, besides the dishes, she had the cream separator to wash. It had many parts including about a dozen cone-shaped discs that had to be disassembled, washed, scalded and placed to dry. Then she had the routine housekeeping tasks: cleaning, and making many beds.

About once a week she attended all the oil lamps – more in winter. The chimneys had to be washed clean of black soot; the wicks trimmed with scissors and the lamps filled with kerosene oil. On Mondays there was the family wash, in early days by washboard, later with benefit of machines of progressive models. Always clothes were hung on the solar dryer.

Cooking and baking was a large task: bread, probably twice a week; cookies, cakes and doughnuts, often; mincemeat with all the ingredients in fall and winter. Even the chickens got cake which Mother made from buckwheat meal and buttermilk and baked in the oven.

Another weekly task, especially large in summer, was making butter from cream – a highly valued dairy product. We put cream on our porridge, our baked apples, and puddings. My father even put it in his tea. Mother kept a little pitcher of it at his place at the table. Most of the cream was accumulated in the cellar until it was ready for churning. The churn was a kind of short wooden barrel set in a wooden frame. It was attached to the frame at two points, one on each side, so it could be whirled around and around. The whirling mechanism was a foot-pedal and a lever. About once a week Mother removed the top cover and poured her accumulated cream into the churn, and clamped the cover tightly.

One summer Claude, Warren and I were assigned to whirl the churn, working in five-minute turns. We sometimes argued about the length of a turn. Between turns we lolled on the veranda bench. Eventually we heard the "breaking" sound inside the churn, i.e., the cream broke up into butter globules and buttermilk. We shouted a great relief. Mother had still much work to complete the process: drain the buttermilk; transfer the milky butter into a big wooden tray; work it with a wooden ladle to extract the residue of buttermilk; press the butter into a wooden mould, then push it out onto a wax paper wrapper.

We failed to consider the burden of work Mother had, until, in later years, trucks from the dairy in Woodstock started picking up the cream. We also failed to appreciate that the butter, when sold represented a good part of her income, and furthermore, that much of her butter money was used to buy clothes and shoes for us. Little wonder, now, that she planned for some of the boys to take sled loads of oats to Esdraelon to be mashed, and for us to pulp turnips to feed with the oats to the cows.

Managing and Creative Ability

Mother managed well, working efficiently through the day, so that after the supper dishes were washed, the kitchen snugged, and the oatmeal simmering in a double boiler, she could sit by the stove on a winter evening with her knitting. This too was work. Her daughter, Kaye Foster, has described it as "work that had to be done to keep the many pairs of hands and feet warm and dry. This was the perpetual task for many mothers of her time." But she was able to do it in a very relaxed way, as Kaye further described it: "She would sit all evening, her needles clicking, barely glancing at sock or mitten."

Kay also recalled Mother's creativity: "Her knitting ability and the quality of her work was legendary. Our mother took delight in using her imagination on all her creations." When she occasionally went to a fabric shop she got immense pleasure from checking out patterns with her sisters, Lottie and Hazel Whitehouse, and selecting pieces of fabric for her creations. Her purchases were few, but she did buy materials to sew for the girls, Kaye and Shirley; hence there were always remnants of fabric.

"If our mother had a hobby, it was the art of quilt making. She didn't go to a fabric shop to pick up templates and select fabric; she used what was readily available in the farmhouse. After the quilt was attached to the frames with string saved from parcels, quilting patterns were decided upon. These were created from ordinary household items, perhaps a flat iron or a plate would be traced on cardboard. Wooden spool ends could be traced for interlocking circles. These designs would be incorporated on background and borders. The leaf design was prevalent.

"In the early years of homemaking, quilt making was a necessary effort on her part to keep the many beds comfortable and attractive for the large family. In those days bleached sugar or flour bags were used for background and for lining quilts.

"In later years her endeavours turned to making quilts for wedding gifts to family, relatives, her children and grandchildren. Many of our homes still display Grandma Corey's quilts." These are monuments both to her artistry and to her caring.

At the time of Mother's death I gathered my memories in a tribute which I presented at her funeral. I recognized her appreciation of beauty in the place where we grew up. Though Mother was initially reluctant to move to E. Knowlesville she came to appreciate the beauty that surrounded us. Sometimes we overlooked the beauty. But it was always there in the bursting buds of spring, the vast greenery of summer, and the blazing celebration of colour in the fall. Mother put beauty into her home-making, in her plants, e.g. geraniums and begonias, in the sweet taste of warm brown bread with baked beans; in her own special apple pies, in whipped cream cake, and in the delicious mixture called mincemeat. Her beauty was expressed, furthermore, in her creations: intricate quilts with many designs and colours, afghans of many patterns, hooked rugs of motley hues. Furthermore there was beauty in her hospitality. Despite much work and activity she always had the time and disposition to extend a warm welcome and share a generous and delicious table with relatives, friends and neighbours.

We all experienced her love and concern. I recall a winter night when she came and woke Warren and me, and told us that Claude had not returned home and she couldn't sleep. He had gone to MacKenzie's for the evening. Could we go and see if he was o.k.? We knew she wouldn't rest until she was assured of his safety. We pulled on clothes, strapped on our snowshoes and hiked over the fields. We opened the door at MacKenzie's: "Is Claude here?" "Yes," replied Fred, "he is upstairs sleeping." As soon as we reported back Mother went to sleep.

Here is another paragraph from my tribute:

All of us know that our mother exerted a great influence for good on us. I say this after many and various experiences: sojourning in several countries, tasting the wisdom of several universities and other institutions of learning, engaging in various kinds of work, talking to people of many walks of life. Looking back on it all, I have to say that nothing I have experienced ever can be as significant as what happened to me in the first 15 years of my life where, in the presence of the beauty of the hills, East Knowlesville, through the fury of winter, the warmth of spring, the heat of summer and the tranquillity of the fall, our mother kneaded and baked bread, cooked potatoes and beef and pork and beans and brown bread, and whipped cream cake, and apple and mince pies and where she washed clothes, and knitted socks and mittens.

Nellie Corey

I conclude with a homely little poem which I wrote for Mother's Day 1975. I take comfort now in having presented it to her while she was still living.

Dear Mother:
These things I remember:
The pancakes you fried,
The rags you dyed,
The mats you hooked,
The dinners you cooked;
The sweet bread you mixed,
The torn clothes you fixed;
The tasty doughnuts you fried,
The loose laces you tied;
The strawberries we picked,
The sweet frosting we licked;
The tracked-up floors you scrubbed,
The glass washboard you rubbed;
The delicious cookies you rolled,
The butter you squeezed from the mould;
The cream we churned,
The nights you yearned,
When a boy hadn't returned;
The eggs you cracked,
The butter you packed;
The burnt wicks you trimmed,
When the lights had dimmed;
The mincemeat we ground,
Intending to keep it around;
The frozen hunks we stole on the sly,
That never got into a pie;
The prayers that were said,
When it was time for bed;
The Bible that was read,
Right after morning bread;
And all the other things you did
Are too many to tell.
But one truth is not hid,
You looked after us well.

Erma Corey Shaw

Erma Eleanor Corey, daughter of Ira T. Corey and Emily Graham, was born at Nackawick, N.B., May 23, 1903. Emily Graham of Maple Ridge, N.B., taught in the Knowlesville School in 1900-01. Thus she met Ira Corey. On July 16, 1902, Emily and Ira were married at the home of her parents, Henry and Eleanor Graham. In the calendar year 1902 Emily taught in Armond. She drove Grandpa's mare, Bess, from Knowlesville.

In 1903 Emily and Ira went to Nackawick. Ira worked on the spring "log drive", for John Quigg, father of Willie and Rev. Perley Quigg. Willie was the husband of Theresa, Emily's sister. Emily stayed at the home of Theresa. There Erma was born. Many anecdotes from Erma's childhood and youth are interspersed in Chapters II through VIII of this book.

When Erma was 16 she went to the Provincial Normal School, Fredericton. When one of us asked our mother, "How did Erma manage to go to Normal School? Where did she get the money?" Mother only partly explained it: "She was determined to go, and she went." Erma reminisced: "As far back as I can remember I had the desire to become a teacher." During her year in Fredericton she was baptized at Brunswick St. Baptist Church, by Rev. G. C. Warren, afterwards Dean of Theology at Acadia School of Theology. Jud Corey knew him there. Erma named Warren Corey after Dr. Warren.

In 1920 Erma began teaching at age 17 in E. Glassville. She boarded with Aunt Mina and Uncle Eb McBrine, next door to the school.[3]

In 1921-22 Erma taught at Armond. Her pupils were: Hilda Henderson; Cecil, William, Ernest, and Clara Brewster; Dorothy Dickinson; Donald, Thelma and Merritt Kimball; Elva and Violet Phillips and perhaps others.

In the fall term of 1922 Erma taught in Rusagonis, a community of small farms in York County, where our uncle, Rev. J.A. Corey, had been pastor.

From January 1923 through June 1924 Erma taught at Windsor, N.B. She boarded with Mr. and Mrs. Henry Smith. Years later, Arthur Orser recollected to Norman Corey: "When the weather was stormy I harnessed my horses, hitched them to my longsled, picked up Erma after school and drove her to Smith's. I didn't want to see her, a lame, handicapped person, wade through the snow." In the summer of 1923 Erma and Grandpa went by train to Hoyt Station to visit the Rev J.A. Corey family (Chapter VII).

In the year 1924-25 Erma taught in her home school, Knowlesville, where some of her pupils had been her schoolmates. Roy Hemphill recollected, "I went to school with Erma and to Erma. So did Ernest and Vernon Whitehouse". On March 5, 1996, Roy played for me a tape – delightful renditions of several poems including, "The Cremation of Sam McGee". He said, "I memorized that when Erma was my teacher." In the fall term Erma drove Dick from Corey's in E. Knowlesville. She stabled him at George W. Whitehouse's. Beginning in January, she boarded with Blanche and George Whitehouse, thus escaping winter travel. For the last half of 1925 Erma took a holiday from teaching and stayed at home in E. Knowlesville.

Approaching Romance

One evening in the fall of 1925 Erma was at the MacKenzie farmhouse having supper. She heard Corey's number ring on the party line and decided to listen. The caller was Carey Dickinson of Simonds, seeking a teacher for the Middle Simonds School. She agreed over the phone to begin in January 1926. Her journey to Simonds was by sleigh. Sandy Brown, working for her father, Ira Corey that winter, hitched a pair; the driving horse Dick, notorious for speed, and a light work mare,

Nell, who could keep up a good trot. Sandy trotted the pair through Esdraelon, Mount Pleasant, and Lansdowne, then down the hill to Peel and across the Saint John River on ice. They emerged on the Simonds side of the river near Harry Hatfield's, thence down river to the old Carleton House, then the home of Mr. and Mrs. Harry Shaw.

Erma's teaching at Middle Simonds continued through May 1927. By agreement with the trustees she left a month early to be married to Allison M. Shaw a farmer and potato inspector, living in Simonds. Allie was a widower, father of seven children; two boys were living at home. The wedding was in the United Baptist Church, Knowlesville, on June 15th, performed by our uncle, Rev. J.A. Corey.

Adventure by Sleigh

In her first winter of marriage Erma experienced some yearnings for home and family in E. Knowlesville. In 1928 the only means of travelling there in winter was by horse and sleigh. Allie had for his travel that winter a large bay work mare, on loan from Jimmie McIsaac of Florenceville. Allie offered to let Erma take the mare for a week. He could travel his potato inspection route between Hartland and Florenceville, by train. Erma's journey on a Monday in February from Simonds to E. Knowlesville was on a clear day. During her visit a heavy snowfall came.

Saturday, the day of Erma's planned return to Simonds, was clear but desperately cold — 40° below zero on the Fahrenheit thermometer. The wind was strong and blustery, packing the snow into hard drifts. Did she have to set out on the journey that day? Those important to her thought not. Allie phoned from Florenceville: "Don't you dare leave!" Her father, Ira Corey, had gone to his logging site on the distant farm woodlot. Afterwards he said, "If I had had any idea you would set out on the journey that day, I would have left the woods and come in and stopped you." Erma's point of view: "It was simply time to go home. I had planned to be away only the six-day week and to be back to my home in Simonds before Sunday. Mrs. Monroe, Allie's former mother-in-law, was at our house and in need of care. Rev. and Mrs. A.W. Brooks had agreed to come to keep house and care for Mrs. Monroe for the week." Erma made one concession. She had planned to leave in the early morning. She decided to wait till near noon to let the weather moderate.

Imagine the scene at the Corey farm: Nellie Corey has several large slabs of hardwood in the kitchen oven. Bob Corey, not yet 14, has harnessed the mare and brought her to the veranda. He has carefully folded her blanket, still retaining some body heat, and put it in the bottom of the sleigh. Nellie brings out the hardwood slabs and tucks them in the folds of the blanket. Erma steps into the sleigh, placing her feet on the warm blanket. She is wearing a heavy, dark brown, bearskin coat, large enough to fit right over her own outer coat. Next, Nellie brings two or three goose-feather pillows and packs them around Erma's legs to further protect her from the severe cold. Finally the heavy buffalo robe is pulled up over her knees and tucked around her. In her heavily mittened hands she picks up the reins. Bob mounts beside her, having slipped his snowshoes under the rear flap cover of the sleigh.

The snow is right up to the running board. The runner braces are dragging. The worst drift of the whole journey is soon encountered, on the corner of the Corey, Alfred LaPage and Osbert Whitehouse properties The mare waded the drift to her belly slowly and nonchalantly. Erma had some apprehension about "the lane", where the road ran between the Whitehouse farm and the Charles Cook farm. Again the mare took the drifts in stride. At Elwood Whitehouse's, Bob having been a companion on the first two miles of the journey, said his quiet goodbye, dismounted, strapped on his snowshoes and returned home.

In the strip of woods between Pat Sarchfield's and the mouth of the S. Knowlesville Road there was a surcease from the wind and the drifts. But the mare was wading again when they passed the Frazier place where Billie London then lived. At a point where no house was in sight there was a near catastrophe. One tug came unhooked. The mare might have lurched forward and broken the hold-back straps, and left Erma in the drift. Obligingly, the mare stopped while Erma leaned over the curved dashboard and hooked the tug. She didn't even have to take her feet out of their warm insulation.

The going became especially heavy past the Archie Robinson and the Wasson farms. But the mare plodded steadily on to Armond Henderson's. Erma reined into the driveway for her first stop and a breather for the mare. Erma unwrapped from the big buffalo robe and went in to warm herself at the well-fired kitchen stove. The welcome was as warm as the wood stove; Erma had been a boarder at the Henderson home when teaching school in Armond. While Erma warmed at the stove the mare cooled in the yard, even with the buffalo thrown over her. In a few moments she was glad to resume the journey.

From that point both horse and driver could take heart. On the road to Windsor there had been enough traffic to enable the mare to break into a little trot, so the section of road from Henderson's' to Windsor was much easier. The Henry Smith home, another former boarding place of Erma's, was her second stopping point. They enjoyed a luxury for that time – a wood burning furnace.

Again, the stop had to be short. There were still miles to travel. Again the mare encountered heavy going up the Windsor hill above Smith's. She was glad when Erma reined into Roy Caldwell's in Lower Windsor for their third stop. Happily Helen was at home and had a good fire in the kitchen stove.

Now the journey has past the half way mark and every step cheered the way to Rockland for the fourth stop. At Enoch

Estabrook's Post Office there was another warm welcome. Again Erma was among friends. For years the Estabrooks had delivered the mail to Grandpa Corey's Post Office in Knowlesville. Erma had known these friendly folks all her growing-up years.

The Rockland break gave the mare needed fresh energy. From there the road ran uphill all the way to Cross Creek. Erma was scheduled for another stop, at Clayton Craig's home, almost opposite the historic Woodford Craig house. But, she said, "I was getting along so well that I kept travelling, eager to reach Hartland."

At Keith and Plummer's store Allie Shaw, the worried husband, was anxiously walking the floor while throwing glances through the window. Imagine his relief when the big bay mare emerged from the Rockland Road onto Hartland's main street. Erma was glad to have a driver to hold the cold reins for the remaining three miles of the 21-mile journey to their home in Simonds.

Four more years passed before the first baby came to Erma and Allie. Meantime Allie endured a very critical illness with a bowel obstruction, and extensive surgery, followed by infection. Erma drove their old Dodge car daily to Woodstock Hospital stopping at Waterville to fill the leaky radiator. After two months in hospital Allie had nine weeks in bed at home. A trained nurse stayed three weeks. Erma then had the care of the patient, applying swabs and dressings. During Allie's illness, Erma's grandfather died in E. Knowlesville.

The first child of Erma and Allie, Alice Emily Shaw, was born March 29, 1932. In the summer of 1933 I was enlisted to help watch the one-year-old girl who could soon run away from Erma.

Loss of Home

Five children followed. When the 6th was age 2 1/2 the

family met disaster. On a cold blustering evening a few days before Christmas, 1943, the old house on the hill burned to the ground. Erma had had a busy day. She had carried water from the puncheon at the barn to heat for laundry. She had hung the wash on the veranda. She had a batch of mincemeat on the stove and was cooking supper. The fire sprang from a broken jug of kerosene at the heating stove in the far hall. Besides most of their household goods, they lost many personal valuables: e.g., two engagement rings, Erma's and her mother's.

 I remember going with Father, Mother, Alice MacKenzie and Kate Hovey, to visit the Shaw family in part of Guy Christian's house. Father presented an envelope of money that he and my brothers had put together. I was then on a Christmas leave from Montreal. In early July 1944, before embarkation, Claude and I visited Erma in hospital in Woodstock. David had been born June 30th. My next visit was in winter of 1946, after returning from overseas. The family was then living in a new house with electric wiring and running water. There was one more child, Annie Mae, born in Hartland, December, 1945, near the second anniversary of the fire. The children of Erma and Allison Shaw, the first six born in Middle Simonds, are:

  Alice Emily, born March 29, 1932
  Margaret Elizabeth, born November 19, 1933
  Eleanor Lucretia, born February 4, 1935
  George Edward, born March 15, 1936
  Mary Jane, born September 25, 1938
  John Allison, born June 4, 1941
  Ira David, born June 30, 1944
  Annie Mae, born December 8, 1945.

 In the growing –up years of the eight children there were many escapades. One, though alarming at the time, is dramatic, in retrospect: One day Annie Mae came in with a bleeding hand – one finger missing. She had been holding a stick of wood for David to cut on the chopping block. Erma accosted David: "Did you cut off her finger? He replied, "I didn't cut 'em all off." Minimizing can be learned at a very early age. They searched but didn't find the finger.

Erma and Allie were devoted parents. Erma made clothes for them, sometimes cutting down and sewing worn garments. They were rewarded with a devoted and appreciative family.

Retirement Years

Allison Shaw, after being superannuated from government employment, worked as a purchasing agent for Harry Greenlaw of Millville, a potato shipper. When their youngest child was nearly 10 Erma returned to teaching. In fall of 1955 she drove a 1/2 ton truck to St. Thomas. In January she returned to Simonds Schoool. In 1926 she had been Bernard Dickinson's first teacher. In 1956 She became the first teacher of his son Sheldon. After three years at Simonds, Erma taught grades 1 and 2 at Somerville, for a year.

Allie lived past age 88; he died October 17, 1966. In January, 1967, Erma went to Bear Point, Shelburne Co., N.S. She kept house for her son-in-law, Rev. Bill Monroe, and two boys, while Margaret was convalescing in the Sanatorium at Kentville, N.S.

Over her 27 years as a widow, Erma's many visits to her children took her to Maine, Massachusetts, Montreal, Kingston, Fredericton and Saint John. In the summer of 1984, with Eleanor, Annie Mae and Dennis Tysick, and their children, Erma motored across the continent. They visited David and family in Vancouver. Erma's children made many visits to Simonds, especially in summer. They travelled far to celebrate both her 80th and her 85th birthdays in Simonds. Many other relatives and friends joined them.

Erma had a strong commitment to maintaining family

ties. At a gathering at her house, July 28, 1967, we made plans to begin Corey family reunions, and launch "The Corey Courier".

Family Memoirs

In autumn of 1992 Erma asked her sisters to help her write biographies of our father's brothers and sisters. It was immediately referred to me. In the second week of November 1992 Margaret and I visited Erma in Simonds. She celebrated our arrival by inviting our siblings to gather for a supper. During that week I began writing family stories from her recollections and from clippings and letters she had preserved. In the ensuing months my sisters and I visited her several more times – at her home and at Alice Long's in Somerville where she made her home that winter. It turned out that Erma had less than a year left to be with us. It is indeed fortunate that in that time she thought of a book on Corey history. The writing fell to me and became a monumental task over the ensuing decade. Erma's memories became invaluable contributions.

In her last winter Erma spent a few weeks in hospital in Woodstock. Mary Jane visited Alice and spent some days with their mother. Erma was told of a growth in her abdomen. Surgery was discussed. She spent some weeks of her last summer at her home, enjoying visits by her children. She remained alert with a clear memory almost to her end. On my last visit with her, I said, "You have a strong faith." She replied, "I want you to put that in the book."

Erma died October 8, 1993, past age 90. At her funeral in Advent Christian Church, Simonds, her son-in-law, Bill Monroe, in his sermon, expressed much appreciation. Burial is in the nearby cemetery, beside Allie. Their children gathered. Some of them still gather for summer holidays at the Shaw home. In August of 2001 Bill Monroe was painting the house.

Children and Grandchildren of Erma and Allison Shaw

Alice Emily Shaw, born March 29, 1932, graduated from Teachers College, Fredericton, and taught school in Carleton Co., N.B. In 1953 Alice married Rev. James William Long at Advent Christian church, Middle Simonds. James was a farmer and pastor of country churches in Carleton Co. They lived in Somerville where "they raised eleven children":

Wanda Grace Long, born March 12, 1954, attended Vocational School in Woodstock, boarding with Maude and Bob Corey. Wanda worked as a secretary in Fredericton. She married Robert Gartley at Wesleyan Church, Woodstock. After living in Moncton they have returned to Woodstock. After a heart attack and open-heart surgery Robert has returned "to work with some limitations." At Richwil Truck Centre, Jacksonville, he is "a mechanic and a reefer specialist" in cold storage and refrigeration. Wanda and Robert have a daughter, Cheyenne Dawn Gartley, born October 2, 1982.

Charles Allan Long, born March 1, 1955, married Muriel Crouse, at United Baptist Church, Waterville. They live in Simonds. Alan is employed by Department of Transport. They have two children: Christina, and Joseph Allan.

James William (Billy) Long, born May 26, 1956, married Wendy Victoria Jones at United Baptist Church, Centreville, N.B. They reside in Charleston. Billy is a self-employed woodcutter. They have three daughters: Shannon, Sarah and Katherine. Shannon entered N.B.B.I. in 1996. In 1999 she married John Blois. Their daughter: Haley Blois. Sarah married Aaron Munn, 1999. They have a son Blake Munn, and a daughter, Brooke Isabel Munn, born January 17, 2002.

Constance (Connie) Jean Long, born December 14, 1957, married Gordon Morrison at Peoples Church, Somerville. They live in Rothesay, N.B. Gordon works for Thornes Hardware, Saint John. Connie teaches Sunday School at Rothesay Baptist Church. They have two sons: Timothy and

Graham Morrison.

Frank Allison Long, born September 19, 1959, worked in farm labor in Somerville. He married Sherry Brewer, September 27, 1997, at Devon Park Baptist Church, Fredericton. They have lived in Zealand, Woodstock and Nackawick, following construction work. They have two children: Gabrielle and Joseph.

Paul Arthur Wilfred Long, born September 9, 1960, married Janet Greer at United Baptist Church, Mount Pleasant. They reside in Somerville. Paul is a finish carpenter; Janet is a nurse at Woodstock Hospital. Their children: Corey and Jillian Long.

John Edward Long, born October 14, 1961, married Nancy Jean Wood at Zion Presbyterian Church, East River St. Mary's, Pictou Co., N.S. They reside in Somerville. John is employed in farm management. Nancy is an elementary teacher's aid in Woodstock. Their children: James William III and Gina Marlene.

Emily Alice Long, born December 4, 1962, married Murray Black, at Wesleyan Church, Somerville. Murray brought to the marriage two children: Lacey and Noah. They reside in Carsonville, Kings Co. Murray is a woods worker. Emily has been teaching grade 1 at Sussex Corner for 17 years. Her only time off was for maternity leave for her two children: Jessica and Danielle.

Barbara Lorraine Long, born January 22, 1964, married Neil Craig, at Peoples Church, Somerville. They reside in Lower Windsor, N.B. Neil is a mechanic at Richwil Truck Centre, Jacksonville. Their children: Marlene, Katrina and Edward.

Gary Brian Long, born April 26, 1968, graduated from N.B.B.I. 1990, and became a missionary in youth work with the Canadian Sunday School Mission. After being Assistant Director at Hampton Bible Camp, he became Director of Cape Breton Bible Camp, Bras d'Or, N.S. in 1995. Gary married Christina Hatt at Rothesay Baptist Church. Their children:

Breanne, Erica, Colby and Jared.

Shawn Anthony Long, born March 29, 1973, is a grandson of Alice and James Long. He was reared as a son. Shawn married Nancy Havens at Wesleyan Church, Somerville. He is employed by Mid Valley Co-op, Jacksonville. Nancy is a social worker with the Department of Health, Woodstock. Their children: Braden Noel, and Derrah Rachelle.

Rev. James William Long died December 29, 1989. Alice Long lives at their home in Somerville.

Margaret Elizabeth Shaw, born November 19, 1933 graduated from Berkshire Christian College, Lennox, Mass. There, at the chapel, she married William Monroe. Among the guests were: Margaret's parents, Erma and Allie Shaw, and Margaret's Uncle Jud Corey and family, then living in Conway, Mass. Bill is an Advent Christian minister. Their first church was at Bear Point, N.S. They were then expecting to be going to India as missionaries. Margaret was diagnosed with tuberculosis and spent about a year in sanatorium in Kentville. Back in New England they served two churches: Springfield, Vt. 14 years, and Friendship, Me., 11 years. They have retired to East Waterford, Me. Bill does interim pastoral work. Margaret and Bill's two sons:

John Monroe graduated from Houghton College, New York State, in 1986. He received a master's degree from Rochester Institute of Technology. He married Lydia Wilson at Free Methodist Church, Rochester, N.Y. where Lydia was Minister of Christian Education. John is Assistant Professor of Computer Science at Roberts Wesleyan College, Rochester. Lydia is at home with their children: Abigail and Aaron.

Philip Monroe graduated from Berkshire Christian College and Westminster Theological Seminary in Philadelphia. In 1990 Philip married Kimberly Vinal at Advent Christian Church, Windsor, Conn. She was Personnel Director, North Park College, Chicago, Ill. In 1999 Philip received a doctorate in psychology from Wheaton College, Ill. He is now chair of the

Psychology Department at Bible Seminary, Hatfield, Pa. Their children: Samuel and Jared.

Eleanor Lucretia Shaw, born February 4, 1935, graduated from Berkshire Christian College, Lennox. She worked as a secretary, first at that college, then at Piedmont Bible College, Winston-Salem, N.C., for 25 years. Since 1994 she has been secretary to the Minister of Music at Calvary Baptist Church, Winston-Salem. Eleanor's adopted son, Paul Ryan Hesman, married Penny Jamison. They have a daughter: Kathryn Joy.

George Edward Shaw, born March 15, 1936, married Ida McLean, at Peoples Church, Somerville. Edward worked as a carpenter and contractor in Framingham, Mass. They also lived in Natick and Marlboro, and in Worcester where he administered the Odd Fellows Nursing Home. In 1985 at Indianapolis, he was installed as Sovereign Grand Master of I.O.O.F. Lodge. His mother, Erma Shaw, John and Jean, and Margaret Monroe attended a banquet in his honour at Natick. Ida, after working several years, suffered a stroke and paralysis. She gained back skills, e.g., in knitting. They have sold their properties in Massachusetts and in Wells, Maine and have bought a house in Dowling Park, Florida. Children of Edward and Ida Shaw:

Susan Shaw, married 2, James Martis at First Congregational Church, Pelham, N.H. Jim is a restaurant owner; Susan is a business contract administrator in Pelham.

Linda Shaw, married David Fair at Mary and Martha Chapel, Sudbury, Mass. They live in Framingham. David sells insurance. Linda does "at home" childcare. Their children: David, Brian and Lydia.

Corey Shaw married Barbara Pettepit at Montigo Bay, Jamaica. They live in Candia, N.H. Corey is an advertising salesman. Barbara is manager of an animal shelter with The Humane Society.

Mary Jane Shaw, born September 25, 1938, married 1, Richard Taylor of Chipman, N.B. They had one daughter,

Malinda, who married Bruce Bellefeuille, at Bethel Baptist Church, St. Laurent, PQ. They moved to Nova Scotia in 1985. Bruce completed his studies for a Master's in Recreation at Acadia in 1987 and became a Recreation Director at a hospital in St. John's Newfoundland. Later they worked in the Halifax-Dartmouth area – Malinda as a special educator in the Halifax-Dartmouth School System. They lived in Beaverbank, N.S. They are now in St. Catharines, Ontario. Bruce is teaching in an alternative school. Their children: Sara and Drew.

Mary Jane married 2, Nicholas Granato at Bethel Baptist Church, St. Laurent. Nick worked with Readers Digest over 26 years in Montreal. After early retirement for his health, they moved to Burlington, Ontario. Mary and Nick have a son and a daughter:

Anthony Granato, after graduating from McGill University in 1996, with a major in English Literature, went to Ansung, S. Korea, to teach English in a Junior High School. Back in Montreal he has been teaching language at McGill and another college. His special interest is teaching English as second language. He has been on a speaking tour promoting a course in teaching language. He spoke at Oxford University.

Tina began college in Montreal, moved to Nova Scotia, lived with Malinda and Bruce, graduated from Dalhousie University with a major in psychology, then went to Mount St. Vincent to obtain a teacher's license. She is now teaching in St. Catherines, Ontario.

John Allison Shaw, born June 4, 1941, married Jean Myshrall at St. Dunstan's Church in Fredericton, N.B. After graduating from U.N.B. in engineering John worked for N.B. Power in Fredericton, and later at Point Lepreau Generating Station. Jean worked at the pharmacy at St. Joseph's Hospital, and later at Saint John Regional Hospital. In 1995 John and Jean went to Atlanta, Ga. John was on an 18-month exchange with a power station there. He resumed work at Point Lepreau until 2001, when he retired from N.B. Power. In August 2001

John and Jean left Saint John for China. John is helping set up a nuclear power plant. In winter of 2002 they were having time to travel, e.g., to Bangkok, Thailand. The three children of John and Jean have scattered:

Graham Shaw graduated from Dalhousie University, 1995; went to Japan and taught English for two years; then took a position with an insurance company in Toronto. In August 1998 Graham married Susannah Fenner, in Toronto. They have a son Ethan Shaw.

David Matthew Shaw, after high school at Millidgeville North, had a course in Retail Meat Cutting at King's Tech., Kentville, N.S. He worked at meat cutting and packaging in the N.S. Valley and in Dartmouth. He has also worked at the Q.E.II hospital complex in Halifax. David has travelled to the Philippines about three times. There he attended Antioch Bible Training Centre. His study included homelitics, hermeneutics and missionology. His experience included work with an orphanage, with homeless street children, and in street meetings. Back home, he has spoken at Tabernacle Life Church, W. Florenceville. David Shaw married Angela McClement, October 13, 2001, at New Covenant Christian Centre, Dartmouth.

Heather Ann Shaw, during high school in Saint John, competed in swimming. She was on summer staff at Camp Medley. In 1995 she began studies at McMaster University, Hamilton, Ontario, in arts and sciences. She took time out for travel to New Zealand. In October, 2001, she attended David's wedding in Dartmouth. She was then teaching in St. Stephen, N.B.

Ira David Shaw, born June 30, 1944, married Lillian Smith. They lived in Simonds. Search for steadier work took him to Vancouver. He married 2, Susan Coombs. They had two children: Tammy, adopted by David; and James. In 1990 David married 3, Dorothy Markham. In Vancouver, David worked in security; now he is building superintendent of a large shopping centre. Dorothy is a store manager for Smith Books. Tammy also lives and works in Vancouver. Jim joined sea cadets, travelled on ships, and took part of his high school while at sea.

Annie Mae Shaw, born December 8, 1945, went from high school to nurses' training in Fredericton. She nursed at Kingston General Hospital, Ontario. On April 13, 1968, Annie Mae married Dennis Tysick, of Kingston, at Advent Christian Church, Middle Simonds, N.B. The reception was at White Swan Inn, Somerville. Dennis was employed in Social Services with the Ontario Department of Health. They have three children:

Mark Tysick married Sharon Willard. Both attended Queens University, Kingston. Sharon received a degree in Law, 1996. They moved to Ottawa. Sharon began articling at the Supreme Court of Canada. Mark graduated from Ottawa University of Medicine with B.Sc. in Nursing 1997. They have moved to New Liskeard, Ontario. Sharon is working with a law firm there. They have three children: Cole, David and Brooklyn Anne.

Laurie Anne Tysick graduated in 1998 from Queens University with a major in Concurrent Education. In 1999 she married Perry Allen Milbury of Simonds, N.B. They both taught at Wesleyan Day School in Sussex N.B. Now both are teaching at Grenville Christian College Brockville, Ontario. It has a boarding school for grades 7 – 12. It includes international students.

Wesley Tysick continued his high school course in a community college, working toward a license in carpentry and construction. He is engaged to Melissa.[4]

1912 Wilfred James Corey 1945

Wilfred Corey, first child of Nellie and Ira Corey, was born September 9, 1912, at the homestead of Grandfather Alfred Corey in Knowlesville. Family tradition is that Alfred named his grandson for Sir Wilfred Laurier, Prime Minister of Canada, 1896 to 1911.

Wilfred Corey attended school in Knowlesville, and East Knowlesville beginning in 1922 when the family moved there.

Before age 10 Wilfred learned to handle horses. Mother used to say that he began so young that he had to climb up on the manager to put the collar and harness on a horse. I recall his quick, adept splicing of a rein or harness strap with copper rivets hammered on a piece of railway track. In his early teens he was handling a pair of horses in winter logging. At age 16 he was driving one of Ira's teams down Newcomb Gulch hauling logs to the mill at South Knowlesville.

He spent several winters of his late teens and early 20's working a team, yarding and hauling logs: One of Ira's teams to Ed White's camp above Divide; Frank Wheeler's team to a Flemming and Gibson camp; Ira's team to N. Branch. Haying took him one summer to Chesley Dingee's, E. Glassville.

Romance came to Wilfred when Lottie Whitehouse invited the Knowlesville teacher to accompany her on a walk one spring evening to the Corey farm in E. Knowlesville. When Lottie and the teacher, Pearl Irving, made a move to return to Knowlesville, Wilfred said, "I'll drive you home." Soon he had the car at the door.

E'er long Pearl had endeared herself to the whole family. She spent a Christmas Eve at the farm. She introduced the game of Black Magic and had us all carried away with fun. She recalls how wonderful it felt to be part of a large family at Christmas time. Kaye recalled that Pearl was in love with all the boys. However she said, years later, "I got the pick of the boys." Pearl and Wilfred had a little time in the living room, but it was punctuated by boots and socks dropping through the heat vent from the boys' room overhead.

Marriage

I have a vivid recollection of seeing Pearl sitting in the car on Main St., Woodstock, in June 1941. I was near to graduating from Woodstock High School. Wilfred was in an office. She told me, with enthusiasm, "We just bought a farm." It was at Lower Brighton. The price of farm, machinery and house with furniture was $1,100. Later she recollected, "We each had saved $500.00. " How did you locate the place? "My father knew Guy Richardson, a neighbour."

Pearl Irving and Wilfred Corey were married in July 1941, at the Baptist Parsonage in Florenceville. Rob and Mrs. Irving and Ira and Nellie Corey were there. Honeymoon was most convenient – at the farm in L. Brighton. The previous owners had even left kitchenware and dishes. To make it more romantic, there was a patch of ripening strawberries.

There was eagerness in the Corey family to help the newly-wed couple in their first major task – haying. They spent part of July with us in E. Knowlesville. Wilfred supervised the haying at Ira Corey's. Father was travelling his new Belgian horse. Pearl kept house while mother, in need of a rest, accepted Kate Hovey's invitation to visit with her. Pearl recalls, "I used the spring-loaded manual washing machine." A boy pushed the washer.

Ira's hay in the barn, we went to Lower Brighton to help Wilfred cut, rake and put his hay in the barn. Claude, Jud and Warren took two pairs of horses, and a wagon with hayrack. There was a big crop of hay; no grain had been planted that season. We had an interesting change. There was time for a dip in the river that marked one border of the farm. The farmhouse was comfortably outfitted with beds, chesterfield, kitchenware and table.

After some early fall ploughing, they closed the place for the winter. Pearl went back to the Irvings in Coldstream and to a teaching position at Bannon. Wilfred went with his father's logging crew to the North Branch, and in the late winter, worked at Juniper Mill. In the winter months Pearl boarded in Bannon. They managed an occasional weekend at the Irving farmhouse. Mr. Irving took his team to a job at McAdam. The young couple planned to have a weekend to themselves. Sadly, a big snowstorm blocked the roads and their plan.

In the spring of 1942 both fathers helped the young couple get outfitted for farming. Pearl said, "My father gave us a cow and a cook stove. Wilfred's father bought him a horse, from Burnham's in Florenceville. Wilfred bought the mate to him. Thus he acquired a pair of westerns, not very well broken. To make it easier for him they made a temporary exchange. Bob and Warren broke one of them with a well-trained horse at the E. Knowlesville farm. Bob got kicked in the abdomen and landed in Bath hospital. He took it all nonchalantly.

In September 1942, Warren and I made another visit to Lower Brighton. We arrived in Hartland by train, from a summer job in Ontario. At suppertime when Wilfred came from ploughing, he said, "We'll dig the potatoes tomorrow." We completed harvesting them on Saturday. I went home that evening. Warren stayed to plough for the next year's crop.

Wilfred Corey with Pearl and baby, Harold Wayne

Pearl and Wilfred had one son: Harold Wayne Corey, born October 1, 1942, while Warren was at the farm. Pearl recalls, "I went directly from the hospital to my mother's with the baby."

In a few days Warren, age 17, arrived in E. Knowlesville from Lower Brighton, driving Wilfred's team. That winter Wilfred worked his team for his father's logging crew on the North Branch. In the late winter he and Warren hauled logs for Pinder in Divide.

Wilfred and Pearl kept close contact with his family

in E. Knowlesville. Kaye Foster kept a photo of Wilfred holding the baby, at about one year. Kaye says, "Harold Wayne was a most beautiful baby with blond curls." Erma recalled, "Wilfred also had hair hanging in ringlets."

A Treasured Farewell

The happy life of Wilfred, Pearl and Harold Corey together was short. The last time I saw Wilfred was at the C.P.R. Station in Woodstock, in early July 1944. I had been home on leave before going overseas. We had had a family gathering at the farm in E. Knowlesville on a Sunday. Knowing that I would be on the train, they drove to Woodstock to say goodbye to me during the "stop". He ran up and touched me on the back as I was about to board the train.

The following winter, 1945, I received a letter in Europe from Mother telling me that Wilfred was in hospital in Fredericton, and that Father and some of my brothers were visiting him. They stayed overnight at Rusagonis with Aunt Alice and Uncle Jud.

Keith Corey recalls working with Wilfred on his farm before he went to hospital: "I went by train from Bristol; Wilfred met me at Hartland. We hauled manure out to his fields on the snow. He was not feeling very well, and became worse." Pearl recalls, "Wilfred became ill with haemorrhaging from his bowel. I travelled to Fredericton on weekends. My father and mother stayed with Harold. Keith did the barn work at the farm." Keith recollects: "There were three or four cows to milk and calves, pigs and a pair of horses to look after."

Pearl recollected attempts at blood transfusion for Wilfred: "Some of his brothers were ready to donate in Fredericton. There was rejection; the types didn't match." After six weeks in Fredericton, Wilfred came home to their farm. Later they took him to hospital in Bath. Norman recollected: "I gave Wilfred blood. At Bath they put me on a bed and rolled it alongside Wilfred's bed for a direct transfusion."

Later they brought Wilfred to Pearl's parents in Coldstream. They set up a bed in their living room. Mr. Irving, in a conversation with me after I returned from overseas, said "Wilfred was in much pain and discomfort. I knew he was not sleeping, so I used to go downstairs and talk to him in the night. He told me, 'I'm not going to get better. I want you to sell the farm and try to get a good price for Pearl.'"

After a few weeks at Irvings' they returned Wilfred to Bath Hospital. Claude arrived home from Europe before Wilfred died on July 2nd, 1945. The family visited often. Pearl was with him to the end. His funeral was in the Knowlesville Baptist Church, conducted by our uncle, Rev. J.A. Corey, who had also visited Wilfred in hospital, giving him spiritual comfort. Norman recollects the pallbearers: six brothers: Bob, Norman, Tom, Claude, Warren and Keith. Wilfred's monument is in Forest Hill Cemetery, Esdraelon. Immediately on returning home from the funeral Mother expressed some of her grief in a letter to me. I received it with the sad news about three weeks later, in Holland.

Pearl, with Harold approaching three, lived with her parents for a year. Then she had her Uncle Harry Irving build her a house in Hartland. She said, "I kept boarders; at one time I had five." In 1947 Pearl married Philip Boyd of Peel. They have a son, Larry Boyd. Later they moved to Peel, where Harold and Larry had fun with a horse and buggy. After Larry began school Pearl returned to teaching, bringing her total years to 29. Pearl has maintained relations with the Corey relatives. She and Philip have attended many family gatherings. At the 1995 Corey Reunion in Knowlesville, in an interview with John Corey, Pearl expressed, to the delight of all present, happy memories of Wilfred and appreciation of the whole Ira branch of Coreys.

Harold Wayne Corey and Family

Harold Wayne Corey attended the two-year course in Industrial Arts in Moncton and became a high school shop teacher in Florenceville and Bristol. Harold married Ellen Harris of Simonds. Their first home was Pearl's house in Hartland. Later Harold used his skill in construction to build a new house at Lansdowne. For a time Harold and family lived next to the family of cousin, Ross Corey. They kept foxes together.

Harold and Ellen have a son, Clifford Wayne Corey, born April 30, 1965, and a daughter, Cynthia Elizabeth, born October 11, 1967.

Clifford graduated from Community College, Moncton, in 1985. He works for the Department of Transport. Clifford married Leisa MacAllister, in 1988. Their Children: Joshua, born September 27, 1988; Ashley, born January 2, 1990; and Jordan, born April 30, 1991. They live near their great-grandmother, Pearl Boyd in Peel. With help from his father, Harold, Clifford built a new house on a piece of land that Philip Boyd gave them from his farm. He says, "It is the best investment I ever made." They visit the Boyds often – daily before they began school in Forenceville. Then Leisa began preparation for a career by enrolling in Business College.

Cynthia Elizabeth Corey married Kenneth Kinney, in 1987. They have a son Adrian, born June 1997. Kenneth is a custodian at Bristol High School. Cynthia, after working in an insurance office in Hartland, is now employed at Thomas Equipment, Centreville. The family is living at Upper Kent and is making plans to sell their house there and move to Bristol.

Ellen and Harold are living in a new house in Wakefield. Harold began constructing it during a "deferred" leave from teaching, 1993-94. In 1995 Harold retired from teaching. In the fall of 1998 his retirement was interrupted by a shock while moose hunting with a friend. Harold lost the normal use of one leg. Ellen visited him regularly in hospital in Saint John,

Woodstock and Fredericton. He also had many visits from other family members and friends. With the help of weeks of therapy he progressed to wheelchair, then crutches, then to walking. He was much encouraged when he recovered his driver's license in the fall of 2000. Until then, Cousin Gary Corey was taking Harold for rides.

Ellen is employed in an insurance office in Hartland. She graduated from Community College, Woodstock, in 1985. Visitors to Ellen and Harold on a summer day enjoy the scenery from their deck overlooking the Saint John River. They enjoy frequent visits from their children and grandchildren. On October 15, 2001 Clifford brought his three children. He picked up Joshua from a football game in Hartland. The writer was a dinner guest with them.

1914 John Robert Corey 1987

On April 23, 1914, at the Alfred Corey homestead, Knowlesville, the second son was born to Nellie and Ira Corey. They named him John Robert after two uncles; his father's Uncle John Kierstead, who was also born on April 23rd, and his mother's Uncle Bob Carr. Bob early acquired the reputation of being quiet and little spoken. In his earliest years this quiet trait saved him from reprimands. Sometimes when his father was out working, Bob would get under the table, undress his feet, let his feelings run riot, and carry on a laughing spree. When Father came home, Nellie would report the pranks and "goings on". Father would say, "You needn't tell me anything about Bob. No foolishness could have come out of him." Mother later came to appreciate Bob's quiet disposition and his trait of carefully choosing his words and his times of speaking. She would say, "Bob never speaks but what he says something."

Erma recollected: Early in his life Bob exhibited an ability to draw and sketch. His sister, Erma, said, "Bob was a great artist. He could draw anything he saw, and was doing it at a very early age," even before he had quite out-grown his baby talk. He seemed to be fascinated with chickens and hens. Fred Fletcher, who visited the family in that era, as well as later, remembered Bob as "the chicken man." When his mother gave Bob a dish of food, he would take it out into the yard, sit down with it and the chicks would come flocking to eat. One of his earliest drawings was "a rooster and hens". He went to the hen house and made careful observations. When he returned to the house his mother asked, "Did you see what you wanted?" He reported, "I couldn't get a very good look at the rooster. He had his pick down eating." The drawing came out very well despite the limited observations. Erma said, "he gave me a group of drawings. Among them was a cluster of lilies that he saw on the front cover of a magazine."

The Corey family's move to E. Knowlesville was fortunate for Bob, eight years old that spring of 1922. A teacher at the E. Knowlesville School quickly recognized Bob's talent. She sent to a mail order house for some special instructions and instruments for drawing. That provided an impetus for a series of productions of beautiful drawings.

Bob never became so immersed in drawing that he forgot the activities of the farm or the community, though it may seem regrettable that Bob's talent for drawing was set aside for the work of farm and forest. In any case, Bob was not averse to the work of farm and forest. He quickly learned to work with tools, implements and horses. Some of his artistry, it seems, translated into carpentry. His handiwork emerged in doors, a pair of horses on the door of the horsebarn, in gates, wagon boxes, pig troughs, ladders, shingled roofs, windmills on the house and the granary and in bird houses in the trees.

Bob never shied away from hard work with his hands. Bob, like many of the youth of his time, grew up to find work in lumber camps by winter and farms by summer. He worked for Charlie Crawford about two years, later for Tom Guthrie a few summers. He never had difficulty in getting employment. If his father needed him for a lumbering operation Bob was quick to work a pair of horses at yarding and "hauling off", at McCrossin Place, at South Branch, and at North Branch. Bob described to the writer the trip from North Branch to Juniper after breaking camp in late February 1942. They drove their horses over an unbroken logging road through the Teague Brook area. They had to take turns being lead team breaking road. Snow fell on the backs of the horses from the heavy-laden fir and spruce boughs that overhung the road.

After a brief stop at the Hemphill/Corey farm, Bob undertook another logging operation at Skeddaddle Ridge. Charles Long had a contract cutting for Sam Bell. Bob took one of Ira's teams to assist in the end-of-winter hauling to Howard Brook. The road came down a steep hill over a cordroy bridge that spanned the deepest part of a gulch. With his first load he let his horses run. Charles Long heard the clink of heels against the runners and ran out from his filing shack. He breathed a sigh of relief when Bob navigated the hill. Subsequently, Bob accepted Charles' counsel to hold back the horses, Jimmie Long recollected.

During their time in E. Knowlesville two sons were born to Maude and Bob Corey:

Gary Wilfred, October 12, 1947, and

John Wayne, April 4, 1949.

Gary still brings up images of his childhood on the E. Knowlesville farm: "The puncheons of water in the woodshed; my mother catching trout from the brook; Keith shooting a deer; Mother and Marjorie rushing with knives; Tom putting me on a horse's back." That farming partnership continued until 1950 when Tom and Marjorie moved to Glassville to start retailing groceries at the former Hovey store.

Gary's recollections go to age five: "Parking the car at the mail box; riding a toboggan down the hill with Dad and John. Dad transporting the neighborhood kids to school in a box shelter with built-in benches carried on bobsleds. Dad, Warren and Keith cutting trees; a limb hitting Dad on the head making a bleeding cut that sent him to Dr. Chestnut in Hartland."

In 1952 Bob and Maude bought a farm at Richmond Corner. Before they moved Bob did fall ploughing there for two weeks. In preparation for the family's move they had Osbert Whitehouse stay there and build cupboards in the kitchen. Colby Orser of E. Knowlesville trucked all their cattle to their new farm. They bought a new 1952 car.

The Corey Family at Richmond Corner

The family enlarged. A third son, Ira Peter, was born July 27, 1955. Ira Corey, grandfather, spent a large part of his last year with them. He died in the farmhouse, March 14, 1957.

John remembers outings with their cousin, Harold Wayne Corey. "We always took him with us on our annual fishing trip on the South Branch. We drove to Foreston, then up to South Ridge, then walked the 'red line' to the stream."

At Richmond Corner, the three boys attended the one-room school that accommodated eight grades. The writer's children, Frederic and Carolyn, attended with them for a few weeks in 1959 when we were between moves. Gary is helping plan a school reunion for August 2002.

John Corey has good memories of his life on the farm at Richmond Corner from age 3 through most of high school. He recalls Bob's care of his fences. Before all the snow melted he shovelled some of it from his fences to prevent sagging of wires and displacing of posts. By tightening the wires he could keep his cattle in the pasture with only two strands of barbed wire. John recollected further, "Gary and I asked to see the inside of the house. The hardwood floors that we had laid upstairs, and everything else in the house, was unchanged". What did change was the way of life for the whole family. Before finishing high school the boys were being lured to other work. Two weeks before he graduated from Woodstock Vocational School in 1966, Gary was offered a job with Department of Public works now Transportation. That summer he began work with the highway crew at $1.40 an hour.

In September, he was approached by the office of technical training. Soon he obtained his license for operating trucks and snowploughs. In March 1967, Gary was sent to Fredericton for a two-month course. It was the beginning of a series of winter courses on his way to becoming an Engineering Technician.

In 1967 John graduated from South Carleton High School, on the Houlton Road. He recognizes that he benefited by the school provisions brought in by Premier Louis Robichaud.

With the boys inclined toward other careers, and the work on the farm not getting any easier, Bob and Maude sold that farm in 1967 and bought a house and moved to Chapel St., Woodstock.

The Family in Woodstock and Beyond

Bob worked on farm machinery for Wilson Equipment. At the big house on Chapel Street, Bob, in a sense, returned to his artistry. Being relieved of the work of field and barn, and having evenings and Saturdays free, he turned his hand to woodwork. He began to make benches, tables and chairs, and birdhouses.

John and Peter benefited from residence in Woodstock. Peter graduated in 1973 from the new Woodstock High School on Connell Road. From there he went to Bethany Bible College, Sussex. John had one year at the new high school before going to Moncton Technical Institute where he earned a diploma in Mechanical Technology. Then he worked for Acadia Pulp and Paper in Nelson Miramichi.

In September 1971 John Corey and Carolyn Montgomery were married at the United Baptist Church,

Hartland. On their honeymoon they stopped in Moncton for Carolyn's graduation in nursing. In Fredericton, their first residence, Carolyn had her first nursing position at Victoria Hospital. John became a student at U.N.B. In 1973 their son Robert was born. Carolyn found that nursing, in addition to caring for a baby, was too much. John got a part-time job.

Ira Peter Corey

Peter lived with John and Carolyn part of a year. Peter had a year of working and travelling following Bethany. He worked with a roofer in Fredericton. He made a trip to Scotland.

During his year at Bethany College, Peter had lessons from Randolph Nicholson, the painter of logging scenes.

In June 1975 Peter married Lee Dunn, daughter of Bertha and Bernie Dunn of South Bay, Saint John. They went to Moncton. At the Technical Institute, Peter began a course in Civil Technology. He also took extra-curricular lessons in painting. John said, "Peter made some rather accomplished paintings."

Sadly and tragically, Peter's life, with great talent and much promise, was cut short. On thanksgiving weekend, 1976, Peter and Lee left Moncton bound for the wedding of Peter's cousin, Ross Corey to Janice Petley, on October 9 at Forenceville. Peter was driving on rain drenched pavement. Near the Moncton end of the Cole's Island cut-off, two cars from Quebec were travelling toward Moncton. The first car passed; the second slid sideways and hit the front end of Peter's car. The collision was fatal for the couple in the colliding car, R.C.M.P. reported.

Peter suffered a severe head injury and bleeding. After momentary alertness he became unconscious. A scan at Moncton Hospital indicated that he was brain dead. Maude and Bob travelled to Moncton and stayed with Peter until he died on

Sunday night. Lee sustained critical injuries in the accident.

Bernie Dunn came to Woodstock, visited with the family and the many relatives and attended the funeral at the house, and the Wesleyan Church. Burial is in Hartland. Lee took several months to recover.

John spoke of Peter's paintings: "Lee kept some. We have two; one, a seaside scene, is at our cottage at Beulah. Gary has one."

Gary Wilfred Corey

Gary came into the Transportation Department when there was a boom in highway construction. In summer of 1967 he worked at soils inspection on a stretch of Trans Canada Highway between Florenceville and River de Chute.

In January 1968, Gary began at U.N.B., a three-month course of training in construction calculating. Over the following three or four years he pursued courses in engineering. I remember Bob telling me that he strongly advised Gary to stick with the courses, though it was difficult at times. He did, until he became a Certified Engineering Technician. Gary worked in highway construction in years 1967 to 1982. Gary married Anne Currie. Their son Jason A. Corey was born September 3, 1972. On the wall of his room, Jason had one of the best drawings of his grandfather, J. Robert Corey – a teddy bear on skates.

John Wayne Corey

John and Carolyn stayed in Fredericton until 1975 when John received from U.N.B. a B.Sc. in mechanical engineering. Then they went to Dalhousie, N.B. John worked for International Paper. In the spring of 1975 Bob and Maude, enroute to Dalhousie, stopped at Four Falls to see me. During the two-year stay of John and Carolyn in Dalhousie their daughter, Elizabeth, was born.

In May 1977 John began work with McCain Foods, Florenceville, N.B. Son, Peter, was born in Florenceville.

Bob's Late Years

In 1979 Bob and Maude sold the big house on Chapel Street and bought a more compact house on Elizabeth Street. Again Bob set up a workshop in the basement with his tools neatly arranged. In this period they enjoyed some leisure including some travel, which increased when Bob retired from Wilson Equipment. They took their trailer often to Beulah. They went with a group to Newfoundland. As Bob's physical energy began to wane he turned to a more sedentary form of artistry – needlepoint. His favourite subject was horses. Several of his artistic productions adorned their walls. He gave some to other members of his family.

J. Robert and Maude Corey

Bob ever remained modest about his artistic ability. At a Corey reunion in Knowlesville we persuaded him to produce a sketch of the old barn at the Alfred Corey homestead. We caught him at a time and a place where he could not escape. We got him seated at a table. We put a newsprint in front of him and a pencil in his hand. "Now please draw the old barn." He quickly called up an image of its shape, and immediately translated the image through the pencil to the paper. A rare moment of artistry. We are preserving the sketch.

In his latter years, Bob experienced some health problems. A heart condition brought him to Saint John. He also suffered a circulation problem in one foot. Eventually he had it amputated in Chalmers Hospital, Fredericton. A few days after the surgery he succumbed from a clot on December 19, 1987.

At Bob's funeral, December 22 in Wesleyan Church, Woodstock, the Minister, Rev. Stillman Cameron, used the text that described Barnabus, "He was a good man." Much to the comfort of the family the pastor expanded on his description of Bob as a good man. This is an attribute that we all cherish for Bob, and will long remember. Interment is in Greenwood Cemetery, Hartland. On August 29, 1992, Maude married Clair Shaw. We continued to be welcomed at Elizabeth St. Bob's brothers have enjoyed the fries of trout caught by Gary.

Gary and John in Later Years

Gary began working as bridge superintendent in 1982 – initially for the winter. It continued until 1990. Gary's next position was Highway Maintenance Superintendent. In 1993 he became the Manager of Maintenance. That year Gary was diagnosed with Parkinson's Disease. He continued on his job without much interruption for the next year, though he also had to deal with divorce papers in 1993.

Gary recalls my shaking his hand at the Corey Christmas gathering at Ross and Janice's restaurant, Florenceville, and saying to him, "Things will get better." I guess I was thinking of overcoming the loneliness of separation. From 1994 through May 2000 Gary maintained his work position, occasionally taking sick leave for a month or two.

Gary recounted further: "In 1997 I applied for long-term disability, but I wasn't ready to give up. I had to prove I could go back to my position as maintenance manager. Later I decided to re-apply for long-term disability, and after a four-month sick leave, began disability benefits."

The year since Gary began disability benefits has been

eventful. In December 2000 he married 2, Donna Billings Beck at Millville. They bought a fifth wheel travel trailer, and have been as far as Pennsylvania, to Mount Carleton, N.B., to Waterville, N.S. to visit his nephew, Robert Corey, and to Montreal to visit Gary's son, Jason.

Jason Andrew Corey

Jason Corey, born 1972, has been pursuing graduate study in music and recording of music. He has the support of both his parents, Gary and Anne, though both have remarried. Jason received a B.A. from St. Francis Xavier University in 1994. Since then he received an M.A. in music from McGill University. Since 1997 he has been working there on a Ph.D. in sound engineering.

In October 2001 Gary, Donna and Jason's grandmother, Maude, visited Jason in Montreal. Together they prepared "a beautiful Thanksgiving dinner." Jason's grandmother wants to go to his graduation in June 2002.

John is now Chief Engineer of Energy Systems. He has corporate responsibility for all McCain plants, which has taken him to England, France, Belgium, Holland, Colombia, Argentina, Australia and Tasmania. He has visited 80% of the McCain plants. Their children in school, Carolyn returned to nursing casually at Bath hospital.

John also works in healthcare – managing his own health. After being diagnosed with a mild heart condition, arrhythmia, John experienced a session of medication, and received a pacemaker. He says, "it was ruining my life." A big factor in John's management of his health is diet. He is a relative vegetarian, allowing "some fish and occasionally a little meat." He says, "Diet has transformed my life. My heart now functions well." Try having breakfast with him, as I did, October 20, 2001. You'll enjoy a variety of fruit.

From their comfortable livingroom in Somerville, John

and Carolyn can look across the Saint John River and see the whole town of Hartland. In the spring of 2000 they moved there from Florenceville.

Children of Carolyn and John Corey

Robert John, born November 18, 1973
Elizabeth Ruth, born September 23, 1975
Peter Edward, born April 4, 1978

Robert John Corey

From Carleton North High School, Bristol, Robbie went to Nova Scotia Agricultural College, Truro. He received a B.Sc., in animal science. At the college he met Pamela Bond, also a degree student. They were married in her home community, Upper Rawdon, N.S., December 17, 1994. Robert worked briefly in acquaculture in Nova Scotia. He also worked for a feed company in New Brunswick, living in Florenceville and travelling over the province, advising farmers.

Robert is now a salesman for Scotian Gold. They live in Waterville N.S. He and Pamela are also building a business of their own, "Pioneer Organics." They sell supplies, e.g., seeds and food, to organic farmers. Their children:
Jessica born February 16, 1996
Luke Robert, born November 18, 1997

Elizabeth Ruth Corey Hoyt

Elizabeth Corey married Jeff Hoyt in August 1998. Both are graduates of Bethany Bible College. They had a year of church ministry in Florida. Then they returned to New Brunswick, first to Moncton, then to Perth, where they have bought a house. Jeff is Assistant Pastor of the Wesleyan Church in Andover. Elizabeth and Jeff have two daughters:

Emily Hoyt and
Alexis Hoyt

Peter Edward Corey

After graduating from Carleton North High School, Peter spent a year at Bethany College, Sussex. Then he went to Nova Scotia Agricultural College, Truro. Thanks to six credits from Bethany College, Peter was able to complete, in three and one half years, his B.Sc. in Acquaculture. In March 2001 he began work with Deer Island Salmon.

On May 12, 2001, right after graduation, Peter married Esther Weatherby. They live in Mace's Bay, N.B. and attend the Baptist Church there. Peter is now working for Heritage Salmon. Peter has interest in humanitarian projects in third world countries. John and Carolyn, after seeing their three children married and settled have begun some trips for pleasure and learning. In summer 2001 they flew to Zambia. There they visited a Wesleyan sponsored hospital with an eye-care clinic. In August 2001, accompanied by Gladys Tracy, they went sight-seeing in Paris.

1914 Alice Corey McKenzie 1971

Alice Marie, first daughter of Nellie and Ira Corey, was born at the Alfred Corey homestead
in Knowlesville, November 8, 1915. With the Corey family, she moved to the former Hemphill farm in E. Knowlesville in the spring of 1922. Alice is listed among the pupils at the E. Knowlesville School in the fall of 1922.

Alice is also on the Glassville school register for 1930 and 1931. Family memory is that she was helping at the home of the Rev. Frank Little who is listed in Glassville History, p.74, for 1929-30. Norman thinks Alice went to Glassville to help Kate Hovey and thence was enlisted to help at the manse.

For some years Alice was the only girl at home among a large family of boys. She was almost 15 when her sister Kathleen was born. Kaye said, "Alice was a second mother to me. She doted on me, curled my hair, made clothes for me and dressed me up. She worked side-by-side with Mum in looking after the family and the house."

At the beginning of July, 1936, Alice Corey married Frederick B. MacKenzie, from the bordering farm. They were married by the Baptist minister in Hartland. Erma and Allie Shaw stood with them. Fred McKenzie had worked in Detroit during the construction boom of late 20's and early 30's. He brought home a new 1930 Chevrolet from Detroit which lasted him 20 years. Locally, he worked in farming and logging, e.g., for Simms and Hemphill families and for Ira Corey at McCrossin fields.

After marriage they lived briefly with the Corey family. One summer they were both at the Jessie Tedford farm, Windsor. Early in their marriage Alice and Fred lived at Howard Brook. Fred became a stationary engineer, overseeing the steam boiler at Smith Brothers' mill. In that time two children were born to Alice and Fred:
    Shirley Anne MacKenzie, 1939
    Frederick Allison MacKenzie, 1940

Alice's first childbirth was difficult. She needed longer than the usual rest period. Pearl Irving stayed with her for a week. Kathleen Corey, not yet nine, stayed longer.

On the Farm

About 1942 the family moved to the MacKenzie farm in E. Knowlesville. They took care of Malcolm MacKenzie, Sr. He had become a widower in the early 30's. Fred kept dairy cows and beef cattle, and grew grain and potatoes. Alice did much of the tending of their extensive garden. Shirley said, "Dad liked to hoe it in evenings after a day of heavier work. Alice canned many vegetables.

Kathleen, who sometimes stayed with her and helped with the housework recalls some of Alice's handiwork: a woodbox from tongue and grooved boards, complete with legs; a door for the bottom of the stairway. She papered and painted. She upholstered furniture. Kaye also described Alice's artistry, e.g., in preparing for a "basket social" she covered a box with crepe paper and decorated it with creeping moss and flowers

Alice was skilful in sewing, embroidery and knitting. She made clothes for herself and for the children. Her daughter, Shirley, recalls that she could lay a garment on a paper, draw the pattern around it, cut the cloth and make the garment. She also could cut an adult jacket to fit a child. Shirley Anne added, "She was a terrific cook. If visitors came she could whip up a meal in amazingly short time."

Visitors

Wilfred MacKenzie came from Michigan with his wife, Ernestine. She saw Alice bring out ingredients for a cake. Ernestine went for a short errand and returned to find the cake out of the oven and being frosted. Shirley Anne has good memories of relatives visiting them. Malcolm MacKenzie, Jr., before going to Africa as a missionary, fascinated them with descriptions of the snakes he anticipated seeing there.

Shirley Anne also described a visit they made to Campobello Island: "Dad made a spontaneous decision one weekend to take us there. We visited Mayford Anthony at Welshpool. Berta was away. Dad hadn't bothered to phone. Mother did the cooking. We stayed two nights. We were fascinated to see the beach when the tide was out."

A delightful memory Shirley Anne has of growing up on the MacKenzie farm was sliding on the hills, including those on the adjacent McEwen place. "Dad made bobsleds, painted red – three connected together. Mother took us out in the evenings in the moonlight. She was a good sport."

Education and Leaving Home

Shirley Anne and Freddie went to the same school that Alice and Fred attended – a short walk from their home. Shirley has photos showing that the pupils from Knowlesville, not having a teacher in their own school one term, joined with the pupils in E. Knowlesville. Later – after Shirley completed grade two – the E. Knowlesville youngsters were transported to Knowlesville School.

After graduating from Juniper High School, Shirley MacKenzie went to Teachers' College, Fredericton. She taught one year at a school in S. Devon. In 1960 she married Earl W. Jacques, son of Rev. Earl L. Jacques of Fredericton.

After finishing grade nine in Juniper, Frederick Allison MacKenzie (Freddie) spent three winters in the Agricultural Course at the Vocational School, Woodstock. Later he spent a year at the auto mechanics course in Moncton. After two more years on the farm in E. Knowlesville he began work in 1962 as a mechanic with J. Clark and Son, Woodstock.

Alice in Later Years

Alice, in the latter part of her life, did not enjoy good health. Her last year or more was fraught with much pain, suffering, and diminishing strength. In a letter dated April 14, 1971 to me in Albany, N.Y., my mother wrote, ".....Alice MacKenzie is in Southern Carleton Hospital, Woodstock. This winter she has been in hospital in Bath, Saint John and Fredericton.... Awful hard on Fred; he is doing everything that can be done for her."

Eventually a large tumour was discovered and removed from her abdomen. Regrettably it was very late in being diagnosed. Shirley and Kathleen, at a critical point, phoned Shirley

Anne who took her mother to hospital in Fredericton.

In a letter dated May 13, 1971, also to me in Albany, Kathleen Foster wrote, "Alice seems to be much the same; she is starting her fourth week home – takes the pills every four hours and eats almost nothing. Shirley Brooks and I spend one day a week with her and have managed to do quite a bit of her house cleaning."

With Mother and other family members, I visited her in the summer of 1971. They prepared a picnic supper. We took her in a car up to the field where Fred was haying. As he ate he expressed his regret: "Alice can't eat." Later, Shirley Brooks recalled, "I went nearly every day; I bathed her and cooked cream of wheat, about the only food she could eat."

In September, 1971, Alice was returned to hospital in Woodstock. I visited her one Saturday there. Maude Corey stayed with her through her last night. Alice died in the hospital on September 25, 1971. Her funeral began with prayers at the McKenzie home in E. Knowlesville. Service at Knowlesville Baptist Church was conducted by Rev. Philip Giberson, assisted by Rev. Otis Shaw. Burial was at Forest Hill Cemetery, Esdraelon.

Fred MacKenzie

In a conversation on December 19, 2001, Shirley Anne said, "Dad stopped living when Mum died." Fred McKenzie remained at the farm in E. Knowlesville for a few years, but soon reduced his farming. He sold his cattle in 1972. Fred had family visitors. Some of Alice's siblings came on Saturday evenings. Fred hosted them with a pot of beans.

In 1977 Erma Shaw and I stopped to visit him enroute to Juniper to visit Mother. Freddie and Shirley Anne visited. Shirley said, "I'd clean his house." It became increasingly difficult. Fred lost interest in housekeeping. He took a few trips, e.g., to Nova Scotia where he bought a new car, casually.

At length he left the farm for a care home, first at Upper Woodstock. When he stopped driving, Freddie took him out for rides. Later Fred was in care at Bath Manor. His end came suddenly at the Carleton Manor, Woodstock. Shirley Ann said, "I received phone calls, but before I could get there he had died."— in November, 1983. His funeral was in Knowlesville Church; burial in Esdraelon.

Shirley Anne MacKenzie Jacques

After residing several years on Argyle St. in Fredericton, Shirley Anne and Earl Jacques moved to Fredericton North, first to an apartment. In Spring 2001 they purchased a house. Shirley and Earle have two daughters and a son:
Tammy Joy, born July 28, 1961,
Peggy Lee, born October 4, 1964,
Anthony Earl Frederick,
born February 13, 1968

Shirley, with Earl and their children, made a return visit to Campobello Island. "We saw the Roosevelt home."

Tammy Jacques married Doug Boyd of Fredericton. He was dealing in computer software. They lived for 1 1/2 years in Chilliwack, B.C. In 1999 they moved to Cambridge, Ontario. They have one daughter Jessica, born 1987. Tammy has been diabetic since age 4 1/2 and needs frequent needle injections.

Peggy Jacques married Laurier (Larry) Latouche, on June 2, 2001. In June they moved to Kitchener, Ontario. Larry works there in carpentry, carpet laying and electrical work. Peggy works in the seafood department of Zehr, though she went to Business College and took some courses in university. Her mother said, "She has to be moving."

In December 2001 Shirley and Earl Jacques motored to Ontario to visit both daughters and deliver baked goods and knitted wear.

Anthony Jacques is living in Grande-Digue, N.B. In

March 2001 he moved there from Harvey, N.B. Anthony is a draftsman working for an engineering firm. He has a large garden, producing many tomatoes and vegetables. He does much canning, pickling and jam-making. Anthony has a fiancée, Patti Doiron. She was at Dalhousie University. She is working as a registered Respiratory Therapist.

In 1968 **Freddie** married Shirley Higgins from Riley Brook on the Tobique River. They have a son and a daughter:

Malcolm MacKenzie, born April 18, 1970

Deborah MacKenzie, born February 12, 1983

Malcolm drives transport trucks over long distances. Now that he drives only in Canada he is able to be home more.

Deborah started school the year her brother finished. In the fall of 2000 Deborah was injured seriously in a collision with a tractor-trailer on the Trans Canada Highway. She spent nine days in hospital in Fredericton, initially in intensive care. They put a screw in her ankle and repaired a dislocated knee. She healed well at home and has only a slight limp. Despite losing time in her last year because of the accident, she graduated from Woodstock High School in June 2001. She is working at Buntings Grocery, and is planning to go to the School of Aesthetics, Moncton.

Freddie MacKenzie worked as a mechanic for J. Clark and Son for 37 years. At the end of 1999 he began retirement. He spent the next year and a half working on their house, which they have owned since 1972.

In summer of 2001 Freddie and Shirley took a three-week trip to Western Canada. After a week in Winnipeg they went to Alberta. At Three Hills they visited his Uncle Malcolm MazKenzie and two of their children, Dan and Beth at nearby Prairie Bible Institute, Drumheller, Alberta. On their return journey Freddie and Shirley stopped at Swift Current and at Ottawa to visit the Parliament Buildings.

In 2000 Freddie sold the E. Knowlesville farm to Crabbe Lumber Co., except for 12 acres of front land. He had been renting the farmland, and had cut wood for himself. Recently he sold the house with two acres to Evan Harrington, Argyle.

Freddie now describes himself as semi-retired; he says he is now ready to start looking for something more to do.

Norman Redlon Corey

Norman Corey, born October 16, 1917, at the Alfred Corey homestead in Knowlesville, had a critical struggle with typhoid pneumonia at about age 4 1/2. At the farm in E. Knowlesville, beginning in 1922, Norman soon regained his strength. He attended school in E. Knowlesville. One winter in his early teens he expanded his school experience. "I went to school in Centre Glassville. I did chores for Olys and Wilma Brown. Olys was working for Clarks at a camp on Elliot Brook." The daughters of Clement and Myrtle Perry remembered Norman. In his growing up years Norman learned to do farm work. Early in life he worked for George W. and Cecil Whitehouse in Knowlesville.[5] About the time W.W II broke out in 1939 Norman was on a harvest excursion in Western Canada. When he returned home that fall he joined his father's logging crew on the South Branch of the Miramichi. The following winter his work in the same place was interrupted by military training.

Military Training

Norman recollected, "In January 1941 I began the 30-day basic training in Fredericton. I was driving one of Dad's teams. I seem to remember January 10th as the morning I left the camp and walked to Glassville. In Glassville I met up with Jack McBrine who was also going for the training. We got a ride to Bristol where we boarded the train. At Hartland, Hilton

Manuel and Arthur Wasson joined us. It was evening when the train arrived in Fredericton.

"At the station, army officers met us. One of them called out names. My name was last of the list called to make up a platoon. Jack McBrine shouted, 'You made a mistake, Sir,' and jumped in with my group too. They let him stay. The four of us from Knowlesville and Glassville: Hilton Manuel, Arthur Wasson, Jack McBrine and I were together in that training period.

"At the end of the 30-day training I went back to the lumber camp and took back the reins of the horses. After a few days I came down with measles, not knowing I had contracted them in Fredericton. In three or four days I was hauling logs again. My brother, Claude, was sleeping with me. He got measles too – a more severe case. When he thought he had recovered he had a relapse. He got to a doctor at Bristol and came back with medicine. I set the alarm clock to give him his medicine, two or three times a night."

Norman made another try at military service. "In the spring I went to Woodstock. At the recruiting station I met with Johnnie McBrine who was also going through the medical tests." One of the doctors examining Norman saw the scar from the surgery when he had pneumonia as a boy. "The doctor sent me to the hospital for x'rays." Norman's physical fitness for military service was questioned.

Farming and Marriage

Norman managed Roy Caldwell's farm in Lower Windsor for several years.

In 1946 Norman married Velma Ellis of Windsor. About that time they bought the Robert Irving farm in East Coldstream. Warren Corey was a partner in the farm, and in their logging. Norman and Velma had one son, Norman Dale Corey, born September 1, 1948, in Hartland, N.B. From the farm, Norman and Velma moved to Windsor, N.B. They bought the former Hatfield store. Velma died there of cancer in 1952.

In 1953 Norman went to Toronto. He worked for Ford Motor Company, in Oakville, for 25 1/2 years. In June 1964 Norman married Marjorie Rogers. Members of Norman's family drove from New Brunswick to Toronto for the church wedding: Bob Corey, Alice MacKenzie, Alice and David Corey, and Paul, Shirley and Jane Brooks.

On September 30, 1980, Norman began an early retirement from Ford Company. His next work was selling real estate in Burlington, Ontario, where they live. In preparation for that work he took upgrading, and then a Real Estate course. After rather strenuous studying he acquired a Real Estate license in 1981, at age 64. Norman continued in real estate for ten years, sometimes attaining highest sales of the month.

Volunteering

In Burlington Norman is a volunteer. "In 1991, I began ten weeks training for 'telephone counselling' at the "Crossroads" program of 100 Huntley St. In May 1992 I began telephone counselling two mornings a week, 8:30 a.m. to 1:00 p.m. People phone in asking for prayer. Also, one morning a week I go to Bethany Residence, a home for handicapped people of various ages. With other volunteers, we do 'ministry' in prayer and song."

Norman's son, Norman Dale Corey, married Diane Breesen. They have a son Scott Andrew Corey, born July 11, 1986. Diane is working for a taxi company. After working as a dispatcher she is now in the office. Dale has his own courier business. He makes deliveries in Mississauga, Niagara and as far as Brockton. Dale, Diane, and Scott live in Mississauga. They visit Norman and Marjorie quite often.

Home-Coming

Throughout the almost half century that Norman has been living in Ontario he has made visits to his family members in Carleton Co. almost yearly. He looks up many long-time friends, e.g., Milo Clark. Norman has spoken at Tabernacle Life Church, Florenceville. He has brought his grandson, Scott Andrew, with him. Marjorie recognizes that, "Norman needs his family." Some years she has accompanied him. In late years she has stayed near her mother, who lived in a nearby apartment. Marjorie's mother died in January 2002, at age 95 1/2.

Norman very much likes to keep in touch with siblings, and to have news from them. He appreciates phone calls. He has been very helpful with recollections for this history.

1919 Thomas Wallace Corey 1975

Tom Corey was born at the Alfred Corey homestead, Knowlesville, on October 16, 1919, the day his brother Norman was age two. I remember Tom as a kind of mentor of my sibling group. When I began school some of the older siblings had already left school. Norman attended briefly.

Tom had much interest in the wildlife, especially birds. He helped us discover birds' nests in the fields and trees. He told us the names: gray birds, juncos, chickadees, snow bunting, sparrows. I think he took much interest in the nature studies in school.

In some ways Tom took his younger siblings under protection. One spring, carrying our lard-pail lunches, we hiked through the field where the sheep pastured. One morning the billy made a run to butt us. Tom instructed us: "We'll all lie on our bellies so he can't hurt us." The billy came close and sniffed us; we lay still. After a few moments the billy and the flock moved away. We picked up our lunch pails and continued to school.

Tom took a good interest in school as long as he was there. At age 15 he quit quite abruptly, without finishing grade eight, and began building a little camp on the edge of our brook. Every time Don Hunter met Tom in the neighbourhood he would ask, "Have you got your camp built yet, Tom?" Warren says Don was hoping to get Tom back. He was a good student; he had learned Algebra. Perhaps Tom was following an inclination to work with his hands and be creative. In his teens he made articles from wood. For example, he was eager to learn how to make snowshoes. Ralph Boyd brought miniature snowshoes to school and gave some instruction on weaving the rawhide mesh into the bows. One winter Tom undertook to make a pair of snowshoes. He cut ash, split it into long strips, boiled water and steamed the ash strips so he could bend them around the frame he had also made.

Quite early in his teens Tom went on a venture down the railway perhaps near Benton or Debec. He was part of a small crew cutting pulp for Kenneth Smith. They slept in a granary on hay. When a night train came roaring by, Tom was frightened. Images of the world coming to an end troubled his waking mind.

Tom early learned all the skills of farming and logging. He hauled high loads of logs out of the McCrossin. He became a good teamster.

As the elder brothers began to work away from home, Tom assumed a leading role. He drove the best team. One spring and summer he experienced a series of runaways that became amusing in retrospect, though embarrassing at the time.

In one episode he had backed the horses into the machine shed and was letting barrels down from the loft onto the sloven wagon. A barrel dropped, frightening the western horses; they took off. In another episode Tom was riding the roller. One horse lowered his head below the pole, hooked his bridle on the end of the pole and pulled his bridle off. Again the horses took off. Tom had to jump off.

The third episode had the whole family in intense anxiety. The team was standing on the barn floor. After we had unloaded the hayrack, Tom noticed that the bridles had been switched. He decided to exchange them. As soon as he slipped one bridle off, the horses took off. The big doors were open. What made the most anxiety, especially for mother standing watching helplessly, was that Gordon, then only about four, was lying on the bottom of the hayrack holding onto rungs. The horses crashed over a fence twice, made about three wild circles over fields and around buildings. Meantime Father opened the sliding doors of the horse barn. Finally they ran into the barn, making a brake on the doorframe.

To all the skills connected to farming and logging, Tom added culinary skills.

Military Training

In the spring of 1941 after concluding a winter as cookee at his father's lumber camp on the South Branch, Tom Corey went to Fredericton for basic training. Clifton Billings, then living in Cloverdale, went at the same time. He recalled, "In April 1941 we got on the train at Hartland and went to Fredericton together. We were good friends throughout the training period in Fredericton." Their friendship extended into travelling together to and from home on some weekend leaves.

Clifton recollected further, "At the completion of the three-month basic training period we had choices about where we might go from Fredericton. We expected to go together to the next posting." But Tom failed medical checks on account of a heart murmur and in July 1941 was discharged.

Perhaps the heart condition was a precursor of a condition more serious than he or any of us were aware.

Tom resumed work in farming and lumbering. He was the cook for his father's crew on the North Branch of the Miramichi in fall and winter of 1941/42. Later he cooked for

Tom Corey and Marjorie Cook

other crews.

In May 1943 he visited me in the Lancaster Hospital. I was a patient there recovering from mumps. He was in Saint John cooking for Clayton Clarke's crew of men who were handling a shipment of fertilizer. For one or more summers Tom worked with Walter Whitehouse at the Victoria Corner farm.

There he met Marjorie Cook. In summer of 1945, Tom, in partnership with his brother Bob, took over the farm in E. Knowlesville from Ira Corey. That fall Tom married Marjorie Cook. In 1950 Tom and Marjorie moved to Glassville having purchased the Hovey store. E'er long Marjorie was managing the store. Tom was in demand as a cook in lumber camps. He cooked for Horace Clarke's crew —perhaps for two winters. The Flemming Company helped facilitate his home visits by lending their jeep. Gordon Corey recalls driving Tom to the camp on Sunday nights.

Children of Marjorie and Tom Corey

Brenda born 1947, lived a few weeks
Roger born May 25, 1950
Ross born August 15, 1955
Neil born August 15, 1958

Tom Corey, with son, Roger

The boys all graduated from Regional High School, then in Florenceville, N.B.

Tom's later phase of work was his own enterprise. He purchased wooded lots or paid stumpage and had men cutting logs and pulp by contract. Gordon recollects that Tom had a bulldozer and a loader.

Tom used some of his resources and contributed generously to two churches; first a small Reformed Baptist meeting place in Glassville. It became part of the Wesleyan denomination and joined with the Bristol congregation. Tom contributed to the building of the new Trinity Wesleyan church in Bristol.

Heart Condition

About 1972 Tom was advised of a heart condition. He found it hard to accept and hard to slow his pace. Carvell Shaw, reporting on a cruising of Erma Shaw's woodlot, said "I couldn't keep up with him." I found no indication that he slowed up; instead it seems he continued apace with his activities. In two springs, 1974 and 1975, we made maple syrup. We tapped trees and gathered sap in a maple stand along the road to Bristol. We boiled it in his yard. Helpers were Chris, Neil and Ross Corey.

Heart failure came suddenly. In early July 1975 on a Friday afternoon Tom hitched his travel trailer to his car and started for Camp Beulah to attend the summer meetings. On the road between Glassville and Bristol he experienced chest pain; he stopped his car and entered his trailer for a rest. His son Ross happened along, stopped to investigate, put him in his vehicle and started for Bath Hospital. Tom died enroute, on July 4, 1975.

Tom's funeral was held in Trinity Wesleyan Church, Bristol, the new church that Tom had helped to build. Marjorie continued to manage the store in Glassville through the summer of 1976. Then she bought a house in Woodstock and moved there in September 1976.

Marjorie Corey married George Murray on June 29, 1993, in Woodstock.

Roger Thomas Corey

After high school Roger went to Moncton Technical Institute, then to a position with Department of Transport, now Navigation Canada, Air Traffic branch. On August 11, 1973

Roger married Judy Bubar, daughter of Katherine and Weldon Bubar, Simonds. They built a house on Magnetic Hill. Judy is a nurse at Moncton City Hospital. They have one son, Matthew Roger Corey, born April 17, 1983.

Matthew attended Wesleyan Academy through grade nine. He had grades 10, 11 and 12 at Riverview High School. He travelled with Roger whose office is in Riverview. Matthew had a summer enterprise: "Power Washing: siding, driveways, decks," in summer of 2001. That fall he went to Atlantic Baptist University, in walking distance from their home.

Roger had a heart bypass in March 1994 at Saint John Regional Hospital. I visited him there. Roger has long been involved with singing groups which has involved much weekend travel. In summer of 2001 he was in a quartet, "Emmaus Road." He brought Judy and Matthew to the Corey gathering at the home of Ross and Janice on August 4; on August 11 his quartet was singing at Rusagonis.

Ross Brent Corey

Ross Corey, h.s. graduation

After one year at University of N.B., Ross returned home and worked in his father's enterprise in woodcutting. In Tom's last years, 1974-75 Ross worked with him. Ross has continued with that enterprise ever since.

On October 9, 1976 Ross married Janice, daughter of Mr. & Mrs. Thomas Petley at United Baptist Church, Florenceville. After a short residence in Simonds they built a house in Lansdowne.

Their company is now called Corewood. Janice is a partner. Ross contracts cutting on private woodlots. He also buys land or pays stumpage. He has two, two-man crews working with skidders, bulldozers and excavators. They work in Carleton County – last summer in Greenfield.

Earlier, Ross, in partnership with Neil, had a furniture store in Florenceville. They also had a restaurant on the edge of the Trans Canada Highway. Janice, who had her own profession as a secretary, became an early-rising cook, making fresh rolls every morning.

Now the building is rented by Fastrax, a trucking company. Corey's also have a storage building with spaces for rent; and an apartment building with eight rental units.

Ross and Janice have a daughter and a son:
>Sarah Dawn Corey, born May 27, 1981, and
>Thomas Ross Corey, born December 19, 1986.

Thomas plays hockey. He has a work shop in the garage.

Coreys of Ira branch at Lansdowne, 1999

He likes to build and paint wood productions. His ambition is to take over the business.

A hobby that Ross pursues in company with his cousin, Kris Foster is searching and gathering parts of abandoned farm machinery. In their entry he has cast iron seats. From the iron ends of a seeder he has made a magazine rack. Janice and Ross have been very hospitable toward Corey relatives. They have hosted home gatherings at Christmas and picnics on their spacious grounds in summer.

Sterling Neil Corey

Neil attended Community College in Saint John and then went to Moncton for a course in heavy equipment. Later, with his brother Ross, he managed a furniture store in Florenceville. He now works for Valley Ridge furniture, Fredericton. He travels to furniture exhibits to make selective purchases of furniture. On July 2, 1983 at Wesleyan Church, Woodstock, Neil married Brenda, daughter of Mr. & Mrs. Edward Currie, Woodstock. They live at Starlight village in Hanwell. They have two sons:

Scott Andrew Corey, born July 29, 1986,
Simon Neil Corey, born November 7, 1990.

The whole family is involved in the Wesleyan Church, Fredericton. Neil serves as sound technician, and Director of Stockade. Simon is in Stockade Boys and in children's choir. Scott is in the youth group. In summer of 2001 they called on Warren Corey in Port Alberni, B.C.

1921 Claude Eugene Corey 1964

Claude was the last of the children of Ira and Nellie Corey born at the Alfred Corey homestead, Knowlesville, September 10, 1921.

One incident that bonded us together in boyhood,

though neither of us was old enough to remember it, was falling into the puncheon of spring water at the E. Knowlesville farm. We held onto the rim of the puncheon until family members returned from picking berries and pulled us out.

The beginning of school for Claude was a frightening, dreaded experience.

Claude, in his teens and later, is remembered for being especially kind and thoughtful; e.g., going to Glassville, perhaps to have a horse shod, and coming back with a milk pitcher from Derrah's store for his mother.

Claude spent his last Christmas before military service at his father's logging camp on the North Branch of the Miramichi. The horses had been taken in boxcars by C.N. Rail. It was not feasible to bring them out for the Christmas break. Claude volunteered to stay at camp and take care of the horses.

My most cherished memories of my brother Claude are the brief contacts we had during military service. In the fall of 1942 Claude went to Fredericton to the basic training camp. When his brother, Jud, came to Fredericton for the same training beginning in February 1943, he visited Claude and a friend, Weldon Bubar, from Coldstream. They were in an army hut hospital recovering from mumps.

Jud and Claude Corey, at Corey farm, 1943

Claude and I had some camaraderie in off-duty hours and on weekends for a few weeks. Soon his basic training was completed and our paths parted.

Claude was sent to far away British Columbia. He was

stationed at Prince George for a time and also on Vancouver Island. Nanaimo was his address for a while. He must have spent a year or more in British Columbia in training and on guard duty. He was granted leaves to come home to New Brunswick. He made the long journey by train probably twice. It took, I think, six days each way. On a trip in the spring of 1944 he stopped in Montreal between trains to see me at Douglas Hall, McGill University. I was in the C.A.U.C.

During one of his leaves we were home together for at least one weekend at the farm in East Knowlesville. A family picture shows Claude and me and all the family members in Carleton County, N.B., and Murray Kenney and family from Maine having a

Last family gathering before embarkation, 1944

Sunday picnic around tables set up in the farmyard.

Our paths crossed again, briefly, in England in early fall of 1944. I had been in signal training – Morse code and radio operation – at Camp Borden, near the little town of Alton since July. As soon as I had received his message I went to his camp at Aldershot, a short train ride away. I made several visits in the few days he was there. We also saw our Uncle Elbridge Brown who was at Aldershot at the same time.

My last visit was on a Sunday afternoon, the day of Claude's departure for the European front. He was marching in parades all over the camp, picking up pieces of equipment and clothing at various points. I followed him as long as I could. We talked each time the parade halted for a break. Those were poignant moments for me, thinking of Claude going as an infantryman into the costly battles then being fought following the allied invasion of the continent that had begun on D-day, in June of that year.

Through that fall I had anxious moments as the newspapers carried reports of casualties and described the desperate engagements Canadians were involved in.

Following is a letter I received in England from Claude in Belgium:

November 6, 1944

Dear Jud:

I received your letter yesterday; it came fast. I was surprised to hear from you so soon and also very glad to get the other letters too as I have not received any mail from home yet, but surely it will come soon. Well, I am out of the front lines for a change; our unit is out for a rest. I had a couple days leave, so I am not fairing too bad. We are staying in private homes here as they have not got any barracks as yet. I should have written yesterday but I didn't get up until ten o'clock; those white sheets and nice bed, as you spoke about, sure (are) nice for a change. Tilley and I have a room to ourselves. It seems almost like home, so I sort of took it easy yesterday. I was to a show last night; it was English spoken....

I also can get ice cream here…; also the Canadian legion is here with candy bars, lifesavers, soap, etc.…So, take it all around I am pretty well off, I think.

Yes, as you say, Papa wrote a very interesting letter. I have written to him a couple of times myself, but as you know I have no reply as yet. He also wrote to me a couple of times in Debert. I am glad to know that they are getting my mail at home. They at least know how I am getting along. I sure have had some strange experiences since my travels in these countries. Sometimes I wonder how I came through alive.

Well Jud, I guess this will be all for now, just a few lines to keep in touch with you. These few lines will let you know I am quite content where I am.

Love, brother, Claude

Excerpts from other letters from Claude:

"My chum Dickinson was transferred to another company but I met Tilley Johnston (you know, Jean Perry's husband). He sure is good company. He and I are in the same platoon." (More on Tilley below).

"I was in this same town about a month ago, that (was) when I was just passing through, as I did not do any fighting in France. I may not have to do any more for a while; I sure hope not."

Claude was in that battle area of Northern Europe all that last winter of the war. In the spring, 1945, I received a letter that he had written from a hospital in the south of England. I think the town was Horsham, which is in West Sussex.

Thinking I was still in England, he said, "Come to see me as soon as you can." The trip to Horsham would have been very easy from my last station in England, Tonbridge, in Kent.

In March of that year, 1945, I had gone to the continent. None of my letters written from the continent had reached him. His letter caught up to me in Holland or Germany. Near the end of the war in the spring of 1945, in Germany or Holland, Claude was shot in the forearm, near his elbow.

Jud Corey, overseas, 1945

In rare moments, after returning home, Claude was able to talk to a few close relatives, including Paul Brooks, about that traumatic brush with death. He said bullets were whizzing all around. After he was shot he was left with only one other person. After a little while that other fellow disappeared. Claude didn't know if he survived or not. All those who were still able, moved forward. Through the long painful hours of that day Claude was left alone in fear. Toward evening a man came and rescued him and took him several miles in a jeep to an emergency hospital.

Later he was taken to the hospital in England where he wrote his letter to me. Before I got back to England on leave, Claude had gone home early in the summer of 1945.

When he reported back to his military unit following a leave at home they discovered pneumonia. Then pleurisy developed. Then they diagnosed tuberculosis. He spent three years, 1945-48, in Saint John, a patient alternately at the D.V.A.

Hospital, Lancaster, and the Sanatorium, East Saint John.

Family members visited him. Father and I came from Juniper on the train to Saint John in winter of 1946. We stayed with Esther and Harold Smith. Warren drove his car taking Keith and me to Saint John that spring. I also visited him on my way to and from Acadia University. Claude also had visits from friends including Jean and Tilley Johnston.

The friendship between Claude Corey and Tilley Johnston must have been especially meaningful to both. In the fall of 1997 I phoned Jean's sister, Jackie O'Brien, in Saint John. Jackie knew about the friendship. She said, "Tilley never stopped talking about Claude." She said both Tilley and Jean were teachers. They taught in the West and finally made their home on Salt Spring Island, B.C.

Jean wrote to me: "Yes Tilley and Claude were in battle together. One story Tilley often laughed about was when they were being shelled and they had a shovel under their packs and as they were crawling under a barbed wire fence Tilley's shovel got caught. Claude extricated him.....We visited Claude in the Sanatorium in Saint John after Tilley came home. Also Tilley visited him in Glassville one summer when we were home. He was fond of Claude." Tilley died in 1990 of "viral pneumonia", on the way back from visiting their daughter in Michigan.

The D.V.A. Hospital where Claude was a patient was on the same street where I now live, Lancaster Ave. In the 90's that hospital was demolished.

Claude's convalescence was long, slow, and somewhat painful. The doctors collapsed one lung to enable it to heal. After three years in Saint John he came home to Carleton County. His treatment continued with periodic appointments at the Bath Hospital for "pneumo" treatment. He described it: They inserted a needle and forced air between the lung and the wall to keep the lung collapsed until healing was complete.

Claude's work after release from hospital was with N.B. Power Commission. As he travelled over a large section of

Carleton County reading meters, he demonstrated "a peculiar ability to enter quickly into friendly relations with people;" he earned a host of friends.

In 1949 Claude married Alice Jones. Most of their married life they resided in Glassville in the house built and occupied by Jim and Kate Hovey. Alice and Claude Corey were blessed with five children:

    David born June 5, 1950,
    Gregory born April 13, 1954,
    Catherine Grace Helen born March 31, 1956,
    Joan Carlene, born June 3, 1959,
    William born July 11, 1962.

To his children Claude brought the ability to love and be loved.

Growing up in Glassville

Kathy, in anticipation of her wedding celebration September 2001, recalled stories of her father's affection in her childhood. When she was five or six, wanting to help him build a garage, she picked up a hammer and nails and tried to nail on a board. "I hit my finger; he carried me into the kitchen and held me a few moments before he went back out."

She recalled another memorable moment of affection from grade two: "I missed the bus one morning. He drove me to school. I asked, 'Can I go with you for the day?' After hesitation he said, 'You should go to school; your mother won't know where you are.' 'We can phone her, and I have my lunch.'" As she coaxed him she felt the warmth of his affection wanting to comply to a child's wish, but knowing that the place for a little girl was in school. To soothe the disappointment he gave her a nickel.

Another memory of Kathy's we'll call "the warmth of affection in the cold of winter." Her Dad went out to scrape off the snow and frost, start the motor, then come back in for a moment. "Before he left he gave me a kiss. His cold cheeks gave me a warm feeling."

Claude liked to be out in the woods and on the brooks, perhaps more so after having been confined for three years. When the boys were bigger he took them fishing. Paul Foster said, "Claude went fishing nearly every Saturday in summer. He was a great fellow to go fishing and hunting with. He had all the equipment organized, e.g., a bundle of kindling wood ready to fry trout".

He did voluntary work at the United Church, e.g., "putting squares on the basement ceiling." Also he was treasurer of the church.

It seems that Claude carried the effects of the war the rest of his life. One January day in 1964 Claude suffered a pain in his chest. He stopped to see Dr Chestnut in Hartland and then tried to continue his work. In mid-afternoon pain forced him to stop reading meters and come home.

In a letter to me Alice recounted the night's experience; he awoke in agony. She phoned Dr. Chestnut who advised, "Call an ambulance and take him to hospital immediately." She had a local nurse come to give him a sedative. They stopped in Bristol to have Dr. Burley give him another sedative. Alice said despite the pain he thought of the ambulance men: "You're doing great, Boys."

Over his nine days in Woodstock hospital the doctors worked to regulate his pulse and rhythm. At one point Alice was hopeful that the crisis was passed. Again his thoughts went out. Alice wrote a letter to me: "Claude has specially and particularly asked me to drop you a line....I brought my pen and paper to the hospital to do just that. He was very pleased to receive your kind note..." On January 24, 1964, Claude died, the result of a massive coronary.

Many people called at the house on Sunday afternoon. To Claude's funeral on Monday, January 27th at the United Church in Glassville, an Acadian woman found a ride from

Juniper. She told family members a story: "When Claude came to read our meter he brought a bag of candy for our little girl."

Claude's monument stands in the United Church Cemetery, Glassville. The foot stone reads: "Cpl. Claude E. Corey 1921-1964, Saint John Fus. (M.g.) C.A." In Europe he served with Winnipeg Rifles. He was perhaps attached to Saint John Fusaliers later. His medals are:

    The France and Germany Star
    The Defence Medal
    The Volunteer Service medal with Clasp
    The War Medal, 1939-45

Alice and the children remained in Glassville until 1968; that spring David graduated from high school in Florenceville. That summer they moved to Fredericton. They were well situated for Fredericton High School and University of New Brunswick. Alice rented rooms to students. There she also began a career in insurance. She was said to be the first woman hired by Metropolitan Life Insurance Co. in Canada.

David Eugene Corey

Two months short of graduation from U.N.B. with a B.Sc., David went into business. Soon he was selling insurance. At an early development stage he was in a partnership: "Corey-Haines Ins." For some years he has had his own company, "Corey Insurance".

On October 1, 1976, David married Pamela Greer at United Baptist Church, Douglas. They lived for a few years in Marysville. Later they built a new house on a hill overlooking Douglas and the Saint John River. They also have a water front property on Eel Lake, Canterbury region.

David and Pam have three children:
    Robin Elaine Corey, born November 26, 1978
    David <u>Blair</u> Corey, born August 26, 1982
    Ashley Pamela Corey, born November 25, 1984.

Gregory Claude Corey

Gregory received a B.Sc. from U.N.B., and an M.Sc., and a Ph.D. from University of Waterloo. He became a chemical scientist. He engaged in research, including "Theoretical Spectroscopy". His research and lecturing took him to Lille, France, to England and the Netherlands. Gregory was a professor at University of Montreal, and at St. Mary's University, Halifax. In recent years Gregory took courses in computer in preparation for engineering. Currently he is working for an engineering firm, Navitrac, International.

Gregory married Georgina Horvath. They have a son, Shannon Lewis. He is an industrial chimney and stack inspector in Toronto. Shannon married Germain Beaudoin.

Georgina has a B.A. from U.N.B., and a B.Ed. from McGill. She has been teaching English as a second language, and also French. She now does supply teaching for Dartmouth School Board. Georgina and Greg live in Cole Harbour, N.S.

Catherine Grace Helen Corey

From Fredericton High School, Kathy became a student at St. Thomas University, Fredericton. After one year she was offered a position as supervisor of a store in Fredericton Mall. Kathy married 1, Scott Greencorn, a U.N.B. student. They were married at United Baptist Church, Douglas, December 8, 1978. They had a daughter and a son:
    Jennifer Lynn Greencorn,
    born January 15, 1982,
    James Linden Greencorn,
    born April 25, 1992.

Early in her work life Kathy entered the insurance business. She is now an insurance broker for York Financial Services Inc., Queen St., Fredericton. In 1997 Blue Cross awarded Kathy a trip to the Bahamas. Joan accompanied her.

David and Gregory Corey, Randy Morehouse,
Alice, Kathy and Billy Corey, Jane Bartlett

On September 29, 2001 at Marysville Community and Heritage Centre, Kathy married 2, Randal Morehouse, an industrial carpenter. Officiating minister was Rev. Paul Brooks. Kathy's mother, her children, her siblings, her nieces and nephews, several of her father's siblings, and spouses, also Randy's mother and stepfather, Bob and Gladys Smalley, and other relatives and friends attended the wedding and reception. Kathy and Randy live in Marysville. Jennifer Greencorn graduated from Fredericton High School in 2000, then spent a year at a School of Aesthetics. She is now an Esthetician in Fredericton.

Joan Corey Bartlett

Joan Carlene Corey graduated from Fredericton High School. On December 27, 1980, Joan married John Bartlett at United Baptist Church, Douglas. John, an engineer, is mechanical superintendent for St. Anne Nackawick Pulp and Paper Mill. Joan and John had a speciality in contract building of houses with modified plans. They did five houses.

Joan and John have two daughters:
Amanda Jane Bartlett,
born March 27, 1986,
Emily Margaret Bartlett,
born February 6, 1990.

Amanda, a grade 10 student at Fredericton High School, is a "track and field" athlete. In the summer of 2001 she was in a group sponsored by the Canadian Legion that went to a "meet" in Sherbrooke, Quebec. On November 11th those athletes, wearing the uniforms the Legion had provided, appeared spontaneously at the cenotaph in Fredericton. She was planning for a fall race in Moncton.

William Gordon Paul Corey

Billy left Fredericton with his mother about 1996. They lived with Greg and Georgina in their new home in Cole Harbour for a while. We had a Corey dinner there in spring of 1997 including: Margaret and Jud; and Chris, Ju and Lisa, home from Thailand. Lisa, then two, entertained the group with singing and dancing. Alice and Billy subsequently moved to Halifax. Billy took courses in Bible study at Victory School of Ministry, which is associated with the Pentecostal Holiness denomination. Alice says Billy "has made a lot of progress" in Halifax. Alice, Billy and Greg came from Halifax for Kathy's wedding in September 2001. They contributed much to the socializing at the reception.

Judson Malcolm Corey

Judson M. Corey, born April 16, 1923, was the first of the children of Ira and Nellie Corey to be born at the E. Knowlesville farmhouse. His experience of growing up on that farm is related in Chapter XVII. Many more experiences and much of his life story is interspersed throughout this book. What is added here, therefore, is not more biography but rather a kind of a resume of education and professional experience:

1938-40, Doaktown High School; Grade 10, prize for highest average.
1941, Junior Matriculaton, Woodstock, New Brunswick, prize for highest standing in Chemistry..
1943-44, McGill University, Montreal; Canadian Army University Course: Science, Mathematics, Engineering.
Summer 1945. Gronigen, Holland, Canadian Legion Educational Services: English, French, History.
1946-51 Acadia University, Wolfville, Nova Scotia:
1949 B.A.; Major in History; Minor in English;
1951 B.D.; Thesis: "The Nativity Narratives".
1953-55 Andover Newton Theological School, Newton Center, Massachusetts:
1955 Master of Sacred Theology; Thesis: "The Central Theme of Ephesians".
Study and experience in clinical pastoral psychology: visiting patients, writing verbatim accounts of conversations for evaluation by supervisor, lectures, study of psychology.
1955-56 New Hampshire State Hospital – clinical work and chaplaincy;
1956 Assistant Chaplain, New Hampshire State Hospital;
1962 Northampton State Hospital – 6 weeks;
1959 Boston City Hospital – 12 weeks.
1967-68 Boston University, Courses in Journalism.

1950-70 ordained Baptist minister; served churches in Nova Scotia, New Brunswick, New Hampshire, Ontario, Massachusetts and New York.
    Edited a six to eight page monthly printed parish paper.
1970-71 State University of New York at Albany.
1971 M.A. in Education; Permanent certification in English (New York State).
School Teaching: Averill Park High School, (N.Y.) substitute; English at Milne School, Albany, N.Y.; High School: Blackville, Newcastle and Plaster Rock, N.B.; Community College, Grand Falls, N.B.;
Social Worker: Alcoholism and Drug Dependency Commission of N.B., 1975-91: group therapy and counselling at Ridgewood Treatment and Rehabilitation Centre.
In January, 2002, "Distinguished Toastmaster recognition" by Toastmasters International for outstanding accomplishments and leadership excellence in the pursuit of the mission of Toastmasters International; has been a member of Saint John Toastmasters since 1976, and more recently of Advanced Dawn Breakers Toastmasters, Sussex, N.B.

Judson M. Corey married 1, Marion Rideout, daughter of Clyde and Mary Long Rideout, Hartland, N.B.; married 2, Margaret Stevens, Saint John, N.B. Judson and Marion had two sons and a daughter:

Frederic Watson Corey, born May 4, 1949,
Carolyn Mary Louise Corey, born April 2, 1951,
Christopher Judson Corey, born June 14, 1957.

Frederic Watson Corey

Frederic Corey was born at Wolfville, N.S. His Dad delivered his mother to the Wolfville Hospital in an old Hudson car. He had to run a front wheel against the curb to stop because the brakes were giving out. Then he went to University Hall, Acadia, to write an English exam. The professor inquired why he was late. He let him stay a little beyond the finish time.

Fred began school in Bow, N.H., continued in elementary school in Port Hope, Ontario, and in Conway, Mass. His high school began in Deerfield Regional High School and continued at Boston Technical High School. He graduated in 1967 and, after a summer job, went to Queen's University, Kingston, Ontario. He received a B.Sc. in Civil Engineering in 1971.

Frederic W. Corey, Queen's University

In Kingston, Fred met Sandra Taylor, daughter of Agatha and Charles Taylor. They were married at the Baptist Church in Kingston, August 27, 1971. Sandra graduated from Frontenac Secondary School in 1970, and from Queen's University in 1973 with Honours in Geography and Sociology.

Fred received from Queen's an M.Sc. in Transportation Engineering in 1973. That spring they moved to Fredericton, N.B. He worked for New Brunswick Department of Highways and Transportation 1973-80.

Fred and Sandra have a daughter and a son born in Fredericton, N.B.: Andrea Corey, born December 29, 1976, Charles Andrew Corey, born December 30, 1978.

In the summer of 1980 the family moved to Winnipeg, Manitoba, where Fred's starting job was Streets Planning Engineer. He is now Streets Project Engineer, Dept. of Public Works. Fred continued participation in Toastmasters International, which he had begun in Fredericton. He has received several recognitions.

Living in Winnipeg

The family lived in Lyndale Dr., in the St. Boniface part of Winnipeg. In 1984 they moved to Vermette, a suburb. There Sandra raised, bred and showed pure-bred bearded collies. Later Sandra enrolled in the Faculty of Education, University of Manitoba. In 1991 she received a B.Ed. She began teaching as a supply. She is now teaching grades 7 and 8 at General Wolfe School. She is an avid quiltmaker. Since 1993 she has participated in rowing. She has been Winnipeg Junior Coach, and Provincial Junior Coach.

Andrea and Charles Corey

Andrea participated for several seasons in the Royal Winnipeg Ballet Dancing School. In 1994 she graduated from College Jeanne-Sauvé (high school) with the Governor General's Medal. That autumn she went to Queen's University, Kingston.

In 1998 Andrea received a degree in Applied Science in Engineering Physics, and went immediately to a job with Ehvert Engineering, Toronto. Later she worked for Mobile Q. She is now with Eloqua Corp., Toronto. Andrea Corey is engaged to Dan Adirim. They are planning to be married in August 2002.

Charles Corey also graduated from College Jeanne-Sauvé in 1996. He has been employed with Angus Reid Polling; he became a supervisor. The company is now called Ipsos-Reid.

At age 15 Charles began rowing on the Red River. He participated on the provincial junior team until age 18. After a year off, he returned to rowing. Charles is now registered as a part-time student at University of Winnipeg.

Carolyn Mary Louise Corey

Carolyn, born in Wolfville, N.S., began kindergarten and finished grades 1 and 2 in Port Hope, Ontario. In Conway, Mass., she completed grammar school and then began Deerfield Regional High School. From 1964-68 she attended Hyde Park High School, Boston. She graduated from Averill Park (New York) High School in 1969. Then she returned to her birthplace and became an arts student at Acadia University. She received a B.A., with a major in English and minor in music, 1973, and a B.Ed., 1974.

At Acadia Carolyn met Gordon Campbell from Tatamagouche, N.S. They both went to Liverpool to teach. Gordon taught English at Liverpool Regional High School. Carolyn taught elementary school in the same region.

Carolyn and Gordon were married at Liverpool United Baptist Church, June 28, 1975. Soon they bought a house in Liverpool. On a Christmas/New Year holiday they flew to Belize to visit an Acadia classmate of Gordon's, Israel Cano.

Carolyn and Gordon have a son, Bryan Allan Campbell, born January 18, 1986 in Liverpool. In 1989-90 Gordon took a sabbatical year from high school teaching, and the family took a trip by van to Mexico and Belize. Bryan had his 4th birthday enroute. On their way south they stopped in Kentucky to visit the Cano family. Israel, dean of a teachers' college in Belize,

Gordon Campbell

was on exchange in Kentucky. The Campbells also visited Cano relatives in Belize.

They went down the east coast of Mexico and returned up the west coast, into California, then eastward through the southern states. In Arkansas they visited the town where Gordon had lived on a farm with his parents and brother. As a boy in Arkansas, Gordon earned his first dollar, picking cotton. They arrived in New Brunswick in April.

Carolyn Corey Campbell

Both Carolyn and Gordon have retired from teaching. They continue to reside in Liverpool. Gordon, an ardent gardener, produces a variety of vegetables and also strawberries. He has also done much genealogical research on his family. Carolyn is an artistic flower gardener. She also maintains an impressive variety of houseplants. She is active in bowling, skating, bicycling, swimming. She plays her piano, and makes quilts.

Bryan Allan Campbell

Bryan attended elementary, junior high and high school in Liverpool. Currently he is in grade 10 at Liverpool Regional High School. He has been in Boy Scouts in Liverpool. One summer he attended a camping program sponsored by the Salvation Army at New Glasgow. He participates in bowling, skating and swimming. Bryan likes all kinds of battery-operated gadgets. He also likes music and singing and is an ardent listener to music.

Christopher Judson Corey

Christopher Corey began school in Conway, Mass., continued elementary at James J. Chittick School, Hyde Park, Mass., attended Algonquin Junior High School in Averill Park, N.Y., and completed grade 8 in Albany, N.Y. He began high school in Blackville, NB., had grade 10 in Plaster Rock, and graduated from S. Victoria High School, Andover, in 1975. That fall he moved into residence at University of New Brunswick, Fredericton. He completed a B.Sc. in Mechanical Engineering in 1981.

Then he went to work on Oil Platform 706 off the coast of Newfoundland, working for Sedco Consortium. Later, in Halifax, he worked for H&R Block preparing income tax returns. He also worked for Lavalin Engineering Co. In Halifax he bought a house with a rental unit.

In 1990 he went to Japan, spent two years teaching English, and enjoyed the many hiking trails in the country. In 1992 he began teaching English in Thailand. There he met and married Suphaphon Chatnok, who is called Ju.

They came to Ontario in 1993. Chris received from Brock University, St. Catherines, a degree in teaching English as a second language. They spent the summer of 1994 picking fruit in the Niagara Peninsula. Early 1995 they returned to Thailand. Chris resumed teaching English. They enjoyed holidays at the Gulf of Thailand.

In 1997 they came to New Brunswick and Nova Scotia for a two-month visit and to sell the house in Halifax. They brought with them a little daughter, age two, with long flowing hair, eagerly learning English, and dancing to the music of the radio.

After one more year in Thailand Chris, Ju and Lisa returned to New Brunswick. Chris spent a 14-month academic year at N.B. Community College, Saint John, learning information technology. During that time their son Kevin was born at S.J.R.H.

Christopher J. Corey, 2001

Since the beginning of 2000 they have been living in Fredericton. Chris worked for E.D.S., a software development company. They have a house in Fredericton with rental units. Lisa began kindergarten in New Brunswick in the fall of 2000.

In January 2001 Ju and Lisa returned to Thailand for five months, taking Kevin. Lisa attended school there. Her mother did volunteer work in the school, initially helping Lisa adjust to the language, and remaining to help the teacher.

Lalita Lisa Corey, born May 17, 1995, started reading before age three. She is now in grade one, French Immersion, and thus speaks some of three languages.

Lisa and Kevin Corey, and Bryan Campbell

Kevin Ittichai Corey, born June 2, 1999, is speaking Thai words and responding to that language. Lisa speaks to him in Thai. She is also teaching him the English alphabet. He is eagerly learning English.

Warren Allan Corey

Warren was born March 7, 1925 at the Corey farmhouse in E. Knowlesville. Memories of our comradeship go back to pre-school days. The story in the preface of this book about our horse stalls is an example of our activity. We built miniature drags, wagons, sleds in imitation of farm implements. In March, 1931, Warren began school in E. Knowlesville. His first teacher in the one-room school was Orland McLeod. Our play and companionship continued until I was away from home in high school.

Our comradeship revived in June 1942 when we joined Clayton Clarke's work crew assembled at the C.P.R. Station in Hartland, N.B. It was a venture far from New Brunswick.

A night on the train brought us to Ottawa where we visited the House of Commons, courtesy of Heber H. Hatfield, M.P. for Carleton-Victoria. A longer train ride, beginning at night and ending at night, brought us to a remote rail station in North-western Ontario. In the darkness we boarded trucks that took us to a comfortable camp with mattresses – unusual for us in a lumber camp. The food was also above our expectations.

The woods work, however, tested the endurance of all the men. Warren and I were in a group cutting bushes for a logging road. Earl Ebbett, Clayton Clarke's assistant, cut and measured a stick and commissioned me to keep a check on the width of the road. Some men cut eight-foot pulp. The mosquitoes were vicious. The venture was short-lived. Most of the men, after a few days, returned to New Brunswick.

An agreement with the Ontario company managing the lumbering, provided free one-way tickets for men who worked three months. A foreman from another camp arrived offering employment on the Black Sturgeon River. Warren and I threw our bags in his pick-up truck. The next morning two fellows arrived asking, "Where are the brothers from New Brunswick?" Dan Gallagher from Johnville and Archie Cummings of Hartland joined us, cutting and splitting firewood – a temporary job.

Soon we were helping build a dam on the Black Sturgeon River. They had dammed half the river. In front of that temporary dam we pried rocks with crowbars and loaded them on horse-drawn drags.

Later we worked on the road hauling and spreading gravel. One morning the teamster received a letter from a buddy in jail. He said, "A friend in need is a friend indeed." He threw the reins to me and took off for Fort William or Port Arthur. Thus, I became the teamster for the gravel crew.

When the mosquito season was over we began cutting pit props by the cord. There, Warren's skills were ahead of mine. While I had spent more time in school, he had become skilful with tools, in this case a Swede saw. He knew how to file it too. He cut more of the small trees than I did. I twitched them out with one horse.

About the end of September our three-month period was up. We took a taxi to Fort William, at the head of Lake Superior. After two nights and two days, including a stop in Montreal, we arrived in Hartland. That was the occasion when we went to the farm at Lower Brighton and helped our brother, Wilfred, harvest his potatoes.

Again our ways parted. I went to a lumber camp – my second winter – as time-keeper and scaler. In early 1943 I was in the Canadian Army. Warren continued to build his skills in farming and logging. At 17 he was yarding logs with a pair of Father's horses at his enterprise on the South Branch. He worked on the Corey farm. His father negotiated an agricultural exemption from military service. He yarded logs for Henry

Pye one winter.

In 1946 Warren, in company with Bud Avery, went on a venture to Western Canada at harvest time. They motored as far as Kamloops.

After a short interval of working with his brothers: Bob, Tom and Keith on the Corey farm, Warren ventured into enterprising. He and Keith bought woodlots from Bob Guthrie and Ian Derrah and logged them. Warren also logged for Billy Haines in East Glassville. He also had a crew with four pairs of horses logging on Tague Brook.

Warren also had a threshing venture. He went from farm to farm with one of Harry Dyer's machines. Keith worked with Warren one season. Later Warren did hay pressing with his own hay press.

In 1952 Warren married Doreen Ellis of Windsor, N.B. Soon they moved onto the Corey farm at E. Knowlesville. Warren had purchased it from his brother Bob who had moved to Richmond Corner.

With all his skills and enterprising in a variety of work, Warren had not fulfilled his interest in venturing. He said, "I always wanted to go west." The trip in 1946 had not reached the Pacific Coast. Doreen's family were living in Port Alberni, B.C.

In 1954 Warren sold the Corey farm to Don Hallet. Warren and Doreen loaded a trailer with household goods. Oliver Branscombe came down to Corey's with the address of his sister Pauline, and Arthur Rudge, past the Rockies in B.C. Warren and Doreen enjoyed a night of hospitality and then resumed their trek westward to Vancouver Island.

In British Columbia Warren adapted to a very different kind of logging, down a mountain. He spoke of overhead lines – "skylines". He worked "in the bush" for fourteen months.

Warren's next venture was as an apprentice carpenter, working with his father-in-law, John Ellis, building the paper mill in Port Alberni.

In 1958 Warren and Doreen returned to Carleton Co., N.B. and took over the Ellis farm in Windsor. While living in Windsor, Warren and Doreen adopted their son, Dale, born June 19, 1959.

In 1965 an urge to venture came over Warren and Doreen again. They sold the farm in Windsor. They took a trip to Ontario, and finding the house-building market unpromising returned to Carleton Co. In Hartland, he built the first house on a new street that was named Corey Street.

In the spring of 1966 Warren and Dorren, again feeling the lure of the West, sold the house in Hartland and returned to Port Alberni, B.C. He went to work for MacMillan Bloedell. Soon he was running a gang saw. Some of his brothers were watching when a TV camera focused on Warren at the controls.

During that time Warren took on an enterprise in building and renovating houses. His mill shift was 1:00 a.m. to 8:00 a.m. After a short morning sleep he took up hammer and saw. He had another sleep in the evening till midnight. Besides carpentry, Warren developed skills in electric wiring, masonry and plumbing. Doreen also developed skills, e.g., joint-filling and dry walls. They built three houses in Port Alberni and renovated ten. After seven and one-half years of long days and working Saturdays and holidays, Warren reflected, "It was time to stop; my stomach bothered me." He took a recess.

Warren and Doreen had visitors in Port Alberni. In 1973 the Fosters: Paul, Kaye, Kris and Stuart, on their cross-country motor trip, spent days with them. Warren took Paul salmon fishing. They left when killer whales approached.

In fall 1981, I visited them. They drove to Nanaimo to meet me at the ferry terminal on Warren's day off. He was then working a day shift in the mill. Every evening we sat in their new house reviewing old stories of growing-up years. Warren was then looking forward to retirement at age 60.

Retirement came in 1985. Immediately they sold their new house in Port Alberni and returned to New Brunswick.

They bought a house in Wakefield. The next spring they moved to a house in Woodstock. Warren had very much wanted to return home to New Brunswick. But maybe making themselves at home again in Carleton County was more difficult than they anticipated.

In September, 1986, Warren and Doreen returned to Vancouver Island. Back in Port Alberni, Warren resumed house building and renovation. Margaret and I visited them in June 1992. Warren and Doreen met us in Nanaimo – glad to see us. They took us to a house Warren had finished. He was building a garage. Together we built, and hoisted onto the plates, the heavy trusses.

That heavy part completed, they took us south on an over-night trip to Victoria. Butchart's Gardens were gorgeous. We also went with them to Parksville on a Sunday morning. At the Kingdom Hall, Warren demonstrated one more skill, that of an accomplished public speaker.

At the time of our visit their son, Dale Corey was in Ontario, near some of his relatives. He found work there but, Warren recollects, it seemed that all the places where he worked closed. He returned to Port Alberni. He became a taxi driver. On one of Wareen's returns from a New Brunswick visit, Dale met him in Nanaimo. Now Dale is driving taxi only part time. He is attending a college, preparing to be a male nurse.

During our 1992 visit Doreen's pace was slowing because of arthritis. Since then she has been con-

Warren Corey and Margaret, Miramichi Lake, 1991

fined to home, except for doctor's appointments. Warren has visited his relatives in New Brunswick in the 90's. On his last visit, 1999, we stayed at Mitchell Corey's cottage on S. Branch of Miramichi. Warren, Keith and I explored Highlands, Divide, E. Knowlesville, including the old farm, and reminisced about many events.

Warren delights to reminisce about the experiences and the activities of our growing-up years —even about the horses we had on the farm, calling them by name. Reminiscing continues – over the phone. I've called him to check on information for this book. On February 13, 2002, when he answered, he said, "I've got my hands into dough." He was making dumplings for the top of their stew – another example of his versatility.

Ira Keith Corey

In the farmhouse in E. Knowlesville, on the cold night of December 21, 1927, a boy was born to Nellie and Ira Corey. They named him Ira Keith Corey. I was four and one half. I remember that we were at a Christmas concert at the E. Knowlesville School. At the close, somebody told us, "Your father has gone home. George Guthrie is taking you home." Apparently Keith was born near midnight. As a small boy he used to give his birthday as "22nd to Cember." So we thought, until the records fixed on December 21st.

Some little anecdotes from Keith's early school days, and his youth: At school he was asked to memorize, "Twenty Froggies Went to School". He procrastinated, perhaps because he was having a little difficulty. Finally the teacher said, "Keith, I want you to be able to recite that poem tomorrow." That evening Keith went to a quiet corner, book in hand, and a tune from Sunday School in his head. He rehearsed all the delightful verses:

> Twenty froggies went to school,
> Down beside a rushing pool;
> Twenty little coats of green,
> Twenty vests, all white and clean.....

Keith's comment decades later was, "Donald Hunter was very surprised when I got up and sang it." Then he recited a verse of another school poem:

> Over in the meadow where the stream runs blue,
> Lived an old mother frog and her little
> froggies two;
> Swim, said the mother; we swim said the two;
> They swam all day where the stream runs blue.

Corey siblings: Keith, Gordon, Warren, Jud, Kaye, Shirley, Norman, 1995

A Dramatic Incident

Keith related to me also an amusing incident that occurred one autumn after the men had gone to their logging camp, and Keith, a teenager, was left at home to do the barn work and manage the livestock. Mother asked for pork. They sent for George Guthrie, who was a kind of handyman who did all kinds of jobs in the community: threshing oats, cutting wood, shoeing horses, shearing sheep and butchering. Keith kindled a fire under the big black pot to boil the water for scalding the pig, while George went up Golden Ridge to fetch another pig from Oscar Rodgers'. The cast iron pot cracked open; the water poured out. Keith hiked across the fields to intercept George at the mouth of the Golden Ridge road and have him go to MacKenzie's to borrow their pot.

As Keith emerged from our field onto the road to Knowlesville, he saw a pair of run-away horses pulling a longsled without even a bottom. He quickly decided not to try to mount the sled for fear of his legs slipping between the ribs of the skeleton sled. He continued toward the intersection of the Golden Ridge road, and found George brushing snow off himself, the sled box upset, the pig about to run away, and the teacher and all the pupils out of school for the excitement. The teacher said, "Boys you're lucky, George!" Haply, a party of hunters, coming from Knowlesville in a car, stopped George's horses and brought them back.

While growing up on the farm in E. Knowlesville, Keith developed lifetime skills. In the little brook that ran through the farm he had no difficulty in catching a good string of trout. Early he learned to stalk a deer. When Fred Fletcher came from New Hampshire, Father – busy with his logging crew – had Keith accompany Fred in the woods. Soon Elbridge Brown, a crew member, began calling Keith, "The Guide."

Helping a Brother

The Corey family is indebted to Keith for timely help to our brother Wilfred, in the last months of life. Fifty-six years later, on an October evening in 2001, as I sat with Keith in the Corey/Caldwell camp on Elliott Brook, he told me the story of which I had previously heard only brief references. Thus I much increased my appreciation of the help Keith gave to Wilfred.

Here is the story Keith recollected: "In the late winter of 1945 I left the farm in East Knowlesville and went to Bristol. I went on the train to Hartland. Wilfred met me. On his farm at Lower Brighton, we hauled manure to the fields. Wilfred was not feeling very well; he got worse. He went to hospital. I stayed to do the barn work. There were three or four cows to milk, and calves, pigs and a pair of horses to look after."

Keith also recollected earlier times on the farm with Wilfred and Pearl. He described their English cherries, saying, "I'd like to have some of them." He recalled harrowing, and Wilfred saying, "Don't work the horses too hard; they haven't worked much through the winter."

"I was also there at harvest time when he hitched his team to the binder. When the whirler started – the revolving slats that pushed the standing grain toward the cutter – the horses took off. Wilfred said, 'I was glad I hadn't hitched the third horse.' He could hardly hold the two."

Working Toward Enterprising

After our parents and our younger siblings moved to Juniper in 1945, Keith worked on the E. Knowlesville farm with Bob and Tom and Warren. They logged in winter. About that time Keith bought a used truck from Barth Wasson. He hauled slab wood to Hartland. Fred MacKenzie was surprised at the number of trips he could make in one day.

Keith also worked for the Flemming Company, around the mill in Juniper, and in logging crews. During that time he met an accident in the woods. The men picked him up and took him to the Bath Hospital. There he met a nurse, Eva May Caldwell. "Eva May Caldwell was born November 27, 1934. She graduated from Bristol High School in 1952. In 1954 she went to Saint John General Hospital and took nursing. Graduated in 1956. She worked at the Bath Hospital, now known as Northern Carleton Hospital." Keith and Eva May were married on October 3, 1958.

Keith's work experience included many employments and enterprises. He worked with his brother, Warren, in custom threshing for a season. "He was a hunting guide for Henderson's Hunting Lodge, South Knowlesville, for two seasons."

Keith did contract work in log and pulp cutting for several years. He began with horses. Later he got a skidder, which he worked for ten years. He also had a truck for hauling pulp. His work was spread over Carleton Co.: Juniper, for Flemmings; Kilfoil for H.J. Crabbe; and up into Victoria Co.: Arthurette, and farther up the Tobique River. One summer he worked at Riley Brook cutting pulp for his brother, Tom Corey, and for Elmer Briggs, who in a partnership had bought about 300 acres of well-wooded land.

In the latter part of his work life Keith looked for other occupations. He took upgrading at St. Andrews and at Grand Falls. He stayed with me and Chris at Four Falls when I was teaching at the Community College in Grand Falls. He went to Saint John Technical School, now known as Community College, where he took autobody repair. After two weeks more in Grand Falls for apprentice work, he began autobody repair. He worked at Hartland, Bath, and Johnville. At length he built his own autobody repair shop in Bristol, Corey's Auto Body on their own property.

Keith and Eva Mae have six children:
Steven Michael Corey, born March 8, 1959,

Rebecca Anne Corey, born May 22, 1960,
Murray Keith Corey, born April 14, 1961,
Brian Kent Corey, born December 18, 1962,
Donald Wayne Corey, born April 18, 1964,
Susan Marie Corey, born December 17, 1965.

Eva May worked early and late – early to the hospital, and late in the evening, keeping house, cooking and caring for the children.

Steven Michael Corey

While a student at Carleton North High School, Steven worked a summer in Knowlesville, helping make broomheads at Hemphill's Mill; again briefly, before he went to work at the H.J. Crabbe Mill in Bristol.

Steven spent one summer working at Lincoln Airport where he did refuelling and mechanical maintenance on spray planes.

During Steven's brief sojourn in Lincoln he met Cathey Mae Clowater of nearby Oromocto. She was educated at Waasis Middle School, at Oromocto Senior High, at U.N.B. one year, and at N.B.C.C., Fredericton, for stenography. Cathey and Steven were married in the chapel of C.F.B. Gagetown, July 5, 1980.

Steven and Cathey first lived at Upper Kent. Steven continued to work for H.J. Crabbe. Cathey worked at Gordon Hunter's law office for two years. Eventually Steven and Cathey built their own home near his parents in Bristol.

On the evening of October 26, 2001, I visited the happy and friendly family in their comfortable home. Cathey said, "here is the lamp you gave us for our wedding." I had forgotten it. Their two boys attend Bristol Elementary School.

Matthew <u>Drew</u> Corey,
born September 22, 1991, and
Dexter John Corey, born August 27, 1993.

Drew likes school very much and also sports: soccer, football, baseball, basketball and swimming. In summer he spends up to five hours a day on his swim team. Dexter is also fond of swimming and likes kickball.

Cathey and Steven take much interest in the boys' school activities. Cathey stops at the school to do voluntary work, e.g., helping with breakfast, before going to the office of MacElwain and Renouf, Florenceville. Cathey has been a legal secretary for the law firm for 19 years. The whole family enjoys canoeing and kayaking on the Miramichi and Tobique Rivers.

Rebecca Anne Bell (Corey)

Rebecca "graduated from Carleton North Senior High in 1978. She worked at McCain Foods as a secretary for the head of personnel until she joined the Canadian Forces in 1983. She works as an Air Traffic Controller. She has been to Egypt twice. She is currently stationed in Baggotville, Quebec, and is living in Chicoutimi, Quebec. Rebecca's son, Alexander Keith Corey (Sandy) was born September 2, 1976. He is living with his grandparents, and working for H.J. Crabbe & Son, Bristol."

Murray Keith Corey

Murray "graduated from Carleton North Senior High School in 1979. He returned to High School in 1983, where he took data processing and a business course. In 1990 he went to Woodstock Community College for upgrading. He completed the upgrading in 1992. In 1993 he started to take a computer programming course at the Community College in Saint John, but failed to complete the course. In 1999 he was in the early stage of starting his own business, 'The Ink Spot'. He planned to print out business cards, invitations, banners, iron-on transfers, and other various items. He enjoys gardening and helping with the maple syrup."

Brian Kent Corey

"Brian worked at the Seed Farm in Foreston several years. He is now working for Alan Vail in the woods. He enjoys the outdoors and loves to hunt and fish. He also likes to snowshoe and spend time at the camp. He is currently living in Gordonsville. Brian's elder daughter, Melissa, was born February 16, 1985 in the Perth Hospital. Jessica Dawn Corey was born on May 26, 1986 in the Perth Hospital." Both girls are in school.

Donald Wayne Corey

After graduating from Carleton North High School in 1982, Donnie piled lumber for H.J. Crabbe and Sons for seven years. Then, he recollected, "In fall of 1991 a young shy Corey boy went to P.E.I. for one year culinary course at Holland College." On P.E.I. Donnie worked as a chef at Rodd's Hotel and Resort, Brudenell and Charlottetown, and at Mill River Resort. In 1994 he returned to New Brunswick. He worked at Beaverbrook Hotel, Fredericton, about three years. Currently he is a sous chef at Holiday Inn at Mactaquac. Donnie and his common-law wife, Kathy Boyd, live in Fredericton. On October 24, 2001, at the Corey/Caldwell Camp, Elliot Brook, Donnie cooked for his Dad, Keith, and his Uncle Jud Corey a mesquit steak with partridge. Served with rice and green beans, it was a rare treat. Days earlier he had cooked a dinner for his brothers, Steven and Brian.

Susan Marie Corey

Susan "graduated from Carleton North Senior High School in 1984. She is living with her parents in Bristol. She has had several baby-sitting jobs. She lived in Fort Frances, Ontario for five years, where she worked at Robin's Donut Shop/Pizza

Nook. She worked at the Bristol Co-op Pre School for two years, 1996-1998. Besides baby-sitting jobs, she has done housework part-time. Susan much enjoys working with children. She enjoys working in the flower and the vegetable gardens. She also enjoys driving the four wheeler.

"Eva May is now fully retired after a forty-year nursing career. She enjoys her grandchildren very much, and helps out with them as much as she can. She also enjoys reading, hunting, fishing and gardening. She also enjoys cooking for her family. They plant a large garden every year. Eva May still makes her own pickles and jams and does her own canning, which she enjoys. They make maple syrup every spring, with Andrew, Eva May's brother. They are frequently visited by their grandchildren and love to see them come."[6]

Anna Kathleen Corey Foster

Anna Kathleen Corey was born on the Corey farm at E. Knowlesville, on September 4, 1930, about three weeks after the passing of both our grandfathers. She was welcomed as the second girl born to Ira and Nellie Corey, following a succession of six boys. She was also welcomed at the E.Knowlesville School where her father and mother took her for an "open house". The new teacher, Miss Ellen J. Blakeney, a lover of children and a Sunday School teacher, extended open arms to the new baby.

In November 1936, Kathleen was again welcomed at that school as a beginning pupil and as the first girl in the school in several years. Donald Hunter, teacher, expressed delight in having one girl instead of an all-boy school. He brought a slab of hardwood from the stove wood supply and placed it under her desk to rest her feet on. The old pine bench was too high for her feet to reach the floor. Most of Kathleen's elementary education was at that school, although she had a few terms at the Knowlesville School. She was very fond of her last teacher, Eva Price.

In the fall of 1945 Kathleen began high school in Juniper. Her parents had moved there to enable her and Shirley and Gordon to attend the school. In Juniper "Kathleen" was soon changed to "Kaye". In 1948 Kaye graduated from Juniper High School with an ambition to teach.

In the fall term of 1948 she taught on "local license" at Biggar Ridge School. There she became confident that she could manage a classroom. With that confidence, and with the support of her brother Claude, she went in January 1949 to the Normal School in Fredericton to fulfil her ambition to teach.

Kaye is still grateful to her brother Claude who had recently come home from three years of convalescence in Saint John, following military service in Europe; he lent to her the money to go to Normal School. After one term in Fredericton, Kaye began teaching grades two and three in Juniper School, in the fall of 1949. In summer of 1950 Kaye was again in Fredericton with her sister Shirley, long-time friend Audrey Manuel, and Alice Hallett. They roomed with Kate and Jim Hovey. In two summer sessions Kaye obtained a permanent license. After two years of teaching, Kathleen Corey married Paul D. Foster, her high school teacher in the Juniper School. He had turned from teacher to insurance agent in Florenceville. They were married in the United Baptist Church, Knowlesville, August 15, 1951. Kaye continued teaching briefly: W. Florenceville, one year; E. Florenceville, fall term. Then she took a maternity leave. Their first son was born June 1953. Kaye resumed teaching for one year, 1954-55, in Bristol.

Paul D. Foster

While he was a student at the Normal School in Fredericton, Paul Foster, son of Talmadge and Leslie Foster, was hired at age 18 by Hugh John Flemming to be principal in Juniper, beginning September 1943. He taught the high school

— all students, all grades. His vice-principal was John Hildebrand, who taught grades 6, 7 and 8.

Paul left teaching in Juniper to start a career in insurance. After that he taught one more term, winter of 1949, at Gagetown, where he took the place of the principal who was on sick leave. In beginning to sell insurance, Paul had the example of his grandfather, Russell Ross.

Early in his insurance career Paul was hired by Continental Life Insurance Co., with head office in Saint John, as a salesman and manager. He said, "I went to see the agents." After a short Saint John experience, Paul started building his own business. His first office was in the house of his parents, Leslie and Talmadge Foster, in Florenceville. In 1956 he moved the family to Maple St. and set up an office there. The second son, Kris was born in 1959. Also that year Paul received his C.L.U., after a five year course of study with the extension department of the University of Toronto.

In October 1961 the Foster family moved to Pine St. into a house built by Kaye's cousin, Fred McBrine, and recently vacated by Doug and Doreen Thorne. "Before we moved in," Paul recollected, "We built an office." About two weeks after their move their third son, Stuart was born.

Sons and Families

Kaye and Paul Foster have three sons:
>Geoffrey Kirk Foster, born June 18, 1953,
>Kris Roderick Foster, born January 1, 1959,
>Stuart Paul Foster, born October 29, 1961.

When Stuart began school in 1967 Kaye began working in the office, an occupation that continued over 25 years. It was a demanding task at times, especially when she had to spend the noon hour getting lunch for the family. However, she was able to follow up personal interests. Along with her sister, Shirley Brooks, Kaye has taken lessons in painting. She has produced some very impressive paintings. Especially noteworthy are scenes of the Corey farm. She has presented one to each of her brothers.

Despite a very busy family and work life, Kaye, with the encouragement of Paul, has frequently entertained – business associates, many friends, and many gatherings of Corey relatives. Another of Kaye's accomplishments is writing 35 plus volumes of family diaries.

Holidays and Trips

While the boys were growing up the family spent many summer days at Miramichi Lake. Paul Foster and John Hildebrand opened a road to the lake, thus initiating access by vehicle, and the subsequent building of many cottages on the lake shore.

Vacationing at the lake was interrupted by and interspersed with trips. They visited my family and me in Nova Scotia, in New Hampshire, in Massachusetts —Conway and Boston, and in New York State.

In summer of 1973 Kaye, Paul, Kris and Stuart, with a small dog, motored across Canada with a trailer camper, all the way to Vancouver Island. At Port Alberni, they visited Warren and Doreen Corey. Warren took Paul fishing. Paul recollected, "We landed one salmon. When whales came, we cleared out."

They also took many winter trips to: London, England, 1967; Bahamas, 1974; Spain, 1985; Hawaii, Australia and New Zealand, 1989; Arizona, 1990 and 91; Europe – 10 countries, 1996. They also took many winter vacations in Florida, relatively short in working years; lengthening to months beginning about 1990.

Retirement

Anticipating spending more time away from business, about 1990 Paul and Kaye acquired a property at Pompano Beach. Paul could approach retirement with a sense of accomplishment. He was "the first New Brunswicker to qualify as both a chartered life underwriter, and as an associate of the Insurance Institute of Canada" (A.I.I.C.).[7]

In 1987 Paul began phasing out his management of his business in favour of the boys – two-thirds then, and the other one-third in 1993.

In 1998 the Fosters' retirement leisure was interrupted. On August 4th we received a phone call from Kaye: "Paul is coming to the hospital in Saint John by ambulance. Geoffrey and I are driving." Paul was critically ill with a heart condition. Twice the hospital called our house in the night. Once Kaye and Geoffrey went to the hospital after midnight. Once I accompanied them in early morning. Then the doctors inserted an oxygen tube, and kept Paul sedated for a few days. Many friends phoned the Corey residence anxiously inquiring about Paul. After a month he went home by car, much to the relief of the family.

On September 15th Paul was brought back to Saint John Regional Hospital, to the cardiac unit; doctors were concerned about fluid on the lungs and about oxygen level. Again Kaye and Geoffrey came to be near Paul. After about two weeks they were able to take him home again. Geoffrey was very attentive to the needs of his father, talking to doctors and helping to manage his medicine at home.

At home, through the autumn with rest and careful exercise, Paul gained strength. In the new year, 1999, they were able to go to Florida. In subsequent summers they have been able to enjoy some time at the lake, especially when Geoffrey has been home and could accompany them.

On August 11, 2001, Paul and Kaye celebrated their golden anniversary with an Open House at St. Leo's Hall, Florenceville. They prepared for 300 guests – friends and relatives. A week later they left on a trip to Alaska. In early January they flew to Florida. At this writing, spring 2002, they are planning to leave there in April for a cruise southward to Panama, through the Canal, and up the Pacific Coast to Vancouver. They expect to fly to Halifax.

The Sons of Kaye and Paul Foster

Geoffrey Kirk Foster

Geoffrey Foster is a scholarly person. He has spent much time and energy on academic pursuits. He went from high school in Florenceville in 1971 to university in Fredericton. He received from U.N.B. a B.A. with Honors in Economics; and a Bachelor of Business Administration, 1976. Early in life, Geoffrey found opportunities for travel. In Vancouver he visited his Great Uncle Edwin Ross, and on Vancouver Island, his Uncle Warren Corey.

Geoffrey's work experience included banking, accounting and investments which took him to Moncton and Saint John. He has also lived in Montreal and Toronto. Between other activities and academic pursuits Geoffrey worked part time in insurance in Florenceville.

After some work experience Geoffrey returned to academic pursuits. He spent some months in Halifax, — a student of St. Mary's University, and a resident at Pine Hill Divinity School, where he socialized with the students. In 1987 Geoffrey received from St. Mary's, a Master of Business Administration.

Geoffrey's main interest in his academic pursuits has been financial planning and investments. He worked, studied and took courses e.g., securities, derivatives and trading. Over several years, Geoffrey worked to achieve the status of

"Chartered Financial Analyst" (CFA). This he completed in 1994.

Geoffrey's latest academic undertaking was a two-year course at the Graduate School of Administration and Management of Harvard University. Geoffrey described his course at Harvard as "an interesting experience, competitive, demanding and tough, but still enjoyable and bringing satisfaction." The Harvard courses, combined with sessions at Charlottesville, Va., enabled Geofffrey to achieve CFA-3 registration.

Philosophy and Values

Geoffrey says, "people are more important than the course work." Through his educational pursuits he has met people from every continent and 50 to 60 countries. At Harvard he was among 60 people from 47 countries. His travels have taken him across U.S.A. to California; to continental Europe: Switzerland, Italy, Germany and Scandinavian Countries; to Britain: Stratford on Avon, and to the exploration of Scottish roots in Enniskillen and Edinburgh. Geoffrey speaks of "being free of constraints", which has enabled him to follow other interests in addition to his degree and certification work. Thus he has expanded his interest in politics, history, literature and music. In Europe he went to a Mozart concert and saw Mozart's birthplace. Geoffrey has collected recordings of historical lectures and of classical music.

Kris Roderick Ross Foster

Kris Foster has made Florenceville and neighborhood his home. He ventured to Rothesay, N.B. in 1976. He graduated from Rothesay Collegiate in 1978. He spent the year 1978-79 at University of New Brunswick, Fredericton. There he roomed with Mitchell Corey. After one year on campus Kris joined Foster Insurance.

On May 14, 1983 at the United Church of Canada, Florenceville, Kris married Wanda Drier, daughter of James and Donna Drier, Bristol.

Wanda graduated from Carleton North High School in 1980. She spent an academic year at Moncton Community College, majoring in "Marketing". She worked for several years for Carleton-Victoria Forest Products Marketing Board. Her recreation has been skiing, yoga and snowmobiling with Kris.

Kris has been an avid fisherman all his life. He took time off school to go with his Uncle Tom Corey and his boys to the Miramichi for smelts. Pursuit of salmon has taken him to the Restigouche River. For lobster he has gone to North Shore. With his cousin, Ross Corey, Kris explores abandoned farms, searching for old farm machinery. From iron seats he is making kitchen stools. He has also made a magazine rack.

The insurance business also takes Kris out onto the farms. Much business is done with farmers. With his brother Stuart he has been managing Foster Insurance since 1987.

Foster family

Property and building has also been a strong interest. They built a new house overlooking the Saint John River from the West Side. Now Kris has nearly finished a new cottage on Miramichi Lake. After the foundation and main structure he has been putting his own handiwork into it.

Wanda and Kris Foster have two daughters:
Erin Kristine Foster,
born February 24, 1985;
Meredith Leslie Foster,
born November 12, 1988.

Wanda gave up her work with Forest Products near the time of Erin's birth. When Meredith was going on seven, Wanda began working with Foster Insurance.

The Daughters

Erin joined the Pathfinders branch of Girl Guides. In 2000 she completed requirements for "The Canada Cord", the highest award in Girl Guides. Then she began working toward the Duke of Edinburgh award. She is very fond of swimming and has become a Certified Life Guard. She took piano lessons for more than four years. She is a fan of recorded music. She also participated in Kung Fu, a martial art, and received her yellow belt. Since her car accident in September 2001, she has had to protect her neck and shoulder.

Since January 2002 Erin has been a resident, grade 11 student at R.C.S. Netherwood, Rothesay, N.B. She enjoys a long weekend at home once a month, plus holidays, e.g., March Break and Easter.

Meredith, a grade eight student, also has many extra-curricular activities: Brownies, basketball, gymnastics, music, swimming and downhill skiing. She is also enthusiastic about computers and has become a "whiz". She also has a strong interest in animals and insects, e.g., cats, snakes, grasshoppers and ladybugs. Meredith is recognized for dry humour and wit.

Her grandmother Foster said, "She is quick to learn and bright in school."

Stuart Paul Foster

Stuart graduated from Carleton North High School in 1980. He studied at U.N.B., Fredericton, for one year then went to Sault Technology Institute, Ontario. In the two-year course he majored in geology, which involved making a collection and labelling many kinds of rocks. There he roomed with Paul Giggie of Bristol.

In Spring 1983 Stuart returned to Florenceville and began work with P.D. Foster Insurance (1982) Ltd. In August 1983 Stuart was married to Patricia Anne Lyall. They have three children:

>Kathleen Patricia Foster,
>born January 20, 1987,
>Cameron Lyall Foster,
>born June 4, 1988,
>Elizabeth Margaret Jane Foster,
>born April 11, 1991.

Stuart is now Office Manager of P.D. Foster Ins. He said, "I like doing business with people in this area. They are good to work with. After business is transacted, they sit and talk about what is happening." Community and personal relations are important to Stuart. At the funeral of his late friend and college roommate, Paul Giggie, Stuart gave the eulogy.

On his desk in the Florenceville office, Stuart can bring up on his screen colourful slides of places he has toured on his motorbike, e.g., Percé Rock on Gaspé Peninsula. He also biked to Upstate New York, sightseeing enroute in the White Mountains and the Green Mountains. His main sport now is golf, having given up hunting.

Trish (Patricia) has been working with children and youth since 1983 except for a short time out when their own

Foster grandchildren: Erin, Meredith, Kate, Elizabeth and Cameron

children were small. Now she is librarian at Centreville Elementary and Centreville Intermediate schools. She also coaches the debating club of Carleton North High School. For the last five years she has taken that club and the Drama Club to England during the March break. They saw "Othello" and other plays in London – six in seven days. Trish also uses her talent with children in church during Story Time.

Kathleen, Cameron and Elizabeth are all avid readers. Cameron and Elizabeth have been "shared reading partners" for kindergarten children. A hardcovered book is a welcome gift for Christmas. Cameron was recognized in their local press as top salesman of crafts, as a fundraiser for his school. The girls are interested in art and crafts, encouraged by Trish.

Shirley Joyce Corey Brooks

Shirely Corey, last daughter of Ira and Nellie Corey, was born at their farmhouse in East Knowlesville on August 3, 1932.

In preparation for the birth, they had engaged Margaret McBrine, a nurse much experienced in "confinement cases" over the Parish of Aberdeen. When the day of birth came, in haying season, the event was managed nonchalantly. Ira, not wanting to interrupt the haying, dispatched a fourteen-year-old boy for the nurse.

Norman recollected: "Papa, busy with haying, sent me, driving Dick, in the buggy, to fetch Mrs McBrine. I went via Esdraelon, thence up toward Glassville. The Fred McBrine family lived on that road. She had her suit case all packed." Shirley's arrival made three girls in a large family of boys. She and sister Kathleen were to develop much companionship. But the summer Shirley was two they were separated for several weeks. It was the summer their youngest brother, Gordon, was born. Maggie and Alex Lindsay, seeing Nellie Corey in Glassville with a babe in arms and a two year old girl, insisted on relieving Nellie of the two year old. Reluctantly, after much persuasion, Nellie let them take Shirley. Twice in early childhood Shirley was reclaimed. The second time was when she was restored to consciousness after being inadvertently walked over by a horse.[8]

Growing up on the farm, Shirley and her sister, like the boys, learned to make their own amusement and find their own excitement. Here is a sample of Shirley's spontaneous fun.

One evening when Mother was waiting to put her to bed she picked up an alder stick that one of her brothers had dropped when he returned from fishing that day. It still had a line and baited hook. Wearing her night dress, Shirley ran down to the bridge, dropped the hook in the brook, pulled out a good-sized trout, and ran up the hill with the trout dangling. When she reached the veranda she remarked, "The time to get the big fish is at night when they have the little ones to bed."

There were also incidents that were not amusing. Shirley went to Glassville to have her hair cut. Jean Hovey accompanied her to Derrah's. Ian asked if she wanted it "shingled" – a strange term to Shirley. She emerged from the store with a boy's haircut.

She was devastated. She recollects, "I cried all night. Next morning I begged to stay home from Sunday School to escape teasing by the boys." Sunday School was a must.

Shirley also had camaraderie with her kid brother, Gordon. The winter they stayed at the logging camp on the S. Branch they iced the path between the office/filing shack and the cookhouse. "When Dad came from his office down that path to the cookhouse for his evening tin of tea, he said, 'Boys that path is slippery. I fell and almost broke my tailbone.'" Shirley and Gordon kept very quiet.

Shirley had most of her first seven grades at the one-room school in E. Knowlesville. She remembers one year at the Knowlesville School, and the teacher, Georgie Philips.

Then, at age 13, Shirley experienced a change of community. In the fall of 1945 she moved with the younger members of her family to Juniper. In that community she especially remembers the youth choir that she and her sister Kaye sang in, and a youth group – both initiated by the Anglican minister, Rev. Mr. Holmes.

In the Juniper School Shirley began grade eight. In 1949 she graduated from Juniper High School. In 1950 she graduated from Normal School in Fredericton. Shirley's first teaching position was at the Glassville School. She boarded with Tom and Marjorie and Alice and Claude Corey.

Shirley immediately began summer School in Fredericton to secure a permanent license. Recalling the summer of 1951 with Kaye, Alice Hallett and Audrey Manuel, she said, "We lived in a house on Gibson St., on the north side of the river. The family was away for the summer". After two summer school sessions at U.N.B. she secured a permanent teacher's license. An early teaching position was at Florenceville.

On July 23, 1952, Shirley Corey married Paul Brooks, son of Rev. William and Mildred Brooks, of Juniper. They were married in the United Baptist Church, Knowlesville. Reception was at the home of Claude and Alice Corey in Glassville.

Early in their marriage Shirley and Paul had a sojourn at Newcastle Bridge. Shirley taught there; Paul worked a bulldozer for the Minto Coal Mine.

Paul developed a variety of skills. His work for the Flemming and Gibson Co., in and around Juniper, involved many phases of logging and lumbering. Later he was self-employed with his own logging truck and loader. He was also self-employed for five years with a grocery store in Juniper. Earlier he had worked in a grocery and meat market in Bath.

In 1974 Paul began a new venture. He became an agent for Metropolitan Life; later he represented Maritime Life.

Shirley taught several years in the Juniper School. She continued to take summer school courses and evening classes, e.g., at Florenceville and Perth to upgrade her license.

Shirley and Paul Brooks have three daughters:
- Jane Rochelle Brooks, born November 13, 1960,
- Lisa Kathleen Brooks, born June 10, 1966,
- Natalie Joy Brooks, born June 22 1968.

They grew up in Juniper and had their first seven grades in Juniper School. Each in turn began grade eight in Florenceville, travelling by bus from Juniper. They all finished Carleton North High School.

More Venture; New Community

In 1986 Paul became an ordained minister. The same year he opened Tabernacle Life Church in W. Florenceville. In 1989 Shirley and Paul sold their house in Juniper and moved to a new house they had built in W. Florenceville. After the move Shirley served as supply teacher a short while, then taught in Centreville for two years.

Daughters and Grandchildren of Shirley and Paul

Jane Brooks

Jane Rochelle Brooks graduated from Carleton North High School in 1978. That fall she became a student at University of N.B., Fredericton. In 1982 she received the Bachelor of Nursing degree from U.N.B. and immediately became a nurse in the Neo-Natal Unit of Dr. Everette Chalmers Hospital in Fredericton. On September 18, 1993, Jane married Teet Vahi, a widower with two daughters, Chaudra and Chantelle. Teet was in the carpentry and construction trade. They built a new house on Dunbar Hill, overlooking the Nashwaak River, near Durham Bridge.

The happy life of Jane and Teet was short; Teet became ill. When he had to give up work, Jane "took a leave of absence from her position to care for him. He received her special care and devotion at home for 14 months. He was unable to recover." A malignant tumour was inoperable. He passed away in August 2000.[9] Teet's funeral was in Smythe St. Cathedral, Fredericton. His brother, Mart Vahi, a Pentecostal pastor and Bishop of Estonia, and a former pastor at Smythe Street, was the preacher.[10] Several other speakers including father-in-law, Paul Brooks, spoke in appreciation and celebration of Teet's life.

At the Chalmers Hospital, Jane had become Nurse Manager. On returning to work in the Neo-Natal Unit, she was asked to prepare and teach a course to beginning nurses on that unit. She has continued involvement in that course. Chaudra Vahi was a student at U.N.B. 2000-2001, then transferred to International School of Arts, Toronto. Chantelle is attending Fredericton High School.

Lisa Kathleen Brooks graduated from Carleton North High School in 1984. On September 15, 1984, she married Dana DeLong, at W. Florenceville. They lived at Bairdsville. They had a daughter and a son:

>Kathleen Lucretia DeLong,
>born August 12, 1988;
>Corey Allison DeLong,
>born March 20, 1990.

Lisa graduated from Community College, Woodstock, in 1994. In November she began work at McCain Foods in the Public Relations Department. She also worked at Dehydrates and Byproducts Dept. In 1994 Lisa married Brent DesRoches at Juniper. Brent is a carpenter. One of his undertakings was enlarging their house – the former McFarland house, in E. Glassville. They raised the roof and extended the house with new rooms. At that attractive home on October 20, 2001, Lisa told me about her work and the children.

Lisa Brooks

Lisa and Brent have a daughter Gina Lynn DesRoches, born January 11, 1996. After a maternity leave, Lisa returned in 1997 to McCain's to the Engineering Department where her cousin, John Corey, also works. Lisa does database work of three types: contract administration, which involves legal forms; environmental data; and time sheet data. The children in 2001-02 school year: Gina, in Kindergarten, Bristol; Corey, grade six, and Kathleen, grade eight in Middle School, Florenceville. Corey is on the basketball team, Florenceville Falcons. They won the Provincial championship in 2002.

Natalie Brooks

Natalie Joy, youngest daughter of Shirley and Paul Brooks, graduated from Carleton North High School in 1987. Then she went to the Community College, Woodstock, for the Bookkeeping Clerk course. She graduated in 1988. For ten years she did bookkeeping and clerical work for her Uncle Weldon Rideout, owner of Arrow Logging, Juniper. On April 20, 1991, Natalie was married to Kevin Lyon of Glassville. They have one son, Brody Jeremiah Lyon, born June 13, 1996. For three years Natalie was employed by Bank of Nova Scotia, Centreville, N.B., until they closed in December 2000. In summer of 2001 Natalie checked out our groceries at the Cooperative Store, Florenceville. On October 26 she collected my payment for potatoes at Mountain View Packers, W. Florenceville. Her work as secretary includes the payroll, and sometimes relieving the manager. She is enjoying the busy atmosphere where potatoes and potato seed are washed, graded, bagged and shipped internationally, daily. Natalie and Brody, now in Kindergarten, are currently living with Shirley and Paul in W. Florenceville.

Shirley and Paul Brooks in Retirement

Shirley retired from teaching in 1992. She continues her interest in painting. The move to Florenceville brought more opportunity. In company with her sister, Kaye Foster, she took lessons. Tabernacle Life Church provided space. Shirley's paintings hang on walls in the Brooks home and sometimes on library walls in art displays. Paul carried on his insurance until 1998. Then he sold his business. Now his energies are devoted to Tabernacle Life Church and related community activities: Sunday services and Bible study; midweek service on Thursday evening; and taking his turn with other ministers in services for seniors at the Manor in Bath.

Gordon Neil Corey

Gordon Neil, the last of the children of Ira and Nellie Corey, was born June 16, 1934, in the farmhouse in E. Knowlesville. Being the youngest of the family, he enjoyed extra affection.

Father held him on his knee in a rocking chair and sang:
"Whoa mule I tell you; whoa der, I say;
Tie a knot in that mule's tail,
And he will run away."
"Possum up a 'cimmon' tree,
Racoon on the ground;
The racoon said, You son-of-a-gun,
Shake them 'cimmons' down."

Father liked to sing: fun songs, hymns – whatever came to mind. Sometimes he sang songs for the whole family:
"It Was from Aunt Dina's Quilting Party I was Seeing Nellie Home"; and,
"Grannie Only Left to Me Her Old Armchair."

Some of the most amusing of Father's songs came out in entertaining Gordon.

Gordon Corey, center, with Jud, Kaye and Shirley, 2001

Gordon was treated with special affection by all the family members. And he was an affectionate boy. One of my best memories of Gordon is an image of him at age five, standing on the platform at C.N.R. Station, Juniper. I was leaving for another term at Doaktown High School. When the conductor shouted, "All board", Gordon put out his hand for a goodbye.

When he started school in E. Knowlesville, Gordon enjoyed the same affection. He sat on Irene Lawson's knee. She brought him an orange every day. Another teacher, Margaret Reeleder, meeting Gordon in adult years, still carried the affection: "Can I kiss you?"

Gordon has not forgotten the affection he received. He recollects, "I had a great relationship with all my brothers." It was expressed in many ways. They gathered a collection for him to buy a pair of snowshoes from Hugh Boyd. Father rehearsed with Gordon an amusing bargaining dialogue to obtain the snowshoes for $3.75. The brothers helped Gordon to devise all kinds of fun: e.g., harnessing a one-year-old filly to pull him on a handsled. He liked horses, machinery and the farm.

Gordon was age 11 when he and two sisters moved with our parents from the farm to Juniper. He recollected, "I couldn't get the farm out of my system. I went there every weekend till the snow came. Bob and Tom let me drive the tractor and horses and run machinery. I yarded wood with one horse."

Gordon was in school in Juniper from grade six into grade nine. School was not his favourite activity. The lure of earning money like other fellows in the neighborhood, and the fascination of trucks, machinery and equipment won out over school.

His first job in Juniper was in the sawmill, at age 14. He recalls, "I took a day off to go hunting. The next day David Cummings said to me, 'Gordon, if you are going to work, you have to work every day.' So I've been working every day ever since."

After his first winter, Gordon began a progression of jobs around the mill and in logging. Early he became a helper on a truck. One morning when a driver didn't show up, Weldon Flemming instructed Gordon, "Get in that truck and start it up!" Before long, Gordon was operating a loader, swinging logs onto trucks, up Tague Brook and on the Nashwaak. While still very young he was operating a bulldozer – one brand new one.

Home, Family and Work in Juniper

In January 1960 Gordon Corey married Esta Grant who grew up in Grant Settlement. She walked the two miles to Canterbury High School. After graduation she experienced a variety of work: Woodstock Hospital; housemaid for a family in Fredericton; then an operator for N.B. Telephone Co. It was while she was working at the Florenceville and Bristol offices that she met Gordon. She got acquainted with Gordon's sister, Kaye Foster, and stayed with them during shift work.

Gordon brought his bride to Juniper. They lived with our mother. Eventually they built an extension onto the house, providing Mother with her own room. Thanks to the care of Esta and Gordon, Mother was able to stay in that home the rest of her life. In her years of failing strength Esta cared for her – a care that extended to Mother's last day.

In 1967 Gordon got his own truck. He hauled logs for Weldon Rideout.

Gordon and Esta had five children:
> Mitchell Gordon, born July 20, 1960
> Sally Louise, born November 22, 1961
> Anthony Neil, born May 4, 1963
> Stephanie Katherine, born November 2, 1968
> Trent Andrew, born March 19, 1972

They all began their education at Juniper School. The first four all went on to Carleton North High School in Bristol. The last, Trent, a boy of 12, had finished grade six and was ready for grade seven in Florenceville when he suffered an accident.

On the evening of July 21, 1984, in Juniper, Trent was fatally injured in a collision with another motor bike. The family was sadly bereaved of an affectionate relationship. His brothers and Sally and Peter gave him gifts and took him places. He was very fond of motor bikes; he had two or three of them. If one got banged up, he got another. He liked hockey and other sports.

The service at Kilcollins Funeral Home, Bath, was attended by many relatives and friends. Trent's monument stands in the United Church Cemetery, Glassville, where many Corey relatives lie.

Graduating and Going to Work

Mitchell Corey was in the first graduating class of Carleton North High School, 1978. Then he went to U.N.B., Fredericton. He had one year of the engineering course. He had interest in going to the Forestry School. He also had interest in work. A summer contracting job led to ongoing contracting and enterprising in the logging industry. He and Charles Kelley bought a skidder from Weldon Rideout.

On July 10, 1982, at the Wesleyan Church, Bristol, Mitchell Corey married Cindy Guthrie, daughter of Sadie and the late Claude Guthrie. Later they built a new house at Highlands.

In 1985 Mitchell and Charles formed Glassville Logging Company. As work expanded they began to coax Gordon: "Come and work with us; come and run the slasher." In 1987 Gordon was persuaded to terminate a 20-year employment with Weldon Rideout and begin work with Mitchell and company. Gordon ran the bulldozer and other equipment.

Anthony was an early employee of Mitchell. After graduating from Carleton North High School, 1981, Anthony drove one of Weldon Rideout's trucks for about a year. Since then he has worked for Mitchell. He has been a trucker, an operator of various machines, and a foreman.

Company employment reached nearly all members of the family. Sally graduated from Carleton North High School in 1979. She worked some summers at the Irving tree nursery. In 1981 Sally Corey married Peter Bulger. He worked for the company almost from its beginning. When Mitchell bought a delimber, Peter operated it. Later Sally took on the task of cooking for six months for Mitchell's crew in the Miramichi area. In 1989 Peter and Sally bought their house in Juniper. In 1994 Sally became the manager of a restaurant which Mitchell bought in Juniper.

Stephanie Corey began working for the company as

soon as she graduated as a secretary from Community College, Woodstock, in 1987. On September 21, 1991, Stephanie married Gerald Lester DeMerchant, son of George and Dorothy DeMerchant, Holmesville. The wedding was at Trinity Wesleyan Church, Bristol. Gerald became an employee of Glassville Logging Co. that year.

Esta Corey, after working at Irving Nursery, Juniper, spring and summer 1978-1985, and as custodian of Juniper School 1985-94, began office work with Stephanie and Cindy for Glassville Logging Co. in 1994. Esta's work included managing the payroll. The last two issues of "Corey Courier" 1995 and 1997, were produced in that office – Stephanie typed them.

Work Ongoing

Mitchell's company is now called Vicon contractors. They do contract work, e.g., for a Newcastle mill and for an Irving company. He cuts logs and wood on various sites, mostly in the Miramichi area, including Renous and Christmas Mountain.

In fall of 2001 Anthony was foreman on the work site of the contract work for Irving Paper at Renous. He was operating the loader and managing the cutting and hauling. He was travelling daily from Florenceville.

Peter Bulger and Gerald DeMerchant continue to work for Mitchell's company. Stephanie is doing the office work for Mitchell. Sally is now working at Mills Convenience Store in Juniper.

Children and Grandchildren

Mitchell and Cindy Corey live at Highlands on the Glassville/Juniper road. Their children:
Matthew Gordon,
born August 13, 1985,

and Amanda Michelle, born January 5, 1988.

Matthew is a student at Carleton North High School, Bristol. He plays on their hockey team. Amanda is a student at Middle School, Florenceville. She has three horses, likes to ride, and competes in horse shows.

Sally and Peter Bulger have a daughter: Kaylie Mary Louise, born May 21, 1987. She is a student at Carleton North High School, Bristol.

Anthony Corey married Karen Campbell on December 23, 1992. They built a new house at Argyle and a shop for Karen's hair salon. About 1998 they moved from Argyle to Florenceville. Karen set up a new hair salon in their new home. Anthony and Karen Corey have a son: Joshua Anthony, born August 20, 1992. He is a student at Florenceville Middle School, and a hockey player.

Stephanie and Gerald DeMerchant have a daughter: Hannah, born prematurely, May 5, 2000, at the Dr. Everett Chalmers Hospital, Fredericton. The baby required hospital care for several weeks before they could bring her home. With loving care and devotion by both Stephanie and Gerald, Hannah has grown to be a pretty little girl.

Gordon and Esta in Retirement

Gordon, semi-retired for a couple of years, has been on call for business errands for Mitchell. Esta is working two days a week for Mitchell and Cindy.

Gordon and Esta maintain valued relations with all the relatives. Norman has divided his visits between Gordon's and the Brooks family. Norman has endeared himself to the children. He recognized, e.g., that Anthony, as a boy, was a lover of the out-of-doors and brought him fishing equipment. There is a strong relationship between Norman, the eldest surviving member of the family, and Gordon, the youngest. Gordon and

Esta are planning a 2002 visit to Norman and family in Burlington.

Gordon and Esta also have close relations with their children and grandchildren. Speaking of his Dad, Anthony said, "He taught me to get up in the morning and go to work." He described Gordon as, "best father, best grandfather, good family man, concerned about everybody in the family; I think the world of him."

Conclusion

In this chapter we have told the stories of the descendants of Ira and Nellie Corey.

The end of this chapter also marks the end of the stories of the descendants of Alfred and Lucretia Corey who lived most of their lives in Knowlesville. Their descendants are scattered over the continent of North America. Some have sojourned much farther. Their work has ranged from scraping floors of cow barns to helping erect skyscrapers.

[1] The Story of Knowlesville, P.107f.;

[2] Ibid., P.142

[3] Narrated in Chapter VIII

[4] Most of the data on the descendants of Erma and Allison Shaw was compiled by Alice Long. The genealogy was printed by Margaret Monroe.

[5] See Chapter VI and VII

[6] Quotations are from Murray Corey's biographies of the siblings, and of the parents in retirement

[7] The Observer, Hartland, N.B., Nov. 21, 1963

[8] See Chapter XVI

[9] Shirley Brooks

[10] Times Globe, Saint John, August 4, 2000

CHAPTER XIX

IN GRATEFUL MEMORY OF MARGARET EVELINE COREY

Margaret in her "Race for the cure" T-shirt

In mid March, 2002, I had reached about this point in the writing of this book. I was looking forward to the pleasure of accomplishment, and celebrating the completion of a decade-long task. Then – an unexpected happening:

Margaret, the person who had been my supporter through the extensive task, and whom I expected to be by my side in the celebration, was diagnosed with a malignant tumor, and a blood clot.

For a while it appeared that all the anticipated satisfaction would vanish. My energy, concentration, and heart for the writing, organizing and planning rapidly diminished. Thank goodness the gathering of stories and data, and the writing was, in the main, accomplished. Two remaining chapters, needed more work. The genealogies needed new format to meet the printer's standards. There was much more proofreading.

From a hospital bed Margaret said to me, "You have to finish your book." Clearly, she was not expecting all my attention. She wanted me to complete the writing that had been in progress through most of our marriage. Through two spring admissions I was able to continue some work on the book, between visits to Margaret in hospital, and after she returned home. By that time I had moved my place of writing from my upstairs study to our dining room table, where I could quickly leave off to respond to Margaret's need for water, juice, pills, or to move to a more comfortable position, or to answer the door bell.

It was a busy and heart-rending time. Friends came to the house; cards and notes came in the mail; people called by phone. The extra-mural nurse – friendly, sensitive and eager to bring comfort, came two or three times a week. I made many trips to hospital to deliver blood samples to the laboratory, to check on effect of blood thinner. In May and June we made many trips to the oncology department of the hospital. Margaret had out-patient radiation treatments, over five weeks.

Through the summer we lived in hope. Margaret very much liked the porch on the front of our house, and had wished the season for using it could be longer. In June we had it winterized with insulation and new windows.

In July we went to Carleton County. Margaret looked forward to the holiday. In company with my brother, Warren, we enjoyed a quiet time in a cottage in Beaufort where the water of the S. Branch of the S.W. Miramichi River flowed quietly by. Margaret enjoyed many trips by car with Warren and me. We visited many relatives; and Warren's long-standing friends. We attended the 50th Wedding Anniversary of Shirley and Paul Brooks. We concluded our holiday with a family picnic, August 3, beside the stream. Then Margaret needed the security of being near the nurses, the doctors and the hospital. On August 4 we returned to Saint John.

Near the end of August we kept an appointment in the oncology department for assessment of the effects of the radiation treatments. The tumor had not been arrested. The oncologist advised us "….a few more weeks or months." I was soon in mourning.

Margaret spoke with courage: "I don't know whether I should focus on living, or on dying." She had much to live for. She dearly loved the grandchildren. They expressed much affection to her. She took great pride in our home. She had put much work and planning into re-decorations and additions. She had welcomed many relatives – her mother, many Corey family members, and friends, and entertained with her cooking and baking. She sent goodies home with the grandchildren.

Margaret remained calm and gracious despite pain, and with all the pain medicine she remained clear-headed. One thing she was very clear about. She did not want to pursue desperate measures. People spoke of other kinds of treatment. We uncovered a book: I Want to Live. She declined to read it, not because she would not have liked to extend her life. Rather, she realistically faced what was happening to her: loss of mobility and of ability to do much even for herself, let alone for others. Furthermore she did not want to spend her precious remaining time on desperate and futile pursuits. She had already declined chemo treatments, seeing it as a prospect of added discomfort.

Yet she did not give up interest in life. We reviewed some of our life together. I read diary notes of a visit we made to Britain – the first ten days of it in company with two grandchildren: Andrea and Charles Corey. She maintained interest in our home. She took pleasure in library books and home renovations. She showed me in a catalogue a new style window curtain with attachments, possible for our large diningroom window.

In retrospect I am humbled, seeing more clearly her unselfishness. When, later, I asked her, "Are you going to order the curtain?" "No, I don't think you would like it." We were able to discuss, briefly, a few practical matters, e.g., a lot in a local cemetery. At that point she thought of her mother. "Mom wouldn't like it to be far away."

In early September medical caregivers began talking to us about regulating Margaret's pain medicine. They advised us that it could best be done in hospital. They gave us the expectation that in a few days she could return home. When she awoke on the morning of Friday, September 13th, she said, "I have to make a decision today," i.e., about going to the hospital. The opening for admission came immediately. When we left home that day we both held to the prospect of an early return.

In hospital, one day she said to me, "I want you to get heat in the porch." But her strength was waning, and her waking hours diminishing. Her affection for me and others, and her sweet disposition held firmly. I tried to be with her for most of her waking hours.

Early on morning of September 25th I received a call from a nurse. I shall be forever grateful that I was able to be with Margaret, expressing my love to her to the end. A nurse assured me that though speech had gone, her hearing had not; neither had her affection gone.

Many other people felt her affection. Members of her church had visited and sent cards over six months. One of them said to me, "To know her, was to love her."

In my grief and search for reconciliation to my loss I have recounted much that Margaret gave to me: companionship, compassion, kindness and sensitivity. I have become more conscious of the enrichment she brought to my life.

Now it occurs to me that the security and comfort of our relationship enabled me to concentrate on the demanding task of writing this book. How graciously she accepted my travels and visits in the pursuit of stories, biographies and genealogies! Sometimes she accompanied me, quickly becoming acquainted with relatives. Several times she stayed home, graciously accepting being alone. Should I regret leaving her alone at times? One thing I can do now is acknowledge my debt to her for the security and support she gave me, that enabled me to pursue this extensive work.

In my grief, I reflected on the line:
"'Tis you, 'tis you must go, and I must bide'".

Margaret's family. Left to right front: George Ruseff, Jud and Margaret Corey, Gloria Williams (mother), Edith Ruseff, Jaclyn Banks, Ron Ruseff

Margaret, 3rd from left, middle row, at Ross Corey's

We cannot explain why some people must go, seemingly prematurely, but my reflection told me there must be purpose in my "biding" into late life. Part of that purpose looms immediately before me, i.e., to complete and celebrate this writing – to be bequeathed to generations to come. I shall go about that task in the strength of the security and confidence Margaret left with me by her love and support. In this sense she is still by my side and will be through the celebration and beyond.

Looking a little farther ahead, I must get back to my part in the work of peace and justice in the world. My prayer is that of St. Francis, "May I this coming day be able to do some work of peace for thee." At this point I make a further dedication of this book to Margaret Stevens Corey.

CHAPTER XX

HOME AND BELONGING

This book is about belonging – to a family and families, to community and communities. Its many stories are of people belonging and being valued within families. We all need to belong, and to have a home.

I count myself fortunate in having experienced that sense of belonging most of the time I was growing up. One boyhood experience served to reinforce, for me, the need and the value of a sense of belonging. That was my experience of going to E. Glassville School at age 11, where, for a time, I experienced the feeling of not belonging.[1]

The culmination of that experience was a memorable homecoming. On a rainy Saturday afternoon in October my two younger brothers, Warren, nine, and Keith, not yet seven, came to our grandmother's, driving our old black mare, Nell. They drove to the orchard where we were spreading manure. Their wagon was a "sweet chariot, come for to carry me home."

I didn't get to go home that day; my uncle persuaded me to stay one more week. Nonetheless, their coming for me was a demonstration of family belonging. The homecoming was a reaffirming of family caring. It was a return to where I was sure I belonged.

I appreciated home, though as a place of continuous abode I was only able to enjoy it through age 15 1/2. Going from home at that early age was not because I wanted to leave. It was a departure, it seemed, I had to make for the pursuit of an education. The story of my leaving the farm in E. Knowlesville and going to Doaktown, I've told in Chapter XI.

In that departure from home, as in the earlier one, I experienced some sense of strangeness and alienation. In Doaktown, I had to face again a strange school, and a strange community. Again, I had some feeling of not belonging.

In another sense, however, I belonged there. Being there was for my benefit. My uncle and aunt, after raising eight children of their own, took me into their home to give me an opportunity that was not available at home. But helping me get started in high school was not the only thing they did for me. In their act of generosity I was assured of continued belonging and being valued.

Reflection on my experience tells me it is not the place we call home that is most important. We can leave home and still have a home, i.e., a sense of belonging. Many of us, over a lifetime, have many places we call home. It is very important, therefore, that through many changes in location we retain a sense of belonging. Also, though the place may change, we can still experience homecoming – an important aspect of the experience of belonging. I came back to my first home many times, and stayed for varying intervals.

If we couldn't have homecomings, we would be deprived of much meaning in life. This reminds me of a story that was told by a worker the summer Warren and I worked on the Black Sturgeon River in Ontario. It is the story of a lumberjack who had drifted from job to job over several years. Finally one summer he hoboed back to his home "down east". The storyteller described how he explored familiar scenes in his hometown. But the nearest he got to a family homecoming was to go round to his family home one evening, and peek in a window. He saw his mother and his sister sitting there. But he couldn't knock on the door and go in. Maybe he thought he no longer belonged.

Even the dog we had on the farm demonstrated the need of belonging. He had a special "belonging" attachment to me, because I was the family member who went, accompanied by Ed Olmstead, to Joe McDermid's, at Highlands, and brought him to our place. Following my departure from home, on many occasions, as Mother described to me afterwards, he sat, or lay, looking in the direction I had left. No matter how many months I was gone, at every homecoming he put on a dramatic welcome.

He also had a strong belonging to the farm. They told me that my brother Wilfred took him to Lower Brighton – I guess as a companion for Harold Wayne. The first time our car drove in their yard, and a door opened, he crawled in and wouldn't budge until they returned home.

My most dramatic experience related to belonging, happened during WW II in Europe. I feared the loss of home and all sense of belonging. The home that I feared losing was no home at all in the sense of a settled abode. Home was wherever we could find a dry comfortable place, e.g., a farmyard, to set up a tent; or a barn with a loft and some hay, perhaps under the same roof as the cows or the horses. It was not any property we could lay claim to. It was a home that pulled up stakes, took wheels and moved at a few hours notice. What then could I lose that could be called home? What I very much feared losing and nearly lost, was my attachment to my group.

The setting of my near loss was in Holland in the spring of 1945. We were camped for a few days in a farmyard. The weather was very mild – a pleasant time to spend the day out-of-doors. My job was in signaling by radio and Morse code –helping maintain communication, and being responsible for some equipment.

One day at noon some of us were told we could have the afternoon off. A truck would take us to town. We could see a movie. The truck would call for us in the evening. When I discovered that the movie was one I had already seen, I decided to explore the town and return to the rendez-vous at the appointed time.

Alas there was no truck, and none of my group members. That evening I felt frustration and bewilderment about failure in rendez-vous – but no great anxiety. After a wait I decided to look for a shelter for the night. I found a barracks that had beds but no bedding, not even a mattress. Sleeping in my uniform prevented the bare wire mesh from cutting too deep an imprint on my body. Having slept in all sorts of places and improvised beds: lumber camps, in hammocks in the hold of a ship, or in an aeroplane hangar, in barns and in tents, I dropped quickly to sleep. In the morning I lost no time getting dressed. A little time in a queue paid off with tea and toast. I inquired the direction of the town where my unit was camped, and got only vague general directions. I set out hitchhiking. After several rides, interspersed with walks, I came upon a British group tenting in a field. It was noon. The fellows were cooking food over an open fire. Cordially they invited me to eat with them. One of the men volunteered to go and talk with his officer and explain my predicament. But there seemed to be a general coldness and strange hesitancy on the part of the officers to help me get back to my unit.

Afterwards I was told that there had been an unfortunate incident in which some of the little reconnaissance planes of the British unit were mistaken for enemy planes, and some of our fellows had taken shots at them. There were no casualties, but the incident was difficult to forget.

What was I going to do? The Brits, in the lower ranks, were more than friendly to the lonely Canuck who had wandered into their camp. The April afternoon was warm and pleasant. The fellows were giving me a kind of tentative home. How could I leave it without some prospect of getting back to where I unquestionably belonged? For some hours I waited, hoping for a more definite move to help me.

In late afternoon one of the fellows who was befriending me told me that one of the officers was about to go on an errand by jeep; he would give me a ride part way. He took me over a tortuous route along farm boundaries, over dirt roads. He had a map. I was confident that he knew his bearings. At length he stopped at the edge of a field. Pointing in the distance he said to me, "If you walk across this field and over that hill at the far side of the field, you should see the farm where your unit is located.

Buoyed with the prospect of arriving back to where I belonged, I walked through the waning day. Then new apprehensions came over me: What if I haven't been given the correct directions? Or, what if they've gone? An overwhelming loneliness, and feeling of isolation and abandonment, came over me.

There were many apprehensions in a war zone. One I hadn't thought of heretofore occurred to me in those moments. How terrible to be abandoned in a foreign country, and suffer the feeling of not belonging to any group or any place. I think that was the nearest I've ever come to identifying with the feeling of a displaced person.

Walking steadily, I arrived at the farmyard just in the nick of time. If I had been ten minutes later I would have been abandoned. The trucks were loaded. One of the fellows had picked up my belongings and thrown them on a vehicle. I climbed aboard, holding to the security of belonging. In the more than half century since that experience, reflection on it has kept me reminded of the importance of belonging. Without a sense of belonging we are deprived. We've all enjoyed a sense of belonging in many groups.

There are many levels of belonging. We belong to our families – the families we grew up with, and our families with spouse and children. We belong to this extensive family – the descendants of Alfred and Lucretia Corey – far more extensive than most of us had imagined, and now strengthened by shared stories.

Our ultimate level of belonging is in the Kingdom of God. For me it is expressed in this prayer:
> In the name of him who had no place to lay his head yet never strayed from the home of thy kingdom, grant that we in our restless wanderings and forced wayfaring may forever keep in

mind that thou art the goal of all travel, the port of all voyages, the home of all pilgrimage, so that our hearts may bear up right bravely, knowing that wherever we may be, on land, or sea, or in the air, coming or going, thou art ever the same, our Father and our God, with peace and power to steady us, and grace to keep our souls. Amen.[2]

[1] The story is told in Chap. VIII

[2] Samuel H. Miller, Prayers for Daily Use (Harper and Brothers, 1957), p.72

CHAPTER XXI

MEMORIALS AND REMEMBERING

Knowlesville people have given me two lists of people the community especially wants to commemorate. But first let us try to express the value of remembering people, and also recognize that for each of us there are people whose memories we want to keep alive.

On March 5, 1996, I visited Lorne and Dorothy Craig at their home in E. Knowlesville. As I sat in that house that day, enjoying the conversation and the hospitality, I had flashbacks of experiences of decades before, and of history that had been narrated to me.

As a boy growing up in that neighborhood, I often visited the family of my mother's sister, Hazel, and George H. Whitehouse who then lived in that house. Their son, Stanley, was born the same year I was. In the decade before I was born, my Uncle, Rev. J.A. Corey and family lived in that house for three years. Their youngest daughter, Mildred, was born there. My uncle married my mother and father in that same house.

Earlier, the house had been occupied by members of the Doucette family. The first, it appears by the records, was Henry N. Doucette, the original grantee of lot 23, range 5; and the last was his nephew, Jacob Doucette.[1]

In structure, the house is as the Doucette family built it and left it, though the Craigs have made changes and renovations. The living room has been extended southward into the space of the former veranda. The old woodshed has been detached and moved to the barnyard. The east window of the kitchen has been replaced by sliding glass doors that open onto a deck. The glass gives a view of the modern barn, the fields and the brook. In place of the wood burning stove is an electric range. From it Dorothy brought freshly baked cookies to us and a carload of her relatives of Juniper and Biggar Ridge: Jim and Irene Hoyt and Georgina Stoddard. The telephone line that originally came from Argyle now comes from Hartland.[2]

Communication now reaches much farther and floods of information come from the whole world; yet the importance of the community and neighboring settlements are not forgotten. Their history and the monuments of their people are being preserved.

On July 31, 1997 I stopped at the Craigs' house again, with a specific purpose in mind, i.e., to gather a little more of the story of the War Memorial in Knowlesville – the planning and the achievement. Lorne did brief me on the monument and revealed satisfaction in the accomplishment.

Before the time of my visit, however, he had expanded his interest in preserving the memories of people who have gone before us. He had moved to other areas of local history. Hence he soon shifted the conversation to a current project.

From their deck he brought an iron grave marker with wrought iron letters, "Robert O'Dell". He had brought it from Golden Ridge for restoration. He had had Dennis DeMerchant make new letters at the shop where he worked in Nackawick. The marker stood on Craigs' deck, waiting to be returned to its gravesite. Land grant maps came on the table: Skedaddle Ridge and Golden Ridge, where once stood pioneer farms and communities long since abandoned.

Soon came an invitation: "If you have a few moments, "I'll show you what we are doing." He drove me past the Hemphill/Corey Farm where I was born – now growing in trees. At the site of the East Knowlesville Schoolhouse we turned up the road to Golden Ridge. On top the first ridge we beheld a beautiful 100-acre field of potatoes in bloom. It is on the Fred Currie farm that we thought was no longer tillable. The left fork of the smoothly graded road took us between the site of the Hugh Boyd farm and the lot where Tom Guthrie pastured cattle for many summers. Past the Richard Boyd homestead, a narrower road changed our direction from east to north and brought us to the Jamison lot.

We stopped where entry posts marked a path into the woods. A short walk brought us to an old cellar, newly excavated. Nearby, stood a stone monument:

    Jane Thorne, died 1870
        Wife of
    Richard Thorne

Also, there are foot stones marking the graves of three children. I marveled that the gravesite that I had mentioned only briefly in **The Story of Knowlesville**, p.63, is now accessible by road and path, so that the stone monument stands in view. However, even when the gravesite was far less accessible, descendants of Richard Thorne were making yearly visits to the grave.

Richard Thorne married 2nd, Rebecca Derrah. They had two children: Richard, Jr., 1875-1925, and Adelaide, 1878-1940. Rebecca is buried in Mount Pleasant. Adelaide married Mansfield Ellis, Bannon. Their children: Clifford, Beulah, Jasper and Preston. The families of Jasper, Preston and Beulah continue to make visits to the gravesites in Golden Ridge.[3]

Lorne turned his car and pointed southward. We passed on our left the site of the Arthur Jordan farms, now the site of beautiful camps belonging to Jordon grandsons

Then passed on our right the site of the farm and log house of Billy Campbell.[4] Cherished is the memory of our faithful mailman who drove his horse in the rains of summer and the storms of winter. As we continued toward the old driving dam on the South Branch, an experience of sixty years earlier came up on my memory screen. It was the memory of walking over fields then only half-grown with bushes, and still pasturing Billy's cows. As our party of four – Billy and I and my two brothers, Warren and Keith – walked toward the South Branch, through fenced fields, fishing rods in hand, Billy told us: "Twelve or fifteen families used to live in this neighborhood."

Now a bulldozed road through woods permits wheel traffic where formerly there was a lane through a pasture partly wooded. Billy's neighboring families have mostly been forgotten. But one name at least lives on: Robert O'Dell.[5] Lorne stopped his car where a footpath leads to the site of the O'Dell homestead. At that site two men and a woman were there working: peeling small trees, laying crushed stone, driving stakes, hammering nails, building little foot bridges with cedar boards stretched across stringers. Some boards were sawn from logs on site. They had uncovered the cellar hole, and made visible the gravesite nearby. Apple trees still grow there. To this gravesite the iron marker that stood on Lorne's deck was soon to be returned. Now carefully restored, the marker also records that Robert's fourteen-year-old daughter died in 1884. To that O'Dell family belongs Lewis O'Dell Carle.[6]

Other memories came back: my father's crews cutting at MacIntosh Brook, McCrossin Place and South Branch. Also Vernon Whitehouse had camps and crews in the area.

The visit to Golden Ridge left me profoundly moved. As I traveled to Juniper I recalled that beautiful piece of extra-canonical literature that was printed in "The Hymnary" and often recited in United Church and Baptist congregations: "Let us now praise famous men: and our fathers that begat us. The Lord hath wrought great glory by them...." It tells of skilled, accomplished people who were honored in their generations.

Then there is a thought-provoking transition: "And some there be which have no memorial: who had perished as though they had never been. And are become as though they had never been born: and their children after them. But these were merciful men: whose righteousness hath not been forgotten."

This ancient wisdom I interpret as a recognition that

while those with high profiles will have monuments erected to their memories, others who perhaps had no great claim to fame, but nonetheless were worthy people who made contributions for those who follow – they tend to be forgotten.

Gray's "Elegy Written in a Country Churchyard", for me is an expression of the same wisdom: i.e., that the virtues and contributions of humble people often go unrecognized:

"Full many a gem of purest ray serene
The dark unfathomed caves of ocean bear:
Full many a flower is born to blush unseen,
And waste its sweetness on the desert air."

Henry David Thoreau also honors the memory of people who have gone before us. Thoreau recognized the people who lived earlier in the neighborhood of Walden Pond. He said, "For human society I was obliged to conjure up the former occupants of these woods." He named: Cato Ingraham, "slave of Duncan Ingraham,.....who built his slave a house, and gave him permission to live in Walden Woods " ; Zilpha, "a colored woman" who, in her little house "spun linen for the townsfolk"; Brister Freeman, "a handy Negro", slave of Squire Cummings once, and Fenda, Brister's "hospitable wife, who told fortunes"; the Stratton family; Nutting and LeGrosse; Wyman the potter who "furnished his townsmen with earthenware" ; Hugh Quoil – "Col. Quoil, he was called, — rumored to have been a soldier at Waterloo."[7]

The two groups of "Former Inhabitants" whom Knowlesville people especially asked the writer to include in this volume are:

The ministers who served Knowlesville Baptist Church.
The soldiers listed on the Knowlesville-Armond War Memorial.

The Ministers who served Knowlesville United Baptist Church:

On 13 October 1862 a Free Christian Baptist Church was organized in Kowlesville by Rev. Cyril Doucette, assisted by Rev. Samuel Hartt.

Rev. C. Doucette	1862-187?
Rev. John Gravenor	1876-188?
Rev. Samuel W. Shaw and Rev. John Gravenor	1888
Lic. Abner McNintch	1889-1890
Rev. Elijah B. Gray	1891-1894
Rev. James J. Barnes	1894-1895
Rev. J. Nobles, Rev. Charles Rideout	1895-1900
Lic. G. Douglas Millbury	1900
Rev. Thomas O. DeWitt	1901
Rev. George W. Foster	1901-1903
Rev. H. Allen Bonnell	1904-1905
G.C.F. Kierstead	1906-1907
Lic. G.W. Camp	1908
Lic. Taylor and Rev. C.B. Lewis	1909-1910
Lic. C.S. Young	1911
Rev. Judson A. Corey	1911-1913[8]
Lic. Roby Brown and Lic. George Peters	1915
Lic. Greenwood and Rev. W.B. Crowell	1916-1917
Rev. Luke Bleakney	1918
Rev. L.J. Tingley and Rev. J. Corey	1919
Mr. Wm. A. Gildart	1921
Evangelist F.W. Foster	1922
Rev. E.A. Trites	1922
Rev. Lew. Wallace	1922
Rev. Mr. Kierstead	1922

Rev. J. Corey	1922
Rev. W.J. Alexander	1923
No pastor	1924
Rev. W.S. Smith	1930
Lic. F.S. Cliffe	1931
Rev. W.S. Smith	1931
Rev. J. Corey	1931
Rev. W.S. Smith	1932
Lic. Agnes Waring	1932-1933
Lic. George Manter Wilson	1935 Acadia grad 1934
Lic. Perry Allaby	1936 Acadia grad 1938
Lic. Harold Pond	1937-1938
Lic. Erle Griffin	1939-1940
Lic. Harold Mitton	1941-1943 Acadia grad 1944
Lic. Willard Smith	1944 Acadia grad 1944
Lic. Lorne Stairs	summer 1947
Lic. John Davey	summer 1948
Lic. Everett Nickerson	summer 1949 Acadia grad 1951
Lic. Malcolm Stairs	summers of 1950 and 1951
Lic. C.R. Barkhouse	1952-1953
Lic. Jack Lockwood	summer 1954
Lic. Lynn Stairs	summer 1955
David Vila	summer 1956
Lic. Robert Steeves	summers of 1958 and 1959
Lic. Ronald McLean	summer 1960 Acadia grad 1968

lic. Brent Robertson	summer 1961
	Acadia grad 1963
Ronald Stanley	1962-1963
Lic. Richard Hallett	summer 1964
Lic. George Allaby	summers 1965 and 1966
	Acadia grad 1968
Lic. Gordon Jones	summer 1967
Lic. Jack Willett	summer 1968
John Tonks	summer 1969
Lic. Isaac Wilkins	summer 1971
	Acadia grad 1968
Brian Wortman	summer 1972
Lic. Otis Derrah	1973-1975 year round
Lic. W. Frenette	summer 1976
Murray Whitehouse	1977-1979 summers
Murray Whitehouse	1980-1988 year round
Lic. Carl O'Donnell	1988-1995
Rev. Brian Wortman	1997-1998
Lic. Carl O'Donnell	1998-1999
Rev. Frederick R. Smith	1999 - 20[9]

Knowlesville-Armond War Memorial

About 1991 a newly-formed committee in Knowlesville sent out a letter:

"The People of Knowlesville & Armond have formed a group to erect a War memorial to honour the men who served and those who died for freedom.

If you were a Knowlesville Veteran or a descendant of a Knowlesville Veteran we would like to hear from you."

The committee chair was Lorne Craig. Secretary was

Clara Brewster. Other members of the committee were: Roy Hemphill, Myrtle Hemphill, Elmer Lapage, Arlie Whitehouse, Beryl de Beaupré and Shawn Shaw.

The committee met many times over a period of two years or more. They worked diligently, following up on many assignments, contacting many people locally and by phone and letter, and obtaining records, e.g., from Ottawa.

Another letter was circulated:

"Work has already started on this project and will be completed in the spring.

As you may know, this is a large undertaking for a community of our size. Private individuals, businesses, and civic organizations in the area are being asked for financial assistance."

Contributions were received from many individuals and groups, including the Canadian Legion, both Florenceville and Hartland branches. People contributed willingly – glad to have a part in the monument.

Summing up the work and accomplishment, Clara Brewster said, "After all the meetings, phone calls, letters, trips to post office, and sticking stamps the work brought a great feeling of satisfaction to all participants."

In the spring of 1993 the following note was circulated:
"The Knowlesville-Armond War Memorial Committee cordially invite you to attend the unveiling of the Memorial Stone.
The ceremonies will be held at 2:30 p.m. on July 10, 1993 at the Knowlesville United Baptist Church and followed by the Legion Service at the Memorial Site."

That day, the monument was unveiled, revealing the following names:

1914 – 1918

Bevan, George *
Brewster, George
Carle, Lewis
Carle, Roy
Dyer, G. Lee
Frost, Arthur *
Harvey, George
Henderson, John *
Jones, Erwin
Kenney, Frank
Kenney, Fred

Keirstead, James
Linder, Ramond
Linder, Samuel *
London, Ivon
MacKenzie, Lee *
Murphy, George
Manuel, Elmer
Shorey, Elwood
Taylor, Harold *
Whitehouse, Earle

N.B. * denotes killed in action

1939 – 1945

- Avery, Alton
- Bell, Joseph
- Boyd, Ralph
- Boyd, Attle
- Branscombe, Paul
- Corey, Claude
- Corey, Judson
- Corey, Norman
- Corey, Thomas
- Craig, Richard
- Fisher, Walter
- Hayden, Ashley
- Hemphill, Arnold
- Hemphill, Harold
- Jones, Willard
- Kimball, Merritt
- Lapage, Elmer
- Lawson, Harold
- Lawson, Jack
- McAfee, Robert
- McLean, Hazen
- Morgan, Ronald
- Olmstead, Douglas
- Olmstead, Edward
- Shorey, Eldon
- Shorey, Weldon
- Whitehouse, Arlie
- Whitehouse, Austin
- Whitehouse, Stanley

A photo of Ed Olmstead was in the possession of the writer. We were schoolmates. Let Ed's photo be representative of many other Knowlesville boys and men who served in the Canadian forces.

Edward Olmstead

Ed contributed the following quotation from Field Marshal Montgomery:

CANADIANS EXCELLED BY NONE – MONTY

TORONTO, May 26 – Field Marshal Montgomery said in a broadcast message to Canada, that "of all the soldiers that have fought under my command in this great war, none are finer than the fighting men from Canada."
"There may be some as good, but there are none finer," he added.
"It is my earnest desire that I may one day visit your great country – if you ask me. I have fought alongside your men in battle and have many friends in the Canadian forces. I feel that I would like to see the country from which came these magnificent men."

Contributed by Edward Olmstead

1950

Brewster, Wilbur
Daye, Jed
Dyer, Donald
Dyer, Robert
Gutherie, Scott *
Jones, Alexander

Morgan, Robert
Orser, Colby
Pencz, Robert
Robinson, Alden
Robinson, Clair

N.B. * denotes killed in action

The day of unveiling was also a day of homecoming to Knowlesville. Many of us who grew up and attended school and church in Knowlesville had a rare meeting. The people of Knowlesville served a generous and delicious supper.

The hospitality continues every year in November when the ladies of Knowlesville welcome members of the Canadian Legion, Hartland Branch, with a dinner. Commendation is expressed to the Legion members. Since the day of unveiling they have come to Knowlesville every year near November 11th for a service at the monument.

1 See, The Story of Knowlesville, p.9f., and p.115f.

2 Ibid., p.105

3 From Mrs. Jasper Ellis (Ella Hallett), via L. Craig

4 See The Story of Knowlesville, p.171f.

5 For names of the families who pioneered homes on the nearby lots, see Annie Dyer's, History of Argyle, p.110.

6 The Story of Knowlesville, p.33

7 Henry David Thoreau, Walden, Chap. 14: "Former Inhabitants;...."

8 For more on Rev. J.A. Corey's ministry to the church and the pastoral circuit, see The Story of Knowlesville, p. 116-122; also Chapter XI of this book

9 This list was provided by Christine Lovelace, Archives Assistant, Vaughn Memorial Library, Acadia University, Wolfville, N.S., in January 1999. It was supplemented and updated by Etta Whitehouse, Treasurer, Knowlesville United Baptist Church.

Charles Allen MacNearney
m. Maud Miller

Robert James Miller, Glassville

GENEALOGIES

Decendants of:
1841 Alfred Corey 1930
and
1842 Lucretia Kierstead 1922

1865 Mina Corey McBrine 1938.	Chapter VIII
1867 Alma Corey Miller 1915.	Chapter IX
1868 Charles H.S. Corey 1945.	Chapter X
1870 Judson Albert Corey 1952.	Chapter XI
1872 Ida Corey McBrine 1953.	Chapter XII
1875 Sarah Corey Fletcher.	Chapter XIII
1879 Alberta Corey Redlon 1955.	Chapter XIV
1882 Laversa Corey Garns 1969.	Chapter XV
1877 Ira Thomas Corey 1957.	Chapter XVI, XVIII.

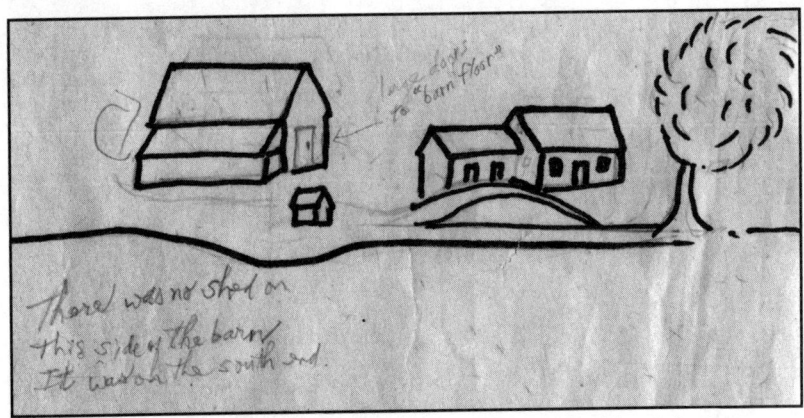

Homestead of Alfred and Lucretia Corey, as sketched by Bob Corey

ARMINA W. COREY – ROBERT E. MCBRINE
                    1865 – 1938   1867 - 1936

1. **ALMA ARMINA MCBRINE** 1892 – 1979
   Clarence Robinson
       MORRILL FREDERICK ROBINSON 1916 - 1997
       Marjorie Brown Lyons
       HAROLD GORDON ROBINSON 1924 - 2001
       Marie DeLong
           CLARENCE HAROLD ROBINSON 1965
           Peggy Norris
               Brianna Rachel Robinson 1995
               Alyssa Jennelle Robinson 2001

2. **GLENNA LUCRETIA MCBRINE** 1894 - 1978
   Joseph Thompson
       ROBERT THOMPSON 1917 - 1971
           ROBERTA THOMPSON SERRANO
           PATRICIA THOMPSON BELL
           MICHAEL THOMPSON

3. **FERNE ELZIVETTA MCBRINE** 1895 - 1975
   Frank David Wheeler
       EDNA KATHLEEN WHEELER 1921 - 2000
       Horace Christman
           JOHN DAVID CHRISTMAN 1945
           Marlene Bitechy
               John David Christman 1973
               Jennifer Ann Christman 1976
           ROBERT WILLIAM CHRISTMAN 1957-1969
       HAZEL ELOISE WHEELER 1923
       George Smith
           SHARON ROBERTA SMITH 1950
           Ross Johnson
       MARY IRENE WHEELER 1924
       Charles Foster
           BARBARA JOAN FOSTER 1948
           JUDITH LEA FOSTER 1955
               David Charles Foster 1985
       FREDERICK JOSEPH WHEELER 1926
       Merna Kathleen Field
           ROBERT FREDERICK WHEELER 1952
           Gail Baltoumas
               Stacy Ann Wheeler 1972
               Sean Thomas Dunn
                   Brittany Ann Dunn 1999
               Jodi Lynn Wheeler 1978
       NELLIE ALBERTA WHEELER 1931
       Edward Stanley DeWitt
           DEBORAH ANN DEWITT 1954
           Kevin Cullen

                             Kristen Marie Cullen 1975
                             Kelly Ann Cullen 1979
                   JODIE LYNNE DEWITT 1961
                   Michael Lemish
                             Connor Michael Lemish 1992
                   DAVID EDWARD DEWITT 1962
                   Shelly Herlihy
                             Craig James DeWitt 1987
                             Peter Joseph DeWitt 1989

   <u>4.</u> **FREDERICK RICE MCBRINE** 1901 - 1983
         Annie Lovely
         Bernice Bell
              CLAUDINE MARGUERITE MCBRINE 1923 – 1978
              Stanley Whitehouse
                   ROBERT WHITEHOUSE 1947
                   Ida Nicholson
                             Calvin Whitehouse 1969
                             Shelly Lunn
                             Carla Dawn Whitehouse 1970
                             Peter Carlisle
                             Christopher Whitehouse 1971
                             Tracy Plant
              MARION LOUISE MCBRINE 1933
              Albert David Bell
                   LAUREL LYNN BELL 1957
                   Ken Neal
                             Kenny Colin Neal 1985
                             Ashley Alyson Neal 1988
                   KATHRYN ANNE BELL 1958
                   Ian Brown
                             Leah Janet Brown 1985
                             Erica Lynne Brown 1988
                             Leslee Anne Brown 1991
                             Andrew Douglas Brown 1994

1786 JOHN MILLER 1857 m. 1798 AGNES McALPINE 1875 in Bothwell, Scotland
1830 HUGH MILLER 1905 – 1821 JANE PENDER 1900

ROBERT JAMES MILLER – ALMA LIZETTE COREY
1862 - 1937   1867 – 1915
AGNES MAUDE MILLER, July 5, 1890 – Oct. 27, 1972
JAMES HUGH MILLER, Sept 20, 1892 – Jan. 14, 1979
WILLIAM JOHN McALPINE MILLER, March 21, 1899 – Sept. 5, 1985
ALMA KATHLEEN MILLER, Sept. 4, 1900 – Sept. 28, 1979
WILMA JEAN MILLER, Feb. 13, 1907 – July 31, 1973

         <u>1.</u> **AGNES MAUDE MILLER** 1890 – 1972

Charles Allen MacNearney 1886 - 1959
   ROBERT EDWIN MacNEARNEY 1916 - 1958
   m.Kathleen S.L. Vaughan, 1939
       DEREK ARCHIBALD MacNEARNEY 1940
       m. Pearl MacMillan
          Ian Robert MacNearney 1966
          m. Sally Marshall
             Alexander Marshall MacNearney 1989
             Heather Jane MacNearney 1991
             Jessie May MacNearney 1993
             James Ian Daniel MacNearney 1996
             John Angus MacNearney 1997
          Craig Donald MacNearney 1968
          Jennifer Lynn MacNearney 1976
       NANCY LOUISE MacNEARNEY 1942
       m. 1961 Colin Moore   (div.)
          Gregory Andrew Moore 1962

Peter James Moore 1965
          m. 1994, Joanne Kelty in Kingston, Ont.
       BEVERLEY KATHLEEN 1948
       m. Frederick Rutledge (div.)
          Leah Elizabeth Rutledge 1975
          Kyle Robert Rutledge (adopted) 1984
   JANET ELIZABETH MacNEARNEY 1918
   m. George Wallace in 1945
       JOHN DOUGLAS MacNEARNEY WALLACE 1948
       m. Catherine White in 1992 in Kelowna, B.C.
       JILL ALLYNE WALLACE 1949
       m. 1985 Robert Miller (div)
          Silas Wallace Miller 1987 in Bathurst, Me.
          Farley Wallace Miller, 1989
       MEREDITH LEIGH WALLACE (1951-1976)
       SHELAGH JEAN WALLACE 1952
       m. Kees Ooderkirk in 1986 (div.)
          Alana Christine 1988
   HUGH M. MacNEARNEY 1920 – 1920
   JOHN DOUGLAS MacNEARNEY 1922 – 1943
   DONALD KEITH MacNEARNEY 1923 – 1924
   ALICE ELAINE MacNEARNEY 1925
   m. 1951 Edward Mitton 1924 – 1997
       THOMAS COURTNEY MITTON 1952
       PETER ALLEN MITTON 1953
       JENNIFER ANNE MITTON 1955
       m. Cyprian Libera b. 1952, in Poland
          Nell Emmeline Libera 1995
   LOIS ALLYNE MacNEARNEY 1926
   m. 1948 John Fiske b. 1926
       PATRICIA JANE FISKE 1949
       JULIANA MAY 1951
       m. Gary Redding in 1980 (div.)
          Jason Redding 1980

       Tyler Redding 1982
     JOHN SUTHERLAND FISKE 1955
     m. 1983, Catherine I. Hall in Berwick
        Jonathan MacNearney Fiske b. 1987 in Halifax
        Kevin Hall Fiske b. 1990 in Halifax
     SHARON LYNN FISKE b. 1957 in Halifax
     JOAN MARIE FISKE b. 1958 in Halifax
     m. 1982, John Garden, in Pine Hill Chapel
        Katie Lynn Fiske b. 1984 inHalifax
        Kyle John Fiske   twins
        Brett Corey Fiske b.1985
  PAULA JANE MacNEARNEY 1928
m. 1951 Gerald A. Fry, in Wolfville, N.S.
     CHARLES ALAN FRY b. 1953 in Ottawa
     m. Pamela L. Alexis in 1985
        Katherine (Tiggy) Antigone .1989, in Tsuba, Japan
        John Paul Alexander, b. 1991 in Dallas, Tx.
     JANICE ELAINE FRY 1954
     m. 1985 David M. Dickson 1953-1994
        Troy Alan Dickson b. 1987 in Maple Ridge, B.C.
        Heather Anne Dickson b. 1991
     LEIGH ANN FRY 1959, in Ottawa
     m. in 1989 Ted Higgins, in B.C.
        Emmalyn Jane Higgins, b. 1990, in Vancouver
        Kathleen Elizabeth Higgins b. 1993 in Vancouver
  ERIC COREY MacNEARNEY 1930
m. Halifax 1956 Anne Isobel Murray, b. 1934
     PAULA CHRISTINE MacNEARNEY 1957
     m. 1982, Paul Christensen, in Windsor Jct.
        Lica Liying Christensen b.1998, in Chatham, N.B.
        Kaj Evan Christensen b.1990, in Moncton, N.B.
        Lars Rowan, b.1992, in Chatham
        Thora Rae Christensen b.1994, in Charlottetown
     JOHN DAVID MacNEARNEY 1960
     m. 1984, Kathleen Telfer, in Wolfville
        Robin May MacNearney 1986
        Douglas Stewart MacNearney 1989, in Antigonish
        Donald Joseph MacNearney 1991
        Rose Ellen 1994
     ALISON KIM MacNEARNEY 1961
     m. David Kalyan, 1987 in Fort McMurray
     b.1966 in Bombay, India
        Jessica Megan Kalyan 1993
        Andrew William Kalyan 1995
        James Michael Kalyan 1996
        John Robert Kalyan

2. **JAMES HUGH MILLER** 1892 – 1979

3. **WILLIAM JOHN McALPINE MILLER** 1899 – 1985

4. **ALMA KATHLEEN MILLER** 1900 – 1979

m. 1923, James A. Hovey, 1896-1959
    JEAN ALMA HOVEY 1926 – 1967
      m. 1949 Basil Flemming, in Juniper
          CAROL JOY FLEMMING 1950
            m. James McAvity Crosby, b.1949
                James Flemming Crosby 1981
                Courtney Jean Crosby 1983
                Frederick William Crosby 1985
                Cecilia Joyce Crosby 1988
          DOUGLAS LESLIE FLEMMING Jan. 1953 – Oct. 1953
          PAMELA JEAN FLEMMING 1954
            m. 1 Stephen Ritchie
            m. 2 Chris Willis in 2001
                Michelle Lee Ritchie 1974
                Sara Renee Jean Ritchie 1978
    EMILY KATHLEEN HOVEY 1929
      m. Fredericton 1950, Leonard Wade b.1922
          DEBRA LYNN WADE 1952
            m. Rudi Drijher, b.1950
                Cailin Elizabeth Drikher 1984
                Daniel James Drijher 1986
                Lukas William Drjher 1988
          DEANNE LEE WADE 1954
            m. John Kennedy b.1954 (div.)
                Robert Andrew Kennedy 1980
                Lesa Kathleen Kennedy 1983
                Adam Harnish Kennedy 1984
          JAMES HOVEY WADE 1956
            m. 1999, Maria Marquis
                Daniel Aaron Mitchell Wade 1989
          CHERYL JOYCE WADE 1960
            m. 2001, Gary Weeks
                Alysha Rae Maya Wade 1995
                Amber Jasmine Wade 1997
                Alannah Cora Wade 1999
    JUNE YVONNE HOVEY 1931
      m. 1953, Gerald A. Covey, b.1928
          HEATHER LYNN COVEY 1958
            m. Michael O'Donnell b.1956 (div.)
                Michael Edward O'Donnell 1984
                Nicholas Gerald Patrick O'Donnell 1985
          STEPHEN EARL COVEY 1961
            m. 1989 Marie Celine LaFonde, b.1961
                Alexandra Pasqual Covey 1991
                Justine Covey 1993
          GREGORY MARK COVEY 1969
    CAROLYN ADELL HOVEY 1936
      m. 1955, Ronald J. Rowe, b.1934
          ROBERT JAMES ROWE 1956
            m. 1979 Carolyn Rand, b.1955
                Matthew Rowe 1980
                Daniel Alexander Rowe 1982

                    Jonathan Rowe 1984
                    Andrew Rowe 1986
          KATHRYN JANE ROWE 1957
          m. 1979 Leo Deveau, b.1956
                    Leah Carolyn Rowe Deveau 1983
                    Danielle Gallant Rowe Deveau 1985
          RANDALL JEFFREY ROWE 1960
          m. 1985, Denise Joyce Currie, b. 1966
                    Jill Elizabeth Rowe 1985
                    Kate Denise Rowe 1987
MARILYN MILLER HOVEY 1939
m. 1963, William R. Hicks, b.1937
          JAMES ANDERSON HICKS 1966
          m. 1992 Krista McElman (div.)
                    Katie Taylor Hicks 1996
          JANET MILLER HICKS 1967
          m. 1993, Benjamin Edward Smith, b.1967
                    Cameron Miller Smith 1996
                    Benjamin William Smith, twins 1998
                    Clayton James Smith 1998
          PETER RAYMOND HICKS 1968
          m. Rhonda Richard, b. 1976
                    Aiden Roger Roy Hicks 2000
          SHARON ELIZABETH HICKS 1971
          m. 1993 Drew Lawrence Simpson, b.1968
                    Grace Marilyn Simpson 1997
                    Sterling Gladwyn Simpson 1999
                    Laughlin James Simpson 2001

5. **WILMA JEAN MILLER** 1907 – 1973
m. 1933, Randall Smallwood Williams, d.1986
          GAIL WILLIAMS 1936
          m.1 1958 John S. Williams, div. 1979
          m.2 Cloyd H. Pfister, 1982
                    ERIC RANDALL WILLIAMS 1959
                    m. 1984, Donna Cummings div. 1996
                              Gabriel N. Williams 1980
                              Randall M. Williams 1982
                              Jennifer B. Williams 1987
                    LORI JEAN WILLIAMS 1961
          LINDA WILLIAMS 1943
          m. 1963, Donald T. VanWart
                    DONALD "VAN" VANWART 1964
                    m. 1988 Jennifer Goehl
                              Austin VanWart twins
                              Jake VanWart 1995
                              Paige VanWart 1997
                    TARA VANWART 1967
                    m. 1994 Michener Chandlee
                              Chiara Bell Chandlee 1996
                    JUSTIN VANWART 1971
                    m. 1997 Daniela Christ

CHARLES HADDEN SPURGEON COREY – ELIZABETH MAE THURBER COREY
July 26,1868 -1945   March 1,1875 – May 4,1959

IVAN GRANT COREY - Feb.29,1896 – Feb.28,1963
EDITH LUCRETIA COREY MITCHELL – July 6,1898 – Nov.22,1962
NOEL CHARLES COREY – May 11,1900 – Oct. 26,1973

1. IVAN GRANT COREY Feb. 29,1896 - 1963
    Elsie Daggett Corey
        MINA COREY Sept.12,1926
        CHARLES DAGGETT COREY May 7,1928
        Lillian Chute Corey
            INEZ COREY OLSON Mar. 11,1952
            Theodore Olson
                Jason Olson 1971
                Trevor Olson 1976
            CARL COREY 1961
        INEZ COREY Feb.14,1930 – Oct. 3,1938
        MELVIN COREY May 15, 1931 – Aug. 9,2001
        Alma Pauline Hooper Corey
            DEBORAH ARLENE COREY JONES Mar.8,1957
            Lester Allen Jones
                Corey Peter Jones May 21,1986
                Jeremy Austin Jones Oct. 18,1991
            ANGELA BENITA COREY OSGOOD Jan.8,1962
            Rich Osgood
            MELVIN IVAN PETER COREY Oct. 27,1964
            Hope Joy Eisenhower Corey
                Heather Jean Corey
                Nov.8,1983 – Oct.22,2000
                Trisha Nichole Corey May 1,1986
                Travis Lee Corey June 13,1990
        LALIA COREY MOREHOUSE Aug.10,1932
        Fred Morehouse
            CONNIE MOREHOUSE GOODINE Aug.7,1952
            Larry Goodine
                Kerry Goodine Aug.6,1980
                Jared Goodine Jan.12,1987
                Rebecca Goodine Nov. 15,1989
            EUNICE MOREHOUSE GILL July 31,1956
                Jason Mollins May 29,1984
            IRA MOREHOUSE Jan.25,1965
            MINA MOREHOUSE July 17,1966
                Mitchell Skidnut Dec. 4,1993
            OWEN MOREHOUSE Nov.,1969
                Breanna Morehouse Jan. 31,2001
        IVAN COREY July 6,1936

        Beverley Porter Corey
              SCOTT COREY July 27,1964
              Susan Corey
                    Joslyn Corey Apr.16,1990
                    Ivan Alfred Corey Apr. 1,1992
                    Brianne Corey June 19,1995

2. **EDITH LUCRETIA COREY MITCHELL** July 8,1898 – Nov.22,1962
     Edgar Mitchell
             DAVID HAROLD MITCHELL 1929
             Winnifred Fitzsimmons Mitchell
                    NORMA GAIL MITCHELL MACKENZIE
                    STEVEN MITCHELL
                    GORDON MITCHELL
             NOEL MITCHELL Sept. 28,1933
             Marie Colwell Mitchell
                    SAMUEL MITCHELL June 30.1971
                    SUSANNE MITCHELL June 6,1975
                    ANDREW MITCHELL Jan.9,1982
             ROBERT MITCHELL Dec.,1935
             Adrienne Brown Mitchell
                    BRENT MITCHELL
                    PHILIP MITCHELL
                    COLEEN MITCHELL
                    PETER MITCHELL

3. **NOEL CHARLES COREY** May 11,1900 – Oct.26,1973
     Bessie Frances Calder Corey
             GERALD GRANT COREY Jan.28,1936
             Elizabeth Ann London Corey
                    CHERYL ANN COREY GERARDI June 30,1964
                      Chris Ron Joseph Gerardi
                          Dakota Scott Joseph Gerardi Nov. 9,1998
                    BLAIR GRANT COREY Aug.30,1972
                        Haley Elizabeth Joy Glaspy Sept.6,1995
                        Brandon David Grant Porter Nov. 23,1998
                        Devin Grant Douglas Porter June 23,2001
             NOEL RANDALL COREY Apr.18,1940
                Judy Paulette Cooke Corey
                    MARK RANDALL COREY July 31,1967 – July 31,1967
                    DEAN DOUGLAS COREY Jan.3,1970
                      Michelle Rose Grant Corey
                    DWIGHT CHARLES COREY Oct. 19,1973
                      Angelisa Sabrina Kathleen Belyea Corey
                        Clarissa Sabrina Victoria Corey May 8,1998
                        Ashten Joshua Corey Nov.30,2001
             HARRY DOUGLAS COREY June 3,1946
                Beverley Edna Schnare Corey
                    CHRISTA BEVERLEY FRANCES COREY Mar.16.1971-

June 24, 1983
DANIEL DOUGLAS COREY Aug. 13, 1975
Karen Joleen Elliott Corey
Abigail Kristine Corey July 27, 1995
KIMBERLEE DAWN COREY Aug. 30, 1979

JUDSON ALBERT COREY – ELIZA ALICE (HOWLETT) COREY
1870 - 1952   1874 - 1955

1. **ALBERTA L. COREY** 1900 – 1964
Mayford Anthony
   ELIZABETH ANTHONY 1927
   Donald Bilensky
      KAREN BILENSKY 1956
      Daniel Long
         Jeffrey Long 1982
         Gregory Long 1983
      BRIAN BILENSKY 1959
      Eleanor Scott
         Christopher Bilensky 1992
         Mitchell Bilensky 1993
   BURDEL ANTHONY 1930
   Doreen Hunter
      JUDITH ANTHONY 1953
      William McCain
         Jeffrey McCain 1975
         Russell McCain 1978
      BARBARA ANTHONY 1957
      Fred Dickinson
         Anthony Dickinson 1980
         Adam Dickinson 1984
      MARK ANTHONY 1960
      Mary-Jean Bettle
         Darren Anthony 1982
         Darlene Anthony 1986
   ROSS ANTHONY 1938
   Jean-Anne Fawcett
      BRENDA JEAN ANTHONY 1962
      Douglas Colquhoun
         Sharis Colquhoun 1987
         Alex Colquhoun 1989
      STEPHEN ROSS ANTHONY 1965
      Lesley Braid
         Owen Ross Anthony

2. **EARLE HOWLETT COREY** 1902 – 1983
   Lois Morgan
      EUGENE COREY 1928
      Marilyn Bennett

                    STEVEN COREY 1953
                    ARLENE COREY 1955
            WILMA COREY 1931
            Charles Kusch
            Robert Eddy

3. **ANNIE RUTH COREY** 1903 - 1990
        Albert Haines
            BEVERLY A. HAINES 1928
            Theresa Hurtley
                    JANE (HURTLEY) HAINES*
                    M. Raymond Ingold
                            Rebecca Ingold 1983
                            Matthew Corey Ingold 1987
                            Benjamine Albert Haines 1990
                    SANDRA (HURTLEY) HAINES*
                    Dale G. Hetrick
                            Sara Jane Hetrick 1982
            KEITH HAINES 1932
            Murial Edwards
                    MARK HAINES* 1956
                    DEBBY HAINES*1965
                    DAVID HAINES 1965
                    MATTHEW HAINES 1967

4. **ESTHER LUCRETIA COREY** 1905 - 1993
        Harold W. Smith
            EARLE W. SMITH 1929
            Ruth King 1930 – 1994
                    Thomas Wayne Smith 1957
                    Brenda Fram 1957
                            Ryan Benjamin Smith 1982
                            Darren Richard Smith 1986
                            Corey Daniel Smith 1989
                    Allan Robert Smith 1959
                    Lori Rae Seifert 1962
                            Joshua Adam Smith 1989
                            Benjamin Allan Smith 1993
                    Nancy Louise Smith 1961
                    Jonathon Underwood 1968
                            Jill Virginia Underwood 1983
                            Christopher Ray Underwood 1986
                            Kaylyn Louise Underwood 1988
                            Joseph Nathan Underwood 1992
                            Lia Underwood 1996
            ALICE JEAN SMITH 1933
            CAROLYN ANN SMITH 1940
            Neil Rempel 1939
                    Jeffrey Mark Rempel 1967
                    Laura Perreaux 1969
                    Debra Michelle Rempel 1969
                    Bradley John Warkentin 1972

       Monika Lynn Rempel 1971
       Timothy Douglas Hooper 1969
         Timothy Michael Hooper 1994
         Madison Taylor Hooper 1995

5. ALFRED JOSHUA COREY 1906 - 1991
 Dorothy Burpee
   ALFRED JON COREY 1938
   Sylvia Blackburn
     BRENDA COREY 1972
     Lonnie Dauphinee
     SALLY A. COREY 1940
     Richard L. Haynes
       Jon Edward Haynes 1965
       Mauree Zocchi
         Anna Z. Haynes 1995
         Alexander Corey Haynes 1998
       Lynda Patrice Haynes 1969
       David Ershoff
         Morgan Alexandra Ershoff 1999
       James Richard Haynes 1971
       Melissa Conmay

6. DAVID WINBURN COREY 1908 - 1998
  Verna M. Stevens
   ELLEN M. COREY 1936
   Thomas J. Lau, M.D.
     THOMAS J. LAU, Jr. 1961 - 1970
     DAVID M. LAU 1963
     Heide Handspeiker
       Brett Lau 1991
     ERIC COREY LAU 1975
     Jennifer Irene Robin
   NEIL D. COREY 1946
   Patricia Coleman
     MATTHEW N. COREY 1974
     JOSHUA THOMAS COREY 1981

7. EDNA VIOLET COREY 1910

8. MILDRED ELLIOTT COREY. 1912 - 1998
 John Johnston
 Clair Shirley
   ELAINE JOHNSTON. 1943
   John Billiard
     CHARLES BILLIARD 1974
     CHRISTINA BILLIARD 1976

 * Adopted

IDA COREY MCBRINE – WILLIAM G. MCBRINE

1872 – 1953   1865 – 1921

   1. **CLARA J. MCBRINE** 1892 – 1992
       P. Whitehouse
       W. Flemming
              CLAUDIA WHITEHOUSE 1910
              J. Lundberg
                  BARBARA LUNDBERG 1929
                  W. Barrington
                      J. Candy Barrington 1948
                      G. Sipprelle
                          Christin Sipprelle 1967
                          V.W. Rosher
                              Emily A 1990
                              Erica 1995
                          Sarah Sipprelle 1976
                      Robert Barrington 1951
                      James Barrington 1952
                      Leslie Bates
                          Alison Bates 1978
                          William Bates 1980
                          Heather Bates 1981
              CLAIRE LUNDBERG 1932
              J. Johnson
                  Thomas Johnson 1959
                  C. Schultz
                      Sean T. Johnson 1989
                      Erik Johnson 1995
                  James Johnson 1960
                  S. Sioles
                  Robert Johnson 1966
                  D. Henry
                      Jennifer Johnson 2000
              JACQUELINE LUNDBERG 1936
              W.E. Imes
                  Paula Imes 1959
                  D. Binner
                      Thomas Binner 1986
                      Rachel Binner 1990
                  Douglas Imes 1961
                  J. Peters
                      Matthew Imes 1992
                      Benjamin Imes 1994
                      Paul Imes 1996
                  Judith Imes 1965
                  D. Stadick
                      Deborah Stadick 1990
                      Robert Stadick 1992
                      Katherine Stadick 1995
                      Scott Stadick 1998
                  Carol Imes 1966
                  R. Sokovich

                              Joseph Sokovich 1993
                              Samuel Sokovich 1995
                              Caleb Sokovich 1997
                              Joshua Sokovich 2000
         JOAN LUNDBERG 1937
         J.P. Koller
                    Joann Koller 1963
                    S. Phillips
                              Andrew Phillips 1994
                    Deborah Koller 1965
                    C. Olsen
                              Joseph Olsen 1990
                              Kathryn Olsen 1992
                              Elizabeth Olsen 1994
                    John Koller 1968
                    J. Quatrale
                              Thomas Koller 1995
                              Matthew Koller 1999
CLARENCE WHITEHOUSE 1911-1988
G. Cummings
         JAN ELIZABETH WHITEHOUSE 1950
         Chas. Good
                    Nicholas Good 1980
                    Aaron Good 1992
         JILL ELAINE WHITEHOUSE 1957
         R.T. French
                    William French 1995
                    Ian French 1996
WALTER WHITEHOUSE 1913
Evelyn Briggs
         LARRY WHITEHOUSE 1944
         R. Sutherland
                    Aaron Whitehouse 1974
                    Michael Whitehouse 1976
         JUDY WHITEHOUSE 1947
         W. Caines
         R. MacDonald
                    Ian Caines 1978
                    Megan Caines 1983
                    Colin Caines 1987
MADELINE WHITEHOUSE 1919
P. Oliver
         SALLY OLIVER 1947
         B. Kindervater
         MARY JANE OLIVER 1948
         M. Phillips
                    James Phillips
                    John Phillips
                    Sarah Phillips
         PAULA OLIVER 1949
         P. Anderson

R. Wilson
    Emily Anderson
       Melissa Anderson 1986
MICHAEL OLIVER 1953
G. McCready
    Joshua Oliver
    Luke Oliver
    Stephen Oliver
RUTH ANN OLIVER 1956
D. Beardsmore
    David Beardsmore
    Jeremy Beardsmore
    Jennifer Beardsmore
    Harley Beardsmore
JUDITH OLIVER 1963
D. Winters
T. Rose
    Jeffrey Winters 1987
    Brandon Winters 1990
    Corey Rose 1998

KATHLEEN WHITEHOUSE 1921
B.J. Thompson
    ROBERT THOMPSON 1951
    JEROME THOMPSON 1953
    MEGAN THOMPSON 1954
    C. Kelley
       Christian Kelley 1983
       Ethan Kelley 1986
    ANDREW THOMPSON 1956
    S. Viel
       Scott Thompson 1980
       Isaac Thompson 1982
    PAUL THOMPSON 1958

RUTH FLEMMING 1923
W. Fawcett
N. Coleman
F. Shute
    LOMIE COLEMAN
    C. MacPherson
       Graeme MacPherson 1992
       Stuart MacPherson 1995
ROBERT FLEMMING 1925
M.A. McMullin
    CATHY FLEMMING 1955
    A. Atkinson
       Julie Atkinson 1981
       Emily Atkinson 1984
       David Atkinson 1986
    JENNIFER FLEMMING 1958
    L. Davis
       Alyson Davis 1990
       Sean Davis 1991

MARY FLEMMING 1933
J. Chesley
    SHAWN CHESLEY 1955
    S. Morrison
        Lindsay Morrison 1982
        Keltie Morrison 1984
    CARI CHESLEY 1957
    W. VanLingen
        Zoe Vanlingen 1994
    ZOE CHESLEY 1959
    B. Frame
        Andrew Frame 1992

2. JUDSON LEROY MCBRINE, SR. 1894 – 1974
Dorothy Bedell McBrine
    JUDSON LEROY MCBRINE JR. 1922 – 1945
    WINNIFRED MCBRINE 1924 – 1995
    Weldon Winchester
    Lloyd Carr
    CLARICE MCBRINE 1926
    Ralph Shorey
    Raymond Irish
        MICHAEL SHOREY 1946
        ROBERTA SHOREY 1947
        RALPH SHOREY 1949
        COLBY SHOREY 1950
        SHARON COREY 1952
        JUDITH SHOREY 1956
        MELODY SHOREY 1957
        SCOTT IRISH 1961
        RAYMOND IRISH 1966
    WILLIAM MCBRINE 1928 (died 8 months)
    JOSEPH FRANKLIN MCBRINE, SR. 1932
    Marie King
        MARK JUDSON MCBRINE 1961
        Linda Cox
            Andrew McBrine 1989
            Stephen McBrine 1990
            Micah McBrine 1993
            Sarah McBrine 1995
            Rebecca McBrine 1995
            Rachel McBrine 1997
        LAUREN JO MCBRINE 1963
        Christopher Sprague
            Hannah Sprague 1996
            Lydia Sprague 2000
        JUDSON LEROY MCBRINE III 1965
        Paula Norton
            Jacob McBrine 1998
        JOSEPH FRANKLIN MCBRINE, JR. 1969
        Lorilee Look
            Vincent Emery McBrine 1983

         Olivia McBrine 1997
       JONATHAN KING MCBRINE 1971
       Becky Washburn
          Daniel McBrine 2000
   JUDITH MCBRINE 1934
   Donald Oliver
      JOEL OLIVER 1957
      MATTHEW OLIVER 1969
   MARY JANE MCBRINE 1937
   James Miller
   John Chick
       JAMES MILLER 1959
       RICHARD MILLER 1961
       KAREN MILLER 1962
       SETH MILLER 1964

3. **NESSIE MCBRINE** 1896 – 1985
 Cecil Avery
   DOROTHY AVERY 1929 – 1989
   P. Seeley
      PETER SEELEY 1953
      S. Migneault
        Jason Seeley 1977
        Michael Seeley 1980
      DONALD SEELEY 1955
      Laurie
        Jennifer Seeley 1985
        Matthew Seeley 1988
      DAVID SEELEY 1958
      Lori Banks
        Sarah Seeley 1994
        Christina Seeley 1997
   ALICE AVERY 1923
   Murray Cooke
   William Craig
      JANE COOKE 1948
      M. Wayne Silsby
        Marc Silsby 1974
        Erin Silsby 1975
        Gregory Silsby 1977
      BILLY CRAIG 1952
      Elizabeth
        Taylor Craig 1988
        Tashia Craig 1991
      MICHAEL CRAIG 1955 – 1976
      CAROL CRAIG 1957 – 1967
   ELIZABETH AVERY 1928
   Walter Gray
      KIMBERLY GRAY 1955
      B Morrison
        Neallie Morrison 1977
        Whitney Morrison 1982

JEFFREY GRAY 1957
C. MacLean
  MacKenzie Gray 1992
  Isaac Gray 1994
  Keegan Gray 1997
  Hunter Gray 1998
ROBERT GRAY 1959
N. Bradley
  Matthew Gray 1991
  Joshua Gray 1992
TIMOTHY GRAY 1962
M. Polchies
  Alexandra Gray 1992
  Samuel Gray 1994
  Benjamen Gray 1996

CECIL AVERY 1933 – 1982
M. MacAffrey
L. Hotchkiss
 JEFFREY AVERY 1957
 JOSHUA AVERY 1974

4. **ELLEN MCBRINE** 1899 – 1984
Harry Lindsay
 MARY LINDSAY 1921 – 1992
 Byron Hand
  JILL HAND 1947
  Robert Greenig
  William Moran
   Jeffrey Greenig 1973
   William Moran 1982
  JUDY HAND 1952
  Robert Light
   Courtney Light 1980
   Jeremy Light 1984
   MacKenzie Light 1986
   Peter Light 1988
  JAYNE HAND 1957
  Joseph Babij
   Rebekah Babij 1983
   Naomi Babij 1984
   Joshua Babij 1986
   Elizabeth Babij 1996
  BYRON HAND 1961
  Jackie
   Christina Hand 1987
JOHN LINDSAY 1926
Marjorie Langin
 JOHN LINDSAY 1950
 Beth Carman
 Ann Campbell
  Jason Lindsay 1981
  Lauren Lindsay 1984

                                    Alexander Lindsay 1987
                            DEBORAH ANNE LINDSAY 1954
                            Luca Rotta-Loria
                                    Andreas Rotta-Loria 1983
                                    Nicolas Rotta-Loria 1991
                    HAROLD LINDSAY 1929 – 1950

5.   VOLA MCBRINE 1902
        Archie Barker
                    WILLIAM BARKER 1924 – 1976
                    Janet Moore
                            PHILIP WM. BARKER* 1949
                            Shirley Gilliland
                                    Marjorie Barker 1981
                                    Megan Barker 1985
                            JUDITH L. BARKER* 1953
                            Dwight Lewis
                                    Kelley Lewis Barker
                                    Andrew Take

6.   KATHLEEN MCBRINE 1904 - 2001
        Percy Williams
                    EDWARD WILLIAMS 1929
                    Nadine Tidd
                            SHERYL WILLIAMS 1956
                            Michael Martin
                                    Lindsay Martin 1985
                                    Kelsey Martin 1988
                                    Taylor Martin 1990
                            JONATHAN WILLIAMS 1958
                            Nancy Fitzpatrick
                                    Geoff Williams 1987
                    ROBERT WILLIAMS 1930 – 1931
                    WILLIAM WILLIAMS 1941
                            Joanie Flitz

7.   GEORGE MCBRINE 1907 – 1972
        Flossie Williams
        Ruth Ross
                    RICHARD MCBRINE 1927
                    Marion Spring
                            DEBORAH MCBRINE 1954
                            RICHARD MCBRINE 1955
                            KENNETH MCBRINE 1957
                            ROBERT MCBRINE
                    JOHN ROSS MCBRINE 1935
                    KENNETH W. MCBRINE 1937

8.   LUCRETIA MCBRINE 1909 – 1990
        Edward McDonnell
                    WILLIAM MCDONNELL 1936
                    Margarette Martin

                    RICHARD MCDONNELL 1962
                    Laurie Jo Harvie
                            Seth McDonnell 1994
                    LIESL MCDONNELL 1969
                    Robert Lilly
                            Jarrod Lilly 1980 (Stepson)
                            Gavin Lilly 1984 (Stepson)
                            Madison Lilly 1999
                            Annabelle Lilly twins
            DONNA McDONNELL 1943
            Donald Bachman
                    JONATHAN BACHMAN 1980

9. **LELAND MCBRINE** 1912
    Marion Lindquist
            RONALD MCBRINE 1936
            Jean Stubbard
                    SEAN MCBRINE 1966
                    SHELLEY WAY 1969
                    Todd Way
                    MATTHEW MCBRINE 1972
                    PATRICIA MCBRINE 1974
            LINDA MCBRINE 1942
            Brian Adkins
                    GRETCHEN ADKINS 1970
                    Tom Leone

10. **LORNE MCBRINE** 1916 – 1963
    Dorothy Garvie
    Pearl Buchanan
            PATRICIA ANNE MCBRNE 1938
            David Wusterbarth
                    DEBBIE WUSTERBARTH
                    ROBERT WUSTERBARTH
                    DENISE WUSTERBARTH
            DAVID MCBRINE 1951
            Deborah Niles
                    CHRISTA LYNN MCBRINE 1973
                    John F. MacKay
                            Amber MacKay 1991
                            Devin Alan MacKay 1995
                    JONATHAN MCBRINE 1977
                    Melissa St. Pierre
        * Adopted

ALFRED COREY b. 1841 – LUCRETIA KIERSTEAD b. 1842

LAVERSA ELLA COREY – LUTHER WALT GARNS
July 1, 1882 – October 22, 1969   November 8, 188 – September 3, 1956

1. **JAMES EDWARD GARNS** 1904 – 1979
    Hazel (Slye)

DAVID GARNS 1925
JOHN LUTHER GARNS 1935
JAMES GARNS

2. **PAUL HENRY GARNS** 1907 – 1959
Mary (Dixon)
JACK GARNS

3. **MALINDA LUCRETIA GAIL (GARNS) BAST** 1909
Gerald Bast
DOUGLAS GARNS BAST

4. **RUTH ELIZABETH (GARNS) MOWEN** 1911
Harry Mowen
HARRY LUTHER MOWEN
HARRIET LAVERSA MOWEN

5. **MIRIAM EDITH GARNS** 1913

6. **ESTHER LAVERSA (GARNS) HARROP** 1915
Obie Harrop
MARIE CATHERINE HARROP 1939
OBIE LEE HARROP 1940
JAMES LOWELL HARROP 1944
PAUL ALFRED HARROP 1949

7. **MARY CATHERINE (GARNS) KREMPELS** August 3, 1917
Robert A. Krempels May 18, 1920
R. DOUGLAS KREMPELS April 3, 1947
Wendy (Hillyard) Dec. 1, 1953
David May 27, 1980
Craig Feb. 24, 1982
Lynnae Sept. 29, 1983
DAVID M. KREMPELS Nov. 18, 1949
Ettamae (Flood Ferguson) Dec. 16, 1948
DEBORAH M. KREMPELS July 31, 1960

8. **ALBERTA MAUD (GARNS) HERSHMAN** 1919
Jacob Hershman
JOAN HERSHMAN 1944
JOHN HERSHMAN 1948
LUCI ANN HERSHMAN 1953

9. **BERNICE LOUISE (GARNS) MCDEARMID** 1922
Andrew McDearmid
CAROL MCDEARMID
ANDREA MCDEARMID
RICHARD MCDEARMID

IRA T. COREY - EMILY GRAHAM COREY
Mar. 3, 1877 - Mar. 14, 1957

ERMA E. Corey   1903 - Oct. 8, 1993

PRINCE W. KENNEY – LUCY
    1830   1827

1.ROLAND KENNEY 1855
  Jane Phillips
      ARTHUR KENNEY 1887 – 1910
        Nellie K. Brown Oct. 30, 1891 – Dec. 1, 1977
            MURRAY ARTHUR KENNEY 1909 – 1979
              Myrtle Haines 1909 – 1989
                  MARY KENNEY Feb.12,1939
                    Carl Avon Grant June 17,1934
                        CARL ARTHUR GRANT Sept. 2,1958
                          Nancy Tardy Dec. 9,1959
                              Jason Lee Grant Nov. 11,1980
                              Jennifer Dawn Grant Jan. 19,1983
                              Adam Carl Grant Dec. 9,1984
                        CALVIN AVON GRANT Nov. 18,1961
                          Virginia Tupper May 12,1960
                              Christa Anne Grant July 29,1983
                              Caleb Tupper Grant Feb. 4,1994
                              Caitlin Adelle Grant Dec. 25,1996
                      CRAIG ALLEN GRANT July 16,1963
                          Stacey Estabrook Apr. 13,1965
                              Celeste Fern Grant Jan. 2,1989
                              Alana Shannon Grant Feb. 19,1991
                      KELLEY JEAN GRANT June 4,1968
                              Chantelle Amber Grant Apr. 20,1986
                              Celina Mary Pangburn July 22,1993
                  GLADYS K. KENNEY Apr. 27,1941
                    Louis P. Keith April 17,1938
                        BRIAN KEITH October 4,1961
                        Carolyn S. Mar.26,1963
                            Kristen A. Keith June 24,1983
                      STEVEN A. KEITH Apr. 28,1966
                CLAUDE M. KENNEY July 17,1942
                Sharon F. Sept. 23,1943
                    JANE E. KENNEY Aug. 18,1965
                    Todd Hart Apr. 26,1961
                        Cooper L. Hart Dec. 13, 2000
                    LYNN M. KENNEY Mar. 14, 1967
                    Dennis R. Appleton May 23, 19499
              H. SHARON KENNEY June 14,1944
              Stephen F. Pangburn June 20,1940
                  DAVID C. PANGBURN Apr. 3, 1971
                  JANELLE PANGBURN July 4, 1984
            GWENDOLYN KENNEY Apr. 11,1947
            SANDRA KENNEY Nov. 10,1948
            Robert Margison Mar. 11,1948

BARBARA KENNEY Nov. 13,1950
Timothy O. Peters Sept. 26,1947
DANIELLE PETERS Nov. 13, 1973
Richard Langley May 24, 1971
Kristen Langley Dec. 16,1999
HEATHER PETERS May 25, 1976
Brad McGuire Mar. 21, 1976
Alexis McGuire Mar. 3, 2000

IRA T. COREY – EMILY GRAHAM COREY
Mar. 3, 1877 – Mar. 14, 1957

ERMA E. Corey 1903 – Oct. 8, 1993

IRA T. COREY – EMILY M. GRAHAM
Mar. 3, 1877 – Mar. 14, 1957   1876 – 1904

ERMA ELEANOR GRAHAM COREY May 23, 1903 – Oct. 8, 1993
Allison Millard Shaw Jan. 25, 1878 – Oct. 17,1966
ALICE EMILY SHAW Mar. 29, 1932
Rev. James Wm. Long Mar. 15, 1931 – Dec. 29, 1989
WANDA GRACE LONG Mar. 12, 1954
Robert Stanley Gartley Dec. 23, 1952
Shawn Anthony Long Mar. 29, 1973
Nancy Lynn Havens June 10, 1971
Braden Noel Long Jan. 15, 1997
Derrah Rachelle Long July 10, 1998
Robert David Gartley Dec. 26, 1978 – Dec. 26, 1978
Cheyenne Dawn Gartley Oct. 2, 1982
CHARLES ALLAN LONG Mar. 1, 1955
Muriel Winnifred Crouse Aug. 7, 1957
Christina Doris Long May 6, 1979
Joseph Allan Long Mar. 2, 1981
JAMES WILLIAM (BILLY) LONG May 26, 1956
Wendy Victoria Jones Dec. 10, 1958
Shannon Victoria Long May 18, 1978
John Harvey Blois Feb. 28, 1976
Halley Grace V. Blois June 24, 2001
Sarah Lois Long Apr. 4, 1980
Aaron Dwight Munn June 6, 1975
Blake Wm. Dwight Munn Apr. 1, 2000
Katherine Louise Long Dec. 14, 1982
CONSTANCE (CONNIE) JEAN LONG Dec.14, 1957
Gordon Paul Morrison Aug.2, 1957
Timothy Paul Morrison Jan. 5, 1988
Graham James Morrison May 13, 1991
FRANK ALLISON LONG Sept. 19, 1959

Sherry Gaye Brewer Apr.11, 1964
    Gabrielle Grace Long July 25, 1998
    Joseph Barry Gideon Long Dec. 6, 1999
PAUL ARTHUR WILFRED LONG Sept. 9, 1960
  Janet Louise Greer Oct. 10, 1961
    Corey MacKenzie Long Mar. 29, 1988
    Jillian Elizabeth Long Apr. 28, 1990
JOHN EDWARD LONG Oct. 14, 1961
  Nancy Jean Wood Feb. 20, 1959
    James William Long III Nov. 21, 1985
    Gina Marlene Long May 19, 1987
EMILY ALICE LONG Dec. 4, 1962
  Albert Murray Black Apr. 16, 1959
    Lacey Black Jan. 11, 1983 *
    Noah Black June 24, 1989 *
    Jessica Emily Black Nov. 16, 1995
    Danielle Louise Black Oct. 27, 1998

*stepchildren

BARBARA LORRAINE LONG Jan. 22, 1964
  Neil Hugh Craig July 4, 1959
    Marlene Rebekah Craig Apr. 10, 1988
    Katrina Alison Craig Oct. 27, 1990
    Edward Winstrom Craig Dec. 12, 1993
GARY BRIAN LONG Apr. 26, 1968
  Christina Shyanne Hatt Mar. 13, 1971
    Breanne Elisabeth Long Apr. 26, 1994
    Erica Katherine Long Feb. 14, 1996
    Colby Alexander Long Sept. 27, 1997
    Jared Gregory Long Sept. 1, 1999

MARGARET ELIZABETH SHAW Nov. 19, 1933
  Rev. William John Monroe June 21, 1929
    WILLIAM JOHN GRAHAM MONROE Jan. 26, 1964
    Lydia Renee Wilson Mar. 2, 1960
      Abigail Elizabeth Monroe Aug. 15, 1995
      Aaron James Monroe Jan. 11, 1998
    PHILIP GALLAGHER MONROE Feb. 17, 1966
    Kimberly Ann Vinal Feb. 26, 1954
      Samuel Philip Monroe Apr. 3, 1998*
      Jared Blakely Monroe May 14, 2000*

ELEANOR LUCRETIA SHAW Feb. 4, 1935
  PAUL RYAN HESMAN Oct. 28, 1963*   *adopted
  Penny Gail Jamison June 24, 1967
    Kathryn Joy Hesman May 26, 1993
GEORGE EDWARD SHAW Mar. 15, 1936
  Ida Marie McLean Mar. 11, 1936
    PETER ALLAN SHAW Oct. 31, 1955 – Oct. 31, 1955
    SUSAN RUTH SHAW June 20, 1957
    Charles Piazza July 2, 1958
      Charles Pasquale Piazza Dec. 15, 1980 – Feb. 7, 1981

SUSAN RUTH SHAW
 James David Martis Jan. 31, 1957 (2nd Husband)
LINDA JEAN SHAW July 24, 1959
 David Gerard Fair July 13, 1956
  David Edward Fair Dec. 5, 1987
  Brian Daniel Fair Feb. 16, 1989
  Lydia Marie Fair Sept. 13, 1996
COREY EDWARD SHAW Apr. 21, 1961
 Barbara Ann Pettepit Mar. 29, 1956
MARY JANE SHAW Sept. 25, 1938
 Richard Taylor
MARY JANE SHAW
 Paul Nicholas Granato Oct. 14, 1945 (2nd Husband)
  MALINDA JANE GRANATO Aug. 30, 1960
   Bruce Bellefeuille Mar. 29, 1953
    Sara Jane Bellefeuille July 8, 1987
    Drew Anthony Bellefeuille Sept. 8, 1989
  ANTHONY AUSTIN GRANATO Oct. 11, 1973
  TINA ELEANOR GRANATO Aug. 28, 1974

JOHN ALLISON SHAW June 4, 1941
 Jean Marilyn Myshrall Feb. 16, 1944
  GRAHAM FRANCIS SHAW Oct. 30, 1970
   Susannah Patricia Fenner Mar. 11, 1971
    Ethan Francis Shaw June 1, 2001
  DAVID MATTHEW SHAW Nov. 3, 1972
   Angela Dawn McClement Mar. 21, 1977
  HEATHER ANN SHAW July 19, 1977
IRA DAVID SHAW June 30, 1944
 Lillian Maplet Smith-
IRA DAVID SHAW
 Susan Josephine Coombs (2nd Wife,1977)
  TAMMY RACHAEL SHAW May 23, 1975*   *adopted
  JAMES MILLARD SHAW July 24, 1978
IRA DAVID SHAW
 Dorothy Francis Markham Mar. 20, 1964 (3rd Wife,1990)
ANNIE MAE SHAW Dec. 8, 1945
 Arnold Dennis Tysick July 8, 1944
  MARK ANTHONY TYSICK May 21, 1972
   Sharon Anne Willard Nov. 30, 1972
    Cole Jeremy Tysick Nov. 18, 1997
    David Anthony Tysick Apr. 18, 2000
    Brooklyn Anne Tysick Oct. 2, 2001
  LAURIE ANNE TYSICK Feb. 3, 1975
   Perry Allen Milbury Oct. 28, 1975
  WESLEY ANDREW TYSICK Mar. 29,1978

IRA T. COREY – NELLIE BROWN KENNY COREY (2nd. Wife, 1912)
Mar. 3, 1877 – Mar.14, 1957 Oct. 30, 1891 – Dec. 1, 1977

WILFRED J. COREY Sept. 9,1912 – July 2, 1945
  Pearl Irving May 8, 1916 -
      HAROLD W. COREY Oct. 1, 1942
        Ellen Harris Aug. 8, 1943
           CLIFFORD COREY Apr. 30, 1965
             Leisa McAllister Aug. 10,1967
                Joshua Wayne Corey Sept. 27,1988
                Ashley Corey Jan. 2, 1990
                Jordan Corey Apr. 30,1991
           CYNTHIA COREY Oct. 11, 1967
             Kenneth Kinney July 18,1962
                Adrian Kinney June 22, 1997
J. ROBERT COREY Apr. 23, 1914 – Dec. 19,1987
  E. Maude Cook May 28,1916
      GARY W. COREY Oct. 12, 1947
        Ann Currie Dec. 31, 1949
           JASON A. COREY Sept. 3, 1972
      GARY W. COREY

        Donna M. Beck May 12, 1942 (2nd Wife)
      JOHN W. COREY Apr. 4, 1949
        Carolyn Montgomery June 7, 1950
           ROBERT J. COREY Nov. 18, 1973
             Pamela L. Bond Nov. 12, 1970
                Jessica L. Corey Feb. 16, 1996
                Luke R. Corey Nov. 18, 1998
           ELIZABETH R. COREY Sept. 23, 1975
             Jeffrey Hoyt Dec. 12, 1970
                Emily E. Hoyt Sept. 19, 2000
                Alexis R. Hoyt Jan. 21, 2002
           PETER E. COREY Apr. 2, 1978
             Esther Weatherby Jan. 21, 1981
      I. PETER COREY July 27, 1955 – Oct. 11, 1976
        Lee Dunn
ALICE M. COREY Nov. 8, 1915 – Sept. 25, 1971
  Fred McKenzie July 1936
      SHIRLEY McKENZIE July 14, 1939
        Earle Jacques
           TAMMY JOY JACQUES July 28, 1961
             Douglas Boyd
                Jessica Boyd Oct. 8, 1987
           PEGGY LEE JACQUES Oct. 4, 1964
             Laurier LaTouche
           ANTHONY EARLE FREDERICK JACQUES Feb.13,1968
      FREDERICK McKENZIE June 14, 1940
        Shirley Higgins
           MALCOLM McKENZIE Apr. 18, 1970
           DEBORAH McKENZIE Feb. 12, 1983

NORMAN R. COREY Oct. 16, 1917
  Velma Ellis   - 1952
      NORMAN DALE COREY Sept. 1, 1948

                Diane Bresen
                      SCOTT ANDREW COREY July 11, 1986

NORMAN R. COREY
  L. Swim (2nd Wife, 1958)
NORMAN R. COREY
  Marjorie Rogers (3rd Wife, 1964)

THOMAS W. COREY Oct. 16, 1919 – July 4, 1975
  Marjorie Cook Aug. 2, 1922
      BRENDA COREY 1947 – 1947
      ROGER T. COREY May 25, 1950
        Judy Bubar Mar. 11, 1952
            MATTHEW THOMAS COREY Apr. 17, 1983
      ROSS COREY Aug. 15, 1955
        Janice Petley Aug. 18, 1955
            SARAH DAWN COREY May 27, 1981
            THOMAS ROSS COREY Dec. 19, 1986
      NEIL COREY Aug. 15, 1958
        Brenda Currie Apr. 4, 1958
            SCOTT ANDREW COREY July 29, 1986
            SIMON NEIL COREY Nov. 7, 1990

CLAUDE E. COREY Sept. 10, 1921 – Jan. 24, 1964
  Alice Jones Dec. 29, 1922
      DAVID EUGENE COREY June 5, 1950
        Pamela Greer July 5, 1955
            ADRIAN NOEL COREY Dec. 20, 1972
            ROBYN ELAINE COREY Nov. 26, 1978
            DAVID BLAIR COREY Aug. 16, 1982
            ASHLEY PAMELA COREY Nov. 25, 1984
      GREGORY COREY Apr. 13, 1954
        Georgina Lewis
      KATHERINE GRACE HELEN COREY Mar. 31, 1956
        Scott Greencorn Sept. 3, 1956
            JENNIFER LYNN GREENCORN Jan. 15, 1982
            JAMES LINDEN GREENCORN Apr. 25, 1992
      KATHERINE GRACE HELEN COREY
        Randy Morehouse (2nd Husband 2001)
      JOAN CARLENE COREY June 3, 1959
        John Bartlett Mar. 25, 1958
            AMANDA JANE BARTLETT Mar. 27, 1986
            Emily Margaret Bartlett Feb. 6, 1990
      WILLIAM COREY July 11, 1962

JUDSON M. COREY Apr. 16, 1923
  Marion Rideout - Dec. 17, 2001
      FREDERIC WATSON COREY May 4, 1949
        Sandra Ann Taylor
            ANDREA LOUISE COREY Dec. 29, 1976
            DANIEL ADIERM COREY
            CHARLES ANDREW COREY Dec. 30, 1978
      CAROLYN MAY LOUISE COREY Apr. 2, 1951
        Gordon Campbell
            BRYAN ALLAN CAMPBELL Jan. 18, 1986

       CHRISTOPHER JUDSON COREY June 14, 1957
        Suphaphon Chatnok
          LALITA LISA COREY May 17, 1995
          KEVIN ITTICHAI Corey June 2, 1999

JUDSON M. COREY
 Margaret Stevens Nov. 18, 1949 – Sept. 25, 2002 (2nd Wife, 1991)
WARREN A. COREY Mar. 7, 1925
 Doreen Ellis   - June 4, 2002
       DALE COREY June 19, 1959

I. KEITH COREY Dec. 21, 1927
 Eva Mae Caldwell
      STEVEN MICHAEL COREY Mar. 8, 1959
       Cathey Clowater
         MATTHEW DREW COREY Sept. 22, 1991
         DEXTER JOHN COREY Aug. 27, 1993
      REBECCA ANNE COREY May 22, 1960
        ALEXANDER KEITH COREY Sept. 2, 1976
      MURRAY KEITH COREY Apr. 14, 1961
      BRIAN KENT COREY Dec. 18, 1962
        MELISSA LYNN COREY Feb. 16, 1985
        JESSICA DAWN COREY May 26, 1986
      DONALD WAYNE COREY Apr. 18, 1964
      SUSAN MARIE COREY Dec. 17, 1965

A. KATHLEEN COREY Sept. 4, 1930
 Paul D. Foster
      GEOFFREY KIRK FOSTER June 18, 1953
      KRIS RODERICK ROSS FOSTER Jan. 1, 1959
       Wanda Dryer
         ERIN KRISTINE FOSTER Feb. 24, 1985
         MEREDITH LESLEY FOSTER Nov. 12, 1988
      STUART PAUL FOSTER Oct. 29, 1961
       Patricia Lyall
         KATHLEEN PATRICIA FOSTER Jan. 20, 1987
         CAMERON LYALL FOSTER June 4, 1988
         ELIZABETH MARGARET JANE FOSTER Apr. 11, 1991

SHIRLEY JOYCE COREY Aug. 3, 1932
 Paul Brooks
      JAYNE ROCHELLE BROOKS Nov. 13, 1960
       Teet Vahi   - 2000
      LISA KATHLEEN BROOKS June 10, 1966
       Dana Delong
         KATHLEEN LUCRETIA DELONG Aug. 12, 1988
         COREY ALLISON DELONG Mar. 20, 1990
      LISA KATHLEEN BROOKS
       Brent DesRoches (2nd Husband)
         GINA LYNN DESROCHES Jan. 11, 1996
      NATALIE JOY BROOKS June 22, 1968

        Kevin Lyon
            BRODY JEREMIAH LYON June 13, 1996

<u>**GORDON NEIL COREY**</u> June 16, 1934
  Esta Grant
    MITCHELL GORDON COREY July 20, 1960
      Cynthia Guthrie
        MATTHEW GORDON COREY Aug. 13, 1985
        AMANDA MICHELLE COREY Jan. 5, 1988
    SALLY LOUISE COREY Nov. 22, 1961
      Peter Bulger
        KAYLIE MARY LOUISE BULGER May 21, 1987
    ANTHONY NEIL COREY May 4, 1963
      Karen Campbell
        JOSHUA ANTHONY COREY Aug. 20, 1962
    STEPHANIE KATHERINE COREY Nov. 2, 1968
      Gerald DeMerchant
        HANNAH KATHERINE DEMERCHANT May 5, 2000
    TRENT ANDREW COREY Mar. 19, 1972 – July 21, 1984

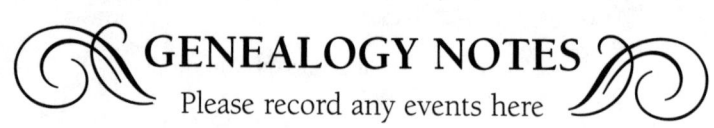
GENEALOGY NOTES
Please record any events here

ABOUT THE AUTHOR

Judson Malcolm Corey, BA,BD, STM, MA, is the grandson of Alfred and Lucretia Corey. His education began in the 1-room school in East Knowlesville, and was enhanced at Doaktown; Woodstock; Montreal; Gronigan, Holland; Wolfville, Nova Scotia; Boston, Mass. and Albany, N.Y. After about 20 years of parish ministry he taught at Blackville, Newcastle, Plaster Rock, Grand Falls and Aroostook, New Brunswick. Then he entered social work. He did counselling and group therapy at Ridgewood Treatment and Rehabilitation Centre. In 2002 Toastmasters International awarded him the D.T.M. This book is the sequel to **The Story of Knowlesville**, published in 1985.

Photo: Universal Portrait Studios